The Early Dated Coins of Europe, 1234-1500

The Early Dated Coins of Europe, 1234-1500

By Robert A. Levinson

THE COIN AND CURRENCY INSTITUTE, INC.

P.O. Box 1057 • Clifton, New Jersey 07014 • USA

(973) 471-1441

www.mail@coin-currency.com

The Early Dated Coins of Europe, 1234-1500

By Robert A. Levinson

SPECIAL NOTICE
Permission is hereby granted for the free use of the numbering system employed in this book by any newspaper, magazine or periodical; and also by any coin dealer or auctioneer in any advertisement, circular, price list or auction catalogue. This permission is granted only when proper acknowledgment is made of the source of this numbering system by mentioning the title of this book and the name of the author whenever and wherever this numbering system is used. Prior written permission is required when this numbering system is used in any publication that is offered for sale.

ISBN 978-0-87184-600-6

Library of Congress Control Number: 2006938330

Printed in the United States of America

DEDICATION

To my wife Maya, who has most willingly indulged me in my hobby/passion/obsession known as medieval numismatics.

ACKNOWLEDGEMENTS

Anyone who is a serious student of numismatics comes to realize that the friendships developed in the study and collecting of coins are just as important, if not more so, than the size or quality of the collection itself. In creating this catalogue, the author has relied (or leaned) heavily on this great network of friends and scholars, many who have provided significant input or efforts into helping bring this catalogue to fruition. Rather than acknowledging all contributions by simply listing names *in seriatum*, I would be remise if I did not say at least a few additional words for those whose especially valuable contributions went beyond what one has a right to expect.

Dr. Gordon A. ("Andy") Singer, U.S.A. – Coin dealer and the "dean" of all medieval numismatics, whose insights and knowledge in this field, which he freely shares with all, are rivaled by none;

Edward Cohen, U.S.A. – A fellow collector *par excellance* whose scholarly assistance regarding the history of the dating of coinage has been invaluable;

John Burnham, U.S.A. – A coin dealer, classically-trained numismatist and mentor who has helped both encourage and mold this project from its earliest days;

Arthur Friedberg, U.S.A. – The renowned author of *Gold Coins of the World* (and numerous other books) who has generously spent his time and considerable energies taking this catalogue from a mere collection of data and writings to its current book form;

Mark Teller and Gus Wing, U.S.A. – Coin dealers whose generous contribution of their time, their library and their priceless contacts in the profession have helped keep this project moving along for nearly 15 years;

James Robert ("Jim Bob") and Deborah ("Deb") Cervin, U.S.A. – The son and daughter-in-law of David Cervin, who so kindly provided me with all of David's research, including all of his correspondence with leading numismatists and museums;

Günther Hild, Germany – Coin dealer and auctioneer (Soester Münzcabinett and Westfälische Auktionsgesellschaft) who has most generously made available his time, his library, his knowledge and his worldwide contacts to provide outstanding assistance in both the German sections of this book and in its overall presentation;

Fritz Rudolf Künker, Germany – Coin dealer and auctioneer (Fritz Rudolf Künker Münzhandlung), and his wonderful team of numismatists (Arne Kirsch, Dr. Andreas Kaiser, Oliver Köpp, Alexandra Elflein, as well as Marion Künker) who together have provided wonderful assistance in the German sections of this catalogue and were always ready with a reference at a moment's notice;

Dr. Hubert Lanz, Germany – Coin dealer and auctioneer (Numismatik Lanz München) who has taken substantial time and effort to patiently educate the author as to the complicated Habsburg relationships and has proofread the same with always valuable comments, not only as to the Habsburg section but for the entire book;

Prof. Dr. Berndt Kluge, Germany - Renowned director of the State Museum of Berlin Coin Cabinet, who has graciously provided his time and numismatic scholarship to assist the author in the examination and study of many of the great rarities in the cabinet.

Claude Roelandt, Belgium – A true numismatic scholar and author who has generously provided his time, his efforts, his photography, his translation skills and his invaluable contacts in the Benelux to greatly assist the research undertaken in those areas;

François de Callataÿ, Belgium – The Director of the Cabinet des Medailles in Brussels, who has so willingly provided for study marvelous access to his museum's magnificent collections;

Jean Elsen, Belgium – Coin dealer and auctioneer (Jean Elsen & ses Fils, S.A.) who along with his sons Olivier and Philippe has always been available to answer questions and provide assistance with the Netherlands sections of this catalogue;

Laurens Schulman, the Netherlands – Coin dealer and auctioneer (Laurens Schulman, B.V.) who has provided excellent assistance in the Northern Netherlands section;

Dr. Alan Walker and Heiner Stotz, Switzerland – Coin dealers and auctioneers (LHS Numismatik AG) who have provided most valuable assistance in the Swiss and Italian sections of this catalogue, especially in locating obscure and out-of-date references;

Dr. Ruedi Kunzmann, Switzerland – President of the Swiss Numismatic Society who has provided substantial assistance in obtaining information on some of the more obscure of the Swiss early dated coins and their references and has proofread the Swiss section;

Lutz Neumann, Switzerland – Coin dealer and auctioneer (UBS, previously Swiss Bank Corporation), who has generously contributed his time in providing reference materials;

Dr. Peter Spufford, Great Britain – Professor, student of Philip Grierson and author of numerous works in the study of medieval coinage and monetary/economic history in the Middle Ages. His indispensable books define numismatic scholarship.

Additionally, the following persons, museums, publishers and organizations have kindly provided assistance or photography, all of which are gratefully acknowledged:

Austria - Dr. Michael Alrum, Kunsthistorisches Museum (Vienna), Landesmuseum Joanneum, Coin Collection (Graz), Karl Peitler, Auktionhaus H.D. Rauch.

Belgium - Prof. dr. Johan van Heesch and Yves Landrain (the Cabinet des Medailles in Brussels), Jean-Luc van der Scheuren, Huberte Renaers, Provinciaal Gallo-Romeins Museum (Tongres), Jean-Luc Dengis, Georges Depreyrot.

France – Michel Prieur (C.G.F.), Dominque Flon, Musée Départemental d'Art Ancien et Contemporain (Épinal), Matthieu Gilles, Drouot Richelieu, Françoise Vinchon.

Germany – Dr. Busso Peus Nachf., Peter Schulten, Verlag Ostfriesische Landschaft, Winifred Bogen, Ruhrlandmuseum Essen, H.-K. Kramer, Günther Felke, U.E.G. Schrock, Collection Bendig (Bremen), Dirk Loebbers.

Netherlands – Drs. Albert Scheffers, Johan Mevius, Christjan van Marissing, Praamstra Books, Gerard Lemmens, Museum Het Valkhof (Nijmegen), Pieter Roelofs, Dr. M.L.F. van der Beek, Karel de Geus, Drs. Arent Pol, Geld- en Bankmuseum (Utrecht), Teylers Museum (Haarlem), Jaarboek voor Munt- en Penningkunde, Amsterdam, Gijs Henzen.

Switzerland - Jean-Paul Divo, Hess-Divo, Leu Numismatik, LHS Numismatik, Jürg Simonett, Rätisches Museum Chur and Münzen & Medaillen GmbH and Münzen & Medaillen Deutschland GmbH, NAC-Spink-Taisei, Peter Hiltbrunner.

Scandanavia - Bjarne Ahlström.

U.S.A. – Dr. Robert Hoge and Francis Campbell (The American Numismatic Society), Victor England and D. Scott VanHorn, PhD. (CNG), Allan Berman, Richard Ponterio, Gordon Haegelin, Harvey Stack, Robert Korver, Steve Ivy, John Mark Osborne, Carla Semola, Jacob Treger, Sanford J. Durst, Sean Breazeal, John S. Davenport (dec'd).

CONTENTS

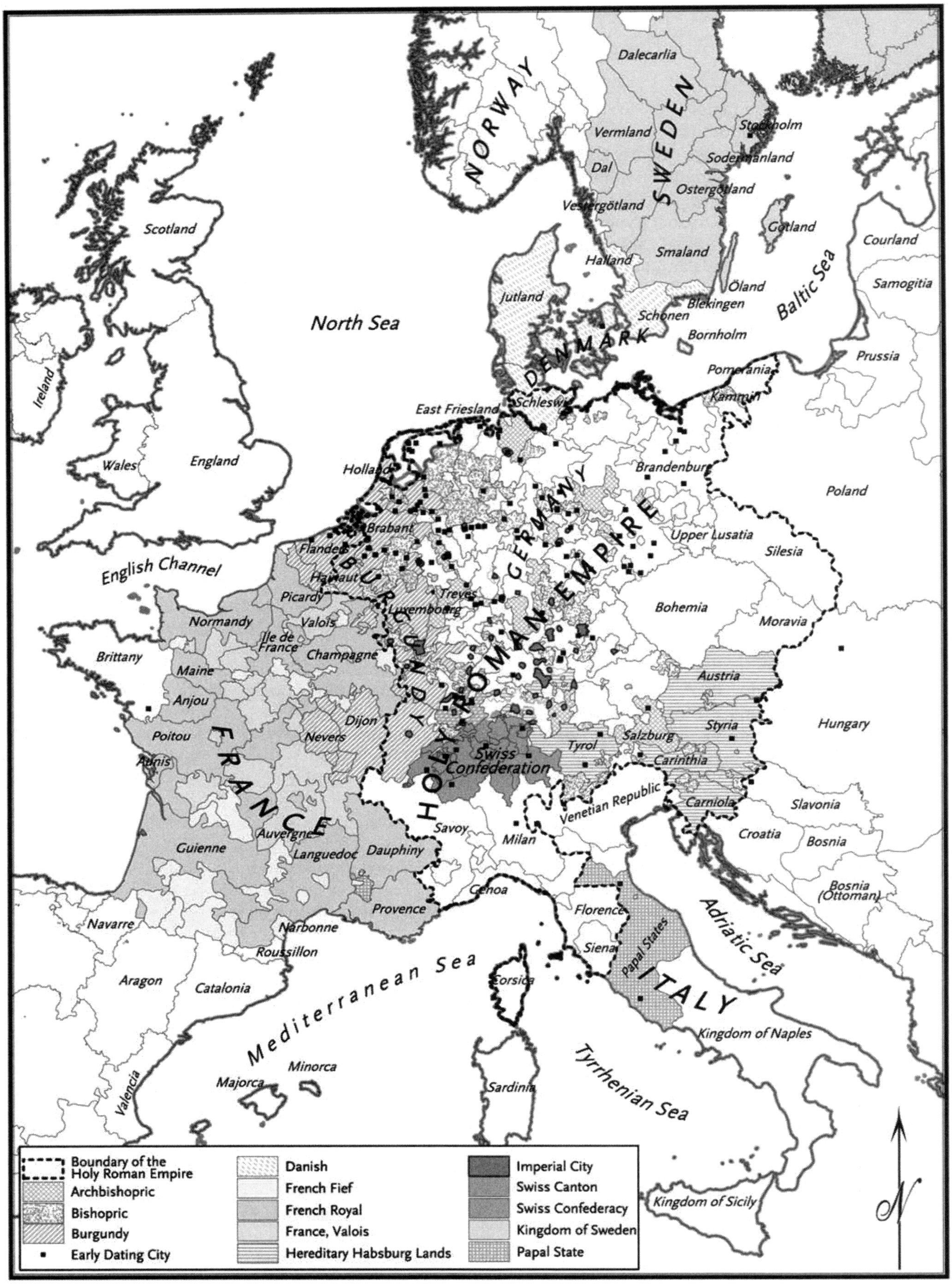
NORWAY
SWEDEN
Dalecarlia
Vermland
Dal
Stockholm
Sodermanland
Ostergötland
Vestergötland
Gotland
Smaland
Halland
Öland
Blekingen
Schonen
Bornholm
Jutland
DENMARK
Courland
Samogitia
Baltic Sea
Prussia
Scotland
Ireland
North Sea
England
Wales
English Channel
East Friesland
Schleswig
Pomerania
Kammin
Holland
Brandenburg
Poland
Brabant
Flanders
Hainaut
Picardy
Treves
Luxembourg
GERMANY
HOLY ROMAN EMPIRE
BURGUNDY
Upper Lusatia
Silesia
Bohemia
Moravia
Normandy
Valois
Ile de France
Champagne
Brittany
Maine
Anjou
Poitou
Aunis
FRANCE
Dijon
Nevers
Austria
Styria
Salzburg
Tyrol
Carinthia
Hungary
Swiss Confederation
Venetian Republic
Carniola
Slavonia
Croatia
Bosnia
Savoy
Milan
Guienne
Auvergne
Languedoc
Dauphiny
Provence
Genoa
Florence
Siena
Papal States
ITALY
Bosnia (Ottoman)
Adriatic Sea
Navarre
Narbonne
Roussillon
Aragon
Catalonia
Mediterranean Sea
Corsica
Kingdom of Naples
Minorca
Majorca
Valencia
Sardinia
Tyrrhenian Sea
Kingdom of Sicily
Boundary of the Holy Roman Empire
Archbishopric
Bishopric
Burgundy
Early Dating City
Danish
French Fief
French Royal
France, Valois
Hereditary Habsburg Lands
Imperial City
Swiss Canton
Swiss Confederacy
Kingdom of Sweden
Papal State
N

PART I. INTRODUCTION

OVERVIEW OF EARLY DATED COINAGE AND ITS HISTORY

The goal of this book is to present for the first time a comprehensive listing, region by region, state by state, mint by mint, of all the known types of dated coins struck in medieval Europe bearing an Anno Domini date of 1500 or earlier. These coins span, albeit very irregularly, the period from 1234 to 1500. In the collecting community these coins are known as early Anno Domini dated coins, or "early dated" coins for short. The coins listed in this book have dates in many different forms yet are all dated to the common era, generally referred to as the date of the birth of Christ, or in Latin "Anno Domini" (the year of our Lord). The treatment of this topic has some boundaries. This book catalogues European coins with Anno Domini dates from 1234-1500 expressed using Roman or modern Arabic-derived numerals. It excludes coins that were intended for circulation in the Islamic world with dates shown in Islamic script.[1]

The interest in the dating of coinage is a natural one. When one begins collecting coins of a particular state, they are usually sorted by oldest to newest. While dates were not always placed on coinage – in fact Anno Domini dating of coins using Latin script did not begin until the mid-13th century - the interest in knowing a coin's date is central to the process of collecting and cataloging. While coins can be assigned to a particular period and even to a particular date by reference to many other clues, such as a coin's type, style, portrait, engraver, event depicted, a mint treaty and so on, an engraved date is the most precise and desired method.

Photo No. 2. Denmark. Roskild Denier 1234 (2x actual size

The idea that coins should bear a date of mintage referencing the time passed since the birth of Christ was not widespread in Europe until the mid-to-late 16th century, and was not even universal in Europe until the early 19th century as certain Italian issues, notably several from Venice, remained undated until that time. While a Christian monk living in North Africa, Dionysus Exiguus, formulated the Anno Domini calendar in the 6th century, it was not until seven hundred years later when European coinage was dated, first by a Danish coin from the bishopric of Roskilde in 1234 (seven pieces current extant, all in museums – see photo #2)

The decision to begin dating coins to an Anno Domini standard was hardly a trend-setter: 138 years passed until the next European coins were dated in 1372, this time simultaneously in the extreme western part of Germany in Charlemagne's capital city of Aachen and in the small Southern Netherlands lordship of Schoonvorst-Sichem, 10 miles to the southeast. Photo #1 above is a stunning example of a 1374 Aachen groschen, effectively the first collectable early dated coin, as all others existing prior to that date are believed to be in museum collections or are no longer extant. The relatively plentiful issuance of dated Aachen coinage in the next fifty years, in contrast with the great rarity of the Schoonvorst-Sichem coinage, has led to the impression, with some validity, that Aachen was the birthplace of dated coinage. Clearly, the 1234 Roskilde piece was a great anomaly – there would not be another dated coin from Scandinavia until 1478. In fact, until 1424, the only European states[2] which struck AD-dated coinage were the bishopric of Roskilde, the city of Aachen, the lordship of Schoonvorst-Sichem and the Holy Roman Emperor in Sicily, but using Islamic script.

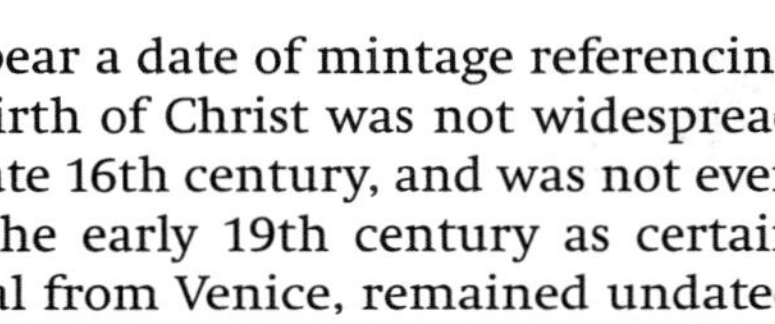

Photo No. 3. Switzerland - St. Gallen. Plappart 1424

However, even the widespread circulation of the Aachen groschens, large attractive coins of good silver which spawned many imitations, did not change the die-engraving habits of most states, and coins for the overwhelming part remained undated.[3] In fact, it was not until 1424 that other states began striking dated coins, most notably hundreds of miles to the south in the bishopric of St. Gallen

---

[1] See Appendix 6 for a listing of the known types of these Islamic script Anno Domini dated coins.
[2] In this catalogue the term "state" is used to describe any authority which issued early dated coins, from the Holy Roman Emperor down to the smallest town.
[3] Aachen's own lower-denomination coinage, issued contemporaneously with its early dated groschens, was itself not dated until 1496.

in Switzerland. In that year, St. Gallen struck dated silver plapparts utilizing modern positional numbers for the date instead of Roman numerals, the first European coin to bear this new dating form (see photo # 3 on the preceding page). The next coins to use these modern numerals were struck in 1456, hundreds of miles distant and more than thirty years hence in the Habsburg duchies of Styria and Austria (see photo #s 4 and 5). Sporadic use of dating on coins, to the point where both dated and undated types were struck by the same state and circulated simultaneously, was the norm, not the exception. The decision to date coins lacked any uniformity and virtually no contemporaneous resource material exists explaining the reasons that mintmasters or rulers decided to begin dating their coinage when it had been previously undated.[4]

Photo No. 4. Styria - Graz. Schinderling 1456

Photo No. 5. Wiener Neustadt. Kreuzer 1456

To logically (and more important - usefully) list in a single book the myriad of types of coinage struck throughout most of Western and Central Europe in the late Middle Ages is an especially daunting task. First, it has been estimated that during the latter half of the Middle Ages, there were over 1000 different mints in Europe alone. Hundreds of states possessed mint rights. The diversity of issuing authorities was staggering: coinage was issued by rulers as lofty as the Holy Roman Emperor and the Pope or as modest as the convent of Essen, ruled by an abbess (see photo #6). Possessing the right to mint was the right to create wealth and gain fiscal stability, so mint rights were not only established at centers of trade and at the sources of bullion, but were also granted as favors, provided as religious donations to ecclesiastical officials, traded for settlements of disputes or sold to raise monies.

Photo No.6 . Essen. Groschen 1474

Approximately 100 of these myriad of distinct states which existed in the late Middle Ages not only struck coinage but placed an Anno Domini date on their coinage and/or countermarked other state's early Anno Domini dated coinage.[5] By 1500, the range of this early dated coinage extended throughout western and central portions of the European continent. Early dated coins were struck as far west as Brittany, as far north as Stockholm, as far south as Sicily and as far east as Kremnitz (Slovakia). Early dated coins were struck at places as isolated as Garz on the island of Rügen in the Baltic Sea between modern-day Poland and Germany and in Krapina, a small town in modern day Croatia, which was granted a mint right for all of six months in 1459 (see photo #7). Appendix 1 provides an alphabetical listing of all of these states and their mints.

Photo No.7. Krapina. Kreuzer 1459

The persons or entities possessing the right to mint coins could not have been more varied. In the Middle Ages, emperors, popes, kings and queens, princes and princesses, dukes and duchesses, counts and countesses, earls and landgraves, barons and baronesses, lords and ladies, electors (male and female) of the Holy Roman Empire, towns, imperial cities, free cities, cantons, archbishoprics, bishoprics, monasteries, nunneries, ecclesiastical officials, minor noble officials, administrators and usurpers all struck coins at a variety of places, creating an exceptionally large field of study.

Only one book has previously approached this subject. Albert Frey, in his seminal 1915 work, *The Dated European Coinage Prior to 1501*, (hereinafter "Frey") was the first and only author to broach this theme. While no doubt an eminent scholar, Frey treated the subject far too superficially. While 543 separate types were listed in his book, smaller denomination coins from the same ruler were often merely footnoted, e.g., "There are also half groschen of the same date." More common than not, legends were absent, the coins themselves were not described, references were generally lacking and ... even dates were misread! Yet, Frey was the sole single reference the auctioneer, collector, dealer and student had to use from 1915 through 1977.

In 1978, David Cervin, who had become interested in the collecting field of early dated coinage about a decade earlier, arranged for Frey to be republished, bringing its arcane subject to the attention of new generations of collectors. Cervin added five supplements to Frey: first, he provided a more thorough listing of the earliest dated coins (those struck before 1425); second, he provided an unscientific listing of what he presumed were the numbers extant (and corresponding prices), based upon surveys of certain museums but not of collections; third, he included eleven plates of photographs; fourth, he provided a summary of rarity; fifth, he included a loose-leaf supplement of some 265 or so

[4] Perhaps the largest and best preserved of medieval mint records are those of the Burgundian Netherlands, the subject of which has been written about extensively by Dr. Peter Spufford of Cambridge, Emeritus Professor of European History at the University of Cambridge and a Fellow at Queens' College, Cambridge. See, for example, Spufford, *Monetary Problems and Policies in the Burgundian Netherlands 1433-1496*, (hereinafter "Spufford, Monetary Problems"). Yet, in correspondence with the author, Dr. Spufford confirms that the tremendous resource materials extant from these time periods give no clue as to why the Burgundian Netherlands, beginning in 1474, started dating coins from the multiple territorial mints under its control. The author has extensively used several of Spufford's scholarly works as essential references.

[5] See section G below for a discussion of early dated countermarked coinage.

types additional to the original 543 listed in Frey. This last supplement also contained a guide to both numbers extant and estimated values, both unfortunately sorely inaccurate. A Second Revised Edition published in 2000 added approximately 80 additional pieces, mainly from the Northern & Southern Netherlands, but inexplicably did not include any of the additional pieces listed in the 1978 reprint.

Regrettably, Cervin chose not to correct the single greatest flaw of Frey, the lack of any coherent organization. Frey listed all coins chronologically, from 1234 – 1500, with no thought as to the context under which the coins were issued. The states were not even listed alphabetically. For example, one finds Frey #347, a Styria 1490 kreuzer, listed next to #348, a Brabant 1490 four-mites. Given that medieval coins are identified and studied by the authority under which they were authorized to be struck, which is in a particular region under a particular ruler, this organizational flaw is troubling. Additionally, scores of erroneous entries in the original Frey, as well as its misidentified dates, were overlooked and thus gained new life in both the 1978 and 2000 reprints.[6]

Given its shortcomings, it has been difficult to use Frey (any edition) as a reference guide if one is a collector by state (as most are), or if he desires to correctly catalog a collection of early dated coins. In 1992, upon the acquisition of his sixth early dated coin, a 1481 four-mites of Brabant, the first early dated copper coin (see photo #8), the author found this important coin noticeably absent from the 1978 Frey reprint. The seller, a prominent dealer specializing in tokens and medals, offhandedly remarked that there were many pieces "not in Frey." Necessity being the mother of invention, the author decided that he would start keeping a list what indeed was "not in Frey." This book is the ultimate result of that innocuous remark made nearly 15 years ago.

Photo No. 8. Brabant. 4 mites 1481

B. THE ARRANGEMENT OF THIS BOOK

This book is divided into four parts: I. Introduction and Discussion; II Catalogue of Coinage; III Discussion of States; and IV Appendices. The format used is quite different than that of Frey. After a number of years of study, and discovering hundreds of types "not in Frey," it became apparent that merely filling in the blanks in Frey and correcting the errors would be inadequate, as the basic organization of Frey made little logical sense. For example, Frey numbers 224 and 225 are an exceedingly rare groschen of Brandenburg and a very common double briquet of Brabant. These two early dated coins truly have little in common other than the first three letters of their respective state's names.

In nearly all auction catalogs and references, coins (dated or not) are listed first by the region in which they are located, such as the Northern Netherlands or Germany, and next by the issuing state. This book follows that same logical division. In Part II, the Catalogue of Coinage, each of the approximate 1,200 or so distinct coin "types" or "subtypes" (both defined below) are divided into eight separate regions: Germany, Southern Netherlands, Northern Netherlands, Habsburg Hereditary Territories and Neighboring Lands, Switzerland, Scandinavia, Italy and France. Within each region, the coins are assigned a unique number, then listed first by date, then chronologically by "state" (issuing authority) and then alphabetically by mint. Thereafter, organization is by denomination (largest to smallest), and within each denomination are listed different types of the same denomination, then subtypes, if any. Under this arrangement, a lower denomination coin from the Saxon mint of Freiberg will be found before a larger denomination coin from the Saxon mint of Leipzig. Commentary follows where appropriate. The listing for each coin includes the full legend and a description of obverse and reverse, as well as an indication of its rarity (see Section J below). Current values are briefly discussed in Section K below and are listed in the accompanying loose-leaf guide. However, sale records, where very notable, are provided in the comments.

Following the Catalogue of Coinage, Part III contains in alphabetical order for each region, a short history/overview of each of the 100 or so different states that minted or countermarked early dated coins. Part III also lists the corresponding unique catalogue number first assigned in Part II, as well as the date, denomination, mint and rarity for each of that state's early dated coins. Those states whose issuance of early dated coins was more prolific (Liège or Aachen, for example) will naturally have a more in-depth overview than the many entities which struck (or countermarked) but one or two early dated coins. The purpose behind Part III is to provide for the reader interested in the coins of a particular state a thorough guide to all of its known early dated types and denominations. By this cross-reference, it is hoped that this book will be more useful to the "state" collector than the original Frey.

To assist in the understanding of early dated coinage, a number of appendices have been provided:

- Appendix 1 – Alphabetical Listing of all States
- Appendix 2 – Abbreviations used on Early Dated Coinage
- Appendix 3 – Latin Religious Inscriptions found on Early Dated Coinage
- Appendix 4 – Patron Saints on Early Dated Coinage

[6] Appendix 7 lists nearly 120 major errors in *Frey* and in the various Cervin supplements. It is necessary to provide this in order to account for the large disparities between *Frey*-listed coinages and those in this catalogue. Additionally, while the 2000 reprint contained a list of "80 new coins from *Gelder-Hoc*," most in fact were already in Frey and now have two separate numbers assigned to each! Still, as one cannot ignore the past 90+ year use of *Frey*, all *Frey* citations are listed in Part II of this catalogue in the references. The criticisms of Cervin's methodology should not be viewed as a criticism of David Cervin himself. Cervin was responsible for creating the "Roman Coin Project", now renamed the David Cervin Roman Coin Project, an admirable program designed to spread the joy of numismatics to young collectors by donating to them Roman coins. Cervin's enthusiasm for numismatics was infectious and the author, who had many pleasant talks with him, cherished his friendship.

References are found in three different parts of this book. In Part II, each early dated coin type listed will have citations to the leading references for that particular coin type. Most commonly these citations will be to reference books but in some cases may be to auction catalogs or articles. Second, in Part III, listed for each of the 100 or so distinct states is the author's opinion of both the best reference source(s) for that state's early dated coinage (concentrating on that particular state) and the best overall regional reference(s) covering the general area, if any.[7] Third, in Part IV, Appendix 7, a bibliography will provide the full names of all references either cited in this book or used by the author in his research. Emphasis will be indicated for those especially vital reference guides such as Krug for Saxony, van Gelder-Hoc for the Burgundian Netherlands, CNA for Habsburg medieval, etc., to which the reader is most confidently directed.

Attempting to thoroughly register a continent's worth of coinage over a roughly 125 year period (apart from the anomalous 1234 Roskilde denier), has been a formidable undertaking. This effort could not have been possible without the very kind and generous assistance of many fine numismatic scholars who are collectors, dealers, auctioneers and friends from both America and Europe. No doubt, given the efforts needed to provide a depth of coverage, limitations of the author's language skills and continued discovery of hoard coins, there will be errors made and/or corrections and updates needed, all of which will be gratefully received and acknowledged. To the extent errors exist, they are those of the author and not of the many contributors.

C. GUIDE TO NUMBERING SYSTEM

No numismatic reference guide is fully satisfactory unless its users can easily reference a particular coin. While some mint records do exist from the medieval times, these records are most often incomplete or missing. There is no optimum way to best assign a unique reference number to a medieval coin type. The choice of this book is to assign the coins of the same region the same prefix and thereafter assign corresponding type and when necessary, subtype numbers.

As the principal distinguishing component in this book is the region, each region is assigned a separate number - Germany I, Southern Netherlands II, Northern Netherlands III, Habsburg Hereditary Territories and Neighboring Lands IV, Switzerland V, Scandinavia VI, Italy VII and France VIII. The numbering system in this book will start with this regional reference. Each distinct coin type within a region will then receive a consecutive number. For example the Aachen 1372 groschen, being the first dated coin of Germany, will have the number of I-1. The 1373 groschen will be I-2. The 1374 groschen of Aachen has two subtypes, which will thus be numbered either I-3a or I-3b. Similarly, the 1498 cadiere d'or of Brittany, being the third dated coin of France (Region VIII) will have the identifying number VIII-3.

D. HOW DISTINCT TYPES ARE DEFINED

Modern coins, being machine struck, bear a pervasive uniformity absent in medieval coinage; hence, all differences or varieties in modern coinage are noteworthy. In contrast, uniformity is the exception in medieval coinage, not the rule. In a compromise between practicality and usefulness on the one hand and thoroughness on the other, this book has listed and assigned unique numbers to what the author considers to be separate "types," with important die variations (as determined from the factors listed below) assigned subtype numbers. However, distinctions consisting of minor differences in spelling, punctuation, abbreviations, legends, designs, devices or engraving forms and styles, are not separately listed as either types or subtypes, as they are more properly classified as minor die variations. It is well beyond the scope of this book to list every die variety of every early dated coin – such an endeavor would require multiple volumes yet add little of valuable substance.

For example, Krug, in his thorough and highly recommended reference on Saxony medieval coinage, *Die Meissnisch-Sachsischen Groschen*, lists 18 separate varieties of the Colditz horngroschen of 1465, 16 varieties of the Freiberg horngroschen of 1466, and 31 varieties of the Schneeberg zinsgroschen of 1499, all with variations as slight as a single letter or single punctuation mark. The Burgundian Netherlands mint in the county of Holland issued double stuivers with Holland abbreviated "HOL" "HO" and "H." The duchy of Brabant was likewise abbreviated on its coins as "BRAB", "BRA", "BR" and "B." Should each be considered a different type and assigned a unique number? While such valuable information is appropriate to record in a single reference guide for a single state, it is not feasible to list in one book every single spelling, punctuation and abbreviation variety known for the dated coins of more than a hundred states spanning more than 125 years.

---

[7] For example, listed as the main specific reference book for Brabant in the Southern Netherlands, is the magnificent 19th century three volume publication, *Histoire Monetaire de Brabant*, by de Witte. The recommended general reference book for Brabant is the essential van Gelder-Hoc, *Les Monnaies des Pays-Bas Bourguignons et Espagnols 1434-1713* (hereinafter "*Gelder-Hoc*"). Full references for all cited works are found in the bibliography in Part IV *infra*.

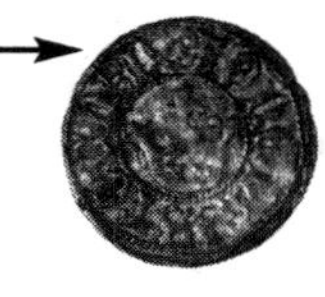

Photo No. 9 . *Sweden. Half Ortug bearing the date "18"*

A typical example of how subtype numbers are assigned in this book is illustrated by the numbers assigned to 1478 Sweden ortugs and half-ortugs, all of which were struck at the Stockholm mint. These remarkable coins, with an immobilized date, continued to be struck in subsequent years bearing the same 1478 date. These were engraved with a number of digits, intending to denote the year 1478, but few of these dies actually achieved their intended purpose. The 1478 dates were expressed on different dies as "1478", "147" "78", "8", "1778" "14" and "878" (see photo # 9). The ortug is provided a type reference number – VI-2 – and its three subtypes, one with normal date of 1478, one with the abbreviated date of "8", and the last with the error date of "147" are assigned respective subtype numbers VI-2(a), VI-2(b) and VI-2(c). The six half-ortug subtypes are assigned numbers VI-3(a) through (f). As this book seeks to provide a compendium of dates in early European coinage, all differences found in the expression of the dates will be noted as separate subtypes.

What is emphasized by the assignment of a subtype number is that out of the myriad of different die varieties known, a few very major ones are notable to such a degree as to warrant their own. Approximately 15% of all types have one or more subtype numbers. This does not mean that there are only 15% of types that have one or more reported die varieties; to the contrary, 95% or more have notable die varieties, which is absolutely typical of medieval coinage with its hand-engraved dies. The decision to label one coin as a distinct "type," and deserving a unique number, while another is labeled but a subtype or still others "mere" die varieties, without their own numbers, is a judgment call on the author's behalf. However, the following rules have been employed to bring some objectivity to each decision:

Photo No. 10a. Brandenburg. Groschen 1500

1. Each distinct date is a "type" and has been assigned its own number. A 1492 dated coin has been assigned a number different from a 1493 dated coin of the same denomination from the same state, mint and ruler;

2. Where the same date is expressed by different means, Roman numerals versus Arabic numerals, medieval numerals versus modern numerals, etc., each has been assigned a separate subtype number. For example, Brandenburg struck groschens and half groschens each with the dates expressed both as "1500" and as "MVC" (1000 + 5 x 100), and both are assigned subtype numbers (compare photo 10a with photo 10b). Similarly, where a date has been expressed with different forms of numbers, such as with a modern "4" as compared to a medieval "4", each has been assigned its own subtype number;

Photo No. 10b. Brandenburg. Groschen MVC

3. Where the same denomination coin of the same state, date and mint has been struck with both full and partial dating, each example has been assigned its own subtype number. Numerous states employed this engraving choice and struck the same date and denomination coin from the same mint with both partial dates and full dates – "1498" and "98" as they appear on Nördlingen half-schillings are common examples. A very few states even struck double digit dated coins as the "standard" die with single digit dated coins as a subsequent (and usually much rarer) die. Saxony horngroschens dated either "66" or "6" and Swedish half ortugs dated either "78" or "8" are such examples. Such date abbreviations can be found in Roman numeral dating, as well. Examples of this are also found on Brandenburg's coinage where the date of 1500, alternatively expressed on some dies as "MVC," is abbreviated as both "MV" and "HV";

4. Denominations with dates found on obverse and reverse as well as mismatched dates are provided distinct subtype numbers. An example is the Brabant double briquet of 1492, the common version has but a single date and an extremely rare version has dates on both sides. Likewise, numerous Saxony coins are known bearing dates on both sides, and in several instances, possess mismatched (muled) dates. All are assigned separate subtype numbers;

Photo No. 11. 1478/1748 Flanders Double Briquet

5. Coins with overdates such 1478/1748 for instance (see photo 11) are noteworthy for this book as they concern dating, and (when known) have been referenced in the commentary but are not issued subtype numbers. Such errors appear fairly commonly on many early dated coins, especially on double briquets and briquets of the Burgundian Netherlands and on Nördlingen half-schillings, where numerous dies were used in the issuance of large numbers of coins;

6. Coins issued under the same ruler but struck in different mint cities are listed as distinct types. The archbishop of Bremen struck large 4 groten coins in the mint cities of Bremen and Vörde. The coins are virtually identical except for their respective obverse legends: "MONETA: NOVA: BREMENSIS" and "MONETA: NOVA: VORDENSIS"; Likewise, the dukes of Cleve issued otherwise identical coins from the mint cities of Cleve and Wesel. All are provided their own unique type numbers;

Photo Nos. 12-14. 1466 Saxony horngroschens of the Wittenberg, Freiberg and Leipzig mints.

7. Coins with mintmarks consisting of symbols are listed as distinct types only when the symbol clearly represents manufacture in a different mint city, as opposed to a different mint in the same city. The best known examples are in Saxony coinage, where the star of Leipzig, the rose of Gotha, the double cross of Colditz, the clover leaf of Wittenberg, the annulet of Ölsnitz and the cross-in-square of Freiberg[8], all represent coinage struck in distinct mint cities under the jurisdiction of the electors and dukes of Saxony (see photo Nos. 12-14). Fortunately, most early dated coins identified their place of manufacture in the legend (as did the higher denomination Saxony coinage), so this distinction rarely arises outside of Saxony;

8. Coins of the same year, state, mint and denomination but with legends identifying one or more different rulers' names are assigned different type numbers. For example, bartgroschens from the Zwickau mint of Saxony were struck with either the joint rulers' initials for Friedrich and Johann or for Friedrich, Johann and Georg. Both are assigned unique type numbers. Brandenburg in its late 15th century coinage listed a variety of rulers names, some alone, some with two names, others with two different names. All have been assigned separate type numbers as these coins have been issued by different authorities;

9. Coins with alternative titles of nobility (as opposed to abbreviations or the absence of titles for spacing reasons), are noteworthy and are listed as subtypes. Examples of this include the 1482 and 1483 double briquets of Brabant, where on a few varieties there is the bold but wholly incorrect assertion that its ruler, Philip the Fair, was also Duke of Lorraine: "MONETA:DVC:AVST:LOT:BRAB:LIM:ZC";

10. Coins with the same date, mint, denomination and ruler but bearing wholly dissimilar obverse or reverse legends are listed as distinct subtypes. In Brabant, obverse legends for the common 1482 and 1483 double patards types were reasonably similar, but the reverse legends were either: "DVP:PATARD:FAB'CAT:I:BRA:1482" ("Double Patard Struck in Brabant in 1482") or "SALVV:FAC:PPL:TVV:DNE:A:1482" ("Oh Lord Make Thy People Safe Year 1482"). In such cases, each is identified as a separate subtype;

11. Off-metal strikes, which are extremely rare in early dated coinage, have been assigned subtype numbers. While later European coinage commonly included patterns, presentation pieces or collector items such as thalers in gold or ducats in silver, early dated coinage was rarely struck in metals other than those intended. The few exceptions consisted mostly of the results of enterprising mint masters cheating on the edicts issued by the governing authorities. Such examples generally occurred due to a breakdown in mint control, often because of civil war, such as that in Liège at the end of the 15th century. For example, a 1494 patard which was normally a base silver coin was also struck from degraded dies in yellow copper (compare photo numbers 15a and 15b below);

Photo No. 15a. 1494 Liège patard (normal issue)

Photo No. 15b. 1494 Liège patard (degraded issue)

12. Coins which bear a date in the 15th century or earlier, but which are known to or reasonably believed to have been struck after the 15th century, are not listed. At best, they have been noted in the commentary. Most spectacular amongst these are the gold 7 ducat strikes of the famous 1486 Tyrol guldenthaler, and the 1479 medaillic marriage thalers of Maximilian and Marie of Brabant, the latter ones listed as Frey #s 196-197. Even Frey admits to their manufacture from dies carved in the 16th century, yet they are still included in that book, a decision not followed herein.

13. Coins issued from the same die but on flans deliberately thicker or heavier than the normal mint standards have been assigned their own type number. In such cases the heavier coins were meant to represent an entirely different denomination. The 1484 half guldiner as a thick strike was equal to a guldiner in weight. Mints in Bern and Basel struck multiple denomination gold and silver coins from the same dies. Most resourceful were the minting authorities of Antegnate in Lombardy, where the same 1494 die was used to strike a four ducat coin in gold, a double testone in silver, and a pattern double testone in bronze (see photo # 16 on the following page). All are assigned unique type

[8] The Saxony mintmark was actually that of a mint master, yet identified the coinage as being struck in a particular mint city. What became confusing is that the mint masters would sometimes change their location taking their mark with them and thus a mintmark identifying a coin with a particular mint city in 1488 might be used by the same master in a different mint city in 1498!

numbers. In contrast, ordinary weight variations are not noted as distinct types, as virtually all early dated coins varied somewhat in that degree and a good deal in some instances;

Photo No. 16. 1494 Antegnate bronze pattern testone

14. Piefоrts, or pattern pieces of greater than normal weight, as well as uniface strikes in off-metals, were often used for presentation pieces or for evaluation of die acceptability. They do not represent different denominations from the standard die. Instead, they represent important historical information regarding minting practices and are thus noted in the commentary without assignation of different type or subtype numbers. There are times where the line between coins of this type and those listed in Paragraph 13 above will indeed be very blurred;

15. Coins where the field devices (usually a shield) interrupt the legend in one die of the same denomination coin and not in another are listed as separate subtypes. Interaction of the legend with the field devices (design) affects the "look" of the entire coin, and thus presents a substantial difference worthy of its own subtype number. See Appendix 5, which provides photographic examples of these differences.

Photo No. 17. 1498 Brandenburg groschen with die engraved backwards

16. Coins possessing significant engraving errors affecting the expression of the date are noted as subtypes. The Aachen groschens with the Roman numeral date of 1302 instead of 1402, the 1498 Brandenburg groschens with the entire reverse legend and date engraved backwards (8941! – see photo #17) and the 1492 Pommeranian schillings from Damm with an backwards "2," are examples of these listed subtypes;

17. Punctuation and spacing dissimilarities in the legend represent minor die varieties only. In such cases the most common form is given. In medieval coinage, such dissimilarities are the norm not the exception;

18. Spelling differences and spelling errors in the legend are commonplace engraving decisions or errors and are not listed here as separate types. Dictionaries had not come into use in the 15th century and earlier and spelling was not standard. It is the most common form of the legend which is provided in the Part II. Differences or errors most often occurred where very large numbers of coins were struck, such as in the highly successful trading communities of the Burgundian Netherlands.[9] The exceptions are where through deliberate spelling or punctuation variations, it is possible to identify separate mint cities. The larger denomination coinage of the Burgundian Netherlands such as the 1487 grand reals d'argent and the 1487 -1488 double griffons present such exceptional cases;

19. Abbreviations in titles of nobility ("D" versus "DVX" for Duke), or dropping entire titles, result from engraving decisions and are not separate types. These variations were quite common in the Burgundian Netherlands, where the ruler's final title of duke of Limburg (abbreviated usually as "LI" or "L") was sometimes dropped. Instead, the Latin abbreviation "Z," representing the word "and" remained with the following strange result: "Duke of Burgundy, Brabant and";

20. Striking errors, such as doubling, offstrikes, planchet defects or weak strikes, have not been listed as types, as they are but manufacturing defects. All are exceedingly common in medieval coinage;

Photo No. 18a (left). 1497 Nördlingen schilling, crude bust
Photo No. 18b (right). 1497 Nördlingen schilling, refined bust

Photo No. 19a (left). 1497 Hamburg ducat, crude engraving
Photo No. 19b (right). 1497 Hamburg ducat, refined engraving

21. Coins bearing significant disparities in the engraving of the design or legend to the point where either the obverse or reverse present a wholly different appearance to the coin are listed as separate subtypes. The starkest examples of these are the two listed subtypes of 1497 Nördlingen schillings. One bears a dumpy, poorly engraved and downright ugly depiction of Holy Roman Emperor Maximilian. The other subtype, with a nearly identical legend, exhibits a splendid Renaissance portrait of the Emperor with slimmed-down features. (compare photo #18a with photo #18b). Similarly, dies for the 1497 Hamburg goldguldens alternatively portrayed both a slim Madonna and Child with attractive lettering versus a portly Madonna and Child with noticeably crude lettering, along with other field device differences (compare photos 19a with 19b). Brandenburg groschens displayed large eagles with plain breasts or ornamented breasts with scepter shields. All are assigned separate subtype numbers. In contrast, coins bearing only minor differences in the devices or in the size or shapes of lettering are not listed as separate types or subtypes;

[9] Mint records summarized in *Gelder-Hoc* disclose the minting of over 6 million dated double briquets from 1474-1477 alone, which would have required a staggering number of dies, all hand-carved by craftsmen who were not necessarily literate.

Photo No. 20. 1403 Aachen groschen with middle-length cross

22. Differences in the length of crosses justify assignment of separate subtype numbers. Crosses are among the most important of all medieval numismatic devices. Crosses on medieval coins provided religious symbolism, legend spacing devices and anti-clipping implements. Most often found on the reverse, crosses on early dated coins were normally either long crosses, which spanned the entire breadth of the coin and divided the legend and devices into quadrants or short crosses which were wholly within the fields and did not interrupt the legends. Very infrequently utilized were middle-length crosses, which divided inner but not outer legends. Aachen groschens dated between 1402 and 1405 present examples of this unusual type (see photo #20). Because the length of the cross visually affects the entire reverse, same denomination coins with different length crosses are assigned separate subtype numbers;

23. Countermarks on early dated coins are assigned their own type number and this book classifies such pieces to be early dated coinage of the state placing the mark. See the discussion in Section G below;

24. Coins whose existence has never been confirmed or for which the author cannot obtain confirmation, have not been listed. Many otherwise excellent reference guides sometimes list early dated coins which do not exist. Even Wolfgang Schulten, in *Deutsche Munzen aus der Zeit Karls V*, one of the finest general reference catalogs ever printed, lists several early dated coins which do not exist. Krumbach, in *Aachener Münzen des Mittelalters*, a very thorough and recent (1995) book on the coinage of Aachen, lists and provides a reference number to a 1376 Aachen groschen of questionable existence, for which no photographs or other objective evidence is present, merely anecdotal evidence reporting its existence.[10] In this book, such unsubstantiated information is noted, if at all, in the commentary (no doubt the publication of the book will bring to light unknown types or those thought unconfirmed, which is a most welcome development). In contrast, coins for which there is strong evidence of prior existence, but which may no longer be extant, such as the 1372 Aachen groschens, are listed and issued type numbers.

E. EARLY DATED EXONUMIA

In the late Middle Ages, there also circulated numismatic-related tokens ("exonumia") which in modern days have been at times mistaken for coinage. Tokens had a wide variety of uses to the public in medieval Europe. Tokens were designed to serve as counting implements ("jetons" or "rechenpfennige"), provided as proof of attendance at meetings ("ratszeichen" or town tokens), given to the poor to trade for food or goods ("armenpfennige" or charity tokens), given by guilds or organizations to signify membership ("mereaux", "jetons de presence" or membership tokens) and so on. The overwhelming majorities of these tokens struck in the 15th century and earlier were undated. However, a very rare few pieces did bear early Anno Domini dates, and thus must be distinguished from coins.

These early tokens, most commonly referred to today as "jetons," were not coins and were not meant to be used as a medium of exchange, despite that some did in fact circulate as small or fractional coinage. This usage occurred when there was a shortage of small denomination coinage, an all-too-frequent occurrence in the late Middle Ages when the profit of seignurage was too minimal to justify the striking of base metal coinage. Many jetons adopted the appearance of contemporary coinage; jetons struck at official mints, such as those issued in the Netherlands by the Burgundian Netherlands rulers, did in fact use designs which often matched the coins of the period, but the legend would identify their limited purpose. For example, here is the reverse inscription on the 1468 jeton of Bruges in Flanders, the Netherlands' first dated jeton: "IECT *P*LES*MAIST*DE*LA*MO*A*BRVG* 1468" (Jeton of the master of the mint of Bruges 1468) - (see photo #21).

Photo No. 21. 1468 jeton of Bruges

Photo No. 22. 1485 Würzburg jeton (obverse) misidentified in Frey as 1487

Principally struck in the Netherlands and mostly cataloged in the leading four-volume work by Dugniolle, *Le Jeton Historique des Dix-Sept Provinces des Pay-Bas,* early dated jetons are far rarer than early dated coinage. There are fewer than 75 total early dated jeton types known, with a number of minor varieties. As jetons were nearly always struck in copper or base metal, deterioration occurred at a greater rate than with precious metals, and few of these very early types were preserved or preserved well. It is beyond the scope of this initial edition to attempt listing all these pieces, and mention is made simply to alert the reader to their existence and to distinguish them from early dated coinage. Frey in fact listed two such pieces, #464, a ratszeichen from Cologne and #294D, a 1485 (misidentified as 1487) jeton from Würzburg (see photo #22).

[10] In correspondence with the author, Krumbach confirmed that he had not seen this coin either and now believes its existence is dubious.

F. LEGENDS AND IDENTIFYING OBVERSE AND REVERSE

The translation of the important identifying Latin legends on early dated coinage is fairly simple.[11] Other than sporadic religious inscriptions most commonly found on larger denomination coinage and on the coinage issued by the Burgundian Netherlands, the legends on early dated coinage encompassed most of the following five topics:

1. The name and title(s) of the immediate sovereign;
2. The name and title(s) of the ruler authorizing the mint right, if different;
3. The place of manufacture;
4. The date, which could be on the obverse or reverse, abbreviated or spelled out, Arabic (modern) or Roman numerals or a combination, and typically with the introductory heading of "ANNO DOMINI" or an abbreviation thereof;
5. The identity of the patron saint, if any.

Any difficulty encountered in interpretation of the legend almost always stems from inconsistent abbreviations. This inconsistency can be traced to a number of factors: lack of standardization of printing and therefore spelling as well (it must be remembered that as the printing press was created only in the middle of this period in 1454), illiterate engravers who were engraving the shapes of the letters, not actual words (the excessively crude Brandenburg dated coinage from 1496-1500 is most illustrative of this), poor engravers, engraving decisions which may have left too little room to express all needed information, and so on. Fortunately, once one understands the abbreviations used, the coins are easily identified. To guide the reader, in Appendix 2 provides a glossary of the most common abbreviations found on early dated coinage. Appendix 3 provides the translation to the Latin religious inscriptions.

The designation of the obverse and reverse on late medieval coinage generally conforms to the following classification: where the coin was issued by nobility (from lords through kings), the side carrying the ruler's name(s) and title(s) is designated as the obverse. The obverse also contains the name of the state, typically found near or at the end of the string of titles. A typical example is illustrated by the obverse legend of a 1475 double briquet of Charles the Rash of Flanders: "KAROLVS:DEI:GRA:DVX:BVRG:CO:FL" (Charles by the Grace of God, Duke of Burgundy, Count of Flanders). The date is sometimes at the end of the obverse legend, but much more commonly found at the end of the reverse legend. It is more infrequently found in the field or on a device such as a shield. The reverse legend on the coinage of nobility is typified by the presence of one of the following: (1) the name of the person or title granting the mint right (most commonly the Holy Roman Emperor); (2) a religious inscription; or (3) the name of the mint. The date then typically follows at the end of the legend, or is in the field.

Free cities, which issued much of the prolific coinage in the Northern Netherlands and Germany during the late Middle Ages, followed a different pattern in their legends. For silver coinage, one side bore the name of the state ("MONETA NOVA DAVENTRIA" as is found on the coinage of Deventer for example), and the other contained the date or (rarely) a religious inscription or both. The former is considered the obverse and the latter the reverse. For gold coinage of free cities, struck from an imperial mint or pursuant to an imperial grant, the date is typically found at the end of the legend which identifies the state (obverse) and Emperor's name would be found on what is typically designated as the reverse. For coinage issued out of the Hereditary Territories, governed directly by the Emperor, the side with the Emperor's name would be designated the obverse while the reverse contains the name of the mint, the date or both.

A companion classification rule is that where the coinage bears a portrait of a ruler (living or dead), that side is referred to as the obverse, even though this may conflict with the rule that the obverse is marked by the name of the state. In contrast, portrayals of saints, a common depiction on early dated coinage (and in the medieval mind persons every bit as important as temporal rulers), are usually found on what is designated to be the coin's reverse, since the accompanying legend almost never lists either the name of state or that of the temporal ruler. Where such exceptions are present, such as on certain coins of Zwolle in the Northern Netherlands – "SANCT:MICHAEL:PAT':ZWOL'" - that side will be listed as the obverse.[12]

Another guideline is that the cross, perhaps the most common single device on medieval coinage, is located on what is designated as the reverse. Very rare instances occur where the cross is properly classified as being on the obverse. This occurs where the patron saint or the Madonna and Child are depicted with no identification of the ruler or state while the side with the cross contains the identifying legend. Following the rules above, the obverse would be the side with the cross. The 1477 parpaiolle issued by the Bishop of Lausanne provide such a rare example (see photo #23).

Photo No. 23. 1477 Lausanne parpaiolle with cross on obverse

[11] While it was not unusual for early dated jetons and tokens to bear legends in common tongues such as French, Flemish or German, no early dated coins bore legends other than in Latin.

[12] Appendix 5 lists the patron saints on early dated coinage and the states associated with each saint.

G. COUNTERMARKS ON EARLY DATED COINAGE

Countermarks, quoting Frey from his other legendary work, *Dictionary of Numismatic Names*, are "a device or lettering, generally made with a punch, on the face of a regular issue, either to give it a new valuation or to indicate its acceptance as a coin of a different country or locality from the one that struck the original [host] piece." The terms "countermarks" and "counterstamps" have been used interchangeably in numismatic literature. This book will use the term "countermark."

Photo No. 24. 1466 Halberstadt countermark on a host Saxony horngroschen of the Leipzig mint

The purpose of the placement of the mark was to indicate the merit or worthiness ("acceptance") of the host coin to circulate in the region, territory or place which marked it. The marking was done by punching a recognizable symbol of the state, such as the gothic "h" of Halberstadt or the thistle of Hamburg, on a circulating coin manufactured outside that state, to indicate that coin was acceptable to circulate within the marking state at its issued value (see photo #24). Countermarking was most often undertaken by smaller cities, especially those in Westphalia in northwestern Germany, where commerce dictated the need for more circulating currency but where local mints did not have the rights to strike their own silver coinage. As with all rules there are exceptions – the highly successful Hanseatic trading cities of Hamburg and Lübeck also countermarked coins – in their cases, they possessed successful mints and rights to strike both gold and silver coinage. Their countermarks were employed to notify merchants which coinage was deemed tolerable to circulate in their respective states.

The fact that a coin bearing a date is countermarked by another state does not indicate exactly the date of the placement of the mark. A 1466 horngroschen of Saxony may have been countermarked by Halberstadt in 1468 or 1473 or later when it first came into circulation in that town. Dates were not impressed onto host coins, only identifying marks. There is but the singular occasion where an existing edict, issued by Ostfriesland in 1491, provides date of the marking. The author therefore recognizes that there is a fair question as to whether countermarks on an early dated host coins should be considered the same as early dated coins of the marking state, but has chosen to list those coins as early dated coins in their own right and the reader can make their own choice of its propriety.

H. DENOMINATIONS OF EARLY DATED COINAGE

Medieval coins rarely had their denomination listed on the coin itself. It was not until the mid-16th century when this placement became common, such as placing the number "3" on a coin to indicate its value of 3 kreuzer. There were a few exceptions, most notable of these were the assignment of denominations by designs in the field – a double briquet of the Burgundian Netherlands featured two (double) lions; a single briquet featured one, and a demi briquet (the denomination of one-half briquet) displayed only the upper half of the lion (see photos 25a-c). Double griffons and single griffons issued in 1487 carried the same symbolic meaning as did Liège coinage struck from 1476-1482.

Photo Nos. 25-a-c (left to right). 1474 Flanders double briquet, single briquet, and demi (half) briquet

There are many reasons that denominations rarely appeared on early dated coinage. First, just as dating was a revolution slow in development and sporadic in application, so was the placement of a denomination. Second, in the Middle Ages, the value was created not by a denomination engraved onto the coin itself (no "full faith and credit" existed as we know it today), but instead by the intrinsic value of the metal contained in the coin. Size did not matter – the amount of good silver in the coin is what set the value.[13] Third, while coins were issued bearing a certain value, that value could change relative to other coins, if the other coins were devalued and relative to itself through its own revaluation during "re-coinage."

Re-coinage was a tactic used by governments to tax money. It was first undertaken by recalling all circulating coins through punitive edicts, then melting the original and then reissuing the now re-coined "same" denomination coin containing less precious metal than before.[14] Coins which had a certain value before a re-coinage edict increased in value and were therefore hoarded, even under penalty of seizure. Thus was born Gresham's axiom that "bad" money

[13] A spitzgroschen of Saxony from the period 1475-1478 was worth twice as much as a half-spitzgroschen, although the latter is twice the size of the former. Differing metal content is the reason for such disparity, a rather significant fact missed by both Frey (#s 162, 178 and 189) and surprisingly by Saurma as well (#s 4394 and 4396) - both of their influential books had it wrong!

[14] Dr. Spufford, in the chapter entitled "The Scourge of Debasement" in his seminal work, *Money and its use in medieval Europe* (at pp. 302-306 - hereinafter "*Spufford Money*"), estimated that majority of the taxes used by France to fund the Hundred Years War were raised by re-coinage and devaluation. He cites that during the year of 1336, 60 gros tournois, the standard large coinage used by France, were struck from each "mark" of silver.

chases away "good" money. In contrast, the same denomination, if re-coined during such a period of inflation, was clearly worth less than before no matter what denomination it was later called, even if assigned a "higher" valuation than before recoinage.

Typically, these devaluations occurred during times of war and uncertainty, and resulted in large numbers of new denominations being issued. For instance, wars and unrest plagued the Netherlands at the end of the 15th century. From the period of 1484-1499, there were no less than seven separate series of coinage struck in the Burgundian Netherlands by Duke Philip the Fair, first under regency of his father Maximilian and second under his own right. Many new denominations were issued at that time, often with confusing results – coins struck containing less silver than before were deemed by the government to circulate at higher exchange rates than coins possessing higher percentages of silver minted only 10 years earlier (or less). However, while citizens affected by these selfish edicts were less puzzled by the myriad of denominations than one would think, they were still no less vocal, especially those who were being paid in coinage now actually worth far less due to the effects of rampant devaluation.[15]

While official devaluation in the Netherlands tended to be minimal as compared to other regions, unofficially the mintmasters sometimes altered the required metal content so de facto the coinage was devalued while de jure it remained unchanged. Smaller denomination coinage required to have certain specified amounts of silver (so-called "black money," given its name because of its quick oxidation from minimal silver content) ended up with little or no silver at all as it was unprofitable for the entrepreneurial mintmasters to coin. It is thus not unusual to see smaller denomination coinage in a variety of hues instead of the dull grayish color that one expects from low silver content billon coinage.

What this all means in the context of this book is that neither denominations nor exchange rates were static. This uncertainty was further compounded by the different regional appellations given early dated coins. A "stuiver," "vlieger," "patard," "double gros," "dopplegrote," and "sou" are all names used at various times and places for the same coin. There exist numerous regional and temporal differences in the names of the denominations. To hopefully provide some clarity, the most commonly used name and alternative name for each of the denominations of the coins in this book will be provided in the commentary for each type. However, there may not exist for every coin a "correct" denomination and differences are bound to occur.

I. METALS USED FOR EARLY DATED COINS

Early dated coins were struck primarily in silver or silver-billon, as silver was the normal medium of exchange in the late Middle Ages. Silver was more useful to the public because typical commercial transactions were far too small to warrant use of gold coinage. Silver coins were struck in fineness from in excess of 90% down to as little as 1%, or even less if the mintmaster, who ran the typical medieval entrepreneurial mint, cheated. The standard coin of the first half of the 15th century was a silver groschen or gros, generally about 24-26 mm in diameter. It was made of good silver of usually 75% or more fineness. The first half of the 15th century was more peaceful than the following half, so recoinage and devaluation was less of a problem.

Early dated coinage was limited to groschens and smaller denomination silver coins until 1436, when double groschens were struck in Cleve (see photo #26), quickly followed by jagers from Groningen and double gros from Liège, both dated 1437. However, a bullion shortage caused numerous mints to close shortly thereafter and larger silver coins were not issued again in any quantity until Saxony began striking very large quantities of good silver horngroschens (see photo #27) in 1465.[16] Sigismund of Tyrol issued the first thick coinage, 1484 half guldiners, impressive large coins

Photo Nos. 26, 27. 1436 Cleve double groschen and 1467 Saxony horngroschen of the Freiberg mint

---

However, by 1355, no less than 480 such gros were being ordered struck from the same "mark," rendering what had been 96% silver coinage less than 20 years earlier devalued to only 20% silver.

[15] Only rarely was devaluation not caused by recoinage, the coinage of East Frisia being the best known example of this. Located at the most northwestern tip of Germany near the Dutch border, this small county modeled the design of its coinage upon that of its highly successful neighbor, the rich trading city of Groningen in the Northern Netherlands. However Groningen in the period of roughly 1470-1490 began a program of severe devaluation. To attract bullion for its mints, East Frisia had to do the same. Due to eventual pressure from Emperor Friedrich III, the succeeding rulers ordered their country's own money to be devalued. As a consequence, a coin that for all intents and purposes appeared to match in size and design the circulating Groningen coinage of the same period was now only worth one-half as much - a stüber was worth a grote, a grote was now only worth a half-grote and so on. Assigning correct denominations in medieval coinage is never an easy task.

[16] This bullion shortage is the subject of an entire chapter in *Spufford Money*, a most highly recommended book.

Photo No. 28. 1484 half guldiner of Tyrol

Photo No. 29. 1486 guldiner of Tyrol

worth one-half a gold gulden, one of the very first dated coins to ever be issued with a realistic portrait (see photo #28). Tyrol even struck from the same dies a few double thickness half-guldiners worth one full gold gulden.

The first thalers, the famous so-called guldiners[17] (see photo # 29), were struck two years later in 1486 at the mint in Hall, also by Sigismund. Fortunately, large quantities of the 1486 guldiners were struck and the coin, highly desirable for both its history and its beauty, regularly appears at auctions several times a year. The striking of larger size silver coins continued to increase so that by the end of the 15th century, thalers, half-thalers and quarter thalers (dickens) were being struck by a number of states, even those as distant as Pommerania.

Photo No. 30. 1436 Cologne goldgulden of the Rhiel mint. The first year Anno Domini dating appeared on a gold coin

Gold coinage was plentiful in the body of Europe in the 14th and 15th centuries; nearly 10% of the known types of early dated coins in this book are gold coins. However, it was not until 1436 that the first dated gold coins were struck (see photo #30). The dating of gold coinage first took place in the Rhineland, where goldguldens were struck to exacting standards under a monetary treaty, the "Rheinischen Münzvertrag" of 1437.[18] An extensive series of these goldguldens were issued by the partners to the treaty, Trier (mint of Coblenz), Cologne (mint of Riehl), the Palatinate (mint of Bacharach) and Mainz (mints of Höchst and Bingen). Each of the dates of 1436, 1437 and 1438 are still collectable today, although not necessarily for each mint.

Photo No. 31. 1487 Holland grand real d'or

The dating of gold coinage was not to prove popular, much the same with that of silver. With the exception of an excessively rare gold gulden dated 1445 from Baar-Mörs, no other early dated gold coinage was struck from 1446 through 1482. In 1482 and 1483 Brabant struck gold florins, but the rest of Europe waited five more years to begin striking dated gold again. In 1487, the first large dated gold coins were struck, a new coinage type issued by Emperor Maximilian, at that time ruling jointly with his father Friedrich III. These aptly-named "grand réals d'or" (the great reals of gold), struck for Maximilian as regent at his Netherlands mints in Holland, Flanders and Gelderland, were testaments to medieval artistry and design (see photo 31). Their issuance was very limited and almost all of the dated gold coinage in the period of 1481- 1490 is very rare to uncollectible.[19]

Photo No. 32. 1500 Frankfurt goldgulden

Beginning 1491, many German states, especially at imperial mints or under imperial grants, began coining goldguldens and all the dates of that decade are collectable today in high grades (see photo #32). Swiss states both struck gold coins from imperial mints and gold coins from dies of large silver coins, creating coins of multiple-gulden weight. Goldguldens of Frankfurt, Nördlingen and Brandenburg-Franconia, as well as ducats of Hamburg, were struck in large quantities and are offered for sale regularly.

Since the circulation of gold in the late Middle Ages was much more limited than that of silver, medieval gold is generally found today in higher grades than silver. Gold was used for international transactions, purchase of lands, ransoms, wars, church donations and so forth. Gold's uses dictated that it was transferred in bulk, and therefore did not

[17] The correct denomination of this coin is a "guldiner," a silver coin worth one goldgulden. The actual name "thaler" was to come later, associated with the large silver coins of Joachimsthal struck in Bohemia in the early 16th century.

[18] The treaty was actually signed in September 1437, but the coins struck by the signatories were first dated in 1436.

[19] Unfortunately, when a new gold coinage such as the grand real d'or was introduced with high standards, it did not last long either figuratively or literally. The pressure to dilute the metal content of the coinage was always too great, with the result that these types of coins were not struck for very long periods. Moreover, their higher gold content made them choice targets for recoinage. The sad result is that very few of these types of magnificent coins survive today.

circulate to any great degree. Gold was also very resistant to deterioration, as nearly all gold was struck to high standards and in several cases (generally associated with the introduction of a new type of coinage), struck in .99+ fineness.

Copper coinage was not a common medium of exchange in the late Middle Ages in the regions that struck early dated coinage. Copper coinage, a mainstay of the late Roman Empire, lost its acceptance in the body of Europe during the Dark Ages and it had not recovered in most cases by the end of the 15th century. Rulers had little interest in coining copper since the profit in doing so was minimal. Thus, smaller denomination coinage either did not exist or was created by halving or quartering existing coinage, a very common occurrence with English coinage in the 11th – 13th centuries (in such cases the long cross on the English silver penny made a useful dividing line between halves – hardly its intended use!). The populace was left to fend on their own to satisfy their needs for low denomination coinage.

Spain, Portugal and Italy struck copper coinage in the 15th century with large degrees of acceptance. However, in the body of Europe, especially in the trading empires of the north centered in the Netherlands where the populace desperately needed access to small denomination coinage, relatively few were struck. The first copper coinage appeared at the end of the 14th century and was struck from that point forward in Flanders, in Brabant and in Liège and by the many feudal lords in the area between Germany and the Netherlands. These small billon coins, struck with a mixture of copper, zinc, lead and with an official silver content of 4% or less, were also known as "black money" ("monnaies noirs" or "deniers noirs").

The metallic composition of small-denomination coinage depended more on a mint's profit-making motive than upon strict allegiance to monetary edicts of the issuing rulers. If the edicts denoting proper quantities of silver had been followed, the cost of coining black money would have resulted in a loss on each coin struck. The issuing mintmasters operated their mints as profit centers and in fact mintmasters were not to be paid until the ruler received his return of costs and profits. Reviews of contemporary mint records determined that at certain mints, "stipulated proportions" of silver required to be used were widely ignored and often both billon pieces and black monies contained no silver at all.[20] Given this background, it is of little surprise that copper was not heavily utilized in the late Middle Ages despite the populace's need for it. It also logically follows that as few copper coins were struck in the regions that dated their coinage, even fewer had dates, and this explains the great rarity of nearly all early dated copper coinage.

The first dated copper coin was the 1481 Brabant four-mites struck by Marie of Burgundy, worth one-sixth of a gros. Officially, it contained 3.6% silver. In practice, it contained an amount from 3.6% downwards. Such pieces can appear blacker or more coppery depending upon the metal content (see photo #8 *supra*). More accessible to collectors today is the 1489 Flanders 2 mites, officially bearing 1.5% silver content (see photo #33). The first dated copper coinage intended to be struck in pure copper was a Brulé ("burnt" or "burnished" in French), struck in 1494 by Liège from its mint in Hasselt (see photo #34).

Photo Nos. 33 (top), 34 (bottom). 1489 Flanders billon double mite and 1494 Liège copper brulé

In Italy, the only other region striking early dated copper coins, an entirely different approach was taken. Instead of issuing copper coinage to be used as small denomination pieces, Italy struck (or cast) magnificent pattern testones, using dies intended for a large thick coins generally of quarter or third-thaler weight. Each of the three pattern testones thus issued featured a classic Renaissance portrait of the ruler, the first of Duke Bentivoglio, Lord of Antegnate in Lombardy and the second two of the Milanese Duke Ludovico Sforza, first with him alone (see photo #35) and second with his late wife Beatrice.[21] The Antegnate piece is very rare, while the Milanese pieces are both of the greatest rarity. All were likely intended as presentation pieces, and the Antegnate coins are often found mounted or with suspension holes.

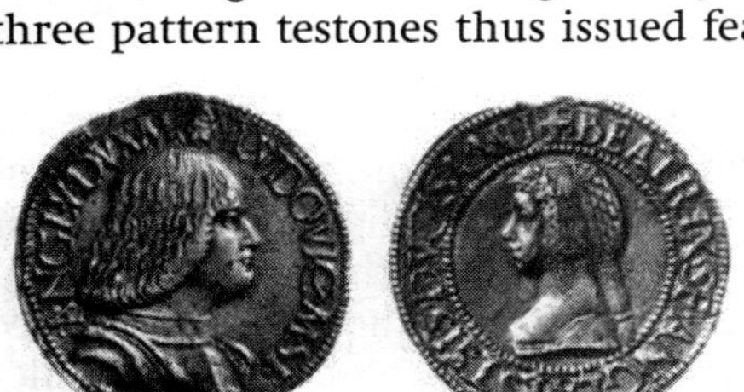

Photo No. 35. 1497 Milan pattern testone

Weights for each of the coins listed in Part II are provided, listed next to the rarity. If the reported specimens are within a 15% range of weight, the standard or most common weight is given. If the reported weights vary beyond this, the range of weights will be provided. The weights of early dated coins almost always vary substantially and do not keep to the strict standards of early modern or modern coinage. There are many reasons for this: the planchets upon which the coins were struck were hand cut, and if not properly weighed at the time of manufacture, would vary in size; most medieval coins are well-worn and the weights reflect varying degrees of wear; chemical reactions from substances in the ground in which coins were buried have leached out both materials and weight; entrepreneurial mint masters cheated in the weights or composition of materials used; clipping has taken its toll of the edges and rims of coins, as

[20] See Spufford's *Monetary Problems* at pp. 42-46. The author previously wrote about this subject in Levinson, "Early Anno Domini Dated Copper Coins," *the Numismatist*, May 1996.

[21] The Antegnate pieces are apparently all cast from the double testone dies, while the Milanese pieces are struck. The author has seen seven Antegnate pieces and owned three – all have been cast.

have striking defects, cracks, etc.

These weight variances were most acute with mid-to-small sized silver coinage, and to the limited extent it was used, copper coinage as well. There exists an exceptionally wide range of variation in the reported weights of silver and copper medieval coins, sometimes as much as 100%. While in early modern or modern coinage improper weight is a reliable indicator of dubious authenticity, in medieval coinage, one has a more difficult time making that conclusion when mid-size or smaller silver coins and copper coins are involved. In contrast, gold had limited circulation and was much more carefully monitored and while there may exist tolerable levels of variation in the weight of gold coinage, it is generally within 10% or less. The same is true of larger silver coinage (dickens, half-guldiners and guldiners/thalers) and silver coinage struck to exacting standards by highly regulated mints such as those in the Burgundian Netherlands.

J. RARITY

This book provides a rarity scale appropriate to the great scarcity of most medieval coins in general, and that of early dated coins in particular. The scale is as follows:[22]

C	=	COMMON (estimated 251 or more pieces collectable)
S	=	SCARCE (estimated 101–250 pieces collectable)
VS	=	VERY SCARCE (estimated 51-100 pieces collectable)
R1	=	RARE (estimated 21-50 pieces collectable)
R2	=	VERY RARE (estimated 11-20 pieces collectable)
R3	=	EXTREMELY RARE (estimated 7-10 pieces collectable)
R4	=	EXCESSIVELY RARE (estimated 4-6 pieces collectable)
R5	=	OF THE GREATEST RARITY (estimated 2-3 pieces collectable)
R6	=	UNIQUE, LIKELY UNIQUE OR UNCOLLECTABLE

First, rarity must be defined in the context of this book's subject. The most "common" early dated coins are double briquets of the Burgundian Netherlands dated between 1474-1481 and several types of Saxony coinage from 1475-1499. The unusually well-preserved mint records of the Burgundian Netherlands reveal a staggering number of double briquets were issued – literally in the millions. While recoinage from later rulers both within and outside the territories took its toll, the numbers extant of the most common of these dates from the larger mints of Brabant and Flanders likely exceed 1000 pieces. The numbers extant of some of the Saxony spitzgroschens dated 1475 and 1477, half schwertgroschens dated 1482 and 1492 and Salzburg batzens dated 1500 likely exceed these numbers as well. However, with but a few exceptions, the numbers decline precipitously from there.[23]

More typical is the other end of the scale. Fully 35% of the coin types and subtypes listed in this book have not been offered for public sale in the last 25 years. Approximately 40% of the known types and subtypes of early dated coins are R4-R6, with six or fewer pieces believed available, with 7% being unique or uncollectable. The discovery of hoards do change numbers extant for a few types, as do collections coming to sale that have been off the market for generations, but the types of greatest rarity have little chance of becoming "merely" rare, much less becoming scarce or common. To determine this rarity rank, auction records have been most heavily utilized, as have records of museum holdings, fixed price lists and anecdotal evidence from the many prominent numismatists and auction companies with whom the author has communicated.

Certain rules have been followed in the assignment of rarity; foremost amongst these is that museum holdings are counted to determine the existence of early dated coin types, but not necessarily their rarity. The reasoning behind this decision is best illustrated by the following examples: the 1478 Swedish ortug with a four digit date is listed in this book as R1. Yet, a hoard of 700+ pieces has been reported to reside in a Swedish museum. If these museum holdings were included, their numbers would change the rarity of this much desired piece to "Common." Yet, all collectors know this coin is certainly not common. Additionally, the first dated coin in this book, the famous 1234 Roskilde denier listed as R6, has seven known specimens, all residing in museums. Including the museum holdings would downgrade its rarity to R3, which makes no sense as this coin has never yet been available to any collector. Accordingly, the absence of a coin from museum holdings is much more useful information than are the number of coins which museums hold, none of which will likely be ever placed on the market for the collector, dealer or auctioneer.

K. PRICES AND VALUES

A loose-leaf supplement has been provided to supply the reader price estimates as of the date of publication. The estimates are listed for the two most common grades, AVF (about very fine) and VF+ (for minor coins) and VF and XF (extremely fine) for gold and silver coins of quarter thaler (dicken) size and larger.[24] As prices are not static, nor are

[22] As explained below, "collectable" for the purposes of this rarity guide, means both currently extant and available to collectors, i.e., not in museum collections.

[23] Cervin's estimates of pieces extant from the Brabant and Flanders mints for 1474-1481 in the 1978 *Frey* range from 7 to 44. It is the author's experience that all of that supplement's estimates of numbers extant are thoroughly unreliable.

[24] These abbreviations represent the grades About Very Fine, Very Fine and Extremely Fine. In German the equivalent grades are Fast Sehr Schön, Sehr Schön and Vorzüglich. In French, Très Beau +, Très Très Beau and Superbe. In Flemish, Bijna Zeer Frai, Zeer Frai and Prachtig.

they reliable in many cases where the coin in question has not surfaced for many years (an all-to-common occurrence in this field of collecting), price estimates printed in a catalog may cause confusion or may be wholly unreliable. In contrast, rarity almost never changes over time with medieval coins. Thus, the rarity information for every numbered type and subtype is printed in the book – this information hopefully will continue to be useful far into the future.

The exceptions to this policy will be the listing in the commentary (below the legend and description) of certain prices deemed to be of exceptional interest to the reader. It will likely interest the reader to know that the most beautiful of all early dated copper coins, the 1497 pattern testone of Milan, portraying Duke Sforza on the obverse and his beloved late wife Beatrice on the reverse (see photo #36), was last sold in 1998 at Leu Numismatik for $22,000, rendering this R5-6 piece out of reach to virtually all collectors. In contrast, the reader may be encouraged to know that the very first collectable early dated coin, the 1374 Aachen groschen (see photo #1 supra), is actually obtainable at "reasonable" prices given its R2 ranking and has been sold at auction several few times in the past decade in the $2500- $4,000 range.

REGION I - Germany

1372

I-1 **Aachen Mint: 1372** **City Jungheit Groschen**

R6 *Weight unknown*

Frey N3, Menadier 92, Krumbach 86.72

KAROLVS:MAG-NVS:INPERAT
Half-length figure of Charlemagne holding imperial orb and sceptre, small shield below

XC:VINCI-XC:REGN-AN:DNI:M-CCC:LXXII-MON-ETA-IVNC-HEIT
Long cross with inner and outer legends

Believed no longer extant.

1373

I-2 **Aachen Mint: 1373** **City Jungheit Groschen**

R6 *Weight unknown*

Frey N4, Frey 1, Menadier 93, Krumbach 86.73

KAROLVS-MAG-NVS:INPERAT
Half-length figure of Charlemagne holding imperial orb and sceptre, small shield below

XC:VINCIT-XC:REGNA-AN:DNI:M:CCC:LXXIII- MON-ETA-IVNC-HEIT
Long cross with inner and outer legends

Possibly no longer extant.

1374

I-3a **Aachen Mint: 1374** **City Jungheit Groschen**

R2 *2.22 g*

Frey N5, Frey 2, Menadier 94, Forschner 61-62, Krumbach 86.74, Coll. Weygand 2318

KAROLVS:MAG-NVS:INPERAT
Half-length figure of Charlemagne holding imperial orb and sceptre, mall shield below

XC:VINCIT-XC:REGNA-AN:DNI:M:CCC:LXXIIII- MON-ETA-IVNC-HEIT
Long cross with inner and outer legends

This coin is generally referred to as the first collectable early dated coin, all others dated prior to it being encased in museum collections or nor longer extant. Examples in the last 10 years have sold from between $2500-$4000.

I-3b **Aachen Mint: 1374** **City Jungheit Groschen**

R5 *2.22 g*

Frey —, Menadier 94e, Forschner 63

same as preceding, but with error date of "MCG:LXXIIII

1375

I-4a **Aachen Mint: 1375** **City Jungheit Groschen**

R2 *2.30 g*

Frey N6, Frey 3, Menadier 95, Forschner 64-66, Krumbach 86.75, Saurma 2802, Coll. Weygand 2319

KAROLVS:MAG-NVS:INPERAT
Half-length figure of Charlemagne holding imperial orb and sceptre, small shield below

XP:VINC-XP:REGN-ANODNI-M CCC:LXXV-MON-ETA-IVNC-HEIT
Long cross with inner and outer legends

I-4b **Aachen Mint: 1375** **City Jungheit Groschen**

R5 *2.30 g*

Frey —, Forschner 65

Same as preceding, but with error date "XCCCLXXV"

I-4c **Aachen Mint: 1375** **City Jungheit Groschen**

R5 *2.30 g*

Frey —, Menadier 95d

Same as preceding, but with error date "MCCC:XXV"

1402

I-5a **Aachen Mint: 1402** **City Aachen Groschen**

R2 *2.32-2.55 g*

Frey N12, Frey 8, Menadier 98, Forschner 67-68, Krumbach 88.02

SCS:KAROL:MA-GNVS:IPERAT'
Facing 3/4 figure of Charlemagne holding imperial orb and sceptre, shield in foreground

ANNO:DOMINI:MILLESIMO:CCCC:SECVNDO-MON-ETA-VRB'-AQVN
Middle-length cross dividing inner legend

I-5b **Aachen Mint: 1402** **City Aachen Groschen**

R5-6

Unpublished?

Same as preceding, but with different vestments and date: "M:CCCC:SECVDO"

An unpublished transitional coin, using "M" instead of "Millesimo" for the date "1000". Specimens known in both a private collection and in the State History Museum of Dresden.

I-5c **Aachen Mint: 1402** **City Aachen Groschen**

R5 *2.40 g*

Unpublished?

Same as above, but with error date "M:CCC:SECVNDO"

1403

I-6 **Aachen Mint: 1403** **City Aachen Groschen**

R *1.73-2.32 g*

Frey N13, Frey 9, Menadier 99, Forschner 69-71, Krumbach 88.03, Saurma 2803, Coll. Weygand 2320

SCS:KAROL:MA-GNVS:IPERAT'

Facing 3/4 figure of Charlemagne holding imperial orb and sceptre, shield in foreground

ANNO:DOMINI:MILLESIMO:CCCC:TERCIO-MON-ETA-VRB'AQVN"

Middle-length cross dividing inner legend

1404

I-7 **Aachen Mint: 1404** **City Aachen Groschen**

R *2.00-2.38 g*

Frey N14, Frey 10, Menadier 100, Forschner 72-75, Krumbach 88.04, Saurma 2804, Coll. Weygand 2321

SCS:KAROL:MA-GNVS:IPERAT'

Facing 3/4 figure of Charlemagne holding imperial orb and sceptre, shield in foreground

ANNO:DOMINI:MILLESIMO:CCCC:QVARTO-MON-ETA-VRB'AQVN

Middle-length cross dividing inner legend

1405

I-8 **Aachen Mint: 1405** **City Aachen Groschen**

R2 *1.86-2.12 g*

Frey N15, Frey 11, Menadier 101, Forschner 76-77, Krumbach 88.05, Saurma 2805, Coll. Weygand 2321

SCS:KAROL:MA-GNVS:IMPERAT

Facing 3/4 figure of Charlemagne holding imperial orb and sceptre, shield in foreground

ANNO:DOMINI:MILLESIMO:CCCC:QVINTO-MON-ETA-VRB'-AQVN

Middle-length cross dividing inner legend

1410

I-9 **Aachen Mint: 1410** **City Aachen Groschen**

R5 *1.90 g*

Frey N18, Frey 13, Menadier 113, Forschner 80, Krumbach 90.10

SCS:KAROL:MA-G':IPERATO'

Half-length figure of Charlemagne holding imperial orb and cathedral, shield in foreground

ANNO:DOMINI:MILLESIMO:CCCC:DEC-MONETA:VRB:AQVES

Short cross not interrupting legend

1411

I-10 **Aachen Mint: 1411** **City Aachen Groschen**

VS *1.64-1.92 g*

Frey N19, Frey 14, Menadier 112, Forschner 81-84, Krumbach 90.11, Saurma 2807, Coll. Weygand 2322

SCS:KAROL:MA-G:IPERATO'
Half-length figure of Charlemagne holding imperial orb and cathedral, shield in foreground

ANNO:DOMINI:MILLESIMO:CCCC:VND- MONETA:VRB':AQVS'
Short cross not interrupting legend

Forschner 82 reports a specimen with an extra "C" in the date, but it notes that a colon engraved on the first "C" has been used to correct the date.

1412

I-11 **Aachen Mint: 1412** **City Aachen Groschen**

R *1.32-1.85 g*

Frey N20, Frey 15, Menadier 114, Forschner 85-88, Krumbach 90.12, Saurma 2808, Coll. Weygand 2322

SCS:KAROL:MA-G:IPERATO'
Half-length figure of Charlemagne holding imperial orb and cathedral, shield in foreground

ANNO:DOMINI:MILLESIMO:CCCC:XII- MONETA:VRB:AQVES'
Short cross not interrupting legend

1413

I-12 **Aachen Mint: 1413** **City Aachen Groschen**

R5 *1.85 g*

Frey N21, Menadier 114b, Forschner 89, Krumbach 90.13

SCS:KAROL:MA-G:IPERATO'
Half-length figure of Charlemagne holding imperial orb and cathedral, shield in foreground

ANNO:DOMINI:MILLESIMO:CCCC:XIII- MONETA:VRB:AQVES'
Short cross not interrupting legend

1418

I-13 **Aachen Mint: 1418** **City Aachen Groschen**

R *1.94 g*

Frey N22, Frey 16, Menadier 115, Forschner 90-91, Krumbach 90.18

SCS:KAROLMA-G:IPERATO'
Half-length figure of Charlemagne holding imperial orb and cathedral, shield in foreground

ANNO:DOMIN:MILLESIMO:CCCC:XVIII- MONETA:VRB:AQVS'
Short cross not interrupting legend

1419

I-14 **Aachen Mint: 1419** **City Aachen Groschen**

C-S *1.71-1.97 g*

Frey N23, Frey 17, Menadier 116, Forschner 92-99, Krumbach 90.19, Coll. Weygand 2323

SCS:KAROL:MA-G:IPERATO'
Half-length figure of Charlemagne holding imperial orb and cathedral, shield in foreground

ANNO:DOMINI:MILESIMO:CCCC:XIX- MONETA:VRB:AQVS'
Short cross not interrupting legend

1420

I-15 **Aachen Mint: 1420** **City Aachen Groschen**

S *1.84 g*

Frey N24, Frey 18, Menadier 117, Forschner 100, Krumbach 90.20, Saurma 2810, Coll. Weygand 2323

SCS:KAROL:MA-G:IPERATO'
Half-length figure of Charlemagne holding imperial orb and cathedral, shield in foreground

ANNO:DOMINI:MILESIMO:CCCC:XX- MONETA:VRB':AQVS'
Short cross not interrupting legend

1421

I-16 **Aachen Mint: 1421** **City Aachen Groschen**

S *1.98 g*

Frey N25, Frey 19, Menadier 118, Forschner 101, Krumbach 90.21, Saurma 2811, Coll. Weygand 2324

SCS:KAROL:MA-G:IPERATO'
Half-length figure of Charlemagne holding imperial orb and cathedral, shield in foreground

ANNO:DOMINI:MILESIMO:CCCC:XXI-MONETA:VRB':AQVS'
Short cross not interrupting legend

1422

I-17 Aachen City
Mint: Aachen
1422 Groschen

R 1.79 g

Frey N26, Frey 20, Menadier 119, Forschner 102, Krumbach 90.22, Saurma 2812, Coll. Weygand 2324

SCS:KAROL:MA-G:IPERATO'
Half-length figure of Charlemagne holding imperial orb and cathedral, shield in foreground

ANNO:DOMINI:MILESIMO:CCCC:XXII-MONETA:VRB':AQVS'
Short cross not interrupting legend

1425

I-18 Aachen City
Mint: Aachen
1425 Groschen

R6 Weight unknown

Frey —, Menadier 120, Krumbach 90.25 Supp.

Same as preceding, but last digits of date "XXV"

While Krumbach originally disputed the existence of this piece, he now reliably reports one in a private collection. The other dates reported in Menadier or Frey which are not listed herein -1406, 1409 and 1430 - have no reliable listings. These dates are misreported or unsubstantiated. The author has twice seen the 1430 date listed for sale in major auction catalogues, but on closer inspection the date has proved to be 1419 instead.

I-19 Cologne Archbishopric
Mint: Riehl
Dietrich (Theodore) II of Mörs, 1414-1463
1425 Groschen

R4 2.03 g

Frey 22, 24A, Noss 330A, Cappe 1101, Saurma 2707, Coll. Weygand 1625

THEO-DIC'A-RCPI':COLO
Long cross with four shields in angles of cross
ANO:DNI:M:CCCC:XXV
Christ on gothic throne with shield below

I-20 Mainz Archbishopric
Mint: Bingen
Konrad III of Dhaun, 1419-1434
1425 Groschen

R6 1.95 g

Frey 23, Geldwesen und Münzpragung in Bingen, S. 18, Anm 38, Und Taf. B12

CONR-ADI:A-RCPI-MAG
Long cross with four shields in angles of cross
A'NO DNI'-:CCCC:XXV
Christ on gothic throne with shield below

Likely only two specimens known, one of which is in a private collection from the sale of the Cervin collection in June 2003.

I-21 Palatinate County and Elector
Mint: Bacharach
Ludwig III, 1410-1436
1425 Groschen

R6 2.14 g

Frey 24, Coll. Noss 92

LVD-W-IC':C'P-R'DV-X:BA
Long cross with four shields in angles of cross

ANO:DNI':M:CCCC:XXV
Christ on gothic throne with shield below

1426

I-22 Cologne Archbishopric
Mint: Riehl
Dietrich (Theodore) II of Mörs, 1414-1463
1426 Groschen

R5 2.13 g

Frey 25, Noss 331, Cappe 1102

A'NO:DNI:M:CCCC:XXVI
Long cross with four shields in angles of cross

THEO-DIC'A-RCPI-COLO
Christ on gothic throne with small shield of Cologne below

1429

I-23 **Aachen** **City**
Mint: **Aachen**
1429 **Groschen**
R5 *1.62 g*
Frey 26A, Menadier 121, Krumbach 90.29

SCS:KAROL:MA-G:INPERAT'
Half-length figure of Charlemagne holding imperial orb and cathedral, shield in foreground

ANNO:DOMINI:MILESIMO:CCCC:XXIX-MONETA:VRBS:AQVES'
Short cross not interrupting legend

I-24 **Göttingen** **City**
Mint: **Göttingen**
1429 **Körtling**
VS *1.40 g*
Frey 26, Schrock 8-9, Saurma 3906

MONE:NOVA:GOTTINGE
Large "G" in either octofoil or 12 foil

ANO:DNI:M:CCCC:XXIX
Large "G" over short cross

1431

I-25 **Mainz** **Archbishopric**
Mint: **Bingen**
Konrad III of Dhaun, 1419-1434
1431 **Groschen**
R5 *Weight unknown*
Frey 27, Riechmann 1789, Saurma 2488

CONRA:AREP:MA
Standing archbishop holding staff with shields of Mainz and family shield at sides

ANNO:DMI:M:CCCC:XXXI- MONETA:BINGE
Short cross with inner and outer legends

1432

I-26 **Cologne** **Archbishopric**
Mint: **Bonn**
Dietrich (Theodore) II of Mörs, 1414-1463
1432 **Groschen**
R5 *2.71 g*
Frey 28, Noss 348, Cappe 1103-04

TH-EODI'-ARC-PI'CO'
Standing archbishop holding staff with two small shields at sides

ANNO:DNI:M:CCCC:XXXII:ET:C'- MONETA:BVNE'
Short cross with inner and outer legends

Also known as a double weisspfennig.

1436

I-27 **Cleve** **Duchy**
Mint: **Cleve**
Adolf II, 1394-1448
1436 **Double Groschen**
R-R2 *3.00 g*
Frey 30, Noss 121, Coll. Weygand 748

ADOLPH:DVX:CLIVEN:Z:CO:DE:MA':KA
Arms of Cleve and the Mark occupying entire field

MONETA:NOV:CLIVENS:ANO:DNI:XXXVI
Long cross within field with W-K-E-C in angles of cross

This is the first Anno Domini dated coin struck with a partial date.

I-28a **Cologne** **Archbishopric**
Mint: **Riehl**
Dietrich (Theodore) II of Mörs, 1414-1463
1436 **Goldgulden**
R3 *3.47 g*
Frey —, Felke 1210, Noss 349, Cappe 1073, FR. 797, De Mey d'or 677

THEO'-ARCP'-COLO'-MO':RI'
Shields of Cologne-Mörs on long cross

ANNO:DNI':M':CCCC:XXXVI
Shields of Mainz, Trier and Palatinate in a trefoil arrangement, two on top and one on top

---

I-28b **Cologne** **Archbishopric**
Mint: **Riehl**
Dietrich (Theodore) II of Mörs, 1414-1463
1436 **Goldgulden**
R5 *3.47 g*
Frey —, Felke 1211

Same as preceding, but with two shields of the trefoil at bottom and one on top

All Rheinland goldguldens with two shields on the bottom and one on top are excessively rare.

I-29 Mainz Archbishopric
Mint: Bingen
Dietrich (Theodore) I of Erbach, 1434-1455
1436 Goldgulden
R6 *3.47 g*
Frey —, FR. 1625, Schelegel 52

THEO'-AREP'-MAGV'-MO'PI'
Shields of Mainz-Erbach on long cross

ANNO:DNI:M:CCCC:XXXVI
Shields of Trier, Cologne and Palatinate in a trefoil arrangement

Unique example found in Frankfurt History Museum.

I-30 Mainz Archbishopric
Mint: Höchst
Dietrich (Theodore) I of Erbach, 1434-1455
1436 Goldgulden
R2 *3.47 g*
Frey 31, Felke 1208-09, FR. 1625, De Mey d'Or 1502, Cappe 604, Schelegel 51, Walther 141

THEO'-AREP-MAGV'-MO':HO'
Shields of Mainz-Erbach on long cross

ANNO:DNI:M:CCCC:XXXVI
Shields of Trier, Cologne and Palatinate in a trefoil arrangement, two on top and one on bottom

---

I-31 Palatinate County and Elector
Mint: Bacharach
Ludwig IV, 1436-1449
1436 Goldgulden
R2 *3.47 g*
Frey 33, Felke 1212, FR 1977, De Mey d'Or 1710

LVDV'-C':P':R'-DVX:B-MO':B'
Shields of Palatinate-Bavaria on long cross

A'NO:DNI':M':CCCC:XXXVI
Shields of Mainz, Trier and Cologne in a trefoil arrangement

I-32a Trier Archbishopric
Mint: Coblenz
Raban of Helmstedt, 1430-1439
1436 Goldgulden
R3 *3.47 g*
Frey 32, Felke 1214-15, Noss 455-57, FR. 3445, De Mey d'Or 2134-34A, Saurma 2616, Coll. Weygand 1892

RABA'-ARCP'-TRE':M-ON':CO'
Shield of Trier-Helmstadt on long cross

ANNO:DNI':M':CCCC:XXXVI
Shields of Mainz, Cologne and Palatinate in a trefoil arrangement, two shields on top and one on bottom

---

I-32b Trier Archbishopric
Mint: Coblenz
Raban of Helmstedt, 1430-1439
1436 Goldgulden
R5 *3.47 g*
Frey —, Felke 1213, 1216

Same as preceding, but with two shields of the trefoil at bottom and one on top

1437

I-33 Cologne Archbishopric
Mint: Riehl
Dietrich (Theodore) II of Mörs, 1414-1463
1437 Goldgulden
VS *3.47 g*
Frey 36, Felke 1224-30, Noss 351-53, Cappe 1071, FR. 797, De Mey d'Or 677, Coll. Weygand 1647

THEO'-ARCP'-COLO'-MO:RI'
Shields of Cologne-Mörs on long cross

A'NO:DNI':M:CCCC:XXXVII
Shields of Trier, Palatinate and Mainz in a trefoil arrangment

---

I-34 Cologne Archbishopric
Mint: Riehl
Dietrich (Theodore) II of Mörs, 1414-1463
1437 Groschen or Weisspfennig
R *1.90 g*
Frey 38, Noss 354, Saurma 2713

THEOD'-ARCPI'-COLON'
Shields of Mainz, Trier and Palatinate in a trefoil arrangement

A':DN':M':CC-CC:XXXVII
St. Peter under canopy, holding staff in right hand and key in left hand

---

I-35 Lübeck City
Mint: Lübeck
1437 Goldgulden
R6 3.47 g
Frey —, Krusy L4, 7

Countermark of double-headed eagle in tiny round shield on a host 1437 Cologne goldgulden of the Riehl mint, No. I-33

This is the earliest dated countermark.

I-36a Mainz Archbishopric
Mint: Bingen
Dietrich (Theodore) I of Erbach, 1434-1455
1437 Goldgulden
R3 3.47 g
Frey —, Felke 1218-19, FR. 1625, Pr. Alexander 158, Saurma 2492

THEO'-AREP'-MAGV'-MO' PI
Shields of Mainz-Erbach on long cross

A'NO:DNI':M':CCCCXXXVII
Shields of Mainz, Cologne and Palatinate-Bavaria in a trefoil arrangement, two on top and one on bottom

---

I-36b Mainz Archbishopric
Mint: Bingen
Dietrich (Theodore) I of Erbach, 1434-1455
1437 Goldgulden
R5 3.47 g
Frey —, Felke 1217

Same as preceding, but with two shields of the trefoil at bottom and one on top

---

I-37 Mainz Archbishopric
Mint: Bingen
Dietrich (Theodore) I of Erbach, 1434-1455
1437 Groschen or Weisspfennig
R3 1.90 g
Frey 44, Saurma 2495

THEOD-ARCPI'-MAGVN'
Shields of Mainz-Erbach in center of shields of Mainz, Cologne and Palatinate-Bavaria in a trefoil arrangement

A'DN':MCC-CC:XXXVII
St. Peter under canopy, holding staff in right hand and key in left hand

---

I-38a Mainz Archbishopric
Mint: Höchst
Dietrich (Theodore) I of Erbach, 1434-1455
1437 Goldgulden
R 3.47 g
Frey 39, Felke 1220-21, 1223, FR. 1625, De Mey d'Or 1502, Schelegel 53, Pr. Alexander 157-58

THEO-AREP-MAGV-MO'HO
Shields of Mainz-Erbach on long cross

ANO:DNI:M:CCCC:XXXVII
Shields of Trier, Cologne and Palatinate in a trefoil arrangement.

I-38b Mainz Archbishopric
Mint: Höchst
Dietrich (Theodore) I of Erbach, 1434-1455
1437 Goldgulden
R5 3.47 g
Frey —, Felke 1222

Same as preceding, but with two shields of the trefoil at bottom and one on top

---

I-39 Palatinate County and Elector
Mint: Bacharach
Ludwig IV, 1436-1449
1437 Goldgulden
VS 3.47 g
Frey 34, Felke 1235-36, Coll. Noss 132, Coll. Mem. 2148, FR. 1977, De Mey d'Or 1710

LVDV'-C':P':R'-DVX:B'-MO':B'
Shields of Palatinate-Bavaria on long cross

A'NO:DNIM':CCCC:XXXVII
Shields of Mainz, Trier and Cologne in a trefoil arrangement

I-40 Palatinate County and Elector
Mint: Bacharach
Ludwig IV, 1436-1449
1437 Groschen or Weisspfennig
R 1.90 g
Frey 35, Coll. Noss 141, Coll. Mem. 2149

MONE'-NOVA-BACH
Shields of Palatinate-Bavaria in center of shields of Mainz, Trier and Cologne in a trefoil arrangement

A':DN':M':CC-CC:XXXVII
St. Peter under canopy, holding staff in right hand and key in left hand

---

I-41 Trier Archbishopric
Mint: Coblenz
Raban of Helmstedt, 1430-1439
1437 Goldgulden
R2 *3.47 g*
Frey 41, Felke 1231-34, Noss 459-61, FR. 3445, De Mey d'Or 2134-34A

RABA-ARCP'-TREV'-MO':CO'
Shield of Trier-Helmstadt on long cross

A'NO:DNI':M:CCCC:XXXVII
Shields of Mainz, Cologne and Palatinate in a trefoil arrangement

---

I-42 Trier Archbishopric
Mint: Coblenz
Raban of Helmstedt, 1430-1439
1437 Groschen or Weisspfennig
R *2.00 g*
Frey 42, Noss 462, Saurma 2619, Coll. Weygand 1887

RABA';-ARCP':TREVE'
Shield of Trier-Helmstadt in center of shields of Cologne, Mainz and Palatinate in a trefoil arrangement

A':DN':M:CC-CC:XXXVII
St. Peter under canopy, holding staff in right hand and key in left hand

1438

I-43 Cologne Archbishopric
Mint: Riehl
Dietrich (Theodore) II of Mörs, 1414-1463
1438 Goldgulden
VS *3.47 g*
Frey 48, Felke 1237-44, Noss 355-59, Cappe 1072, FR. 797, De Mey d'Or 677, Coll. Weygand 1648

THEO'-ARCP'-COLO'-MO':RI'
Shields of Cologne-Mörs on long cross

A'NO:DNI':M':CCCC:XXXVIII
Shields of Trier, Palatinate and Mainz in a trefoil arrangment

---

I-44 Cologne Archbishopric
Mint: Riehl
Dietrich (Theodore) II of Mörs, 1414-1463
1438 Groschen
VS *1.90 g*
Frey 49, Noss 360, Saurma 2714, Coll. Weygand 1626

THEOD'-ARCPI'-COLON'
Shields of Cologne-Mörs in center of shields of Mainz, Trier and Palatinate in a trefoil arrangement

A':D':M':CC-CC:XXXVIII
St. Peter under canopy, holding staff in right hand and key in left hand

---

I-45 Halberstadt City
Mint: Halberstadt
1438 Groschen or Weisspfennig
R5 *1.90 g*
Frey —, Krusy H1, 9b

Countermark of small crowned lowercase "h" on a host 1438 Cologne groschen of the Riehl mint. See No. I-44.

I-46 Hamburg City
Mint: Hamburg
1438 Goldgulden
R6 *3.47 g*
Frey —, Krusy H2, 6

Countermark of nesselblatt (thistle flower) in triangular shield on a host 1438 Palatinate goldgulden of the Bacharach mint. See I-51 below.

I-47 Limburg County
Mint: Broich
Dietrich (Theodore) I, 1410-1439
1438 Turnosgroschen
R6 *1.89 g*
Frey —, Berghaus-Spiegel 59

TEODRICVS:DE-LIMBORCH
Half-length figure of Charlemagne holding imperial orb and

cathedral, shield in foreground

ANNO:MILLESIMO:CCCC:*X*X*X*V°III-MONETA:NOVA:DE:BR
Short cross not interrupting legend

This coin copies the Aachen groschens of the preceding decades.

I-48 Mainz Archbishopric
Mint: Bingen
Dietrich (Theodore) I of Erbach, 1434-1455
1438 Goldgulden
R6 *3.47 g*
Frey 47A, FR. 1625, Schlegel p. 92

THEO'-AREP'-MAGV'-MO'BI'
Shields of Mainz-Erbach on long cross

A'NO*DNI*M*CCCC*XXXVIII
Shields of Trier, Cologne and Palatinate-Bavaria in a trefoil arrangement

Leu lists this piece as likely unique.

I-49 Mainz Archbishopric
Mint: Bingen
Dietrich (Theodore) I of Erbach, 1434-1455
1438 Groschen or Weisspfennig
R3 *2.00 g*
Frey —, Pr. Alexander 161

THEOD-ARCPI'-MAGVN'
Shields of Mainz-Erbach in center of shields of Mainz, Cologne and Palatinate-Bavaria in trefoil arrangement

A'DM'MCC-*CCXXXVIII
St. Peter under canopy, holding staff in right hand, key in left hand

A 1438 Mainz thaler is a Becker forgery.

I-50 Mainz Archbishopric
Mint: Höchst
Dietrich (Theodore) I of Erbach, 1434-1455
1438 Goldgulden
R2 *3.47 g*
Frey 47, Felke 1249-50, FR. 1625, Pr. Alexander 159, Schelegel 54, Walther 143

THEO'-AREP'-MAGV'-MO'HO'
Shields of Mainz-Erbach on long cross

ANO:DNI':M:CCCC:XXXVIII
Shields of Trier, Cologne and Palatinate-Bavaria in a trefoil arrangement

---

I-51 Palatinate County and Elector
Mint: Bacharach
Ludwig IV, 1436-1449
1438 Goldgulden
S *3.47 g*
Frey 50, Felke 1251-54, Coll. Noss 135, Coll. Mem. 2150, FR. 1977, De Mey d'Or 1710, Saurma 2424

LVDV'-C':P':R'-DVX:B'-MO':B'
Shields of Palatinate-Bavaria on long cross

A'NO:DNI':M':CCCC:XXXVIII
Shields of Mainz, Trier and Cologne in a trefoil arrangement

I-52a Palatinate County and Elector
Mint: Bacharach
Ludwig IV, 1436-1449
1438 Groschen or Weisspfennig
VS *2.00 g*
Frey 51, Coll. Noss 142, Coll. Mem. 2151, Saurma 2426

LVDV'-C4:P':RE'-DVX:B'
Shields of Palatinate-Bavaria in center of shields of Mainz, Trier and Cologne in a trefoil arrangement

A':DN':M':CC-CC:XXXVIII
St. Peter under canopy, holding staff in right hand and key in left hand

---

I-52b Palatinate County and Elector
Mint: Bacharach
Ludwig IV, 1436-1449
1438 Groschen or Weisspfennig
R4-5 *1.96 g*
Unpublished?

MONE-NOVA-BACH
Shields of Palatinate-Bavaria in center of shields of Mainz, Trier and Cologne in a trefoil arrangement

A':DN':M':CC-CC:XXXVIII
St. Peter under canopy, holding staff in right hand and key in left hand

I-53 **Trier** **Archbishopric**
Mint: **Coblenz**
Raban of Helmstedt, 1430-1439
1438 **Goldgulden**
R2 *3.47 g*
Frey 45, Felke 1245-48, Noss 463-64, FR. 3445, De Mey d'Or 2134-34A, Coll. Weygand 1893

RABA'-ARCP'-TREV'-MO':CO'
Shield of Trier-Helmstadt on long cross

A'NO:DNI':M':CCCC:XXXVIII
Shields of Mainz, Cologne and Palatinate in a trefoil arrangement

---

I-54 **Trier** **Archbishopric**
Mint: **Coblenz**
Raban of Helmstedt, 1430-1439
1438 **Groschen or Weisspfennig**
VS *2.00 g*
Frey 46, Noss 465, Saurma 2620, Coll. Weygand 1888

RABA'-ARCP'-TREVE'
Shield of Trier-Helmstadt in center of shields of Cologne, Mainz and Palatinate in a trefoil arrangement

A':DN':M':CC-CC:XXXVIII
St. Peter under canopy, holding staff in right hand and key in left hand

1441

I-55 **Cleve** **Duchy**
Mint: **Cleve**
Adolf II, 1394-1448
1441 **Double Blanken**
R6 *4.31 g*
Frey 55A, Noss 125

ADOLPH':DVX:CLIVEN':Z:COMES:MR
Helmeted diagonal shields of Cleve and the Mark

MONETA:NOVA:CLIVENS':A'NO:DNI:XLI
Cross with fleur-de-lys in angles of cross

The single known specimen is in the State Museum of Berlin

I-56 **Cleve** **Duchy**
Mint: **Cleve**
Adolf II, 1394-1448
1441 **Blanken**
R4-5 *2.28-2.50 g*
Frey 55B, Noss 126

ADOLPH':DVX:CLIVEN':COMES:MR'
Helmeted diagonal shields of Cleve and the Mark

MONETA:NOVA:CLIVEN':A'NO:DNI:XLI
Cross with fleur-de-lys in angles of cross

I-57 **Cleve** **Duchy**
Mint: **Cleve**
Adolf II, 1394-1448
1441 **Half Blanken**
R4-5 *1.67 g*
Frey 55C, Noss 128

ADOLP':DVX:CLIVEN':Z:COME':MR
Helmeted diagonal shields of Cleve and the Mark

MONETA:NOVA:CLIVEN':A':XLI
Cross with fleur-de-lys in angles of cross

I-58 **Cleve** **Duchy**
Mint: **Huissen**
Adolf II, 1394-1448
1441 **Blanken**
R5 *2.08 g*
Frey —, Noss 127

ADOLPH':DVX:CLIVEN':Z:COMES-MR'
Helmeted diagonal shields of Cleve and the Mark

MONETA:NOVA:HVESSEN'A'NO:DNI:XLI
Cross with fleur-de-lys in angles of cross

I-59 **Cleve** **Duchy**
Mint: **Huissen**
Adolf II, 1394-1448
1441 **Half Blanken**
R5 *1.52 g*
Frey —, Noss 129

ADOLP':DVX:CLIVEN':Z:COME':MR'
Helmeted diagonal shields of Cleve and the Mark

MONETA:NOVA:HVESSEN':A':XLI
Cross with fleur-de-lys in angles of cross

I-60 **Jülich-Berg** **Duchy**
Mint: **Schoonvorst**
Gerhard, 1437-1475
1441 **Groschen**

R4 *1.75 g*
Frey 55, Lucas 16, Noss 145, Menadier 20, Van der Chijs 29.13, Coll. Weygand 257

GERARD:DVX:IVL:Z:MON:Z:CO:RAB
Shields of Jülich-Berg and Ravensberger in trefoil

ANNO:DOMINI:MILESIMO:CCCCXLI- MONETA:NOVA:SCOENV
Short cross with inner and outer legend

Lucas erroneously lists this piece as a demi gros.

1442

I-61 **Göttingen City**
Mint: Göttingen
1442 Körtling
R6 *Weight unknown*
Frey —, Schrock 10

MONE:NOVA:GOTTIN
Large "G" in octofoil

ANO:DNI:M:CCCC:XXXXII
Large "G" over short cross

Sole known example in the Lower Saxony Coin Cabinet at the Deutsches Bank in Hannover.

I-62 **Jülich-Berg Duchy**
Mint: Schoonvorst
Gerhard, 1437-1475
1442 Groschen
R5 *1.80 g*
Frey 55D, Lucas 16a, Noss 145

GERARD:DVX:IVL:Z:MON:Z:CO:RAB
Shields of Jülich-Berg and Ravensberger in trefoil

ANNO:DOMINI:MILESIMO:CCCCXLII- MONETA:NOVA:
SCOENVO
Short cross with inner and outer legends

1443

I-63 **Cologne Archbishopric**
Mint: Riehl
Dietrich (Theodore) II of Mörs, 1414-1463
1443 Groschen or Weisspfennig
R2 *1.90 g*
Frey 59, Noss 377, Cappe 1113

THEOD'-ARCPI'-COLON'
Shields of Cologne-Mörs in center of shields of Mainz, Trier and Palatinate in a trefoil arrangement

A'NO:DM:C-CCCC:XLIII
St. Peter under canopy, holding staff in right hand and key in left hand

Well-struck examples of this date are extremely rare.

I-64 **Jülich-Berg Duchy**
Mint: Schoonvorst
Gerhard, 1437-1475
1443 Groschen
R4 *1.75 g*
Frey 56, Lucas 16b, Noss 146, Van der Chijs 29.13

GERARD:DVX:IVL:Z:MON:Z:CO:RAB
Shields of Jülich-Berg and Ravensberger in trefoil

ANNO:DOMINI:MILESIMO:CCCC:
XLIII- MONETA:NOVA:SCOENV
Short cross with inner and outer legends

I-65 **Mainz Archbishopric**
Mint: Bingen
Dietrich (Theodore) I of Erbach, 1434-1455
1443 Groschen or Weisspfennig
R2 *1.90 g*
Frey 57, Pr. Alexander 162, Cappe 637, Coll. Walther 133

MONE-NOVA-BING'
Shields of Mainz-Erbach in center of shields of Mainz, Cologne and Palatinate-Bavaria in a trefoil arrangement

A'NO:D':M'-CCCC:XLIII
St. Peter under canopy, holding staff in right hand and key in left hand

Well-struck examples of this date, with clear separation of the digits of the date are excessively rare.

I-66 **Palatinate County and Elector**
Mint: Bacharach
Ludwig IV, 1436-1449
1443 Groschen or Weisspfennig
R2 *2.00 g*
Frey 58, Coll. Noss 143

MONE*-*NOVA*-*BACH'
Shields of Palatinate-Bavaria in center of shields of Mainz, Trier and Cologne in a trefoil arrangement

A'*DN'*M*C-CCC*XLIII

St. Peter under canopy, holding staff in right hand and key in left hand

1444

I-67 Brunswick City
Mint: Brunswick
1444 Groschen or Weisspfennig
R4 2.00 g
Frey —, Coll. Noss 145, Krusy B 5,7g

Countermark of lionshield on a host 1444 Palatinate groschen of the Bacharach mint. See I-73 below.

I-68 Brunswick City
Mint: Brunswick
1444 Groschen or Weisspfennig
R4 2.00 g
Frey —, Krusy B5, 8b

Countermark of lionshield on a host 1444 Trier groschen of the Coblenz mint. See I-74 below.

This countermark differs from the other Brunswick countermarks on early dated coins by the presence of the lion's tongue.

I-69a Cologne Archbishopric
Mint: Riehl
Dietrich (Theodore) II of Mörs, 1414-1463
1444 Groschen or Weisspfennig
C 1.90 g
Frey 64, Noss 378, Cappe 1106, Saurma 2715, Coll. Weygand 1656

THEOD'-ARCPI'-COLON'
Shields of Cologne-Mörs in center of shields of Mainz, Trier and Palatinate in a trefoil arrangement

A'NO:D':M:C-CCC:XLIIII
St. Peter under canopy, holding staff in right hand and key in left hand

---

I-69b Cologne Archbishopric
Mint: Riehl
Dietrich (Theodore) II of Mörs, 1414-1463
1444 Groschen or Weisspfennig
R2 1.90 g
Frey 61, Noss 379

MONE'-NOVA-RILE'
Shields of Cologne-Mörs in center of shields of Mainz, Trier and Palatinate in a trefoil arrangement

A'NO:D':M:C-CCC:XLIIII
St. Peter under canopy, holding staff in right hand and key in left hand

---

I-70 Halberstadt City
Mint: Halberstadt
1444 Groschen or Weisspfennig
R4 2.00 g
Frey —, Krusy H1, 9f

Countermark of small crowned lowercase "h" on a host 1444 Trier groschen of the Coblenz mint. See I-74 below.

I-71 Jülich-Berg Duchy
Mint: Schoonvorst
Gerhard, 1437-1475
1444 Groschen
R2 1.80 g
Frey 66, Lucas 16c, Noss 147, Menadier 22, Saurma 2981, Coll. Weygand 258

GERARD:DVX:IVL:Z:MON:Z:CO:RAB
Shields of Jülich-Berg and Ravensberger in trefoil

ANNO:DOMINI:MILESIMO:CCCC:
XLIIII- MONETA:NOVA:SCOENVO
Short cross with inner and outer legends

I-72 Mainz Archbishopric
Mint: Bingen
Dietrich (Theodore) I of Erbach, 1434-1455
1444 Groschen or Weisspfennig
R 1.90 g
Frey 63, Cappe 638, Walther 134

MONE-NOVA-BING'
Shields of Mainz-Erbach in center of shields of Mainz, Cologne and Palatinate-Bavaria in a trefoil arrangement

A'NO:D':M-CCCC:XLIIII
St. Peter under canopy, holding staff in right hand and key in left hand

I-73 Palatinate County and Elector
Mint: Bacharach
Ludwig IV, 1436-1449
1444 Groschen or Weisspfennig
C 2.00 g
Frey 62, Coll. Noss 144, Coll. Mem. 2152, Saurma 2427

MONE-NOVA-BACH'
Shields of Palatinate-Bavaria in center of shields of Mainz, Trier and Cologne in a trefoil arrangement

A':DN':M:C-CCC:XLIIII
St. Peter under canopy, holding staff in right hand and key in left hand

---

I-74 Trier Archbishopric
Mint: Coblenz
Jakob I of Sierk, 1439-1456
1444 Groschen or Weisspfennig
S 2.00 g
Frey 65, Noss 474, Saurma 2628, Coll. Weygand 1899

MONE'-NOVA-COVE'
Shield of Trier-Sierk in center of shields of Mainz, Cologne and Palatinate-Bavaria in a trefoil arrangement

A':DN':M:C-CCC:XLIIII
St. Peter under canopy, holding staff in right hand and key in left hand

1445

I-75 Brunswick City
Mint: Brunswick
1445 Groschen or Weisspfennig
R4 1.90 g
Frey —, Krusy B5, 7f

Countermark of lionshield on a host 1445 Mainz groschen of the Bingen mint. See I-77 below.

I-76 Cologne Archbishopric
Mint: Riehl
Dietrich (Theodore) II of Mörs, 1414-1463
1445 Groschen or Weisspfennig
S 1.90 g
Frey 67, Noss 380, Cappe 1107, 1114, Saurma 2716, Coll. Weygand 1627

MONE'-NOVE-RILE'
Shields of Cologne-Mörs in center of shields of Mainz, Trier and Palatinate in a trefoil arrangement

A'NO:DNI'M:CCCC:XLV
St. Peter under canopy, holding staff in right hand and key in left hand

---

I-77 Mainz Archbishopric
Mint: Bingen
Dietrich (Theodore) I of Erbach, 1434-1455
1445 Groschen or Weisspfennig
S 1.90 g
Frey 68, Pr. Alexander 163, Cappe 640, Coll. Walther 135

MONE-NOVA-BING'
Shields of Mainz-Erbach in center of shields of Mainz, Cologne and Palatinate-Bavaria in a trefoil arrangement

A'NO:DNI'-M:CCCC:XLV
St. Peter under canopy, holding staff in right hand and key in left hand

---

I-78 Palatinate County and Elector
Mint: Bacharach
Ludwig IV, 1436-1449
1445 Groschen or Weisspfennig
S 1.90 g
Frey 69, Coll. Noss 146, Coll. Mem. 2153, Coll. Weygand 2087

MONE'-NOVA-BACH'
Shields of Palatinate-Bavaria in center of shields of Mainz, Trier and Cologne in a trefoil arrangement

A'NO':DNI'M':CCCC:XLV
St. Peter under canopy, holding staff in right hand and key in left hand

1446

I-79 Cologne Archbishopric
Mint: Riehl
Dietrich (Theodore) II of Mörs, 1414-1463
1446 Groschen or Weisspfennig
VS 1.90 g
Frey 73, Noss 381, Cappe 1115, Saurma 2717, Coll. Weygand 1656

MONE'-NOVA*-RILE'
Shields of Cologne-Mörs in center of shields of Mainz, Trier and Palatinate in a trefoil arrangement

A'DNI':M:CCCC:XLVI
St. Peter under canopy, holding staff in right hand and key in left hand

---

I-80 **Göttingen** **City**
Mint: **Göttingen**
1446 **Körtling**
R6 *0.90 g (fragment missing)*
Unpublished?

MONETAºNOVAºGOTTING
Large "G" in octofoil

ANOºDNIºMCCCCºXXXXVI
Large "G" over short cross

A recent hoard piece and presumably unique. First sold at Künker in 2002, now in author's collection.

1447

I-81 **Cologne** **Archbishopric**
Mint: **Riehl**
Dietrich (Theodore) II of Mörs, 1414-1463
1447 **Groschen or Weisspfennig**
S *2.00 g*
Frey 76, Noss 382, Cappe 1109, Saurma 2718, Coll. Weygand 1656

MONE'-NOVA-RILE'
Shields of Cologne-Mörs in center of shields of Mainz, Trier and Palatinate in a trefoil arrangement

A'DNI':M:CCCC:XLVII
St. Peter under canopy, holding staff in right hand and key in left hand

---

I-82 **Mainz** **Archbishopric**
Mint: **Bingen**
Dietrich (Theodore) I of Erbach, 1434-1455
1447 **Groschen or Weisspfennig**
R2 *1.90 g*
Frey 76, Pr. Alexander 164, Coll. Walther 136

MONE-NOVA-BING'
Shields of Mainz-Erbach in center of shields of Mainz, Cologne and Palatinate-Bavaria in a trefoil arrangement

A'DNI'M-CCCC:XLVII
St. Peter under canopy, holding staff in right hand and key in left hand

---

I-83 **Palatinate** **County and Elector**
Mint: **Bacharach**
Ludwig IV, 1436-1449
1447 **Groschen or Weisspfennig**
S *2.00 g*
Frey 77, Coll. Mem. 2154

MONE'-NOVA-BACH'
Shields of Palatinate-Bavaria in center of shields of Mainz, Trier and Cologne in a trefoil arrangement

A'DNI':M:CCCC:XLVII
St. Peter under canopy, holding staff in right hand and key in left hand

1448

I-84 **Cologne** **Archbishopric**
Mint: **Riehl**
Dietrich (Theodore) II of Mörs, 1414-1463
1448 **Groschen or Weisspfennig**
VS *1.90 g*
Frey 78, Noss 383-84, Cappe 1110, Saurma 2719, Coll. Weygand 1657

MONE*-NOVA*-RILE'
Shields of Cologne-Mörs in center of shields of Mainz, Trier and Palatinate in a trefoil arrangement

A:DN':M:CC-CCXLVIII
St. Peter under canopy, holding staff in right hand and key in left hand

---

I-85 **Palatinate** **County and Elector**
Mint: **Bacharach**
Ludwig IV, 1436-1449
1448 **Groschen or Weisspfennig**
VS *1.90 g*
Frey 80, Coll. Noss 148, Coll. Mem. 2155

MONE'-NOVA-BACH'
Shields of Palatinate-Bavaria in center of shields of Mainz, Trier and Cologne in a trefoil arrangement

A':DN':M:CC-CC:XLVIII
St. Peter under canopy, holding staff in right hand and key in left hand

---

I-86 **Trier** **Archbishopric**
Mint: **Coblenz**
Jakob I of Sierk, 1439-1456
1448 **Groschen or Weisspfennig**

VS *1.90 g*
Frey 79, Noss 475, Saurma 2629, Coll. Weygand 1900

MONE'-NOVA-COVE'
Shield of Trier-Sierk in center of shields of Mainz, Cologne and Palatinate-Bavaria in a trefoil arrangement

A':DN':M:CC-CC:XLVIII
St. Peter under canopy, holding staff in right hand and key in left hand

1449

I-87 **Cologne** **Archbishopric**
Mint: **Riehl**
Dietrich (Theodore) II of Mörs, 1414-1463
1449 **Groschen or Weisspfennig**
VS *1.90 g*
Frey 82, Noss 385, Cappe 1111, Coll. Weygand 1657

MONE'-NOVA-RILE'
Shields of Cologne-Mörs in center of shields of Mainz, Trier and Palatinate in a trefoil arrangement

A':DN':M:C-CCC:XLIX
St. Peter under canopy, holding staff in right hand and key in left hand

I-88 **Palatinate-** **County and Elector**
Mint: **Bacharach**
Ludwig IV, 1436-1449
1449 **Groschen or Weisspfennig**
R *2.00 g*
Frey 81, Coll. Noss 150

MONE'-NOVA-BACH'
Shields of Palatinate-Bavaria in center of shields of Mainz, Trier and Cologne in a trefoil arrangement

A':DN:M:CC-CC:XLIX
St. Peter under canopy, holding staff in right hand and key in left hand

1450

I-89 **Cologne** **Archbishopric**
Mint: **Bonn**
Dietrich (Theodore) II of Mörs, 1414-1463
1450 **Groschen or Weisspfennig**
R4 *1.45 g*
Frey 83, Cappe 1112

MONE'-NOVA-BVNE'
Shields of Cologne-Mörs in center of shields of Mainz, Trier and Palatinate in a trefoil arrangement

A'DN':M:C-CCC:L
St. Peter under canopy, holding staff in right hand and key in left hand

I-90 **Cologne** **Archbishopric**
Mint: **Riehl**
Dietrich (Theodore) II of Mörs, 1414-1463
1450 **Groschen or Weisspfennig**
R *1.90 g*
Frey 83A, Noss 386, Coll. Weygand 1657

MONE'-NOVA-RILE'
Shields of Cologne-Mörs in center of shields of Mainz, Trier and Palatinate in a trefoil arrangement

A'NO:DNI'-M:CCCC:L
St. Peter under canopy, holding staff in right hand and key in left hand

1457

I-91 **Saxony** **Duchy and Elector**
Mint: **Gotha**
Wilhelm III, Duke of Saxony & Landgrave of Thuringen, 1445-1482
1457 **Groschen**
R5 *Weight unknown*
Frey 95, Krug 1305-06, Haupt Table. 42,10

W:DI:GRACIA:DVX:SAXONIE
Triple-stranded flowery short cross in quatrefoil, shield of Duke of Saxony at top

GROSSVS:LANTG:TVRING:1ꭓ٦Λ
Crowned lion above Landsberger shield with roses at sides

Struck by Wilhelm III, Duke of Saxony and Landgrave of Thuringen. Krug 1306 is a much smaller die - 24mm versus 28mm.

I-92 **Saxony** **Duchy and Elector**
Mint: **Leipzig**
Friedrich II, 1428-1464
1457 **Turnosgroschen**
R3 *Weight unknown*
Frey 94, Krug 849-59, Haupt Table. 40.4

F:DI:GRACIA:TVRINGE:LANG-ANNO:M:CCCC:LVII
Inner and outer legends with short cross in center and Landsberger shield at top

GROSSVS:MARCH:MISNENSIS
Inscription surrounding elaborate Thuringen helmet
Struck in the name of Friedrich II as Elector and Landgrave.

1463

I-93 Paderborn City
Mint: Paderborn
1463 Jager
R5 *2.50 g*
Frey —, Krusy P1, 24

Countermark of shield with cross inside with three vertical bars below on a host 1463 Groningen jager. See below under Region III, Northern Netherlands, III-36.

1465

I-94 Göttingen City
Mint: Göttingen
1465 Körtling
R *1.20 g*
Frey 110A, Schrock 11

MONE*NOVA*GOTTINGE
Large "G" in octofoil

ANO*DNI*M*CCCC*LXV
Large "G" over short cross

I-95 Saxony Duchy and Elector
Mint: Colditz
Elector Ernst with Dukes Albrecht and Wilhelm III, 1465-1482
1465 Horngroschen
S *2.70 g*
Frey 109, Krug 1392-1409

E:A:D:G:DVCS:SAX:TVR:L:MARCH:HIS
Ornate helmet of Saxony over leaning shield of Saxony - doublecross mintmark of Colditz at beginning of legend

W:D:G:DVX:SAX:TVR:L:MARCH:HIS:65
Ornate helmet of Thuringen over leaning shield of Thuringen - double-cross mintmark of Colditz at beginning of legend

Colditz horngroschens of this date used a "sideways" 5, an unusual engraving found in only a few other types.

I-96a Saxony Duchy and Elector
Mint: Freiberg
Elector Ernst with Dukes Albrecht and Wilhelm III, 1465-1482
1465 Horngroschen
S *2.70 g*
Frey 109, Krug 1354-60

E:A:D:G:DVCS:SAX:TVR:L:MARCH:HIS 6┐
Ornate helmet of Saxony over leaning shield of Saxony - cross in square mintmark of Freiberg at beginning of legend

W:D:G:DVX:SAX:TVR:L:MARCH:HIS
Ornate helmet of Thuringen over leaning shield of Thuringen

I-96b Saxony Duchy and Elector
Mint: Freiberg
Elector Ernst with Dukes Albrecht and Wilhelm III, 1465-1482
1465 Horngroschen
R4 *2.70 g*
Frey —, Krug 1361

Same as preceding, but date is "65" with a sideways modern "5" instead of a medieval "5"

1466

I-97 Göttingen City
Mint: Göttingen
1466 Körtling
VS *1.30 g*
Frey 116, Schrock 12, Saurma 3907

MONE:NOVA:GOTTINGE
Large "G" in octofoil

ANO':DNI"M:CCCC:LXVI
Large "G" over short cross

I-98a Halberstadt City
Mint: Halberstadt
1466 Horngroschen
R2 *2.70 g*
Frey —, Krusy H1, 13e

Countermark of large crowned lowercase "h" on a host 1466 Saxony horngroschen of the Leipzig mint. See I-103a below.

I-98b **Halberstadt** **City**
Mint: **Halberstadt**
1466 **Horngroschen**
R2 *2.70 g*
Frey —, Krusy H1, 8b

Same as preceding, but with an uncrowned smaller lowercase "h"

I-98c **Halberstadt** **City**
Mint: **Halberstadt**
1466 **Horngroschen**
R3 *2.70 g*
Frey —, Krusy H1, 13d

Countermark of a large crowned lowercase "h" on a host 1466 Saxony horngroschen of the Colditz mint. See I-100 below.

I-99 **Hesse** **Landgraviate**
Mint: **Eschwege?**
Ludwig II, 1458-1471
1466 **Dreihelmgroschen**
R4 *2.63-2.90 g*
Frey 117, Schutz 299-300

L:D:G:LANTGRAVIVS:HASSIE:66
Four part shield with annulets at sides and either an annulet or leaves at top of shield

G:L:H'COMIT:DE CYGENH:ET:NY
Horned helmet of Hesse flanked by helmets of Nidda and Ziegenhain, leaning shield of Saxony

Named for the three helmets on the reverse field.

I-100 **Saxony** **Duchy and Elector**
Mint: **Colditz**
Elector Ernst with Dukes Albrecht and Wilhelm III, 1465-1482
1466 **Horngroschen**
R *2.70 g*
Frey 111, Krug 1410-12

E:A:D:G:DVCS:SAX:TVR:L:MARCH:HIS
Ornate helmet of Saxony over leaning shield of Saxony - doublecross mintmark of Colditz at beginning of legend

W:D:G:DVX:SAX:TVR:L:MARCH:HIS:66
Ornate helmet of Thuringen over leaning shield of Thuringen - double-cross mintmark of Colditz at beginning of legend

I-101a **Saxony** **Duchy and Elector**
Mint: **Freiberg**
Elector Ernst with Dukes Albrecht and Wilhelm III, 1465-1482
1466 **Horngroschen**
S *2.70 g*
Frey 111, Krug 1370-74, 76-77

E:A:D:G:DVCS:SAX:TVR:L:MARCH:HIS 66
Ornate helmet of Saxony over leaning shield of Saxony - cross in square mintmark of Freiberg at beginning of legend

W:D:G:DVX:SAX:TVR:L:MARCH:HIS
Ornate helmet of Thuringen over leaning shield of Thuringen - cross in square mintmark of Freiberg at beginning of legend

I-101b **Saxony** **Duchy and Elector**
Mint: **Freiberg**
Elector Ernst with Dukes Albrecht and Wilhelm III, 1465-1482
1466 **Horngroschen**
R *2.70 g*
Frey —, Krug 1362-69, 1375

Same as preceding, but with single digit date of "6"

I-101c **Saxony** **Duchy and Elector**
Mint: **Freiberg**
Elector Ernst with Dukes Albrecht and Wilhelm III, 1465-1482
1466 **Horngroschen**
R5 *2.85 g*
Frey —, Krug 1378

Mule - same as preceding, but with date of "65" on obverse and "66" on reverse

The description in Krug 1378 does not match the photograph.

I-102 **Saxony** **Duchy and Elector**
Mint: **Gotha**
Elector Ernst with Dukes Albrecht and Wilhelm III, 1465-1482
1466 **Horngroschen**
R3 *2.70 g*
Frey 111, Krug 1465-66

E:A:D:G:DVCS:SAX:TVR:L:MARCH:HIS
Ornate helmet of Saxony over leaning shield of Saxony - rose mintmark of Gotha at beginning of legend

W:D:G:DVX:SAX:TVR:L:MARCH:HIS:66
Ornate helmet of Thuringen over leaning shield of Thuringen - rose mintmark of Gotha at beginning of legend

---

I-103a **Saxony** **Duchy and Elector**
Mint: **Leipzig**
Elector Ernst with Dukes Albrecht and Wilhelm III, 1465-1482
1466 **Horngroschen**
C *2.70 g*
Frey 111, Krug 1428-41

E:A:D:G:DVCS:SAX:TVR:L:MARCH:HIS
Ornate helmet of Saxony over leaning shield of Saxony - 5 pointed star mintmark of Leipzig at beginning of legend

W:D:G:DVX:SAX:TVR:L:MARCH:HIS:66
Ornate helmet of Thuringen over leaning shield of Thuringen - 5 pointed star mintmark of Leipzig at beginning of legend

---

I-103b **Saxony** **Duchy and Elector**
Mint: **Leipzig/Colditz**
Elector Ernst with Dukes Albrecht and Wilhelm III, 1465-1482
1466 **Horngroschen**
R5 *2.70 g*
Frey 111, Krug 1442

E:A:D:G:DVCS:SAX:TVR:L:MARCH:HIS
Ornate helmet of Saxony over leaning shield of Saxony - 5 pointed star mintmark of Leipzig at beginning of legend - 1466 legend

W:D:G:DVX:SAX:TVR:L:MARCH:HIS:65
Ornate helmet of Thuringen over leaning shield of Thuringen - double-cross mintmark of Colditz at beginning of legend

A fascinating mule of two different mints and two different dates. As Leipzig did not strike 1465 dated horngroschens, this piece was struck at the earliest in 1466 and muled to the reverse 1465 dated legend of a Colditz groschen.

I-104 **Saxony** **Duchy and Elector**
Mint: **Ölsnitz**
Elector Ernst with Dukes Albrecht and Wilhelm III, 1465-1482
1466 **Horngroschen**
R4 *2.65 g*
Frey 111, Krug 1469-70

E:A:D:G:DVCS:SAX:TVR:L:MARCH:HIS
Ornate helmet of Saxony over leaning shield of Saxony - annulet mintmark of Ölsnitz at beginning of legend

W:D:G:DVX:SAX:TVR:L:MARCH:HIS:66
Ornate helmet of Thuringen over leaning shield of Thuringen - annulet mintmark of Ölsnitz at beginning of legend

---

I-105 **Saxony** **Duchy and Elector**
Mint: **Wittenberg**
Elector Ernst with Dukes Albrecht and Wilhelm III, 1465-1482
1466 **Horngroschen**
R3 *2.85 g*
Frey 111, Krug 1471-74

E:A:D:G:DVCS:SAX:TVR:L:MARCH:HIS
Ornate helmet of Saxony over leaning shield of Saxony - clover mintmark of Wittenberg at beginning of legend

W:D:G:DVX:SAX:TVR:L:MARCH:HIS:66
Ornate helmet of Thuringen over leaning shield of Thuringen

I-106 **Wernigerode** **City**
Mint: **Wernigerode**
1466 **Horngroschen**
R6 *2.70 g*
Frey —, Krusy W5, 3a

Countermark of crowned "W" on a host 1466 Saxony horngroschen of the Leipzig mint, No. I-103a above.

1467

I-107 **Göttingen** **City**
Mint: **Göttingen**
1467 **Körtling**
R4 *1.20 g*
Frey 121, Schrock 13

MONE*NOVA*GOTTINGE
Large "G" in octofoil

ANO*DNI*M*CCCC*LXVII
Large "G" over short cross

I-108 Hesse Landgraviate
Mint: Cassel
Ludwig II, 1458-1471
1467 Horngroschen
R2 2.50-2.80 g
Frey 118, Schutz 301, Hoffmeister 129-32, Saurma 2238

L:D:G:LANTGRAVIVS:HASS
Lion shield under helmet of Hesse with rose initial mark

G:L:H:COMIT:DE:CYGENHA 6Λ
Shield of Ziegenhain under helmet of Ziegenhain, with rose initial mark

Issued by Ludwig II of Cassel (Kassel).

I-109a Hesse Landgraviate
Mint: Eschwege
Ludwig II, 1458-1471
1467 Horngroschen
R2 2.50-2.80 g
Frey 117, Schutz 302

L:D:G:LANTGRAVIVS:HAS
Lion shield under helmet of Hesse with three leaf initial mark

G:L:H:COMIT:DE:CYGENH:6Λ
Shield of Ziegenhain under helmet of Ziegenhain with three leaf initial mark

Schulten lists two other early dated coins of Hesse, but their existence is not confirmed.

I-109b Hesse Landgraviate
Mint: Eschwege
Ludwig II, 1458-1471
1467 Horngroschen
R4 2.50 g
Frey 117, Schutz 303

Same as preceding, but with error date of "6"

I-110 Hesse-Marburg Landgraviate
Mint: Uncertain
Heinrich III, 1458-1483
1467 Horngroschen
R3 2.70 g
Frey 119, Schutz 341, Hoffmeister 109-12, Saurma 2238

H:D:G:LANTGRAVAVIVS:HAS
Lion shield under helmet of Hesse

G:L:H:COMIT':DE:CYGENH 6Λ
Shield of Ziegenhain under helmet of Ziegenhain with fleur-de-lys initial mark

Issued by Heinrich III of Marburg.

I-111 Saxony Duchy and Elector
Mint: Colditz
Elector Ernst with Dukes Albrecht and Wilhelm III, 1465-1482
1467 Horngroschen
S 2.70 g
Frey 120, Krug 1413-20

E:A:D:G:DVCS:SAX:TVR:L:MARCH:HIS
Ornate helmet of Saxony over leaning shield of Saxony - doublecross mintmark of Colditz at beginning of legend

W:D:G:DVX:SAX:TVR:L:MARCH:HIS:6Λ
Ornate helmet of Thuringen over leaning shield of Thuringen - double-cross mintmark of Colditz at beginning of legend

---

I-112a Saxony Duchy and Elector
Mint: Freiberg
Elector Ernst with Dukes Albrecht and Wilhelm III, 1465-1482
1467 Horngroschen
S 2.70 g
Frey 120, Krug 1379-82

E:A:D:G:DVCS:SAX:TVR:L:HARCH:HIS:6Λ
Ornate helmet of Saxony over leaning shield of Saxony - cross in square mintmark of Freiberg at beginning of legend

W:D:G:DVX:SAX:TVR:L:MARCH:HIS
Ornate helmet of Thuringen over leaning shield of Thuringen - cross in square mintmark of Freiberg at beginning of legend

I-112b Saxony Duchy and Elector
Mint: Freiberg
Elector Ernst with Dukes Albrecht and Wilhelm III, 1465-1482
1467 Horngroschen
R4 2.70 g
Frey 120, Krug 1383

Same as preceding with date "6Λ" at end of obverse legend and "66" at end of reverse legend

---

I-113 Saxony Duchy and Elector
Mint: Leipzig
Elector Ernst with Dukes Albrecht and Wilhelm III, 1465-1482
1467 Horngroschen
S 2.70 g
Frey 120, Krug 1443-51

E:A:D:G:DVCS:SAX:TVR:L:MARCH:HIS
Ornate helmet of Saxony over leaning shield of Saxony - 5 pointed star mintmark of Leipzig at beginning of legend

W:D:G:DVX:SAX:TVR:L:MARCH:HIS:6Λ
Ornate helmet of Thuringen over leaning shield of Thuringen - 5 pointed star mintmark of Leipzig at beginning of legend

---

I-114 Wernigerode City
Mint: Wernigerode
1467 Horngroschen
R6 2.70 g
Frey —, Krusy W5, 3b

Countermark of crowned "W" on a host 1467 Saxony horngroschen of the Leipzig mint. See I-113 above.

1468

I-115 Erfurt City
Mint: Erfurt
1468 Groschen
R2 2.80 g
Frey 127, Leitzmann 395-97, Posern-Klett 417-19, Saurma 4636

GROSSVS:NOVVS:ERFFORDENSIS
Shield of Erfurt set inside quatrefoil

SANCTVS:MARTINVS:EPISCOPVS:68
St. Martin on horseback with beggar below, all in quatrefoil

I-116 Halberstadt City
Mint: Halberstadt
1468 Horngroschen
R4 2.70 g
Frey —, Krusy H1, 13f

Countermark of large crowned "h" on a host 1468 Saxony horngroschen of the Colditz mint. See I-118 below.

I-117 Hesse-Marburg Landgraviate
Mint: Uncertain
Heinrich III, 1458-1483
1468 Horngroschen
R2 2.75 g
Frey 125, Schutz 342, Hoffmeister 113, Saurma 2276

H:D:G:LANTGRAVIVS:HAS
Lion shield under helmet of Hesse

G:L:H:COMIT':DE:CYGENH' 68
Shield of Ziegenhain under helmet of Ziegenhain with fleur-de-lys initial mark

---

I-118 Saxony Duchy and Elector
Mint: Colditz
Elector Ernst with Dukes Albrecht and Wilhelm III, 1465-1482
1468 Horngroschen
R 2.70 g
Frey 126, Krug 1421-25

E:A:D:G:DVCS:SAX:TVR:L:MARCH:HIS
Ornate helmet of Saxony over leaning shield of Saxony - doublecross mintmark of Colditz at beginning of legend

W:D:G:DVX:SAX:TVR:L:MARCH:HIS:68
Ornate helmet of Thuringen over leaning shield of Thuringen - double-cross mintmark of Colditz at beginning of legend

---

I-119 Saxony Duchy and Elector
Mint: Freiberg
Elector Ernst with Dukes Albrecht and Wilhelm III, 1465-1482
1468 Horngroschen
S 2.90 g
Frey 126, Krug 1384-88

E:A:D:G:DVCS:SAX:TVR:L:MARCH:HIS 68
Ornate helmet of Saxony over leaning shield of Saxony - cross in square mintmark of Freiberg at beginning of legend

W:D:G:DVX:SAX:TVR:L:MARCH:HIS
Ornate helmet of Thuringen over leaning shield of Thuringen - cross in square mintmark of Freiberg at beginning of legend

---

I-120a Saxony Duchy and Elector
Mint: Leipzig
Elector Ernst with Dukes Albrecht and Wilhelm III, 1465-1482
1468 Horngroschen
VS *2.90 g*
Frey 126, Krug 1452-56

E:A:D:G:DVCS:SAX:TVR:L:MARCH:HIS
Ornate helmet of Saxony over leaning shield of Saxony - 5 pointed star mintmark of Leipzig at beginning of legend

W:D:G:DVX:SAX:TVR:L:MARCH:HIS:68
Ornate helmet of Thuringen over leaning shield of Thuringen - 5 pointed star mintmark of Leipzig at beginning of legend

---

I-120b Saxony Duchy and Elector
Mint: Leipzig/Colditz
Elector Ernst with Dukes Albrecht and Wilhelm III, 1465-1482
1468 Horngroschen
R4 *2.80 g*
Frey 126, Krug 1457-58

E:A:D:G:DVCS:SAX:TVR:L:MARCH:HIS
Ornate helmet of Saxony over leaning shield of Saxony - 5 pointed star mintmark of Leipzig at beginning of legend

W:D:G:DVX:SAX:TVR:L:MARCH:HIS:68
Ornate helmet of Thuringen over leaning shield of Thuringen - double-cross mintmark of Colditz at beginning of legend

A mule of Leipzig and Colditz. Two dies are known, one with the date on obverse and one with the date on reverse.

1469

I-121 Halberstadt City
Mint: Halberstadt
1469 Stüber
R6 *Weight unknown*
Frey —, Krusy H1, 12d

Countermark of large angular crowned lowercase "h" on a host 1469 Deventer stuiver. See below under Region III, Northern Netherlands, III-49

This coin was countermarked by both Halberstadt and Hildesheim and is thus listed as an early dated coin of both. While both used a lower-case "h" as a mark, the Halberstadt "h" is angular, long and thin, while the Hildesheim mark is short and rounded.

I-122 Halberstadt City
Mint: Halberstadt
1469 Horngroschen
R4 *Weight unknown*
Frey —, Krusy H7, 8c

Countermark of large gothic lowercase "h" on a host 1469 Saxony horngroschen of the Leipzig mint. See I-127 below.

I-123 Hildesheim City
Mint: Hildesheim
1469 Stüber
R6 *Weight unknown*
Frey —, Krusy H7, 6b

Countermark of small rounded lowercase "h" on a host 1469 Deventer stuiver. See below under Region III, Northern Netherlands, III-49.

This coin was countermarked by both Halberstadt (see I-121 above) and Hildesheim.

I-124 Saxony Duchy and Elector
Mint: Colditz
Elector Ernst with Dukes Albrecht and Wilhelm III, 1465-1482
1469 Horngroschen
R *2.80 g*
Frey 132, Krug 1426-27

E:A:D:G:DVCS:SAX:TVR:L:MARCH:HIS
Ornate helmet of Saxony over leaning shield of Saxony - doublecross mintmark of Colditz at beginning of legend

W:D:G:DVX:SAX:TVR:L:MARCH:HIS:69
Ornate helmet of Thuringen over leaning shield of Thuringen - double-cross mintmark of Colditz at beginning of legend

---

I-125 Saxony Duchy and Elector
Mint: Freiberg
Elector Ernst with Dukes Albrecht and Wilhelm III, 1465-1482
1469 Horngroschen
VS *2.80 g*
Frey 132, Krug 1389-91

E:A:D:G:DVCS:SAX:TVR:L:MARCH:HIS 69
Ornate helmet of Saxony over leaning shield of Saxony - cross in square mintmark of Freiberg at beginning of legend

W:D:G:DVX:SAX:TVR:L:MARCH:HIS
Ornate helmet of Thuringen over leaning shield of Thuringen - cross in square mintmark of Freiberg at beginning of legend

I-126 **Saxony** **Duchy and Elector**
Mint: **Gotha**
Elector Ernst with Dukes Albrecht and Wilhelm III, 1465-1482
1469 **Horngroschen**
R3 *2.80 g*
Frey 132, Krug 1467-68

E:A:D:G:DVCS:SAX:TVR:L:MARCH:HIS
Ornate helmet of Saxony over leaning shield of Saxony - rose mintmark of Gotha at beginning of legend

W:D:G:DVX:SAX:TVR:L:MARCH:HIS:69
Ornate helmet of Thuringen over leaning shield of Thuringen - rose mintmark of Gotha at beginning of legend

---

I-127 **Saxony** **Duchy and Elector**
Mint: **Leipzig**
Elector Ernst with Dukes Albrecht and Wilhelm III, 1465-1482
1469 **Horngroschen**
S *2.70 g*
Frey 132, Krug 1459-63

E:A:D:G:DVCS:SAX:TVR:L:MARCH:HIS
Ornate helmet of Saxony over leaning shield of Saxony - 5 pointed Star mintmark of Leipzig at beginning of legend

W:D:G:DVX:SAX:TVR:L:MARCH:HIS:69
Ornate helmet of Thuringen over leaning shield of Thuringen - 5 pointed star mintmark of Leipzig at beginning of legend

One die is known with date on the obverse.

1471

I-128 **Göttingen** **City**
Mint: **Göttingen**
1471 **Körtling**
R4 *1.20 g*
Frey 142A, Schrock 14

MONE*NOVA*GOTTINGE
Large "G" in octofoil

ANNO*DNI*M*CCCC:LXXI
Large "G" over short cross

I-129 **Jülich-Berg** **Duchy**
Mint: **Düren**
Gerhard, 1437-1475
1471 **Groschen or Bausche**
R4 *1.70 g*
Frey 142, Noss 165a-d, Saurma 2980, Thomsen 6168, Coll. Weygand 256

GERARDVS:-DVX:IVL':Z-M
Duke holding sword behind quartered shield of Ravensburg

ANNO:DNI':MILESMO'M:CCCC:LXXI-MONE':NOVA:DVIREN'
Short cross with inner and outer legends

Despite its extreme rarity, four different dies are reported by Noss.

1473

I-130 **East Frisia** **County**
Mint: **Emden or Norden**
Theda Cirksena, 1466-1483
1473 **Witten**
R3 *0.62 g*
Frey —, Kappelhoff 79

MO'TEDE:COITIS:OSTFRISIE
Shield with standing lion facing left

AN:D-M:CC-CC:LX-XIII
Long cross with stars in angles of cross

This is the first dated coin of East Frisia (Ostfriesland), located in the northwesternmost part of Germany next to northern Holland. Almost without exception, the coins of East Frisia are found poorly struck and well-worn.

I-131 **Göttingen** **City**
Mint: **Göttingen**
1473 **Körtling**
R5 *1.20 g*
Frey —, Schrock 15

MONE*NOVA*GOTTINGE
Large "G" in octofoil

ANO*DNI*M*CCCCLXX3
Large "G" over short cross

This is the first example of a mixed numeral dated coin.

I-132 **Limburg** **County**
Mint: **Broich**
Heinrich I, 1443-1486
1473 **Stuiver**
R4 *2.28-2.76 g*
Frey —, Berghaus-Spiegel 77a-b

HENRICVS-CO*DE*LIMB'
Swan facing left over leaning banded shield of Groningen

ANNO:-DOMIIII-M:CCCC-LXXIII:
Thick double-stranded long cross with letter "B" in center for Broich mint

This coin copies the Groningen stuiver.

1474

I-133 East Frisia County
Mint: Emden or Norden
Theda Cirksena, 1466-1483
1474 Witten
R4 0.62 g
Frey 157, Kappelhoff 80, Saurma 3301

TEDE COITIS' OSTFRISIE
Shield with standing lion facing left

AN' D'-M CC-CC LX-XIIII
Long cross with stars in angles of cross

I-134 Erfurt City
Mint: Erfurt
1474 Uniface Hohlpfennig
R4 0.30 g
Frey —, Leitzmann 405, Posern-Klett 425

ΛȢ
Date over spokes of wheel

An early dated bracteate!

I-135 Essen Convent
Mint: Essen
Sophie IV of Gleichen, 1459-1489
1474 Groschen
R6 1.85 g
Frey —, Kramer 30.11

SOPIA:DE.GELICHE.ABBA'ASS'
Sitting lion facing left with shield as collar on neck

ANNO-DNI.M-CCCCL-XXIIII
Long cross over four-part shield

Unique example in the Ruhrland Museum of Essen. Essen has the distinction of being the only convent to issue early Anno Domini dated coins.

I-136a Limburg County
Mint: Broich
Heinrich I, 1443-1486
1474 Stuiver
R4 2.27-2.62 g
Frey 160C, Berghaus-Spiegel 78a-b

HENRICVS:COM-ES:DE:LIMBOR'
Swan facing left over leaning banded shield of Groningen

ANNO:-DNI:M-CCCC:L-XXIIII:
Thick double-stranded long cross with letter "B" in center for Broich mint

This coin copies the Groningen stuiver.

I-136b Limburg County
Mint: Broich
Heinrich I, 1443-1486
1474 Stuiver
R6 2.53 g
Frey —, Berghaus-Spiegel 79

HENRICVS:COM-ES:DE-LIMBORC
Swan facing left over leaning shield of Limburg with double-tailed lion advancing left

ANNO:-DNI:M-CCCC:L-XXIIII:
Thick double-stranded long cross with letter "B" in center for Broich mint

This coin copies the Leeuwarden stuiver.

1475

I-137 Cleve Duchy
Mint: Cleve
Johann I, 1448-1481
1475 Groschen
C 2.00 g
Frey 166, Noss 144, Coll. Weygand 769-70

IOHS'*DVX*CLIV''-Z*CO'*DE*MARK'
Shield of Cleve over small diagonal shield of the Mark

ANNO*DNI*M*CCCC*LXXV
Shield of Cleve-Mark on long cross with circles in quadrants

I-138 Cleve Duchy
Mint: Cleve
Johann I, 1448-1481
1475 Half Groschen
S 1.40 g
Frey 166A, Noss 145, Coll. Weygand 772-74

IOHS':DVX:CLIV':CO':MARK
Shield of Cleve with star above

ANNO-DNI':M-CCCC-LXXV
Shield of Cleve-Mark on long cross with stars in angles

I-139 East Frisia County
Mint: Emden or Norden
Theda Cirksena, 1466-1483
1475 Witten
R3 0.62 g
Frey 167, Kappelhoff 81

MO' TEDE COITIS' OSTFRISIE
Shield with standing lion facing left

AN' D'-M CC-CC L-XXV
Long cross with stars in angles

I-140 Saxony Duchy and Elector
Mint: Colditz
Elector Ernst, Dukes Albrecht and Wilhelm III, with Electress Margaretha, 1475-1482
1475 Spitzgroschen
R 1.60 g
Frey —, Krug 1593-1600

E:W:A:D:G:DVCS:SX:TV:L:MA:HS
Shield of Duke of Saxony with double-cross mintmark of Colditz at beginning of legend

M:GROSSVS:NOVVS:MAR:HIS Λ ˥
Landsberger shield in trefoil, no reverse mintmark

Jointly issued by Margaretha, Electress of the Holy Roman Empire, along with Ernst, Albrecht and Wilhelm III. The letter "M" on the reverse, representing "Margaretha," distinguishes this coin.

I-141 Saxony Duchy and Elector
Mint: Colditz
Margaretha (alone), 1475-1482
1475 Margaretha Spitzgroschen
R3 1.60 g
Frey 162B, Krug 1607

M:D:G:DVCISSA:SX:TV:L:MA:HS
Shield of Saxony with double-cross mintmark of Colditz at beginning of legend

GROSSVS:NOVVS:MARCH:HIS Λ ˥
Landsberger shield in trefoil with double-cross mintmark of Colditz at beginning of legend

Issued by Electress Margaretha alone.

I-142 Saxony Duchy and Elector
Mint: Colditz
Elector Ernst with Dukes Albrecht and Wilhelm III, 1465-1482
1475 Half Spitzgroschen
R 1.90 g
Frey 162, Krug 1549-50

E:W:A:D:G:DVCS:SAX:TV:L:HAR:HS
Shield of Duke of Saxony with double-cross mintmark of Colditz at beginning of legend

GROSSVS:NOVVS:MARCH:HIS: Λ ˥
Standing lion in shield advancing left, with double-cross mintmark of Colditz at beginning of legend

The half spitzgroschen, although significantly larger than the spitzgroschen, contained but half of its silver content.

I-143 Saxony Duchy and Elector
Mint: Colditz
Elector Ernst, Dukes Albrecht and Wilhelm III, with Electress Margaretha, 1475-1482
1475 Half Spitzgroschen
R2 1.90 g
Frey 162, Krug 1603-06

E:W:A:D:G;DVCS:SAX:TV:L:MAR:HIS
Shield of Duke of Saxony in trefoil with double-cross mintmark of Colditz at beginning of legend

M:GROSSVS:NOVVS:MARCH:HS Λ ˥
Standing lion in shield, advancing left

Jointly issued with Margaretha ('M'), along with Ernst, Albrecht and Wilhelm.

I-144 Saxony Duchy and Elector
Mint: Colditz
Margaretha (alone), 1475-1482
1475 Half Margaretha Spitzgroschen
R4 1.90 g
Frey 162B, Krug 1608-09

M:D:G:DVCISSA:SAX:TV:L:MAR:HS
Shield of Duke of Saxony in trefoil with double-cross mintmark of Colditz at beginning of legend

GROSSVS:NOVVS:MARCH:HIS Λ ˥
Standing lion in shield advancing left with double-cross mintmark of Colditz at beginning of legend

Issued by Margaretha alone.

I-145 Saxony Duchy and Elector
Mint: Freiberg
Elector Ernst with Dukes Albrecht and Wilhelm III, 1465-1482
1475 Spitzgroschen

C *1.40-1.60 g*

Frey —, Krug 1493-97

E:W:A:D:G:DVCS:SX:TV:L:HA:HS
Shield of Duke of Saxony with cross-in-square mintmark of Freiberg at beginning of legend

GROSSVS:NOVVS:MARCH:HS Λ ˥
Landsberger shield in trefoil with cross-in-square mintmark of Freiberg at beginning of legend

Gothic lettering on these pieces engraved the letter "M" in "Marchio" and "Meissen" as an "H", so the abbreviations were either "HA" or "HS." These were struck by Dukes Ernst, Albrecht and Wilhelm III.

I-146a Saxony Duchy and Elector
Mint: Freiberg
Elector Ernst with Dukes Albrecht and Wilhelm III, 1465-1482
1475 Half Spitzgroschen

VS *1.75-2.10 g*

Frey 162, Krug 1541-45

E:W:A:D:G:DVCS:SAX:TV:L:HAR:HS
Shield of Duke of Saxony with cross-in-square mintmark of Freiberg at beginning of legend

GROSSVS:NOVVS:MARCH:HIS: Λ ˥
Standing lion in shield advancing left, with cross-in-square mintmark of Freiberg at beginning of legend

---

I-146b Saxony Duchy and Elector
Mint: Freiberg/Leipzig
Elector Ernst with Dukes Albrecht and Wilhelm III, 1465-1482
1475 Half Spitzgroschen

R4 *1.90 g*

Frey 162, Krug 1546

E:W:A:D:G:DVCS:SAX:TV:L:HAR:HS
Shield of Duke of Saxony with cross-in-square mintmark of Freiberg at beginning of legend

GROSSVS:NOVVS:MARCH:HIS: Λ ˥
Standing lion in shield advancing left, with 6 pointed star mintmark of Leipzig at beginning of legend

Mule of Freiberg and Leipzig mintmarks.

I-147 Saxony Duchy and Elector
Mint: Gotha
Elector Ernst with Dukes Albrecht and Wilhelm III, 1465-1482
1475 Half Spitzgroschen

R3 *1.90 g*

Frey 162, Krug 1547-48

E:W:A:D:G:DVCS:SAX:TV:L:HAR:HS
Shield of Duke of Saxony with rose mintmark of Gotha at beginning of legend

GROSSVS:NOVVS:MARCH:HIS: Λ ˥
Standing lion in shield advancing left, with rose mintmark of Gotha at beginning of legend

---

I-148 Saxony Duchy and Elector
Mint: Leipzig
Elector Ernst with Dukes Albrecht and Wilhelm III, 1465-1482
1475 Spitzgroschen

C *1.60 g*

Frey —, Krug 1504-17

E:W:A:D:G:DVCS:SX:TV:L:HA:HS
Shield of Duke of Saxony with 6 pointed star mintmark of Leipzig at beginning of legend

GROSSVS:NOVVS:MARCH:HS Λ ˥
Landsberger shield in trefoil with 6 pointed star mintmark of Leipzig at beginning of legend

---

I-149 Saxony Duchy and Elector
Mint: Leipzig
Elector Ernst with Dukes Albrecht and Wilhelm III, 1465-1482
1475 Half Spitzgroschen

S *1.90 g*

Frey 162, Krug 1551-56

E:W:A:D:G:DVCS:SAX:TV:L:HAR:HS
Shield of Duke of Saxony with 6 pointed star mintmark of Leipzig at beginning of legend

GROSSVS:NOVVS:MARCH:HIS: Λ ˥
Standing lion in shield advancing left, with 6 pointed star mintmark of Leipzig at beginning of legend

I-150 Saxony Duchy and Elector
Mint: Zwickau
Elector Ernst with Dukes Albrecht and Wilhelm III, 1465-1482
1475 Spitzgroschen

R2 *1.60 g*
Frey —, Krug 1518-20

E:W:A:D:G:DVCS:SX:TV:L:HA:HS
Shield of Duke of Saxony with crescent and annulet mintmark of Zwickau at beginning of legend

GROSSVS:NOVVS:MARCH:HSΛ ⅂
Landsberger shield in trefoil with cresent and annulet mintmark of Zwickau at beginning of legend

1476

I-151 Mörs County
Mint: Mörs
Vincent I, 1448-1493
1476 Stüber

R4 *2.20 g*
Frey 176A, Noss 31, Moers in Nummis 28, Coll. Weygand 1275 (1466 sic)

VINC':CO':MOERS:ET:SA'-MONETA:NOVA:MOERSSENCIS
Four-part shield of Mörs-Saarwerden circled by inner and outer legends

ANO-DI'M-CCCC-LXXVI
Medium length cross dividing legend with 12 shields circling legend

This coin copies the Utrecht jagers (with a value of 1 2/3 stuivers) of David of Burgundy, Bishop of Utrecht, who issued such coins from 1474-1479. The German name for "stuiver" is "stüber."

1477

I-152 Mörs County
Mint: Mörs
Vincent I, 1448-1493
1477 Stüber

R3 *2.06 g*
Frey —, Noss 32, Moers in Nummis 29-30

VINC':CO':MOERS':ET:SAR'- MONETA:NOVA:MOERSSEN
Four-part shield of Mörs-Saarwerden circled by inner and outer legends

A'NO-D'MC-CCCL-XXVII
Medium length cross dividing legend with 12 shields circling legend

I-153 Paderborn City
Mint: Paderborn
1477 Double Stüber

R4 *2.60 g*
Frey —, Krusy P1, 24a, JMP XXXIX 1952, #22a

Countermark of shield with cross inside with three vertical bars below on a host 1477 Utrecht jager, No. III-94

I-154 Saxony Duchy and Elector
Mint: Colditz
Elector Ernst, Dukes Albrecht and Wilhelm III, with Electress Margaretha, 1475-1482
1477 Spitzgroschen

R3 *1.40-1.60 g*
Frey 178, Krug 1601-02

E:W:A:D:G:DVCS:SX:TV:L:MA:HS
Shield of Duke of Saxony with clover and half-rose mintmark of Colditz

M:GROSSVS:NOVVS:MARCH:HSΛ Λ
Landsberger shield in trefoil, no reverse mintmark

Issued by Margaretha along with Ernst, Albrecht and Wilhelm.

I-155 Saxony Duchy and Elector
Mint: Freiberg
Elector Ernst with Dukes Albrecht and Wilhelm III, 1465-1482
1477 Spitzgroschen

C *1.50 g*
Frey 178, Krug 1498-1502

E:W:A:D:G:DVCS:SX:TV:L:HA:HS
Shield of Duke of Saxony with cross-in-square mintmark of Freiberg at beginning of legend

GROSSVS:NOVVS:MARCH:HSΛ Λ
Landsberger shield in trefoil with cross-in-square mintmark of Freiberg at beginning of legend

Issued by Dukes Ernst, Albrecht and Wilhelm III.

I-156 Saxony Duchy and Elector
Mint: Zwickau
Elector Ernst with Dukes Albrecht and Wilhelm III, 1465-1482
1477 Spitzgroschen

C *1.60 g*
Frey 178, Krug 1521-26

E:W:A:D:G:DVCS:SX:TV:L:HA:HS

Shield of Duke of Saxony with crescent and annulet mintmark of Zwickau at beginning of legend

GROSSVS:NOVVS:MARCH:HS Λ Λ
Landsberger shield in trefoil with cresent and annulet mintmark of Zwickau at beginning of legend

Issued by Dukes Ernst, Albrecht and Wilhelm III.

I-157 Warburg City
Mint: Warburg
1477 Double Stüber
R4 *2.60 g*
Frey —, Krusy W2,8a, JMP XXXIX 1952, #23

Countermark of a large double lily in diamond on a host 1477 Utrecht jager, No. III-94

I-158 Werl City
Mint: Werl
1477 Double Stüber
R5 *2.60 g*
Frey —, Krusy W4, JMP XXXIX 1952., #21

Countermark of cross in shield with tiny diagonal crosses in upper quadrants on a host 1477 Utrecht jager, No. III-94

1478

I-159 Mörs County
Mint: Mörs
Vincent I, 1448-1493
1478 Jager
R6 *2.30 g*
Unpublished?

MONETA:NOVA:MOERSSENCIS
Double-headed eagle over two diagonal shields

SIT:NO-ME:DOM-INI:BE-NEDICT -ANO-DO:MC-CCCLX-XXVIII
Long cross dividing inner and outer legends, stars in quadrants

This coin copies the Groningen jager. Likely unique (author's collection).

I-160a Mörs County
Mint: Mörs
Vincent I, 1448-1493
1478 Stüber
R3 *2.28 g*
Frey —, Noss 36, Moers in Nummis 32-33, Coll. Weygand 1277

MONET:NOVA:MOERSSENES
Large double-headed eagle over diagonal shield of Mörs

ANNO-DOMINI-M:CCCCL-XXVIII
Thick long cross with letter "S" in center

Misidentified in "Moers in Numis" as a jager.

I-160b Mörs County
Mint: Mörs
Vincent I, 1448-1493
1478 Stüber
R4 *2.18 g*
Frey 195A, Noss 33, Coll. Weygand 1276

VINC':CO':MOER':ET:SAR'- MONETA:NOVA:MOERSSENCIS
Four-part shield of Mörs-Saarwerden circled by inner and outer legends

ANOD-I:MCC-CCLX-XVIII
Medium length cross dividing legend with 12 shields circling legend

---

I-161 Paderborn City
Mint: Paderborn
1478 Double Stüber
R3 *2.70 g*
Frey —, Krusy P1, 24b-d, JMP XXXIX 1952, #22b, Van der Chijs 18.27

Countermark of shield with cross inside with three vertical bars below on a host 1478 Utrecht jager, No. III-104

I-162 Saxony Duchy and Elector •
Mint: Freiberg
Elector Ernst with Dukes Albrecht and Wilhelm III, 1465-1482
1478 Spitzgroschen
R2 *1.60 g*
Frey 189, Krug 1503

E:W:A:D:G:DVCS:SX:TV:L:HA:HS
Shield of Duke of Saxony with cross-in-square mintmark of Freiberg at beginning of legend

GROSSVS:NOVVS:MARCH:HS ᴧ 8
Landsberger shield in trefoil with cross-in-square mintmark of Freiberg at beginning of legend

---

I-163 Saxony Duchy and Elector
Mint: Zwickau
1478 Spitzgroschen
C *1.60 g*
Frey 189, Krug 1527-40

E:W:A:D:G:DVCS:SX:TV:L:HA:HS
Shield of Duke of Saxony with clover leaf mintmark of Zwickau at beginning of legend

GROSSVS:NOVVS:MARCH:HS ᴧ 8
Landsberger shield in trefoil with clover leaf mintmark of Zwickau at beginning of legend

---

I-164 Saxony Duchy and Elector
Mint: Zwickau
Elector Ernst with Dukes Albrecht and Wilhelm III, 1465-1482
1478 Half Spitzgroschen
VS *2.10 g*
Frey 189, Krug 1557-62

E:W:A:D:G:DVCS:SAX:TV:L:HAR:HS
Shield of Duke of Saxony with clover leaf mintmark of Zwickau at beginning of legend

GROSSVS:NOVVS:MARCH:HIS ᴧ 8
Standing lion in shield advancing left, with clover leaf mintmark of Zwickau at beginning of legend

---

I-165 Soest City
Mint: Soest
1478 Double Stüber
R5-6 *2.70 g*
Frey —, Krusy S10, 46a-b, JMP XXXIX 1952, #20

Countermark of key with four teeth on host Utrecht 1478 jager, No. III-104

I-166 Warburg City
Mint: Warburg
1478 Double Stüber
R3 *3.00 g*
Frey —, Krusy W2,9b-c, JMP XXXIX 1952, #24a, Van der Chijs 18.26

Countermark of a small double lily in diamond on a host 1478 Utrecht jager, No. III-104

1479

I-167 Cleve Duchy
Mint: Cleve
Johann I, 1448-1481
1479 Braspfennig
S *3.40-3.70 g*
Frey 206, Noss 149, Saurma 2928, Coll. Weygand 766-67

IOHS'*DVX*CLIVENS'*ET*CO'*MARK'
Large helmet of Cleve from which hangs shields of Cleve and the Mark

ANNO-DOMI'-M:CCCC-LXXIX
Double-stranded long cross with fleur-de-lys in angles of cross

---

I-168 Cleve Duchy
Mint: Cleve
Johann I, 1448-1481
1479 Half Braspfennig
R2 *2.02-2.25 g*
Frey 207, Noss 150

IOHS':DVX:CLIV':CO':MARK
Large helmet of Cleve from which hangs shields of Cleve and the Mark

ANNO-DNI':M-CCCC-LXXIX
Double-stranded long cross with fleur-de-lys in angles of cross

---

I-169 Hesse-Marburg Landgraviate
Mint: Wolfhagen
Heinrich III, 1458-1483
1479 Pfennig
R5 *1.17 g*
Frey 208, 208B, Schutz 343, Hoffmeister 114*

MONETA*WOLFHAGEN
Small bust under castle towers

ANNO*DNI'*M*CCCCLXXXIX
Bearded Landgrave standing, holding sword and imperial orb

This is an exceedingly rare denomination for an early dated coin. Two dies are known, one with the final "x" in the date partially obscured by having been engraved over the initial cross mark.

I-170 **Paderborn** **City**
Mint: **Paderborn**
1479 **Double Stüber**
R4 *2.60 g*
Frey —, Krusy P1, 24e

Countermark of shield with cross inside with three vertical bars below on a host 1479 Utrecht jager, No. III-115

I-171 **Warburg** **City**
Mint: **Warburg**
1479 **Double Stüber**
R4 *3.00 g*
Frey —, Krusy W2, 9d, JMP XXXIX 1952, #24a

Countermark of a small double lily in diamond on a host 1479 Utrecht jager, No. III-115

1480

I-172 **Mörs** **County**
Mint: **Mörs**
Vincent I, 1448-1493
1480 **Stüber**
R4 *2.10 g*
Frey 215, Noss 34, Moers in Nummis 31

VINC':CO':MOERS':ET:SA'- MONETA:NOVA:MOERSSENCIS
Four-part shield of Mörs-Saarwerden circled by inner and outer legends

ANO-DIM-CCCC-LXXX
Medium length cross dividing legend with 12 shields circling legend

1481

I-173 **Brandenburg** **Margraviate and Elector**
Mint: **Angermuende**
Johann Cicero, 1486-1499
1481 **Groschen**
R4 *2.20 g*
Frey 224, Bahrfeldt 42

IOHAN • DG • MARCHI:BRANDEBVR
Large eagle

MONETA:NOVA:MARCHI:BRAND:81
Cross with shields in angles of cross

Struck by Johann prior to becoming elector. Also known as a "statthalter (governor) groschen." While reported in Frey to be unique, there are three separate dies for this coin listed in Bahrfeldt and four examples were known to Bahrfeldt.

I-174 **Göttingen** **City**
Mint: **Göttingen**
1481 **Körtling**
R3 *1.20 g*
Frey 231A, Schrock 16

MONE*NOVA*GOTTINGE
Large "G" in octofoil

ANO*DNI*M*CCCCLXXXI
Large "G" over short cross

I-175 **Jever** **Lordship**
Mint: **Jever**
Edo Wimken II, 1468-1511
1481 **Örtchen**
R4 *0.68 g*
Frey 231, Kappelhoff 125, Saurma 3336

EDO-WIMK:CAPITAN-IEV
Lion shield of Jever

ANNO-DNI M-CCCCL-XXXI
Long cross with "I-E-V-E" in angles of cross

1482

I-176 **Cleve** **Duchy**
Mint: **Cleve**
Johann II, 1481-1521
1482 **Stüber**
R2 *2.80 g*
Frey 235A, Noss 181, Schulten 1465, Coll. Weygand 780

IOHS':DVX:CLIVENS':Z:CO':DE:MARK
Swan with outstretched wings behind shield of Cleve and the Mark

ANNO-DNI':M-CCCC-LXXXII
Flowery long cross with "C-L-I-V" in angles of cross

Also known as a "swanstüber" for the graceful swan whose wing cradles the ducal shield.

I-177 Cleve Duchy
Mint: Wesel
Johann II, 1481-1521
1482 Braspfennig
R2 3.67 g
Frey 235, Noss 156-57, Schulten 1455, Coll. Weygand 820

IOHS':DVX:CLIVENS':ET:CO':MARK'
Large helmet of Cleve from which hangs shields of Cleve and the Mark

ANNO-DNI':M-CCCC:L-XXXII
Double-stranded long cross with fleur-de-lys in angles of cross

---

I-178 Cologne Archbishopric
Mint: Deutz
Hermann IV of Hesse, 1480-1508
1482 Turnose
VS 2.90 g
Frey 237, Noss 478-79, Cappe 1175-78, Schulten 1605, Coll. Weygand 1683

HERMANNI:ARCHI:EPI':COLONIEN'-TVRON'-TVICN'
Tower shield of Tours over leaning shield of Cologne-Hesse-Zegenhain-Cologne with inner and outer legends

SIT:NOMEN:DONINI: BENEDICTVM-AN'*M*CCCC*LXXXII
Short cross with inner and outer legends

While often listed as rare, this coin regularly surfaces at auction sales and can be obtained in higher grades.

I-179 Halberstadt City
Mint: Halberstadt
1482 Bausche
R4 1.71 g
Frey —, Krusy H1, 7f

Countermark of small lowercase "h" on a host 1482 Jülich-Berg bausche of the Mülheim mint. See I-182 below.

I-180 Hannover City
Mint: Hannover
1482 Groschen
R4 2.00 g
Frey 236, Buck/M 84

MONETA°NOVA°HONOVERENVIS
Lion on ramparts of castle advancing left between city towers

BE'DICTA°SIT°SANCTA°TRINIT'- 1-ꭓ-8-2
Short cross with shield of Hannover in center and date in angles of cross

The reported early dated Hannover thalers are all fake.

I-181 Jever Lordship
Mint: Jever
Edo Wimken II, 1468-1511
1482 Half Witte
R5 0.62 g
Frey —, Kappelhoff 124, De Mey Im 684

MO'T EDE CPITIS OSTRI
Lion in shield facing right

ANO-MCC-CC.LX-XXII
Long cross with stars in angles of cross

I-182 Jülich-Berg Duchy
Mint: Mülheim
Wilhelm IV, 1475-1511
1482 Bausche
C-S 1.80 g
Frey 233, Noss 178-79, Schulten 1428, Saurma 2986, Coll. Weygand 275-77

WILHEL'*DVX-IVL*Z*MON

Half-length figure of duke holding sword behind quartered arms of Jülich-Berg, small shield of Ravensberg in center

MONETA*NOVA*MOLHEM-AN'*M*CCCC*LXXXII
Short cross with inner and outer legends

I-183 Jülich-Berg Duchy
Mint: Mülheim
Wilhelm IV, 1475-1511
1482 Half Bausche
R3 0.83 g
Frey 233A, Noss 180a-d, Schulten 1429, Coll. Weygand 281

WILHEL'*DVX-IVL'*Z*MON'
Half-length figure of duke holding sword behind quartered arms of Jülich-Berg, small shield of Ravensberg in center

MONETA*NOVA*MOLHEM - 1-Ջ-8-Z
Short cross with date in angles of cross

I-184 Saxony Duchy and Elector
Mint: Freiberg
Elector Ernst with Dukes Albrecht and Wilhelm III, 1465-1482
1482 Half Schwertgroschen
R 2.20 g
Frey 232, Krug 1617-18

E:W:A:D:G:DVCS:SAX:TV:LA:HAR:HIS
Elector's shield of crossed swords in trefoil, cross-in-square mintmark of Freiberg at beginning of legend

GROSSVS:NOVVS:DVCVM:SAXONI82
Shield of Landsberg-Meissen in trefoil with cross-in-square mintmark of Freiberg at beginning of legend

The schwertgroschen was equivalent in value to a half spitzgroschen, 40 to the gulden.

I-185 Saxony Duchy and Elector
Mint: Zwickau/Schneeberg
Elector Ernst and Duke Albrecht, 1482-1485
1482 Half Schwertgroschen
C 2.20 g
Frey 232, Krug 1610-18, Coll. Krug 570

E:A:D:G:DVCS:SAX:TV:LA:MAR:HS
Elector's shield of crossed swords in trefoil, clover leaf mintmark of Zwickau-Schneeberg at beginning of legend

GROSSVS:NOVVS:DVCVM:SAXONI82
Shield of Landsberg-Meissen in trefoil with clover leaf mintmark of Zwickau-Schneeberg at beginning of legend

The "2" in the date is often engraved into a tiny space before the initial marks and as a result, is often misread. These coins were struck until 1485 with an immobolized date.

1483

I-186 Cleve Duchy
Mint: Cleve
Johann II, 1481-1521
1483 Stüber
R 2.70 g
Frey —, Noss 182, Schulten 1465, Thomsen 6172

IOHS':DVX:CLIVENS':Z:CO':DE:MAKRA
Swan with outstretched wings behind shield of Cleve and the Mark

ANNO-DNI':M-CCCC:L-XXXIII
Flowery long cross with "C-L-I-V" in angles of cross

I-187a East Frisia County
Mint: Emden
Enno I, 1483-1491
1483 Stüber
R2 2.73 g
Frey 249, 249A, Kappelhoff 89, Schulten 2538

ENNO CO' FRI-*-SIE OI'GE'TAL'
Harpyie eagle with stars at sides, two small shields at feet

DA PAC-EM DNI'-IN DIEB-VS NRIS'-AN'M-CCCC-*LXX-XIII*
Long cross with inner and outer legends, shield in center with alternating harpyies and lions

This coin is also known as a double grote.

I-187b East Frisia County
Mint: Emden
Enno I, 1483-1491
1483 Stüber (devalued)
R6 2.70 g
Frey —, Krusy 03, 1

Countermark of harpyie eagle shield on a host 1483 stüber

(devalued to grote). See I-187a immediately preceding.

In 1491 Count Edzard issued an edict ordering this coin, issued by his older brother Count Enno, to be marked for devaluation. This is the only example of an early dated coin counterstamped by its own country, a practice employed widely by the Spanish empire 150 years later.

I-188 **East Frisia County**
Mint: Emden
Enno I, 1483-1491
1483 Groten
R3 *2.50 g*
Frey —, Kappelhoff 88, Schulten 2539

ENNO:CO':F'SIE-OI'GENTAL'83
Harpyie eagle with stars at sides, leaning quartered shield at feet

DA- PA-CE' DNI'-IN' DIE-B' NR'83
Double-stranded long cross with letter "E" in center

This coin copies the Groningen stuiver.

I-189 **East Frisia County**
Mint: Emden
Enno I, 1483-1491
1483 Half Groten
R2 *1.12 -1.40 g*
Frey —, Kappelhoff 84-85, Schulten 2540

ENNO COM' FRISIE OI'GENTAL
Harpyie eagle in shield

DA PA-CE' DNI-IN DIE-B' NR' 83
Long cross with lion shield of Jever in center

I-190 **Göttingen City**
Mint: Göttingen
1483 Körtling
R4 *1.20 g*
Frey 253A, Schrock 17

MONE:NOVA:GOTTINGE
Large "G" in octofoil

ANO*DI*M*CCCCLXXXIII
Large "G" over short cross

I-191 **Hannover City**
Mint: Hannover
1483 Groschen
R6 *2.08 g*
Frey —, Buck/M 84.1

MONETAºNOVAºHONOVERENCIS
Lion on ramparts of castle advancing left between city towers

BE'DICTAºSITºSANCTAºTRIN'º - 1ʎ83
Short cross with shield of Hannover in center and date in angles of cross

Possibly unique. Reported as the piece from Collection Knigge Hannover.

I-192 **Jever Lordship**
Mint: Jever
Edo Wimken II, 1468-1511
1483 Groten
R4 *2.08 g*
Frey —, Kappelhoff 132, Schulten 1400

EDO WIMK' CAPITAL IEVER
Crested helmet above lion shield of Jever

ANNO -DNI'M-CCCC L-XXXIII
Thick long cross with "I-E-V-E" in angles of cross, star in center

I-193 **Jülich-Berg Duchy**
Mint: Mülheim
Wilhelm IV, 1475-1511
1483 Bausche
S *1.80 g*
Frey 253, Noss 181a-r, Schulten 1428, Saurma 2987, Thomsen 6171, Coll. Weygand 278-79

WILHEL'*DVX-IVL*Z*MON
Half-length figure of duke holding sword behind quartered arms of Jülich-Berg, small shield of Ravensberg in center

MONETA*NOVA*MOLHEM-AN'*M*CCCC*LXXXIII
Short cross with inner and outer legends

I-194 **Jülich-Berg Duchy**
Mint: Mülheim
Wilhelm IV, 1475-1511
1483 Half Bausche
R5 *0.83 g*
Frey —, Noss 182, Schulten 1429, Coll. Weygand 282

WILHEL'*DVX-IVLºZºMON
Half-length figure of duke holding sword behind quartered arms of Jülich-Berg, small shield of Ravensberg in center

MONETA*NOVA*MOLHEM - 1-4-S-3
Short cross with date in angles of cross

The "8" in the date is in the form of an "S."

I-195 **Stolberg County**
Mint: Wernigerode
Heinrich IX, 1455-1497
1483 Groschen
R3 *2.00*
Frey 250, Friederich 69-74, Schulten 3420

GRAVC°HENRICI°IN°STOLBERG
Stag facing left in trefoil shield of Stolberg

GROS°DOMI°IN°WERNIGERODE 83
Helmeted shield of Wernigerode with two trout

In 1483 and in 1485, these groschens had a very large flan. Thereafter, it was reduced considerably.

1484

I-196 **Cleve** **Duchy**
Mint: **Cleve**
Johann II, 1481-1521
1484 **Stüber**
VS *2.70 g*
Frey 259, Noss 183, Schulten 1465

IOHS':DVX:CLIVENS':Z:CO':DE:MARK
Swan with outstretched wings behind shield of Cleve and the Mark

ANNO-DNI':M-CCCC:L-XXXIIII
Flowery long cross with "C-L-I-V" in angles of cross

I-197 **Göttingen** **City**
Mint: **Göttingen**
1484 **Körtling**
R *1.20 g*
Frey —, Schrock 18, Schulten 1004

MONE*NOVA*GOTTINGE
Large "G" in octofoil

A*D*M*CCCC*LXXXIIII
Large "G" over short cross

I-198 **Jülich-Berg** **Duchy**
Mint: **Mülheim**
Wilhelm IV, 1475-1511
1484 **Bausche**
S *1.80 g*
Frey 254, Noss 183a-g, Schulten 1428, Coll. Weygand 280

WILHEM'*DVX-IVL*Z*MON
Half-length figure of duke holding sword behind quartered arms of Jülich-Berg, small shield of Ravensberg in center

MONETA*NOVA*MOLHEM-AN'*M*CCCC*LXXXIIII
Short cross with inner and outer legends

1485

I-199 **Cleve** **Duchy**
Mint: **Cleve**
Johann II, 1481-1521
1485 **Stüber**
VS *2.40 g*
Frey 271, Noss 184-86, Schulten 1465, Riechmann 342, Coll. Weygand 781-83

IOHS':DVX:CLIVENS':Z:CO':DE:MARK
Swan with outstretched wings behind shield of Cleve and the Mark

ANNO-DNI':M-CCCC-LXXXV
Flowery long cross with "C-L-I-V" in angles of cross

I-200 **Cleve** **Duchy**
Mint: **Wesel**
Johann II, 1481-1521
1485 **Stüber**
S *2.80 g*
Frey 272, Noss 158a, Schulten 1464, Coll. Weygand 798

IOHS':DVX:CLIVENS':Z:CO':MAR'
Swan with outstretched wings behind shield of Cleve and the Mark

AN':D-N':M:C-CCC:L-XXXV
Flowery long cross with "W-E-S-A in angles of cross

I-201 **Göttingen** **City**
Mint: **Göttingen**
1485 **Körtling**
R2 *1.30 g*
Frey 273A, Schrock 19

MONE*NOVA*GOTTINGE
Large "G" in octofoil

ANO*DNI*M*CCCCLXXXV
Large "G" over short cross

I-202 **Jever** **Lordship**
Mint: **Jever**
Edo Wimken II, 1468-1511
1485 **Groten**
R4 *2.30 g*
Frey —, Kappelhoff 133, Schulten 1400

EDO WIMK' CAPITAL' IEVER
Crested helmet above leaning lion shield of Jever

ANNO-DNI'M-CCCCL-XXXV
Thick long cross with "I-E-V-E" in angles of cross, star in center

---

I-203 **Stolberg** **County**
Mint: **Wernigerode**
Heinrich IX, 1455-1497
1485 **Groschen**
R5 *2.00 g*
Frey 273E, Friederich 75, Schulten 3420

GRAVE • HENRICI • IN • STOLBERG
Stolberg shield of stag facing left in trefoil

GROS • DOMI • IN • WERNGERODE 8ᒣ
Helmeted shield of Wernigerode with two trout

1486

I-204 **Cleve** **Duchy**
Mint: **Cleve**
Johann II, 1481-1521
1486 **Stüber**
VS *2.80 g*
Frey 282, Noss 187-88, Schulten 1465, Coll. Weygand 784-85

IOHS':DVX:CLIVENS':Z:CO:MARK'
Swan with outstretched wings behind shield of Cleve and the Mark

ANNO-DNI':-M:CC-CC:86
Flowery long cross with "C-L-I-V" in angles of cross

Noss 188 is a variety without the "C-L-I-V."

I-205 **East Frisia** **County**
Mint: **Emden**
Enno I, 1483-1491
1486 **Doppelgrote**
R2 *2.20 g*
Frey 282A, Kappelhoff 90, Schulten 2538

ENNO CO' FRI-*-SIE OI'GE'TAL'
Crowned harpyie eagle above small leaning shields of East Frisia and Jever

DE*PAC-EM*DNI'IN*DIEB-VS*NRIS'-AN'M-CCCC- LXX-XVI
Long cross with inner and outer legends, shield in center with alternating harpyies and lions

---

I-206 **East Frisia** **County**
Mint: **Emden**
Enno I, 1483-1491
1486 **Half Groten**
R3 *1.20 g*
Frey —, Kappelhoff 86, Schulten 2540

ENNO COM' FRISIE OI'GENTAL'
Harpyie eagle in shield

DA*PA-CE' DNI-IN*D'IE-D'*NR*86
Long cross with lion shield of Jever in center

I-207 **Göttingen** **City**
Mint: **Göttingen**
1486 **Körtling**
VS *1.30 g*
Frey 282B, Schrock 20, Schulten 1004

MONE*NOVA*GOTTINGEN
Large "G" in octofoil

ANO*DNI*M*CCCC*LXXXVI
Large "G" over short cross

I-208 **Jever** **Lordship**
Mint: **Jever**
Edo Wimken II, 1468-1511
1486 **Groten**
R4 *2.00 g*
Frey —, Kappelhoff 134, Schulten 1400

EDO WIMK' CAPITAL' IEVER
Crested helmet above lion shield of Jever

ANNO-DNI'M-CCCCL-XXXVI
Thick long cross with "I-E-V-E" in angles of cross, star in center

---

I-209 **Jever** **Lordship**
Mint: **Jever**
Edo Wimken II, 1468-1511
1486 **Half Groten**
R4-5 *1.38 g (chipped flan)*
Frey —, Kappelhoff 130, Schulten 1401

EDO WIMKE CAPITAL' IEVE
Crested helmet above lion shield of Jever

ANNO-DNI M-CCCCL-XXXVI
Shield with Jever lion

I-210 **Jever** **Lordship**
Mint: **Jever**
Edo Wimken II, 1468-1511
1486 **Witten**
R4 *0.57 g*
Frey —, Kappelhoff 126, De Mey Im 683, Schulten 1402

EDO WIMK' CAPITAL' IEVE'
Lion shield of Jever

ANNO-DNI M-CCCCL-XXXVI
Long cross with "I-E-V-E" in angles of cross

1487

I-211a **Essen** **Convent**
Mint: **Borbeck**
Sophie IV of Gleichen, 1459-1489
1487 **Half Groschen**
R4 *0.85 g*
Frey 294A, Kramer 34.1, Grote 17a-b, Schulten 845

EOFAI*D*G*GELIG*ABDIEE'*D*ES
Double-stranded flowery short cross

ANNO.DNI.H.CCCC.LXXVII
Standing lion facing left

I-211b **Essen** **Convent**
Mint: **Borbeck**
Sophie IV of Gleichen, 1459-1489
1487 **Half Groschen**
R5 *0.85 g*
Frey —, Kramer 34.2

BENEDICTV'*SIT*NOMEN*DMI*
Double-stranded flowery short cross

ANNO*DNI*M*CCCCL • XXXVII
Standing lion facing left

I-212 **Göttingen** **City**
Mint: **Göttingen**
1487 **Körtling**
R5-6 *1.30 g*
Frey 294C, Schrock 21

MONE*NOVA*GOTTINGEN
Large "G" in octofoil

ANO*DNI*M*CCCCL • XXXΛ
Large "G" over short cross

I-213 **Jever** **Lordship**
Mint: **Jever**
Edo Wimken II, 1468-1511
1487 **Witten**
R5 *0.90 g*
Frey —, Kappelhoff 127, De Mey Im 683

EDO WIMK' CAPITAL' IEV
Lion shield of Jever

ANNO-DNI M-CCCCL-XXXΛ
Long cross with "I-E-V-E" in angles of cross

I-214 **Limburg** **County**
Mint: **Hohenlimburg**
Johann, 1484-1511
1487 **Half Stüber**
R4 *1.21-1.66 g*
Frey —, Berghaus-Spiegel 82-83, Van der Chijs 29.2, Schulten 1767 (text)

IOHS • COMES • DE • LIMBORH'
Half-length figure of double-tailed lion advancing left

ANNO*DNI*M*CCCC*LXXXVII
Double-stranded flowery short cross

This coin copies the Nijmegen half stuiver. Varieties are with and without a rose under the exergue. The latter, listed as Berghaus-Spiegel 82, is likely unique.

1488

I-215 **Cleve** **Duchy**
Mint: **Cleve**
Johann II, 1481-1521
1488 **Stüber**
R *2.33 g*
Frey 313, Noss 189, Schulten 1465

IOHS':DVX:CLIVENS':Z:CO':DE:MAR'
Swan with outstretched wings behind shield of Cleve and the Mark

ANNO-DNI'-MCC-CC:88
Long cross with letters "C-L-I-V" in angles of cross

I-216 **Cleve** **Duchy**
Mint: **Wesel**

Johann II, 1481-1521
1488 Stüber
R 2.54 g
Frey 314, Noss 159, Schulten 1464

IOHS':DVX:CLIVENS':Z:CO':MARK'
Swan with outstretched wings behind shield of Cleve and the Mark

ANNO-DNI'-M:CC-CC:88
Long cross with letters "W-E-S-A" in angles of cross

I-217a East Frisia County
Mint: Emden
Enno I, 1483-1491
1488 Doppelgrote
R3 2.30-2.70 g
Frey 315, Kappelhoff 91-92, Schulten 2538

ENNO CO'FRI-*-SIE OI'GE'TAL'
Harpyie eagle over small leaning shields of East Frisia and Jever

DA*PAC-EM*DNE-IN*DIEB-VS*NRIS'-ANNO-DOMI-'M*CC-CC*88
Long cross with inner and outer legends, shield in center with alternating harpyies and lions

---

I-217b East Frisia County
Mint: Emden
Enno I, 1483-1491
1488 Doppelgrote
R3 2.67 gr
Frey–, Kappelhoff 91

ENNO' CO'FRI-*-SIE'OI'GE'TAL
Harpyie eagle over small leaning shields of East Frisia and Jever

DA*PAC-EM*DNI-IN*DIEB-VSNRIS- AN'M-CCCC-*LXX-XVIII
Long cross with inner and outer legends, shield in center with alternating harpyies and lions

---

I-218 East Frisia County
Mint: Emden
Enno I, 1483-1491
1488 Half Groten
R3 1.20 g
Frey —, Kappelhoff 87, Schulten 2540

ENNO COM' FRISIE OI'GENTAL'
Harpyie eagle in shield

DA PA-CE' DNI-IN' DIE-B' NR'88
Long cross with lion shield of Jever in center

I-219 Einbeck City
Mint: Einbeck
1488 Körtling
R6 1.45 g
Frey —, Schrock Einbeck p. 45 (1480 - sic!)

MONE:NOVA:EMBECEN
Gothic "E" over short cross

ANNO:DNI:M:CCCC:LXXX:8
Gothic "E" over short cross

Unique first dated coin of Einbeck, formerly in Schrock's personal collection, now in collection of the author. Misidentified by Schrock in his book as a 1480 körtling. Sold at Künker in 2003 for $7800.

I-220 Essen Convent
Mint: Borbeck
Sophie IV of Gleichen, 1459-1489
1488 Half Groschen
R5 0.85 g
Frey 320A, Kramer 34.3-4, Grote 17c, Schulten 845

SOFAI*D*GELIG*ABDIEE'*D*ES
Double-stranded flowery short cross

ANNO*DNI*M*CCCC*LXXXVIII
Standing lion facing left

Two dies are known for this excessively rare piece.

I-221 Göttingen City
Mint: Göttingen
1488 Körtling
R 1.40 g
Frey 320C, Schrock 22, Schulten 1004

MONE*NOVA*GOTTINGEN
Large "G" in octofoil

ANO*DNI*M*CCCCLXXX8
Large "G" over short cross

Well-struck pieces of this date are extremely rare.

I-222 Jever Lordship
Mint: Jever
Edo Wimken II, 1468-1511
1488 Half Groten
R4 1.57 g
Frey —, Kappelhoff 131, Schulten 1401

EDO WIMKE CAPITAL' IEVE
Crested helmet above leaning lion shield of Jever

ANNO-DNI -CCCCL-XXX8
Thick long cross with stars in angles

I-223 Limburg County
Mint: Hohenlimburg
Johann, 1484-1511
1488 Double Stüber
R4 2.38 g
Frey —, Berghaus-Spiegel 84, Van der Chijs 29.1, Schulten 1765

MONETA*NOVA*LIMBORGH
Seated facing lions with three stars in field, three roses below exergue

ANNO*DNI*M*CCCC*LXXXVIII
Shield of Limburg on flowery short cross

I-224a Limburg County
Mint: Hohenlimburg
Johann, 1484-1511
1488 Stüber
R4 1.46-1.97 g
Frey 320B, Berghaus-Spiegel 85a-c, Schulten 1767 (plates)

MONETA*NOVA*LIMBORGH
Full-length lion advancing left

ANNO*DNI*M*CCCC*LXXXVIII
Double-stranded flowery short cross

Only four known examples according to Peus.

I-224b Limburg County
Mint: Hohenlimburg
Johann, 1484-1511
1488 Stüber
R5 1.33 g
Frey —, Berghaus-Spiegel 86

ANNO*DNI*M*CCCC*LXXXVIII
Full-length lion advancing left

SITNOHEN*DNI*BENEDICTV'
Double-stranded flowery short cross

Probably a mule.

I-225 Pommerania Duchy
Mint: Garz
Bogislaus X, 1474-1523
1488 Schilling
R4 1.30 g
Frey —, Bahrfeldt P. #25, p.19

BVGSLAVS D G DVX STETE
Griffin facing left

NOHE-TAHO-VAGA-RCE 8
Shield of Rügen on long cross

Single digit dated coin with "8" representing 1488.

I-226 Saxony Duchy and Elector
Mint: Freiberg
Elector Friedrich III, Johann and Duke Albrecht, 1486-1500
1488 Half Schwertgroschen
R3 2.10 g
Frey 319, Krug 1698

A:F:H:D':G':DVCS:SAX;TV:LA:MAR:HS
Elector's shield of crossed swords in trefoil, long cross mintmark of Freiberg at beginning of legend

GROSSVS:NOVVS:DVCVM:SAXONI82
Shields of Landsberg-Meissen in trefoil, long cross mintmark of Freiberg at beginning of legend

Extremely rare mule with legend of 1486 but 1482 date. Friedrich became elector in 1486.

I-227a Saxony Duchy and Elector
Mint: Schneeberg
Elector Friedrich III, Johann and Duke Albrecht, 1486-1500
1488 Half Schwertgroschen
C 2.30 g
Frey 319, Krug 1684-91

F:A:H:D:G:DVCS:SAX:TV:L:MAR:HS
Elector's shield of crossed swords in trefoil, clover leaf mintmark of Schneeberg at beginning of legend

GROSSVS:NOVVS:DVCVM:SAXOI88
Shield of Landsberg-Meissen in trefoil with clover leaf mintmark of Schneeberg at beginning of legend

---

I-227b **Saxony** **Duchy and Elector**
Mint: **Schneeberg**
Elector Friedrich III, Johann and Duke Albrecht, 1486-1500
1488 **Half Schwertgroschen**
R3 *2.30 g*
Frey —, Krug 1695-96

F:A:H:D:G:DVCS:SAX:TV:L:HAR:HS
Elector's shield of crossed swords in trefoil, clover leaf mintmark of Schneeberg at beginning of legend

GROSSVS:NOVVS:DVCVM:SAXONI82
Shield of Landsberg-Meissen in trefoil with clover leaf mintmark of Schneeberg at beginning of legend

Mule of 1488 obverse legend with 1482 date.

I-227c **Saxony** **Duchy and Elector**
Mint: **Schneeberg**
Elector Friedrich III, Johann and Duke Albrecht, 1486-1500
1488 **Half Schwertgroschen**
R2 *2.30 g*
Frey —, Krug 1691-94

E:A:D:G:DVCS:SAX:TV:LA:HAR:HS
Elector's shield of crossed swords in trefoil, clover leaf mintmark of Schneeberg at beginning of legend

GROSSVS:NOVVS:DVCVM:SAXOI88
Shield of Landsberg-Meissen in trefoil with clover leaf mintmark of Schneeberg at beginning of legend

Mule of 1482 obverse legend with 1488 date.

1489

I-228 **Aachen** **City**
Mint: **Aachen**
1489 **Turnosgroschen**
R2 *1.42 -1.93 g*
Frey 329, Menadier 123, Forschner 113-14, Krumbach 94.89, Schulten 1, Coll. Weygand 2325

S:KAROL:MA:IPERA
Half-length figure of Charlemagne holding imperial orb and cathedral.

ANO:DNI:MILESIMO:CCCC:LXXXIX-MONETA:VRB:AQVEN
Short cross with inner and outer legends

I-229 **Cleve** **Duchy**
Mint: **Wesel**
Johann II, 1481-1521
1489 **Half Stüber**
R2 *2.01 g*
Frey 323, Noss 160, Schulten 1476, Saurma 2940, Coll. Weygand 799

IOHS':DVX:CLIVE'S:Z:CO':MAR'
Arms of Cleve and the Mark occupying entire field

MO':NO'-WESA-LIE':A':-D':1489
Long cross with fleur-de-lys in angles of cross, star in center

Struck both in Wesel and in Unna. This legend identifies Wesel.

I-230 **Cologne** **Archbishopric**
Mint: **Deutz**
Hermann IV of Hesse, 1480-1508
1489 **Turnosgroschen**
R *2.50 g*
Frey 336C, Noss 480-01, Cappe 1179, Schulten 1606

H'MAI:ARCHI-EPI':COLONIE'
St. Peter behind shield of Cologne

BENEDICTVS:SIT:DEVS:IN:SECVLA:SECV- GRO-S'TV-ICIE-1489
Shield of Cologne-Hesse-Nidda-Cologne over cross interrupting inner legend

---

I-231 **Cologne** **Archbishopric**
Mint: **Deutz**
Hermann IV of Hesse, 1480-1508
1489 **Albus**
S *1.90 g*
Frey 321, Noss 482-83, Cappe 1180, Schulten 1607, Coll. Weygand 1684-85

H'MAI'A-EPI':COL
St. Peter holding staff and key behind large quartered shield of Cologne-Hesse-Ziegenhain-Cologne

MONE':NOVA:TVICIENS':1489
Shields of Cologne-Hesse-Nidda-Ziegenhain forming a cross

I-232 Dortmund City
Mint: Dortmund
1489 Four Mites
R6 Weight unknown
Frey —, JMP XXXIX 1952, #40

Countermark of single headed eagle on a host 1489 Louvain four mites

This unique coin is located at the Cabinet des Medailles in Brussels. The host coin is itself excessively rare.

I-233 Erfurt City
Mint: Erfurt
1489 Uniface Hohlpfennig
R5 Weight unknown
Frey —, Leitzmann 404, Posern-Klett 421

A*M*ꝝ*ꝝ*9 (surrounding shield of Erfurt)
Shield of Erfurt

The date on this coin is somewhat conjectural. Given the style, it is clearly not of the first half of the 15th century. It is believed that the first "4" represents the centuries and the second is an erroneous use of a "4" instead of an 8. Stylistically, the coin fits the assigned date of 1489, while Posern-Klett assigns this piece to "1450 or later."

I-234 Göttingen City
Mint: Göttingen
1489 Körtling
S 1.10 g
Frey 330, Schrock 23, Schulten 1004

MONE*NOVA*GOTTINGE
Large "G" in octofoil

ANO*DNI*M*CCCC*LXXXIX
Large "G" over short cross

I-235 Jever Lordship
Mint: Jever
Edo Wimken II, 1468-1511
1489 Stüber
R4 2.00 g
Frey 324, Kappelhoff 135, Schulten 1400?, Saurma 3335

EDO WIMK' CAPITAL' IEVER
Crested helmet above leaning lion shield of Jever

ANNO-DNI'M-CCCC-LXXX9
Thick long cross with "I-E-V-E "in angles of cross, star in center

---

I-236 Jever Lordship
Mint: Jever
Edo Wimken II, 1468-1511
1489 Witten
R4 0.72 g
Frey —, Kappelhoff 128, De Mey Im 683, Schulten 1402

EDO WIMK' CAPIT' IN IEV'
Lion shield of Jever

ANN'-DN'M-CCCC-LXXX9
Long cross with "I-E-V-E" in angles of cross

I-237 Jülich-Berg Duchy
Mint: Mülheim
Wilhelm IV, 1475-1511
1489 Double Bausche
S 2.50-2.81 g
Frey 322, 322A, Noss 187a-t, Schulten 1427, Saurma 2990, Coll. Weygand 269

WILHELM*DVX*IVLIAC'*Z*MONTE
Seated lion facing left wearing cape

MONE-NOVA-MULH-EM*1489
Quartered arms of Jülich-Berg and Ravensburg on long cross

I-238 Jülich-Berg Duchy
Mint: Mülheim
Wilhelm IV, 1475-1511
1489 Half Weisspfennig
R3 1.07 g
Frey 322, Noss 188a-e, Schulten 1434, Saurma 2993, Coll. Weygand 283

WILHELM:DVX-IVLIAC:Z:MOH
St. Hubertus standing with sword behind quartered arms of

Jülich-Berg and Ravensburg

MONETA*NOVA*MULHE'*1489
Short cross with inner and outer legends

I-239 Mainz Archbishopric
Mint: Uncertain
Berthold of Henneberg, 1484-1504
1489 Schilling
R5 Weight unknown
Frey –, Pr. Alexander 205, Schulten 1942

BERT':ARCH'EPIS':PRIN':EE'
Quartered arms of Mainz, Romhild, Henneberg and Mainz

S-PET':A-POS':1489
St.. Peter holding key and cross behind shield of Palatinate-Mainz

---

I-240 Mark County
Mint: Unna
Johann II, 1481-1521
1489 Half Stüber
R6 1994 g
Frey –, Noss 160 (note), Schulten 1477

IOHS':DVX:CLIVE'S:Z:CO'MAR'
Arms of Cleve and the Mark occupying entire field

MO':NO' –VNNA –ANNO–D*1489
Long cross with fleur-de-lys in angles of cross, star in center

In 1489, the county of Mark was ruled by the Duke of Cleve.

I-241 Osnabrück Bishopric
Mint: Osnabrück
Konrad IV of Reitberg, 1482-1508
1489 Half Stüber
R6 1.95 g
Frey –, Kennepohl 164, Schulten 2510

CONRADVS:EPVS:OSNABVRG'
Quartered arms of Osnabruck and Rietberg

MONE-NOVA-OSNA-BVRG-1-ꝝ-8-9
Long cross with date in angles of cross

I-242 Palatinate County and Elector
Mint: Heidelberg?
Philip I, 1449-1508
1489 Goldgulden
R6 3.18 g
Frey –, FR. 1981

PHILIP-P'C'P'R'-DVXºB-AVAR'- 1ꝝ-89
Date above quartered arms of Palatinate-Bavaria

MONE'NOVA-AVRE'RENE'
Christ on gothic throne with shield of Mainz at feet

Probably unique. Sold by Künker in March 2001.

I-243 Pommerania Duchy
Mint: Garz
Bogislaus X, 1474-1523
1489 Schilling
C 1.20 g
Frey 325, Dannenberg 377, Schulten 2770

BVGSLASºDºGºDVXºSTETIN
Griffin facing left

MOHE-TA NO-VAGA-RE 89º
Shield of Rügen on long cross

1490

I-244 Aachen City
Mint: Aachen
1490 Turnosgroschen
R3 1.90 g
Frey 338, Menadier 123d, Forschner 115, Krumbach 94.90, Schulten 1

S:KAROL:MA:IPERA
Half-length figure of Charlemagne holding imperial orb and cathedral.

ANO:DNI:MILESIMO:CCCC:LXXXX-MONETA:VRB:AQVEN
Short cross with inner and outer legends

I-245 Cleve Duchy
Mint: Cleve
Johann II, 1481-1521
1490 Braspfennig
R3 4.00 g
Frey 341A, Noss 190, Schulten 1457

IOHS':DVX:CLIVENS':Z:CO':DE:MA-R'
Helmeted diagonal shields of Cleve and the Mark with the shield of Cleve interrupting legend

MONETA:NOVA:CLIVENS':M:CCCC:XC
Cross with fleur-de-lys in angles of cross

I-246 Cleve Duchy
Mint: Cleve
Johann II, 1481-1521
1490 Stüber
VS 2.80 g
Frey 341, Noss 191-92, Schulten 1468, Coll. Weygand 786-88

IOHS':DVX:CLIVENS':Z:CO':DE:MAR'
Shield of Cleve in center of field

MO':NO'-CLIVN'-M:CC-CC:XC
Shield of the Mark on long cross

I-247 Cleve Duchy
Mint: Wesel
Johann II, 1481-1521
1490 Braspfennig
R3 4.25 g
Frey 342A, Noss 162, Schulten 1456

IOHS':DVX:CLIVENS':ET:CO':MARK'
Helmeted diagonal shields of Cleve and the Mark

MONETA:NOVA:WESALIE:M:CCCC:XC
Cross with fleur-de-lys in angles of cross

I-248 Cleve Duchy
Mint: Wesel
Johann II, 1481-1521
1490 Stüber
VS 2.80 g
Frey 342, Noss 163-64, Schulten 1467, Coll. Weygand 801-03

IOHS:DVX:CLIVENS':CO':MARK
Shield of Cleve in center of field

MO':NO-WESA-LIE:M:C-CCC:XC
Shield of Mark on long cross

I-249 Cleve Duchy
Mint: Wesel
Johann II, 1481-1521
1490 Half Albus
R3 1.24 g
Frey —, Noss 165, Schulten 1486

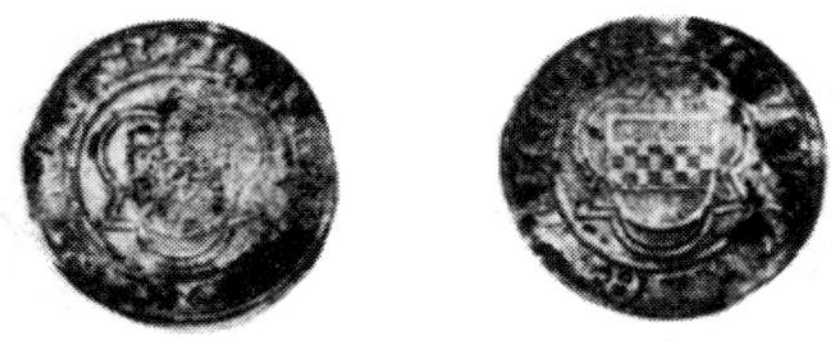

IOHS':DVX:CLIVENS':Z:CO':MARK
Shield of Cleve in trefoil

MO':NO'-WESA-LIE:M:C-CCC:XC
Shield of Mark in trefoil

I-250a Göttingen City
Mint: Göttingen
1490 Körtling
S 1.20 g
Frey 337, Schrock 24, Schulten 1004

MONE*NOVA*GOTTING
Large "G" in octofoil

ANNO*DNI*M*CCCC:XC
Large "G" over short cross

I-250b Göttingen City
Mint: Göttingen
1490 Körtling
R5 1.20 g
Frey —, Schrock 7
Same as preceding, but with error date of "ANNO:DNI:M*CCCC*X"

This date is not 1410, but an erroneous engraving of the date of 1490.

I-251 Mainz Archbishopric
Mint: Mainz
Berthold of Henneberg, 1484-1504
1490 Goldgulden
R5 3.40 g
Frey 340, FR. 1629, De Mey d'Or 1507, Pr. Alexander 206, Schulten 1940, Cappe 692

BERTO-LO'AR-CHIE'M-OGVNT'- 1ꝝ-90
Quartered arms of Romhild-Henneberg with arms of Mainz in center, over long cross with date above shield

MONE'NOVA-AVRE'RENE'
Christ on gothic throne with shield of Palatinate-Mainz at feet

I-252 **Mark** **County**
Mint: **Unna**
Johann II, 1481-1521
1490 **Stüber**
R6 *2.80 g*
Frey —, Menadier M. 95, Coll. Lejeune 1352, Schulten 1478

IOHS'DVX xCLIVENSxZxCO'xMARK
Shield of Cleve

MO'NO-VNNE-NS'MC-CCCXC
Shield of Mark on long cross

This coin copies the stüber issued by the Count's mints at Wesel and Cleve under his joint title as Duke of Cleve. As with the other coins of the Mark, this is of the greatest rarity.

I-253 **Palatinate** **County and Elector**
Mint: **Heidelberg**
Philip I, 1449-1508
1490 **Goldgulden**
R5 *3.40 g*
Frey 339, FR. 1981, De Mey d'Or 1716, Schulten 2655

PHILIP-P'C'R'H'-DVX:B-AVAR'- 14-90
Date above quartered arms of Palatinate-Bavaria

MONETA:NOVA-AVRE:HEID'
Christ on gothic throne with shield of Palatinate-Mainz at feet

---

I-254 **Palatinate-Zweibrücken** **County**
Mint: **Veldenz**
Alexander, 1489-1514
1490 **Schilling**
R6 *Weight unknown*
Frey 339A, Berlin Blaetter #5, 1870, p. 156, Pl 61, #2, Schulten 2712

ALLEXA'-C.P.R.DX B'
St. Peter with shield of Palatinate-Bavaria below

MONETA:NOVA:VELDS' 1ꝗ90
Shields of Palatinate and Bavaria formed in triangle

I-255a **Saxony** **Duchy and Elector**
Mint: **Freiberg**
Elector Friedrich III, Johann and
Duke Albrecht, 1486-1500
1490 **Half Schwertgroschen**
R2 *2.20 g*
Frey 343, Krug 1713

F:A:H:D:G:DVX:SAX:TV:L:IIAR:IIS:90
Elector's shield of crossed swords in trefoil, (new) rose mintmark of Freiberg at beginning of legend

GROSSVS:NOVVS:DVCVM:SAXONI
Shield of Landsberg-Meissen in trefoil with new rose mintmark of Freiberg at beginning of legend

In 1490, the new mintmaster of Freiberg adopted the rose mintmark which was previously used on Gotha's early dated coins.

I-255b **Saxony** **Duchy and Elector**
Mint: **Freiberg**
Elector Friedrich III, Johann and
Duke Albrecht, 1486-1500
1490 **Half Schwertgroschen**
R4 *2.20 g*
Frey —, Krug 1714

F:A:H:D:G:DVX:SAX:TV:L:MAR:MS:90
Elector's shield of crossed swords in trefoil, new rose mintmark of Freiberg at beginning of legend

GROSSVS:NOVVS:DVCVH:SAXONI9
Shield of Landsberg-Meissen in trefoil with new rose mintmark of Freiberg at beginning of legend

Variety with dates on both obverse and reverse and exceptionally crude lettering.

I-256a **Saxony** **Duchy and Elector**
Mint: **Zwickau**
Elector Friedrich III, Johann and
Duke Albrecht, 1486-1500
1490 **Half Schwertgroschen**
S *2.00 g*
Frey 343, Krug 1699-1710, Schulten 2966

F:A:H:D:G:DVCS:SAX:TV:L:MAR:HS
Elector's shield of crossed swords in trefoil, clover leaf mintmark of Zwickau at beginning of legend

GROSSVS:NOVVS:DVCVM:SAXONI90
Shield of Landsberg-Meissen in trefoil with clover leaf mintmark of Zwickau at beginning of legend

The "0" in the date is very tiny. Three dies are known with the date at the end of the obverse legend. See Krug 1708-10.

I-256b **Saxony** **Duchy and Elector**
Mint: **Zwickau**
Elector Friedrich III, Johann and
Duke Albrecht, 1486-1500
1490 **Half Schwertgroschen**
R3 *2.00 g*
Frey —, Krug 1711-12

E:A:D:G:DVCS:SAX:TV:LA:MAR:HS
Elector's shield of crossed swords in trefoil, clover leaf mintmark of Zwickau at beginning of legend

GROSSVS:NOVVS:DVCVM:SAXONI90
Shield of Landsberg-Meissen in trefoil with clover leaf mintmark of Zwickau at beginning of legend

Mule with legend of Ernst from 1482 and date of 1490. Ernst died in 1486.

I-256c Saxony Duchy and Elector
Mint: Zwickau/Freiberg
Elector Friedrich III, Johann and Duke Albrecht, 1486-1500
1490 Half Schwertgroschen
R4 *2.00 g*
Frey —, Krug 1715

F:A:H:D:G:DVCS:SAX:TV:LA:HA:HIS
Elector's shield of crossed swords in trefoil, clover leaf mintmark of Zwickau at beginning of legend

GROSSVS:NOVVS:DVCVH:SAXONI90
Shield of Landsberg-Meissen in trefoil with new rose mintmark of Freiberg at beginning of legend

Mule of Zwickau and Freiberg.

1491

I-257 Aachen City
Mint: Aachen
1491 Broad Mariengroschen
R5 *2.60-3.00 g*
Frey 354, Menadier 126, Forschner 118, Krumbach 97.91, Schulten 3, Saurma 2815

VRBS:AQVEN:REGNI:SEDES:CAPVT:OIM:1ꝶ91
Crowned Madonna and Child and Charlemagne with cathedral in between, date in exergue

CIVITATV:ET:PROVINCIARVM:GALLIE
City shield of Aachen over flowery cross

I-258 Aachen City
Mint: Aachen
1491 Mariengroschen
VS *2.27-2.96 g*
Frey 353, Menadier 125, Forschner 116-17, Krumbach 98.91, Schulten 2

VRBS:AQ-VENSIS-REGNI:SE-CES:1ꝶ91
City shield of Aachen over flowery long cross

AVE:REGNA:SELORV:MATER:REGIS:AGELOR'
Crowned Madonna and Child

This coin is excessively rare in higher grades. It is almost always found very worn and poorly struck.

I-259a Cologne Archbishopric
Mint: Deutz
Hermann IV of Hesse, 1480-1508
1491 Goldgulden
R *3.25 g*
Frey 350, Noss 484b-d, Cappe 1181-82, FR. 803, De Mey d'Or 691, Schulten 1603, Saurma 1447, Coll. Weygand 1676

H'MAI'ARC-HIEPI'COL'
Christ on gothic throne, shield of Hesse-Ziegenhain below

MO'AV'-RENE-'S'1ꝶ91
Quartered arms of Cologne-Hesse-Nidda-Cologne in trefoil with three small shields of Mainz, Trier and Palatinate at triangle points

---

I-259b Cologne Archbishopric
Mint: Deutz
Hermann IV of Hesse, 1480-1508
1491 Goldgulden
R2 *3.25 g*
Frey 350, Noss 484a, Cappe 1183, FR. 803, De Mey d'Or 691 , Schulten 1603, Saurma 1447

Same as preceding, but with the date shown as 1491

I-260a East Frisia County
Mint: Emden
Edzard I, 1491-1528
1491 Stüber
R5? *Weight unknown*
Frey 355A, Schulten 2550, Coll. Roeper, Part II, No. 2094

(Uncertain)
Harpyie eagle occupying field with four surrounding stars

(Uncertain)
Long cross with fleur-de-lys in angles of cross

I-260b **East Frisia County**
Mint: Emden
Edzard I, 1491-1528
1491 Stüber
R6 *2.91 g*
Frey —, Kappelhoff 99, Schulten 2551

MO'-EDZARD'*CO-FRI'*OI'E'TAL'
Four part shield with alternating harpyies and eagles, star above

DA*PA'-CE*DNI'-DIEB'*N-*IS*91
Thick double-stranded long cross with star in center and fleur-de-lys in angles

Schulten states that only one example is known of this type.

I-261 **East Frisia County**
Mint: Emden
Edzard I, 1491-1528
1491 Krummsteert
R *2.30-2.85 g*
Frey 355, Kappelhoff 98, Schulten 2555

EDZARD'*COMES*FRI'*OI'ENTA'
Harpyie occupying field with four surrounding stars

DA*PACE*DNE'*IN*DIEB'*NRIS*91
Short cross with fleur-de-lys in angles of cross

I-262 **East Frisia County**
Mint: Emden
Edzard I, 1491-1528
1491 Half Krummsteert
R4 *1.60 g*
Frey —, Kappelhoff 97, Schulten 2556

EDZARD'*COMES*FRI'*ORIETA'
Harpyie eagle in quatrefoil

DA*PACE'*DN'*IN*DIEB'NRS'91
Short cross with fleur-de-lys in angles of cross

I-263 **Frankfurt City and Imperial mint**
Mint: Frankfurt
Friedrich III (Emperor), 1452-1493
1491 Goldgulden
R *3.25 g*
Frey 364, J & F 124, 2043, FR. 940, De Mey d'Or 975A, Schulten 850

MONE'ºNOVA-FRANCF 1ꭗ91
John the Baptist holding lamb and book, small shield of Weinsberg at feet

FRIDRIC':RO'AN':IMPE'ATO
Imperial orb in trefoil

The Imperial mint at Frankfurt was the most prolific issuer of early dated gold coins. As might be expected, amongst all the dated issues there are a variety of variations of spellings, abbreviations and spacing devises found.

I-264 **Göttingen City**
Mint: Göttingen
1491 Körtling
VS *1.20 g*
Frey 358, Schrock 25, Schulten 1004

MONE*NOVA*GOTTINGE
Large "G" in octofoil

ANO*DNI*M*CCCC*XCI
Large "G" over short cross

I-265 **Hildesheim City**
Mint: Hildesheim
1491 Sechsling
R2 *1.10 g*
Frey —, Buck/B. 12, Schulten 1278, 1285, Saurma 4022

MO:NO:HILDEN:M:CCCCXCI
Shield of Hildesheim

SAC'*BERWARDV*P
Half-length figure of St. Bernward standing, holding cross

Also known as Bernwardsgroschen. Schulten lists this coin both as a groschen (S. 1278) and as a sechsling (S. 1285).

I-266 **Jever Lordship**
Mint: Jever
Edo Wimken II, 1468-1511
1491 Groten
R4-5 *Weight unknown*
Frey —, De Mey Im 661, Schulten 1403?

MONE' EDONIS CAPITALIS IEVER
Standing lion facing left

ANNO-DNI:M-CCCC-XCI
Long cross with shield of Jever in center

I-267 Mainz Archbishopric
Mint: Mainz
Berthold of Henneberg, 1484-1504
1491 Goldgulden
R3 3.25 g
Frey 352, FR. 1630, De Mey d'Or 1508, Schulten 1941

BERTO-LO'ARC'-EPI MO'
Quartered arms of Mainz, Romhild, Henneberg and Mainz set in trefoil with small shields of Cologne, Trier and Palatinate at triangle points

MONE:NO'-AVRE:1ꝝ91
Christ on gothic throne with shield of Mainz at feet

I-268 Nördlingen Imperial City
Mint: Nördlingen
Friedrich III (Emperor), 1452-1493
1491 Goldgulden
R 3.25 g
Frey 359, Herzfelder 9, FR. 1794, De Mey d'Or 1645, Schulten 2405

MONETA:NOV'-NORDLI' 1ꝝ91
John the Baptist holding lamb and book, small shield of Weinsberg at feet

FRIDRICVS:ROMAN:IMPERATOR
Imperial orb in trefoil

I-269 Palatinate County and Elector
Mint: Heidelberg
Philip I, 1449-1508
1491 Goldgulden
R2 3.25 g
Frey 350, FR. 1982, De Mey d'Or 1717, Schulten 2656

PHS*CO*PR'-DVX*BAVA'
Christ on gothic throne with small shield of Palatinate-Bavaria at feet

MO':AV-RENE-1ꝝ91
Conjoined shields of Mainz, Cologne and Trier arranged in trefoil with shield of Palatinate-Bavaria in center

This piece is often misattributed to Cologne.

I-270 Pommerania Duchy
Mint: Damm
Bogislaus X, 1474-1523
1491 Schilling
R2 1.14 g
Frey 357, Schulten 2769

BVGSLAVSºDºGºDVXºSTETIN
Griffin facing left

MON-ETAºN-OVAD-AM 91
Shield of Rügen on long cross

Nearly all listed examples of this date are misattributed 1495 schillings with a medieval "5" in the date "9˥."

I-271 Saxony Duchy and Elector
Mint: Zwickau
Elector Friedrich III, Johann and Duke Albrecht, 1486-1500
1491 Half Schwertgroschen
R3 2.00 g
Frey —, Krug 1716-18, Schulten 2966

F:A:H:D:G:DVCS:SAX:TV:L:MAR:MIS
Elector's shield of crossed swords in trefoil, clover leaf mint-mark of Zwickau at beginning of legend

GROSSVS:NOVVS:DVCVM:SAXONI9I
Shield of Landsberg-Meissen in trefoil with clover leaf mint-mark of Zwickau at beginning of legend

One die is known with the date on the obverse instead. See Krug 1718.

I-272 Trier Archbishopric
Mint: Coblenz
Johann II of Baden, 1456-1503
1491 Goldgulden
R4 3.25 g
Frey 351, FR. 3450, De Mey d'Or 2143, Noss 540, Schulten 3509

IOHAN'-ARCEP'-TREVE'
Shield of Trier-Baden in trefoil with three small shields in triangle points

MONE':NOV'-AV'RE:1ꝝ91
Christ on gothic throne with small shield of Trier-Baden at feet

Schulten 3510 lists 1491 and 1492 dated goldguldens of a completely different type but no confirmation is available of their existance.

1492

I-273 Aachen City
Mint: Aachen
1492 Broad Mariengroschen

R5 2.60-2.90 g

Frey 371, Menadier 127, Forschner 119, Krumbach 97.92, Schulten 3, Saurma 2816, Coll. Weygand 2326

VRBS:AQVEN:REGNI:SEDES:CAPVT:OIM:1ꝶ92
Crowned Madonna and Child and Charlemagne with cathedral in between, date in exergue

CIVITATV':ET:PROVINCIARVM:GALLIE
City shield of Aachen over flowery cross

I-274 Cleve Duchy
Mint: Cleve
Johann II, 1481-1521
1492 6 Stüber

R4-5 6.00 g

Frey 385, Noss 195, Schulten 1452

IOHS':DVX:CLIVENS':Z:CO':DE:MAR-K'
Elaborate helmets of Cleve and the Mark over shields of Cleve and the Mark

MONETA:NOVA:CLIVENS':M:CCCC:XCII
Quartered arms of Cleve and the Mark on flowery cross

I-275 Cleve Duchy
Mint: Cleve
Johann II, 1481-1521
1492 Braspfennig

R2 3.30 g

Frey 385A, Noss 196-97, Schulten 1458

IOHS':DVX:CLIVENS':Z:CO':DE:MARK
Large helmet of Cleve from which hangs shields of Cleve and the Mark

MON:NO-CLIVEN-M:CCC-C:XCII
Double-stranded flowery cross with fleur-de-lys in angles and rhombus in center with four leaf clover

---

I-276 Cleve Duchy
Mint: Wesel
Johann II, 1481-1521
1492 Stüber

VS 3.26 g

Frey 384, Noss 167a, Schulten 1469, Coll. Weygand 795-96

IOHS':DVX:CLIVENS':ET:CO':MARK'
Large helmet of Cleve from which hangs shields of Cleve and the Mark

MONE-NOVA-WESA-LIE:92
Double-stranded long cross with rhombus in center and fleur-de-lys in angles

---

I-277 Cleve Duchy
Mint: Wesel
Johann II, 1481-1521
1492 Half Stüber

R2 2.14 g

Frey 384A, Noss 168, Schulten 1479

IOHS':DVX:CLIVE':Z:CO':MARK'
Crested helmet of Cleve from which hangs small shields of Cleve and the Mark

MONE'-NOVA-WESA-LIE:92
Double-stranded long cross with fleur-de-lys in angles of cross

---

I-278a Frankfurt City and Imperial mint
Mint: Frankfurt
Friedrich III (Emperor), 1452-1493
1492 Goldgulden

VS 3.25 g

Frey 396E, J & F 125-26, FR. 940, De Mey d'Or 978, Schulten 850

MONE'ºNOVA-FRANCF'º **I** ꝶ9Z
John the Baptist holding lamb and book, small shield of Weinsberg at feet

FRIDRICVS':ROMAN':IMPE'A'
Imperial orb in trefoil

The number 2 in the date appears as a "Z."

I-278b Frankfurt City and Imperial mint
Mint: Frankfurt
Friedrich III (Emperor), 1452-1493
1492 Goldgulden

R2 3.25 g

Frey —, De Mey d'Or 975a, FR. 940 var.

Same as preceding, but with double digit date "92"

I-279 Göttingen City
Mint: Göttingen
1492 Körtling
S 1.20 g
Frey 396, Schrock 26, Schulten 1004

MONE:NOVA:GOTTINGEN
Large "G" in octofoil

ANO:DNI:M:CCCC:XCII
Large "G" over short cross

I-280 Mainz Archbishopric
Mint: Mainz
Berthold of Henneberg, 1484-1504
1492 Goldgulden
R2 3.25 g
Frey 375, FR. 1630, De Mey d'Or 1508, Pr. Alex 207, Schulten 1941,

BERTO-LO'ARC'-EPI MO'
Conjoined shields of Cologne, Jülich and Trier set in trefoil with four-part shield in center

MONE:NOV'-AV:RE:1492
Christ on gothic throne, small shield of Mainz at feet

I-281 Mainz Archbishopric
Mint: Mainz
Berthold of Henneberg, 1484-1504
1492 Half Groschen
R2 1.10 g
Frey 376, Pr. Alexander 208, Schulten 1943

BERT'+ARCH+EPS+PRINC'+ELEC'
Four part shield inside polyfoil

S+-PET:AP-OSTO'L • 1492
St. Peter holding staff and key behind shield of Mainz-Palatinate

Also known as a schilling.

I-282 Mark County
Mint: Hörde
Johann II, 1481-1521
1492 Braspfennig
R6 3.31 g
Frey—, Coll. Weygand 1114, Coll. Lejeune 1352, Schulten 1459

IOHS*DVX*CLIVENS*ET*CO*MARK'
Large helmet of Cleve from which hangs shields of Cleve and the Mark

MONE-TA*NO-VA*HO-RDE*9Z
Double-stranded long cross with fleur-de-lys in angles

This coin copies the braspfennig issued from the Duke's Cleve mints located in Cleve and Wesel. There are likely only two extant examples - one in the State Museum of Berlin and the other, which was sold by Münzen & Medaillen GmbH of Stuttgart in 2006 for $8,500.

I-283 Neuss City
Mint: Neuss
1492 Double Groschen
R2 3.00 g
Frey 386, Noss 7, Schulten 2386, Coll. Weygand 2526-27

MONE:NOVA:CIV-IT:NVSSIENSIS
Large crown and two shields set in trefoil

SIT:NOMEN:DNI:BENEDICTV:149Z
Short cross with flowers in angles of cross

I-284 Nördlingen Imperial City
Mint: Nördlingen
Friedrich III (Emperor), 1452-1493
1492 Goldgulden
R 3.25 g
Frey 381, Herzfelder 10, FR. 1794, Schulten 2405

MONETA:NOV-NORDLI':1492
John the Baptist holding lamb and book, small shield of Weinsberg at feet

FRIDRICVS:ROMAN:IMPERATO'
Imperial orb in trefoil

I-285 Palatinate County and Elector
Mint: Heidelberg
Philip I, 1449-1508
1492 Goldgulden
R2 3.25 g
Frey 373, FR. 1982, De Mey d'Or 1717, Schulten 2656

PHS*CO*PR'-DVX*BAVA'
Christ on gothic throne with small shield of Palatinate-Bavaria at feet

MO'AV*-*RENE*-*S*1Ꝝ92
Quartered arms of Palatinate-Bavaria in trefoil with three small shields of Mainz, Trier and Cologne at triangle points

---

I-286 Palatinate County and Elector
Mint: Uncertain
Philip I, 1449-1508
1492 Half Groschen
R2 1.00 g
Frey 374, Schulten 2663

PHILI+-C+P+P-ELEC'+
Four part shield of Palatinate-Mainz in polyfoil

S PET'+A-POSTOL'+1492
St. Peter holding key and cross behind shield of Palatinate-Mainz

Also known as a schilling.

I-287 Palatinate County and Elector
Mint: Uncertain
Philip I, 1449-1508
1492 Half Albus
R 1.00 g
Frey 374A, Schulten 2664

PHILI*-C*P*P*-ELEC'*
Lion in shield facing left with surrounding shields of Palatinate, Bavaria and Regalienfeld at perimeter

S-PET'*-A*1Ꝝ92
St. Peter holding key and cross behind shield of Palatinate-Mainz

---

I-288a Pommerania Duchy
Mint: Damm
Bogislaus X, 1474-1523
1492 Schilling
S 1.20 g
Frey 367, Dannenberg 380, Schulten 2769

BVGSLAVSºDºGºDVXºSTETIN
Griffin facing left

MONE-TANO-VAºDH-AM 92
Shield of Rügen on long cross

I-288b Pommerania Duchy
Bogislaus X, 1474-1523
Mint: Damm
1492 Schilling
VS 1.20 g
Frey —, Dannenberg 380 var.

Same as preceding, but "2" is backwards

I-289a Pommerania Duchy
Mint: Garz
Bogislaus X, 1474-1523
1492 Schilling
R 1.20 g
Frey 378, Dannenberg 378, Schulten 2770

BVGSLAVSºDºGºDVXºSTETIN
Griffin facing left

MONE-TAºNO-VAºGA-RE 92
Shield of Rügen on long cross

I-289b Pommerania Duchy
Mint: Garz
Bogislaus X, 1474-1523
1492 Schilling
R4 1.30 g
Frey 377, Dannenberg 412, Schulten 2767

DVX:BVGSLAVS:STETTIN
Griffin facing left

LATG-RAVV-ILSE-IOR92
Shield of Rügen on long cross

A commemorative coin struck by Bogislaus in 1498 after pilgrimage to the Holy Land.

I-290 Saxony Duchy and Elector
Mint: Freiberg
Elector Friedrich III, Johann and Duke Albrecht, 1486-1500
1492 Half Schwertgroschen
VS 2.00 g
Frey 383, Krug 1735-40, Schulten 2962 (Annaberg)

F:A:H:D:G:DVCS:SAX:TV:LA:HA:HIS
Elector's shield of crossed swords in trefoil, rose mintmark of Freiberg at beginning of legend

GROSSVS:NOVVS:DVCVH:SAXONI92
Shield of Landsberg-Meissen in trefoil with rose mintmark of Freiberg at beginning of legend

---

I-291 Saxony Duchy and Elector
Mint: Zwickau/Schneeberg
Elector Friedrich III and Johann, 1486-1525
1492 Bartgroschen
VS 2.40 g
Frey —, Krug 1841-1867, Schulten 2972

FRED'E-LC:IO:-DVCVS:S/AXO
Bust of Elector Friedrich III facing right with sword on shoulder

GROSSVSºNOVVSºZWICKAVIE-14-9Z
Crowned helmet of the Duke of Saxony with date at sides of helmet

Issued by Friedrich and Iohann. Die types with the number "2" are much scarcer than with the letter "Z" representing a "2." Unmounted specimens in higher grades are extremely rare.

I-292 Saxony Duchy and Elector
Mint: Zwickau/Schneeberg
Elector Friedrich III, Johann and Duke Georg, 1486-1500
1492 Bartgroschen
VS 2.40 g
Frey 382, Krug 1868-81, Coll. Krug 585, Schulten 3035

FRID'E-IºGER-DVCS-ºSA/XOI
Bust of Elector Friedrich III facing right with sword on shoulder

GROSSVSºNOVVSºZWICKAVI-14-9Z
Crowned helmet of the Duke of Saxony with date at sides of helmet

Issued by Friedrich, Johann and Georg. Extremely rare in higher grades.

I-293 Saxony Duchy and Elector
Mint: Zwickau/Schneeberg
Elector Friedrich III, Johann and Duke Albrecht, 1486-1500
1492 Half Schwertgroschen
C 2.00 g
Frey 383, Krug 1719-34, Schulten 2966

F:A:H:D:G:DVCS:SAX:TV:L:HAR:HIS
Elector's shield of crossed swords in trefoil, clover leaf mintmark of Zwickau at beginning of legend

GROSSVS:NOVVS:DVCVM:SAXONI92
Shield of Landsberg-Meissen in trefoil with clover leaf mintmark of Zwickau at beginning of legend

These coins with the Zwickau mintmark were struck in both Zwickau and Schneeberg.

I-294a Stolberg County
Mint: Wernigerode
Heinrich IX, 1455-1497
1492 Groschen
R2 2.10 g
Frey 372, Friederich 76, 78-81, Schulten 3420, Saurma 4288

GRAVE • HENRICI • IN • STOLBERG
Stolberg shield of stag facing left in trefoil

GROS • DNI' • IN • WERNGERODE 9Z
Short, triple stranded flowery cross with Wernigerode shield at top

Beginning 1492, the flan of these groschens became much smaller.

I-294b Stolberg County
Mint: Wernigerode
Heinrich IX, 1455-1497
1492 Groschen
R3 2.10 g
Frey —, Friederich 77, Schulten 3420

Same as preceding, but with single digit date of "Z" (2)

I-295 **Worms** **Bishopric**
Mint: **Mainz**
Johann of Dalberg, 1482-1503
1492 **Schilling**
R5 *1.00 g*
Frey 376, Joseph 237, Schulten 3637

IO+CAMER+EPISCO+VORMACI
Quartered arms of Worms-Dalberg in quatrefoil

S+PET'+PA-TRON'+1ꝝ9Z
St. Peter behind shield of Worms

This coin copies contemporary coinage of Mainz and the Palatinate.

1493

I-296a **Cologne City** **City**
Mint: **Cologne**
1493 **Blanken**
R5-6 *2.84 g*
Frey 412, Noss 34, Cappe 1272-73, Schulten 1665

SIT:NOMEN:DOMINI:BENEDICTV'1ꝝ93- CIVITAS:COLONIEN'
Short cross with inner and outer legends

IASP:MELCHIOR:BALTHAS'
Elaborate flowery triple-stranded short cross

I-296b **Cologne City** **City**
Mint: **Cologne**
1493 **Blanken**
R5 *2.82 g*
Frey 412, Noss 35, Cappe 1274, Schulten 1666

SIT:NOMEN:DOMINI:BENEDICTV:1ꝝ93- CIVITAS:COLONIEN'
Short cross with inner and outer legends

IASPA-MELCR'-BALTH'
City shield of Cologne with three horizontal crowns

I-297a **Frankfurt** **City and Imperial mint**
Mint: **Frankfurt**
Friedrich III (Emperor), 1452-1493
1493 **Goldgulden**
VS *3.25 g*
Frey 398, J & F 127, 2044, FR. 940, De Mey d'Or 978, Schulten 850

MON'E°NOVA-FRANCF'1ꝝ93
John the Baptist holding lamb and book, small shield of Weinsberg at feet

FRIDRICVS°ROMAN'°IMPERA'
Imperial orb in trefoil

I-297b **Frankfurt** **City and Imperial mint**
Mint: **Frankfurt**
Friedrich III (Emperor), 1452-1493
1493 **Goldgulden**
R *3.25 g*
Frey —, J & F 127k-n, 2575c, FR. 940 var.

Same as preceding, but with double digit date "93"

I-298 **Göttingen** **City**
Mint: **Göttingen**
1493 **Körtling**
R2 *1.10 g*
Frey 412A, Schrock 27, Schulten 1004

MONETA:NOVA:GOTTINGEN
Large "G" in octofoil

ANNO:DNI:M:CCCC:XCIII
Large "G" over short cross

Körtlings dated 1493-1500 tend to be very weakly struck and are excessively rare in higher grades.

I-299 **Hildesheim** **City**
Mint: **Hildesheim**
1493 **Sechsling**
R2 *0.96-1.57 g*
Frey 410, Buck/B. 13, Schulten 1278, 1285, Thomsen 6949

MO':NOVA:HILDESE':XCIII
Shield of Hildesheim

SAC'*BERWARDV'*P'*
Half-length figure of St. Bernward standing, holding cross

I-300 **Jever** **Lordship**
Mint: **Jever**
Edo Wimken II, 1468-1511
1493 **Double Krummsteert**
R5 *1.69 g (chip missing)*
Frey —, Kappelhoff 141, Schulten 1404

MONE'EDONIS CAPITAL___R
Standing lion facing left

ANNO -DNI M- CCCC -XCIII
Long cross with shield of Jever in center

I-301 Lüneburg City
Mint: Lüneburg
1493 Goldgulden
R6 3.25 g
Frey —, Krusy L5, 2

Countermark of letter "A" in a tiny round shield on a host 1493 Frankfurt goldgulden

---

I-302 Mainz Archbishopric
Mint: Mainz
Berthold of Henneberg, 1484-1504
1493 Goldgulden
R2 3.25 g
Frey 412C, FR. 1630, De Mey d'Or 1508, Cappe 695, Coll. Walther 165, Schulten 1941

BERTO-LO'ARC':-EPI MO'
Quartered arms in trefoil with small shields of Trier, Cologne and Palatinate at triangle points

MONE*NO'-AVRE*1ጰ93
Christ on gothic throne, small shield of Mainz at feet

I-303 Mainz Archbishopric
Mint: Mainz
Berthold of Henneberg, 1484-1504
1493 Half Groschen
R2 1.00 g
Frey 405, Pr. Alexander 209, Coll. Walther 166, Schulten 1943

BERT+ARCH+IPS+PRINC+ELE
Quartered arms of Mainz, Romhild, Henneberg and Mainz

SºPETºA-POSTº1ጰ93
St. Peter holding key and cross behind shield of Mainz-Palatinate

---

I-304 NördlingenImperial City
Mint: Nördlingen
Friedrich III (Emperor), 1452-1493
1493 Goldgulden
R 3.25 g
Frey 397, Herzfelder 11, FR. 1794, Schulten 2405

MONETA:NOV-NORDLI':1ጰ93
John the Baptist holding lamb and book, small shield of Weinsberg at feet

FRIDRICVS:ROMAN:IMPERATO'
Imperial orb in trefoil

I-305 Palatinate County and Elector
Mint: Heidelberg
Philip I, 1449-1508
1493 Goldgulden
R 3.25 g
Frey 406A, 412D, FR. 1982 var, De Mey d'Or 1717 var., Schulten 2656

PHILI-P-C PR-DVX PA
Shield of Palatinate-Bavaria in trefoil with small shields of Mainz, Trier and Cologne at triangle points

MONE:NOV-AV'RE'-1ጰ93+
Christ on gothic throne with shield of Palatinate-Bavaria at feet

Both Friedberg and De Mey d'Or list the legends for the 1491 and 1492 as applying to all pieces struck from 1491-1500. However, there are different legends on the goldguldens struck after 1492.

I-306 Palatinate County and Elector
Mint: Uncertain
Philip I, 1449-1508
1493 Half Groschen
R 1.00 g
Frey 406, 406B, 412E, Schulten 2663, Coll. Mem. 2178

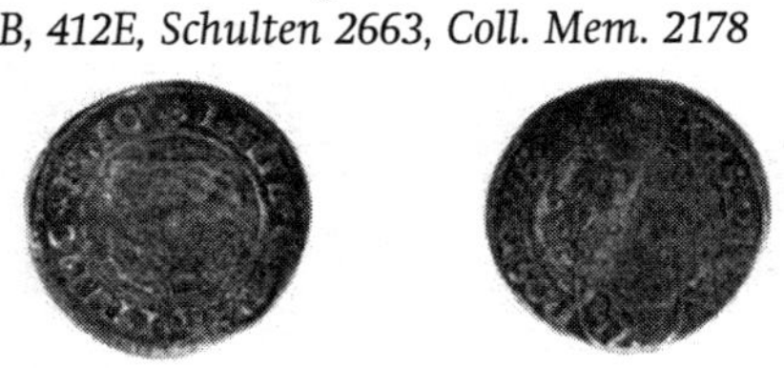

PHIL'+CO'+PAL'+PRINC'+ELEC'
Quartered arms of Mainz-Bavaria

S:PET:A-POST:1493
St. Peter holding key and cross behind shield of Palatinate-Mainz

---

I-307 Pommerania Duchy
Mint: Damm
Bogislaus X, 1474-1523
1493 Schilling
VS 1.20 g
Frey 401, Dannenberg 381, Schulten 2769

BVGSLAVSºDºGºDVXºSTETIN
Griffin facing left

MONE-TAºNO-VAºDH-AM 93
Shield of Rügen on long cross

I-308 Saxony Duchy and Elector
Mint: Zwickau/Schneeberg
Elector Friedrich III and Johann, 1486-1525
1493 Bartgroschen
R3 2.40 g
Frey 407, 412F, Krug 1882-86, Merseberger 355, Schulten 2972

FRID'-ELEC:I:-DVCS:-SAXO
Bust of Elector Friedrich III facing right with sword on shoulder

GROSSVS:NOVVS:ZWICKAVIE- 14-93
Crowned helmet of the Duke of Saxony with date at sides of helmet

---

I-309 Schwarzburg County
Mint: Königsee
Günther XXXVI, 1488-1493,
Balthasar II of Leutenberg 1463-1521
and Heinrich XXXI, 1493-1526
1493 Groschen
R3 2.00 g
Frey 408, Schulten 3360, Fischer 49, Reichmann 1738

GºBºHºCOMITES-SWARZBVRG 93
Shield with large helmet interrupting field

GROSSVS*MAIOR*KONIGISSEE-N
Standing knight with sword

I-310 Schwarzburg County
Mint: Königsee
Günther XXXVI, 1488-1493,
Balthasar II of Leutenberg 1463-1521
and Heinrich XXXI, 1493-1526
1493 Half Groschen
R2 2.10 g
Frey 409, Schulten 3362, Fischer 50a-c, Riechmann 1930, #175

G*B*N*COMITES*SWARZBVRGEN 93
Crowned standing lion advancing left

GROSSVS*NOVVS*KONIGISSEENSIS
Elaborate flowery short cross in quatrefoil with periods in angles

---

I-311 Stolberg County
Mint: Wernigerode
Heinrich IX, 1455-1497
1493 Groschen
R4 2.10 g
Frey 411, Friederich 82-84, Schulten 3420

GRAVE • HENRICI • IN • STOLBERG
Stolberg shield of stag facing left

GROS • DNI • IN • WERNGERODE 93
Short, triple stranded flowery cross with Wernigerode shield at top

1494

I-A312 Cleve Duchy
Mint: Cleve
Johann II, 1481-1521
1494 Braspfennig
R6 3.18 g
Unpublished?

IOHS DVX CLIVENS ET CO MARK
Large helmet of Cleve from which hangs shields of Cleve and the Mark

MON NO-CLIVEN-MCCCCXCIIII
Double-stranded long cross with fleur-de-lys in angles of cross

---

I-312 Cleve Duchy
Mint: Wesel
Johann II, 1481-1521
1494 4 Möhrchen
R3 0.68 g
Frey —, Noss 171, Schulten 1492

IOHS':DVX-CLIVE':Z:M
Helmeted stag's head above shield of Cleve

MON'-NO':W-ESAL'- I ꝝ9ꝝ
Long cross with fleur-de-lys in angles of cross

This denomination was equivalent to four heller. Schulten also lists quarter groschen and pfennigs dated 1493, but both are believed to be undated.

I-313 Erfurt City
Mint: Erfurt
1494 Uniface Scherf
R4 *0.30 g*

Frey 422, Schulten 838

9 º 4
Date divided by wheel with five spokes

I-314 Frankfurt City and Imperial mint
Mint: Frankfurt
Maximilian I (Emperor), 1493-1519
1494 Goldgulden
VS *3.25 g*
Frey 416, J & F 128, FR. 941, De Mey d'Or 979, Schulten 851

MO'ºNO'ºFR-ANC'ºF'º I ꝝ9ꝝ
John the Baptist holding lamb and book, small shield of Weinsberg at feet

MAXIMILIANVSºROMA'ºREX
Imperial orb in trefoil

I-315 Göttingen City
Mint: Göttingen
1494 Körtling
R2 *1.10 g*
Frey 423A, Schrock 28, Schulten 1004

MONETA:NOVA:GOTTINGE
Large "G" in octofoil

ANO:DNI:M:CCCC:XCIIII
Large "G" over short cross

I-316 Hildesheim City
Mint: Hildesheim
1494 Sechsling
R *1.00-1.43 g*
Frey 419, Buck/B.14 , Schulten 1278, 1285

MO':NOV:HILDESE:XCIIII
Shield of Hildesheim

SAC'*BERWARDV'*P'*
Half-length figure of St. Bernward standing, holding cross

I-317 Mainz Archbishopric
Mint: Mainz
Berthold of Henneberg, 1484-1504
1494 Goldgulden
R6 *3.25 g*
FR 1630, Schulten 1941

BERTO-LD AR-EPI'
Quartered arms of Mainz, Romhild, Henneberg and Mainz set in trefoil with small shields of Cologne, Trier and Jülich at triangle points

MONE'NOV'-AV.RE I ꝝ9ꝝ
Christ on throne, small shield of Mainz at feet

Sold at the famous Saurma auction in 1898 by L. & L. Hamburger.

I-318 Nördlingen Imperial City
Mint: Nördlingen
Maximilian I (Emperor), 1493-1519
1494 Goldgulden
R3 *3.25 g*
Frey 417, Herzfelder 12, FR. 1795, Schulten 2406

MONETA:NOV-NORDLI: I ꝝ9ꝝ
John the Baptist holding lamb and book, small shield of Weinsberg at feet

MAXIMILIANVS:ROMAN':REX
Imperial orb in trefoil

I-319 Palatinate County and Elector
Mint: Uncertain
Philip I, 1449-1508
1494 Half Groschen
R3 *1.00 g*
Frey 421, 421A, Schulten 2663

PHIL*CO'*PAL'*PRINC'*ELEC'
Quartered arms of Palatinate-Bavaria

SºPETº'ºA-POSTº I ꝝ9ꝝ
St. Peter holding key and cross behind shield of Palatinate-Mainz

I-320 **Pommerania** **Duchy**
Mint: **Damm**
Bogislaus X, 1474-1523
1494 **Schilling**
S *1.36 g*
Frey 415, Dannenberg 382, Schulten 2769

BVGSLVSºDºGºDVXºSTETIN
Griffin facing left

MON-ETA:N-OVA:D-AM 9ꝝ
Shield of Rügen on long cross

I-321 **Saxony** **Duchy and Elector**
Mint: **Schneeberg**
Elector Friedrich III, Johann and Duke Albrecht, 1486-1500
1494 **Half Schwertgroschen**
R5 *2.02 g*
Frey —, Krug 1741

F:A:H:D:G:DVCS:SAX:TV:LA:HA:HIS
Elector's shield of crossed swords in trefoil, clover leaf mintmark of Schneeberg at beginning of legend

GROSSVS:NOVVS:DVCVH:SAXO 9ꝝ
Shield of Landsberg-Meissen in trefoil with clover leaf mintmark of Schneeberg at beginning of legend

This is the only known Saxony coin dated 1494.

I-322 **Württemberg** **County**
Mint: **Tübingen**
Eberhard V, 1457-1496
1494 **Schilling**
R5 *1.56 g*
Frey 423, Coll. Ebner III,8, Klein 28a-b, Schulten 3650

EBERH+COM+&+WIRT+SENIOR
Quartered arms of Württemberg and Mompelgard

ATTE-MPTO 1ꝝ-9ꝝ
Date divided by palm tree

One of the few pieces ever offered in a public sale brought $36,000 in the Meister & Sonntag auction of October, 2006.

1495

I-323 **Erfurt** **City**
Mint: **Erfurt**
1495 **Uniface Pfennig**
R4 *0.30 g*
Frey —, Schulten 831

1495 - E
Shields and wheel with spokes, date above and letter "E" below

I-324 **Erfurt** **City**
Mint: **Erfurt**
1495 **Uniface Scherf**
R3 *0.30 g*
Frey —, Leitzmann 406, Schulten 838

9 º 5
Date divided by wheel with five spokes

I-325 **Frankfurt** **City and Imperial mint**
Mint: **Frankfurt**
Maximilian I (Emperor), 1493-1519
1495 **Goldgulden**
S *3.25 g*
Frey 428, J & F 129, FR. 941, De Mey d'Or 979, Schulten 851

MO'ºNO'ºFR-ANC'F'º1ꝝ95
John the Baptist holding lamb and book, small shield of Weinsberg at feet

MAXIMILIANVSºROMA'ºREX
Imperial orb in trefoil

Schulten reports the existance of a 1495 goldgulden under the title of Friedrich III, but no photograph or other confirmation is available.

I-326 **Göttingen** **City**
Mint: **Göttingen**
1495 **Körtling**
R3 *1.20 g*
Frey 426, Schrock 29

MONETA:NOVA:GOTTIN
Large "G" in octofoil

ANO:DNI:M:CCCC:XCV"
Large "G" over short cross

I-327 **Hildesheim** **City**
Mint: **Hildesheim**
1495 **Sechsling**
R *1.11-1.39 g*
Frey 431, Buck/B. 15, Schulten 1278, 1285

MO:NOV:HILDESEII:XCV+
Shield of Hildesheim

SAC*BERWARDV*P'
Half-length figure of St. Bernward standing, holding cross

I-328 **Mainz** **Archbishopric**
Mint: **Mainz**
Berthold of Henneberg, 1484-1504
1495 **Goldgulden**
R5-6 *3.25 g*
FR. 1630, Schulten 1941

BER-ARC'-EP'M
Quartered arms of Mainz, Romhild, Henneberg and Mainz set in trefoil with small shields of Cologne, Trier and Jülich at triangle points

MONE'NOV'- AV'RE'1ጸ95
Christ on gothic throne with shield of Mainz at feet

The date on this coin, with a "lightning strike" 5, is often misidentified.

I-329 **Mainz** **Archbishopric**
Mint: **Mainz**
Berthold of Henneberg, 1484-1504
1495 **Half Groschen**
R2 *1.00 g*
Frey 427, Coll. Walther 167, Schulten 1943

BERT+AREP'+PPI+ELEC"
Quartered arms of Mainz, Romhild, Henneberg and Mainz

S-PET+-+A'149-5
St. Peter holding key and cross behind shield of Mainz-Palatinate

---

I-330 **Mainz** **Archbishopric**
Mint: **Mainz**
Berthold of Henneberg, 1484-1504
1495 **Uniface Pfennig**
R5 *Weight unknown*
Frey —, Schulten 1944

1495
Date over shield of Mainz

I-331 **Nördlingen** **Imperial City**
Mint: **Nördlingen**
Maximilian I (Emperor), 1493-1519
1495 **Goldgulden**
R3 *3.25 g*
Frey 430, Herzfelder 13, FR. 1795, Schulten 2406

MONETA:NOV-NORDLI:1ጸ95
John the Baptist holding lamb and book, small shield of Weinsberg at feet

MAXIMILIANVS:ROM:REX
Imperial orb in trefoil

I-332 **Nördlingen** **Imperial City**
Mint: **Nördlingen**
Maximilian I (Emperor), 1493-1519
1495 **Half Schilling**
R6 ? *1.20 g*
Unpublished?

MONETA:NOVA:NORDLING' 1ጸ95
Large imperial eagle

MAXIMILIANVS:ROMANOR:REX
Shield of Weinsberg in trefoil

Example in author's collection.

I-333 **Palatinate** **County and Elector**
Mint: **Uncertain**
Philip I, 1449-1508
1495 **Half Albus**
VS *1.00 g*
Frey 425, 425A, Schulten 2664, Noss 199, Coll. Mem. 2179

PHIL'+CO-PAL'+P-RI'+ELE'
Lion shield surrounded by three small shields of Mainz, Bavaria and Regalianfeld

S-PET':A-POS':149-5
St. Peter holding key and cross behind shield of Palatinate-Mainz

This is the variety with a sideways or lazy "4." The date is found as either "14-95" or "149-5."

I-334 **Pommerania** **Duchy**
Mint: **Damm**
Bogislaus X, 1474-1523
1495 **Schilling**
S *1.20 g*
Frey 424, Dannenberg 383, Schulten 2769

BVGSLAVS DVX STETTIN
Griffin facing left

MON-ETAN-OVA:D-AM 9ᒣ-
Shield of Rügen on long cross

Schulten reports a 1495 schilling from the Stettin mint but it is not confirmed. This date is often mistaken for 1497.

I-335a Saxony Duchy and Elector
Mint: Freiberg
Elector Friedrich III, Johann and Duke Albrecht, 1486-1500
1495 Half Schwertgroschen
VS 1.90 g
Frey —, Krug 1763-65

F:A:H:D:G:DVX:SAX:TV:L:MAR:MS
Elector's shield of crossed swords in trefoil, rose mintmark of Freiberg at beginning of legend

GROSSVS:NOVVS:DVCVM:SAXONI9⅂
Shield of Landsberg-Meissen in trefoil with rose mintmark of Freiberg at beginning of legend

---

I-335b Saxony Duchy and Elector
Mint: Freiberg
Elector Friedrich III, Johann and Duke Albrecht, 1486-1500
1495 Half Schwertgroschen
R5 1.90 g
Frey —, Krug 1770

F:A:H:D:G:DVX:SAX:TV:L:HAR:HIS:9⅂
Elector's shield of crossed swords in trefoil, rose mintmark of Freiberg at beginning of legend

F:A:H:D:G:DVCS:SAX:TV:L:HA:HIS
Elector's shield of crossed swords in trefoil, rose mintmark of Freiberg at beginning of legend

Mule of two obverses!

I-335c Saxony Duchy and Elector
Mint: Freiberg/Schneeberg
Elector Friedrich III, Johann and Duke Albrecht, 1486-1500
1495 Half Schwertgroschen
R5 1.90 g
Frey —, Krug 1766

F:A:H:D:G:DVX:SAX:TV:L:MAR:MS9⅂
Elector's shield of crossed swords in trefoil, rose mintmark of Freiberg at beginning of legend

GROSSVS:NOVVS:DVCVH:SAXONI92
Shield of Landsberg-Meissen in trefoil with clover leaf mintmark of Schneeberg at beginning of legend

Fascinating mule of 1495 Freiberg obverse and 1492 Schneeberg reverse!

I-335d Saxony Duchy and Elector
Mint: Freiberg/Schneeberg
Elector Friedrich III, Johann and Duke Albrecht, 1486-1500
1495 Half Schwertgroschen
R4 1.90 g
Frey —, Krug 1767-68

F:A:H:D:G:DVX:SAX:TV:L:MAR:MS
Elector's shield of crossed swords in trefoil, rose mintmark of Freiberg at beginning of legend

GROSSVS:NOVVS:DVCVH:SAXONI9⅂
Shield of Landsberg-Meissen in trefoil with clover leaf mintmark of Schneeberg at beginning of legend

Mule of 1495 Freiberg and Schneeberg mints.

I-336a Saxony Duchy and Elector
Mint: Schneeberg
Elector Friedrich III, Johann and Duke Albrecht, 1486-1500
1495 Half Schwertgroschen
C 2.00 g
Frey —, Krug 1742-47, 1750-56, 1760-61, Schulten 2964

F:A:H:D:G:DVX:SAX:TV:L:MAR:MS
Elector's shield of crossed swords in trefoil, clover leaf mintmark of Schneeberg at beginning of legend

GROSSVS:NOVVS:DVCVM:SAXONI9⅂
Shield of Landsberg-Meissen in trefoil with clover leaf mintmark of Schneeberg at beginning of legend

The date is found alternatively at the end of the legend on either the obverse or reverse side.

I-336b Saxony Duchy and Elector
Mint: Schneeberg
Elector Friedrich III, Johann and Duke Albrecht, 1486-1500
1495 Half Schwertgroschen
VS 1.80 g
Frey —, Krug 1748-49, 1757-59, Schulten 2964

F:A:H:D:G:DVX:SAX:TV:L:MAR:MS9⅂
Elector's shield of crossed swords in trefoil, clover leaf mintmark of Schneeberg at beginning of legend

GROSSVS:NOVVS:DVCVM:SAXONI9⅂
Shield of Landsberg-Meissen in trefoil with clover leaf mintmark of Schneeberg at beginning of legend

A scarcer die type with dates on both obverse and reverse.

1496

I-337a Aachen City
Mint: Aachen
1496 Quarter Groschen
R2 0.60 g
Frey 439A, Menadier 128a-b, Krumbach 99.96, Schulten 5

MONETA:VRBIS:AQVENSIS - 1Ꝝ96
Flowery short cross with date in angles of cross

AVE:GRAC:PLENA:C:TEC
Madonna and Child with shield of Aachen below

Excessively rare in higher grades.

I-337b Aachen City
Mint: Aachen
1496 Quarter Groschen
R4-5 0.60 g
Frey —, Menadier 128c
Same as preceding, but with error date of "1-Ꝝ-6-9"

I-338 Brandenburg Margraviate and Elector
Mint: Angermuende
Johann Cicero, 1486-1499
1496 Groschen
R 2.30 g
Frey 437, Bahrfeldt 43-44, 46-47, Weyl 144-47, Schulten 250

IOH'SºD:GºMARCHIOºBRAºELEC'
Large eagle

MONE-ANNO-DOMI-1Ꝝ96
Long cross with four shields in angles of cross

Numerous legend varieties exist.

I-339a Brandenburg Margraviate and Elector
Mint: Uncertain
Johann Cicero, 1486-1499
1496 Half Groschen
R 1.15 g
Frey 437A, Bahrfeldt 59, Weyl 148-49, Schulten 259

IOH'SºD:GºMARCHIOºBRAºELEC
Large eagle with sceptre shield on breast

MONE-ANNO-DOMI-1Ꝝ96
Long cross with four shields in angles of cross

Numerous legend varieties exist.

I-339b Brandenburg Margraviate and Elector
Mint: Uncertain
Johann Cicero, 1486-1499
1496 Half Groschen
R2 1.15 g
Frey —, Bahrfeldt 63-64

IOH'SºDºG:MARCHIOºDRAºELEC
Large eagle with plain breast

MONE-ANNO-DOMI-1Ꝝ96
Long cross with sceptre shield in center

Bahrfeldt 63 is an excessively rare variety with periods in the four angles of cross of the reverse field.

I-340 Cleve Duchy
Mint: Wesel
Johann II, 1481-1521
1496 Half Albus
R3 0.90 g
Frey 448B, Noss 172, Schulten 1486

IOHS:DVX:CLIVENS':Z:CO:MAR'
Shield of Cleve in trefoil

MO':NO':WESALIE:A:M:CCCC:96
Shield of the Mark in trefoil

I-341 Erfurt City
Mint: Erfurt
1496 Uniface Pfennig
R3 0.30 g
Frey 440, Posern-Klett 426-28, Schulten 831

1496 - E
Shields with wheel and spokes, date above and letter "E" below

---

I-342 Erfurt City
Mint: Erfurt
1496 Uniface Scherf
R3 0.30 g
Frey —, Leitzmann 407, Schulten 837-38

9 º 6
Date divided by wheel with five spokes

I-343 Frankfurt City and Imperial mint
Mint: Frankfurt
Maximilian I (Emperor), 1493-1519

1496 Goldgulden

R 3.25 g

Frey 432, J & F 130, FR. 941, De Mey d'Or 979, 2046, Schulten 851

MO'ºNO'ºFR-ANCF'º1ጸ96

John the Baptist holding lamb and book, small shield of Weinsberg at feet

MAXIMILIANVSºROMAºREX

Imperial orb in trefoil

I-344 Göttingen City
Mint: Göttingen
1496 Körtling

R4 1.10 g

Frey 448A, Schrock 30

MONETA:NOVA:GOTTING

Large "G" in octofoil

ANO:DNI:M:CCCC:XCVI

Large "G" over short cross

I-345 Mainz Archbishopric
Mint: Mainz
Berthold of Henneberg, 1484-1504
1496 Half Groschen

R 1.00 g

Frey 433, Pr. Alexander 210-11, Coll. Walther 168, Schulten 1943

BERT'+AREP'+PRI'+ELECT

Quartered arms of Mainz, Romhild, Henneberg and Mainz

S-+PET'+-A'+1496

St. Peter holding key and cross behind shield of Mainz-Palatinate

---

I-346 Mühlhausen City
Mint: Mühlhausen
1496 Uniface Pfennig

R3 0.20 g

Frey —, Posern-Klett 639-40, Schulten 2248

M - 9-6

Winged shield of Mühlhausen dividing date with letter "M" above

The die varieties have either annulets or stops on the sides of the letter "M".

I-347 Nördlingen Imperial City
Mint: Nördlingen
Maximilian I (Emperor), 1493-1519
1496 Goldgulden

R3 3.25 g

Frey 434, Herzfelder 14, FR. 1795, Schulten 2406

MONETA:NOV-NORDLI:1ጸ96

John the Baptist holding lamb and book, small shield of Weinsberg at feet

MAXIMILIANVS:ROMAN:REX

Imperial orb in trefoil

I-348 Nördlingen Imperial City
Mint: Nördlingen
Maximilian I (Emperor), 1493-1519
1496 Schilling

R4 2.50 g

Frey 434A, Herzfelder 15, Schulten 2407

MONETA:NOOIA:NORDLING:1ጸ96

Crude, thick and unattractive crowned bust of Maximilian facing left

MAXIMILIANV-ROMANOR:REX

Large crowned imperial eagle with Weinsberg shield at feet

I-349 Nördlingen Imperial City
Mint: Nördlingen
Maximilian I (Emperor), 1493-1519
1496 Half Schilling

R3 1.00 g

Frey 434B, Herzfelder 16, Schulten 2408

MONETA:NOVA:NORDLING:96

Large imperial eagle

MAXIMILIANVS:ROMANRVM:REX

Shield of Weinsberg in trefoil

I-350 Palatinate County and Elector
Mint: Uncertain
Philip I, 1449-1508
1496 Half Albus

S 1.00 g

Frey 435, 435A, Schulten 2664

PHILI+-C.P.P.+-ELEC'

Lion shield surrounded by three small shields of Mainz, Bavaria and Regalianfeld

S-PET'+AP-OS+1ጸ96

St. Peter holding key and cross behind shield of Palatinate-Mainz

---

I-351 Palatinate-Mosbach-Newmarket County
Mint: Newmarket
Otto II, 1461-1499
1496 Goldgulden

R4 3.25 g

Frey 442, FR. 2046, De Mey d'Or 1724, Gotz 138, Schulten 2743

OTTO:C:P:RENI-DVX:BAVARIE
Madonna with sunrays emitting from sides, shield of Bavaria at feet

MONETA:NOVA:AVR':NOVIFOREN:1ꝝ96
Quartered arms of Palatinate-Bavaria in trefoil

I-352 Pommerania Duchy
Mint: Damm
Bogislaus X, 1474-1523
1496 Schilling
S *1.20 g*
Frey 436, Dannenberg 384, Schulten 2769

BVGSLVSºDVXºSTETTIN
Griffin facing left

MON-ETAºN-OVAºD-AM 96
Shield of Rügen on long cross

I-353 Saxony Duchy and Elector
Mint: Freiberg
Elector Friedrich III, Johann and Duke Albrecht, 1486-1500
1496 Zinsgroschen
R4 *2.50 g*
Frey 441, Krug 2044

FRI**AL*IO*D*G*DVCES*SAXO
Thuringen helmet over leaning Elector's shield, rose mintmark of Freiberg at end of legend

GROSSVS:NOVVS:DVCVM:SAXONIE96
Saxony helmet over leaning Saxony shield

I-354 Saxony Duchy and Elector
Mint: Leipzig
Elector Friedrich III, Johann and Duke Albrecht, 1486-1500
1496 Zinsgroschen
C *2.50 g*
Frey 441, Krug 1887-1900, Schulten 2958-59

FRI:AL:IO:D':G':DVCES:SAXONIE*
Thuringen helmet over leaning Elector's shield, star mintmark of Leipzig at end of legend

GROSSVS:NOVVS:DVCVM:SAXONIE96
Saxony helmet over leaning Saxony shield

I-355 Würzburg Bishopric
Mint: Würzburg
Lorenz of Bibra, 1495-1519
1496 Schilling
R3 *2.10 g*
Frey 438, Helmschrott 7, Schulten 3712

LAVRE'ºEPSºHERBN'ºFRAºDVX - 1ꝝ96
Shield of Franconia with date above

SANCTVSº-KILIANVS
St. Kilian standing, holding sword and sceptre

1497

I-356a Brandenburg Margraviate and Elector
Mint: Frankfurt
Johann Cicero, 1486-1499
1497 Half Groschen
R5 *1.10 g*
Frey 450A, Bahrfeldt 58

IOHSºDºGºHARºBRAºELECT
Large eagle with sceptre shield on breast

MONETAºANNOºDOMIº1ꝝ9Λ
Four part shield

I-356b Brandenburg Margraviate and Elector
Mint: Frankfurt
Johann Cicero, 1486-1499
1497 Half Groschen
R3 *1.10 g*
Frey 450A, Bahrfeldt 61, Weyl 152, Schulten 257-58

IOHS:DºGºMARºBRAºCLECT'
Large eagle with sceptre shield on breast

MON-ANNO-DOMI-1ꝝ9Λ
Short cross with four shields in angles of cross

I-356c Brandenburg Margraviate and Elector
Mint: Frankfurt
Johann Cicero, 1486-1499
1497 Half Groschen
R3 *1.20 g*
Frey 450A, Bahrfeldt 65

IOH'SºDºGºMARCHIOºDRAºELEC
Large eagle with plain breast

MONE-ANNO-DOMI-1Ꝝ9Λ
Long cross with sceptre shield in center

I-357a Brandenburg Margraviate and Elector
Mint: Uncertain
Johann Cicero, 1486-1499
1497 Groschen
R2 *2.20 g*
Frey 450, Bahrfeldt 50, 52, Weyl 151, Schulten 251

IOHSºD:GºMARCHOIºBRAºELEC
Large eagle with sceptre shield on breast

MONETA:ANNO:DOMMIº1Ꝝ9Λ
Short cross with four shields in angles of cross

Varieties known with plain and flowery crosses.

I-357b Brandenburg Margraviate and Elector
Mint: Uncertain
Johann Cicero, 1486-1499
1497 Groschen
R3 *2.20 g*
Frey 450, Bahrfeldt 48, Weyl 150, Schulten 250

IOH'SºD:GºMARCHIOºBRAºELEC
Large eagle with sceptre shield on breast

MONE-ANNO-DOMI-1Ꝝ9Λ
Long cross with four shields in angles of cross

I-358a Brandenburg-Franconia Margraviate
Mint: Swabia
Friedrich IV, 1495-1515
1497 Goldgulden
S *3.25 g*
Frey 449, Schrötter 450-56, FR. 306, Schulten 193

FRIDRICI:D:G:-MARCH:BRAN
John the Baptist holding lamb and book, dog's head at feet

MONE:NOV:AVR-SWOBACH:1Ꝝ9Λ
Short cross with four shields in angles of cross

I-358b Brandenburg-Franconia Margraviate
Mint: Swabia
Friedrich IV, 1495-1515
1497 Goldgulden
VS *3.25 g*
Frey 449, FR. 306, Schulten 193

Same, but date shown as 149Λ

I-359 Cleve Duchy
Mint: Cleve
Johann II, 1481-1521
1497 Stüber
R2 *2.53 g*
Frey —, Noss 198, Schulten 1465, Coll. Weygand 789-90

IOHS':DVX:CLIVENS':Z:CO':DE:MARKA
Swan with outstretched wings behind shield of Cleve and the Mark

ANNO-DNI':M-CCCC-XCVII
Flowery long cross with "I-E-V-E" in angles of cross

I-360 Frankfurt City and Imperial mint
Mint: Frankfurt
Maximilian I (Emperor), 1493-1519
1497 Goldgulden
VS *3.25 g*
Frey 451, J & F 131, 2047, FR. 941, De Mey d'Or 979, Saurma 2160, Schulten 851

MO'ºNO'ºFR-ANCF'º1Ꝝ9Λ
John the Baptist holding lamb and book, small shield of Weinsberg at feet

MAXIMILIANVSºROMA'ºREX
Imperial orb in trefoil

I-361 Göttingen City
Mint: Göttingen
1497 Körtling
R3 *1.20 g*
Frey 464B, Schrock 31

MONETA:NOVA:GOTTIN
Large "G" in octofoil

ANO:DNI:M:CCCC:XCVII
Large "G" over short cross

I-362a Hamburg City
Mint: Hamburg
1497 Ducat
S *3.45 g*
Frey 454, FR. 1100, De Mey d'Or 1157, Gaedechens 82-85, Schulten 1079

MONETA N'-O':HAMBVRG
Madonna and Child over shield of Hamburg

AVE:PLEN-GRACIA:1ꝝ9Λ
Madonna and Child with thistle flower shield at feet

This type is characterized by a thinner Madonna and closer-spaced lettering and a wider oval containing the Madonna.

I-362b Hamburg City
Mint: Hamburg
1497 Ducat
C *3.45 g*
Frey 454, FR. 1100, De Mey d'Or 1156, Gaedechens 86-88, Schulten 1080,

MONETA N'-O':HAMBVRG
Madonna and Child over shield of Hamburg

AVE:PLEN-GRACIA:1ꝝ9Λ
Madonna and Child with thistle flower shield or crescent moon at feet

This type is characterized by a heavy Madonna and widely-spaced lettering. The absence of the city mark of a thistle flower shield or "nesselblatt" in some of these types may indicate a later striking from the end of the 16th century, according to Gaedechens.

I-363 Lübeck City
Mint: Lübeck
1497 Ducat
R5 *3.45 g*
Frey —, Krusy L4, 7

Countermark of double-headed eagle in tiny round shield on a host 1497 Hamburg ducat

Schulten 1803 lists a 1492 double schilling of Lübeck whose existence is doubtful.

I-364 Mainz Archbishopric
Mint: Mainz
Berthold of Henneberg, 1484-1504
1497 Goldgulden
R5 *3.25 g*
Frey 464A, FR. 1630, Schulten 1941

MONE:NO'-AVRE:1ꝝ9Λ
Four-part shield of Mainz, Romhild, Henneberg and Mainz in trefoil with small shields of Cologne, Trier and Palatinate at triangle points

BERTO-LO'ARC'-EPI MO'
Christ on gothic throne, small shield of Mainz at feet

I-365 Mühlhausen City
Mint: Mühlhausen
1497 Uniface Pfennig
R4 *0.20 g*
Frey —, Posern-Klett 642-44

M - 9-Λ
Winged shield of Mühlhausen dividing date with letter "M" above

---

I-366a Nördlingen Imperial City
Mint: Nördlingen
Maximilian I (Emperor), 1493-1519
1497 Goldgulden
R2 *3.25 g*
Frey 457, Herzfelder 17, FR. 1795, Schulten 2406

MONETA:NOV-NORDLI:1ꝝ9Λ
John the Baptist holding lamb and book, small shield of Weinsberg at feet

MAXIMILIANVS:ROMANO:REX
Imperial orb in trefoil

I-366b Nördlingen Imperial City
Mint: Nördlingen
Maximilian I (Emperor), 1493-1519
1497 Goldgulden
R4 *3.25 g*
Frey —, De Mey d'Or 1645, Schulten 2405
MONETA:NOV-NORDLI 1497
John the Baptist holding lamb and book, small shield of Weinsberg at feet

FRIDRICVS:ROMAN:REX
Imperial orb in trefoil

Mule issued under the name of Friedrich III, who died four years earlier.

I-366c Nördlingen Imperial City
Mint: Nördlingen
Maximilian I (Emperor), 1493-1519
1497 Goldgulden
R3 *3.25 g*

Same as preceding but with date "9Λ"

I-367a **Nördlingen Imperial City**
Mint: Nördlingen
Maximilian I (Emperor), 1493-1519
1497 Schilling
R3 *2.5 g*
Frey –, Herzfelder 19, Schulten 2407

MONETA:NOVA:NORDLING:1ጸ9Λ
Crude, thick and unattractive crowned bust of Maximilian facing left

MAXIMILIANV-ROMANOR:REX
Large crowned imperial eagle with Weinsberg shield at feet

I-367b **Nördlingen Imperial City**
Mint: Nördlingen
Maximilian I (Emperor), 1493-1519
1497 Schilling
R3 *2.5 g*
Frey –, Herzfelder 19v

MONETA:NOVA:NORDLING:149Λ
Attractive and thin Renaissance bust of Maximilian facing left

MAXIMILIANVS-ROMANOR:REX
Large uncrowned imperial eagle with Weinsberg shield at feet

I-368 **Nördlingen Imperial City**
Mint: Nördlingen
Maximilian I (Emperor), 1493-1519
1497 Half Schilling
S *1.10 g*
Frey 458, Herzfelder 20-21, Schulten 2408

MONETA:NOVA:NORDLING:1ጸ9Λ
Large imperial eagle

MAXIMILIANVS:ROMANOR:REX
Shield of Weinsberg in either trefoil or sixfoil

An overdate of "98/97" is known.

I-369 **Palatinate County and Elector**
Mint: Heidelberg
Philip I, 1449-1508
1497 Goldgulden
R2 *3.25 g*
Frey 452, Noss 196, FR. 1982 var., De Mey d'Or 1717 var, Schulten 2656

PHIL'-C'PAL-+P'ELE
Shield of Bavaria-Palatinate in trefoil with three small shields Mainz, Cologne and Trier at triangle points

MO'NE:AV-RENE-1ጸ9>
Christ on gothic throne with shield of Palatinate-Bavaria at feet

I-370 **Pommerania Duchy**
Mint: Damm
Bogislaus X, 1474-1523
1497 Schilling
R5? *1.20 g (estimated)*
Frey –, Dannenberg 385

BVGSLAVS DVX STETTINE
Griffin facing left

MON':ETAN-OVAD-AM9Λ
Shield of Rügen on long cross

Nearly all known examples of this piece are misidentified 1495 schillings with a medieval "5" (ᒣ). The author has never seen a genuine piece. Although the legend and date are fully described in Dannenberg, no photo or line drawing is provided.

I-371 **Würzburg Bishopric**
Mint: Würzburg
Lorenz of Bibra, 1495-1519
1497 Schilling
R *2.10 g*
Frey 464D, Helmschrott 7, Schulten 3712

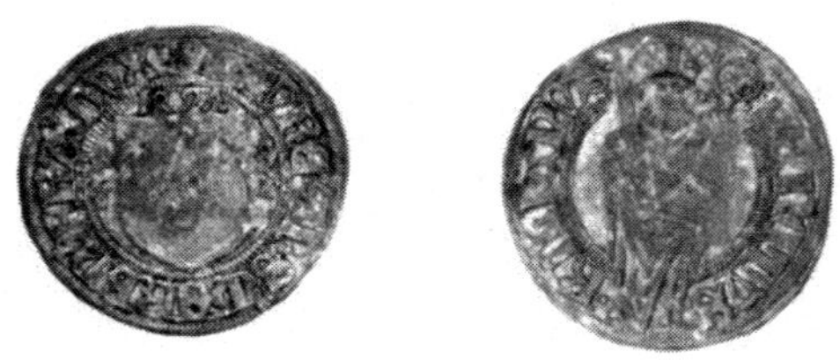

LAVRE'ºEPS'ºHERBN'ºFRA'ºDVX - 1ጸ9Λ
Shield of Franconia with date above

SANCTVS-KILIANVS
St.. Kilian standing, holding sword and sceptre

1498

I-372a **Aachen City**
Mint: Aachen
1498 Quarter Groschen
R4 *0.60 g*
Frey 481A, Menadier 129b, Forschner 12, Krumbach 99.98, Schulten 5

MONETA:VRBIS:AQVENSIS - 1ጸ98
Flowery short cross with date in angles of cross

AVE:GRAC:PLENC:C:TE
Madonna and Child with shield of Aachen below

A piefort of this date is known. See Schulten 6.

I-372b **Aachen** **City**
Mint: **Aachen**
1498 **Quarter Groschen**
R4-5 *0.60 g*
Frey —, Menadier 129c

Same as preceding, but with error date of "1-ጸ-8-9" and backwards "N's" in legend

---

I-373 **Brandenburg** **Margraviate and Elector**
Mint: **Berlin?**
Joachim I and Albrecht, 1499-1515
1498 **Groschen**
R *2.20 g*
Frey —, Bahrfeldt 84, Weyl 177, Schulten 267

IOACH ET ALB MARCH BRAN'DG
Large eagle with sceptre shield on breast

MONETA:ANNO:DOMINI 1ጸ98
Short thick cross with four shields in angles of cross

Struck by Joachim and Albrecht.

I-374a **Brandenburg** **Margraviate and Elector**
Mint: **Frankfurt**
Johann Cicero, 1486-1499
1498 **Half Groschen**
R *1.20 g*
Frey 468A, Bahrfeldt 60, Weyl 60, Schulten 259

IOHSºDºGºMARCHIOºDRAºELE
Large eagle with sceptre shield on breast

MONE-TANN-ODNI-1ጸ98
Long cross with four shields in angles of cross

Struck by Johann Cicero alone, as with subtypes b and c as well.

I-374b **Brandenburg** **Margraviate and Elector**
Mint: **Frankfurt**
Johann Cicero, 1486-1499
1498 **Half Groschen**
R3 *1.20 g*
Frey —, Bahrfeldt 62

IOHSD:G:HAREHIOºDRAºCLC
Large eagle with sceptre shield on breast

MONE-TANN-ODNI-1ጸ98
Long cross with sceptre shield in center

I-374c **Brandenburg** **Margraviate and Elector**
Mint: **Frankfurt**
Johann Cicero, 1486-1499
1498 **Half Groschen**
R3 *1.20 g*
Frey —, Bahrfeldt 66

IOHSºD:G:MARCHIOºBRAºCLCE
Large eagle with plain breast

MONC-ANNO-DOMI-1ጸ98
Long cross with sceptre shield in center

I-375a **Brandenburg** **Margraviate and Elector**
Mint: **Uncertain**
Johann Cicero, 1486-1499
1498 **Groschen**
R2 *2.20 g*
Frey —, Bahrfeldt 45,49, Weyl 153, Schulten 250

IOHSºD:GºMARCIOºDRAºELEC
Large eagle with sceptre shield on breast

MONE-T ANN-O DNI-1ጸ98
Long cross with four shields in angles of cross

Struck by Johann Cicero alone.

I-375b **Brandenburg** **Margraviate and Elector**
Mint: **Uncertain**
Johann Cicero, 1486-1499
1498 **Groschen**
VS *2.20 g*
Frey 468, Bahrfeldt 51a-e, g-h, 53-55, Weyl 154-59, Schulten 251

IOHSºDGºMARCHIOºBRAºELEC
Large eagle with sceptre shield on breast

MONETAºANNOºDOMINIº1ꝝ98
Short cross with four shields in angles of cross

Struck by Johann Cicero alone. Varieties are known with both short cross and flowery cross, and with/without flower on shield. Bahrfeldt 54 is an extremely rare variety with "MONETA NOWA" instead of "MONETA ANNO DOMI".

I-375c Brandenburg — Margraviate and Elector
Mint: Uncertain
Johann Cicero, 1486-1499
1498 — Groschen
R4 — 2.20 g
Frey —, Bahrfeldt 51f

Same as preceding, but with entire reverse engraved backwards showing a date of "89ꝝ1"

A spectacular error of major interest.

I-376 Brandenburg-Franconia — Margraviate
Mint: Swabia
Friedrich IV, 1495-1515
1498 — Goldgulden
S — 3.25 g
Frey 469, Schrötter 457-67, FR. 306, De Mey d'Or 441, Schulten 193

FRIDRICI:D:G'-MARCH':BRAN'
John the Baptist holding lamb and book, dog's head at feet

MONE:NOV:AVR-SWOBACH:1ꝝ98
Short cross with four shields in angles of cross

A variety with the date on the obverse instead of the reverse is reported in Schrötter #467, but no photograph or drawing is available.

I-377 Einbeck — City
Mint: Einbeck
1498 — Körtling
R4 — 1.20 g
Frey —, Buck 7a-b, Schrock Einbeck, p. 45, Schulten 807

MONE:NOVA:EMBEC:SN
Gothic "E" over short cross

ANNO:DNI:M:CCCCXCVIII
Gothic "E" over short cross

I-378 Erfurt — City
Mint: Erfurt
Friedrich IV, 1495-1515
1498 — Uniface Scherf
R3 — 0.30 g
Frey 472, Leitzmann 415, Posern-Klett 434, Schulten 838

9 º 8
Date "98" on top of Erfurt shield of wheel with five spokes

I-379 Frankfurt — City and Imperial mint
Mint: Frankfurt
Maximilian I (Emperor), 1493-1519
1498 — Goldgulden
VS — 3.25 g
Frey 470, J & F 132, FR. 941, De Mey d'Or 979, Schulten 851

MO'ºNO'ºFR-ANCF'º1ꝝ98
John the Baptist holding lamb and book, small shield of Weinsberg at feet

MAXIMILIANVSºROMAºREX
Imperial orb in trefoil

I-380 Göttingen — City
Mint: Göttingen
1498 — Körtling
R3 — 1.20 g
Frey —, Schrock 32, Schulten 1004

MONETA:NOVA:GOTTIN
Large "G" in octofoil

ANO:DNI:M:CCCC:XCVIII
Large "G" over short cross

I-381 Lippe — Lordship
Mint: Lemgo
Bernhard VII, 1431-1511
1498 — Mite
R6 — 0.39 g
Frey 481, Ihl 24, Schulten 1780

NOBIL:BERNHARD:LIP
Rose shield of Lippe

MON-NOV-LEM-EGE - 1ꝝ98
Long cross with date in angles of cross

Also known as a 1/6 stuiver.

I-382 Nördlingen Imperial City
Mint: Nördlingen
Maximilian I (Emperor), 1493-1519
1498 Goldgulden
R 3.25 g
Frey 466, Herzfelder 22, FR. 1795, De Mey d'Or 1647, Schulten 2406

MONETA:NO-NORDLIN:98
John the Baptist holding lamb and book, small shield of Weinsberg at feet

MAXIMILIAN':ROMANOR:REX
Imperial orb in trefoil

Herzfelder 23 reports a possible die type with the full date of "1498" yet notes it may be a gilded schilling.

I-383 Nördlingen Imperial City
Mint: Nördlingen
Maximilian I (Emperor), 1493-1519
1498 Schilling
R3 2.20 g
Frey 481D, Herzfelder 24, Schulten 2407

MONETA:NOVA:NORDLING:1498
Attractive and thin Renaissance bust of Maximilian facing left

MAXIMILIAN-ROMANOR REX
Large crowned imperial eagle with Weinsberg shield at feet

I-384a Nördlingen Imperial City
Mint: Nördlingen
Maximilian I (Emperor), 1493-1519
1498 Half Schilling
VS 1.10 g
Frey 467, Herzfelder 26, Schulten 2408

MONETA:NOVA:NORDLING:1498
Large imperial eagle

MAXIMILIANVS:ROMANOR:REX
Shield of Weinsberg in trefoil

I-384b Nördlingen Imperial City
Mint: Nördlingen
Maximilian I (Emperor), 1493-1519
1498 Half Schilling
R 1.10 g
Frey 467, Herzfelder 25, Schulten 2408

same as preceding, but date "98"

I-385 Osnabrück Bishopric
Mint: Osnabrück
Konrad IV of Reitberg, 1482-1508
1498 Braspfennig
R4 2.80 g
Frey —, Kennepohl T 14, 173a, Krusy 02, 11c-d, JMP XXXIX 1952, # 25

Countermarks of two separate wheels with 6 spokes on a host 1498 Utrecht Braspfennig, No. III-262

I-386 Palatinate-Mosbach-Newmarket County
Mint: Newmarket
Otto II, 1461-1499
1498 Goldgulden
R5 3.25 g
Frey —, FR. 2046, Gotz 139, Schulten 2743

OTTO:C:P:RENI-DVX:BAVARIE
Madonna with sunrays emitting from sides, shield of Bavaria at feet

MONETA:NOVA:AVR':NOVIFORE:1ꝶ98
Quartered arms of Palatinate-Bavaria in trefoil

I-387 Saxony Duchy and Elector
Mint: Annaberg
Elector Friedrich III, Johann and Duke Albrecht, 1486-1500
1498 Schreckenberger
R3 4.30 g
Frey —, Krug 2090-93, Schulten 2954

FRIDERICVS*ALBERTVS:IOHANNES*D
Angel above Elector's shield of crossed swords, clover mint-mark of Annaberg at beginning of legend

GROSSVS:NOVVS:DVCM:SAXONIE - 1ꝝ98
Large four-part shield with small shield of Duke of Saxony at center with four digit date above shield

Schulten lists schreckenbergers with dates of 1495 and 1496 but none are known dated before 1498. The 1500 dated piece listed by Schulten is also not confirmed.

I-388 **Saxony** **Duchy and Elector**
Mint: **Freiberg**
Elector Friedrich III, Johann and Duke Albrecht, 1486-1500
1498 **Half Schwertgroschen**
R3 *1.90 g*
Frey —, Krug 1771-72

F:A:H:D:G:DVCS:SAX:TV:L:MAR:MS
Elector's shield of crossed swords in trefoil, rose mintmark of Freiberg at beginning of legend

GROSSVS:NOVVS:DVCVM:SAXONI98
Shield of Landsberg-Meissen in trefoil with rose mintmark of Freiberg at beginning of legend

The date can be found either at the end of the obverse legend as in Krug 1771 or the reverse legend as in Krug 1772.

I-389 **Saxony** **Duchy and Elector**
Mint: **Leipzig**
Elector Friedrich III, Johann and Duke Albrecht, 1486-1500
1498 **Goldgulden**
R4 *3.25 g*
Frey —, Krug 2183, FR. 2928, De Mey d'Or 1926, Schulten 2950

FRI:AL:IO:DG-DVCV:SAX
John the Baptist standing, holding lamb and book, two small shields of Elector and Duke of Saxony at his feet

MONE:NOVA:AVR:LIPCENSIS:1ꝝ98
Imperial orb in quatrefoil

Rarest date and type for the goldguldens issued by Friedrich, Albrecht and Johann.

I-390 **Saxony** **Duchy and Elector**
Mint: **Leipzig**
Elector Friedrich III, Georg and Johann, 1486-1525
1498 **Goldgulden**
R2 *3.25 g*
Frey —, Krug 2193-94, FR. 2929, De Mey d'Or 1927, Schulten 2974

FRI:GE:IO:D-G:DVCV:SAX
John the Baptist standing, holding lamb and book, two small shields of Elector and Duke of Saxony at his feet

MONE:AVR:LIPCENSIS:1ꝝ98
Imperial orb in quatrefoil

One of several types dated prior to the period of joint rule.

I-391a **Saxony** **Duchy and Elector**
Mint: **Schneeberg**
Elector Friedrich III, Johann and Duke Albrecht, 1486-1500
1498 **Zinsgroschen**
C *2.30 g*
Frey 465, Krug 1990-2007, Schulten 2961

FRI:AL:IO:D':G':DVCES:SAXONIE
Thuringen helmet over leaning Elector's shield, star mintmark of Schneeberg sometimes at end of legend

GROSSVS:NOVVS:DVCVM:SAXONIE98
Saxony helmet over leaning Saxony shield, with or without star mintmark at end of legend

---

I-391b **Saxony** **Duchy and Elector**
Mint: **Schneeberg**
Elector Friedrich III, Johann and Duke Albrecht, 1486-1500
1498 **Zinsgroschen**
R3 *3.25 g*
Frey 465, Krug 2008

FRI:AL:IO:D':G':DVCES:SAXONIE98
Thuringen helmet over leaning Elector's shield, star mintmark of Schneeberg before date

GROSSVS:NOVVS:DVCVM:SAXONIE98
Saxony helmet over leaning Saxony shield, with star mintmark at end of legend

Rare die with date on both obverse and reverse.

I-392 **Werl** **City**
Mint: **Werl**
1498 **Braspfennig**
R5-6 *2.80 g*
Frey —, Krusy W4, 14B, JMP XXXIX 1952, #27

Countermarks of two separate crosses in shield with point in upper left quadrant on a host 1498 Utrecht braspfennig, No. III-262

I-393 **Würzburg Bishopric**
Mint: Würzburg
Lorenz of Bibra, 1495-1519
1498 Schilling
R *2.00 g*
Frey 481C, Helmschrott 7, Schulten 3712

LAVRE' EPS'ºHERBN'ºFRA'ºDVX- 1ꝝ98
Shield of Franconia with date above

SANCTVSº-KILANVS
St. Kilian standing, holding sword and sceptre

1499

I-394 **Brandenburg** **Margraviate and Elector**
Mint: Berlin?
Joachim I and Albrecht, 1499-1515
1499 Groschen
R *2.20 g*
Frey 515, Bahrfeldt 85, Weyl 178-79, Schulten 267

IOACH:ETºALBºMARCHºBRANºDG
Large eagle with sceptre shield on breast

MONETAºANNOºDOMINIº1ꝝ99
Thick short cross with four shields in angles of cross

Struck by Joachim and Albrecht.

I-395 **Brandenburg** **Margraviate and Elector**
Mint: Frankfurt
Johann Cicero, 1486-1499
1499 Groschen
R *2.20 g*
Frey 515, Bahrfeldt 56-57, Weyl 161, Schulten 255

IOHSºDºGºMARCHIOºDRAºCLCE
Large eagle with sceptre shield on breast

MONE+T ANN+O DNI+1ꝝ99
Short cross with four shields in angles of cross

Struck by Johann Cicero alone. Varieties are known with and without rose on the cross.

I-396a **Brandenburg** **Margraviate and Elector**
Mint: Frankfurt
Joachim I, 1499-1535
1499 Groschen
R *2.20 g*
Frey 515, Bahrfeldt 123, Weyl 180, Schulten 254

IOACHIMºDºGºMARCHIOºB
Large eagle with sceptre shield on breast

MONETAºNOºVAºFRANº1ꝝ99
Flowery cross with four shields in angles of cross

Struck by Joachim alone.

I-396b **Brandenburg** **Margraviate and Elector**
Mint: Frankfurt
Joachim I, 1499-1535
1499 Groschen
R4 *2.20 g*
Frey —, Bahrfeldt 123/121

IOACHIM :D:G:MARCHIO:B
Large eagle with sceptre shield on breast

HONETA:NOWA:FRAN:1ꝝ99
Thick short cross with four shields in angles of cross

Mule with obverse legend of a Joachim groschen and reverse legend used in joint coinage of Joachim and Albrecht.

I-397a **Brandenburg** **Margraviate and Elector**
Mint: Frankfurt
Joachim I and Albrecht, 1499-1515
1499 Groschen
VS *2.20 g*
Frey —, Bahrfeldt 121-22a-b

IOACHIHºAºDºGºHARºCHIºB
Large eagle with sceptre shield on breast

MONETAºNOWAºFRANº 1ꝝ99
Thick short cross with four shields in angles of cross

Struck by Joachim and Albrecht.

I-397b **Brandenburg** **Margraviate and Elector**
Mint: Frankfurt
Joachim I and Albrecht, 1499-1515
1499 Groschen
R4 *2.20 g*
Frey —, Bahrfeldt 122c

Same as preceding, but with error date of "199"

I-398 **Brandenburg** **Margraviate and Elector**
Mint: **Frankfurt**
Johann Cicero, 1486-1499
1499 **Half Groschen**
R2 *1.20 g*
Frey 515A, Bahrfeldt 67, Weyl 162, Schulten 259

IOHSºD:G:MARCHIOºBRAºCLCE
Large eagle with plain breast

MONC-ANNO-DOMI-1ጸ99
Sceptre shield over long cross

Struck by Johann Cicero alone.

I-399 **Brandenburg** **Margraviate and Elector**
Mint: **Uncertain**
Johann Cicero, 1486-1499
1499 **Groschen**
R4 *2.20 g*
Frey 515, Schulten 250

IOHSºDGºMARCIOºDRAºELEC
Large eagle with sceptre shield on breast

MONE-T ANN-O DNI-1ጸ99
Long cross with four shields in angles of cross

Struck by Johann Cicero alone. Bahrfeldt does not list this date, so the rarity of this piece is not entirely certain.

I-400 **Brandenburg** **Margraviate and Elector**
Mint: **Uncertain**
Joachim I and Albrecht, 1499-1515
1499 **Half Groschen**
R4 *2.20 g*
Frey —, Bahrfeldt 266, Schulten 282

IOACHIºETºALBºMARCHºBRAN
Large eagle with sceptre shield on breast

MONC-ANNO-DOMI-1ጸ99
Sceptre shield over long cross

Struck by Joachim and Albrecht.

I-401 **Brandenburg-Franconia** **Margraviate**
Mint: **Swabia**
Friedrich IV, 1495-1515
1499 **Goldgulden**
S *3.25 g*
Frey 505, Schrötter 468-77, FR. 306, Schulten 193

FRIDRICH:D:G:MARCH:BRAN'
John the Baptist holding lamb and book, dog's head at feet

MONE':NOVA:AVR':SWOBACH':1ጸ99
Short cross with four shields in angles of cross

I-402 **Breisach** **City**
Mint: **Breisach**
1499 **Dicken**
R5 *Weight unknown*
Frey 498, Berstett 61, Schulten 537

MONETA:BRISACNIENSIS*1ጸ99
Shield of Breisach on flowery cross in quatrefoil

S'*STEPHANVS;PROTHOMART'*
Stoning of St. Stephen

I-403 **Breisach** **City**
Mint: **Breisach**
1499 **Groschen**
R6 *Weight unknown*
Frey —. Berstett 62

MONETA BRISACH. 99
Double-headed eagle with shield below

GLORIA IN EXCELSI. D.
Flowery short cross in circle

Possibly no longer extant.

I-404 **Bremen** **Archbishopric**
Mint: **Bremen**
Johann III, 1497-1511
1499 **4 Groten**
S *3.20 g*
Frey 497, Jungk 108-114, Schulten 564

IOHS*DEI*GR-ARC*EPI'*B
St. Peter seated on throne, holding book and key, small shield of Rode below

MONETA*NOVA*BREMENSIS 1ጸ99
Large key in field

I-405 **Bremen** **Archbishopric**
Mint: **Vörden**
Johann III, 1497-1511
1499 **4 Groten**
S-VS *3.20 g*
Frey —, Jungk 125-132, Schulten 566

IOH'S*DEI*GR*-ARC*EPI*BR*
St. Peter seated on throne, holding book and key, small shield of Rode below

MONETA*NOVA*VORDENSIS*1Ꝝ99
Large key in field

A rare variety is known with the reverse legend starting at the bottom of the coin.

I-406 **Brunswick City**
Mint: Brunswick
1499 Large Groschen
R5 *3.33-3.79 g*
Frey —, Jesse 1, Schulten 518

MONETAºNOVAºBRVNSWICSº1Ꝝ99
Shield with standing lion facing left

SANCTVS-AVCTORº
Saint holding model of church

I-407 **Brunswick City**
Mint: Brunswick
1499 Autorgroschen
R5 *2.30 g*
Frey 512, Jesse 2, Schulten 519

MONETAºNOVAºBRVNSWICENSIS
Standing lion in field, facing left

SANCTVS-AVCTORº1Ꝝ99
Saint holding model of church

I-408 **Brunswick City**
Mint: Brunswick
1499 Kleiner Groschen
R *1.60 g*
Frey —, Jesse 4, Schulten 525

MONETAºNOVAºBRVNSWICENSº
Shield with standing lion facing left

ANNOºDOMINIºMºCCCCºXCIX
City towers (six) of Brunswick in field

I-409 **Colmar City**
Mint: Colmar
1499 Dicken
R4 *7.20 g*
Frey 511, E&L 2, Schulten 634, De Mey Al 7

MONETA:NO':C-OLMAR:1Ꝝ99
Large eagle with small shield below

S:MARTI-N:PATRO
St. Martin on horseback, giving alms

I-410 **Colmar City**
Mint: Colmar
1499 Groschen
R5 *3.70 g*
Frey 511A, E&L 4, Schulten 637, De Mey Al 9

GROSSVS:NO':ECU:COLMARIE
Large eagle with small shield below

SANCTVS:MARTINVS:EPISCO':ET-:PA-TRO-N:1-Ꝝ99
Inner legend quartered by short cross, unbroken outer legend

I-411a **Colmar City**
Mint: Colmar
1499 Plappart
R5 *1.96 g*
Frey —, E&L 5, Schulten 638, De Mey Al 11

MONETA:NO:C-OLMAR:1Ꝝ99
Large eagle with small shield below

S:MARTI-N:PATRON
Standing St. Martin with skeleton at left

I-411b **Colmar City**
Mint: Colmar
1499 Plappart
R5 *1.82 g*
Frey —, E&L 12, Schulten 640, De Mey Al 10

MONETA:NO-COLMARI:1Ꝝ99
Large eagle with small shield below

SANCTVS*MARTINVS:EP
Plain cross

I-412 Einbeck City
Mint: Einbeck
1499 Körtling
R3 *1.20 g*
Frey 500, Buck 8a-d, Schrock Einbeck p. 45, Schulten 807

MONE:NOVA:EMBEC:SN
Gothic "E" over short cross

ANNO:DNI:M:CCCC:XCIX
Gothic "E" over short cross

I-413a Erfurt City
Mint: Erfurt
1499 Uniface Pfennig
R4 *0.30 g*
Frey —, Schulten 831

1499 - E
Shields with wheel and spokes, date above and letter "E" below

---

I-413b Erfurt City
Mint: Erfurt
1499 Uniface Pfennig
R4 *0.30 g*
Frey —, Schulten 832 (photo #2)

9-9
Wheel with spokes inside shield with 9-9 on sides of shield and "E" above

---

I-414 Frankfurt City and Imperial mint
Mint: Frankfurt
Maximilian I (Emperor), 1493-1519
1499 Goldgulden
VS *3.25 g*
Frey 496, J & F 133, 2048, FR. 941, De Mey d'Or 979, Schulten 851

MO'ºNO'ºFR-ANCF'º1Ꝝ99
John the Baptist holding lamb and book, small shield of Weinsberg at feet

MAXIMILIANVSºROMAºREX
Imperial orb in trefoil

I-415 Freiburg In Breisgau City
Mint: Freiburg
1499 Dicken
R5 *7.32 g*
Frey 510, Berstett 142, Schulten 896

GROSSVS:FRIBVRG:BRISGA':1Ꝝ99
Raven's head facing left

AVE:MAR-IA:GRA':P'
Madonna and Child seated

Despite the legend of "GROSSVS," this coin is clearly a dicken and bears dicken weight.

I-416a Freiburg In Breisgau City
Mint: Freiburg
1499 Groschen
R5 *3.95 g*
Frey —, Schulten 899?

MO'ºNO'ºFRIBVRGºIºBRISE':1Ꝝ99
Ravenshead shield in sixfoil

AVEºMARIA - GRACIAºPLE
Madonna and Child seated

Schulten lists a batzen which may be intended to be this coin. However, with a reported weight of 3.95 grams, it should instead be labeled a groschen, the same as Schulten 902. A sale in 1995 confirms its existance. Schulten also reports a 1498 vierer whose existance has not been confirmed.

I-416b Freiburg in Breisgau City
Mint: Freiburg
1499 Groschen
R5 *3.84 g*
Frey 501A, Berstett 143, 221, Schulten 902

GROSS:FRIBVERG:BRISGA' 1Ꝝ99
Ravenshead shield in sixfoil

AVE.MARIA-GRACIA.PLE
Madonna and child

A klippe of this date is known.

I-417 Göttingen City
Mint: Göttingen
1499 Körtling
R3 *1.20 g*
Frey 515E, Schrock 33, Schulten 1004

MONETA:NOVA:GOTTING
Large "G" in octofoil

ANO:DNI:M:CCCC:XCIX
Large "G" over short cross

I-418 Henneberg County
Mint: Schleusingen
Wilhelm V, 1480-1559
1499 Groschen
R5 2.30 g
Frey —, Heus 146, Schulten 1146

WILºDºCOME-HENBERº1ꝝ99
Hen shield with large helmet above

IºVINCITºOM-NIAºVIRTVSº
Large helmet interrupting field with small Würzburg shield below

This coin was meant to copy the Saxony groschens of the same period.

I-419 Lippe Lordship
Mint: Lemgo
Bernhard VII, 1431-1511
1499 Stuiver
R5-6 1.90 g
Frey 482, Ihl 25, Coll. Weweler 143, Schulten 1776

NOBILIS*BERNARD*D'LIPP'
Rose shield of Lippe

MONE-NOVA-LEME-GENS-1-ꝝ-9-9
Long cross with date in angles of cross

Possibly only 2 known.

I-420 Mainz Archbishopric
Mint: Mainz
Berthold of Henneberg, 1484-1504
1499 Goldgulden
R6 3.25 g
Frey 464A, FR. 1630, Schulten 1941

BERTO-LO'ARC'-EPI MO'
Four-part shield of Mainz, Romhild, Henneberg and Mainz in trefoil with small shields of Cologne, Trier and Palatinate at triangle points

MONE:NO'-AVRE:1ꝝ99
Christ on gothic throne, small shield of Mainz at feet

I-421a Nördlingen Imperial City
Mint: Nördlingen
Maximilian I (Emperor), 1493-1519
1499 Half Schilling
R 1.40 g
Frey 499, 499A, Herzfelder 28, Schulten 2408

MONETA:NOVA:NORDLING':1499
Large imperial eagle

MAXIMILIANVS:ROMANORVM:REX
Shield of Weinsberg in trefoil

I-421b Nördlingen Imperial City
Mint: Nördlingen
Maximilian I (Emperor), 1493-1519
1499 Half Schilling
R2 1.40 g
Frey 499, 499A, Herzfelder 27, Schulten 2408

Same as preceding, but date "99"

I-422 Öttingen County
Mint: Öttingen
Wolfgang I and Joachim, 1477-1520
1499 Schilling
R6 Weight unknown
Frey —, Loffelholz 27, Schulten 2589

MEDIVS:SOGIDVS:OTING:1499
Shield of Öttingen with cross in center set in trefoil

MONE:NOVA:ARGEN 1499
Helmet of Öttingen with bracken head with "W" and "I" on sides of head representing Counts Wolfgang and Joachim

Believed no longer extant.

I-423 Öttingen County
Mint: Öttingen
Wolfgang I and Joachim, 1477-1520
1499 Half Schilling
R6 Weight unknown
Frey —, Schulten 2590

MEDIVS:SOGIDVS:OTING;1499 (?)
Shield of Öttingen with cross in center in quatrefoil

MONE:NOVA:ARGEN 1499 (?)
Helmet of Öttingen with bracken head with "W" and "I" on sides of head representing Counts Wolfgang and Joachim

This piece is believed extant, but no photographs or line drawings are available.

I-424 Pommerania Duchy
Mint: Damm
Bogislaus X, 1474-1523
1499 Schilling
S 1.30 g
Frey 507, Dannenberg 386, Schulten 2769

BVGSLVSºDVXºSTETTIN

Griffin facing left

MON-ETA:N-OVA:D-AM 99
Shield of Rügen on long cross

Schulten reports a 1498 schilling from the Damm mint but without verification of its existance.

I-425 Pommerania Duchy
Mint: Stettin
Bogislaus X, 1474-1523
1499 Goldgulden

R4 *Weight unknown*
Frey 509, Dannenberg 371, FR. 2077, De Mey d'Or 1741A, Schulten 2765

BOGSL-AVS:D:G:-DVX:ST-ETINE- 9-9
Long cross on four-part shield with date above shield

CONSERVA-NOS:DO:NA
Madonna and Child holding sceptre

I-426 Pommerania Duchy
Mint: Stettin
Bogislaus X, 1474-1523
1499 Schilling

VS *1.20 g*
Frey 508, Dannenberg 387, Schulten 2768

BVGSLAVSºDVXºSTETIN
Griffin facing left

MON-NOVº-STE-TNº99
Shield of Rügen on long cross

The photo for Schulten 2768 is of a witten, not a schilling.

I-427 Pommerania Duchy
Mint: Stettin
Bogislaus X, 1474-1523
1499 Witten

R2 *0.60 g*
Frey —, Dannenberg 413

BOGSLAVS DVX STET
Griffin facing left

MON-ETA-STE-TI99
Lowercase letter "b" on shield over long cross

I-428a Saxony Duchy and Elector
Mint: Annaberg
Elector Friedrich III, Johann and Duke Albrecht, 1486-1500
1499 Schrenkenberger

R2 *4.30 g*
Frey 502A, Krug 2094-97, Schulten 2954

FRIDERICVS:ALBERTVS:IOHANNES
Angel above Elector's shield of crossed swords, clover mintmark of Annaberg at beginning of legend

GROSSVS:NOVVS:DVCVM:SAXONIE - 1ꝶ99
Large four-part shield with small shield of Duke of Saxony at center with four digit date above shield

This coin, as well as subtype b below, were struck by Friedrich, Albrecht and Johann.

I-428b Saxony Duchy and Elector
Mint: Annaberg
Elector Friedrich III, Johann and Duke Albrecht, 1486-1500
1499 Schrenkenberger

R2 *4.30 g*
Frey 502A, Krug 2098-2106, Schulten 2954

FRIDERICVS*ALBERTVS*IOHANNES*
Angel above Elector's shield of crossed swords, either clover or crescent/star mintmark of Annaberg at beginning of legend

GROSSVS:NOVVS:DVCVM:SAXONIF - 99
Large four-part shield with small shield of Duke of Saxony at center, crescent/star mintmark at beginning of legend with date above shield

---

I-429 Saxony Duchy and Elector
Mint: Annaberg
Elector Friedrich III, Georg and Johann, 1486-1525
1499 Schrenkenberger

R4 *4.30 g*
Frey —, Krug 2107, Schulten 2954

FRIDERICVS:GEORGIVS:IOHANN
Angel above Elector's shield of crossed swords, either clover or star mintmark at beginning of legend

GROSSVS:NOVVS:DVCVM:SAXONI - 1ꝶ99
Large four-part shield with small shield of Duke of Saxony at center, clover leaf mintmark at beginning of legend with date above shield

I-430 **Saxony** **Duchy and Elector**
Mint: **Leipzig**
Elector Friedrich III, Johann and Duke Albrecht, 1486-1500
1499 **Goldgulden**
R2 *3.25 g*
Frey 501, Krug 2184-86, FR. 2928, De Mey d'Or 1926, Schulten 2950

FRI:AL:IO:DG-DVCV:SAX
John the Baptist standing, holding lamb and book, two small shields of Elector and Duke of Saxony at his feet

MONE:NOVA:AVR:LIPCENSIS:1ጸ99
Imperial orb in quatrefoil

Struck by Friedrich, Albrecht and Johann

I-431 **Saxony** **Duchy and Elector**
Mint: **Leipzig**
Elector Friedrich III, Georg and Johann, 1486-1525
1499 **Goldgulden**
R2 *3.25 g*
Frey —, Krug 2195-98, FR. 2929, De Mey d'Or 1928, Schulten 2974

FRI:GE:IO:D-G:DVCV:SAX
John the Baptist standing. holding lamb and book, two small shields of Elector and Duke of Saxony at his feet

MONE:NOVA:AVR:LIPCENSIS:1ጸ99
Imperial orb in quatrefoil

Struck by Friedrich, Georg and Johann

I-432 **Saxony** **Duchy and Elector**
Mint: **Schneeberg**
Elector Friedrich III, Johann and Duke Albrecht, 1486-1500
1499 **Zinsgroschen**
C *2.50 g*
Frey —, Krug 2009-39

FRI:AL:IO:D':G':DVCES:SAXONI
Thuringen helmet over leaning Elector's shield, star mintmark of Schneeberg sometimes at end of legend

GROSSVS:NOVVS:DVCVM:SAXONI99
Saxony helmet over leaning Saxony shield, with star mintmark sometimes at end of legend or before date or missing

Common type in the name of Friedrich, Johann and Albrecht.

I-433 **Saxony** **Duchy and Elector**
Mint: **Schneeberg**
Elector Friedrich III, Georg and Johann, 1486-1525
1499 **Zinsgroschen**
R3 *2.50 g*
Frey —, Krug 2040-43

FRI*GE*IO*D*G*DVCES*SAXO
Thuringen helmet over leaning Elector's shield, star mintmark of Schneeberg sometimes at end of legend

GROSSVS:NOVVS:DVCVM:SAXONI99
Saxony helmet over leaning Saxony shield

Excessively rare die in the name of Friedrich, Johann and Georg.

I-434 **Saxony** **Duchy and Elector**
Mint: **Schneeberg/Freiberg**
Elector Friedrich III, Johann and Duke Albrecht, 1486-1500
1499 **Half Schwertgroschen**
R4 *1.90 g*
Frey 502, Krug 1773

F:A:H:D:G:DVCS:SAX:TV:L:HAR:HIS
Elector's shield of crossed swords in trefoil, clover leaf mintmark of Schneeberg at beginning of legend

GROSSVS:NOVVS:DVCVM:SAXON99
Shield of Landsberg-Meissen in trefoil with rose mintmark of Freiberg at beginning of legend

Mule of Freiberg and Schneeberg mints.

I-435 **Thann** **City**
Mint: **Thann**
1499 **Dicken**
R3 *7.35 g*
Frey 504, E&L 4, Schulten 3490, De Mey Al. 4, Coll. Voltz 777

MONETA:NO:TANNENSIS:1ጸ99
Shield of Thann on flowery cross inside quatrefoil

S'*THEOBA-LDVS:EPS*
St. Theobald seated, holding staff

I-436 Thann City
Mint: Thann
1499 Groschen
R4 3.45 g
Frey –, E&L 2, Schulten 3491, De Mey Al 5

GROSSVS:NO:TANNENSIS:1ꝝ99
Shield of Thann inside polyfoil

S'*THEO'-ALDVS:EPS
St. Theobald standing, holding staff

I-437 Würzburg Bishopric
Mint: Würzburg
Lorenz of Bibra, 1495-1519
1499 Schilling
R3 2.10 g
Frey –, Helmschrott 7, Schulten 3712

LAVRE'ºEPSºHERBN'ºFRA'ºDVX- 1ꝝ99
Shield of Franconia with date above

SANCTVS-KILIANVS
St. Kilian standing, holding sword and sceptre

1500

I-438a Brandenburg Margraviate and Elector
Mint: Frankfurt
Joachim I and Albrecht, 1499-1515
1500 Groschen
R 2.30 g
Frey –, Bahrfeldt 90-91

IOCHIM.A.D.G.MARGI.BRANDEN
Large eagle with sceptre shield on breast

MONETAºANNO:DOMINI1ɼ00
Short thick cross with four shields in angles of cross

Struck by Joachim and Albrecht. Bahrfeldt assigns these two types to the mint of Frankfurt because of the distinct lettering and abbreviations which match the coins struck with the name of that mint.

I-438b Brandenburg Margraviate and Elector
Mint: Frankfurt
Joachim I and Albrecht, 1499-1515
1500 Groschen
VS 2.30 g
Frey –, Bahrfeldt 126-28

IOCHIMºAºDºGºMARGIºBRANDEN
Large eagle with sceptre shield on breast

MONETAºNOVAºFRANCFORTºMºVC
Short cross with four shields in angles of cross

Struck by Joachim and Albrecht. Numerous legend variations exist. The date is expressed both as "MºVC" as well as "HºVC." This is not a date variation but an engraving variation, as the letter "H" was often used in place of the letter "M" on these crudely engraved coins. However, the error dates listed as Bahrfeldt 124 and 125, where the date is expressed as "HC" instead of MVC or HVC, are listed as separated subtypes below.

I-438c Brandenburg Margraviate and Elector
Mint: Frankfurt
Joachim I and Albrecht, 1499-1515
1500 Groschen
R3 2.30 g
Frey –, Bahrfeldt 124-25

Same as preceding, but with error date "HV" for "MVC"

I-439 Brandenburg Margraviate and Elector
Mint: Frankfurt
Joachim I and Albrecht, 1499-1515
1500 Half Groschen
R2 1.00 g
Frey –, Bahrfeldt 273-74, 78, Schulten 284

IOACHIM'ALB'DºGºMAR'BRAN
Large eagle with plain or crossed-hatched breast

HON-FRAC-FORTº-ºHVC
Shield with sceptre on long cross

Struck by Joachim and Albrecht. Multiple die variations exist.

I-440 Brandenburg Margraviate and Elector
Mint: Frankfurt
Joachim I, 1499-1535
1500 Half Groschen
R6 Weight unknown
Frey –, Bahrfeldt 275

IOACHIºMARCHIOºELECºBRAN
Large eagle with plain breast

MONE-ºFRAC-FOR-HºVC
Sceptre shield over long cross

Struck by Joachim's name alone. Bahrfeldt reported this coin no longer extant.

I-441a **Brandenburg** **Margraviate and Elector**
Mint: **Berlin?**
Joachim I and Albrecht, 1499-1515
1500 **Groschen**
S *2.20 g*
Frey 530, Bahrfeldt 86-88, Weyl 181-84, 88, Schulten 267-70

IOACH ET ALB MARCH BRAN'DG
Large eagle with sceptre shield on breast

MONETAºANNO:DOMINI1ɼ00
Short thick cross with four shields in angles of cross

Struck by Joachim and Albrecht. Numerous legend variations exist.

I-441b **Brandenburg** **Margraviate and Elector**
Mint: **Berlin?**
Joachim I and Albrecht, 1499-1515
1500 **Groschen**
S *2.20 g*
Frey —, Bahrfeldt 89

IOACHI:ET.ALB:MAR:BARN
Large eagle with sceptre shield on breast

MONETAºANNOºDOMINº1 ˥00
Short thick cross with four shields in angles of cross

Struck by Joachim and Albrecht.

I-441c **Brandenburg** **Margraviate and Elector**
Mint: **Uncertain**
Joachim I and Albrecht, 1499-1515
1500 **Groschen**
R3 *2.20 g*
Frey —, Bahrfeldt 108

IOACHI ET ALB MARCHºBRANDG
Large eagle with sceptre shield on breast

MONETAºNOVAºARGE'TAºANNOº1500
Short thick cross with four shields in angles of cross

Struck by Joachim and Albrecht.

I-442a **Brandenburg** **Margraviate and Elector**
Mint: **Uncertain**
Joachim I, 1499-1535
1500 **Groschen**
R *2.20 g*
Frey —, Bahrfeldt 92, Weyl 186-87, Schulten 299-300

IOACHIMºDEIºGRAºMAR'BRANDE'
Large eagle with sceptre shield on breast

MONETAºANNOºDOMINIº1ɼ00
Short thick cross with four shields in angles of cross

Struck by Joachim alone.

I-442b **Brandenburg** **Margraviate and Elector**
Mint: **Uncertain**
Joachim I, 1499-1535
1500 **Groschen**
R2 *2.20 g*
Frey —, Bahrfeldt 109

IOACHIMºDEIºGRAºMAR'BRANDE'
Large eagle with sceptre shield on breast

MONET:NOVAºARGENTAºANNO 1500
Short thick cross with four shields in angles of cross

Struck by Joachim alone.

I-443a **Brandenburg** **Margraviate and Elector**
Mint: **Uncertain**
Joachim I and Albrecht, 1499-1515
1500 **Half Groschen**
R *1.00 g*
Frey —, Bahrfeldt 267a-c, Weyl 185, Schulten 282

IOACHIºETºALBºMARCHºBRAN
Large eagle with sceptre shield on breast

MONE-ANNO-DOMI-1ɼ00
Sceptre shield over long cross

Struck by Joachim I & Albrecht. Major legend variations exist due to exceptionally crude lettering. This is the "common" type with a backwards medieval "5".

I-443b **Brandenburg** **Margraviate and Elector**
Mint: **Uncertain**
Joachim I and Albrecht, 1499-1515
1500 **Half Groschen**
R4 *1.00 g*
Frey —, Bahrfeldt 267d

Same as preceding, but with normal medieval 5 in date

I-444 **Brandenburg-Franconia** **Margraviate**
Mint: **Swabia**
Friedrich IV, 1495-1515
1500 **Goldgulden**
S *1.00 g*
Frey 528, Schrötter 478-85, FR. 306, De Mey d'Or 441, Schulten 193

FRIDRICI:D:G:-MARCH:BRAN
John the Baptist holding lamb and book, dog's head at feet

MONE:NOV:AVR-SWOBACH:1500
Short cross with four shields in angles of cross

I-445 **Brunswick** **City**
Mint: **Brunswick**
1500 **Autorgroschen**
R5 *2.25 g*
Frey 536, Jesse 3, Schulten 519

MONETA°NOVA°BRVNSWICENSIS
Standing lion in field, facing left

SANCTVS°AVCTOR°1ᒣ00
Saint holding model of church

I-446 **Brunswick** **City**
Mint: **Brunswick**
1500 **Kleiner Groschen**
R *1.50 G*
Frey —, Jesse 5, Schulten 525

MONETA°NOVA°BRVNSWICENS
Standing lion in shield, facing left

ANNO°DOMINI°M°CCCCC
City towers (five) of Brunswick in field

I-447 **Cleve** **Duchy**
Mint: **Cleve**
Johann II, 1481-1521
1500 **Stüber**
R3 *2.65 g*
Frey —, Noss 205, Schulten 1470

IOHS':DVX:CLIVENS':ET:CO':MARK
Conjoined shields of Cleve and the Mark

REDD-ITE:D-EC:Q':D'-SV':1ᒣ00
Double-stranded long cross

I-448 **Einbeck** **City**
Mint: **Einbeck**
1500 **Körtling**
R3 *1.10 g*
Frey 527, Buck 9a-d, Schrock Einbeck p.45, Schulten 807

MONE:NOVA:EMBEC'
Gothic "E" over short cross

ANNO:DNI:M:CCCCC
Gothic "E" over short cross

I-449 **Frankfurt** **City and Imperial mint**
Mint: **Frankfurt**
Maximilian I (Emperor), 1493-1519
1500 **Goldgulden**
VS *3.25 g*
Frey 529, J & F 134, FR. 941, De Mey d'Or 979, 2049, Schulten 851

MO'°NO'°FR-ANCF'°1500
John the Baptist holding lamb and book, small shield of Weinsberg at feet

MAXIMILIANVS°ROMA REX
Imperial orb in trefoil

I-450 **Göttingen** **City**
Mint: **Göttingen**
1500 **Körtling**
R *1.20 g*
Frey 521, Schrock 34, Schulten 1004

MONETA:NOVA:GOTTING
Large "G" in octofoil

ANO:DOMINI:M:CCCCC
Large "G" over short cross

I-451 **Henneberg County**
Mint: Schleusingen
Wilhelm V, 1480-1559
1500 Groschen
R5 *2.40 g*
Frey —, Heus 147a-b, Schulten 1146

WIL:D:G:COM-ES:HENBERG:1500
Hen shield with large helmet above

I°VINCIT:OM-NIA:VIRTVS
Large helmet interrupting field with small Würzburg shield below

---

I-452 **Henneberg County**
Mint: Schleusingen
Wilhelm V, 1480-1559
1500 Half Groschen
R6 *1.46 g*
Frey —, Heus 152, Schulten 1148

WILHELMVS:COMES:HENBERG - 1500
Shield of Henneberg with date above

CONCORDIA:RES:CRESCVNT
Divided shield with standing lion facing right and large letter "H"

Possibly unique. The weight of the only confirmed known piece may be slightly low due to a hole.

I-453 **Jülich-Berg Duchy**
Mint: Mülheim
Wilhelm IV, 1475-1511
1500 Double Bausche
S *2.20-2.60 g*
Frey 538, Noss 192a-n, Schulten 1427, Saurma 2991, Coll. Weygand 273

WILHELN'*DVX*IVLIAC'*Z MONTE'
Seated lion facing left

MONE'-NOVA-MVLH-EM*1700
Quartered arms of Jülich-Berg and Ravensburg on long cross

Unusual version of the number "5" is used in this date, identical to a modern "7."

I-454 **Mühlhausen City**
Mint: Mühlhausen
1500 Uniface Pfennig
R4 *0.20 g*
Frey —, Schulten 1248

M - 15-00
Winged shield of Mühlhausen dividing date with letter "M" above

---

I-455 **Nördlingen Imperial City**
Mint: Nördlingen
Maximilian I (Emperor), 1493-1519
1500 Goldgulden
R *3.25 g*
Frey 526, Herzfelder 29, FR. 1795, De Mey d'Or 1647, Schulten 2406

MONETA:NOV':NORDLI:1500
John the Baptist holding lamb and book, small shield of Weinsberg at feet

MAXIMILIAN:ROMANORN:REX
Imperial orb in trefoil

While Friedberg and De Mey d'Or both list a 1499 goldgulden, its existence is not confirmed.

I-456 **Nördlingen Imperial City**
Mint: Nördlingen
Maximilian I (Emperor), 1493-1519
1500 Half Schilling
R3 *1.30 g*
Frey 525, Herzfelder 30, Schulten 2408

MONETA:NOVA:NORDLING:1500
Large imperial eagle

MAXIMILIANVS:ROMANOR:REX
Shield of Weinsberg in trefoil

Schulten lists hellers dated 1498 and 1500 but their existence is doubtful.

I-457 **Palatinate County and Elector**
Mint: Heidelberg
Philip I, 1449-1508
1500 Goldgulden
R4 *3.25 g*
Frey —, De Mey d'Or 1717 var., Schulten 2656

PHIL'*-C*PAL*-*P*ELE*
Large shield of Mainz-Bavaria with three small shields of Cologne arranged in triangle

MO':AV-RENE-1500
Christ on gothic throne with shield below

I-458 **Palatinate-Upper Palatinate** **County**
Mint: **Newmarket**
Elector Philip I, 1500-1508
1500 **Goldgulden**
R3 *3.25 g*
Frey 535, FR. 1983, De Mey d'Or 1720, Gotz 146, Schulten 2657

PHILIP:PAL':ELECT':IMPE'1500
Letter "P" above three shields forming triangle

AVE:GR:PLE-NA:DN:TECV'
Standing Madonna and Child surrounded by rays

Struck for the region of Oberpfalz. Die varieties are known, despite its great rarity.

I-459a **Pommerania** **Duchy**
Mint: **Stettin**
Bogislaus X, 1474-1523
1500 **Half Mark**
R5 *Weight unknown*
Frey —, Dannenberg 374, Schulten 2766

BVGSL-AVS DV-X STET-IN M V C
Shield of Pommerania on long cross

CONSERVA*-*NOS DOMINA
Standing Madonna and Child surrounded by rays

According to Peus, only three examples exist with this date variety. This innovative date of MVC stands for 1000+5x100.

I-459b **Pommerania** **Duchy**
Mint: **Stettin**
Bogislaus X, 1474-1523
1500 **Half Mark**
R4 *Weight unknown*
Frey —, Dannenberg 375

BVGSLA-VSºDVX-STETTI-ENº1500
Shield of Pommerania on long cross

CONSERVA*-*NOS DOMINA
Standing Madonna and Child surrounded by rays

I-460a **Pommerania** **Duchy**
Mint: **Stettin**
Bogislaus X, 1474-1523
1500 **Schilling**
VS *1.40 g*
Frey —, Dannenberg 388, Schulten 2768

BVGSLAVS DVX STETIN
Griffin facing left

MON-NOV':STE'-M:V:C
Shield of Rügen on long cross

I-460b **Pommerania** **Duchy**
Mint: **Stettin**
Bogislaus X, 1474-1523
1500 **Schilling**
VS *1.20 g*
Frey —, Dannenberg 389, Schulten 2768

BVGSLAVS DVX STETTIENSIS
Griffin facing left

MONE-NOVA-STET-IN.1500
Shield of Rügen on long cross

I-461 **Pommerania** **Duchy**
Mint: **Stettin**
Bogislaus X, 1474-1523
1500 **Witten**
S *0.60 g*
Frey —, Dannenberg 414, Schulten 2771

BVGSLAVS DVX STETIN
Griffin facing left

MON.-NOV'.-STE'.-M.V.C.
Gothic lower-case "b" on shield over long cross

I-462 **Saxony** **Duchy and Elector**
Mint: **Annaberg**
Elector Friedrich III, Johann and
Duke Albrecht, 1486-1500
1500 **Half Guldiner**
R3 *8.93 g*
Frey 532, Haupt, Table 52.5, Merseberger 341, Schulten 2953

FRID-ALB-FR:IO-HAN
Large elaborate helmet on Saxony shield with small shields at sides interrupting legend

MONE-ARGEN-DVCV-SAXON-15-00
St. John standing, holding lamb, with two shields at sides interrupting legend, date in field at sides of Saint

Struck by Friedrich, Albrecht and Johann.

I-463 Saxony Duchy and Elector
Mint: Annaberg
Elector Friedrich III, Georg and Johann, 1486-1525
1500 Half Guldiner

R3 *8.93 g*
Frey 532, Haupt, Table 52.6, Merseberger 365, Schulten 2984

FRID:-GEO-R:IO-HAN:
Large elaborate helmet on Saxony shield with small shields at sides interrupting legend

MONE-ARGEN-DVCV-SAXON-15-00
St. John standing, holding lamb, with two shields at sides interrupting legend, date in field at sides of Saint

Struck by Friedrich, Georg and Johann.

I-464a Saxony Duchy and Elector
Mint: Leipzig
Elector Friedrich III, Johann and Duke Albrecht, 1486-1500
1500 Goldgulden

R3 *3.25 g*
Frey 531, Krug 2187, De Mey d'Or 1926, Schulten 2950

FRI:AL:IO:DG-DVCV:SAX
John the Baptist standing, holding lamb and book, two small shields of Elector and Duke of Saxony at his feet

MONE:NOVA:AVR:LIPCENSIS:1500
Imperial orb in quatrefoil

Struck in the name of Friedrich, Albrecht and Johann.

I-464b Saxony Duchy and Elector
Mint: Leipzig
Elector Friedrich III, Johann and Duke Albrecht, 1486-1500
1500 Goldgulden

R5 *3.25 g*
Frey —, Krug 2188

MO:AVREA-LIPCENS
John the Baptist standing. holding lamb and book, single small shield of Duke of Saxony at his feet

MONE:NOVA:AVR:LIPCENSIS:1500
Imperial orb in quatrefoil

Excessively rare mule with two reverse legends.

I-465 Saxony Duchy and Elector
Mint: Leipzig
Elector Friedrich III, Georg and Johann, 1486-1525
1500 Goldgulden

R4-5 *3.25 g*
Frey —, FR. 2615, De Mey d'Or 1928, Schulten 2974

FRI:GE:IO:D-G:DVCV:SAX
John the Baptist standing, holding lamb and book, two small shields of Elector and Duke of Saxony at his feet

MONE:NOVA:AVR:LIPCENSIS:1500
Imperial orb in quatrefoil

Excessively rare type struck in the name of Friedrich, Georg and Johann. Unreported in Krug.

I-466 Stolberg County
Mint: Stolberg
Heinrich IX and Botho II, 1498-1508
1500 Groschen

R4 *2.00 g*
Frey 539, Friederich 85, Schulten 3423

H:S:H:I:ET:BODO:CO:I:STALBERG'
Stolberg shield with stag facing left, helmet below

GROSSVS:NOVVS:COIT:I:STALBERG1˥00
Flowery cross with four shields in angles of cross

I-467 Würzburg Bishopric
Mint: Würzburg
Lorenz of Bibra, 1495-1519
1500 Goldgulden

R4 *3.25 g*
Frey —, FR. 3619, De Mey d'Or 2229, Schulten 3710

LAVRENC:EPS:HERBN:FRA:DVX:1500
Quartered shield of Franconia

MONE:NOVA-AVR:WIRCEP'
St. Kilian behind small shield of Franconia

I-468 Würzburg Bishopric
Mint: Würzburg
Lorenz of Bibra, 1495-1519
1500 Schilling

R4 *2..00 g*
Frey —, Helmschrott 7, Schulten 3712

LAVRE':EPS':HERBN':FRA:DVX- 1500
Shield of Franconia with date above

SANCTVS-KILIANVS
St. Kilian standing, holding sword and sceptre

REGION II - Southern Netherlands

1372

II-1 Schoonvorst-Sichem Lordship
Mint: Schoonvorst
Renaud II, 1369-1396
1372 Gros
R6 Weight unknown
Frey N5, Frey 2, Van der Chijs 28.1, Menadier 12, Lucas 9, RBN 1857, Pl. 23, #35

RENARD:DNS:DE SCOVORST Z SIC
Shield with nine large pellets on polyfoil

ANNOD-IMINI-MCCC:-:LXXII- MON-ETA-SCOV-ORST
Long cross with inner and outer legends

Likely only one piece currently extant. Frey lists this piece as unique. However, Lucas lists a variety 9a. The extant example is located at Limburgs Museum in Maastricht.

1390

II-2 Schoonvorst-Sichem Lordship
Mint: Schoonvorst
Renaud II, 1369-1396
1390 Gros
R5-6 2.0 g
Frey 7, Van der Chijs 29.5, Menadier 13, Coll. Weygand 1340

RENARD:DNS:DE:SCHOVORST Z SIC
Shield with nine large pellets on polyfoil

ANNOD-OMINI-M:CCC:LXXXX- MON-ETA-SCOV-ORST
Long cross with inner and outer legends

1391

II-3 Schoonvorst-Sichem Lordship
Mint: Schoonvorst
Renaud II, 1369-1396
1391 Gros
R 2.10 g
Frey 8, Van der Chijs 28.3, 29.6, Menadier 14, Lucas 11, Coll. Weygand 1341-44

RENARD:DNS:DE:SCHOVORST Z SICH
Shield with nine large pellets on polyfoil

ANNOD-OMINI-M:CCC:-LXXXXI- MON-ETA-SCOV-ORST
Long cross with inner and outer legends

1392

II-4 Schoonvorst-Sichem Lordship
Mint: Schoonvorst
Renaud II, 1369-1396
1392 Gros
R4-5 2.10 g
Frey 9, Menadier 15, Lucas 12

RENARD:DNS:DE:SCHOVORST Z SICH
Shield with nine large pellets on polyfoil

ANNOD-OMINI-M:CCC:-:*XCII-MON-ETA-SCOV-ORST
Long cross with inner and outer legends

1393

II-5 Schoonvorst-Sichem Lordship
Mint: Schoonvorst
Renaud II, 1369-1396
1393 Gros
R3 1.90 g
Frey N10, Frey 7, Van der Chijs 28.4, Menadier 16, Lucas 13, Saurma 2795, Stephanik 5205, Coll. Weygand 1345

RENARD:DNS DE:SCHOVORST:Z:SICH
Shield with nine large pellets on polyfoil

ANNOD-OMINI-M:CCC:-XCIII-MON-ETA-SCOV-ORST
Long cross with inner and outer legends

1394

II-6 Schoonvorst-Sichem Lordship
Mint: Schoonvorst
Renaud II, 1369-1396
1394 Gros
R6 2.17 g
Frey N11

RENARD*DNS:DE:SCHOVORST:Z:SICH
Shield with nine large pellets on polyfoil

ANNOD-OMINI-M:CCCX-CIIII MON-ETA-SCOV-ORST
Long cross with inner and outer legends

Likely only three known, one of which is in the ANS collection. This date was unknown to both Lucas and Menadier.

1437

II-7 Liège Bishopric
Mint: Uncertain
John of Heinsberg, 1419-1455
1437 Double Gros
R4 2.95-3.29 g
Frey 43, CH. 310, Dengis 645

IOHS':EPS':LEODIEN:DX':BVLLO':Z:COM:LOS'
Arms of Heinsberg occupying entire field with small shield in center

ANNO:DOMINI:MILLESIO:CCCCXXXVII
Cross

1438

II-8 Liège Bishopric
Mint: Uncertain
John of Heinsberg, 1419-1455
1438 Double Gros
R3 3.20 g
Frey —, CH. 310, Dengis 645

IOH:EPS:LEODIEN:DX:BULLO:Z:COM:LOS
Arms of Heinsberg occupying entire field with small shield in center

ANNO:DOMINI:MILLESIO:CCCCXXXVIII
Cross

II-9 Liège Bishopric
Mint: Uncertain
John of Heinsberg, 1419-1455
1438 Demi Gros
R4-5 0.73-0.87 g
Frey 51A, CH. 311, Dengis 646

IOH:EPS:LEOD:DX:BULLO:Z:CO:LOS
Arms of Heinsberg occupying entire field with small shield in center

ANNO:DOMINI:M:CCCCXXXVIII
Short cross

II-10 Liège Bishopric
Mint: Uncertain
John of Heinsberg, 1419-1455
1438 Quarter Gros
R5 0.68 g
Frey —, CH. 312, Dengis 647

IOH:EPS:LEOD:DX:BUL:CO:LO
Arms of Heinsberg occupying entire field with small shield in center

ANNO:DNI:M:CCCCXXXVIII
Cross

1474

II-11 Brabant Duchy
Mint: Antwerp
Charles the Rash, 1467-1477
1474 Double Briquet
C 3.06 g
Frey 155, GH 34-1, DW 507, Van der Chijs 17.7, Stephanik 4694

KAROL:DEI:GRA:DVX:BG:BRA:Z:LI
Two seated facing lions with briquet in center

SALVV:FAC:PPLM:TVV:DNE:A:1ጸΛጸ
Shield of Burgundy on flowery cross

A briquet, also known as a fire-steel, was a hand-held metal tool used to create sparks for the fireplace. When represented on a coin, it often has sparks coming from its sides, looking like small dolphins or fish.

II-12 Brabant Duchy
Mint: Antwerp
Charles the Rash, 1467-1477
1474 Briquet
S 3.06 g
Frey 155A, GH 35-1, DW 508

KAROL:DEI:GRA:DVX:BG:Z:LI
Seated lion holding shield of Burgundy

BENEDIC:HEREDITATI:TVE:A: **I** ጸΛጸ
Triple-stranded cross in flowery wreath

II-13 **Brabant** **Duchy**
Mint: **Antwerp**
Charles the Rash, 1467-1477
1474 **Demi Briquet**
VS *0.87 g*
Frey 155B, GH 36-1, DW 509

KAROL:DI:GRA:DX:BG:BRA:Z:LI
Head of lion facing left

BENEDIC:AIA:MEA:DNO:A: **I ጸ Λ ጸ**
Flowery wreath on short cross

For the illiterate public, the number of lions on the coin represented the denomination of the coin. With the demi briquet, only a "half" lion is present.

II-14 **Flanders** **County**
Mint: **Bruges**
Charles the Rash, 1467-1477
1474 **Double Briquet**
C *3.06 g*
Frey 160A, GH 34-3, D.d.P Pl. 13, 65, De Mey Fl. 416

KAROLVS:DEI:GRA:DVX:BVRG:CO:F
Two seated facing lions with briquet in center

SALVVM-FAC:POP-VLV:TVV:-DNE **I ጸ Λ ጸ**
Shield of Burgundy on flowery cross

II-15 **Flanders** **County**
Mint: **Bruges**
Charles the Rash, 1467-1477
1474 **Briquet**
S *3.06 g*
Frey 160B, GH 35-3a, D.d.P 13, 66, De Mey Fl. 417-20

KAROLVS:DEI:GRA:DVX:BVRG:CO:FL
Seated lion holding shield of Burgundy

BENEDIC:HEREDITATI:TVE: **I ጸ Λ ጸ**
Triple-stranded cross in flowery wreath

II-16 **Flanders** **County**
Mint: **Bruges**
Charles the Rash, 1467-1477
1474 **Demi Briquet**
VS *0.87 g*
Frey 612, GH 36-3, D.d.P Pl. 13, 67, De Mey Fl. 421-22

KAROL:DEI:GRA:DVX:BVR:CO:F
Half-length figure of lion advancing left

BENEDIC:AIA:MEA:DNO: **I ጸ Λ ጸ**
Flowery wreath on short cross

1475

II-17 **Brabant** **Duchy**
Mint: **Antwerp**
Charles the Rash, 1467-1477
1475 **Double Briquet**
C *3.06 g*
Frey 165, GH 34-1, DW 507, Stephanik 4695-96

KAROL:DEI:GRA:DX:BG:BRA:Z:LI
Two seated facing lions with briquet in center

SALVV:FAC:PPLM:TVV:DNE:A: **I ጸ Λ 5**
Shield of Burgundy on flowery cross

The illustration is of an overdate of 1475/55.

II-18 **Brabant** **Duchy**
Mint: **Antwerp**
Charles the Rash, 1467-1477
1475 **Briquet**
VS *3.06 g*
Frey 165A, GH 35-1, DW 508, Van der Chijs 17.6

KAROL:DEI:GRA:DVX:BG:BRA:Z:LI
Seated lion holding shield of Burgundy

BENEDIC:HEREDITATI:TVE:A: **I ጸ Λ 5**
Triple-stranded cross in flowery wreath

II-19 **Brabant** **Duchy**
Mint: **Antwerp**
Charles the Rash, 1467-1477
1475 **Demi Briquet**
VS *0.87 g*
Frey 165B, GH 36-1, DW 509

KAROL:DI:GRA:DX:BG:BRA:Z:LI
Half-length figure of lion advancing left

BENEDIC:AIA:MEA:DNO:A: I ꝸ Λ5
Flowery wreath on short cross

II-20a **Flanders** **County**
Mint: **Bruges**
Charles the Rash, 1467-1477
1475 **Double Briquet**
C *3.06 g*
Frey 167A—, GH 34-3c, D.d.P 13, 65, De Mey Fl. 414-15

KAROLVS:DEI:GRA:DVX:BVRG:CO:FL
Two seated facing lions with briquet in center

SALVVM-FAC:POP-VLV:TVV:-DNE: I ꝸ Λ5
Shield of Burgundy on flowery cross

II-20b **Flanders** **County**
Mint: **Bruges**
Charles the Rash, 1467-1477
1475 **Double Briquet**
R2 *3.06 g*
Frey —, GH 34-3c, D.d.P 13, 65, De Mey Fl. 414-15

Same as preceding but with a sideways "5."

II-21 **Flanders** **County**
Mint: **Bruges**
Charles the Rash, 1467-1477
1475 **Briquet**
VS *3.06 g*
Frey 620, GH 35-3a, D.d.P 13, 66, De Mey Fl. 420

KAROLVS:DEI:GRA:DVX:BVRG:CO:FL
Seated lion holding shield of Burgundy

BENEDIC:HEREDITA:TVE: I ꝸ Λ5 (sideways 5)
Triple-stranded cross in flowery wreath

1476

II-22 **Brabant** **Duchy**
Mint: **Antwerp**
Charles the Rash, 1467-1477
1476 **Double Briquet**
C *3.06 g*
Frey 174, GH 34-1, DW 507, Stephanik 4697-99

KAROL:DEI:GRA:DX:BG:BRA:Z:LI
Two seated facing lions with briquet in center

SALVV:FAC:PPLM:TVV:A: I ꝸ Λ6
Shield of Burgundy on flowery cross

II-23 **Brabant** **Duchy**
Mint: **Antwerp**
Charles the Rash, 1467-1477
1476 **Briquet**
S *3.06 g*
Frey 174A, GH 35-1, DW 508, Stephanik 4700-01

KAROL:DEI:GRA:DVX:BG:BRA:Z:LI
Seated lion holding shield of Burgundy

BENEDIC:HEREDITATI:TVE:A: I ꝸ Λ 6
Triple-stranded cross in flowery wreath

II-24 **Brabant** **Duchy**
Mint: **Antwerp**
Charles the Rash, 1467-1477
1476 **Demi Briquet**
VS *0.87 g*
Frey 174B, GH 36-1, DW 509

KAROL:DI:GRA:DX:BG:BRA:Z:LI
Half-length figure of lion advancing left

BENEDIC:AIA:MEA:DNO: I ꝸ Λ6
Flowery wreath on short cross

II-25 **Liège** **Bishopric**
Mint: **Uncertain**
Louis of Bourbon, 1456-1482
1476 **Double Patard**
R2 *2.48-3.22 g*
Frey 175, CH. 346-47, Dengis 696-97

LVDO'*DE*BORB*EPS'*LEOD'*DVX:BVL
Two seated facing lions

SALVV'—:FAC*PO—TW'*:DN'—LXXVI
Shield of Bourbon on ornate long cross which interrupts legend

The location of the primary mint for Liège was not certain. The smaller mint of Hasselt identified all of its coinage in the legends.

II-26 Liège Bishopric
Mint: Hasselt
Louis of Bourbon, 1456-1482
1476 Patard
R2 2.21-3.13 g
Frey 176B, CH. 351-52, Dengis 701

MO:EPI:LEODIEN:FACTA:HASSELT
Seated lion holding shield of Bourbon

BNDIC:HEREDITATI:TVE:LXXVI
Ornate triple-stranded short cross

1477

II-27 Brabant Duchy
Mint: Antwerp
Marie of Burgundy, 1477-1482
1477 Double Briquet
C 3.06 g
Frey 627, GH 39-1, DW 516-17, Stephanik 4703

MARIA:DEI:G:DVCISS:BG:BR:Z:LI
Two seated facing lions with briquet in center

SALVV:FAC:PPLM-TVV:DNE A•: I 8 Λ Λ
Shield of Burgundy on flowery cross

II-28 Brabant Duchy
Mint: Antwerp
Marie of Burgundy, 1477-1482
1477 Briquet
S 3.06 g
Frey 181, GH 40-1, DW 519

MARIA:DEI:G:DVCISS:BG:BRAB':Z:LI
Seated lion holding shield of Burgundy

BENEDIC:HEREDITATI:TVE:A I 8 Λ Λ
Triple-stranded flowery short cross

II-29a Flanders County
Mint: Bruges
Marie of Burgundy, 1477-1482
1477 Double Briquet
C 3.06 g
Frey 181, 181A, GH 39-3, D.d.P pL. 18, 70, De Mey Fl. 431

MARIA:DVCISSA:BG:COMIT:FLAD
Two seated facing lions with briquet in center

SALVV:FAC:PPLM:TVV:DNE: I 8 Λ Λ
Shield of Burgundy on flowery cross

An overdate of 1477/6 is known.

II-29b Flanders County
Mint: Bruges
Marie of Burgundy, 1477-1482
1477 Double Briquet
R5 3.06 g
Unpublished?

MARIA:DVCISSA:BG:COMIT:FLAD
Two seated facing lions with briquet in center

SALVV:FAC:PPLM:TVV:DNE:1 Λ Λ
Shield of Burgundy on flowery cross

An error date which is located at the Cabinet des Medailles in Brussels.

II-30 Flanders County
Mint: Bruges
Charles the Rash, 1467-1477
1477 Briquet
R5 3.06 g
Unpublished?

KAROLVS:DEI:GRA:DVX:BVRG:CO:FL
Seated lion holding shield of Burgundy

BENEDIC:HEREDITA:TVE: I 8 Λ Λ
Triple-stranded flowery short cross

Issued in the name of Charles a year after his death. No documentation exists of coins issued in his name at the Bruges mint for this year. Examples sold in Münz Zentrum in 1991 and in Cervin collection in 2003.

II-31 **Flanders** **County**
Mint: **Bruges**
Marie of Burgundy, 1477-1482
1477 **Briquet**
R5 *3.06 g*
Frey —, JMP 1987, p.189

MARIA:DVCISSA:BG:COMIT:FLAND
Seated lion holding shield of Burgundy

BENEDIC:HEREDITATI:TVE': I ꝝ Λ Λ
Triple-stranded flowery short cross

Until 1987, no briquets were known to have been struck for Marie at the Bruges mint with this date.

1478

II-32 **Brabant** **Duchy**
Mint: **Antwerp**
Marie of Burgundy, 1477-1482
1478 **Double Briquet**
C *3.06 g*
Frey 185, GH 39-1b DW 517, Van der Chijs 17.2, Stephanik 4704-05

MARIA:DEI:G:DVCISS:BG:BR:Z:LI
Two seated facing lions with briquet in center

SALVV:FAC:PPLM-TVV:DNE:A•:1ꝝΛ8
Shield of Burgundy on flowery cross

II-33 **Brabant** **Duchy**
Mint: **Antwerp**
Marie of Burgundy, 1477-1482
1478 **Briquet**
S *3.06 g*
Frey 185A, GH 40-1b, DW 520, Van der Chijs 18.3-4, Stephanik 4706

MARIA:DEI:G:DVCISS:BG:BRAB:Z:LI
Seated lion holding shield of Burgundy

BENEDIC:HEREDITATI:TVE:A:1ꝝΛ8
Triple-stranded flowery short cross

II-34 **Flanders** **County**
Mint: **Bruges**
Marie of Burgundy, 1477-1482
1478 **Double Briquet**
C *3.06 g*
Frey 185C, GH 39-3b, D.d.P no.88

MARIA:DVCISSA:BG:COMIT:F
Two seated facing lions with briquet in center

SALVV:FAC:PPLM:TVV:DNE:1ꝝΛ8
Shield of Burgundy on flowery cross

An strange overdate of 1478/1748 is known, as well as several others.

II-35 **Flanders** **County**
Mint: **Bruges**
Marie of Burgundy, 1477-1482
1478 **Gros**
C *1.87 g*
Frey 185E, GH 43-3, De Mey Fl. 445-47, D.d.P Pl. 18, 73

MARIA:DVCISSA:BG:CO:FLA
Large ornate letter "M" in quatrefoil

BENEDIC:AIA:MEA:DNO 1ꝝ78
Flowery short cross

II-36 **Liège** **Bishopric**
Mint: **Uncertain**
Louis of Bourbon, 1456-1482
1478 **Double Patard**
R *2.39-3.82 g*
Frey 190, CH. 348, 350, Dengis 698, 700

LVDO*DE*BORB*EPS*LEOD*DVX*BVL
Two seated facing lions

SALVV*FAC*PO*TVVM*DNE*LXXVIII
Shield of Bourbon on ornate short cross which does not interrupt legend

---

II-37 **Liège** **Bishopric**
Mint: **Hasselt**
Louis of Bourbon, 1456-1482
1478 **Patard**
R *2.08-3.03 g*
Frey 195, CH. 351-52, Dengis 701-02

MO*EPI*LEODIEN*FACTA*HASSELT
Seated lion holding shield of Bourbon

BNDIC*HEREDITATI*TVE*LXXVIII
Ornate triple-stranded short cross

1479

II-38 Brabant Duchy
Mint: Antwerp
Marie of Burgundy, 1477-1482
1479 Double Briquet
C *3.06 g*
Frey 205, GH 39-1b, DW 517, Van der Chijs 17.2, Stephanik 4708

MARIA:DEI:G:DVCISS:BG:BR':Z:LI
Two seated facing lions with briquet in center

SALVV:FAC:PPLM-TVV:DNE:A•:1ꝝ∧9
Shield of Burgundy on flowery cross

II-39 Brabant Duchy
Mint: Antwerp
Marie of Burgundy, 1477-1482
1479 Briquet
VS *3.06 g*
Frey 205A, GH 40-1b, DW 520, Stephanik 4710

MARIA:DEI:G:DVCISS"BG:BR:Z:LI
Seated lion holding shield of Burgundy

BENEDIC:HEREDITATI:TVE:A•:1ꝝ∧9
Triple-stranded flowery short cross

II-40 Flanders County
Mint: Bruges
Marie of Burgundy, 1477-1482
1479 Double Briquet
S *3.06 g*
Frey 205C, GH 39-3b, D.d.P No. 88-89, De Mey Fl. 435, 437

MARIA:DVCISSA:BG':COMIT:FL
Two seated facing lions with briquet in center

SALVV:FAC:PPLM:TVV:DNE 1ꝝ∧9
Shield of Burgundy on flowery cross

II-41 Flanders County
Mint: Bruges
Marie of Burgundy, 1477-1482
1479 Gros
C *1.87 g*
Frey 205E, GH 41-3a, D.d.P 18, 73, De Mey Fl. 447

MARIA*DVCISSA*BG*CO*FL
Large ornate letter "M" in quatrefoil

BENEDIC*AIA*MEA*DNO* 1ꝝ79
Flowery short cross

II-42a Liège Bishopric
Mint: Uncertain
Louis of Bourbon, 1456-1482
1479 Double Patard
R *2.19-3.13 g*
Frey 208, CH 347, Dengis 697

LVDO*DE*BORB'*EPS'*LEOD'DVX*BVL'
Two seated facing lions

SALVV'*—FAC*P'*—TVV'*D'*—LXXIX
Shield of Bourbon on ornate long cross interrupting legend

II-42b Liège Bishopric
Mint: Uncertain
Louis of Bourbon, 1456-1482
1479 Double Patard
R *2.21-3.13 g*
Frey 208, CH. 350, Dengis 700

LVDO:DE:BORB:EPS:LEOD:DVX:BVL
Two seated facing lions

SALVV*FAC*PO*TVVM*DNE*LXXIX
Shield of Bourbon on ornate short cross not interrupting legend

---

II-43 Liège Bishopric
Mint: Uncertain
Louis of Bourbon, 1456-1482
1479 Patard
R2 *2.13-3.19 g*
Frey 208A, CH. 354, Dengis 704

MO*LVDOVIC*EPS*LEODIENSIS
Seated lion holding shield of Bourbon

BNC*HEREDITATI*TVE*LXXIX
Ornate triple-stranded short cross

II-44 **Liège** **Bishopric**
Mint: **Hasselt**
Louis of Bourbon, 1456-1482
1479 **Patard**
R *2.08-3.22 g*
Frey 203, CH. 353, Dengis 702-03

MO*EPI*LEODIEN*FACTA*HASSELT
Seated lion holding shield of Bourbon

BNDIC*HEREDITATI*TVE*LXXIX
Ornate triple-stranded short cross

1480

II-45 **Brabant** **Duchy**
Mint: **Antwerp**
Marie of Burgundy, 1477-1482
1480 **Double Briquet**
S *3.06 g*
Frey 210, GH 39-1b, DW 517, Stephanik 4709

MARIA:DEI:G:DVCISS:BG:BR:Z:LI
Two seated facing lions with briquet in center

SALVV:FAC:PPLM-TVV:DNE A•:1ꝝ80
Shield of Burgundy on flowery cross

II-46 **Brabant** **Duchy**
Mint: **Antwerp**
Marie of Burgundy, 1477-1482
1480 **Briquet**
S *3.06 g*
Frey 210A, GH 40-1b, DW 520, Stephanik 4711

MARIA:DEI:G:DVCISS:BG:BR:Z:LI
Seated lion holding shield of Burgundy

BENEDIC*HEREDITATI*TVE*A*1ꝝ80
Triple-stranded flowery short cross

II-47 **Brabant** **Duchy**
Mint: **Antwerp**
Marie of Burgundy, 1477-1482
1480 **Gros**
R *1.87 g*
Frey 210B, GH 41-1a, DW 522, Van der Chijs 35.1, Stephanik 4713

MARIA:DVCISSA:BG:BRAB:Z:LI
Large ornate letter "M" in quatrefoil

BENEDIC:AIA:MEA:DNO:A•:1ꝝ80
Flowery short cross

II-48 **Brabant** **Duchy**
Mint: **Antwerp**
Marie of Burgundy, 1477-1482
1480 **Demi Gros**
R3 *1.08 g*
Frey 662, GH 42-1, DW 524-25, Van der Chijs 35.2

MARIA:DVCISS:BG:BR:Z:LI
Stylized, rectangular letter "M"

IN:NOMINE:DOMINI:1ꝝ80
Flowery short cross

II-49 **Flanders** **County**
Mint: **Bruges**
Marie of Burgundy, 1477-1482
1480 **Double Briquet**
VS *3.06 g*
Frey 211, GH 39-3b,c, D.d.P No. 88-91, De Mey Fl. 437-40

MARIA:DVCISSA:BG:COMIT:FL
Two seated facing lions with briquet in center

SALVV:FAC:PPLM:TVV:DNE 1ꝝ80
Shield of Burgundy on flowery cross

II-50a **Flanders** **County**
Mint: **Bruges**
Marie of Burgundy, 1477-1482
1480 **Briquet**
R *3.06 g*
Frey 211A, GH 40-3, D.d.P Pl. 18, 71-72, De Mey Fl. 441-43

MARIA:DVCISSA:BG:COMIT:FL
Seated lion holding shield of Burgundy

BENEDIC:HEREDITATI:TVE 1ꝝ80
Triple-stranded flowery short cross

II-50b **Flanders** **County**
Mint: **Bruges**
Marie of Burgundy, 1477-1482
1480 **Briquet**
R4 *3.06 g*
Frey 654, GH 40-3 var., De Mey Fl. 444

MARIA:DVCISSA:BG:COMIT:FLA
Seated lion holding shield of Burgundy

SALVV:FAC:PPLM:TVV:DNE 1ꝝ80
Triple-stranded flowery short cross

This is a hybrid piece with the obverse design of a briquet and the reverse legend of a double briquet.

II-51 **Flanders** **County**
Mint: **Bruges**
Marie of Burgundy, 1477-1482
1480 **Gros**
VS *1.87 g*
Frey 211B, GH 41-3a,b, D.d.P Pl. 18, 74, De Mey Fl. 447-48

MARIA*DVCISSA*BG*CO*FL
Large ornate letter "M" in quatrefoil

BENEDIC*AIA*MEA*DNO 1480
Flowery short cross

II-52a **Liège** **Bishopric**
Mint: **Uncertain**
Louis of Bourbon, 1456-1482
1480 **Double Patard**
R *2.65 g*
Frey —, CH. 347, Dengis 697

LVDO*DE*BORB*EPS*LEOD*DVX*BVL
Two seated facing lions

SALVV*—FAC*PO'—TVVM*D'*—LXXX
Shield of Bourbon on ornate long cross

II-52b **Liège** **Bishopric**
Mint: **Uncertain**
Louis of Bourbon, 1456-1482
1480 **Double Patard**
R3 *2.90 g (average)*
Frey —, Dengis 700

Same as preceding, but with short cross not interrupting legend

---

II-53 **Liège** **Bishopric**
Mint: **Uncertain**
Louis of Bourbon, 1456-1482
1480 **Patard**
R2 *2.13- 3.09 g*
Frey 222B, CH. 354, Dengis 704

MO*LVDOVIC*EPS*LEODIENSIS
Seated lion holding shield of Bourbon

BNC*HEREDITATI*TVE*LXXX
Ornate triple-stranded short cross

1481

II-54 **Brabant** **Duchy**
Mint: **Antwerp**
Marie of Burgundy, 1477-1482
1481 **Double Briquet**
C *3.06 g*
Frey 225, GH 39-1c, DW 518, Stephanik 4707

MARIA:DEI:G:DVCISS:BG:BR:Z:LI
Two seated facing lions with briquet in center

SALVV:FAC:PPLM-TVV:DNE A•:1ꝝ81
Shield of Burgundy on flowery cross

II-55 **Brabant** **Duchy**
Mint: **Antwerp**
Marie of Burgundy, 1477-1482
1481 **Briquet**
VS *3.06 g*
Frey 225A, GH 40-1c, DW 521

MARIA:DEI:G:DVCISS:BG:BR:Z:LI
Seated lion holding shield of Burgundy

BENEDIC:HEREDITATI:TVE:A•:1ꝝ81
Triple-stranded flowery short cross

An overdate of 1481/0 is known.

II-56 Brabant Duchy
Mint: Antwerp
Marie of Burgundy, 1477-1482
1481 Gros
VS 1.87 g
Frey 225B, GH 41-1b, DW 523

MARIA:DVCISSA:BG:BR:Z:LI
Large ornate letter “M” in quatrefoil

BENEDIC:AIA:MEA:DNO:A•:1ᛟ81
Flowery short cross

II-57 Brabant Duchy
Mint: Antwerp
Marie of Burgundy, 1477-1482
1481 Demi Gros
R4 1.98 g
Frey 674, GH 42-1, DW 525

MARIA:DVCISS:BG:BR:Z:LI
Stylized, rectangular letter “M”

IN:NOMINE:DOMINI:1ᛟ81
Flowery short cross

II-58 Brabant Duchy
Mint: Antwerp
Marie of Burgundy, 1477-1482
1481 Four Mites
R 1.21 g
Frey 675, GH 47-1, DW 528, Van der Chijs 18.6

MARIA:DEI:G:DVCISS:BG:BR:LI
Large ornate letter “M”

SIT:NO-ME:DOI-BENEDI-CT:1ᛟ81
Long cross

This is the first early dated copper coin. Struck originally as a billon coin of only 3.6% silver, over time the amount of silver contained in this piece diminished to trace amounts only.

II-59 Flanders County
Mint: Bruges
Marie of Burgundy, 1477-1482
1481 Double Briquet
R 3.06 g
Frey 225C, GH 39-3c, D.d.P No. 90-91, De Mey Fl. 439-40

MARIA:DVCISSA:BG:COMIT:F
Two seated facing lions with briquet in center

SALVV:FAC:PPLM:TVV:DNE 1481
Shield of Burgundy on flowery cross

II-60 Flanders County
Mint: Bruges
Marie of Burgundy, 1477-1482
1481 Gros
R 1.87 g
Frey 672, GH 41-3b, De Mey Fl. 448

MARIA*DVCISSA*BG*CO*FL
Large ornate letter “M” in quatrefoil

BENEDIC*AIA*MEA*DNO 1ᛟ81
Flowery short cross

II-61a Liège Bishopric
Mint: Uncertain
Louis of Bourbon, 1456-1482
1481 Double Patard
VS 2.19-3.13 g
Frey 226, CH. 347, Dengis 697

LVDO*DE*BORB*EPS*LEOD*DVX*BVL
Two seated facing lions

SALVV'*FAC*P'*—TV'*D—LXXXI
Shield of Bourbon on ornate long cross

II-61b Liège Bishopric
Mint: Uncertain
Louis of Bourbon, 1456-1482
1481 Double Patard
R2 1.92-3.82 g
Frey —, Dengis 698-700

Same as preceding, but with short cross on reverse which does not interrupt legend

---

II-62 Liège Bishopric
Mint: Uncertain
Louis of Bourbon, 1456-1482
1481 Patard
R 2.13-3.09 g
Frey —, CH. 354, Dengis 704

MO*LVDOVIC*EPS*LEODIENSIS
Seated lion holding shield of Bourbon

BNC*HEREDITATI*TVE*LXXXI
Ornate triple-stranded short cross

1482

II-63 Brabant Duchy
Mint: Antwerp
Philip the Fair (Minority), 1482-1492
1482 Florin d'or
R4 3.40 g
Frey —, GH 50-1, DW 531, FR. 37, De Mey d'Or 417, Delmonte 75

MON:AR-DV:AVS-TR:BRA-BANCIE
Shield of Austria-Burgundy on long cross

SANCTVS:-:ANDREAS1ꝶ82
St. Andreas standing behind large cross

II-64a Brabant Duchy
Mint: Antwerp
Philip the Fair (Minority), 1482-1492
1482 Double Briquet
R 3.06 g
Frey —, GH 52-1a, DW 539, Van der Chijs 19.7

MON':ARCHIDVCV:AV':BVR':BRA':LI':Z
Two seated facing lions with briquet in center

DVP:PATARD:FAB'CAT:I:BRA:1ꝶ82
Shield of Austria-Burgundy on flowery cross

Struck in the name of the infant Duke Philip upon the death of Marie of Burgundy in 1482

II-64b Brabant Duchy
Mint: Antwerp
Philip the Fair (Minority), 1482-1492
1482 Double Briquet
VS 3.06 g
Frey 244B, GH 52-1c, DW 541, Van der Chijs 19.8

MON'.AR.DV.AVSTRIE.BRABANCIE
Two seated facing lions with briquet in center

SALVV.FAC.PPLM.TVV.DNE.A.1ꝶ82
Shield of Burgundy on flowery cross

II-64c Brabant Duchy
Mint: Antwerp
Philip the Fair (Minority), 1482-1492
1482 Double Briquet.
R4 3.06 g
Frey —, GH 52-1c Supp.

MONETA:DVC:AVST:LOT:BRA:LI:ZC
Two seated facing lions with briquet in center

SALVV.FAC.PPLM.TVV.DNE.A.1ꝶ82
Shield of Burgundy on flowery cross

Extremely rare variety with title of Duke of Lorraine ("Lot") included, a quest for which Charles gained his nickname (the "Rash") and lost his life.

II-65a Brabant Duchy
Mint: Antwerp
Philip the Fair (Minority), 1482-1492
1482 Briquet
R2 3.06 g
Frey 241, GH 53-1b, DW 543, Van der Chijs 19.9

MONETA*AR*DV*AVSTRIE*BRABANSIE
Seated lion holding shield of Austria-Burgundy

BENEDIC*HEREDITATI*TVE*A•1ꝶ82
Triple-stranded flowery short cross

Struck for Philip during his minority.

II-65b Brabant Duchy
Mint: Antwerp
Philip the Fair (Minority), 1482-1492
1482 Briquet
R 3.06 g
Frey —, GH 53-1a, DW 540, Van der Chijs 19.10, Stephanik 4716

MON'*ARCHIDVCV'*AV*BVRG*BRAB*LI
Seated lion holding shield of Austria-Burgundy

SIMP*PATARD*FAB'CAT*I*BRA'*1ꝶ82
Flowery short cross

Struck for Philip during his minority.

II-66 Liège Bishopric
Mint: Uncertain
Louis of Bourbon, 1456-1482
1482 Double Patard
R2 1.92-3.82 g
Frey 234, CH. 350, Dengis 700

LVDO*DE*BORB*EPS*LEOD*DVX*BVL
Two seated facing lions

SALVV*FAC*PO*TVVM*DNE*LXXXII
Shield of Bourbon on ornate short cross

1483

II-67 Brabant Duchy
Mint: Antwerp
Philip the Fair (Minority), 1482-1492
1483 Florin d'or
R4 *3.40 g*
Frey —, GH 50-1, DW 531, FR. 37, De Mey d'Or 417, Delmonte 75

MON • AR-DV • AVS-TR • BRA-BANCIE
Shield of Austria-Burgundy on long cross

SANCTVS:-:1ꝝ83-:ANDREAS
St. Andreas standing behind large cross

II-68a Brabant Duchy
Mint: Antwerp
Philip the Fair (Minority), 1482-1492
1483 Double Briquet
R *3.06 g*
Frey 245, GH 52-1b, DW 541, Van der Chijs 19.10, Stephanik 4717

MON' • AR • DV • AVSTRIE • BRABANCIE
Two seated facing lions with briquet in center

SALVV:FAC:PPLM:TVV:DNE:A • :1ꝝ83
Shield of Austria-Burgundy on flowery cross

II-68b Brabant Duchy
Mint: Antwerp
Philip the Fair (Minority), 1482-1492
1483 Double Briquet
R3 *3.06 g*
Frey —, GH 52-1c, DW 542

MONETA:DVC:AVST:LOT:BRA:LI:ZC
Two seated facing lions with briquet in center

SALVV.FAC.PPLM.TVV.DNE.A.1ꝝ83
Shield of Burgundy on flowery cross

Type with title of Lorraine included.

II-69 Brabant Duchy
Mint: Antwerp
Philip the Fair (Minority), 1482-1492
1483 Briquet
R2 *3.06 g*
Frey —, GH 53-1b, DW 543, Stephanik 4718-19

MONETA • AR • DV • AVSTRIE • BRABANSIE
Seated lion holding shield of Austria-Burgundy

BENEDIC • HEREDITATI • TVE • A • 1ꝝ83
Triple-stranded flowery short cross

II-70 Brabant Duchy
Mint: Antwerp
Philip the Fair (Minority), 1482-1492
1483 Gros
R3 *1.87 g*
Frey 253F, GH 55-1, DW 544, Van der Chijs 19.11

MONETA:AR:DV:AVSTRIE:BRABANSIE
Large ornate letter "M" in quatrefoil

BENEDIC • AIA • MEA • DNO • A • 1ꝝ83
Flowery short cross

II-71 Brabant Duchy
Mint: Antwerp
Philip the Fair (Minority), 1482-1492
1483 Demi Gros
R4 *1.80 g*
Frey —, GH 56-1, DW 546

MON • AR • DV • AVSTRIE • BRAB
Stylized, rectangular letter "M"

IN • NOMINE • DOMINI • A • 1ꝝ83
Flowery short cross

II-72 Liège, Family of Mark Bishopric
Mint: Liège
John of the Mark (Claimant), 1482-1484
1483 Double Patard
R5 *2.68 g*
Frey 248, CH. 372, Dengis 739

IOHS*DEI*GRA*POSTULAT*LEODI'

Two facing seated lions

SIT*NOME*DNI*BNEDICTV*LXXXIII
Shield of the Mark on ornate short cross

II-A72 Liège, Family of Mark Bishopric
Mint: Liège
William of the Mark (Administrator), 1482-1484
1483 Demi Stoeter
R5-6 *1.33-1.61 g*
Frey —, Dengis 732

WILHEL:DE:MAR:MAB'.LEOD
Realistic bust of William of the Mark facing right with long beard and cap

ANO—DNI—LXX-XIII
Shield of Mark-Virenbourg over triple-stranded long cross

II-73 Liège, Family of Mark Bishopric
Mint: Liège
John of the Mark (Claimant), 1482-1484
1483 Patard
R5-6 *Weight unknown*
Frey —, CH. 373, RBN 1873 p.396, Dengis 740

IOHS*DEI*GRA*POSTULAT*LEODIE'
Seated lion holding shield of the Mark

SIT*NOME*DNI*BENEDICT*LXXXIII
Ornate short cross

Likely only one or two known.

II-74 Liège, Family of Mark Bishopric
Mint: Liège
John of the Mark (Claimant), 1482-1484
1483 Demi Patard
R5 *.83-1.67 g*
Frey —, CH. 374, Dengis 741

IOHS*DEI*GRA*POSTULAT*LE'
Lion advancing left behind shield of the Mark

ANNO*DNI*M*CCCC*LXXXIII
Ornate short cross (Type shown of 1484)

A unique copper pattern of this piece was sold at the Dupriez sale in Brussels in 1910.

1484

II-75 Brabant Duchy
Mint: Antwerp
Philip the Fair (Minority), 1482-1492
1484 Gros
R *1.87 g*
Frey 264D, GH 55-1, DW 544, Van der Chijs 19.11

MON • AR • DV • AVSTRIE • BRABANCIE
Large ornate letter "M" in quatrefoil

BENEDIC • AIA • MEA • DNO • A • 1ጸ8ጸ
Flowery short cross

II-76 Liège, Family of Hornes Bishopric
Mint: Uncertain
John of Hornes, 1484-1505
1484 Double Patard
R5 *3.00 g*
Frey 257, CH. 390, Dengis 757

IOHIS*ELECT*COFMAT*LEODIEN
Two seated facing lions

SALW*FAC*PO*TVVM*DNE*LXXXጸ
Shield of Hornes on ornate cross

This coin bears the first partially-dated, mixed numeral (Roman and Arabic) date.

II-77a Liège, Family of Hornes Bishopric
Mint: Uncertain
John of Hornes, 1484-1505
1484 One-Third Patard
R2 *0.61-1.10 g*
Frey —, CH. 409, Dengis 760

IOIH:ELE:COFMAT:LOEDIEN
Two leaning shields of Hornes

MISER:NRI:Q:PASSUS:ES:P:NOB- 1-ጸ-8-ጸ
Ornate cross with date in angles

Issued before John was confirmed by the Pope as his duly-elected bishop.

II-77b Liège, Family of Hornes Bishopric
Mint: Uncertain
John of Hornes, 1484-1505
1484 One-Third Patard
R5 *0.77 g*
Frey —, CH. 409, Dengis 760

Same as preceding but with error date "1-ጸ-ጸ-8"

II-77c Liège, Family of Hornes Bishopric
Mint: Uncertain
John of Hornes, 1484-1505
1484 One-Third Patard

R5-6 *0.61-1.10 g*
Frey —, CH. 409, Dengis 789

Same as preceding but with obverse legend: IOHS'*DE*HORN*EPS*LEODI'

Issued after John's confirmation as bishop.

II-78 **Liège, Family of Mark Bishopric**
Mint: Uncertain
William of the Mark (Administrator), 1482-1484
1484 Double Patard
R6 *2.71 g*
Frey —, Dengis 730, RBN 1905, p. 175-77

WILHEL:D:MARH'MAB'LEO'B
Facing 3/4 length armored highly realistic figure of William of the Mark

ANO-DNI-LXX-XIIII
Shield of Mark-Virnenbourg over triple-stranded long cross

This spectacular coin is of the usurper, William of the Mark, whose only title was "Mambour," or lay administrator. It was unknown until 1905. The first known piece, a holed specimen in the Duke of Arenberg's collection, was lost after World War I. A unique example is now extant from a small treasure find in 1995 and was sold at Elsen in 1999 for $13,000. As William of the Mark was a usurper, upon his execution in 1486, his coins were not likely to escape the melting pot. (Now in author's collection).

II-79 **Liège, Family of Mark Bishopric**
Mint: Liège
William of the Mark (Administrator), 1482-1484
1484 Stoeter
R4 *2.54-2.86 g*
Frey 256, CH. 370, Dengis 731

WILHEL:D:MARK:MAB:LEOD
Realistic bust of William of the Mark facing right with long beard and cap

ANO:DONI:LXXXIIII
Shield of Mark-Virnenbourg over triple-stranded long cross

An excessively rare coin, equal in value to two patards, portraying a facing renaissance bust of the usurper, William of the Mark. One of the first renaissance portraits on an early dated coin. A unique variety of this coin with the obverse legend *WIHEL:D MAN H:MAB LIOD* was sold in the famous Dupriez sale in Brussels in 1910. Another die with small varieties is also reliably reported. Fakes from dies cut in the 19th century have recently surfaced.

II-80 **Liège, Family of Mark Bishopric**
Mint: Liège
William of the Mark (Administrator), 1482-1484
1484 Demi Stoeter
R4 *1.40 g*
Frey 256, CH. 371, Dengis 732

WILHEL:D:MAR:MAB:LEO
Realistic bust of William of the Mark facing right with long beard and cap

ANO:DNI:LXXXIIII
Shield of Mark-Virnenbourg over triple-stranded long cross

II-A81 **Liège, Family of Mark Bishopric**
Mint: Liège
William of the Mark (Administrator), 1482-1484
1484 Demi Patard
R6 *1.99 g*
Frey —, Dengis 735

WILHEL*D*MARET*CO*ARB
Lion advancing left behind shield of the Mark

ANNO:DNI:M:CCCC:LXXXIIII
Ornate short cross

Also known as a demi-aidant. Unique specimen from the Glaumont hoard in 1926 but unpublished until 1978. This is the only known coin of William without his bust.

II-81 **Liège, Family of Mark Bishopric**
Mint: Liège
John of the Mark (Claimant), 1482-1484
1484 Demi Patard
R4 *1.17 g*
Frey 255, CH. 374, Dengis 741

IOHS:DEI:GRA:POSTULAT:LE
Lion advancing left behind shield of the Mark

ANNO:DNI:M:CCCC:LXXXIIII
Ornate short cross

Issued by William's son, John of the Mark.

1485

II-82 **Brabant Duchy**
Mint: Antwerp
Philip the Fair (Minority), 1482-1492
1485 Double Briquet
VS *3.06 g*
Frey 267, GH 52-1b var., DW 541 var.

MON' • AR • DV • AVSTRIE • BRABANCIE
Two seated facing lions with briquet in center

SALVV:FAC:PPLM:TVV:DNE:A • :1ꭓ85
Shield of Austria-Burgundy on flowery cross

II-83 **Brabant** **Duchy**
Mint: **Antwerp**
Philip the Fair (Minority), 1482-1492
1485 **Briquet**
R2 *3.06 g*
Frey 267A, GH 53-1b, DW 543 var

MONETA • AR • DV • AVSTRIE • BRABANSIE
Seated lion holding shield of Austria-Burgundy

BENEDIC • HEREDITATI • TVE • A • 1ꭓ85
Triple-stranded flowery short cross

II-84 **Liège, Family of Hornes** **Bishopric**
Mint: **Hasselt**
John of Hornes, 1484-1505
1485 **Patard**
R6 *1.85 g*
Frey —, CH. Supp. 27a, Dengis 799

IOHS:DE:HORNE:EPISCOPVS:LEODIENSIS:E:
Quartered arms of Hornes and Looz

SI:DEVS: - NOBISCV': - QVIS:CONT - NOS:1ꭓ85
Thick long cross with fleur-de-lys and lions in angles of cross

The "5" in the date employs the "lightning strike" style.

II-85 **Liège, Family of Hornes** **Bishopric**
Mint: **Uncertain**
John of Hornes, 1484-1505
1485 **One-Third Patard**
R4 *0.61-1.85 g*
Frey 269, CH. 409,

IOIH:ELE:COFMAT:LEODIEN
Two leaning shields of Hornes

MISER:NRI:Q:PASSUS:ES:P:NOB- 1-ꭓ-8-5
Ornate cross with date in angles

II-86 **Liège, Family of Mark** **Administrator**
Mint: **Uncertain**
William of the Mark (Administrator), 1482-1484
1485 **Stoeter**
R6 *2.65 g*
Frey —, CH. p. 213, Dengis 733, RBN. 1864, p. 447

WILHEL:D,MAREHA:Z:ARB
Realistic bust of William of the Mark facing right, with long beard and cap

ANO-DNI-MLX-XXV
Shield of Mark-Virnenbourg over triple-stranded long cross

Struck in the Arenberg territories outside of Liège. Possibly no longer extant.

II-87 **Liège, Family of Mark** **Administrator**
Mint: **Uncertain**
William of the Mark (Administrator), 1482-1484
1485 **Demi Stoeter**
R6 *1.55-1.89 g*
Frey —, CH. p. 213-14, Dengis 734

WILHEL*D*MARHA*Z*A'B"
Realistic bust of William of the Mark facing right, with long beard and cap

ANO-DNI-MLX-XXV
Shield of Mark-Virnenbourg over triple-stranded long cross

Likewise struck in the Arenberg territories outside of Liège . Two pieces currently extant, one in the Cabinet des Medailles in Brussels and the other in the Museum of Tongres (Tongeren).

1486

II-88 **Liège, Family of Hornes** **Bishopric**
Mint: **Uncertain**
John of Hornes, 1484-1505
1486 **Double Patard**
R2 *2.31-3.03 g*
Frey —, CH. 404-05, Dengis 785-86

IO:D:HOR:EP:LEOD:DV:BVL:COIT:L
Shield of Hornes

SI:DEUS:NOBSCU:QUIS:COTA:NOS:86
Very ornate flowery short cross

II-89 **Liège, Family of Hornes** **Bishopric**
Mint: **Uncertain**
John of Hornes, 1484-1505
1486 **Patard**
R *1.17-1.95 g*
Frey —, CH. 408, Dengis 788

IOHS:DE:HORN:EPS:LEODIEN
Shield of Hornes

SI:DEVS:NOBSC:QVIS:COT:NOS:86
Very ornate flowery short cross

II-90a **Liège, Family of Hornes** **Bishopric**
Mint: **Uncertain**
John of Hornes, 1484-1505
1486 **Double Heaume**
R *2.33-2.82 g*
Frey —, CH. 413, Dengis 793

IO:D:HOR:EP:LEOD:DV:BVL:COIT:L
Leaning shield of Hornes surmounted by elaborate helmet

SI:DVS:NOBS:QVS:COTA:NOS:1ꝝ86
Long cross with alternating lions and fleur-de-lys in angles

II-90b **Liège, Family of Hornes** **Bishopric**
Mint: **Uncertain**
John of Hornes, 1484-1505
1486 **Double Heaume**
R5 *2.60 g (est.)*
Frey —, Dengis 793 note

IOHS'DE'HORN ELEC'CO'FMA'LEODIE:
Same as preceding but with title prior to confirmation

II-91a **Liège, Family of Hornes** **Bishopric**
Mint: **Uncertain**
John of Hornes, 1484-1505
1486 **One-Third Patard**
R3 *0.49-1.08 g*
Frey 279, CH. 410, Dengis 790

IOHS:DE:HORN:EPS:LEODIE
Two leaning shields of Hornes

SI:DEUS:NOBSC:QUIS:CO:T:N-1-ꝝ-8-6
Ornate short cross with date in angles

II-91b **Liège, Family of Hornes** **Bishopric**
Mint: **Uncertain**
John of Hornes, 1484-1505
1486 **One-Third Patard**
R2 *0.87-0.95 g*
Frey 279, CH. 411, Dengis 791

IOHS'*DE*HORN*EPS'*LEODI'
Two leaning shields of Hornes

SI.DEVS.NOBS'C'QVIS.CO'T'N.86
Ornate short cross

1487

II-92 **Brabant** **Duchy**
Mint: **Antwerp**
Philip the Fair (Minority), 1482-1492
1487 **Florin d'or**
R6 *3.71 g*
Frey —, GH 66-6, DW 533, Van der Chijs 18.3, FR. 41, Delmonte 345

SANCT*ANDREA*FILIOS*PROTEG'*TVOS 1ꝝ8Λ
St. Andreas holding book, standing beside large cross

AMA*IVSTVCIA*PACE*Z*DEFENDE*PPLM'*TVVM
Shield of Austria-Burgundy on flowery cross

Note: Gelder Hoc 66-6 attributes this piece, also known as a ducat of Burgundy, to Holland.

II-93 **Brabant** **Duchy**
Mint: **Antwerp and Malines**
Philip the Fair (Minority), 1482-1492
1487 **Silver Real**
R3 *7.20 g*
Frey 285, GH 67-1, DW 556-57, Van der Chijs 19.13

CVSTODIAT • C'ATOR • O'IM • HV'ILE • S'VV • SVV • 1ꝝ8Λ
Half-length figure of Maximilian as Holy Roman Emperor facing right, holding sword and imperial orb

DET • TIBI • MATRIS • V'TVTE • ET • IN • CELIS • GLORIAM
Elaborate large joint monogram of initials of Maximilian as regent and his son Philip

This stunning 35 mm coin of 8 stuivers, struck by Maximilian for his infant son Philip, is the first large silver coin of the Netherlands.

II-94 **Brabant** **Duchy**
Mint: **Antwerp**
Philip the Fair (Minority), 1482-1492
1487 **Double Griffon**
R2 *3.60 g*
Frey 284, 284A, GH 68-1a, DW 558, Van der Chijs 19.14, Stephanik 4730-32

MO'*ARGT*RO*RG*Z*PHI*AR*DV'*AV'*BGB'
Two facing griffins holding briquet with initial mark of hand

SALVV'*FAC*DNE*PPLM'*TVV'* 1ጸ8Λ
Shield of Austria-Burgundy on flowery cross

This is identified to Antwerp by the hand initial mark.

II-A94 **Brabant** **Duchy**
Mint: **Malines**
Philip the Fair (Minority), 1482-1492
1487 **Double Griffon**
R2 *3.60 g*
Frey —, GH 68-1 b, c, DW 559-60

Same as preceding, but with initial mark of crown on obverse and German eagle on reverse

---

II-95a **Flanders** **County**
Mint: **Bruges**
Philip the Fair (Minority), 1482-1492
1487 **Gold Real**
R5-6 *14.82 g*
Frey —, GH 64-5a, FR. 195, De Mey d'Or 849, D.d.P Pl. 15, 15, De Mey Fl. 475, Delmonte 499

MAXIMILIAN:DEI:GRA:RP,A:REX:SEMP:AVGV
Emperor seated on gothic throne

TENE:MENSVRAM:ET:RESPICE:FINEM:*1ጸ8Λ
Crowned eagle shield of Holy Roman Emperor

II-95b **Flanders** **County**
Mint: **Bruges**
Philip the Fair (Minority), 1482-1492
1487 **Gold Real**
R5-6 *14.82 g*
Frey —, GH 64-5b, FR. 195. De Mey d'Or 848, De Mey Fl. 476, Delmonte 499

Same as preceding, but date reads as M:CCCCLXXXVII

II-96 **Flanders** **County**
Mint: **Bruges**
Philip the Fair (Minority), 1482-1492
1487 **Double Griffon**
R6 *3.60 g*
Unpublished?

MONET'ºRO'ºREG'ºZºPHI'ºARCHID'ºAV'ºGº
Two facing griffins holding briquet

SALVV:FAC:DOMINE:POPVLVM:TVVM: 1ጸ8Λ
Shield of Austria-Burgundy on flowery cross

A unique piece attributed to Flanders by the crown initial mark and the style of the lettering. Sold at Schulman in 2002 (author's collection).

II-97 **Flanders** **County**
Mint: **Bruges**
Philip the Fair (Minority), 1482-1492
1487 **Griffon**
R6 *1.80 g*
Unpublished?

DENA*SIMPLEX*GRIFON*NOMINAT* 1ጸ8Λ
Griffin facing left holding briquet

DEVM:PLVS:AMA:QVAM:ARGENTVM:
Shield of Austria-Burgundy on flowery cross

A unique piece attributed to Flanders by punctuation and type. Sold at Schulman in 2002. No other dated single griffons from any state or mint exist (author's collection).

1488

II-98 **Brabant** **Duchy**
Mint: **Brussels**
Philip the Fair (Minority), 1482-1492
1488 **Quadruple Patard**
R5-6 *3.58 g*
Frey —, GH 162, DW 567-68

PHS:DEI:GRACIA:DVX:BRAB:Z:LIMB:1ꝝ88
St. Michael slaying dragon, carrying shield with the letter "B"

DA:PACEM:DOMINE:IN:DIEBVS:NOSTRIS
Four-part lion shield of Brabant-Limburg on a flowery cross

A marvelous piece but with no recent auction history.

II-99 Brabant Duchy
Mint: Brussels
Philip the Fair (Minority), 1482-1492
1488 Double Patard
R5 3.25 g
Frey 298, GH 163, DW 569-70, Van der Chijs 20.20

PHS:DEI:GRA:DVX:BRAB:1ꝝ88
St. Michael holding cross with shield of Brabant below

INVOCA-VI:DEV-ADIVTO-RE:MEV
Long cross with letter "B" in center, lions of Brabant in angles

Struck in Brussels during revolt against Maximilian.

II-100 Brabant Duchy
Mint: Louvain
Philip the Fair (Minority), 1482-1492
1488 Double Patard
R6 3.12 g
Unpublished

PHS:DEI:GRA:DVX:BRABANT:LY
Four-part shield of Brabant-Limburg

ANNO:DOMINI:M:CCCC:LXXXV.I.I.I
Flowery cross with small shield of Louvain in center

A unique and previously unpublished specimen, sold by Elsen in 2006. Examples are known with the date of 1489, with the date being recut from 1488. However, until now, a coin from the original die was not known. This coin is also known as a triple sol.

II-101 Brabant Duchy
Mint: Malines
Philip the Fair (Minority), 1482-1492
1488 Demi Noble d'or
R 3.40 g
Frey 299, GH 75-1, DW 534, Van der Chijs 18.4, FR. 39, De Mey d'Or 419, Delmonte 81

MO:RO:RE:Z:PHI:ARDVC:AVS:BG:BRA
Emperor Maximilian in boat holding sword with small shield of Austria-Burgundy in foreground

REFORMATIO:GVERRE:PAX:EST:ANNO:1ꝝ88
Ornate triple-stranded short cross in polyfoil with crowns in angles

---

II-102 Brabant Duchy
Mint: Malines
Philip the Fair (Minority), 1482-1492
1488 Double Patard
R 2.99 g
Frey 300, GH 77-1, DW 566, Van der Chijs 20.21

MONETA+DVCIS+BRANBANCIE+Z+LIM'
Four-part lion shield of Brabant-Limbourg

REFORMACIO+GVERRE+PAX+EST+1ꝝ88
Thick flowery short cross with mintmark in center

II-103 Flanders County
Mint: Ghent
Philip the Fair (Minority), 1482-1492
1488 Florin St. Jean
R3 3.30 g
Frey —, GH 142a, FR. 238, De Mey d'Or 858, D.d.P Pl. 16. 25, De Mey Fl. 612-14, Delmonte 501

PHS*-D'*G'*D'-B'*CO'*-*FLA'*- G-A-N-D
Shield of Austria-Burgundy on flowery cross with G-A-N-D around shield

BATISTA:PROSPER:ADESTO:1ꝝ88
John the Baptist standing behind shield of Flanders

II-104 Flanders County
Mint: Ghent
Philip the Fair (Minority), 1482-1492
1488 Patard
R 3.00 g
Frey 310, GH 143a-c, D.d.P No. 28-32, De Mey Fl. 620-23

PHS'*D-G*D'*B-CO*FL-ANDIE- G-A-N-D
Shield of Austria-Burgundy on flowery cross with G-A-N-D around shield

EQVA*LIBERTAS*DEO*GRATA*1ꝝ88
Lion advancing left

There are dies with and without the name of "Gand" around shield. All were struck in Ghent during revolt from 1488-1491.

II-A105 Liège, Family of Hornes Bishopric
Mint: Uncertain
John of Hornes, 1484-1505
1488 One-Third Patard
R5 *0.80 g (est.)*
Frey —, Dengis 790
IOHS:DE:HORN:EPS:LEODIE
Two leaning shields of Hornes

SI:DEUS:NOBSC:QUIS:CO:T:N- I ꝝ-8-8
Ornate short cross with date in angles

II-105 Liège, Family of Mark Bishopric
Mint: Uncertain
Everard of the Mark (Protector), 1488-1489
1488 Double Patard
R4 *2.29-3.28 g*
Frey 306, CH. 378, Dengis 752-53

EVERARD:DE:MARC:PROT:LEO
Lion advancing left behind shield of the Mark

ANNO*DNI*MCCCC*LXXXVIII
Ornate short cross with boar at top

II-A106 Liège, Family of Mark Bishopric
Mint: Liège
Everard of the Mark (Protector), 1488-1489
1488 Patard
R6 *2.40 g*
Frey —, Dengis 751

EVERARD'D.MAR':PROT'LEO
Shield of Mark-Arenberg occupying entire field
ANNO-DNI-M-CCCC-LXXX8
Very ornate short cross with "E" in center

II-106 Liège, Family of Mark Bishopric
Mint: Liège
Everard of the Mark (Protector), 1488-1489
1488 Demi Patard
R5 *1.19-1.74 g*
Frey 307, CH. 379-80, Dengis 748-49

EVERA:D:MARC:PROT:LEO
Lion advancing left behind shield of the Mark

ANNO:DNI:M:CCCC:LXXX8
Flowery cross

According to Elsen, only 2 or 3 in private hands. There are types with the boar symbol alternately on the obverse and reverse.

II-107 Liège, Family of Mark Bishopric
Mint: Liège
Everard of the Mark (Protector), 1488-1489
1488 Demi Patard
R4 *1.19 g*
Frey —, CH. 381, Dengis 750

EVRA:D:MAR:PROT:L
Shield of the Mark

ANO:DNI:M:CCCC:XXX:8
Thick ornate short cross

A misengraving of the date of 1488.

1489

II-108 Brabant Duchy
Mint: Antwerp
Philip the Fair (Minority), 1482-1492
1489 Florin d'or
R5 *3.40 g*
Frey —, GH 80-1, DW 536, Van der Chijs 18.5, FR. 41, De Mey d'Or 421, Delmonte 78

PHI:ARDHIDV-AVST-BVRG:BRA
St. Andre carrying long cross behind shield of Austria-Burgundy

MAXIMILI-AN:REX-ROMANO-PAT:1ꝝ89
Crowned shield of the Emperor on long cross

II-109 Brabant Duchy
Mint: Antwerp
Philip the Fair (Minority), 1482-1492
1489 Demi Florin d'or
R5 *1.70 g*
Frey 333, GH 81-1, DW 537, Van der Chijs 18.6, FR. 42, De Mey d'Or 422, Delmonte 79

PHI:ARCHID-AV-BVRG-BRA
St. Andre carrying long cross behind shield of Austria-Burgundy

MAXIMILIAN:REX:ROMANO:PATE-1ꝶ89
Crowned shield of the Emperor dividing date

II-110 Brabant Duchy
Mint: Antwerp
Philip the Fair (Minority), 1482-1492
1489 Quadruple Patard
R3 *6.27 g*
Frey 331, GH 82-1, DW 576, Van der Chijs 20.23, Stephanik 4715

PH'I:ARCHIDVCIS:AVSTRIE:BVRGDIE:BRABA
Philip standing behind five part shield of Austria-Burgundy, all within polyfoil

MAXIM'-LIA'ºREX-ROMAN'º-PAT'º1ꝶ89
Crowned shield of the Emperor on flowery long cross

II-111 Brabant Duchy
Mint: Antwerp
Philip the Fair (Minority), 1482-1492
1489 Double Patard
R4 *3.71 g*
Frey 332, GH 83-1, DW 577, Van der Chijs 20.24

PH'I:ARCHIDVC:AVSTRIE:BVRGDIE:BRAB
Shield on flowery short cross

MAXIMILIANVS:REX:ROMANOR':PATER:1ꝶ89
Crowned shield of Emperor in trefoil

II-112 Brabant Duchy
Mint: Antwerp
Philip the Fair (Minority), 1482-1492
1489 Patard
R3 *3.06 g*
Frey 332A, GH 84-1, DW 578, Van der Chijs 20.25

PHI'ARCHIDVCISºAVSTRIEºBVRG'DIEºBRA
Arms occupying entire field

MAXIMI-LIAN REX-ºROMANO'-ºPAT'º1ꝶ89
Crowned shield of Emperor on long cross

II-113 Brabant Duchy
Mint: Antwerp
Philip the Fair (Minority), 1482-1492
1489 Gros
VS *1.80 g*
Frey 333B, GH 85-1, DW 579-80, Van der Chijs 20.26

PH'IºARCHIDVCºAVSTRIEºBVRG'ºBRA
Shield of Austria-Burgundy occupying entire field

MAXIMILIANºREXºROMANO'ºPAT'º1ꝶ89
Flowery short cross with alternating lions and crowns in angles and mintmark in center

---

II-114 Brabant Duchy
Mint: Antwerp
Philip the Fair (Minority), 1482-1492
1489 Demi Gros
R4 *1.11 g*
Frey —, GH 86-1

PHIºARCHIDVCºAVSºBVRGºB
Shield of Austria-Burgundy occupying entire field

MAXIMILIANºREXºROºPATº1ꝶ89
Flowery short cross with mintmark in center

II-115 Brabant Duchy
Mint: Brussels
Philip the Fair (Minority), 1482-1492
1489 Patard
R5 *1.75 g*
Frey —, GH 164, DW 571

PHS:DEI:GRACIA:DVX:BRAB
St. Michael carrying the shield of Brabant-Limburg

PAX-OPTIM-A:RER-VM 1ꝶ89
Long cross with letter "B" in center

Struck in Brussels during revolt against Maximilian.

II-116 Brabant Duchy
Mint: Louvain
Philip the Fair (Minority), 1482-1492
1489 Double Patard
R5 *2.90 g*
Frey –, GH 159, DW 573

PHS:DEI:GRA:DVX:BRABAN:Z:LI
Shield of Brabant-Limbourg in trefoil

ANNO:DOMINI:M:C:C:C:C:LXXXXVIIII
Flowery cross with a small shield of Louvain in center

Struck in Louvain during the revolt against Maximilian.

II-117 Brabant Duchy
Mint: Louvain
Philip the Fair (Minority), 1482-1492
1489 4 Mites
R5 *1.31 g*
Frey –, GH 161, DW 575, Van der Chijs 36.5, JMP XXXIX 1952, #40

PHS:DEI:GRA:DVX:BRABAN:Z:LY
Shield of Louvain in quatrefoil

ANNO-:DOMI-NI:+-:1ꝝ89
Long cross

Struck in Louvain during the revolt against Maximilian.

II-118 Flanders County
Mint: Furnes
Philip the Fair (Minority), 1482-1492
1489 Quadruple Patard
R6 *Weight unknown*
Frey –, De Mey Fl. 503

MO:RO:RE:Z:PHI:ARCV:AVS:BG:CO:FLA
Large eagle with outstretched wings behind shields of Holy Roman Emperor and Austria-Burgundy

REFORMACIO:GVERRE:PAX:EST:A:1ꝝ89
Large thick flowery short cross with fleur-de-lys in center

Possibly unique. Struck at the small provincial mint at Furnes, most likely in order to avoid the revolt. A wonderful piece.

II-119 Flanders County
Mint: Ghent
Philip the Fair (Minority), 1482-1492
1489 Double Briquet
R2 *3.06 g*
Frey 332B, GH 146a, D.d.P Pl. 17, 35, De Mey Fl. 628-29

PHS*DEI*GRA*DVX*B'*COMES*FLANDR
Two seated facing lions with briquet in between, letters "GANDA" below

FIAT*PAX*IN*VIRTVTE*TVE*ET*HAB'*1489
Shield of Flanders on flowery cross

Struck in Ghent during the revolt against Maximilian.

II-120 Flanders County
Mint: Ghent
Philip the Fair (Minority), 1482-1492
1489 Double Mite
R *1.08 g*
Frey 334B GH 151, D.d.P Pl. 18, 44, De Mey Fl. 644

PHS'*DEI*GRA*DVX*B'*CO'*FL'
Lion in shield of advancing left

IN*DOMINO*CONFIDO*1489
Short thick cross with mintmark in center

A copper-billon coin.

II-121 Liège, Family of Hornes Bishopric
Mint: Uncertain
John of Hornes, 1484-1505
1489 Double Patard
R *2.53-2.85 g*
Frey –, CH. 406, Dengis 787

IO:D:HOR:EP:LEOD:DV:BVL:CO:L
Shield of Hornes

SI:DEVS:NOBSCV:QVIS:COTR:NOS:1ꝝ89
Very ornate flowery short cross

II-122a Liège, Family of Hornes Bishopric
Mint: Uncertain
John of Hornes, 1484-1505
1489 Double Heaume
R2 *2.31-3.01 g*
Frey 336E, CH. 415, Dengis 795

IO:D:HOR:EP:LEOD:DV:BVL:COT:L
Shield of Hornes surmounted by elaborate helmet

SI:DVS:NOBS:QVS:COTA:NOS:1489
Long cross with alternating lions and fleur-de-lys in angles

Undated varieties exist as well.

II-122b Liège, Family of Hornes Bishopric
Mint: Uncertain
John of Hornes, 1484-1505
1489 Double Heaume
R3 3.00 g
Frey 336E, CH. 415 notes

Same as above, but date is "1ꝝ89."

II-123 Liège, Family of Mark Bishopric
Mint: Liège
Everard of the Mark (Protector), 1488-1489
1489 Double Patard
R4 3.08 g
Frey 326, CH. 383-84, Dengis 752-53

EVERAR:D:MARC:PROT:LEO
Shield of Mark-Arenberg with small boar above

ANNO*DNI*M*CCCC*LXXXIX
Very ornate short cross with "E" in center

II-124 Liège, Family of Mark Bishopric
Mint: Liège
Everard of the Mark (Protector), 1488-1489
1489 Patard
R5 2.40 g
Frey —, CH. 382, Dengis 751

EVERAR:D:MAR:PROT:LEO
Arms of Mark-Arenberg occupying entire field

ANNO:DNI:M:CCCC:LXXXIX
Long cross

1490

II-125 Brabant Duchy
Mint: Antwerp
Philip the Fair (Minority), 1482-1492
1490 Double Florin d'Or
R6 5.06 g
Frey —, GH 79-1, DW 535, FR. 40, De Mey d'Or 420, Delmonte 77

PHI:ARCH-IDVC:AV-STRIE:B-VRG:BRAB
Helmeted shield of Austria-Burgundy on flowery long cross

MAXIMILIANVS:REX:ROMANOR:PATER:1ꝝ90
Maximilian in polyfoil holding orb and sceptre behind shield of Holy Roman Empire

---

II-126 Brabant Duchy
Mint: Antwerp
Philip the Fair (Minority), 1482-1492
1490 Gros
R 1.80 g
Frey 348A, GH 85-1, DW 580

PHI • ARCHIDVCIS • AVSTRIE • BVRG • BRA
Arms of Austria-Burgundy occupying entire field

MAXIM'L-IAN • REX-ROMANO-PAT'1ꝝ90
Flowery short cross with alternating lions and crowns in angles and mintmark in center

---

II-127 Brabant Duchy
Mint: Antwerp
Philip the Fair (Minority), 1482-1492
1490 Four Mites
R3 1.43 g
Frey 348, GH 93-1, DW 584, Van der Chijs 35.6, Stephanik 4722

PHS*ARCHIDVC*AVSTRIE*BVRG*BRAB
Arms of Austria-Burgundy occupying entire field

MAXIML-IAN*REX*-ROMANO-PAT1ꝝ90
Long cross

A copper coin intended to be struck in billon.

1491

II-128 Flanders County
Mint: Ghent
Philip the Fair (Minority), 1482-1492
1491 Patard

R3 2.88 g

Frey —, GH 154a,b, D.d.P Pl. 18, 45-46, De Mey Fl. 650-51

PHS*D*G*ARCHID*AVST*B*Z*CO*FLA 1ꝝ91
Shield of Austria-Burgundy occupying entire field

FIAT-PAX*I'-VIRTV-TE*TVA - G-A-N-D
Shield of Flanders with lion advancing left on triple-stranded long cross with letters G-A-N-D around shield

Struck during Ghent's revolt against Maximilian.

1492

II-129 Brabant Duchy
Mint: Antwerp
Philip the Fair (Majority), 1492-1506
1492 Florin d'or

R5 3.26 g

Frey —, GH 96-1, DW 538, FR. 43, De Mey d'Or 423, Delmonte 80

PHI:ARCI-DVC:AV:BG:B:Z
Christ enthroned with shield of Brabant at feet

MO:-RO:-REG:-:1ꝝ92
Crowned shield of Holy Roman Empire with surrounding shields of Austria, Burgundy and Hungary in quatrefoil

---

II-130a Brabant Duchy
Mint: Antwerp
Philip the Fair (Majority), 1492-1506
1492 Double Briquet

VS 2.91 g

Frey 387, GH 97-1, DW 586, Van der Chijs 36.6

PHS*ARCHDVCIS*AVSTRIE*BVRGVNDIE*BRAB
Two seated facing lions with briquet in center with mintmark below

SALVVM*FAC*POPVLVM*TVVM*DOMINE*1ꝝ92
Shield of Austria-Burgundy on flowery short cross with mintmark in center

II-130b Brabant Duchy
Mint: Antwerp
Philip the Fair (Majority), 1492-1506
1492 Double Briquet

R3 2.91 g

Frey —, GH 97-1, DW 587

PHS*ARCHDVX*AVSTRIE*BVRGVNDIE*BRA'1ꝝ92
Two seated facing lions with briquet in center with mintmark below

SALVVM*FAC*POPVLVM*TVVM*DOMINE*1ꝝ92
Shield of Austria-Burgundy on flowery short cross with mintmark in center

This coin has a highly unusual die variety with date found on both obverse and reverse.

II-131 Brabant Duchy
Mint: Antwerp
Philip the Fair (Majority), 1492-1506
1492 Briquet

VS 2.88 g

Frey 387A, GH 98-1, DW 588, Van der Chijs 21.30, Stephanik 4725

PHS+ARCHIDVX+AVSTRIE+BVRGVNDIE+BRABANC
Seated lion holding shield of Austria-Burgundy

BENEDIC+HEREDITATI+TVE+ANNO+DNI+1ꝝ92
Triple-stranded flowery short cross with mintmark in center

II-132 Flanders County
Mint: Ecluse
Philip the Fair (Majority), 1492-1506
1492 Double Patard

R5 2.85 g

Frey 387B, GH 156, D.d.P 4, 60, De Mey Fl. 654-55

PHS*DEI*GR'*ARCHID'*AVST*ET*CO'*FLA - S-L-V-S
Shield of Austria-Burgundy on flowery short cross with S-L-V-S around shield

AB*INIMICIS*MEIS*LIBE'*ME*DE*1ꝝ92
Lion seated next to castle of Ecluse

The two coins from the mint of Ecluse have extremely artistic designs. Sadly, both are of the greatest rarity with no recent auction history..

II-133 **Flanders** **County**
Mint: **Ecluse**
Philip the Fair (Majority), 1492-1506
1492 **Patard**
R5 *2.85 g*
Frey —, GH 157, D.d.P 4, 61, De Mey Fl. 656-67

PHS:D':G:-:AVST:ET:CO':FLA- S-L-V-S
Shield of Austria-Burgundy on short cross with "S-L-V-S" surrounding shield

AB:INIMICIS:MEIS;LIBEA:ME:DEVS:1ꝝ92
Castle of Ecluse

1494

II-134 **Liège, Family of Hornes** **Bishopric**
Mint: **Hasselt**
John of Hornes, 1484-1505
1494 **Brulé**
R2 *1.40 g*
Frey 418, CH. 423, Dengis 802 De Mey M.C.L.63

IOHS':EPS':L-E-OD'*DVX*B'*C*L'
Shield of Hornes over smaller shields of Bouillon and Looz

MON'-FCA-HAS-1ꝝ9ꝝ
Ornate long cross with alternating lions and crosses in angles

One of the tiny handful of early dated copper coins, this piece may be the only Southern Netherlands copper coin intended to be struck without any silver and therefore not a billon piece with trace silver. In fact its name "brulé" means burnt or fiery, representing its bright copper finish.

II-135a **Liège, Family of Hornes** **Bishopric**
Mint: **Liège**
John of Hornes, 1484-1505
1494 **Patard**
R *1.14-1.78 g*
Frey —, CH. 417, Dengis 797-98

IOHS:EPS:LEOD:DVX:BVL:CO:LO
Shield of Hornes

SI:DEV:NOBC:QS:CON:NOS:9ꝝ
Double-stranded long cross with alternating lions and horns in angles of cross

II-135b **Liège, Family of Hornes** **Bishopric**
Mint: **Liège**
John of Hornes, 1484-1505
1494 **Patard**
R2 *1.29 g (est.)*
Frey —, CH. 417 var., Dengis 797

Same as preceding, but struck in yellow copper with a badly degraded die

Chestret notes that because of the civil wars in Liège, this nominally silver coin was also struck in yellow copper or in very debased billon.

II-A135 **Liège, Family of Hornes** **Bishopric**
Mint: **Liège**
John of Hornes, 1484-1505
1494 **Brulé**
R5 *1.40 g*
Frey —, Dengis 803, RBN 1896, p. 404, Pl. XI

IOHS • EPS • L-EOD • DVX • BVL • CO • LOS
Shield of Hornes

SIDEV'—NOB'C—QSCON—NOS9ꝝ
Double-stranded long cross with alternating lions and horns in angles of cross

1496

II-136 **Brabant** **Duchy**
Mint: **Antwerp**
Philip the Fair (Majority), 1492-1506
1496 **Toison D'Argent**
VS *3.40 g*
Frey 445, GH 110-1, DW 605, Van der Chijs 22.8, Stephanik 4740-41

PH'S*DEI*GRA'*ARCHID'*AVSTE*DVX*BG'*B
Crowned shield of Austria-Burgundy interrupting legend over flowery short cross

INICIVM*SAPIENSIE*TIMVR*DOMINI*ANNO*1ꝝ96
Golden fleece under two large briquets

II-137 **Brabant** **Duchy**
Mint: **Antwerp**
Philip the Fair (Majority), 1492-1506
1496 **Double Briquet**
S *3.10 g*
Frey 446, GH 111-1a, DW 608, Van der Chijs 22.10, Stephanik 4748

PH'S'+DEI+GRA'+ARCHID'+AVSTE'+DVX+BG'+B'
Crowned shield of Austria-Burgundy interrupting legend, all inside polyfoil

OMNIS+SPIRITVS+LAVDET+DOMINI+ANNO+1ꝝ96
Triple-stranded flowery short cross with mintmark in center

1497

II-138 Brabant Duchy
Mint: Antwerp
Philip the Fair (Majority), 1492-1506
1497 Toison D'Argent
R 3.40 g
Frey 462, GH 110-1, DW 605, Stephanik 4742

PH'S*DEI*GRA'*ARCHID'*AVSTE*DVX*BG'*B
Crowned shield of Austria-Burgundy interrupting legend over flowery short cross

INICIVM*SAPIENSIE*TIMVR*DOMINI*ANNO*1ꝝ9Λ
Golden fleece under two large briquets

II-139 Brabant Duchy
Mint: Antwerp
Philip the Fair (Majority), 1492-1506
1497 Double Patard
R 3.10 g
Frey —, GH 111-1a, b

PH'S'+DEI+GRA'+ARCHID'+AVSTE'+DVX+B+B+
Crowned shield of Austria-Burgundy interrupting legend, all inside polyfoil

OMNIS+SPIRITVS+LAVDET+DOMINI+ANNO+1ꝝ9Λ
Triple-stranded flowery short cross with mintmark in center

II-140a Namur County
Mint: Namur
Philip the Fair (Majority), 1492-1506
1497 Double Mite
R2 0.70 g
Frey 463, GH 129-7, Chalon 217

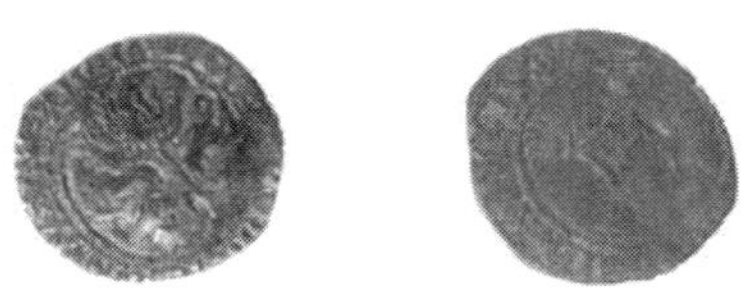

PHS+ARCHID+AVST+DVX+BG+CO+N
Standing lion facing left

IN+DOMINO+CONFIDO+AO+1ꝝ97
Short cross with briquet in center

II-140b Namur County
Mint: Namur
Philip the Fair (Majority), 1492-1506
1497 Double Mite
R5 0.70 g
Frey —, Chalon 218

IN+DOMINO+CONFIDO+ANNO+1ꝝ97
Standing lion facing left

PHS+ARCHID+AVST+DVX+BG+CO+N
Short cross with briquet in center
An excessively rare variety with the obverse and reverse legends reversed.

1498

II-141 Brabant Duchy
Mint: Antwerp
Philip the Fair (Majority), 1492-1506
1498 Toison D'Argent
VS 3.40 g
Frey 479, GH 110-1, DW 605, Stephanik 4743

PH'A*DEI*GRA'*ARCHID'*AVSTE*DVX*BG"*B
Crowned shield of Austria-Burgundy interrupting legend over flowery short cross

INICIVN*SAPIENSIE*TIMVR*DOMINI*ANNO*1ꝝ98
Golden fleece under two large briquets

Stephanik reports that a coin exists with the error date "1448" but no photo or other confirmation is available.

II-142 Brabant Duchy
Mint: Antwerp
Philip the Fair (Majority), 1492-1506
1498 Double Patard
C 3.10 g
Frey —, GH 111-1b, Stephanik 4749-50

PHS*DEI*GRA*ARCHID*AVST*DVX*B*B
Crowned shield of Austria-Burgundy interrupting legend, all inside polyfoil

OMNIS*SPIRITVS*LAVDET*DOMINVM*AN*1ꝝ98
Triple-stranded flowery short cross with mintmark in center

1499

II-143 Brabant Duchy
Mint: Antwerp
Philip the Fair (Majority), 1492-1506
1499 Toison d'or

R4 4.49 g

Frey 494, GH 114-1, DW 596, Van der Chijs 35.1, FR. 45, De Mey d'Or 425, Delmonte 83

PHS:DEI:GRA:ARCHD-AVSTE:DVX:BG:B'
Shield of Austria-Burgundy carried by two lions, golden fleece below

DILICITE:IVSTICIA:QVI:INDICATIS:TRA:1Ꝝ99
Large triple-stranded cross in stylized quatrefoil

II-144 Brabant Duchy
Mint: Antwerp
Philip the Fair (Majority), 1492-1506
1499 Florin d'or

VS-R 3.30 g

Frey 493, GH 115-1a, DW 597, Van der Chijs 21.4, FR. 46, De Mey d'Or 427, Delmonte 85, Stephanik 4737-38

PHS:DEI:GRA:ARCHID:AVSTRIE:DVX:BVRG:BR
Triple-stranded flowery short cross with lion in center

SANCTE:PHE:INTER:CEDE:PRO:NOBIS 1Ꝝ99
St. Philip behind shield holding cross and book

II-145 Brabant Duchy
Mint: Antwerp
Philip the Fair (Majority), 1492-1506
1499 Toison D'Argent

VS 3.40 g

Frey 495, GH 110-1, DW 605

PH'S*DEI*GRA*ARCHID*AVSTE*DVX*BG'*B
Crowned shield of Austria-Burgundy interrupting legend over flowery short cross

INICIVM*SAPIENSIE*TIMVR*DOMINI*ANNO*1Ꝝ99
Golden fleece under two large briquets

II-146a Brabant Duchy
Mint: Antwerp
Philip the Fair (Majority), 1492-1506
1499 Double Patard

C 3.10 g

Frey –, GH 111-1, Stephanik 4751

PHS+DEI+GRA+ARCHID+AVST+DVX+B+B
Crowned shield of Austria-Burgundy interrupting legend, all inside polyfoil

OMNIS*SPIRITVS*LAVDET*DOMINVM*AN*1Ꝝ99
Triple-stranded flowery short cross with mintmark in center

II-146b Brabant Duchy
Mint: Antwerp
1499 Double Patard

C 3.10 g

Frey –, GH 119-1, DW 609

PHS*DEI*GRA*ARCHID*AVST*DVX*BG*B
Crowned shield of Austria-Burgundy entirely within field

OMNIS*SPIRITVS*LAVDET*DOMINVM*A*1Ꝝ99
Triple-stranded flowery short cross with mintmark in center

II-147 Namur County
Mint: Namur
Philip the Fair (Majority), 1492-1506
1499 Florin d'or

R 3.30 g

Frey –, GH 115-7, Chalon 207, FR. 351, De Mey d'Or 1593, Delmonte 423

PHS:DEI:GRA:ARCHIDV:AVST:DVX:BVR:CO:NA
Triple-stranded flowery short cross with crowns and briquets in angles

SºPHILIPE:IN:TERC:PRO:NOBIS:1Ꝝ99
St. Philip holding sceptre above five-part crowned shield

II-148 Namur County
Mint: Namur
Philip the Fair (Majority), 1492-1506
1499 Double Patard
S 3.10 g
Frey —, GH 119-7, Chalon 211

PHS':DEI"GRA':ARCHIDV"AVS"DVX"BVR:CO':N'
Crowned shield of Austria-Burgundy entirely within field

OMNIS:SPVS:LAVDET:DOMINVM:1ጸ99:NA'
Triple-stranded flowery cross with mintmark in center

II-149 Namur County
Mint: Namur
Philip the Fair (Majority), 1492-1506
1499 Patard
S 3.06 g
Frey 506, GH 120-7, Chalon 16

PHS:DEI:GRA:ARCHIDV:AVS:DVX:BVR':CO':NA
Crowned shield of Austria-Burgundy entirely within field, but with no polyfoil

SIT:NOM-EN:DNI':-BENEDIC-TV':1ጸ99
Ornamented long cross in quatrefoil with mintmark in center

II-150 Namur County
Mint: Namur
Philip the Fair (Majority), 1492-1506
1499 Double Mite
R3 0.70-1.07 g
Frey —, GH 129-7, Chalon 219

PHS+ARCHID+AVST+DVX+BG+CO+N
Lion advancing left

IN+DOMINI+CONFIDO+AO+1ጸ99
Short thick cross with briquet in center

II-A150a Tournai City
Mint: Tournai
1499 Patard
R5? 2.50 g
Unpublished?

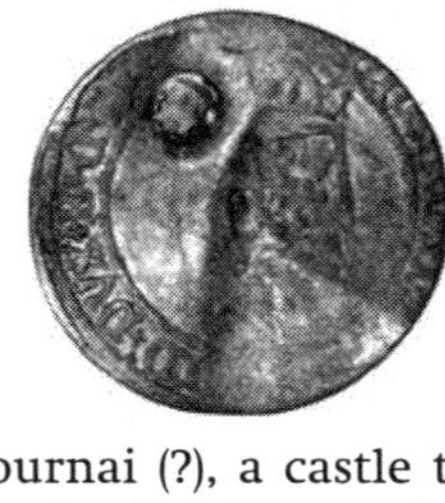

Countermark of Tournai (?), a castle tower, on a host 1499 Holland patard. See Region III-271a below, Van Gelder-Hoc 120-6A.

II-A150b Tournai City
Mint: Tournai
1499 Patard
R5? 2.20 g
Unpublished?

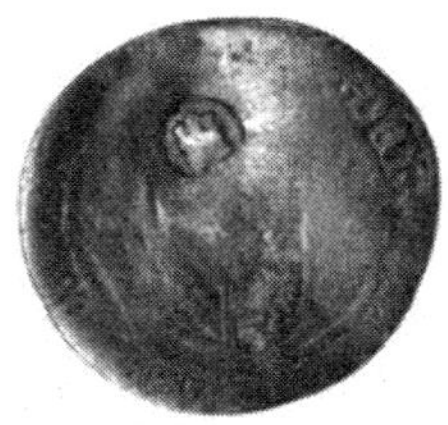

Countermark of Tournai (?), a castle tower, on a host 1499 Holland patard. See Region III-271b below, Van Gelder-Hoc 172-6.

II-B150 Tournai City
Mint: Tournai
1499 Patard
R5 2.30 g
Unpublished?

Countermark of Tournai (?), a castle tower, on a host 1499 Namur patard. See II-149 above, Van Gelder-Hoc 120-7.

1500

II-151 Brabant Duchy
Mint: Antwerp
Philip the Fair (Majority), 1492-1506
1500 Toison d'or
R5 4.49 g
Frey —, GH 114-1, DW 596, FR. 45, De Mey d'Or 425

PHS:DEI:GRA:ARCHD-AVSTE:DVX:B:Z
Shield of Austria-Burgundy carried by two lions, golden fleece below

DILICITE:IVSTICIA:QVI:INDICATIS:TRA:1500
Large triple-stranded cross in stylized quatrefoil

II-152 Brabant Duchy
Mint: Antwerp
Philip the Fair (Majority), 1492-1506
1500 Toison D'Argent
VS *3.40 g*
Frey –, GH 117-1, DW 605, Van der Chijs 22.8

PH'S*DEI*GRA'*ARCHID'*AVSTE*DVX*BG'*B
Crowned shield of Austria-Burgundy entirely within field over flowery cross

INICIVM*SAPIENSIE*TIMVR*DOMINI*ANNO*1500
Golden fleece under two large briquets

II-153a Brabant Duchy
Mint: Antwerp
Philip the Fair (Majority), 1492-1506
1500 Double Patard
VS *3.10 g*
Frey –, GH 111-1b

PHS*DEI*GRA*ARCHID*AVST*DVX*B*B
Crowned shield of Austria-Burgundy interrupting legend, all inside polyfoil

OMNIS*SPIRITVS*LAVDET*DOMINVM*ANNO*1500
Triple-stranded flowery short cross with mintmark in center

II-153b Brabant Duchy
Mint: Antwerp
Philip the Fair (Majority), 1492-1506
1500 Double Patard
C *3.10 g*
Frey –, GH 119-1, DW 609, Stephanik 4752-54

PHS*DEI*GRA*ARCHID*AVSTE*DVX*BVRG*BRA
Crowned shield of Austria-Burgundy entirely within field

OMNIS*SPIRITVS*LAVDET*DOMINI*ANNO*1500
Triple-stranded flowery short cross with mintmark in center

II-154 Brabant Duchy
Mint: Maastricht
Philip the Fair (Majority), 1492-1506
1500 Florin d'or
R4 *3.30 g*
Frey –, GH 115-2a, Van der Chijs 21.6, FR. 49, De Mey d'Or 430, Delmonte 88

PHS:DEI:GRA:ARCHID-AVST:DVX:BG:B
St. Philip behind shield holding cross and book

MO:AV:FACTA:TRAIECTI:IN:VROENHOF:1500
Short flowery cross with two crowns and two fleur-de-lys in angles, mintmark in center of cross

---

II-155 Brabant Duchy
Mint: Maastricht
Philip the Fair (Majority), 1492-1506
1500 Demi Florin d'or
R4 *1.65 g*
Frey –, GH 116-2, DW 604, Van der Chijs 21.7, FR. 50, De Mey d'Or 431, Delmonte 89

PHS:DEI:GRA:ARCHID-AVST:DVX:BG:B
St. Philip behind shield holding cross and book

MO:AV:FACTA:TRAIECTI:IN:VROENHOF:1500
Short flowery cross with two crowns and two fleur-de-lys in angles, mintmark in center of cross

---

II-156 Brabant Duchy
Mint: Maastricht
Philip the Fair (Majority), 1492-1506
1500 Toison D'Argent
R *3.40 g*
Frey –, GH 118-2a, DW 607, Van der Chijs 22.9

PHS'*DEI*GRA*ARCHIC-AVSTE*DVX*BVRG'*B*Z
Crowned shield of Austria-Burgundy surrounded by collar of the order of the golden fleece

MO'FACT*-*TRAIECE*-*IN*VROE'*-*HOF-1500
Flowery long cross with mintmark in center

II-157 Brabant Duchy
Mint: Maastricht
Philip the Fair (Majority), 1492-1506
1500 Double Patard
S *3.10 g*
Frey –, GH 119-2a, DW 610

PHS*DEI*GRA*ARCHID*AVST*DVX*BVRG*B
Crowned shield of Austria-Burgundy entirely within field

MONETA*FACTA*TRIECT*IN*VROEHOF*1500
Triple stranded flowery cross with mintmark in center

II-158 **Brabant** **Duchy**
Mint: **Maastricht**
Philip the Fair (Majority), 1492-1506
1500 **Patard**
VS *3.06 g*
Frey —, GH 120-2a, DW 613, Stephanik 22.12

PHS*DEI*GRA*ARCHID*AVSTE*DVX*BVRG*BRA
Crowned shield of Austria-Burgundy entirely within field but with no polyfoil

MON*FAC-TIECT*-IN*VRO-H*1500
Ornamented long cross in quatrefoil with mintmark in center

II-159 **Tournai** **City**
Mint: **Tournai**
1500 **Patard**
R5 *3.06 g*
Unpublished

Countermark of Tournai (?), a castle tower, on a host 1500 Brabant patard of Maestricht mint. See II-158 above, van Gelder-Hoc 120-2a

REGION III - Northern Netherlands

1424

III-1 **Anholt-Batenburg** **Barony**
Mint: **Anholt**
Gijsbert I of Anholt/II of Bronkhorst, 1408-1432
1424 **Groschen**
R6 *Weight unknown*
Frey N28

GISGBERT:DE:-BATENBO'
Half-length figure of Charlemagne holding imperial orb and cathedral, small shield below

ANNO:DOMINI:MILESIMO:CCCC:XXIIII-MONETA:DE:AENOLT
Short cross with inner and outer legends

This coin copies the Aachen groschens of this period. The two known pieces are found at the Cabinet des Medailles of Brussels and the Koninklijk Kabinet of the Netherlands.

1427

III-2 **Anholt-Batenburg** **Barony**
Mint: **Anholt**
Gijsbert I of Anholt/II of Bronkhorst, 1408-1432
1427 **Groschen**
R6 *1.20 g (fragment missing)*
Frey 25A, RBN 1870, pl. 7, TMP 1895, p. 187

S.KAR:GISEB-ERT:DE:BA
Half-length figure of Charlemagne holding imperial orb and cathedral, small shield below

ANNO:DOMINI:MILESIMO:CCCCXXVII-MONETA:DE:AENHOL'
Short cross with inner and outer legends

Unique specimen located at the Teylers Museum in Haarlem, the Netherlands.

1436

III-3 **Anholt-Batenburg** **Barony**
Mint: **Anholt**
Theodore of Bronckhorst, 1432-1451
1436 **Groschen**
R6 *2.06 g*
Blätter fur Münzefründe, 1913 pp. 5370-71

THEODRICVS: - DE:BRON' - *
Half-length figure of Charlemagne holding imperial orb and cathedral, small shield below

ANNO:DNI':MILESIMOCCCC:XXXVI - MONETA:NOVA:DE:BA
Short cross with inner and outer legends

1437

III-4 **Groningen City**
Mint: Groningen
1437 Jager
R4 *2.16 g*
Frey 37, Puister 251a, Van der Chijs 10.44

MONETA:NOVA:GRONIGENSIS
Double-headed eagle in quatrefoil with upright shield of Groningen below

SIT:NOMEN:DOMINI:BENEDICTVM- ANO:DNI:M:CCCC:XXXVII
Short cross with stars in angles of cross, inner and outer legends

---

III-5 **Groningen City**
Mint: Groningen
1437 Half Jager
R5 *1.00 (est.)*
Frey 37A, Puister 252a

MONETA:NOVA:GRONIGENSIS
Double-headed eagle in quatrefoil with upright shield of Groningen below

SIT:NOMEN:DOMINI:BENEDICTVM- ANO:DNI:M:CCCC:XXXVII
Short cross with stars in angles of cross, inner and outer legends

1438

III-6 **Groningen City**
Mint: Groningen
1438 Jager
R3 *2.16 g*
Frey 52, Puister 251b, Van der Chijs 10.44

MONETA:NOVA:GRONIGENSIS
Double-headed eagle in quatrefoil with upright shield of Groningen below

SIT:NOMEN:DOMINI:BENEDICTVM-ANO:DNI:M:CCCC:
XXXVIII
Short cross with stars in angles of cross, inner and outer legends

1439

III-7 **Groningen City**
Mint: Groningen
1439 Jager
R2 *2.16 g*
Frey 53, Puister 251c, Van der Chijs 10.45, Stephanik 3451-52

MONETA:NOVA:GRONIGENSIS
Double-headed eagle in quatrefoil with upright shield of Groningen below

SIT:NOMEN:DOMINI:BENEDICTVM-ANO:DNI:M:CCCC:XXXIX
Short cross with stars in angles of cross, inner and outer legends

---

III-8 **Groningen City**
Mint: Groningen
1439 Half Jager
R5 *1.00 g*
Frey —, Puister 252b, Van der Chijs 10.46

MONETA:NOVA:GRONIGENSIS
Double-headed eagle in quatrefoil with upright shield of Groningen below

SIT:NOMEN:DOMINI:BENEDICTVM-ANO:DNI:M:CCCC:XXXIX
Short cross with stars in angles of cross, inner and outer legends

1440

III-9 **Groningen City**
Mint: Groningen
1440 Jager
R5 *2.16 g (est.)*
Frey 54, Puister 251d

MONETA:NOVA:GRONIGENSIS
Double-headed eagle in quatrefoil with upright shield of Groningen below

SIT:NOMEN:DOMINI:BENEDICTVM-ANO:DNI:M:CCCC:XXXX
Short cross with stars in angles of cross, inner and outer legends

1445

III-10 Baar-Mörs County
Mint: Baar or Cologne
Walram of Mörs
(Contestant to Bishopric) 1415-1456
1445 Goldgulden
R4 *3.47 g (est.)*
Frey 70, FR. 1, De Mey d'Or 266, Delmonte 680, Stephanik 4481

MONETA*NOVA*AVREA*BAER
Shields of Utrecht-Baar, Utrecht-Lathem and Utrecht-Mörs in trefoil arrangement

ANNO-DOMI-CCC-CXLV
Shield of Utrecht-Mörs on long cross

The Netherlands' first dated gold coin.

1454

III-11 Groningen City
Mint: Groningen
1454 Stuiver
R3 *1.30 g*
Frey 84, Puister 259a, Van der Chijs 10.47, Stephanik 3453-54

MONETA:NOVA-GRONIGENSIS
Double-headed eagle with shield of Groningen placed diagonally below

ANNO.-DOMIN-MCCCC-LIIII
Long cross with "G" in center

III-12 Groningen City
Mint: Groningen
1454 Half Stuiver
R4 *1.60 g*
Frey 84A, Puister 1.265, Van der Chijs 10.48, 19.2, Stephanik 3455

MONETA:GR-ONIGENSIS
Double-headed eagle with shield of Groningen placed diagonally below

ANN-O:M:C-CCC:L-IIII
Long cross with small point in center

1455

III-13 Bolsward City
Mint: Bolsward
1455 Stuiver
R5 *2.20 (est.)*
Frey —, Puister-Fr. 2.002a

MONETA:NOVA:DE:BOLSWER'
Double-headed eagle

ANNO-DOMN'-MCCCC-LV:+
Long cross with letter "B" in center

III-14 Bolsward City
Mint: Bolsward
1455 Quarter Stuiver
R5-6 *Weight unknown*
Frey —, Puister-Fr. 2.004

MONETA:DEºBOLSW__
Double-headed eagle inside shield

___-___-MCC-CCLV
Long cross with letter "B" in center

III-15 Bolsward City
Mint: Bolsward
1455 Plak
R5 *0.80 g*
Frey 87, Puister-Fr. 2.005, Van der Chijs 4.1, Stephanik 3105

MONETA:DE:BOLSW-
Double-headed eagle

ANO-:DNI:-MCC-CCLV
Long cross with "B-O-L-S" in angles

Both Van der Chijs and Frey mistake this coin for a quarter stuiver (escalin). A plak equaled 1/6 stuiver.

III-16 Groningen City
Mint: Groningen
1455 Jager
R2 *2.36 g*
Frey 85, Puister 253a, Van der Chijs 10.49, Stephanik 3456

MONETA:NOVA:GRONIGENSIS
Double-headed eagle in quatrefoil with shield of Groningen placed diagonally below

CTV:SIT-NOMEN-DOMINI-BENEDI - A'NO:DNI':M:CC:CCLV
Long cross with inner and outer legends, stars in angles of cross

In contrast to virtually all dated coins struck in this decade, Groningen jagers of this date are found in surprisingly high condition and several have recent auction records.

III-17 Groningen City
Mint: Groningen
1455 Stuiver
R3 *2.60 g*
Frey —, Puister 259b, 260b, Van der Chijs 10.50-51, Stephanik 3457

MONETA:NOVA:GRONIGENSIS
Double-headed eagle with shield of Groningen placed diagonally below

ANNO-DOMI:-NI:M:C-CCC:LV
Long cross with either star or letter "G" in center

III-18 Groningen City
Mint: Groningen
1455 Half Stuiver
R4 *1.40 g*
Frey —, Puister 1.266a, Van der Chijs 10.52

MONETA:NOV-A:GRONIGENIS
Double-headed eagle with shield of Groningen placed diagonally below

ANNO-DOMI-NIMC-CCC:LV
Long cross with star in center

1456

III-19 Bolsward City
Mint: Bolsward
1456 Stuiver
R5 *2.20 (est.)*
Frey 88, Puister-Fr. 2.002b, Van der Chijs 4.2

MONETA:NOVA:DE:BOLSWER'
Double-headed eagle

ANNO-DOMN-:M:CCCC-:LVI+
Long cross with letter "B" in center

III-20 Bolsward City
Mint: Bolsward
1456 Half Stuiver
R4-5 *1.80 g*
Frey 89, Puister-Fr. 2.003, Van der Chijs 4.3, Stephanik 3106

MONETA:DE:BOLSWERDIA
Double-headed eagle

ANNO-:DOMI-N:MCC-CC:LVI
Long cross with "B-O-L-S" in angles, letter "B" in center of cross

---

III-21 Groningen City
Mint: Groningen
1456 Jager
R3 *2.10 g*
Frey 90, Puister 1.253b, Van der Chijs 10.53

MONETA:NOVA:GRONIGENSIS
Double-headed eagle in quatrefoil with shield of Groningen placed diagonally below

CTV:SIT-NOMEN-DOMINI-BENEDI - ANO-DNI-M:CC-CCLVI
Long cross with inner and outer legends, stars in angles of cross

1457

III-22 Bolsward City
Mint: Bolsward
1457 Jager

R4 1.70 g
Frey 93, Puister-Fr. 2.001, Van der Chijs 4.4

MONETA:NOVA:BOLSWERDIA
Double-headed eagle

SIT:NOMEN:DOMINE:BENEDIC':-ANNO:DO':MCCCCLVII
Short cross with inner and outer legends

III-23 Bolsward City
Mint: Bolsward
1457 Stuiver

R5 2.20 (est.)
Frey —, Puister-Fr. 2.002c

MONETA:NOVA:DE:BOLSWER'
Double-headed eagle

ANNO-DOMN'-MCCCC-LVII
Long cross with letter "B" in center

III-24 Groningen City
Mint: Groningen
1457 Half Stuiver

R5 1.40 g
Frey 92, Puister 1.266b, Stephanik 3458

MONETA:NOV-A:GRONIGENIS
Double-headed eagle with shield of Groningen placed diagonally below

ANNO-DOMI-NI:MC-CCCLVII
Long cross with star in center

1458

III-25 Deventer City
Mint: Deventer
David of Burgundy, 1455-1496
1458 Plak

R5 0.60 g
Frey —, JFD 12

MONETA*DE*DAVEN-
Eagle

ANNO*DNI*M:CCCC:LVIII
Long cross

III-26 Deventer City
Mint: Deventer
David of Burgundy, 1455-1496
1458 Half Plak

R5 Weight unknown
Frey —, JFD 66

MONETA:NOVA:DAVETRIE
Eagle

ANNON*DNI*MCCCCLVIII
Short cross

III-27 Groningen City
Mint: Groningen
1458 Jager

R4-5 2.20 g (fragment missing)
Frey 97B, Puister 254a

MONETA:NOVA:GRONIGENSIS
Double-headed eagle in quatrefoil with shield of Groningen placed diagonally below

CTV:SIT-NOMEN-DOMINI-BENEDI - A'NO-DNI'M-CCCC-LVIII
Long cross with inner and outer legends, stars in angles of cross

---

III-28 Groningen City
Mint: Groningen
1458 Half Stuiver

R5 1.40 g
Frey 97A, Puister 266c

MONETA:NOV-A:GRONIGENIS
Double-headed eagle with shield of Groningen placed diagonally below

ANNO-DOMI-NI:M-CCCC-LVIII
Short cross with star in center

1459

III-29 Groningen City
Mint: Groningen
1459 Jager

R4 2.60 g (est.)
Frey 99, Puister 1.253c, 254b, Van der Chijs 19.22

MONETA:NOVA:GRONIGENSIS
Double-headed eagle in quatrefoil with shield of Groningen placed diagonally below

CTV:SIT-NOMEN-DOMINI-BENEDI - ANO-DNI:M-CCCC-LIX
Long cross with inner and outer legends

III-30 **Groningen City**
Mint: Groningen
1459 Half Stuiver
R5 *1.40 g*
Frey 99A, Puister 266d

MONETA:NOV-A:GRONIGENS
Double-headed eagle with shield of Groningen placed diagonally below

ANNO'-DNI:M-CCCC-LIX
Long cross with star in center

1460

III-31 **Groningen City**
Mint: Groningen
1460 Jager
R4 *2.60 g*
Frey 100, Puister 1.254b, Van der Chijs 10.54, Stephanik 3459

MONETA:NOVA:GRONIGENSIS
Double-headed eagle in quatrefoil with shield of Groningen placed diagonally below

CTV:SIT-NOMEN-DOMINI-BENEDI - ANO-DNI-M:CCC-CLX
Long cross with inner and outer legends, three stars and one clover in angles of cross

---

III-32 **Nijmegen City**
Mint: Nijmegen
1460 One-Eighth Stuiver
R6 *0.30 g*
Frey –, De Beeldenaar 15 (1991-1992) p.337

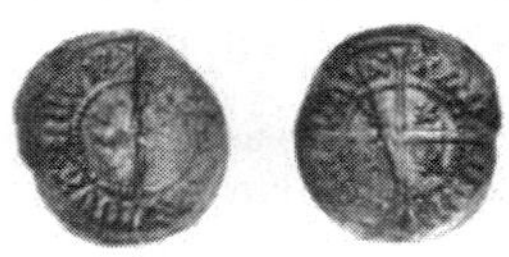

MONETA:NOVA:NOVIMA
Standing lion facing left

ANO-DNI-MCC-CCIX
Long cross

This recently discovered piece, whose Roman Numeral date reads "MCC-CCIX", is all likelihood an engraving error for "MCCCCLX". Nijmegen appointed its first mintmaster in 1457, and its first dated coin of 1462 is similar in style. This unique coin, sold by L. Schulman in May 1990, is now in the Het Valkhof Museum in Nijmegen.

1461

III-33 **Groningen City**
Mint: Groningen
1461 Jager
R4 *2.50 g*
Frey 102, Puister 1.254d, Van der Chijs 10.55, Stephanik 3460-61

MONETA:NOVA:GRONIGENSIS
Double-headed eagle in quatrefoil with shield of Groningen placed diagonally below

CVTSIT:NOMEN:DOMINI:BENEDI-ANO-DNI-M:CCC-CLXI
Long cross with inner and outer legends, three stars and one clover in angles of cross

1462

III-A34 **Deventer City**
Mint: Deventer
1462 Quarter Stuiver
R6 *.60 gr.*
Unpublished?

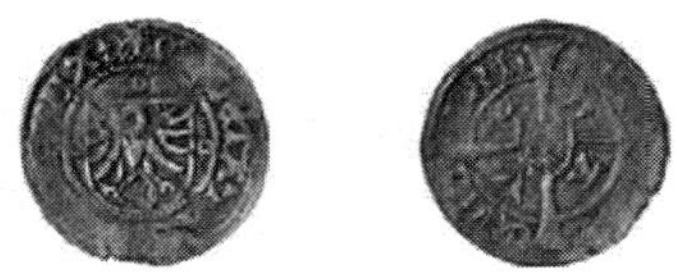

MONETA:D____NTRIA
Eagle shield with annulets at sides and top

ANO-___-____-CCCC-LXII
Long cross with shield in center, D-A-V-E in angles of cross

III-34 **Groningen City**
Mint: Groningen
1462 Jager
R2 *2.50 g*
Frey 103, Puister 1.254e, Van der Chijs 11.56, Stephanik 3462

MONETA:NOVA:GRONIGENSIS
Double-headed eagle in quatrefoil with shield of Groningen placed diagonally below

CTV:SIT-NOMEN-DOMINI-BENEDI - ANO-DNI':M-CCCC-LXII
Long cross with inner and outer legends, three stars and one clover in angles of cross

An overdate of 1462/1 is known.

III-35 **Nijmegen City**
Mint: Nijmegen
1462 One-Eighth Stuiver
R5 *Weight unknown*
Frey –, Nijmegen Museum 1

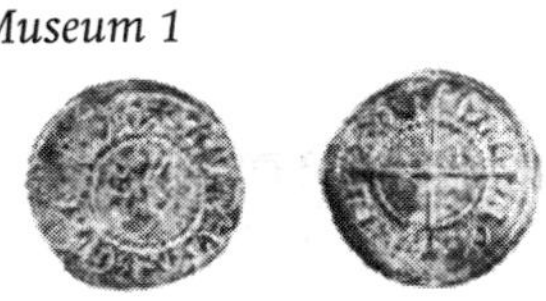

MONETA:NOVA:NOVIMA
Standing lion facing left

ANO-DNI-MCC-LXII
Long cross

Also known as a quarter groschen. The date on this and on the 1463 one eighth stuiver is engraved wrong.

1463

III-36 Groningen City
Mint: Groningen
1463 Jager
R3 *2.50 g*
Frey 104, Puister 1.253f, Van der Chijs 11.58, Stephanik 3463-64

MONETA:NOVA:GRONIGENSIS
Double-headed eagle in quatrefoil with shield of Groningen placed diagonally below

CTV:SIT-NOMEN-DOMINI-BENEDI - ANO-DNI:M-CCCC-LXIII
Long cross with inner and outer legends, four stars or three stars and one clover in angles of cross

---

III-37 Nijmegen City
Mint: Nijmegen
1463 One-Eighth Stuiver
R5 *Weight unknown*
Frey 105, Van der Chijs 1.7

MONETA:NOVA:NOVIMA
Standing lion facing left

ANO-DNI-MCC-LXIII (sic)
Long cross

1465

III-38 Groningen City
Mint: Groningen
1465 Jager
R2 *2.10-2.50 g*
Frey 110, Puister 1.253e, Van der Chijs 11.59

MONETA:NOVA:GRONIGENSIS
Double-headed eagle in quatrefoil with shield of Groningen placed diagonally below

CTV:SIT-NOMEN-DOMINI-BENEDI - A'-DNI'-M:CC-CC:L-XV
Long cross with inner and outer legends, stars in angles of cross

III-39 Groningen City
Mint: Groningen
1465 Half Stuiver
R4 *1.30 g*
Frey —, Puister 1.266e, Van der Chijs 11.60

MONETA:NOV'-GRONIGENIS
Double-headed eagle with shield of Groningen placed diagonally below

ANNO-DOMI-NI:M:C-CCC:LXV
Short cross with star in center

1466

III-40 Deventer City
Mint: Deventer
David of Burgundy, 1455-1496
1466 Jager
R3 *2.50 g*
Frey 112, 117A, JFD 16a,b, Van der Chijs 17.11-12, De Mey Ut. 295, Stephanik 1841

MONETA:NOVA-DE:DAVENTRIE
Eagle above shields of Deventer and the Oversticht

GLORIA-IN:EX-CELSIS-DEO:ET- ANNO-DNI:M-CCCC-LXVI
Long cross with shield in center, inner and outer legends

The Oversticht was land belonging to the bishopric of Utrecht under whose authority Deventer coins were issued, located across the river Ijssel.

III-41 Deventer City
Mint: Deventer
David of Burgundy, 1455-1496
1466 Gros
VS *1.60 g*
Frey 113, JFD 17, Van der Chijs 17.13

MONETA*NOVA-DAVETRIE
Eagle above shields of Deventer and the Oversticht

ANNO-MILLE-SIO*CC-CCLXVI
Shield of Burgundy on long cross

III-42 Deventer City
Mint: Deventer
David of Burgundy, 1455-1496
1466 Plak
R 0.90 g
Frey 114, JFD 13

MONE*NOVA-DE*DAVENT
Eagle above shield of the Oversticht

ANNO-DNI:M-CCCC-LXVI
Long cross

III-43 Deventer City
Mint: Deventer
David of Burgundy, 1455-1496
1466 Half Plak
R3 0.50 g
Frey 115, JFD 14

MONE*NOVA-DE*DAVENT
Eagle above shield of the Oversticht

ANNO:DNI:M:CCCC:LXVI
Short cross

III-44 Deventer City
Mint: Deventer
David of Burgundy, 1455-1496
1466 Quarter Plak
R4-5 0.20 g
Frey —, JFD 15

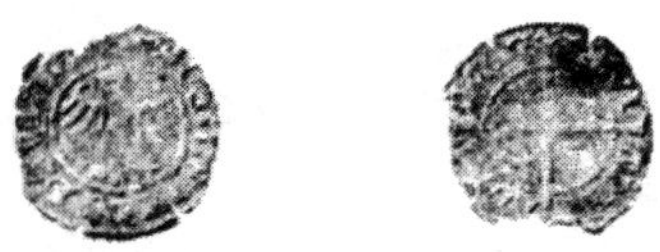

MONE*NOVA-DE*DAVENT
Eagle above shield of the Oversticht

ANN-DNI:M-CCCC-LXVI
Long cross

1467

III-45 Groningen City
Mint: Groningen
1467 Stuiver
R4 2.90 g
Frey 122, Puister 1.260b, Van der Chijs p. 470, Stephanik 3465

MONETA:NOVA-GRONIGENSIS
Double-headed eagle with shield of Groningen placed diagonally below

ANNO-DOMIN-M:CCC-C-LXVII
Long cross with star in center

III-46 Groningen City
Mint: Groningen
1467 Half Stuiver
R4 1.30 g (est.)
Frey 124A, Puister 266f, Stephanik 3466

MONETA:NOV'-GRONIGENIS
Double-headed eagle with shield of Groningen placed diagonally below

ANNO-DOMI-NI:M:C-CCC:LXVII
Long cross with star in center

1468

III-47 Deventer City
Mint: Deventer
David of Burgundy, 1455-1496
1468 Stuiver
R 2.30 g
Frey 130, 130A, JFD 18, De Mey Ut. 296, Van der Chijs 17.14, Stephanik 1842

MONETA*NOVA-DE*DAVENTRIA
Eagle shield of Deventer over small leaning shield of the Oversticht

ANNO-DOMIN-M:CCCC-LXVIII
Shield of Burgundy on long cross

1469

III-48 Deventer City
Mint: Deventer
David of Burgundy, 1455-1496
1469 Stuiver
R2 2.10 g
Frey 131, 131A, 133B, JFD 19, De Mey Ut. 296, Van der Chijs 17.15, Stephanik 1843

MONETA*NOVA-DE*DAVENTRIA
Eagle shield of Deventer over small leaning shield of the Oversticht

ANNO-DOMIN-M:CCCC-LXVIIII
Shield of Burgundy on long cross

The Cervin supplement of Frey listed this same coin under three different numbers!

III-49 Groningen City
Mint: Groningen
1469 Stuiver
R3 2.80 g
Frey 133A, Puister 1.260-61, Van der Chijs 19.23

MONETA:NOVA-GRONIGENSIS
Double-headed eagle with shield of Groningen placed diagonally below

ANNO-DOMIN-M:CCCC-LXIX
Long cross with star or clover in center

1470

III-50 Deventer City
Mint: Deventer
David of Burgundy, 1455-1496
1470 Stuiver
R 2.10 g
Frey 136, Van der Chijs 29.1, JFD 20, De Mey Ut. 296, Stephanik 1844

MONETA*NOVA-DE*DAVENTRIA
Eagle shield of Deventer over small leaning shield of the Oversticht

ANNO-DOMIN-M:CCC-C:LXX
Shield of Burgundy on long cross

III-51 Deventer City
Mint: Deventer
David of Burgundy, 1455-1496
1470 Gros
R2 1.80 g
Frey 136 A, B, JFD 21, Van der Chijs 17.16, De Mey Ut. 297

MONETA*NOVA-DE*DAVENTRIA
Eagle shield of Deventer over small leaning shield of the Oversticht

ANNO-MILLE-SIO:CC-CC:LXX
Shield of Burgundy on long cross

III-52 Groningen City
Mint: Groningen
1470 Stuiver
R2 2.80 g
Frey 137, Puister 1.260e, Van der Chijs 11.61, Stephanik 3467

MONETA:NOVA-GRONIGENSIS
Double-headed eagle with shield of Groningen placed diagonally below

ANNO-DOMIN-M:CCCC-LXX
Long cross with star in center

1471

III-53 Deventer City
Mint: Deventer
David of Burgundy, 1455-1496
1471 Stuiver
VS 2.20 g
Frey 141, JFD 22, Van der Chijs 17.17, De Mey Ut. 296

MONETA*NOVA-DE*DAVENTRIA
Eagle shield of Deventer over small leaning shield of the Oversticht

ANNO-DOMIN-M:CCC-CLXXI
Shield of Burgundy on long cross

III-54 Deventer City
Mint: Deventer
David of Burgundy, 1455-1496
1471 Gros
R 1.50 g
Frey 141A, B, 142B, JFD 23a-c, Van der Chijs 17.18, De Mey Ut. 297

MONETA*NOVA-DE*DAVENTRIA
Eagle above shields of Deventer and the Oversticht

ANNO-MILO-CCCC-LXXI
Shield of Burgundy on long cross

III-55 Groningen City
Mint: Groningen
1471 Stuiver
R 2.80 g
Frey 138, Puister 1.262, Van der Chijs 11.62, Stephanik 3468

MONETA:NOVA-GRONIGE'SIS
Double-headed eagle with shield of Groningen placed diagonally below

ANNO-DOMIN-M:CCC-CLXXI
Long cross with rose in center

III-56 **Leeuwarden** **City**
Mint: **Leeuwarden**
1471 **Stuiver**
R5-6 *Weight unknown*
Frey —, Puister-Fr. 4.006a

MONETA:NOVA-LEWERDEN'SIS
Double-headed eagle over diagonal lion shield

ANNO-DOMIN-MCCCC-LXXI
Double stranded long cross with rose in center

1472

III-57 **Bolsward** **City**
Mint: **Bolsward**
1472 **Stuiver**
R3 *2.40 g*
Frey 147, Puister-Fr. 2.007a, Van der Chijs 4.5, Stephanik 3107

MONETA:NOVA:BOLSWERDEN
Double-headed eagle

ANNO:-DOMI':-:MCCCC:-LXXII
Long cross with letter "B" in center

III-58 **Deventer** **City**
Mint: **Deventer**
David of Burgundy, 1455-1496
1472 **Stuiver**
VS *2.30 g*
Frey 143, JFD 24, Van der Chijs 17.19, De Mey Ut. 296, Stephanik 1845-46

MONETA*NOVA-DE*DAVENTRIA
Eagle shield of Deventer over small leaning shield of the Oversticht

ANNO-DOMIN-M:CCCC-LXXII
Shield of Burgundy on long cross

III-59 **Deventer** **City**
Mint: **Deventer**
David of Burgundy, 1455-1496
1472 **Gros**
R2 *1.60 g*
Frey 143A, B, JFD 25, Van der Chijs 17.20, De Mey Ut. 297

MONETA*NOVA-DAVENTRIE
Eagle above shields of Deventer and the Oversticht

ANNO-MILO-CCCC-LXXII
Shield of Burgundy on long cross

III-60 **Groningen** **City**
Mint: **Groningen**
1472 **Stuiver**
VS *2.80 g*
Frey 146, Puister 1.259c, Van der Chijs 11.63, 19.24, Stephanik 3469

MONETA:NOVA-GRONIGENSIS
Double-headed eagle with shield of Groningen placed diagonally below

ANNO-DOMIN-M:CCCC-LXXII
Long cross with letter "G" in center

III-61 **Leeuwarden** **City**
Mint: **Leeuwarden**
1472 **Stuiver**
R5 *2.60 g*
Frey 149, 149A, Puister-Fr. 4.006b, Van der Chijs 5.1

MONETA:NOVA:LEWERDEN'SIS
Double-headed eagle over diagonal lion shield

ANNO:-DOMIN:-M:CCCC-:LXXII
Double stranded long cross with rose in center

1473

III-62 **Deventer** **City**
Mint: **Deventer**
David of Burgundy, 1455-1496
1473 **Stuiver**
R *2.30 g*
Frey 152, 152C, JFD 26, Van der Chijs 17.21, De Mey Ut. 96, Stephanik 1847

MONETA*NOVA-DE:DAVENTRIA
Eagle shield of Deventer over small leaning shield of the Oversticht

ANNO-DOMIN-M:CCCC-LXXIII
Shield of Burgundy on long cross

III-63 Deventer City
Mint: Deventer
David of Burgundy, 1455-1496
1473 Gros
R 1.60 g
Frey 152A, B, C, JFD 27a-d, Van der Chijs 18.22

MONETA*NOVA-DAVENTRIA
Eagle above shields of Deventer and the Oversticht

ANNO-MILO-CCCC-LXXIII
Shield of Burgundy on long cross

III-64 Groningen City
Mint: Groningen
1473 Stuiver
R 2.60 g
Frey 151, Puister 1.259d, Van der Chijs 11.64, Stephanik 3470-71

MONETA:NOVA-GRONIGENSIS
Double-headed eagle with shield of Groningen placed diagonally below

ANNO-DOMIN-M:CCCC-LXXIII
Long cross with letter "G" in center

III-65 Leeuwarden City
Mint: Leeuwarden
1473 Stuiver
R5 2.60 g
Frey 150, Puister-Fr. 4.006c, Van der Chijs 5.3

MONETA:NOVA:LEWERDENS
Double-headed eagle over diagonal lion shield

ANO:D-OMIN':M-CCCC:L-XXIII
Double stranded long cross with rose in center

1474

III-66 Bolsward City
Mint: Bolsward
1474 Stuiver
R4 2.10 g
Frey 154, Puister-Fr. 2.007c, Van der Chijs 4.6, Stephanik 3108

MONETA:NOVA:BOLSWERDEN
Double-headed eagle

ANNO-:DOMIN-:MCCCC-LXXIIII
Long cross with letter "B" in center

III-67 Bolsward City
Mint: Bolsward
1474 Half Stuiver
R5 0.97 g
Frey 154A, Puister-Fr. 2.008a, RBN 1865, p. 379

MONETA+NOVA+BOLSWERDE
Double-headed eagle

ANNO-DNI+M-CCCC+L-XXIIII
Long cross with letter "B" in center

III-68 Deventer City
Mint: Deventer
David of Burgundy, 1455-1496
1474 Stuiver
VS 2.30 g
Frey 160D, JFD 28, Van der Chijs 29.5, De Mey Ut. 296

MONETA*NOVA-DE*DAVENTRIA
Eagle shield of Deventer over small leaning shield of the Oversticht

ANNO-DOMIN-M:CCCC-LXXIIII
Shield of Burgundy on long cross

III-69a Gelderland Duchy
Mint: Nijmegen
Charles the Rash, 1467-1477
1474 Double Briquet
R3 3.06 g
Frey 602, GH 34.2a, Van der Chijs 12.6

KAROL:DEI:GRA:DVX:BVR:GELD
Two seated facing lions with briquet in center

SALVV:FAC:PPLM:TVVM:1ꝜΛꝜ
Shield of Burgundy on flowery cross

III-69b Gelderland Duchy
Mint: Nijmegen
Charles the Rash, 1467-1477
1474 Double Briquet
R6? 3.06 g
Unpublished

Same as preceding but with very large lions on the obverse interrupting the inner circle around the legend and a much smaller than normal shield on the reverse.

Sold by L. Schulman in April 2001.

III-70 Gelderland Duchy
Mint: Nijmegen
Charles the Rash, 1467-1477
1474 Briquet
R3 3.06 g
Frey 158, GH 35-2a-b, Van der Chijs 12.11, Roest 235-37

KAROLVS:DEI:GRA:DVX:BVRG:Z:GEL
Seated lion holding shield of Burgundy

BENEDIC:HEREDITATI:TVE:1:Ꝝ:Λ:Ꝝ
Triple stranded flowery short cross

III-71 Gelderland Duchy
Mint: Nijmegen
Charles the Rash, 1467-1477
1474 Half Briquet
R2 0.87 g
Frey 159, GH 36.2, Van der Chijs 12.12, Roest 238-39, Stephanik 3849-51

KAROL:DI:GRA:DVX:BVRG:GEL
Half-length figure of lion advancing left

BENEDIC:AIA:MEA:DNO:1ꝜΛꝜ
Flowery cross

III-72 Groningen City
Mint: Groningen
1474 Stuiver
VS 2.60 g
Frey 156, Puister 1.259e, Van der Chijs 11.65, Stephanik 3472-74

MONETA:NOVA-GRONIGENSIS
Double-headed eagle with shield of Groningen placed diagonally below

ANNO-DOMIN-M:CCCC-LXXIIII
Long cross with letter "G" in center

III-73 Utrecht Bishopric
Mint: Wijk-bij-Duurstede
David of Burgundy, 1455-1496
1474 Jager
R2 2.50 g
Frey 153, Van der Chijs 29.6, De Mey Ut. 315

MONETA:NOVA:TRAIECTENS- ANNO:DNI':M:CCCC:LXXIIII
Burgundy shield with inner and outer surrounding legends

MEM-E'TO-DNE'*D-AVID
Short cross quartering legend, surrounded by 13 fleur-de-lys in small circles

1475

III-74 Bolsward City
Mint: Bolsward
1475 Stuiver
R4 2.00 g
Frey 164, Puister-Fr. 2.007d, Van der Chijs 18.1, Stephanik 3109

MONETA:NOVA:BOLSWERDEN':
Double-headed eagle

ANNO-:DOMIN:-:MCCCC-LXXV
Long cross with letter "B" in center

III-75 **Gelderland Duchy**
Mint: **Nijmegen**
Charles the Rash, 1467-1477
1475 **Double Briquet**
R1-2 *2.00 g*
Frey 161B, GH 34-2b-c, Van der Chijs 12.7-10, Roest 240-47

KAROLVS:DEI:GRA:DVX:BVRG:Z:GELR
Two seated facing lions with briquet in center

SALVVM:FAC:PPLM:TVVM:DNE:1ꝸΛ˥
Shield of Burgundy on flowery cross

III-76 **Gelderland Duchy**
Mint: **Nijmegen**
Charles the Rash, 1467-1477
1475 **Briquet**
R4 *3.06 g*
Frey 161, GH 35-2c

KAROLVS:DEI:GRA:DVX:BVRG:Z:GEL
Seated lion holding shield of Burgundy

BENEDIC:HEREDITATI:TVE:1:ꝸ:Λ:˥
Triple-stranded cross in flowery wreath

III-77 **Gelderland Duchy**
Mint: **Nijmegen**
Charles the Rash, 1467-1477
1475 **Half Briquet**
R2 *0.87 g*
Frey 167B, GH 36-2, Van der Chijs 12.12, Roest 248-50

KAROL:DI:GRA:DVX:BVRG:GEL
Half-length figure of lion advancing left

BENEDIC:AIA:MEA:DNO:1ꝸΛ˥
Flowery cross

III-78 **Groningen City**
Mint: **Groningen**
1475 **Stuiver**
VS *2.80 g*
Frey 163, Puister 1.259f , Van der Chijs 11.66, Stephanik 3475

MONETA:NOVA-GRONIGENSIS
Double-headed eagle with shield of Groningen placed diagonally below

ANNO-DOMIN-M:CCCC-LXXV
Long cross with letter "G" in center

III-79 **Utrecht** **Bishopric**
Mint: **Wijk-bij-Duurstede**
David of Burgundy, 1455-1496
1475 **Jager**
R5 *2.40 g*
Frey —, De Mey Ut. 315

MONETA*NOVA*EPIS*TRAIECTEN' - ANNO*DNI' *M°CCCC*LXXV
Burgundy shield with inner and outer surrounding legends

MEM-E'TO-DNE'*D-AVID
Short cross quartering legend, surrounded by 13 fleur-de-lys in small circles

1476

III-80 **Bolsward** **City**
Mint: **Bolsward**
1476 **Stuiver**
R4 *2.50 g*
Frey 170, Puister-Fr. 2.007e, Van der Chijs 4.7

MONETA:NOVA:BOLSWERDEN'
Double-headed eagle

ANNO-:DOMIN-:MCCCC-LXXVI
Long cross with letter "B" in center

III-81 **Deventer** **City**
Mint: **Deventer**
David of Burgundy, 1455-1496
1476 **Half Plak**
R3 *0.45 g*
Frey 172, JFD 29, Van der Chijs 12.18

MON*NOV-D*DAVEN
Eagle above shield of the Oversticht

ANNO*DNI'M*CCCC*LXXVI
Short cross

Stephanik labels this coin as a piece of 3 mites.

III-82 Gelderland Duchy
Mint: Nijmegen
Charles the Rash, 1467-1477
1476 Half Briquet
R2 0.87 g
Frey 168A, GH 36-2b, Van der Chijs 29.11, Roest 252-53

KAROL:DI:GRA:DVX:BVRG:GEL
Half-length figure of lion advancing left

BENEDIC:AIA:MEA:DNO:1ጸ Λ6
Flowery cross

Roest reported a 1476 double briquet of Charles the Rash, but it has not been confirmed.

III-83 Groningen City
Mint: Groningen
1476 Jager
R4-5 2.70 g (est.)
Frey —, Puister 1.255a, Stephanik 3476

MONETA:NOVA:GRONIGENSIS
Double-headed eagle with two small diagonal shields below

SIT:NO-ME:DO-MINI-BE-NEDICT-ANNO-DNI'M-CCCC-LXXVI
Long cross with inner and outer legends, "G-R-O-N" in center of angles of cross

---

III-84 Groningen City
Mint: Groningen
1476 Stuiver
VS 2.80 g
Frey 171, Puister 1.259g, Van der Chijs 12.67, Stephanik 3477-78

MONETA:NOVA-GRONIGENSIS
Double-headed eagle with shield of Groningen placed diagonally below

ANNO-DOMIN-M:CCCC-LXXVI
Long cross with letter "G" in center

III-85 Sneek City
Mint: Sneek
1476 Stuiver
R5 Weight unknown
Frey —, Puister-Fr. 5.003a

MONETA:NOVA:SNEKENSIS
Sneek shield of half-eagle on left and three verticle crownson right

ANNO-DOMIN-MCCCC-LXXVI
Thick long cross with letter "S" in center

III-86 Utrecht Bishopric
Mint: Wijk-bij-Duurstede
David of Burgundy, 1455-1496
1476 Jager
R 2.60 g
Frey 173, Van der Chijs 18.23, De Mey Ut. 315

MONETA*NOVA*EPIS*TRAIECTEN' -
ANNO*DNI'*M*CCCC*LXXVI
Burgundy shield with inner and outer surrounding legends

MEM-E'TO-DNE'*D-AVID
Short cross quartering legend, surrounded by 13 fleur-de-lis in small circles

1477

III-87 Bolsward City
Mint: Bolsward
1477 Stuiver
R4 Weight unknown
Frey 183, 183, Puister-Fr. 2.007f, Van der Chijs 4.8*

MONETA:NOVA:BOLSWERDEN
Double-headed eagle

ANNO-:DOMIN-:MCCCC-LXXVII
Long cross with letter "B" in center

III-88 Deventer City
Mint: Deventer
David of Burgundy, 1455-1496
1477 Half Plak
R6? 0.40 g
Unpublished

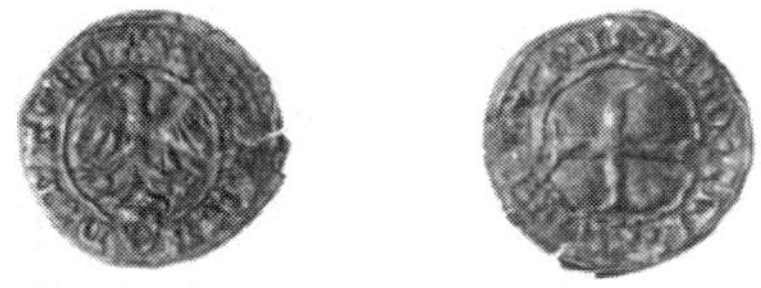

MO:N:NOVA-D:DEVENT
Eagle above shield of the Oversticht

ANNO*DNI'M*CCCC*LXXVII
Short Cross

In author's collection.

III-89 Gelderland Duchy
Mint: Nijmegen
Charles the Rash, 1467-1477
1477 Half Briquet
R5 *0.87 g*
Frey 628, GH 36-2b

KAROL:DI:GRA:DVX:BVRG:GEL
Half-length figure of lion advancing left

BENEDIC:AIA:MEA:DNO:1 ℵ Λ Λ
Flowery cross

III-90 Groningen City
Mint: Groningen
1477 Jager
VS *2.70 g*
Frey 177, Puister 1.255b, Van der Chijs 12.68, 19.26, Stephanik 3479

MONETA:NOVA:GRONIGENSIS
Double-headed eagle with two small diagonal shields below

SIT:NO-ME:DO-MINI-BE-NEDICT-ANNO-DNI'M-CCCC-LXXVII
Long cross with inner and outer legends, "G-R-O-N" or stars in center of angles of cross

---

III-91 Groningen City
Mint: Groningen
1477 Stuiver
R3 *2.80 g (est.)*
Frey —, Puister 1.259h, Van der Chijs 12.69

MONETA:NOVA-GRONIGENSIS
Double-headed eagle with shield of Groningen placed diagonally below

ANNO-DOMIN-M:CCCC-LXXVII
Long cross with letter "G" in center

III-92 Nijmegen City
Mint: Nijmegen
1477 Quarter Stuiver
R4 *0.70 g*
Frey 183A, Nijmegen Museum 7a-c, Van der Chijs 1.8

MONETA:NOVA:NOVAMAGEN
Double-headed eagle shield of Nijmegen with shield on breast of eagle

ANNO-DNI:M-CCCC-LXXVII
Long cross

III-93 Sneek City
Mint: Sneek
1477 Stuiver
R5 *Weight unknown*
Frey 183, Puister-Fr. 5.003b, Van der Chijs 22.1, Stephanik 3114

MONETA:NOVA:SNEKENSIS
Sneek shield of half-eagle and three verticle crowns

ANNO-DOMIN-MCCCC-LXXVII
Thick long cross with letter "S" in center

III-94 Utrecht Bishopric
Mint: Wijk-bij-Duurstede
David of Burgundy, 1455-1496
1477 Jager
VS *2.60 g*
Frey 182, Van der Chijs 18.24, De Mey Ut. 315, Stephanik 1860

MONETA:NOVA:EPIS':TRAIECTENS-
ANNO:DNI':M:CCCC:LXXVII
Burgundy shield with inner and outer surrounding legends

MEM-E'TO-DNE'*D-AVID
Short cross quartering legend, surrounded by 13 fleur-de-lys in small circles

1478

III-95 Bolsward City
Mint: Bolsward
1478 Stuiver
R4-5 *2.40 g*
Frey —, Puister-Fr. 2.007g

MONETA NOVA:BOLSWERDEN
Double-headed eagle

ANNO-DNIºM-CCCCºL-XXVIII
Long cross with letter "B" in center

III-96 Bolsward City
Mint: Bolsward
1478 Half Stuiver
R5 *1.00 g (est.)*
Frey 184, Puister-Fr. 2008b, Van der Chijs 4.9

MONETA:NOVA:BOLSWERDE'
Double-headed eagle

ANNO-DNI:M-CCCCL-XXVIII
Long cross with letter "B" in center

III-97 **Deventer** **City**
Mint: **Deventer**
David of Burgundy, 1455-1496
1478 **Half Plak**
R6? *.40 g (est.)*
Unpublished?

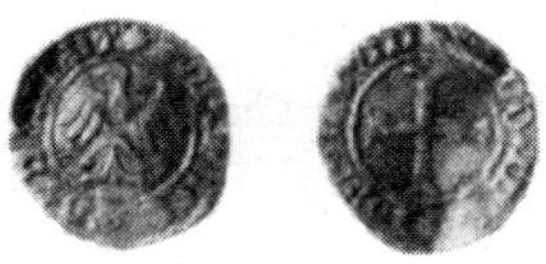

MON*NOVA-DE DEVENT
Eagle above shield of the Oversticht

ANNO*DNI'M*CCCC*LXXVIII
Short cross

Sold by L. Schulman in April 1995.

III-98 **Gelderland, Family of Egmont Duchy**
Mint: **Roermond**
Charles of Egmont (Minority), 1477-1480
1478 **Jager**
R5-6 *Weight unknown*
Frey —, RBN 1872 #102

KAROL:DVX:GELR:IVLI:CO:ZV- ANNO:DNI:MCCCCLXXVIII
Small shield of Gelderland surrounded by inner and outer legends

MEM-ETO-MFI-LIDI
Short cross quartering legend, surrounded by 13 fleur-de-lys in small circles

This excessively rare coin copies the design of the Utrecht jagers of David of Burgundy.

III-99 **Gelderland, Family of Egmont Duchy**
Mint: **Roermond**
Charles of Egmont (Minority), 1477-1480
1478 **Stuiver**
R *2.50 g*
Frey 194, 194A, Van der Chijs 14.2

KAROL:DVX:GEL:IVL:Z:CO:ZV
Quartered arms of Gelderland

ANNO-DNI:M:-:CCCC-LXXVIII
Thick flowery short cross

Egmont family coins are usually found poorly struck and very worn.

III-100 **Holland** **County**
Mint: **Dordrecht**
Marie of Burgundy, 1477-1482
1478 **Double Briquet**
VS *3.06 g*
Frey 635, GH 39-4a, Van der Chijs 14.6-8, 37.22-23

MARIA*DVCISSA*BG*COMIT*HOL
Two seated facing lions with briquet in center

SALVV*FAC*PPLM*TVV*DNE 1ꝸΛ8
Shield of Burgundy on flowery cross

III-101 **Holland** **County**
Mint: **Dordrecht**
Marie of Burgundy, 1477-1482
1478 **Briquet**
R *3.06 g*
Frey 188, GH 40-4a, Van der Chijs 16.09-10

MARIA*DVCISSA*BG*COMIT*HO
Seated lion holding shield of Burgundy

BENEDIC*HEREDITATI*TVE 1ꝸ78
Triple-stranded flowery short cross

III-102 **Holland** **County**
Mint: **Dordrecht**
Marie of Burgundy, 1477-1482
1478 **Gros**
VS *1.87 g*
Frey 639, GH 41-4a, Van der Chijs 16.16

MARIA*DVCISSA*BG*CO*HO
Large ornate letter "M" in quatrefoil

BENEDIC*AIA*MEA*DNO 1ꝸ78
Flowery short cross

III-103 **Sneek** **City**
Mint: **Sneek**
1478 **Stuiver**
R5 *Weight unknown*
Frey —, Puister-Fr. 5.003c

MONETA:NOVA:SNEKENSIS
Sneek shield of half-eagle and three verticle crowns

ANNO-DOMIN-MCCCC-LXXVII
Thick long cross with letter "S" in center

III-104 **Utrecht** **Bishopric**
Mint: **Wijk-bij-Duurstede**
David of Burgundy, 1455-1496
1478 **Jager**
S *3.10 g*
Frey 186, Van der Chijs 18.26, De Mey Ut. 315, Stephanik 1861

MONETA:NOVA:EPIS':TRAIECTENS-ANNO-DNI':M:CCCC:LXXVIII
Burgundy shield with inner and outer surrounding legends

MEM-E'TO-DNE'*D-AVID
Short cross quartering legend, surrounded by 13 fleur-de-lys in small circles

---

III-105 **Utrecht City** **City**
Mint: **Utrecht**
1478 **Muter**
R4-5 *0.68 g*
Frey 187, 187A, Van der Chijs 25.4, De Mey Ut. 372

CIVITAS:TRAIECTENSIS
City shield of Utrecht in octofoil

ANNO-MCCC-C:LXX-VIII
Long cross with four roses in angles of cross

1479

III-106 **Deventer** **City**
Mint: **Deventer**
David of Burgundy, 1455-1496
1479 **Quarter Plak**
R3 *0.25 g*
Frey 199, JFD 30 (sic. Half Plak)

MO'NOVA:DE:DAVENTRI
Eagle above shield of the Oversticht

ANN'DNI'M:CCCC:LXXIX
Short cross

A uniface lead pattern striking of a reverse die exists for this coin. The die used to create this pattern was not used as the official issue was smaller. This is one of several dies probably made at the mint.

III-107a **Deventer, Campen & Groningen**
Tri-City Monetary Alliance
Mint: **Campen**
1479 **Stuiver**
R3 *2.60 g*
Frey 208E, JFD DKZ 2a, Van der Chijs 9 (Campen) and Van der Chijs 12.71 (Groningen)

MONE-TANO-VACA-MPEN
Shield of Campen over long triple-stranded cross

AN'DN-MCCCC-LXXIX
Conjoined shields of Deventer, Campen and Groningen interrupting legend, set in trefoil, letter "C" in center

---

III-107b **Deventer, Campen & Groningen**
Tri-City Monetary Alliance
Mint: **Campen**
1479 **Stuiver**
R5 *2.60 g*
Frey 208E, JFD DKZ 2b

MONE'-NOVA-CAMP
Conjoined shields of Deventer, Campen and Groningen interrupting legend, set in trefoil, letter "C" in center

ANNO-DNI'M-CCCC-LXXIX
Shield of Campen over triple-stranded long cross

It is apparent that this coin represents an engraving error with the obverse and reverse legends switched. A lead pattern strike of the obverse of this coin is known.

III-108 **Deventer, Campen & Groningen**
Tri-City Monetary Alliance
Mint: **Deventer**
1479 **Stuiver**
R4 *2.70 g*
Frey 198, JFD DKZ 1a-b, Van der Chijs 9 (Deventer) and Van der Chijs

12.70 (Groningen)

MONE':NOVA:DE:DAVENTRIA
Conjoined shields of Deventer, Campen and Groningen, within field, arranged in trefoil, letter "D" in center

ANNO-DNI'M-CCCC-LXXIX
Shield of Deventer on long cross

III-109 Deventer, Campen & Groningen
Tri-City Monetary Alliance
Mint: Deventer
1479 Half Stuiver
R4 *Weight unknown*
Frey —, JFD DKZ 3a-b

MONE':NOVA:DE:DAVENTRIA
Conjoined shields of Deventer, Campen and Groningen arranged in trefoil, letter "D" in center

ANNO-DOMIN'-MCCCC-LXXIX
Shield of Deventer on long cross

III-110 Gelderland, Family of Egmont Duchy
Mint: Zutphen
Charles of Egmont (Minority), 1477-1480
1479 Stuiver
R2 *2.40 g*
Frey 208C, Van der Chijs Type 14.2-3, Roest 259-60

KAROL:DVX:GEL:IVL:Z:CO:ZV
Two-part shield of Gelderland

ANNO:-DNI:M-:CCCC:-LXXIX:+
Long cross with lions in angles of cross

III-111 Holland County
Mint: Dordrecht
Marie of Burgundy, 1477-1482
1479 Double Briquet
VS *3.06 g*
Frey 200, GH 39-4b, Van der Chijs 15.1-2

MARIA*DVCISSA*BG*COMIT*HO
Two seated facing lions with briquet in center

SALVV*FAC*PPLM*TVV*DNE 1Ꭓ79
Shield of Burgundy on flowery cross

The "9" on this and the next two coins appears as a flattened "8".

III-112 Holland County
Mint: Dordrecht
Marie of Burgundy, 1477-1482
1479 Briquet
R *3.06 g*
Frey 200A, GH 40-4a-b, Van der Chijs 16.11-12

MARIA*DVCISSA*BG*COMIT*HO
Seated lion holding shield of Burgundy

BENEDIC*HEREDITATI*TVE 1Ꭓ79
Flowery triple-stranded short cross

III-113 Holland County
Mint: Dordrecht
Marie of Burgundy, 1477-1482
1479 Gros
S *1.87 g*
Frey 200B, GH 41-4a, Van der Chijs 16.17

MARIA*DVCISSA*BG*CO*HO
Large ornate letter "M" in quatrefoil

BENEDIC*AIA*MEA*DNO 1Ꭓ79
Flowery short cross

III-114 Nijmegen City
Mint: Nijmegen
1479 Quarter Stuiver
R4 *0.70 g (est.)*
Frey —, Nijmegen Museum 7d-e

MONETA:NOV:NOVAMAGEN
Shield of Nijmegen

ANNO-DNI:M-CCC-LXXIX
Long cross

III-115 Utrecht Bishopric
Mint: Wijk-bij-Duurstede
David of Burgundy, 1455-1496
1479 Jager
R2 *2.60 g*
Frey 201, Van der Chijs 18.28, De Mey Ut. 315, Stephanik 1862

MONETA:NOVA:EPIS:TRAIECTENS-ANNO:DNI':M:CCCC:LXXIX
Burgundy shield with inner and outer surrounding legends

MEM-E'TO-DNE':D-AVID
Short cross quartering legend, surrounded by 13 fleur-de-lys in small circles

---

III-116 Zutphen City
Mint: Zutphen
1479 Albus
R6 *2.50 g*
Frey —, Beek 1

MON'NOVA-ZVTPHANE'
Lion shield of Schwarzbourg over small leaning shield of Zutphen

ANO:M-CCC-C:L-XXIX
Ornate triple-stranded long cross with small shield of Gelderland in center

Possibly only one specimen known, in the City Museum of Zutphen. See III-125 for a similar example.

III-117 Zutphen City
Mint: Zutphen
1479 Half Albus
R4 *1.60 g*
Frey 202, Beek 2, Stephanik 4291

MONE:NOVA-ZVTPHANES
Lion shield of Schwarzbourg over small leaning shield of Zutphen

AN:D-M:CC-CC:L-XXIX
Ornate triple-stranded long cross with small shield of Gelderland in center

1480

III-118 Campen City
Mint: Campen
1480 One-Eighth Stuiver
R5 *0.26 g*
Frey 218, Van der Chijs 15.14

MONE NOVA CAMPEN
Shield of the Oversticht

AN'D-MCC-CCL-XXX
Thick long cross

III-119 Deventer City
Mint: Deventer
David of Burgundy, 1455-1496
1480 Half Plak
R6
Unpublished?

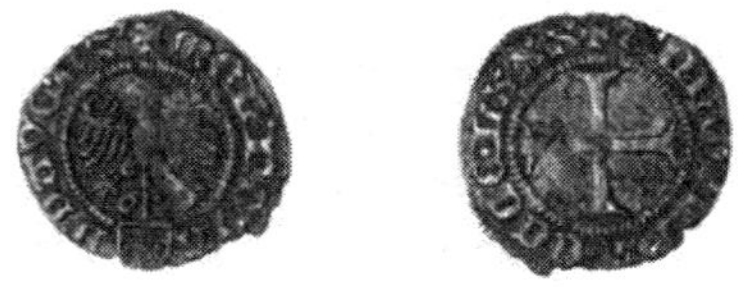

MON'NOVA-D'DAVENT'
Eagle above shield of the Oversticht

ANNO DNI M CCCC LXXX
Cross

Van der Chijs 12.23 and JFD 34 list this type, but only with the date 1481. Sold by L. Schulman in November 1999 (author's collection).

III-120 Gelderland Duchy
Mint: Uncertain
Marie of Burgundy, 1477-1482
1480 Gros
R2 *1.87 g*
Frey 212A, GH 41-2, Van der Chijs 12.4

MARIA*DVCISSA*B'G'*Z*GELRIE
Large ornate letter "M" in quatrefoil

BENEDIC*AIA*MEA*DNO*1ꝝ80
Flowery short cross

III-121 Gelderland, Family of Egmont Duchy
Mint: Zutphen
Charles of Egmont (Minority), 1477-1480
1480 Stuiver
R *2.35 g*
Frey 212, Van der Chijs 14.3, Roest 261-63

KAROL:DVX:GEL:IVL:Z:CO:ZV
Shield of Gelderland

ANNO:-DNI:M-:CCCC:-LXXX
Long cross with lions in angles of cross

III-122 Holland County
Mint: Dordrecht
Marie of Burgundy, 1477-1482
1480 Double Briquet
VS 3.06 g
Frey 216, GH 39-4b, Van der Chijs 15.4

MARIA*DVCISSA*BG*COMIT*H
Two seated facing lions with briquet in center

SALVV*FAC*PPLM*DNE 1480
Shield of Burgundy on flowery cross

III-123 Holland County
Mint: Dordrecht
Marie of Burgundy, 1477-1482
1480 Briquet
R3 3.06 g
Frey 216A, GH 40-4b, Van der Chijs type 16.12-13

MARIA*DVCISSA*BG*COMIT*HO
Seated lion holding shield of Burgundy

BENEDIC*HEREDITATI*TVE*1480
Triple-stranded flowery short cross

III-124 Holland County
Mint: Dordrecht
Marie of Burgundy, 1477-1482
1480 Gros
VS 1.87 g
Frey 216B, GH 41-4a, Van der Chijs 16.18

MARIA*DVCISSA*BG*CO*HO
Large ornate letter "M" in quatrefoil

BENEDIC*AIA*MEA*DNO 1480
Flowery short cross

III-125 Zutphen City
Mint: Zutphen
1480 Albus
R2 2.50 g
Frey 209, 209A, Beek 3, Van der Chijs 6.1, Stephanik 4292

MON'NOVA-ZVTPHANE'
Lion shield of Schwarzbourg over small leaning shield of Zutphen

A'M-CCC-CL-XXX
Ornate triple-stranded long cross with small shield of Gelderland in center

A piefort is known. See Beek 3a and Van der Chijs p. 102.

III-126 Zutphen City
Mint: Zutphen
1480 Half Albus
R3 1.60 g
Frey 209B, Van Beek 4, Stephanik 4293

MONE:NOVA-ZVTPHANES
Lion shield of Schwarzbourg over small leaning shield of Zutphen

A-N':D'-M:CC-CC:L-XXX
Ornate triple-stranded long cross with small shield of Gelderland in center

---

III-127 Zutphen City
Mint: Zutphen
1480 One-Eighth Albus
R4 0.20 g
Frey —, Van Beek 5, Van der Chijs 7. Supp.

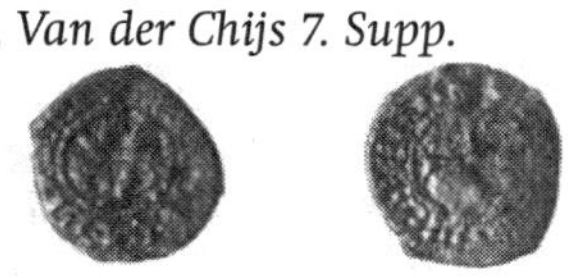

MO'NO'ZVTPHAN
Standing lion facing left

AN'D'MCCCCLXXX
Short cross

1481

III-128 Deventer City
Mint: Deventer
David of Burgundy, 1455-1496
1481 Stuiver
R4 2.40 g
Frey 231B, JFD 31, Van der Chijs 12.20

MONE:NOVA-D-DAVENTRIA
Eagle above shields of Deventer and the Oversticht

AN:D-N-M:C-CCC:L-XXXI
Flowery triple-stranded long cross

III-129 Deventer City
Mint: Deventer
David of Burgundy, 1455-1496
1481 Half Stuiver
R4 1.50 g
Frey 228, JFD 32, Van der Chijs 12.21

MONE':NOVA:DE:DAVENTRIA
Eagle above shield of the Oversticht

ANNO:DOMINI:M:CCCC:LXXXI
Flowery triple-stranded short cross

III-130 Deventer City
Mint: Deventer
David of Burgundy, 1455-1496
1481 Plak
R4 0.60 g
Frey —, JFD 33, Van der Chijs 12.22

MON:NOVA:D:DAVENT
Eagle above shield of the Oversticht

AN'D-MCC-CCL-XXXI
Long cross

III-131 Deventer City
Mint: Deventer
David of Burgundy, 1455-1496
1481 Half Plak
R4-5 0.50 g
Frey —, JFD 34, Van der Chijs 12.23

MON:NOVA:D:DAVENT
Eagle above shield of the Oversticht

ANNO:DN'MCCCCLXXXI
Short cross

III-132 Holland County
Mint: Dordrecht
Marie of Burgundy, 1477-1482
1481 Double Briquet
VS 3.06 g
Frey 227, GH 39-4a-b, Van der Chijs 15.5-6

MARIA*DVCISSA*BG*COMIT*HO
Two seated facing lions with briquet in center

SALVV*FAC*PPLM*TVV*DNE 1481
Shield of Burgundy on flowery cross

III-133 Holland County
Mint: Dordrecht
Marie of Burgundy, 1477-1482
1481 Briquet
VS 3.06 g
Frey 227A, GH 40-4a-b, Van der Chijs 16.13, 37.25

MARIA*DVCISSA*BG*COMIT*HO
Seated lion holding shield of Burgundy

BENEDIC*HEREDITATI*TVE 1481
Triple stranded flowery short cross

A modern "4" was used on the double briquet, briquet and gros. Subsequent dies for the rest of the 15th century reverted to the use of "ꝝ" instead of "4".

III-134 Holland County
Mint: Dordrecht
Marie of Burgundy, 1477-1482
1481 Gros
R 1.87 g
Frey 227B, GH 41-4a-b, Van der Chijs 16.19

MARIA*DVCISSA*BG*CO*HO
Large ornate letter "M" in quatrefoil

BENEDIC*AIA*MEA*DNO 1481
Flowery short cross

1482

III-135 Groningen City
Mint: Groningen
1482 Stuiver
VS 2.40 g
Frey 242, Puister 1.259i, Stephanik 3480

MONETA:NOVA-GRONIGENSIS
Double-headed eagle with shield of Groningen placed diagonally below

ANNO-DOMIN-M:CCCC-LXXXII
Long cross with letter "G" in center

III-136a Holland County
Mint: Dordrecht
Marie of Burgundy, 1477-1482
1482 Double Briquet

R *3.06 g*
Frey 240, GH 39-4a, Van der Chijs 15.7

MARIA*DVCISSA*BG*COMIT*HOL
Two seated facing lions with briquet in center

SALVV*FAC*PPLM*TVV*DNE 1482
Shield of Burgundy on flowery cross

Struck in Marie's name after her death.

III-136b Holland County
Mint: Dordrecht
Marie of Burgundy, 1477-1482
1482 Double Briquet
R *3.06 g*
Frey —, GH 39-4a, Van der Chijs 15.8

Same as preceding, but date "1 ꝝ 8 2."

III-137 Holland County
Mint: Dordrecht
Marie of Burgundy, 1477-1482
1482 Briquet
R *3.06 g*
Frey 240A, GH 40-4a, Van der Chijs 16.14

MARIA*DVCISSA*BG*COMIT*HOL
Seated lion holding shield of Burgundy

BENEDIC*HEREDITATI*TVE 1ꝝ82
Triple-stranded flowery short cross

Struck in Marie's name after her death.

III-138 Utrecht Regency
Mint: Utrecht
Engelbert of Cleve (Regent), 1482
1482 Braspenning
R4-5 *2.51-3.15 g*
Frey 244, Van der Chijs 20.2, De Mey Ut. 338

ENGELBERT':DE:CLIVIS:Z:DE:MARKA
Helmeted elk over shields of Cleve and Mark

MON':NO-VA:TRA-IECTEN-LXXXII
Long cross with fleur-de-lys in angles of cross, mintmark in center

Struck by Engelbert of Cleve during his forced regency over the city of Utrecht. A braspenning was worth one and a quarter stuivers.

III-139 Utrecht Bishopric
Mint: Wijk-bij-Duurstede
David of Burgundy, 1455-1496
1482 Double Briquet
R2 *2.80 g*
Frey 243, Van der Chijs 18.29, De Mey Ut. 318, Stephanik 1852

MONETA:NOVA:EPI:TRAIECTENS'
Two seated facing lions with tinder box in between

MEMENTO:DOMINE:DAVID:1ꝝ82
Shield of Burgundy on fiery short cross

III-140 Utrecht Bishopric
Mint: Wijk-bij-Duurstede
David of Burgundy, 1455-1496
1482 Briquet
R2 *2.29-2.89 g*
Frey —, Van der Chijs 18.30, De Mey Ut. 319, Stephanik 1853-54

MONETA:NOVA:EPI':TRAIECTENS'
Lion facing left, holding shield of Burgundy

MEMENTO:DOMINE:DAVID:1ꝝ82
Fiery triple- stranded short cross

1483

III-141 Holland County
Mint: Dordrecht
Marie of Burgundy, 1477-1482
1483 Double Briquet
R2 *3.06 g*
Frey 246, GH 39-4a, Van der Chijs type 15.8

MARIA*DVCISSA*BG*COMIT*HOL
Two seated facing lions with briquet in center

SALVV*FAC*PPLM*TVV*DNE 1ꝝ83
Shield of Burgundy on flowery cross

Struck in Marie's name after her death.

III-142 Utrecht Bishopric
Mint: Wijk-bij-Duurstede
David of Burgundy, 1455-1496
1483 Briquet
R3-4 *2.00 g*
Frey 247, Van der Chijs 18.32, De Mey Ut. 319

MONETA • NOVA • EPI • TRAIECTENS'
Seated lion holding shield of Burgundy

MEMENTO • DOMINE • DAVID • 1ꝝ83
Fiery triple-stranded short cross

III-143 Utrecht City City
Mint: Utrecht
1483 Stuiver
R5-6 *Weight unknown*
Frey –, De Mey Ut. 380, JMP 1952, p.91

S':MARTINVS:EPS':Z:PATRONVS
St. Martin riding on horseback

AN':DN-I:MCC-CCLX-XXIII
Ornamented long cross with "V-T-R-E" in angles

1484

III-144 Holland County
Mint: Dordrecht
Philip the Fair (Minority), 1482-1492
1484 Gros
R2 *1.87 g*
Frey 265A, GH 55-6, Van der Chijs 17.7

MO:ARCHIDVC:AVST:BG:CO:HOLL
Large ornate letter "M" in quatrefoil

BENEDIC:AIA:MEA:DNO:1ꝝ8ꝝ
Flowery short cross

III-145 Nijmegen City
Mint: Nijmegen
1484 Half Stuiver
R2 *1.70 g*
Frey 264, Nijmegen Museum 8a, Van der Chijs 1.9

MONETA:NOVA:NOVIMAGEN'
Lion advancing left, holding shield of Nijmegen

ANNO:DNI':M:CCCC:LXXXIIII
Ornate triple-stranded short cross

1485

III-146 Campen City
Mint: Campen
1485? One-Eighth Stuiver
R6 *Weight unknown*
Unpublished?

(obliterated)
Shield of Campen with small shield of the Oversticht in foreground

ANOD-NIMC-CCCL-X_XV
Double stranded long cross with letter "G" (!) in center

A large edge chip has removed what appears to be a middle "X" in the date. It is possible, given the size of the missing chip, that the date is actually 1495. Sold by Coin Investment BV of the Netherlands in September 1999.

III-147 Franeker City
Mint: Franeker
1485 Half Stuiver
R5 *1.60 g*
Frey 273, Puister-Fr. 3.004a, Van der Chijs 6.1

MONET:NOVA:FRANKEREN
Lion advancing left

ANNO:DNI:M:CCCC:148V (sic)
Flowery double-stranded short cross

Highly unusual form of date with Roman then Arabic then Roman numerals!

III-148a Groningen City
Mint: Groningen
1485 Jager
R 2.00 g
Frey 270, Puister 1.258a, Van der Chijs 12.73

MONET:NOV-GRONINGENS
Double-headed eagle in quatrefoil with two small diagonally placed shields below, letter "G" at bottom

SIT:NO-ME'DN-I:BEN-EDICT- A'M-CCC-CLX-XXV
Long cross with inner and outer legends

III-148b Groningen City
Mint: Groningen
1485 Jager
R 2.40 g
Frey —, Puister 1.257, Van der Chijs 12.72

MONET:NOV-GRONINGENS
Double-headed eagle in quatrefoil with two small diagonally placed shields below

SIT:NOMEN:DNI:BENEDICTV- A'M-CCC-CLX-XXV
Middle-length cross with eagle shield in center

III-149 Groningen City
Mint: Groningen
1485 Stuiver
VS 2.20 g
Frey 270A, Puister 1.264a, Van der Chijs 12.74

MONETA:NOV-GRONIGE'SIS
Double-headed eagle with upright shield of Groningen below
ANNO DOMINI MCCCCLXXXV
Short thick cross with letter "G" in center

III-150 Holland County
Mint: Dordrecht
Philip the Fair (Minority), 1482-1492
1485 Double Briquet
R2 3.06 g
Frey 266, GH 52-6, Van der Chijs 17.8-9, Stephanik 449

MO:ARCHIDVCV:AVST:BG:CO:HOL
Two seated facing lions with briquet in center

SALVV:FAC:PPLM:TVV:DNE:1ꝝ85
Shield of Austria-Burgundy on flowery cross

III-151 Holland County
Mint: Dordrecht
Philip the Fair (Minority), 1482-1492
1485 Half Briquet
R3 1.87 g
Frey —, GH 54-6, Van der Chijs 18.11-12, Stephanik 451

MO • ARCHIDVCV • AVST • BG • CO • HOL
Half-length figure of lion advancing left

BENEDIC • ANIA • MEA • DNO • 1ꝝ85
Flowery short cross

III-152 Nijmegen City
Mint: Nijmegen
1485 Half Stuiver
R 1.80 g
Frey 268, Nijmegen Museum 8b-d, De Voogt 10, Van der Chijs 1.10, Stephanik 4207

MONETA:NOVA:NOVIMAGEN
Lion advancing left, holding shield of Nijmegen

ANNO:DOMI':M:CCCC:LXXXV
Ornate triple-stranded short cross

III-153 Utrecht Bishopric
Mint: Wijk-bij-Duurstede
David of Burgundy, 1455-1496
1485 Three-Quarters Stuiver
R3 2.35 g
Frey 273C/286, Van der Chijs 18.33-34, De Mey Ut. 321, Stephanik 1863-64

MONETA-EPISCOPI-TRAIECTE
Quartered arms of Utrecht-Burgundy

MEMET-O:DNE-DAVID-1ꝝ8ꞁ
Thick long cross with rosace in center

Both Frey references to this coin are inaccurate. Frey 273C describes this as a stuiver and Frey 286 provides the inaccurate date of 1487 by misreading the medieval "5." This is the only known early dated coin bearing this highly unusual denomination.

1486

III-154 Campen City
Mint: Campen
1486 Quarter Stuiver
R5-6 *Weight unknown*
Frey —, JMP 1987 p.177

MONETA*NOVA*CAMP
Shield of Campen

ANN-O • DN-MCC-CC86- C-A-M-P
Long cross with letters in angles of cross, shield in center

Likely only two or three known.

III-155 Franeker City
Mint: Franeker
1486? Half Stuiver
R5-6 *1.20 g*
Frey —, Van der Chijs 6.2

MON':NOVA:FRANKEREN'
Lion advancing left

ANNO:DNI:M:CCCC:1ꝝ8—
Flowery double-stranded short cross

Van der Chijs theorizes the last digit of this coin to be a "6".

III-156 Groningen City
Mint: Groningen
1486 Jager
R *1.60-1.95 g*
Frey 278A, Puister 1.258b, Van der Chijs 12.75-76, Stephanik 3435-38

MO:NOVA-GRONIGES
Double-headed eagle in quatrefoil with two small diagonally placed shields below

SIT:NO-ME:DN-I:BEN-EDICT- A'M-CCC-CLX-XXVI
Long cross

A variety has the obverse legend of "MONET:NOV-GRONINGENS." See Van der Chijs 12.76

III-157 Groningen City
Mint: Groningen
1486 Stuiver
VS *1.70 g*
Frey 278, Puister 1.264b, Van der Chijs 13.77, Stephanik 3439-40

MONETA:NOV-GRONIGESIS
Double-headed eagle with upright shield of Groningen below

ANNO:DOMINI:MCCCCLXXXVI
Double-stranded short cross with letter "G" in center

III-158 Holland County
Mint: Dordrecht
Philip the Fair (Minority), 1482-1492
1486 Double Briquet
R2 *3.06 g*
Frey 281, GH 52-6, Van der Chijs 17.9

MO:ARCHIDVCV:AVST:BG:CO:HOL
Two seated facing lions with briquet in center

SALVV:FAC:PPLM:TVV:DNE: **I** ꝝ86
Shield of Austria-Burgundy on flowery cross

The "8" is created on this coin by two large annulets.

III-159 Holland County
Mint: Dordrecht
Philip the Fair (Minority), 1482-1492
1486 Briquet
R2 *3.06 g*
Frey —, GH 53-6, Van der Chijs 17.10

MO:ARCHIDVCV:AVST:BG:CO:HOL
Seated lion holding shield of Austria-Burgundy

BENEDIC:HEREDITATI:TVE: **I** ꝝ 8 6
Flowery triple-stranded short cross

III-160 Holland County
Mint: Dordrecht
Philip the Fair (Minority), 1482-1492
1486 Half Briquet
R 1.87 g
Frey 282D, GH 54-6, Van der Chijs 18.13-14

MO • ARCHIDVCV • AVST • BG • CO • HOL
Half-length figure of lion advancing left

BENEDIC • ANIA • MEA • DNO • 1ꝶ86
Flowery short cross

III-161 Nijmegen City
Mint: Nijmegen
1486 Half Stuiver
R 1.80 g
Frey 280, Nijmegen Museum 8e-l , Van der Chijs 23.7, De Voogt 11c, Stephanik 4208

MONETA:NOVA:NOVIMAGEN'
Lion advancing left, holding shield of Nijmegen

ANNO:DNI':M:CCCC:LXXXVI
Ornate triple-stranded short cross

1487

III-162a Franeker City
Mint: Franeker
1487 Half Stuiver
R4 1.60 g
Frey 294, Puister-Fr. 3.004c, Van der Chijs 6.3

MONEºNOVºFRANIKAREN
Lion advancing left

ANNO:DOMINI: I ꝶ 8 Λ
Ornate double-stranded flowery short cross

III-162b Franeker City
Mint: Franeker
1487 Half Stuiver
R5 1.60 g
Frey —, Puister-Fr. 3.005, Van der Chijs 6.4

MON':NOVA:FRANKAREN'
Lion advancing left

SIGNO:CRVCIS:SALVEMVR 1ꝶ8Λ
Flowery short cross

III-163 Gelderland Duchy
Mint: Zaltbommel
Philip the Fair (Minority), 1482-1492
1487 Gold Real
R6? 14.82 g
Frey —, GH 64-3, FR. 65, De Mey d'Or 1116, Delmonte 614

MAXIMILIANVS:DEI:GRATIA:ROMANOR:REX:SEMP:AVG
Emperor seated on gothic throne

TENE:MENSVRAM:ET:RESPICE:FINEM:M:CCCC:LXXXVII
Crowned eagle shield of Holy Roman Emperor

Specimen in the Teylers Museum in the Netherlands.

III-164 Gelderland Duchy
Mint: Zaltbommel
Philip the Fair (Minority), 1482-1492
1487 Silver Real
R5 7.10 g
Frey 288, GH 67-3, Van der Chijs 12.7, Roest 288

CUSTODIAT*CREATOR*ONIV*HVMILE'*SERVV*SVV*1ꝶ8Λ
Half-length figure of Maximilian as Holy Roman Emperor facing right, holding sword and imperial orb

DET*TIBI*MATRIS*VTVTE-ET*IN*CELIS*GLORIAM
Large joint elaborate monogram of initials of Maximilian as regent and his son Philip

A cover photo for this book. The photographed example was sold at Künker in 2005.

III-165 Gelderland Duchy
Mint: Zaltbommel
Philip the Fair (Minority), 1482-1492
1487 Double Griffon
R4 3.60 g
Frey —, GH 68-5, Van der Chijs 13.8, Roest 289

MONET:ARGENTEA:RO':REG':Z:PH:ARCHID:AV:G
Two facing griffins holding briquet

SALVV:FAC:DOMINE:POPVLV:TVVM:1ꝶ8Λ
Shield of Austria-Burgundy on flowery cross

III-166 Gelderland Duchy
Mint: Zaltbommel
Philip the Fair (Minority), 1482-1492
1487 One-Sixth Griffon?
R6 Weight unknown
Frey—, Van der Chijs 29.10

SEXTV*P____R____CNI_DIAT
large letter "M" suspended from crown

DI_PLV-___-V ARGE-TV 1ꝶ8Λ
Three-part shield of Austria-Burgundy over long cross

A highly unusual denomination described in Van der Chijs p. 99 and with a fragmentary line drawing at 29.10, but bearing a clear date. Gelder-Hoc 71-3 lists as a gros a coin with the same designs but a very different legend. The legend would suggest the denomination. This coin is likely no longer extant.

III-167 Groningen City
Mint: Groningen
1487 Jager
R5 1.65 g
Frey 283, Puister 1.258c, Van der Chijs 13.78

MO:NOVA-GRONIGE
Double-headed eagle in quatrefoil with two small diagonally placed shields below

SIT:N-O:DNI-BENE-DICTV-A'MC-CCCL-XXX-VII
Long cross

III-168 Holland County
Mint: Dordrecht
Philip the Fair (Minority), 1482-1492
1487 Gold Real
R3 14.82 g
Frey 287, GH 64-6, Van der Chijs 17.1-2, FR. 129, De Mey d'Or 1196, Delmonte 749, Stephanik 445

MAXIMILIANVS:DEI:GRA:ROMANORV:REX:SEP:AVG
Emperor seated on gothic throne

TENE:MENSVRAM:ET:RESPICE:FINEM:M:CCCC:LXXXVII
Crowned eagle shield of Holy Roman Emperor

This magnificent coin is the largest early Anno Domini dated gold coin struck originally as a gold piece, as opposed to a striking from thaler dies, as with the guldenthaler gold strike.

III-169 Holland County
Mint: Dordrecht
Philip the Fair (Minority), 1482-1492
1487 Ducat
R5 3.71 g
Frey —, GH 66-6, FR. 132, De Mey d'Or 1198, Delmonte 751

SANCTA:ANDREAS:FILIOS:PROTEGETVOS:1ꝶ8Λ
St. Andreas holding book, standing beside large cross

AMA:IVSTICIAM:PACE:Z:DEFENDE:PPLM:TVVM
Shield of Austria-Burgundy on flowery cross

III-170 Holland County
Mint: Dordrecht
Philip the Fair (Minority), 1482-1492
1487 Silver Real
R4 7.20 g
Frey 294E, GH 67-6, Van der Chijs 18.21, Stephanik 446

CVSTODIAT*C'ATOR*ONIV*HVILE*SERVVM*SVV*1ꝶ8Λ
Half-length figure of Maximilian as Holy Roman Emperor facing right, holding sword and imperial orb

DET*TIBI*M'TVTE-ET*IN*CELIS*GLORIAM
Elaborate large joint monogram of initials of Maximilian as regent and his son Philip

The Gelderland and Holland silver reals, according to Van Gelder & Hoc, are virtually indistinguishable, with minor punctuation identifying each.

III-171 Holland County
Mint: Dordrecht
Philip the Fair (Minority), 1482-1492
1487 Double Griffon
R3 3.60 g
Frey 290, GH 68-6a, Van der Chijs 18.22

MO*ARGETEA*RO*REG*Z*PHI*ARCHID*AV*B*CO*H
Two facing griffins holding briquet

SALVV*FAC*DOMINE*POPVLVM**TVV*1ጸ8Λ
Shield of Austria-Burgundy on flowery cross

III-172 Holland County
Mint: Dordrecht
Philip the Fair (Minority), 1482-1492
1487 Half Gros
R5-6 1.10 g
Frey —, GH 72-6, Van der Chijs 19.27

SEXTE*PL*SIMPLEX*GRIFONI*NOIAT
Large ornate letter "M" in quatrefoil

DEV*PLV-S*AMA*Q-VA*ARGE-TV*1ጸ8Λ
Shield of Austria-Burgundy on long cross

While this coin's inscription proclaims it is worth "one-sixth of a griffon," it is actually worth only one-eighth, since the griffon was equal to four groschen. See the commentary in van Gelder & Hoc, p. 44.

III-173 Leeuwarden City
Mint: Leeuwarden
1487 Jager
R5-6 Weight unknown
Frey —, Puister-Fr. 4.010

MO'NO'ºCIVIT-A-T LEWERDEN
Double-headed eagle over two diagonal shields

SIT*NO-MEN*D-OMI BN-CDICTV-*D-OMI'*-MCC-CC*87
Long cross over shield of Leeuwarden with inner and outer legends

One confirmed known piece in the Netherlands National Coin Museum.

III-174a Leeuwarden City
Mint: Leeuwarden
1487 Stuiver
R4 2.30-2.69 g
Frey 292, Puister-Fr. 4.014, Van der Chijs 5.5, Stephanik 3118,

MONETA:NOVA:LEWERDEN
Lion facing left, holding shield of Leeuwarden

ANNO:DOMINI:M:CCCC:87
Ornate triple-stranded short cross

III-174b Leeuwarden City
Mint: Leeuwarden
1487 Stuiver
R5 Weight unknown
Frey —, Puister-Fr. 4.011

MONETA NO-LEWERDEN
Double-headed eagle over diagonal lion shield

ANNO-DOMI-NIMC-CCC87
Double-stranded long cross with rose in center

III-175 Leeuwarden City
Mint: Leeuwarden
1487 Half Stuiver
R4 0.90 g
Frey 293, Puister-Fr. 4.013, Van der Chijs 5.6

MONETA:NOVA:LEWERDEN'
Lion in shield

ANNO-DOMI-NI:MC-CCC87
Shield with double-headed eagle on long cross

1488

III-176 Campen City
Mint: Campen
1488 Quarter Stuiver
R5 0.60 g
Frey 309, Van der Chijs 15.15

MONETA*NOVA*CAMP
Shield of Campen with small shield of the Oversticht in foreground

ANN-O • DN-MCC-CC88- C-A-M-P
Long cross with letters in angles of cross, shield in center

III-177 Campen City
Mint: Campen
1488? One-Eighth Stuiver
R6 *Weight unknown*
Unpublished?

MONE NOVA CAMPEN
Shield of the Oversticht

AN'D-MCC-CCL-XXX8(?)
Thick long cross

From a recent auction. The last digit of the date is not entirely clear.

III-178 Deventer City
Mint: Deventer
Friedrich III, 1452-1493
1488 Goldgulden
R2 *3.25 g*
Frey 304, JFD 36a-b, Van der Chijs 11.2, FR. 20, De Mey d'Or 736, Delmonte 1079

MON:DE:DAVENTRIA 88
St. Lebuinus seated, holding staff and book with small eagle shield at feet

FREDRIC:ROMANORV:IMPER'
Imperial orb in trefoil

III-179 Deventer City
Mint: Deventer
David of Burgundy, 1455-1496
1488 Quarter Stuiver
R4 *1.10 g*
Frey —, JFD 37, Van der Chijs 12.24, Stephanik 2529

MONETA:DE:DAVENTRIA
Eagle shield of Deventer over small leaning shield of the Oversticht

ANN-O:DN-M:CC-CC88- D-A-V-E
Long cross with letters in angles of cross

III-180 Deventer City
Mint: Deventer
David of Burgundy, 1455-1496
1488 One-Eighth Stuiver
R5 *0.60 g*
Frey —, JFD 38, Van der Chijs 13.2

MONETA:DE:DAVENTRIA
Eagle above shield of the Oversticht

ANNO-O:DN-M:CC-CC88
Small shield of the Oversticht on long cross

III-181 Deventer, Campen & Zwolle
Tri-City Monetary Alliance
Mint: Campen
1488 Stuiver
R3 *2.60 g*
Frey 308, JFD DKZ 5, Van der Chijs 9.2

MONE-NO:VA-CAMP
Conjoined shields of Campen, Deventer and Zwolle set in trefoil, letter "C" in center

ANN-O:DN-M:CC-CC:88
Shield of Campen over triple-stranded long cross

III-182 Deventer, Campen & Zwolle
Tri-City Monetary Alliance
Mint: Campen
1488 Half Stuiver
R3 *1.78 g*
Frey —, JFD DKZ 8, Van der Chijs 10.5

MONE-NOVA-CAMP
Conjoined shields of Campen, Deventer and Zwolle set in trefoil, letter "C" in center

ANN-O:DN-M:CC-CC:88
Shield of Campen over triple-stranded long cross

III-183 Deventer, Campen & Zwolle
Tri-City Monetary Alliance
Mint: Campen
1488 Quarter Stuiver
R5 *1.30 g (est.)*
Frey —, JFD DKZ 11

MONE-NOVA-CAMP
Conjoined shields of Campen, Deventer and Zwolle set in trefoil, letter "C" in center

ANN-DNI-M:CC-CC88
Shield of Campen over triple-stranded long cross

III-184a Deventer, Campen & Zwolle
Tri-City Monetary Alliance
Mint: Deventer
1488 Stuiver
R3 *2.50 g*
Frey —, JFD DKZ 4, Van der Chijs 9.1

MONE-NO'DE-DAVE
Conjoined shields of Deventer, Campen and Zwolle set in trefoil, interrupting legend, with letter "D" in center

ANN-O:DN-M:CC-CC88
Shield of Deventer over triple-stranded long cross

III-184b Deventer, Campen & Zwolle
Tri-City Monetary Alliance
Mint: Deventer
1488 Stuiver
R6? *2.20 g*
Unpublished?

MONETAºNOVAºDEºDEVENTRIA
Conjoined shields of Deventer, Campen and Zwolle set in trefoil, within field, letter "D" in center

ANN-O:DN-M:CC-CC88
Shield of Deventer over triple-stranded long cross

A transitional piece with the obverse of 1479 and reverse of 1488. In author's collection.

III-185 Deventer, Campen & Zwolle
Tri-City Monetary Alliance
Mint: Deventer
1488 Half Stuiver
R2 *1.78 g*
Frey —, JFD DKZ 7, Van der Chijs 10.4

MONE-NO'DE-DAVE
Conjoined shields of Deventer, Campen and Zwolle set in trefoil, letter "D" in center

ANN-O:DN-M:CC-CC:88
Shield of Deventer over triple-stranded long cross

III-186 Deventer, Campen & Zwolle
Tri-City Monetary Alliance
Mint: Deventer
1488 Quarter Stuiver
R4 *1.30 g*
Frey —, JFD DKZ 10

MON'-NOVA-DAVE
Conjoined shields of Deventer, Campen and Zwolle set in trefoil, letter "D" in center

ANN-O:DN-M:CC-CC:88
Shield of Deventer over triple-stranded long cross

A different die of great rarity exists with the obverse legend "MON-NOV-DEVE".

III-187 Deventer, Campen & Zwolle
Tri-City Monetary Alliance
Mint: Zwolle
1488 Stuiver
R4 *2.30 g*
Frey —, JFD DKZ 6, Van der Chijs 9.3

MONE-NOVA-ZWOL
Conjoined shields of Zwolle, Deventer and Campen set in trefoil, letter "Z" in center

ANN-O:DN-M:CC-CC:88
Shield of Zwolle over triple-stranded long cross

III-188 Deventer, Campen & Zwolle
Tri-City Monetary Alliance
Mint: Zwolle
1488 Half Stuiver
R4 *1.78 g*
Frey —, JFD DKZ 9, Van der Chijs 10.6

MONE-NOVA-ZWOL
Conjoined shields of Zwolle, Deventer and Campen set in trefoil, letter "Z" in center

ANN-O:DN-M:CC-CC:88
Shield of Zwolle over triple-stranded long cross

III-189 Deventer, Campen & Zwolle
Tri-City Monetary Alliance
Mint: Zwolle
1488 Quarter Stuiver
R5 *1.30 g (est.)*

Frey —, JFD DKZ 12

MON'-NOV'Z-WOLL
Conjoined shields of Zwolle, Deventer and Campen set in trefoil, letter "Z" in center

ANN-DNI-MCC-CC88
Shield of Zwolle over triple-stranded long cross

III-190 Franeker City
Mint: Franeker
1488 Half Stuiver
R5 *1.40 g*
Frey 303A, Puister-Fr. 3.004d, Van der Chijs 6.5

MON:NOVA:FRANKAREN
Lion advancing left

ANNO:DOMINI:1ꝶ88
Flowery short cross

III-191 Gelderland Duchy
Mint: Zaltbommel
Philip the Fair (Minority), 1482-1492
1488 Half Noble d'or
R5 *3.40 g*
Frey —, GH 75-4, FR. 66, De Mey d'Or 1117, Delmonte 615

MO:RO:REG:Z:PHI:ARDVC:AVS:BG:BR:Z:GEL
Emperor Maximilian in boat holding sword with small shield of Austria-Burgundy in foreground

REFORMATIO:GVERRE:PAX:EST:ANNO:1ꝶ88
Ornate triple-stranded short cross in polyfoil with crowns in angles

---

III-192 Gelderland Duchy
Mint: Zaltbommel
Philip the Fair (Minority), 1482-1492
1488 Double Griffon
R5 *3.60 g*
Frey —, GH 68-4, Roest 298

MO • ARGE • RO • RG • Z • PHI • AR DV • AV • BG
Two facing griffons holding briquet

SALVV • FAC • DOMINE • POPVLVM • TVV • 1ꝶ88
Shield of Austria-Burgundy on flowery cross

III-193 Gelderland Duchy
Mint: Zaltbommel
Philip the Fair (Minority), 1482-1492
1488 Double Patard
R2 *2.99 g*
Frey 312, GH 77-4, Van der Chijs 14.1, Stephanik 3857

MON'*DVCIS*GELRIE*ET*COMIT'*ZVT
Four part shield of Gelderland-Jülich

REFORMACIO*GVERRE*PAX*EST*88
Thick ornate short cross with mintmark in center

III-194 Groningen City
Mint: Groningen
Friedrich III, 1452-1493
1488 Goldgulden
R4 *3.25 g*
Frey 301, Puister 282, Van der Chijs 13.80, FR. 81, De Mey d'Or 1078, Delmonte 1142, Stephanik 3442

MONE:AVRE-GRONI'GE'S:88
John the Baptist holding lamb with letter "G" between feet

FREDRIC:ROMANORV':IMPE
Imperial orb in trefoil

III-195 Groningen City
Mint: Groningen
1488 Half Plak
R6 *0.60 g*
Frey 302, Puister 1.231, Van der Chijs 13.79

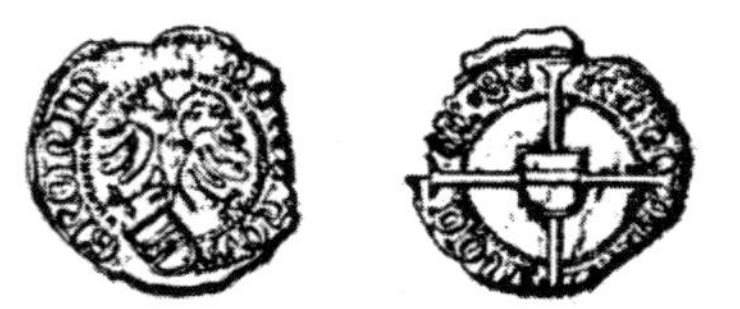

MONE:NOVA:GRONIN
Double-headed eagle with shield of Groningen placed diagonally below

ANNO-DOMI-M:CC-CC:88
Long cross with shield in center

Likely no longer extant.

III-196 Holland County
Mint: Dordrecht
Philip the Fair (Minority), 1482-1492
1488 Half Noble d'or
R2 *3.40 g*
Frey 295, GH 75-6b, Van der Chijs 17.5-6, FR. 131, Delmonte 752, Stephanik 447-48

MO+RO+REG+Z+PHI+ARDVC+AVS+BG+BR+CO+HO
Emperor Maximilian in boat holding sword with small shield of Austria-Burgundy in foreground

REFORMACIO+GVERRE+PAX+ANNO+1ጸ88
Ornate triple-stranded short cross in polyfoil with crowns in angles

---

III-197 Holland County
Mint: Dordrecht
Philip the Fair (Minority), 1482-1492
1488 Double Griffon
R3 3.60 g
Frey 296, GH 68-6b, Van der Chijs 19.23, Stephanik 464

MO • ARGENTEA • RO • REG • Z • PHI • ARCHIDV • AV • B • CO • H
Two facing griffons holding briquet

SALVV • FAC • DOMINE • POPVLVM • TVV • 1ጸ88
Shield of Austria-Burgundy on flowery cross

III-198 Holland County
Mint: Dordrecht
Philip the Fair (Minority), 1482-1492
1488 Double Patard
R4 2.99 g
Frey 297, GH 77-6, Van der Chijs 19.36

MO*NOVA*COMITIS*HOLLA*Z*ZE
Four part lion shield

REFORMACIO*GVERRE*PAX*EST*1ጸ88
Thick ornate short cross with mintmark in center

III-199 Nijmegen City
Mint: Nijmegen
1488 Half Stuiver
R3 1.80 g (est.)
Frey 311, Nijmegen Museum 8m, Van der Chijs p. 264

MONETA:NOVA:NOVIMAGEN'
Lion advancing left, holding shield of Nijmegen

ANNO:DNI':M:CCCC:LXXXVIII
Triple-stranded flowery short cross

III-200 Zwolle City
Mint: Zwolle
1488 Plak
R4 0.80 g
Frey —, Wiel 6, Van der Chijs 17.5, Stephanik 2806

MON':NOV':ZWOLLENS
Shield of Zwolle

ANN-DNI-MCC-CC88
Long cross with "Z-W-O-L" in angles of cross

III-201 Zwolle City
Mint: Zwolle
1488 Quarter Plak
R5 0.25 g
Frey —, Wiel 9

Photo 2x actual size

MON:NOV:ZWOL
Shield of Zwolle

ANN-DNI-MCC-CC88
Long cross with rosettes in angles of cross

1489

III-202 Franeker City
Mint: Franeker
1489 Double Stuiver
R5 2.28 g
Frey —, Puister-Fr. 3.003a

MON:NOVA:FRANIKARENSIS
Quartered arms with four lions facing left

ANNO DOMINI MILLESI'O *4*89
Flowery short cross

Franeker was one of the very few states to strike a mixed letter and modern numeral date, as in this specimen.

III-203 Gelderland Duchy
Mint: Zaltbommel
Philip the Fair (Minority), 1482-1492
1489 Gros
R5 1.80 g
Frey —, GH 85-4, JMP 1951, p. 114, Egg 88

PHI:ARCHIDVC:AVSTRIE:BVR:GELR
Five part shield of Austria-Burgundy occupying entire field

MAXIMILIA:REX:ROMA'O:PAT:1ꝝ89
Flowery cross with crowns and lions in angles and mintmark in center

---

III-204 Groningen City
Mint: Groningen
1489 Plak
R4 Weight unknown
Frey 336F, Puister 1.223a

MON:NOV-GRONINGE
Double-headed eagle with shield of Groningen placed diagonally below

AN:'O-MCC-CCLX-XXIX
Long cross with eagle shield in center

III-205 Holland County
Mint: Dordrecht
Philip the Fair (Minority), 1482-1492
1489 Florin d'or
R6 3.40 g
Frey 336, GH 80-6, Van der Chijs 37.29, FR. 132a, Delmonte 753

PHI:ARCHIDVC:AV:BG:B:CO:HOL:ZZ
Saint Andre holding long cross behind shield of Austria-Burgundy

MAXIMIL-IAN+REX-ROMANO-PAT+1ꝝ89
Crowned shield of Holy Roman Empire on long cross

III-206 Holland County
Mint: Dordrecht
Philip the Fair (Minority), 1482-1492
1489 Patard
R3 3.06 g
Frey 335, GH 84-6, Van der Chijs 19.37-38

PHIºARCHIDVCISºAVSTRIEºBVRºBRºC'ºHOºZZ
Arms of Austria-Burgundy occupying entire field

MAXIMI-LIANºREX-ROMANO-PATº1ꝝ89
Crowned shield of Holy Roman Empire on long cross

III-207 Holland County
Mint: Dordrecht
Philip the Fair (Minority), 1482-1492
1489 Gros
R2 1.80 g
Frey 335B, GH 85-6, Van der Chijs 20.39, 41-43, Stephanik 452

PHIºARCHIDVCºAVSTºBVRGºCOºHºZ
Arms of Austria-Burgundy occupying entire field

MAXIMILIANºREXºROMANORºPATº1ꝝ89
Flowery short cross with alternating lions and crowns in angles and mintmark in center

---

III-208 Nijmegen City
Mint: Nijmegen
1489 Stuiver
R4 2.60 g
Frey 334, Nijmegen Museum 9, Van der Chijs 1.11

MONETA*NOVA*NOVIMAGENSIS
Seated lion holding shield of Nijmegen

ANNO-DNI'*M-CCCC*L-XXXIX
Thick double-stranded long cross with fleur-de-lys in angles and mintmark in center

---

III-209 Nijmegen City
Mint: Nijmegen
1489 Half Stuiver
R2 1.80 g (est.)
Frey 334A, Nijmegen Museum 8n, Van der Chijs 1.12, De Voogt 13, Stephanik 4209

MONETA*NOVA*NOVIMAGEN'
Lion advancing left, holding shield of Nijmegen

ANNO+DNI+M+CCCC+LXXXIX
Triple-stranded flowery short cross

III-210 Nijmegen City
Mint: Nijmegen
1489 Quarter Stuiver
R4-5 Weight unknown
Frey —, Nijmegen Museum 10, De Voogt 15

MON*NOVA*NOVIMAGEN
Double-headed eagle with shield on breast

ANNO-DNIM-CCCC-LXXX9
Long cross

1490

III-211 Franeker City Mint: Franeker
1490 Double Stuiver
R5 *2.24 g*
Frey —, Puister-Fr. 3.003b, Van der Chijs 6.7

MON:NOVA:FRANIKARENSIS
Quartered arms with four lions facing left

ANNO DOMINI MILLESI'O *ꝶ*90
Flowery short cross

III-212 Franeker City Mint: Franeker
1490 Half Stuiver
R6 *1.40-1.60 g (est.)*
Frey —, Puister-Fr. 3.004f

MONEºNOVºFRANIKAREN
Lion advancing left

ANNO:DOMINI__O'ꝶ.90
Double-stranded flowery short cross

The likely sole known example is in the Netherlands National Coin Museum.

1491

III-213 Franeker City Mint: Franeker
Friedrich III, 1452-1493
1491 Goldgulden
R4-5 *3.34 g*
Frey 361, Puister-Fr. 3.002a, FR. 31, RBN 1873, p.301, Delmonte 1032, Stephanik 3116

MONE*NOVA*-*AVR*FRA 91
John the Baptist holding lamb and book with lion mintmark in legend between feet

FREDRIC'RO'.AN'.IMPE'ATO'
Imperial orb in trefoil

III-214 Groningen City Mint: Groningen
1491 Stuiver
R3 *2.30 g*
Frey 362, Puister 1.260e, Van der Chijs 13.81, Stephanik 3481

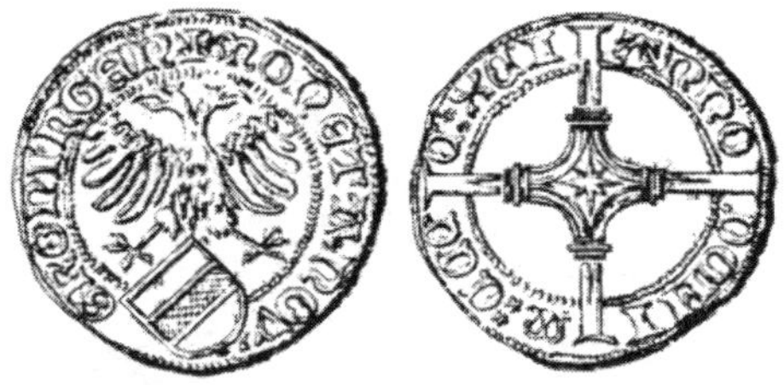

MONETA:NOV-GRONINGEN
Double-headed eagle with shield of Groningen placed diagonally below
ANNO-DOMI-M:CCC-C:XCI
Long cross with star in center

Van der Chijs erroneously refers to this piece as a jager instead of a stuiver.

III-215 Groningen City Mint: Groningen
1491 Half Stuiver
R4 *Weight unknown*
Frey —, Puister 1.266g, Van der Chijs 13.82

MON':NOVA-GRONINGE'
Double-headed eagle with shield of Groningen placed diagonally below

ANNO-DOMI-M:CCC-C:XCI
Long cross with star in center

III-216 Groningen City Mint: Groningen
1491 Plak
R4 *1.05 g*
Frey 363, Puister 1.223, Van der Chijs 13.83, 19.27

MON':NOVA-GRONINGE'
Double-headed eagle with shield of Groningen placed diagonally below

AN':D-NI':M-CCCC-XCI
Long cross with eagle shield in center

III-217 Groningen City
Mint: Groningen
1491 Half Plak
R4-5 *0.45 g*
Frey —, Puister 1.232a, Van der Chijs 13.84

MON':NOVA-GRONINGE'
Double-headed eagle with shield of Groningen placed diagonally below

ANNO:DOMI:M:CCCC:XCI
Short cross with shield of Groningen at center

III-218 Leeuwarden City
Mint: Leeuwarden
1491 Half Stuiver
R6 *Weight unknown*
Frey —, Puister-Fr. 4.012, RBN 1869, p. 180

MON'*NOVA*-*LEWARDIE
Double-headed eagle over diagonal lion shield

ANNO-DOMI'-MCCCC-C*XCI
Double-stranded long cross

Likely no longer extant.

1492

III-219 Deventer City
Mint: Deventer
David of Burgundy, 1455-1496
1492 Stuiver
R4-5 *2.30 g*
Frey 396D, JFD 40

MONETA:NOVA-DE:DAVENTRIA
Eagle above shields of Deventer and the Oversticht

AN:D-NI:M-CCCC-XCII
Thick triple-stranded long cross

III-220 Franeker City
Mint: Franeker
Friedrich III, 1452-1493
1492 Goldgulden
R5 *3.25 g (est.)*
Frey 380, Puister-Fr. 3.002b, FR. 31, De Mey d'Or 975a, Delmonte 1032, Stephanik 3117

MONE'*NOVA*-*AVR'*FRA' 9Z
John the Baptist holding lamb and book with lion mintmark in legend between feet

FREDRIC'*RO'AN'*IMPE'ATO'
Imperial orb in trefoil

III-221 Gelderland Duchy
Mint: Malines
Philip the Fair (Majority), 1492-1506
1492 Double Briquet
R *2.80 g*
Frey 391, GH 97-4, Van der Chijs 14.3, Roest 306-17, Stephanik 3855

PHS:ARCHIDVX:AVSTRIE:BVRG:Z:GEL
Two seated facing lions with briquet in center with mintmark below

SALVVM:FAC:POPVLUM:TVVM:DNE 1ꝝ9Z
Shield of Austria-Burgundy on flowery short cross with mintmark in center

An overdate of 1492/4 is known..

III-222 Gelderland Duchy
Mint: Malines
Philip the Fair (Majority), 1492-1506
1492 Briquet
R *2.70 g*
Frey 39B, GH 98-4b, Van der Chijs 14.4-6, Roest 318-34, Stephanik 3856, 58

PHS*ARCHIDVX*AVSTRIE*BVRG*Z*GELR
Lion seated left, holding shield of Austria-Burgundy

BENEDIC*HEREDITATI*TVE*AN*1ꝝ9Z
Triple-stranded flowery short cross with mintmark in center

Roest #334 reports a piece with a backwards "2," but no confirmation is available.

III-223 Groningen City
Mint: Groningen
1492 Stuiver
R5 *2.30 g (est.)*
Frey —, Puister 1.260f

MONETA:NVO-GRONINGEN
Double-headed eagle with shield of Groningen placed diagonally below

ANNO-DOMI-M:CCC-C:XCII
Long cross with star in center

III-224 Groningen City
Mint: Groningen
1492 Kromstaart
R3 1.86 g
Frey 388, Puister 1.214a, Van der Chijs 13.85, Stephanik 3444-45

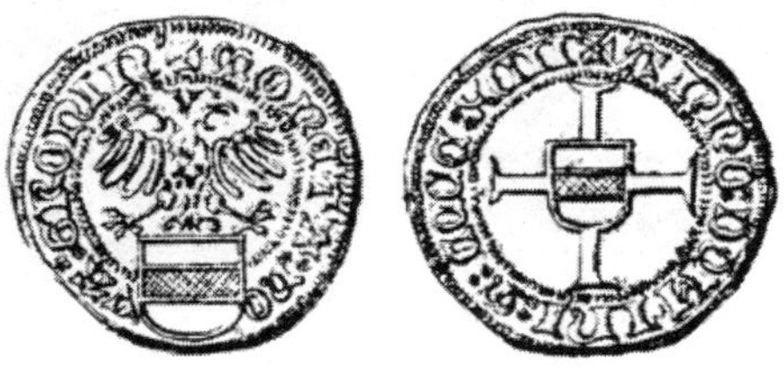

MONETA:NO-VA:GRONIN'
Double-headed eagle with upright shield of Groningen below

ANNO:DOMINI:M:CCCC:XCII
Short cross with shield of Groningen at center

III-225 Holland County
Mint: Dordrecht
Philip the Fair (Majority), 1492-1506
1492 Double Briquet
R 2.90 g
Frey 390, GH 97-6, Van der Chijs 21.15

PHS:ARCHIDVX:AVST:BVR:CO:HOLLA:Z:Z
Two seated facing lions with briquet in center and mintmark below

SALVV:FAC+POPVLVM+TVVM+DNE+1ꝝ9Z
Shield of Austria-Burgundy on flowery short cross with mintmark in center

---

III-226 Holland County
Mint: Dordrecht
Philip the Fair (Majority), 1492-1506
1492 Briquet
R2 2.70 g
Frey 390A, GH 98-6, Van der Chijs 22.16-17, Stephanik 487

PHS+ARCHIDVX+AVST+BVR+CO+HOLLA+Z
Lion seated left, holding shield of Austria-Burgundy

BENEDIC+HEREDITATI+TVE+1ꝝ9Z
Triple-stranded flowery short cross with mintmark in center

III-227 Holland County
Mint: Dordrecht
Philip the Fair (Majority), 1492-1506
1492 Gros
R4-5 1.78 g
Frey 390B, GH 100-6, Tijdschrift 1902, p. 286

PHS*ARCHIDVX*AVST*BG*CO*HO*Z*Z
Arms of Austria-Burgundy occupying entire field

BENEDI-C*ANIA-MEA*DN-O*1ꝝ9Z
Long cross with alternating lions and fleur-de-lys in angles and mintmark in center

---

III-228 Leeuwarden City
Mint: Leeuwarden
1492 Stuiver
R5 *Weight unknown*
Frey 393, Puister-Fr. 4.016a, Van der Chijs 5.7

MONETA:NOVA:LEWERDENSIS
Lion seated left holding shield of Leeuwarden

ANNO:DOMINI:M:CCCC:XCII
Flowery short cross

A unique variety has the letters "L•E•W•E•" in angles of cross.

III-228b Leeuwarden City
Mint: Leeuwarden
1492 Stuiver
R5 *Weight unknown*
Frey —, Puister-Fr. 4.015

MONETA:NOVA:LEWERDENSIS
Lion seated left holding shield of Leeuwarden

ANNO:DOMINI:M:CCCC:XCII' -L-E-W-E
Flowery short cross with letters in angles of cross

III-229 Leeuwarden City
Mint: Leeuwarden
1492 Quarter Stuiver
R6 *0.68 g (fragment missing)*
Unpublished?

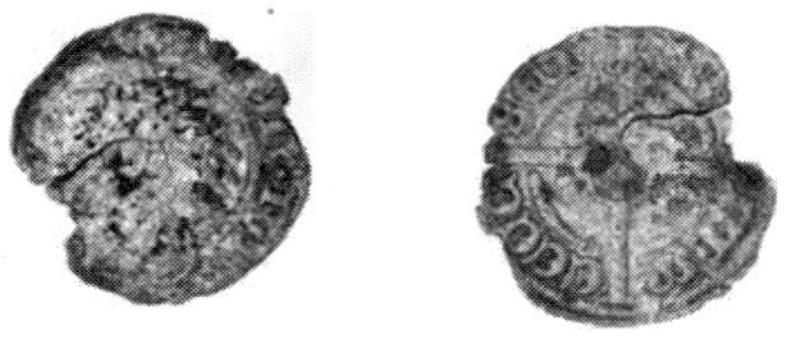

MON*-NOV* - ____D'
Lion seated left holding shield of Leeuwarden

AN__-NI*M-CCCC-XCII
Long Cross with eagle shield in center

From a 1986 hoard. Likely unique (author's collection).

III-230 Sneek City
Mint: Sneek
1492 Jager
R5 *2.50 g*
Frey 389, Puister-Fr. 5.005, Van der Chijs 5.3, Stephanik 3115

MONETA:NOVA:SNEKENSIS-ANNO:DNI:M:CCCC:X:CII
Sneek shield with inner and outer legends

DA:PA-CE':DN'-I:DIEB-NRIS-QZ:NO-E:A9Q-PVGT-P':NO
Long cross with inner and outer legends

III-231 Utrecht Bishopric
Mint: Wijk-bij-Duurstede
David of Burgundy, 1455-1496
1492 Florin d'or
R4 *3.20 g*
Frey 394, Van der Chijs 17.6, De Mey Ut. 332, FR. 193, De Mey d'Or 2170

MO':NO'-AVR':E-PI:TRA-IECT:'92
Shield of Burgundy on long cross

ELEGIT:DA-VIT:S'W:SVV'
King David seated on gothic throne, playing harp with shield of Utrecht at feet

---

III-232 Utrecht Bishopric
Mint: Wijk-bij-Duurstede
David of Burgundy, 1455-1496
1492 Half Florin d'or
R4 *1.68 g*
Frey 394A, Van der Chijs 16.5, De Mey Ut. 333, FR. 192, De Mey d'Or 2171

MONE:NO:AV:EPI:TRAIE:'9Z
Shield of Burgundy in octofoil

ESTVLIT:EV:DE:GREGIB:I:O
Half-length figure of King David playing harp with shield of Utrecht below

---

III-233 Utrecht Bishopric
Mint: Wijk-bij-Duurstede
David of Burgundy, 1455-1496
1492 Briquet
R *2.15-2.75 g*
Frey 395, Van der Chijs 18.35-36, De Mey Ut. 335

MONETA:NOVA:EPI':TRAIECTE'
Seated lion holding shield of Burgundy

INVENI:DAVID:SEVV':MEV:149Z
Fiery triple-stranded short cross

III-234 Utrecht Bishopric
Mint: Wijk-bij-Duurstede
David of Burgundy, 1455-1496
1492 Gros
R *1.65 g*
Frey 396, 396A, 396B, Van der Chijs 19.37, De Mey Ut. 336, Stephanik 1855

MON':NO':EPI:TRAIECTE':149Z
Arms of Burgundy occupying entire field

MEMOR:ESTO:VERBI:TVI
Flowery short cross

III-235 Zwolle City
Mint: Zwolle
1492 Stuiver
R5 *2.70 g*
Frey 392, Wiel 4, Van der Chijs 17.4

SANCT:MICHAEL:PAT':ZWOL'
St. Michael slaying monster, shield of Zwolle below

ANN-O:DNI'-M:CC-CC:92
Triple-stranded flowery long cross with shield of Zwolle in center

1493

III-236 Leeuwarden City
Mint: Leeuwarden
1493 Stuiver
R6 Weight unknown
Frey 399, Puister-Fr. 4.016b, Van der Chijs 5.8

MONETA:NOVA:LEWERDENSIS
Lion seated left holding shield of Leeuwarden

ANNO:DOMINI:M:CCCC:XCIII
Flowery short cross

Likely no longer extant.

III-237 Sneek City
Mint: Sneek
1493 Half Stuiver
R6 Weight unknown
Frey 400, Puister-Fr. 5.006, Van der Chijs 5.4

MONETA:NOVA:SNEKENSIS
Sneek shield of half-eagle and three verticle crowns

ANNO-DNI:M:-CCCC:-XCIII
Thick long cross

Possibly no longer extant.

1494

III-238 Utrecht Bishopric
Mint: Hasselt
David of Burgundy, 1455-1496
1494 Gros
R2 1.39-1.80 g
Frey 420, 420A, Van der Chijs 19.38-39, De Mey Ut. 302, Stephanik 1849-50

MON':NO':EPI:TRAIECT':1ꝝ9ꝝ
Arms of Burgundy occupying entire field

FIAT:M-ISERIC-ORTVA-DOMIN
Long cross with alternating lions and fleur-de-lys in angles, shield of Utrecht in center

---

III-239 Utrecht Bishopric
Mint: Hasselt
David of Burgundy, 1455-1496
1494 Half Gros
R2 1.00 g
Frey 420B, Van der Chijs 19.40, De Mey Ut. 303

MON':NO:EPI:TRAIECT 9ꝝ
Arms of Burgundy occupying entire field

INVENI:DAVID:SERVV':M
Short cross with shield of Utrecht in center

III-240 Utrecht Bishopric
Mint: Hasselt
David of Burgundy, 1455-1496
1494 Quarter Gros
R3 0.46 g
Frey 420C, Van der Chijs 19.41, De Mey Ut. 304, Stephanik 1872

MO':NO':EPI:TRAIEC 9ꝝ
Short cross with alternating lions and fleur-de-lys in angles, with lion in center of cross

INVENI:DAVID:SERVV':ME
Arms of Burgundy occupying entire field

1495

III-241 Deventer City
Mint: Deventer
David of Burgundy, 1455-1496
1495 Plak
R4 0.44 g
Frey 431B, JFD 41

MONET*DE*DAVENTR
Eagle

ANN-DNI-MCC-CC95
Long cross with shield of Oversticht in center

III-242 Holland County
Mint: Dordrecht
Philip the Fair (Majority), 1492-1506
1495 Briquet
R4 2.88 g
Frey 431C, GH 98-6, Van der Chijs 22.18, 38.37

PH'S*ARCHI*DVX*AVST*BVR'*COMES*HOLL+
Lion seated left, holding shield of Austria-Burgundy

BENEDIC*HEREDITATI*TVE*ANNO*1ꝶ95
Thick triple-stranded flowery short cross with mintmark in center

The die for this coin used the "lightning strike" form of 5.

III-243 Zwolle City
Mint: Zwolle
1495 Half Plak
R3 *0.40 g*
Frey —, Wiel 7, Van der Chijs 17.6

MONETA:NOVA:ZWOLLE'
Shield of Zwolle

ANN-DNI-MCC-CC95
Long cross with shield of Zwolle in center

III-244 Zwolle City
Mint: Zwolle
1495 Quarter Plak
R5 *0.25 g*
Frey —, Wiel A9

MON:NOV:ZWOL
Shield of Zwolle

ANO:DNI:MCC:CC95
Short cross

1496

III-245 Gelderland, Family of Egmont Duchy
Mint: Uncertain
Charles of Egmont (Majority), 1492-1538
1496 Double Briquet
VS *3.70 g*
Frey 447, Van der Chijs 16.20, Roest 383-86

KAROL'DV-*GEL'*IVL'*CO-3
Elaborate helmeted shield of Gelderland

EQVITAS*IVDICIA*TVA*DOMINE*96
Short cross with alternating lions and fleur-de-lys in angles

A beautifully engraved coin of low grade silver and rarely found well struck. Extremely rare in high grades.

III-246 Holland County
Mint: Dordrecht
Philip the Fair (Majority), 1492-1506
1496 Toison D'Argent
R *3.40 g*
Frey 443, GH 110-6, Van der Chijs 22.19

PHS+DEI+GRA+ARCIDVX+AVS+B+CO+HO
Crowned shield of Austria-Burgundy interrupting legend over flowery short cross

INICIVM+SAPIENCIE+TIMOR+DOMINI+ANO+1ꝶ96
Golden fleece under two large briquets

III-247 Holland County
Mint: Dordrecht
Philip the Fair (Majority), 1492-1506
1496 Double Patard
S *3.00 g*
Frey 444, GH 111-6, Van der Chijs 22.20-22, Stephanik 488-90

PHS+DEI+GRA+ARCID+AVS'+BG+CO+HOL'
Crowned shield of Austria-Burgundy interrupting legend, all inside polyfoil

OMNIS+SPIRITVS+LADVET+DOMINVM+ANNO+1ꝶ96
Flowery triple-stranded short cross with mintmark in center

1497

III-248 Holland County
Mint: Dordrecht
Philip the Fair (Majority), 1492-1506
1497 Double Patard
R4 *3.00 g*
Frey —, GH 111-6

PHS+DEI+GRA+ARCHID+AVST+DVX+BG+CO+H
Crowned shield of Austria-Burgundy interrupting legend, all inside polyfoil

OMNIS+SPIRITVS+LAVDET+DOMINVM+ANO+1ꝶ97
Thick flowery short cross with mintmark in center

III-249 Holland County
Mint: Dordrecht
Philip the Fair (Majority), 1492-1506
1497 Patard

R5 *2.90 g*
Frey —, GH 112-6d (Supp)

PHS+DEI+GRA+ARCID+AVS+BG'+CO'+HOL'
Crowned shield of Austria-Burgundy interrupting legend but with no polyfoil

SIT+NO-MEN+DO-MI+BNEDIC-TV+1ꝝ97
Ornate long cross with mintmark in center, all in quatrefoil

III-250 Utrecht Bishopric
Mint: Hasselt or Wijk-bij-Duurstede
Frederick IV of Baden, 1496-1517
1497 Stuiver
R4 *2.60 g*
Frey 461, Van der Chijs 21.5, De Mey Ut. 345

MO'*NO'*FRE'*DE:BADE:EPI:TRA':149Λ
Shield of Utrecht-Bade in polyfoil

SALVV-FAC:PO-PVLV:TV-VM:DN
Long cross with lion in center, all in ornate quatrefoil

III-251 Utrecht Bishopric
Mint: Hasselt or Wijk-bij-Duurstede
Frederick IV of Baden, 1496-1517
1497 Half Stuiver
R6 *Weight unknown*
Frey —, Van der Chijs 21.6

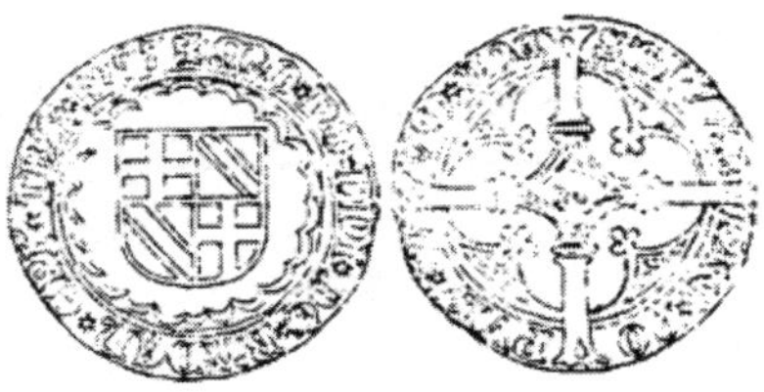

MO'*NO'*FRE'*DE:BADE:EPI:TRA':1497
Shield of Utrecht-Bade in polyfoil

SALVV-FAC:PO-PVLV:TV-VM:DN
Long cross with lion in center, all in ornate quatrefoil

Likely no longer extant. This coin differs from the previous in size and its use of the modern "7".

III-252 Utrecht Bishopric
Mint: Hasselt or Wijk-bij-Duurstede
Frederick IV of Baden, 1496-1517
1497 Duit
R5-6 *Weight unknown*
Frey —, Notes of Prof. Enno van Gelder

No photo or description is available of this coin. However, its existence was confirmed in 1977 by the reknowned Professor Enno van Gelder of the Netherlands. Likely only one or two known.

III-253 Zwolle City
Mint: Zwolle
1497 Half Plak
R3 *0.40 g*
Frey 459, Wiel A7, Van der Chijs 17.6

MONETA:NOVA:ZWOLL'
Shield of Zwolle

ANN-DNI-MCC-CC97
Long cross with shield of Zwolle in center

III-254 Zwolle City
Mint: Zwolle
1497 Quarter Plak
R4-5 *0.20 g*
Frey 460, Wiel 10, Van der Chijs 17.7

MON:NOVA:ZWOLLE'
Shield of Zwolle

AN.....M:CCCC:97
Short cross

1498

III-255 Deventer City
Mint: Deventer
Maximilian I, 1493-1517
1498 Goldgulden
R5-6 *3.32 g*
Frey 477, JFD 42, Van der Chijs 11.4, FR. 21

MONETA*DE*DA-VENT*1ꝝ98
St. Lebuinus seated, holding staff and book with small eagle shield at feet

MAXIMILIANVS*ROMANORV*REX
Imperial orb in trefoil

III-256 Frisia Governorship
Mint: Franeker
Albert of Saxony, 1498-1506
1498 Thaler
R6? *3.25g (est.)*
Frey 476, Van der Chijs 6.1

ALBERTVS:DVX:SAXONIE:GVB:FRISIE

Large shield with arms of Saxony and Frisia over flowery short cross

DEI:GRACIA:REGES:REGNAT -1498
Lions holding crowned shield with double headed eagle inside and date below

It is not entirely clear if this coin was actually struck in the year of its date or ia a later pattern.

III-257 Groningen City
Mint: Groningen
1498 Jager
R *2.34 g*
Frey 473, Puister 1.253f, Van der Chijs 13.86, Stephanik 3482

MONETA:NOVA:GRONIGENSIS
Double-headed eagle in quatrefoil with shield of Groningen placed diagonally below

CTV:SIT-NOMEN-DOMINI-BENEDI - AN:D-N:MC-CCC:X-CVIII
Inner and outer legends with stars in center

III-258 Groningen City
Mint: Groningen
1498 Stuiver
S *2.30 g*
Frey 474, 474A, Puister 1.260g, Van der Chijs 13.87-89, Stephanik 3483-84

MONE:NOVA-GRONINGENSES
Double-headed eagle with shield of Groningen placed diagonally below

ANNO-DOMIN-M:CCCC-XCVIII
Long cross with star in center

III-259a Groningen City
Mint: Groningen
1498 Kromstaart
R2 *2.10 g*
Frey —, Puister 1.214c, Van der Chijs 13.91

MONETA:NO-VA:GRONING'
Double-headed eagle with upright shield of Groningen below

ANNO:DOMINI:M:CCCC:XCVIII
Short cross with shield of Groningen at center

III-259b Groningen City
Mint: Groningen
1498 Kromstaart
R4 *2.10 g*
Frey 475, Puister 1.215a, Van der Chijs 13.90

SIT:NOMEN-DNI:BENEDIC'
Double-headed eagle with upright shield of Groningen below

ANNO:DOMINI:M:CCCC:XCVIII
Short cross with shield of Groningen in center

The obverse legend of this piece and its 1499 counterpart is an obvious engraving error since the name of Groningen appears nowhere.

III-260 Groningen City
Mint: Groningen
1498 Plak
R3 *0.50 g*
Frey —, Puister 1.223c, Van der Chijs 13.92

MON:NOV-GRONINGE
Double-headed eagle with shield of Groningen placed diagonally below

AN:O-OMI:M-CCCC-XCVIII
Long cross with eagle shield in center

III-261 Groningen City
Mint: Groningen
1498 Half Plak
R4 *0.40 g*
Frey —, Puister 1.232b, Van der Chijs 13.93

MON:NOVA-GRONINGE
Double-headed eagle with shield of Groningen placed diagonally below

ANN:DNI:M-CCCC:XCVIII
Short cross with shield of Groningen in center

III-262 Utrecht Bishopric
Mint: Hasselt or Wijk-bij-Duurstede
Frederick IV of Baden, 1496-1517
1498 Braspenning
VS *2.80 g*
Frey 478, Van der Chijs 21.7-10, De Mey Ut. 346

MONE':FREDRICI:EPI':TRAIEC'TE
Crowned and helmeted shields of Utrecht-Bade and Bade

ANNO-DOMIN-MCCCC-XCVIII
Long cross with fleur-de-lys in angles with mintmark in center of cross

---

III-263 Utrecht Bishopric
Mint: Hasselt or Wijk-bij-Duurstede
Frederick IV of Baden, 1496-1517
1498 Duit
R5-6 *Weight unknown*
Frey —, De Mey Ut. 354 note

Likely only one or two known, only in museum collections.

1499

III-264 Deventer City
Mint: Deventer
Frederick IV of Baden, 1496-1517
1499 Double Stuiver
R4 *3.50 g*
Frey 483, JFD 43, Van der Chijs 13.3-4

MONETA:NOVA:DE:DAVENTRIA
Eagle above shields of Deventer and the Oversticht, shields not interrupting legend

ANN-DOM-INI-1Ꝝ99
Eagle shield over flowery cross

III-265 Deventer City
Mint: Deventer
Frederick IV of Baden, 1496-1517
1499 Stuiver
R5 *3.15 g (est.)*
Frey 515D, JFD 44

MO'*NO'*-*DE*DAV*-ENTRIA*
Large shield dividing reverse field into three sections, small shields at bases

SANCT:LE-BUIN:1Ꝝ99
St. Lebuinus in foreground holding shield and mitre with view of city in background, small shield of Deventer below

---

III-266 Groningen City
Mint: Groningen
1499 Jager
VS *2.70 g*
Frey 485, Puister 1.253g, Van der Chijs 14.98-99, Stephanik 3485

MONETA*NOVA*GRONINGENS
Double-headed eagle in quatrefoil with shield of Groningen placed diagonally below

SIT+NO-ME'*DNI-BENED-ICTVM-AN'D-NI'*M-CCCC-XCIX
Long cross with stars in angles of cross

III-267 Groningen City
Mint: Groningen
1499 Stuiver
S *2.10-2.70 g*
Frey 486, Puister 1.260h, Van der Chijs 14.100-03, Stephanik 3486-96

MONETA:NOV-GRONINGEN'
Double-headed eagle with shield of Groningen placed diagonally below

ANNO-DNI:M-CCCC-XCIX
Long cross with star in center

III-268a Groningen City
Mint: Groningen
1499 Kromstaart
R3 *2.10 g (est.)*
Frey —, Puister 1.214d, Van der Chijs 14.104

MONETA:NO-VA:GRONIN'
Double-headed eagle with upright shield of Groningen below

ANNO:DOMIN:M:CCCC:XCIX
Short cross with shield of Groningen in center

III-268b Groningen City
Mint: Groningen
1499 Kromstaart
R3 2.30 g (est.)
Frey —, Puister 1.215b, Van der Chijs 14.105, Stephanik 3446-67

SIT:NOMEN-DNI:BENEDIC
Double-headed eagle with upright shield of Groningen below

ANNO:DOMINI:M:CCCC:XCIX
Short cross with shield of Groningen in center

III-269a Holland County
Mint: Dordrecht
Philip the Fair (Majority), 1492-1506
1499 Toison D'Argent
VS 3.40 g
Frey 487, GH 117-6, Van der Chijs 22.24-25, Stephanik 491-94

PHS+DEI+GRA+ARCID+AVS+DVX+BG+CO+HO
Crowned shield of Austria-Burgundy entirely within field over flowery cross

INICIVM+SAPIENCIE+TIMOR+DNI+ANNO+1ꝝ99
Golden fleece under two large briquets

III-269b Holland County
Mint: Dordrecht
Philip the Fair (Majority), 1492-1506
1499 Toison D'Argent
R2 3.40 g
Frey 488, GH 118-6, Van der Chijs 22.26, Stephanik 495

PHS+DEI+GRA+AR-CID+AVS+BG+C'+HO
Crowned shield of Austria-Burgundy surrounded by collar of the order of the golden fleece

INICIVM-SAPIEC-E+TIMOR-DNI+1ꝝ99
Flowery cross

III-270a Holland County
Mint: Dordrecht
Philip the Fair (Majority), 1492-1506
1499 Double Stuiver
C 3.10 g
Frey 489, GH 119-6a-b, Van der Chijs 22.27-31, Stephanik 496-504

PHS+DEI+GRA+ARCID+AVS+DVX+BG+C'+HO-
Crowned shield of Austria-Burgundy interrupting legend, all inside polyfoil

OMNIS+SPIRITVS+LAVDET+DNM+ANNO+1ꝝ99
Thick flowery short cross with mintmark in center

Struck for Philip during his lifetime.

III-270b Holland County
Mint: Dordrecht
Charles V, 1506-1555
1499 Double Stuiver
C 3.10 g
Frey 490, GH 171-6, Van der Chijs 23.43

MONET+ARCID+AVS+DVX+BG+C'+HOL'
Crowned shield of Austria-Burgundy entirely within field

OMNIS+SPIRITVS+LAVDET+DNM+ANNO+1ꝝ99
Thick flowery short cross with mintmark in center

Struck by Charles V in the name of his father after Philip's death.

III-271a Holland County
Mint: Dordrecht
Philip the Fair (Majority), 1492-1506
1499 Stuiver
C 3.06 g
Frey —, GH 120-6a-c, Van der Chijs 23.36-39, Stephanik 505-10

PHS+DEI+GRA+ARCID+AVS+DVX+BG+C'+HO
Shield of Austria-Burgundy in plain field

SIT+NOM-EN+DNI-BNEDIC-TM+1ꝝ99
Ornamented long cross in quatrefoil with mintmark in center

Struck for Philip during his lifetime.

III-271b Holland County
Mint: Dordrecht
Charles V, 1506-1555
1499 Stuiver
C 3.06 g
Frey 489A, GH 172-6, 13, Van der Chijs 23.44-48

MONET'+NOVA+ARCID+AVS+DVX+BG'+C'+HO
Crowned shield of Austria-Burgundy entirely within field

SIT+NOM-EN+DNI-BNEDIC-TM+1Ꝝ99
Ornamented long cross in quatrefoil, mintmark in center

This piece was struck after the death of Philip by Charles V, who retained the same style of coinage as his father.

III-272 Nijmegen City
Mint: Nijmegen
1499 Half Stuiver
R3 1.30 g
Frey 491, 515C, Nijmegen Museum 13, Van der Chijs 1.13

MONETA:NOVA:NOVIMAGENSI'
Lion advancing left, holding shield of Nijmegen

ANNO-DNI:M-CCCC-XCIX
Long cross with alternating lions and fleur-de-lys in angles

III-273 Nijmegen City
Mint: Nijmegen
1499 One-Eighth Stuiver
R5 Weight unknown
Frey —, Nijmegen Museum 14, De Voogt 19

MON:NOVA:NOVIMAGEN'
Double-headed eagle in shield

ANO-DNIM-___C-XCIX
Long cross with "N-O-V-A" in angles of cross

III-274 Utrecht Bishopric
Mint: Hasselt or Wijk-bij-Duurstede
Frederick IV of Baden, 1496-1517
1499 Quarter Stuiver
R3 0.90 g
Frey 492, Van der Chijs 21.11, De Mey Ut. 350, Stephanik 1886

MO'*FRED*DE*BAD*EPI*TR
Arms occupying entire field

ANNO*DOMINI*M*CCCC99
Fiery cross with rose in center

III-275 Zwolle City
Mint: Zwolle
1499 Double Stuiver
R4-5 3.30-3.56 g
Frey 484, Wiel 3, Van der Chijs 17.3

S':MICHAEL:PATO:ZWOL'
St. Michael between two gothic pillars slaying monster with shield of Zwolle below

ANNO:DOMINI:M:C:C:C:C:XCIX
Shield of Zwolle on flowery short cross

III-276 Zwolle City
Mint: Zwolle
1499 Stuiver
R5 1.60 g
Frey —, Wiel 5, Van der Chijs 16 Supp.

SANCTY:MICHAEL:PAT':ZWOL'
St. Michael slaying monster, large shield of Zwolle at left

ANNO-DNI'M-CCCC-XCIX
Long cross with shield of Zwolle at center

III-277 Zwolle City
Mint: Zwolle
1499 Half Plak
R5 0.40 g
Frey —, Wiel 8

MON:NOVA:ZWOLLE
Shield of Zwolle

ANO-DNI-MCC-CC99
Long cross with shield of Zwolle in center

1500

III-278 Deventer City
Mint: Deventer
Frederick IV of Baden, 1496-1517

1500 Double Stuiver
R4 3.00 g
Frey 523, JFD 45, Van der Chijs 13.4, Stephanik 2186

MON:NOVA-D-DAVENTRIA
Eagle above shields of Deventer and the Oversticht, shields interrupting legend

ANN-DOM-INI-1500
Eagle shield of Deventer over triple stranded long cross

III-279 Deventer City
Mint: Deventer
Frederick IV of Baden, 1496-1517
1500 Stuiver
R5 3.15 g
Frey 524, JFD 46, Van der Chijs 12.25

MO':NO-DE:DAV-ENTRIA
Trefoil containing large shield of Deventer with two small shields on sides

SCS:LEB-UIN:1500
St. Lebuinus holding staff with shields of Deventer and Oversticht below

The Netherlands national coin museum owns a piefort of this coin.

III-280 Frisia Governorship
Mint: Franeker
Albert of Saxony, 1498-1506
1500 Double Stuiver
R4-5 3.50 g
Frey 518, JMP III, 1916

GVBERNATO'-*PHRISI'*1500
Double-headed eagle over shield of Friesland

ALB'TVS*DVX*SAXO'*ZE'-BNDICTV*SIT*NOMEN*
DNI*NRI*DEI*IHV*XPI'
Short cross with inner and outer legends

III-281 Frisia Governorship
Mint: Franeker
Albert of Saxony, 1498-1506
1500 Stuiver
R3 2.20 g
Frey 516, Van der Chijs 6.5

ALB'TVS:DVX:SAXO':Z:GVBNA:PHR'
Double-headed eagle over diagonal shield

DEI:GR-ACIA:R-EGES:RE-GNANT- ANN'-DOMI-I'M:C-CCCC
Long cross

III-282 Utrecht Bishopric
Mint: Hasselt or Wijk-bij-Duurstede
Frederick IV of Baden, 1496-1517
1500 Quarter Stuiver
R4 0.90 g (est.)
Frey —, De Mey Ut. 351, Stephanik 2186

MON*FREDRICI*EPI*TRAET
Arms occupying entire field

ANNO*DOMINI*MCCCCC
Short cross with mintmark in center

REGION IV - Habsburg Hereditary Territories & Neighboring Lands

1456

IV-1a Austria Duchy
Mint: Wiener Neustadt
Friedrich III (Emperor 1452), 1440-1493
1456 Kreuzer
R3 0.76-1.04 g
Frey 91C, CNA Fa 33, Pohl 27, Szego 2L35

FRIDERIC'ºRO'ºIMPERA'
Four small shields arranged in a cross

ANNO DOMINI 1456
Elaborate monogram of Friedrich, Holy Roman Emperor, with the letters "AEIOV"

IV-1b Austria Duchy
Mint: Wiener Neustadt
Friedrich III (Emperor 1452), 1440-1493
1456 Kreuzer
R4 0.60 g
Frey 91C, CNA Fa 33 var.

FRID-ERIC-IMP-ARA
Four small shields arranged in a cross with a long cross between shields quartering legend

ANNO DOMINI 1ጸℸ6
Elaborate monogram of Friedrich, Holy Roman Emperor, with the letters "AEIOV"

IV-2 **Styria** **Duchy**
Mint: **Graz**
Friedrich III (Emperor 1452), 1440-1493
1456 **Uniface Pfennig**
R *0.32-0.58 g*
Frey 91A, CNA Fb 5a, Pohl 14, 15a, Szego 2L20

5-F-R-I-6
initials in trefoil surrounding banded shield
Uniface

The "5" is sideways, the "6" semi-upright. This is first partially dated coin using a modern "5".

1457

IV-3 **Austria** **Duchy**
Mint: **Wiener Neustadt**
Friedrich III (Emperor 1452), 1440-1493
1457 **Kreuzer**
R6 *0.89 g*
Frey —, CNA Fa 34

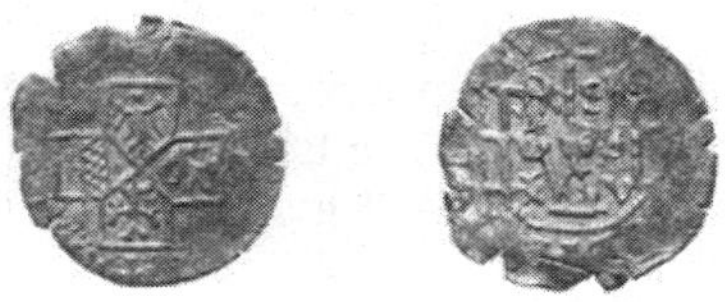

FRIDERIC':RO':IMPERA
Four small shields arranged in a cross

ANNO DOMINI 1ጸℸΛ
Elaborate monogram of Friedrich, Holy Roman Emperor, with the letters "AEIOV"

1458

IV-4 **Austria** **Duchy**
Mint: **Wiener Neustadt**
Friedrich III (Emperor 1452), 1440-1493
1458 **Kreuzer**
R2 *0.90 g*
Frey 97C, CNA Fa 35, Szego 2L35

FRIDERIC':RO':IMPERA'
Four small shields arranged in a cross

ANNO:DOMINI 1ጸ:ℸ:8:
Elaborate monogram of Friedrich, Holy Roman Emperor, with the letters "AEIOV"

IV-5a **Styria** **Duchy**
Mint: **Graz**
Friedrich III (Emperor 1452), 1440-1493
1458 **Kreuzer**
VS *0.68-0.90 g*
Frey 96, CNA Fb 6, Pohl 26, Pichler T1,#30

FRI:D:G:RO:IMPERATOR
Double-headed eagle inside shield, finely engraved with delicate lettering

MONETA:IN:GRECZ:1ጸℸ8
Four part shield with fine lettering, medieval "5"

IV-5b **Styria** **Duchy**
Mint: **Graz**
Friedrich III (Emperor 1452), 1440-1493
1458 **Kreuzer**
R3 *0.76 g*
Frey —, CNA Fb 6a

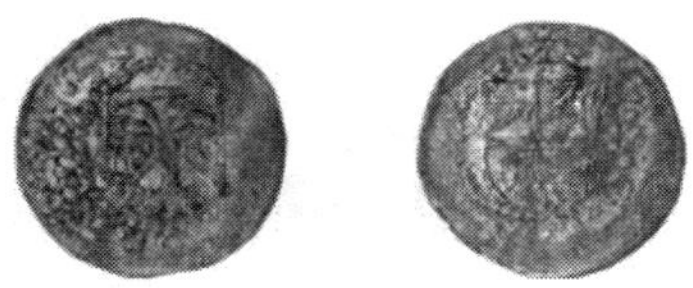

MONETA:IN:GRECZ:1ጸ58
Double-headed eagle inside shield, crude lettering and devices

FRI:D:G:R:IMPERATOR
Four part shield with crude details and lettering,

Type with a weakly struck "8" often appearing as a "3". This coin is distinguished from the previous by opposite obverse and reverse legends, the use of a modern "5" in place of a medieval "5" and by a much cruder die.

IV-5c **Styria** **Duchy**
Mint: **Graz**
Friedrich III (Emperor 1452), 1440-1493
1458 **Kreuzer**
R4 *0.68-0.90 g*
Frey —, CNA Fb 6b

FRI:D:G:R:IMPERATOR
Four part shield, crude lettering and devices

MONETA:IN:GRECZ:1ጸℸ8
Double eagle inside shield, crude lettering and devices

This coin has the legends reversed from the previous subtype.

IV-5d **Styria** **Duchy**
Mint: **Graz**
Friedrich III (Emperor 1452), 1440-1493
1458 **Kreuzer**
R5 *0.68-0.90 g*
Frey —, CNA Fb 6b var

FRI:D:G:R:IMPERATOR
Four part shield, crude lettering and devices

MONETA:IN:GRECZ: ጸℸ
Double eagle inside shield, crude lettering and devices

A variety with even cruder die features. In error, the first and last digits of the date were not engraved so the date reads as "ጸℸ". This error was misinterpreted by Frey to be a "1445" dated coin.

IV-5e **Styria** **Duchy**
Mint: **Graz**
Friedrich III (Emperor 1452), 1440-1493
1458 **Kreuzer**
R5 *0.94 g*
Frey —, CNA Fb 6c

MONETA:IN:GRECZ:1ꭗ58
Double-headed eagle inside shield, crude lettering and devices

MONETA:IN:GRECZ:1ꭗ58
Four part shield, crude lettering and devices

Highly unusual error subtype with reverse legends on both sides.

IV-6 **Styria** **Duchy**
Mint: **Graz**
Friedrich III (Emperor 1452), 1440-1493
1458 **Uniface Pfennig**
R4 *0.32-0.58 g*
Frey 97, CNA Fb 5b, Szego 2L21

5-F-R-I-8
Initials in trefoil surrounding banded shield

Both the "8" and the "5" are engraved sideways.

1459

IV-7 **Austria** **Duchy**
Mint: **Wiener Neustadt**
Friedrich III (Emperor 1452), 1440-1493
1459 **Kreuzer**
R3 *0.65-0.82 g*
Frey 99B, CNA Fa 36, Pohl 29, Szego 2L35

FRIDERIC':RO':IMPERA'
Four small shields arranged in a cross

ANNO DOMINI 1ꭗ⌉9
Elaborate monogram of Friedrich, Holy Roman Emperor, with the letters "AEIOV"

This coin, as well as the Styria and Krapina coins of the same date, represents the first time that a modern "9" was used on early dated coinage.

IV-8a **Krapina** **Barony**
Mint: **Krapina**
Jan von Vitovec, ?-1469
1459 **Kreuzer**
R5 *0.72-0.96 g*
Frey —, CNA Fb 41, Pohl p. 137

FRI'...RO:IMPERATOR
Double-headed eagle inside shield

MONETA:IN :KRAPINA:9
Four part shield of Austria

Issued by Jan von Vitovec, baron in Krapina, under the authority of Emperor Friedrich III. This is the only early dated coin struck in what is now modern-day Croatia.

IV-8b **Krapina** **Barony**
Mint: **Krapina**
Jan von Vitovec, ?-1469
1459 **Kreuzer**
R6 *0.54 g*
Unpublished?

FRI'...RO:IMPERATOR
Double-headed eagle inside shield

MONETA:IN :KRAPINA:⌉9
Four part shield of Austria

Type with two digit date. This is the only example of a single digit dated coin where the die with a single digit date is more common than the companion type with a double digit date. Sold at Lanz in 1998 to a museum.

IV-9 **Styria** **Duchy**
Mint: **Graz**
Friedrich III (Emperor 1452), 1440-1493
1459 **Uniface Pfennig**
R4 *0.32-0.58 g*
Frey 98, CNA Fb 5c, Pohl 17, Szego 2L21

5-F-R-I-9
Initials in trefoil surrounding banded shield

The "5" appears sideways.

1460

IV-10a **Austria** **Duchy**
Mint: **Vienna**
Friedrich III (Emperor 1452), 1440-1493
1460 **Pfennig**
R4 *0.36-0.60 g*
Frey 101B, CNA Fa 11, Szego 2L39

6 I 0 (at top) "F P' (on sides) and either "TW" or "W" at bottom. Initials in crude trefoil surrounding Austrian banded shield with date "60" above, divided by "I" (Imperator)

The condition of these tiny pieces is rarely strong enough for full attribution.

IV-10b **Austria** **Duchy**
Mint: **Vienna**
Friedrich III (Emperor 1452), 1440-1493
1460 **Pfennig**

R4 *0.52-0.72 g*
Frey —, CNA Fa 12, Szego 2L40

Same as preceding, but with Vienna cross shield instead of a banded cross.

IV-11 Austria Duchy
Mint: Wiener Neustadt
Friedrich III (Emperor 1452), 1440-1493
1460 Kreuzer
R4 *0.50 g*
Frey —, CNA Fa 37, Pohl 28 (Piefort), Szego 2L35

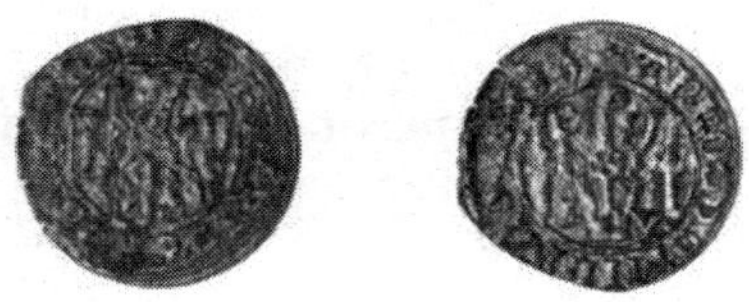

FRIDERIC':RO':IMPER'
Four small shields arranged in a cross

ANNO:DOMINI:1:ꝝ:6:0
Elaborate monogram of Friedrich, Holy Roman Emperor, with the letters "AEIOV"

This coin was also struck as a piefort. The weight of this "dickstuck," or thick (piefort) kreuzer is 4.48g versus .5 for the normal struck piece.

IV-12 Tyrol County
Mint: Meran
Sigismund, 1439-1490
1460 Kreuzer
R2 *0.90 g*
Frey —, CNA J45, 40-43, Morosini 74

SI-GIS-MVN-DVS
Long cross intersecting diagonal short cross

COMES:60:TIROL

Crowned eagle facing left.

IV-13 Styria Duchy
Mint: Graz
Friedrich III (Emperor 1452), 1440-1493
146? Groschen
R5 *1.94 g*
Frey —, CNA Fb 7

FRI:D:G:ROM:IMPERAT
Crowned double-headed eagle

GROSVS:IN:M:GREC3 14:6:
Stylized panther advancing left

The last digit on this very unusual coin was never engraved. Being of the same weight as the achters dated 1467 on, it appears stylistically that this coin was struck between 1460-1466.

IV-14 Styria Duchy
Mint: Graz
Friedrich III (Emperor 1452), 1440-1493
146? Kreuzer
R5 *1.22 g*
Frey —, CNA Fb 8

FRI:D:G:RO:___RATO
Double-headed eagle
MON: IN :M:GRECZ:1:4:6
Stylized panther advancing left

The last digit was never engraved. Given the style of this coin, it appears to have been struck between 1460-1466.

1467

IV-15 Austria Duchy
Mint: Vienna
Friedrich III (Emperor 1452), 1440-1493
1467 Kreuzer
R2 *0.90 g*
Frey 124, CNA Fa 15, Pohl 49, Szego 2L58

FRIDERICV:IMPER'
Double-headed eagle

A-EI-OV:1ꝝ6Λ
Double cross

IV-16 Styria Duchy
Mint: Graz
Friedrich III (Emperor 1452), 1440-1493
1467 Sechzehner
R3 *3.82 g*
Frey 123, CNA Fb 10, Saurma 718

FRI:D:G:ROMANORVM:IMPERA
Double-headed eagle with rosette between heads

GROSSVS:IN:GEC:ANNO:1:ꝝ:6:7
Conjoined shields of Old Austria, New Austria, Styria, Kärnten and Krain with letters "AEIOV" in center

IV-17 **Styria** **Duchy**
Mint: **Graz**
Friedrich III (Emperor 1452), 1440-1493
1467 **Achter**
R2 *1.92 g*
Frey 123A, CNA Fb 14, Pichler P. 112, No. 3 (note)

FRI:D:G:ROM:IMPER'
Double-headed eagle

MONETA:IN:G:1ꝝ6Λ
Conjoined shields of Old Austria, Styria and Kärnten

1468

IV-18 **Austria** **Duchy**
Mint: **Vienna**
Friedrich III (Emperor 1452), 1440-1493
1468 **Kreuzer**
R2 *0.80 g*
Frey 128, CNA Fa 16, Pohl 49, Szego 2L58

FRIDERICV':IMPER'
Double-headed eagle

A-EI-OV-1ꝝ68
Double cross

IV-19 **Styria** **Duchy**
Mint: **Graz**
Friedrich III (Emperor 1452), 1440-1493
1468 **Achter**
R *1.62-1.98 g*
Frey 128A, CNA Fb 15, Pichler P. 112, #2

FRI:D:G:ROMA:IMPER'
Double-headed eagle

MONETA:IN:G:1ꝝ68
Conjoined shields of old Austria, Styria and Kärnten

1469

IV-20 **Styria** **Duchy**
Mint: **Graz**
Friedrich III (Emperor 1452), 1440-1493
1469 **Sechzehner**
R3 *3.40-3.72 g*
Frey 133, CNA Fb 11, Pichler P. 112, #3

FRI:D:G:ROMANORVM:IMPERA:
Double-headed eagle with rosette between heads

GROSSVS:IN:GEC:ANNO:1:ꝝ:6:9
Conjoined shields of Old Austria, New Austria, Styria, Kärnten and Krain with letters "AEIOV" in center

1470

IV-21 **Austria** **Duchy**
Mint: **Wiener Neustadt**
Friedrich III (Emperor 1452), 1440-1493
1470 **Kreuzer**
C *0.90 g*
Frey 135, CNA Fa 45, Pohl 42, Szego 2L51

FRIDIC':ROMAN'*IP':
Double-headed eagle

MON-NOV'-CIV'-1ꝝΛ0
Double cross

IV-22 **Styria** **Duchy**
Mint: **Graz**
Friedrich III (Emperor 1452), 1440-1493
1470 **Sechzehner**
R3 *3.38-3.70 g*
Frey 134, CNA Fb 12, Pichler P. 112, #5

FRI:D:G:ROMANORVM:IMPERA:
Double-headed eagle with rosette between heads

GROSSVS:IN:GEC:ANNO:1ꝝΛ0
Conjoined shields of Old Austria, New Austria, Styria, Kärnten and Krain with letters "AEIOV" in center

---

IV-23 **Styria** **Duchy**
Mint: **Graz**
Friedrich III (Emperor 1452), 1440-1493
1470? **Achter**
R? *1.80 g*
Frey 134A, CNA–

FRI:D:G:ROM:IMPERA
Double-headed eagle

MONETA-IN:G:1ꝝΛ0
Conjoined shields of old Austria, Styria and Kärnten

The last digit on this coin is very weak, and a strong strike of the "0" has not been seen by the author.

1471

IV-24 Austria Duchy
Mint: Wiener Neustadt
Friedrich III (Emperor 1452), 1440-1493
1471 Kreuzer
C *0.69-0.98 g*
Frey 140, CNA Fa 46, Pohl 42a, Szego 2L51

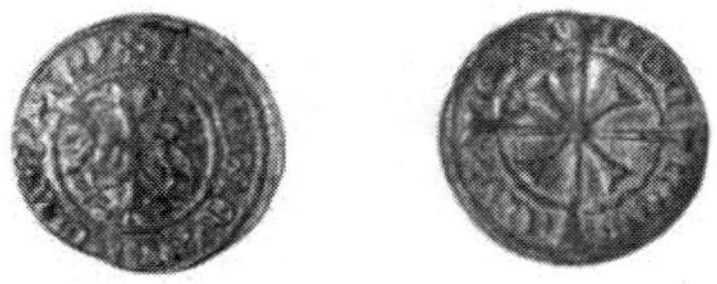

FRIDRIC'ROMAN'*IP'
Double-headed eagle

MON-NOV'-CIV'-1ꝝΛ1
Double cross

IV-25 Styria Duchy
Mint: Graz
Friedrich III (Emperor 1452), 1440-1493
1471 Sechzehner
R2 *3.78 g*
Frey 139, CNA Fb 13, Pichler P. 112, #6, Saurma 719

FRI:DEI:GRA:ROMANORVM:IMPE:
Double-headed eagle with rosette between heads

GROSSVS:IN:GEC:ANNO:1ꝝΛ1
Conjoined shields of Old Austria, New Austria, Styria, Kärnten and Krain with letters "AEIOV" in center

The obverse legend uses a ꝝ punch as the letter "R" in the abbreviation "GRA".

IV-26 Styria Duchy
Mint: Graz
Friedrich III (Emperor 1452), 1440-1493
1471 Achter
R2 *1.80 g*
Frey 139A, CNA Fb 17, Pichler P. 113, #10

FRI:D:G:ROMA:IMPE':RA:
Double-headed eagle

MONETA:I-N:G':1ꝝΛ1
Conjoined shields of Austria, Styria and Kärnten

1472

IV-27 Austria Duchy
Mint: Wiener Neustadt
Friedrich III (Emperor 1452), 1440-1493
1472 Kreuzer
R3 *0.80 g*
Frey 144, CNA Fa 47, Pohl 43, Szego 2L51

FRIDRIC'ROMAN':*P':
Double-headed eagle

MON-NOV'-CIV'1ꝝΛ2
Double cross

IV-28 Styria Duchy
Mint: Graz
Friedrich III (Emperor 1452), 1440-1493
1472 Achter
R2 *1.73 g*
Frey 145, CNA Fb 18, Pichler P. 113, #13, 14, Saurma 720

FRI:D:G:ROMA:IMPER':
Double-headed eagle

MONETA:IN:G:1ꝝΛ2
Conjoined shields of Austria, Styria and Kärnten

1473

IV-29 Styria Duchy
Mint: Graz
Friedrich III (Emperor 1452), 1440-1493
1473 Achter
R3 *1.60 g*
Frey —, CNA Fb 19, Pichler P. 114, #15

FRI:D:G:ROMA:IMPERA'
Double-headed eagle

MONETA-IN:G:1ꝝΛ3
Conjoined shields of Austria, Styria and Kärnten

The letter "R" in "IMPERA" is made from a "ꝝ" punch.

1474

IV-30 **Austria** **Duchy**
Mint: **Vienna**
Friedrich III (Emperor 1452), 1440-1493
1474 **Pfennig**
R6 *0.58 g*
Frey 160E, CNA Fa 17, Pohl 48, Szego 2L57

Λꝸ
Shield between date with letter "W" above

This likely unique coin is not fully struck so the details are minimal.

IV-A30 **Styria** **Duchy**
Mint: **Graz**
Friedrich III (Emperor 1452), 1440-1493
1474 **Achter**
R6 *1.75 g*
Unpublished ?

FRI:D:G:ROMA:IMPER':
Double-headed eagle

MONETA:IN:G:1- -ꝸ
Conjoined shields of Austria, Styria and Kärnten

Unique coin located at the State Museum of Berlin.

1477

IV-31 **Görz** **County**
Mint: **Lienz**
Leonhard, 1462-1500
1477 **Kreuzer**
R3 *0.90 g*
Frey 180, CNA K 41a

LEONH:COM:GORICI
Shield of Görz

MON-NOV-LVE'-1ꝸ77
Double cross

An overdate of 1477/79 is known.

1478

IV-32a **Görz** **County**
Mint: **Lienz**
Leonhard, 1462-1500
1478 **Kreuzer**
R *0.90 g*
Frey —, CNA K 41b, CNI 9v, M-T 540

LEONH:COM:GORICI
Shield of Görz

MON-NOV-LVE'-1ꝸΛ8
Double cross

A piefort is reported of 7.86 g. See CNA p.373. The "7" in the date is sometimes engraved as a sideways "V".

IV-32b **Görz** **County**
Mint: **Lienz**
Leonhard, 1462-1500
1478 **Kreuzer**
R3 *0.90 g*
Frey —, CNA K 41b var.

Same as preceding, but with modern 7 in the date

1479

IV-33 **Görz** **County**
Mint: **Lienz**
Leonhard, 1462-1500
1479 **Kreuzer**
R3 *0.90 g*
Frey —, CNA K 41c, CNI VI

LEONH:COM:GORICI
Shield of Görz

MON-NOV-LVE'-1ꝸ79
Double cross

1480

IV-34a **Styria** **Duchy**
Mint: **Graz**
Friedrich III (Emperor 1452), 1440-1493
1480 **Kreuzer**
R3 *0.90 g*
Frey 221, CNA Fb 23, Schulten 4069

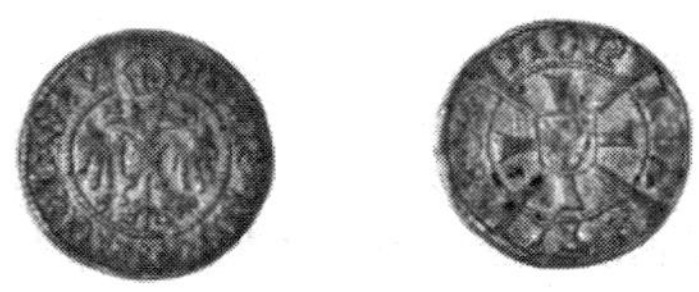

FR':R:IMP:A:E:I:O:V
Crowned double-headed eagle

MON-NOV-STI-*8:C*
Double cross with legend in angles of cross and panther shield in center

The date on this type is shown as either "8 * C" or *8C.* with the "0" in both cases being struck unclosed similar to the letter "C." Almost all pieces sold as a 1480 are misindentified 1489's, such as the coin pictured in Frey, where the "9," with a tiny tail, appears flattened.

IV-34b **Styria** **Duchy**
Mint: **Graz**
Friedrich III (Emperor 1452), 1440-1493
1480 **Kreuzer**
R5 *0.90 g*
Unpublished?

Same, but with a backwards "C" representing the "0"

Likely only two specimens known, one in author's collection.

1481

IV-35 **Austria** **Duchy**
Mint: **Vienna**
Friedrich III (Emperor 1452), 1440-1493
1481 **Groschen**
R4 *2.56 g*
Frey —, CNA Fa 21, Pohl 54, Szego 2L65

FRIDERIC':RO:IMPAT':A:E:I:O:V
Crowned double-headed eagle

NOVVS:GROSSVS:AVSTRIE:1481
Four shields forming a cross inside quatrefoil

IV-36 **Austria** **Duchy**
Mint: **Vienna**
Friedrich III (Emperor 1452), 1440-1493
1481 **Kreuzer**
R2 *1.00 g*
Frey 223, 229, CNA Fa 23, Pohl 52, Szego 2L62, Schulten 4068

FRID':RO':IMP':AEIOV
Crowned double-headed eagle

MONE:NOVA:AVST':81
Short cross with four shields in angles of cross

1482

IV-37 **Austria** **Duchy**
Mint: **Vienna**
Friedrich III (Emperor 1452), 1440-1493
1482 **Groschen**
R6 *Weight unknown*
Frey —, CNA Fa 22

FRIDERIC':RO:IMPAT:A:E:I:O:V
Crowned double-headed eagle

NOVVS:GROSSVS:AVSTRIE:1482
Four small shields of Austria, Styria, Krain and Kärnten inside a quatrefoil, forming a cross

IV-38 **Austria** **Duchy**
Mint: **Vienna**
Friedrich III (Emperor 1452), 1440-1493
1482 **Kreuzer**
S *0.90 g*
Frey 244A, CNA Fa 24, Szego 2L63, Schulten 4067

FR:R:INP:A:E:I:O:V
Crowned double-headed eagle

MO'-NOV-AVS-*8Z*
Double cross with banded shield of Austria in center

IV-39 **Styria** **Duchy**
Mint: **Graz**
Friedrich III (Emperor 1452), 1440-1493
1482 **Kreuzer**
C *1.00 g*
Frey 238, CNA Fb 22, Schulten 4069

FR':R:IMP:A:E:I:O:V
Crowned double-headed eagle

MON-NOV-STI-*8Z*
Double cross with legend in angles of cross and panther shield in center

1483

IV-40 **Austria** **Duchy**
Mint: **Vienna**
Friedrich III (Emperor 1452), 1440-1493
1483 **Kreuzer**
S *0.90 g*
Frey 253B, CNA Fa 25, Szego 2L63

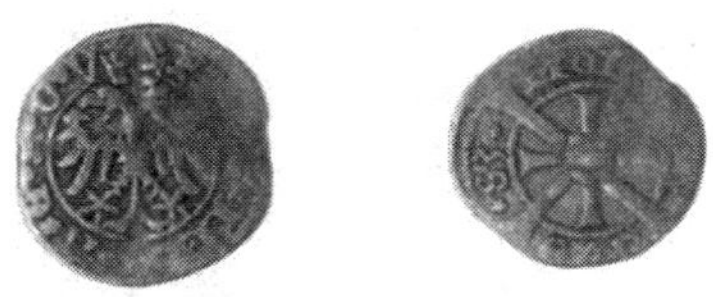

FR:R:IMP:A:E:I:O:V
Crowned double-headed eagle

MO'-NOV-AVS-*83*
Double cross with banded shield of Austria in center

IV-41 **Styria** **Duchy**
Mint: **Graz**
Friedrich III (Emperor 1452), 1440-1493
1483 **Kreuzer**
VS *0.90 g*
Frey 252, 253C, D, CNA Fb 24

FR':R:IMP:A:E:I:O:V
Crowned double-headed eagle

MON-NOV-STI-*8*3*
Double cross with legend in angles of cross and panther shield in center

1484

IV-42 Austria Duchy
Mint: Vienna
Friedrich III (Emperor 1452), 1440-1493
1484 Kreuzer
R 0.90 g
Frey —, CNA Fa 26, Szego 2L63, Schulten 4067

FR:R:IMP:A:E:I:O:V
Crowned double-headed eagle

MO'-NOV-AVS-*8Ꭿ*
Double cross with banded shield of Austria in center

IV-43a Styria Duchy
Mint: Graz
Friedrich III (Emperor 1452), 1440-1493
1484 Kreuzer
R 0.90 g
Frey 263, 265B, CNA Fb 25, Schulten 4069

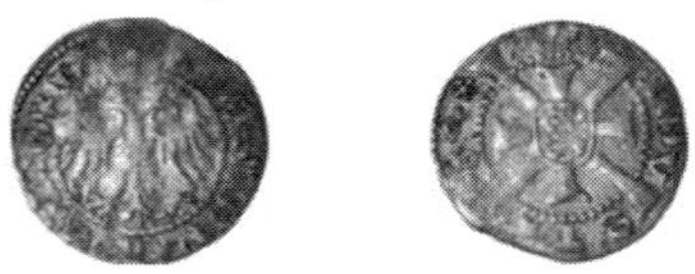

FR':R:IMP:A:E:I:O:V
Crowned double-headed eagle

MON-NOV-STI-*84*
Double cross with legend in angles of cross and panther shield in center

---

IV-43b Styria Duchy
Mint: Graz
Friedrich III (Emperor 1452), 1440-1493
1484 Kreuzer
R 0.90 g
Frey —, CNA Fb 25 var.a

Same as preceding, but with the date shown as "8Ꭿ."

IV-43c Styria Duchy
Mint: Graz
Friedrich III (Emperor 1452), 1440-1493
1484 Kreuzer
R 0.90 g
Frey —, CNA Fb 25a (1)

Same as preceding, but with a backwards 4 in the date

IV-44 Tyrol County
Mint: Hall
Sigismund, 1439-1490
1484 Dick Half Guldiner
R4 31.70 g
Frey 260, M.D. 80-82, Schulten 4422

SIGISMVNDVS*ARCHIDVX*AVSTRIE*
Crowned half-length figure of the Archduke facing right and holding staff

1484
Knight on horseback galloping right, 14 shields circling field, with date below

A coin of guldiner weight struck on a half guldiner planchet with weight of 30.55 - 31.92 gr. as opposed to the normal half guldiner weight of 15.09 - 16.18 gr., as catalogued by Moeser-Dworschak.

IV-45a Tyrol County
Mint: Hall
Sigismund, 1439-1490
1484 Half Guldiner
R 15.60 g
Frey 261, M.D. 65-79, Schulten 4425

SIGISMVNDVS*ARCHIDVX*AVSTRIE*
Crowned half-length figure of the Archduke facing right and holding staff

1484
Knight on horseback galloping right, 14 shields circling field, with small date below

---

IV-45b Tyrol County
Mint: Hall
Sigismund, 1439-1490
1484 Half Guldiner
R3-4 15.60 g
Frey —, M.D. 62-64, Schulten 4425

Same as preceding, but with a very large date and a scarf on the back of the knight's helmet.

1485

IV-46 Austria Duchy
Mint: Vienna
Friedrich III (Emperor 1452), 1440-1493
1485 Kreuzer
S *1.00-1.50 g*
Frey 273B, CNA Fa 27, Szego 2L64, Schulten 4067

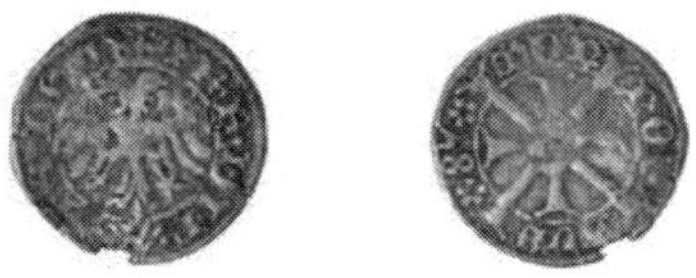

FR:R:IMP:AEIOV
Crowned double-headed eagle

MON-NOV-AVS-* 8 ㄱ*
Double cross with banded shield of Austria in center

The lack of spacing between the motto AEIOV is highly unusual.

IV-47 Styria Duchy
Mint: Graz
Friedrich III (Emperor 1452), 1440-1493
1485 Kreuzer
VS *1.10 g*
Frey —, CNA Fb 26, Schulten 4069

FR'R:IMP'A:E:I:O:V
Crowned double-headed eagle

MON-NOV-STI-*8* ㄱ
Double cross with legend in angles of cross and panther shield in center

1486

IV-48a Styria Duchy
Mint: Graz
Friedrich III (Emperor 1452), 1440-1493
1486 Kreuzer
R *1.10 g*
Frey 275, 277, CNA Fb 27, Schulten 4069

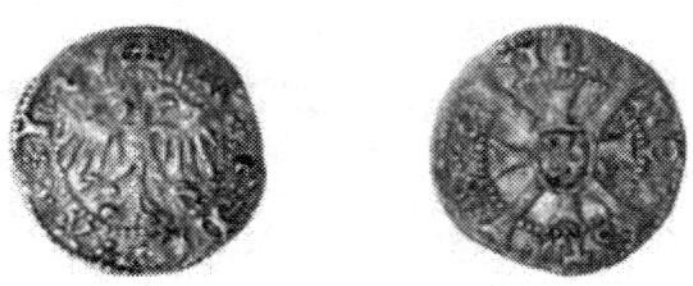

FR'R:IMP'A:E:I:O:V
Crowned double-headed eagle

MON-NOV-STI-*8*6*
Double cross with legend in angles of cross and panther shield in center

---

IV-48b Styria Duchy
Mint: Graz
Friedrich III (Emperor 1452), 1440-1493
1486 Kreuzer
R3 *1.00 g*
Frey —, CNA Fb 27a

Same as preceding, but with backwards "6" in the date

IV-49a Tyrol County
Mint: Hall
Sigismund, 1439-1490
1486 Guldiner
VS *31.60 g*
Frey 274, M.D. 86-97, Davenport 8087

SIGISMVNDVS*-ARCHIDVX AVSTRIE
Full length, front-facing figure of the Archduke, holding sword and septer, helmet and designs in field with inner obverse border

1486
Knight on horseback galloping right surrounded by 16 small shields, small date below

Although often listed as rare or very rare, this subtype of the first dated thaler is one of the more common early dated coins to appear at auctions, averaging 5 -7 or more appearences each year. However, its popularity cannot be underestimated. There exists a posthumous striking from a die engraved by a different mintmaster with the shield of Austria-Enns reversed, for which three examples are extant, the last to sell at a Swiss Bank Corporation auction in 1997 for $14,500.

IV-49b Tyrol County
Mint: Hall
Sigismund, 1439-1490
1486 Guldiner
R3 *31.60 g*
Frey —, M.D. 84-85, Davenport 8086

SIGISMVNDVS*-ARCHIDVX AVSTRIE
Full length 3/4 facing figure of the Archduke, holding sword and septer, helmet, designs in field with no inner border

1486
Knight on horseback galloping right surrounded by 16 small shields, very large date below and scarf on knight's helmet.

It is from this die that gold strikes of 7 ducat weight were made, but all after 1500.

IV-49c **Tyrol** **County**
Mint: **Hall**
Sigismund, 1439-1490
1486 **Guldiner**
R5 *31.36 g*
Frey —, M.D. 83, Davenport 8085

Same as preceding, but on obverse archduke is facing front, there are no designs in the field, while on reverse there are fourteen shields and a small date

1487

IV-50 **Styria** **Duchy**
Mint: **Graz**
Friedrich III (Emperor 1452), 1440-1493
1487 **Goldgulden**
R6 *3.22 g*
Frey —, CNA Fb 21a

FRIDER'*87-RO'*IMP'
Standing emperor holding sceptre and imperial orb

MONE'*NOVA*AVREA*STIRIE
Flowery cross with four shields in angles of cross

Unique example in Landesmuseum Joanneum in Graz.

IV-51a **Styria** **Duchy**
Mint: **Graz**
Friedrich III (Emperor 1452), 1440-1493
1487 **Kreuzer**
R3 *0.90 g*
Frey 291, CNA Fb 28, Schulten 4069

FR':R:IMP:A:E:I:O:V
Crowned double-headed eagle

MON-NOV-STI-*8>*
Double cross with legend in angles of cross and panther shield in center

The digit "7" is engraved as a sideways "V".

IV-51b **Styria** **Duchy**
Mint: **Graz**
Friedrich III (Emperor 1452), 1440-1493
1487 **Kreuzer**
R2 *0.90 g*
Frey —, CNA Fb 28 var.

Same as preceding, but with a backwards "7" in the date: "8<"

IV-51c **Styria** **Duchy**
Mint: **Graz**
Friedrich III (Emperor 1452), 1440-1493
1487 **Kreuzer**
R5 *1.00 g*
Unpublished?

Same as preceding, but with
"7" in the date engraved as "V": "8V"

1488

IV-52 **Styria** **Duchy**
Mint: **Graz**
Friedrich III (Emperor 1452), 1440-1493
1488 **Kreuzer**
R *0.90 g*
Frey 320, CNA Fb 29, Schulten 4066

FR':R:IMP:A:E:I:O:V
Crowned double-headed eagle

MON-NOV-STI-*88*
Double cross with legend in angles of cross and panther shield in center

An overdate of 1488/4 is known.

1489

IV-53 **Styria** **Duchy**
Mint: **Graz**
Friedrich III (Emperor 1452), 1440-1493
1489 **Kreuzer**
S *0.90 g*
Frey 327, 328, CNA Fb 30, Schulten 4069

FRI':R:IMP:A:E:I:O:V
Crowned double-headed eagle

MON-NOV-STI-:*89*
Double cross with legend in angles of cross and panther shield in center

1490

IV-54	**Styria**	**Duchy**
	Mint:	**Graz**
	Friedrich III (Emperor 1452), 1440-1493	
	1490	**Kreuzer**
R		*0.80 g*

Frey 344, 347, CNA Fb 31, Schulten 4069

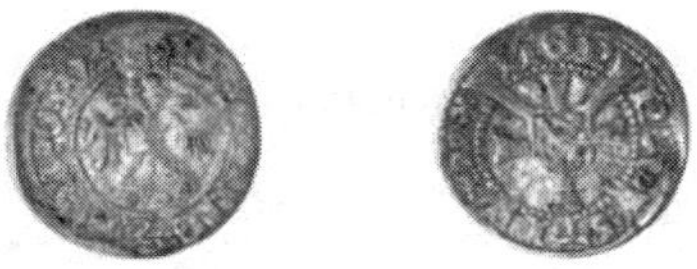

FRI':R:IMP:A:E:I:O:V
Crowned double-headed eagle

MON-NOV-STI-*90*
Double cross with legend in angles of cross and panther shield in center

The "0" in the date is very tiny.

1491

IV-55	**Styria**	**Duchy**
	Mint:	**Graz**
	Friedrich III (Emperor 1452), 1440-1493	
	1491	**Kreuzer**
R-R2		*0.90 g*

Frey 365, 366B, CNA Fb 32

FRI':R:IMP:A:E:I:O:V
Crowned double-headed eagle

MON-NOV-STI-*91*
Double cross with legend in angles of cross and panther shield in center

1493

IV-56	**Styria**	**Duchy**
	Mint:	**Graz**
	Friedrich III (Emperor 1452), 1440-1493	
	1493	**Kreuzer**
R3		*0.90 g*

Frey 402, CNA Fb 33

FRI':R:IMP:A:E:I:O:V
Crowned double-headed eagle

MON-NOV-STI-*93*
Double cross with legend in angles of cross and panther shield in center

1495

IV-57	**Tyrol**	**County**
	Mint:	**Hall**
	Maximilian I, 1493-1519	
	1495	**Königsguldiner**
R5		*3.20 g*

Frey —, Egg 1, Davenport 8001, Schulten 4440

MAXIMILIANºROMA'ºREXºSEMPERºAVGVST:1-495
Half-length figure of Maximilian as Holy Roman Emperor facing right, holding sword and imperial orb

(No legend)
Large Habsburg eagle with two shields on breast, 20 shields in circle around field

1498

IV-58	**Görz**	**County**
	Mint:	**Lienz**
	Leonhard, 1462-1500	
	1498	**Triple Kreuzer**
R5		*1.60 g*

Frey —, CNA K 43, CNI VI,S63,#1, M-T 545, Schulten 3940

LEON • COM • GORI • ET • TIR
Realistic bare-headed bust of Count facing right

MON • -NOVA-PALA-CORI- 1ꝶ-98
Long cross with shields of Görz and Tyrol below, divided date above

An extremely fine specimen of this coin sold in 1998 at Hess-Divo for $20,000.

1499

IV-59	**Hungary**	**Kingdom**
	Mint:	**Kremnitz**
	Wladislaw II, 1490-1516	
	1499	**Thaler**
R4		*Weight Unknown*

Frey 503, Huszár 793, CNH 266, Davenport 8249 , Egg p. 100

MONETA*WLADISLAI*REGIS*VNGARIE*
Ornamented shield

LADISLVS*REX-*SANCTVS-1ºꝶº9º9
St. Ladislaus on horseback

This coin was also struck in gold from the thaler dies. See Huszár 739 and CNH 266.

1500

IV-60 Hungary Kingdom
Mint: Kremnitz
Wladislaw II, 1490-1516
1500 Thaler
R4 *11.50-58.50 g*
Frey 540, Huszár 794, CNH 267 A-B, Davenport 8250-51

MONETA*WLADISLAI *D*G*REGIS*VNGARIE*1500
Large shield of Hungary with ornaments above, "Kremitz" at left and "Tvrso" at right

SANCTVS*-*LADISLAVS*REX*VNGARIE
St. Ladislaus on horseback, facing left, small Madonna and shield above, border of lilies

Gold strikes from this die have been reported. See Huszár 739 and CNH 267. Piefort with a weight of 58.50 g are also known.

IV-61 Hungary Kingdom
Mint: Kremnitz
Wladislaw II, 1490-1516
1500 Pattern Silver Gulden
R6 *14.80 g*
Frey —, CNH. 286, Huszár 824

WLADISLAVD:G:REX-VNGARIE:ET:BOHEMIE
Crowned Madonna in field of rays

SANCTVS LADIS-LAVS REX-15-00
Crowned St. Ladislaus holding orb and battleaxe with shields at sides and date in field

---

IV-62 Salzburg Archbishopric
Mint: Salzburg
Leonhard von Keutschach, 1495-1519
1500 Ducat
R2 *3.45 g*
Frey —, Probzst 64, FR. 579, Schulten 4234

LEONARD9D+G+ARCHIEPI+SAL-1500
Shield of Salzburg in quatrefoil with date above shield

SANCT9:RV-DBERT9EPS
St. Rupert above radish shield of family Keutschach

An extremely rare variety exists without the initials "D.G".

IV-63 Salzburg Archbishopric
Mint: Salzburg
Leonhard von Keutschach, 1495-1519
1500 Goldgulden
R *3.25 g*
Frey 520, Probzst 77, FR. 580, Schulten 4235

LEONARD9:ARCHIEPI:SALZE-1500
Date above four-part shield

SANCT9R-VDBERT':EPS
St. Rupert above radish shield of family Keutschach

IV-64 Salzburg Archbishopric
Mint: Salzburg
Leonhard von Keutschach, 1495-1519
1500 Batzen
C *3.20 g*
Frey 534, Probzst 99, Schulten 4255

LEONARD9:ARCHIEPI:SALCZ-1500
Conjoined shields of Salzburg and Family Keutschach with date above

SANCT9:RVDBERTVS:EPVS
Half-length figure of St. Rupert

This same coin was struck as a piefort of 13.56 g (Probszt 100/Schulten 4257) and in gold (Schulten 4256). The illustration is of the unique piefort (Auction H.D. Rauch 2006)

IV-65 Salzburg Archbishopric
Mint: Salzburg
Leonhard von Keutschach, 1495-1519
1500 Uniface Pfennig
S *0.36 g*
Frey —, Probzst 125, Schulten 4260

1500 - L
Date above joint shields, "L" below

IV-66 Salzburg Archbishopric
Mint: Salzburg
Leonhard von Keutschach, 1495-1519
1500 Heller
R2 *0.28 g*
Frey —, Probzst 138, Schulten 4262

1500
Date above radish shield in quatrefoil

Shield in quatrefoil

REGION V - Switzerland

1424

V-1 **St. Gallen** **City**
Mint: **St. Gallen**
1424 **Plappart**
R4 *1.85 g*
Frey N27, Frey 21, Ilke 275, HMZ 714, Coll. Swiss 2, 1381-82

MONETA:NOVA:SANT:GALLI
Shield on floriated cross inside quatrefoil

SANTTVS:GAL-LVS:1ꝝ2ꝝ
St. Gall standing with club striking bear

This is the first coin with a modern Arabic-numeral date. Types exist with a large and small bear.

1477

V-2a **Lausanne** **Bishopric**
Mint: **Lausanne**
Benoit of Montferrand, 1476-1491
1477 **Parpaiolles**
R5-6 *2.58 g*
Frey —, Dolivo 69, HMZ 986

MOGEFERRANDO EPS LAVS ETC-1-4-7-7
Cross in quatrefoil with date in angles

REGINA CELI LETARE ALLE
Madonna and Child seated behind very large shield of Montferrand, all within field

The earliest examples of the modern "4" are found on these parpaiolles.

V-2b **Lausanne** **Bishopric**
Mint: **Lausanne**
Benoit of Montferrand, 1476-1491
1477 **Parpaiolles**
R6 *Weight unknown*
Frey —, Dolivo 70

Same as preceding, but reverse shield is tiny and interrupts legend

In the Schweizerisches Landesmuseum in Zürich.

1484

V-3 **Lucerne** **City**
Mint: **Lucerne**
1484 **Spagürli**
R6 *0.73 g*
Frey —, Wielandt 25, HMZ 589

LVCERNENSIS + 8ꝝ
Shield of Lucerne in trefoil

MONETA NOVA +
Flowery short cross

Also known as three heller. Unique example located in the Swiss Landesmuseum in Zürich. Two different obverse dies exist, even though only one extant coin is known.

1488

V-4 **Chur** **Bishopric**
Mint: **Chur**
Orlieb of Brandis, 1458-1491
1488 **Plappart**
R6 *2.15 g*
Frey —, HMZ 388, Museum Chur p. 38-39

MONE-T'EPI - CVRI-ENIS
Four part shield on long cross

AVE*REGI - NA:CELORV - 88
Madonna and Child

Also known as half batzen. This unique piece is found in the museum of the Castle of Szoresco in Milan.

1491

V-5 **Basel** **City and Imperial mint**
Mint: **Basel**
Friedrich III, 1452-1493
1491 **Goldgulden**
R2 *3.25 g*
Frey 356, Winterstein 190-93, Ewig 1, HMZ 58, FR. 11, De Mey d'Or 279, Coll. Swiss 1, 543

MONETA-BASILI:1ꝝ91
Madonna and Child standing, shield of Weinsberg at feet

FRIDRICVS:ROMANO':IMP
Imperial orb in trefoil

1492

V-6 **Basel** **City and Imperial mint**
Mint: **Basel**
Friedrich III, 1452-1493
1492 **Goldgulden**
R2 *3.25 g*
Frey 370, Winterstein 194-96, Ewig 3, HMZ 58, FR. 11, De Mey d'Or 279, Coll. Swiss 1, 544-45

MONETA-BASIL':1ᴧ92
Madonna and Child standing, shield of Weinsberg at feet

FRIDRICVS:ROMANO':IMPR'
Imperial orb in trefoil

A single piece with slightly different lettering is known.

V-7 **Bern** **City**
Mint: **Bern**
1492 **4 Goldgulden**
R4 *13.40 g*
Frey —, Geiger 38c, FR. 92, De Mey d'Or 315, Coll. Swiss 1, 354

MONETA:NO:BERNENSIS
Shield of Bern between letters "B" and "E", eagle above

SºVINCEN-NCIVS 1492
Saint Vincent holding quill pen

Struck from dicken dies with a weight of 13.35 gr. Choice examples of the coin have sold for in excess of $20,000.

V-8 **Bern** **City**
Mint: **Bern**
1492 **3 Goldgulden**
R5 *9.96 g*
Frey —, Geiger 38b, FR. 93, De Mey d'Or 316,

MONETA:NO:BERNENSIS
Shield of Bern between letters "B" and "E", eagle above

SºVINCEN-NCIVS 1492
Saint Vincent holding quill pen

Struck from dicken dies.

V-9 **Bern** **City**
Mint: **Bern**
1492 **2 Goldgulden**
R5 *6.60 g (est.)*
Frey —, FR. 94, De Mey d'Or 317

MONETA:NO:BERNENSIS
Shield of Bern between letters "B" and "E", eagle above

SºVINCEN-NCIVS 1492
Saint Vincent holding quill pen

Struck from dicken dies.

V-10 **Bern** **City**
Mint: **Bern**
1492 **Double Dicken**
R5 *14.01 g*
Frey —, Geiger 39, Lohner 262, Coll. Swiss 1, 355

MONETA:NO:BERNENSIS
Shield of Bern between letters "B" and "E", eagle above

SºVINCEN-NCIVS 1492
Saint Vincent holding quill pen

The dicken weight was slightly over 7 gr. The double dicken had a weight of 14.01 gr. A heavy double dicken with a weight of 18.87 gr, listed as likely unique, was sold by Leu in 2001.

V-11 **Bern** **City**
Mint: **Bern**
1492 **Dicken of 1/3 Gulden Weight**
R4 *9.50 g*
Frey —, Geiger 40, Lohner 340, HMZ 164, Coll. Swiss 1, 353

MONETA:NO:BERNENSIS
Shield of Bern between letters "B" and "E", eagle above

SºVINCEN-NCIVS 1492
Saint Vincent holding quill pen

V-12 **Bern** **City**
Mint: **Bern**
1492 **Dicken of 1/4 Gulden Weight**
R2 *7.32 g*
Frey 369, Geiger 38, Lohner 341, HMZ 164, Coll. Swiss 1, 352, Saurma 1764

MONETA:NO:BERNENSIS
Shield of Bern between letters "B" and "E", eagle above

SºVINCEN-NCIVS 1492
Saint Vincent holding quill pen

1493

V-13 **Basel** **City and Imperial mint**
Mint: **Basel**
Friedrich III, 1452-1493
1493 **Goldgulden**
R2 *3.15 g*
Frey —, Winterstein 197-206, Ewig 4, HMZ 58, FR. 11, De Mey d'Or 279, Coll. Swiss 1, 546

MONETA'-BASIL':1ᛟ93
Madonna and Child standing, shield of Weinsberg at feet

FRIDRICVS:ROMANO':IMP
Imperial orb in trefoil

Issued in the name of Friedrich

V-14 **Basel** **City and Imperial mint**
Mint: **Basel**
Maximilian I, 1493-1519
1493 **Goldgulden**
R4 *3.20 g*
Frey 404, Winter. 207, HMZ 58, FR. 12, De Mey d'Or 279

MONETA-BASIL':1ᛟ93
Madonna and Child standing, shield of Weinsberg at feet

MAXIMILIANVS:ROM:R
Imperial orb in trefoil

Issued in the name of Maximilian

V-15 **Bern** **City**
Mint: **Bern**
1493 **Guldiner**
R2 *29.40 g*
Frey 403, Geiger 41, Lohner 166, HMZ 163, Davenport 8721, Coll. Swiss 1, 359

SANCTVSºVIN-CENCIVSº1493
St. Vincent holding book and pen

Bear facing left with eagle of Holy Roman Empire above, arc of seven canton shields above, surrounded by circle of 20 canton shields

1494

V-16 **Bern** **City**
Mint: **Bern**
1494 **Heavy Guldiner**
R4 *39 g*
Frey —, Geiger 42b, Davenport 8720, Coll. Swiss 1, 362

SANCTVS*VIN-CENCIVS*1494
St. Vincent holding book and pen

Bear facing left with eagle of Holy Roman Empire above, arc of seven canton shields above, surrounded by circle of 20 canton shields

Struck with a weight averaging 39 gr., as opposed to 29 gr. for the guldiner.

V-17 **Bern** **City**
Mint: **Bern**
1494 **Guldiner**
R *29 g*
Frey 414, Geiger 42, Lohner 168-69, HMZ 163, Davenport 8721, Coll. Swiss 1, 360-61

SANCTVS*VIN-CENCIVS*1494
St. Vincent holding book and pen

Bear facing left with eagle of Holy Roman Empire above, arc of seven canton shields above, surrounded by circle of 20 canton shields

1495

V-18 **Chur** **Bishopric**
Mint: **Chur**
Heinrich VI of Höwen, 1491-1503
1495 **Plappart**
R6 *1.58 g*
Frey —, HMZ 391, 2 HMZ Bulletin p. 49

MONE-EPI-CVRI-ENCIS - 95
Four part shield on long cross with date above shield

AVE*REGI - NA * CLORVM
Madonna and Child

Unique piece in Rätisches Museum of Chur.

1498

V-19 **Sitten** **Bishopric**
Mint: **Sitten**
Nicholas Schiner, 1497-1499
1498 **Thaler**
R3 *29.33 g*
Frey 471, Coll. Swiss 2, 1641, HMZ 1022, Davenport 8786

NICOLAVS*EPS*SEDVNENS'++PRE'+ET+CO+1498
Bishop holding sword, kneeling at feet of the throned emperor

Circle of 16 shields around field with Bishop's cap with ribbons over arms

In 2002 Leu sold a specimen listed as possibly the finest known for $20,000.

1499

V-20 **Basel** **City**
Mint: **Basel**
1499 **4 Ducats**
R5 *15.84 g*
Frey —, Ewig 121, De Mey d'Or 281A

MONETA:BASILIENSIS:1ᛟ99
Two basilisks facing holding shield of Basel

AVE:MARIA:GRACIA:P'
Madonna and Child standing

Struck on dicken dies.

V-21 **Basel** **City**
Mint: **Basel**
1499 **Heavy Thaler**
R5 *27.86 g*
Frey —, Voltz IV/2, V/1, Coll. Swiss 3, 2369, Coll. Brand 1985, #163

MONETA:BASILIENSIS:1ᛟ99
Basilisks holding shield of Basel

AVE:MARIA:GRACIA:P'
Madonna and Child standing

Struck on dicken dies with weight of nearly four dicken. The Brand specimen sold for over $36,000 in the Leu Oct. 2003 Collection Swiss sale.

V-22 **Basel** **City**
Mint: **Basel**
1499 **Dicken**
R2 *7.20 g*
Frey 513, Ewig 321, Voltz IV/2-V/I, HMZ 59, Coll. Swiss 3, 2370-71, Saurma 1751

MONETA:BASILIENSIS:1ᛟ99
Two basilisks facing holding shield of Basel

AVE:MARIA-GRACIA:P'
Madonna and Child standing

V-23 **Basel** **City**
Mint: **Basel**
1499 **Heavy Groschen**
R5 *4.85 g*
Frey —, Ewig 367, Voltz III/2-V/3, Coll. Swiss 3, 2372, HMZ 60

GROSSVS:BASILIENS':1ᛟ99
Shield of Basel in six-foil

SALVE:REGI-NA:MISE'
Madonna and Child emanating rays

Struck in the weight of a heavy half dicken on a groschen die.

V-24 **Basel** **City**
Mint: **Basel**
1499 **Turnosgroschen**

R4 *3.89 g*
Frey 514, Ewig 369, HMZ 60

GROSSVS:BASILIENS':99
Shield of Basel in polyfoil

SALVE:REGINA:MISERICORDIE::VITA- DVL-CED-OES-PES
Mid-length cross quartering inner legend

A lighter weight groschen of 3.89 gr. compared to 4.66-4.85 for the groschen of half-dicken weight. Restrikes in gold and in silver from original dies were made in 1901 to commemorate the 400th anniversary of Basel's entry into the Swiss coinage federation in 1501.

1500

V-25 **St. Gallen** **City**
Mint: **St. Gallen**
1500 **Dicken**
R3 *9.26 g*
Frey 537, HMZ 719, Coll. Swiss 1, 624

MONETA*NOVA*SANCTI*GALI
Standing bear advancing left

SANCTVS*OTHMARVS*1500
Large eagle occupying entire field

V-26 **St. Gallen** **City**
Mint: **St. Gallen**
1500 **Batzen**
R4 *3.26 g*
Frey —, HMZ 721, Ilke Supp. I, 139, HMZ 721, Coll. Swiss 2, 1384

MONETA*NOVA*SANCTI*GALLI
Standing bear advancing left

0 SANC-TVS*O-THMA-RVS*150
Long cross dividing legend with eagle in center

The date on this strangely engraved coin starts in the last quadrant of the cross with "150" and ends with the "0" in the first quadrant!

V-27 **St. Gallen** **City**
Mint: **St. Gallen**
1500 **Plappart**
R4 *1.88 g*
Frey —, HMZ 722, Ilke 278, Coll. Swiss 2, 1385

MONETA*NO*SACT*GA
Standing bear advancing left

SANCTVS*OTHMARVS*1500
Large eagle occupying entire field

REGION VI - Scandinavia

VI-1 **Roskilde** **Bishopric**
Mint: **Roskilde**
Niels Stigsens, 1225-1249
1234 **Denier**
R6 *0.53-1.00 g*
Frey N1, Nordisk Numismatisk Unions Medlemsblad N. 5-6, August 2003, p. 88-90, National Museum Yearbook 1997, p. 211, Lindahl, Coins of the Valdemars

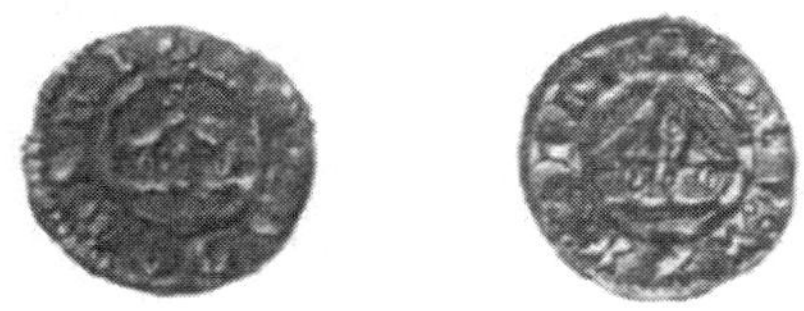

ANNO DOMINI
Crude bishop's hat

M:CC:XXXIIII
Crown

Seven total extant, all in Scandanavian museums. The first Anno Domini dated coin struck in Europe using a Latin inscription. Two different dies are known.

1478

VI-2a **Sweden** **Kingdom**
Mint: **Stockholm**
Sten Sture the Elder, 1471-1497, 1501-1503
1478 **Ortug**
R *1.40 g*
Frey 193, Lagerqvist 2a,b,d, Galster 219

SCS:ERICVS:REX
Facing crowned bust of king

NONETA:STOCK:1ꝝΛ8
Shield of three crowns

Lagerqvist types a, b and d vary only by the presence of a letter "S" over the shield rightside up (2a), sideways (2b) or completely absent (2d).

VI-2b **Sweden** **Kingdom**
Mint: **Stockholm**
Sten Sture the Elder, 1471-1497, 1501-1503
1478 **Ortug**
R2 *1.40 g*
Frey —, Lagerqvist 2c,e

SCS:ERICVS:REX
Facing crowned bust of king

NONETA:STOCK:8:0
Shield of three crowns

A large annulet resembling a "0" found next to the "8" in type 2e has caused a false reported date of "1480." See, e.g., Frey 222 and 222a. Lagerqvist type 2c has a small annulet.

VI-2c **Sweden** **Kingdom**
Mint: **Stockholm**
Sten Sture the Elder, 1471-1497, 1501-1503
1478 **Ortug**
R5 *1.40 g (est.)*
Frey —, Coll. Bruun #259

SCS:ERKVS:REX
Facing crowned bust of king

NONETA:STOCK 1ꝶΛ
Shield of three crowns

An error date with the last digit of 8 dropped.

VI-3a **Sweden** **Kingdom**
Mint: **Stockholm**
Sten Sture the Elder, 1471-1497, 1501-1503
1478 **Half Ortug**
R2 *1.00 g*
Frey 193A, Lagerqvist 8, Galster 221a

SCS:ERICVS:REX
Facing crowned bust of king

MONETA:STOCK:Λ 8 8
Large crown

A design of two large annulets, one above the other, has been mistaken for an "8", for a false reported date of 1488. See Frey 316.

VI-3b **Sweden** **Kingdom**
Mint: **Stockholm**
Sten Sture the Elder, 1471-1497, 1501-1503
1478 **Half Ortug**
R *0.80 g*
Frey —, Lagerqvist 9b

SCS:ERICVS:REX
Large "S" occupying entire field

MONETA:STOCK:Λ8:
Large crown

VI-3c **Sweden** **Kingdom**
Mint: **Stockholm**
Sten Sture the Elder, 1471-1497, 1501-1503
1478 **Half Ortug**
R4 *1.00 g*
Frey —, Lagerqvist 9a

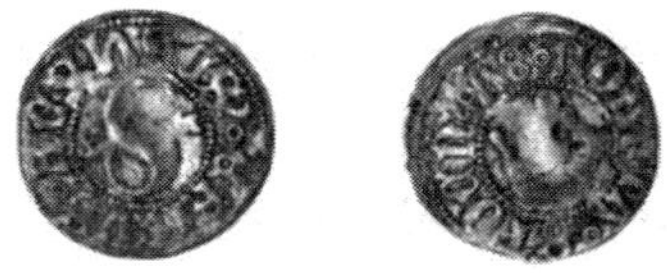

SCS:ERICVS:REX 1Λ
Large "S" occupying entire field

MONETAºSTOCK'ºΛ8
Large crown

Error date of "1Λ" on obverse instead of "14", and "Λ 8" on reverse. The date, as thus engraved, is "1ΛΛ8".

VI-3d **Sweden** **Kingdom**
Mint: **Stockholm**
Sten Sture the Elder, 1471-1497, 1501-1503
1478 **Half Ortug**
R6 *0.80 g*
Frey —, Lagerqvist 9e

SCS:ERICVS:REX:
Large "S" occupying entire field

NONETAºSTOCK' 1ꝶ
Large crown

Partial date of "14" on reverse represents full date of "1478". Only three pieces are reportedly extant, two of which are in museum collections.

VI-3e **Sweden** **Kingdom**
Mint: **Stockholm**
Sten Sture the Elder, 1471-1497, 1501-1503
1478 **Half Ortug**
R *1.10 g*
Frey —, Lagerqvist 9c, Galster 222

SCS:ERICVS:REX
Large "S" occupying entire field

NONETAºSTOCK'8
Large crown

The single digit date "8" represents "1478".

VI-3f **Sweden** **Kingdom**
Mint: **Stockholm**
Sten Sture the Elder, 1471-1497, 1501-1503
1478 **Half Ortug**
R6 *Weight unknown*
Frey —, Lagerqvist 9d

SCS:ERICVS:REX:8

Large "S" occupying entire field

NONETA:STOCK':Λ8
Large crown

A fascinating error date, caused by muling of the abbreviated dates on the obverse of "8" and "78" on the reverse. According to Swedish Auctionhouse B. Ahlstrom, no sales records exist for this hybride coin.

1496

VI-4 Denmark Kingdom
Mint: Copenhagen
Hans I, 1481-1513
1496 Gold Triple Noble
R6 44.72 g
Frey —, FR. 1, De Mey d'Or 724, Galster 25, Schou 1

IOH':DEI:GRA:REX:DANOR:IVSSIT:ME:FIERI:AN':1Ꭶ96
King seated on large gothic throne

DEXTERA:DNI:EXALTA:ME:DEXTRA:DNI:FECIT:VIRTV
Crowned five-part shield

Believed unique.

VI-5 Denmark Kingdom
Mint: Copenhagen
Hans I, 1481-1513
1496 Gold Noble
R6 14.75 g
Frey 448, FR. 3, De Mey d'Or 726, Galster 24, Schou 2-3

IOH':DEI:TRA:REX:DANOR:OVSSOT:HE:FOERO:AM':1Ꭶ96
King seated on large gothic throne

DEXTERA:DNI:EXALTA:ME:DEXTRA:DNI:FECIT:VIRTV
Crowned five-part shield

Two known, both in museum collections.

REGION VII - Italy

1480

VII-1 Forli Lordship
Mint: Uncertain
Hieronymus Riaria, 1480-1488
1480 Ducato d'oro
R6 Weight unknown
Frey —, CNI 1, FR. 346, De Mey d'Or 799, Biaggi 812

HYER:REARIVS:FORLIV:ET:IMVL:DYN
Two-headed eagle with arms on breast

IN:ADIVT:MEVM:IN:A:MCCCCLXXX
Facing bishop, raising right hand

Bearing a Roman numeral date, this coin, issued by the lords of Forli, is the first early dated Italian coin. The extreme rarity of this coin is suggested by the absence in CNI of any photographs.

1494

VII-2 Antegnate Lordship
Mint: Bologna
Giovanni (John) II, Bentivoglio, 1494-1509
1494 4 Ducats
R5 13.57 g
Frey —, CNI 1, FR. 57, De Mey d'Or 136, Biaggi 86

IOANNES:BENTIVO-LVS:II:BONONIENSIS
Renaissance bust of duke facing right wearing berretto

MA-XIMILIANI-IMPERATORIS-MVNVS-MCCCCLXXXX-IIII
Legend in six horizontal lines occupying entire field

The mint right was granted to Giovanni for his aid to Maximilian during the French invasion of Italy.

VII-3 Antegnate Lordship
Mint: Bologna
Giovanni (John) II, Bentivoglio, 1494-1509
1494 Mezzo Ducato
R5 1.72 g
Frey —, CNI 30, FR. 58, De Mey d'Or 137, Biaggi 89

IOANNI:II:BENTIVO
Quartered arms of Bentiviglio family

MA-XIMIMILIANI-IMPERA-MVN-VS:MCCCC-LXXXX-IIII
Legend in six horizontal lines occupying entire field

VII-4 **Antegnate Lordship**
Mint: Bologna
Giovanni (John) II, Bentivoglio, 1494-1509
1494 Double Testoni Piefort
R5 *19.29 g*
Frey –, CNI 32, Gnecchi 99, Biaggi 90

IOANNES°BENTIVO-LVS-II°BONONIENSIS
Renaissance bust of duke facing right wearing berretto

MA-XIMILIANI-IMPERATORIS-MVNVS-MCCCCLXXXX-IIII
Legend in six horizontal lines occupying entire field

VII-5 **Antegnate Lordship**
Mint: Bologna
Giovanni (John) II, Bentivoglio, 1494-1509
1494 Mezzo Testone
R5 *4.85 g*
Frey –, CNI 48

IONNES°BENTIVO-LVS-BONONIENSIS
Renaissance bust of duke facing right wearing berretto

MA-XIMILLANI-IMPERA°MVN-MCCCC-LXXXX-IIII
Legend in six horizontal lines occupying entire field

All other dies of this denomination are undated.

VII-6a **Antegnate Lordship**
Mint: Bologna
Giovanni (John) II, Bentivoglio, 1494-1509
1494 Giulio
R4 *2.30 g*
Frey –, CNI 49-54, Gnecchi 103, Biaggi 94

IOANNES°BENTIVOL-VS II°BONONIENSIS
Renaissance bust of duke facing right wearing berretto

MA-XIMILIANI-IMPERA°MVN-VS°MCCCC-LXXXX-IIII
Legend in six horizontal lines occupying entire field

VII-6b **Antegnate Lordship**
Mint: Bologna
Giovanni (John) II, Bentivoglio, 1494-1509
1494 Guilio
R5 *2.30 g*
Frey –, CNI 55-57, Biaggi 95

IB-SB
Helmeted arms occupying field

MA-XIMILIA-NI°IMP°-MVNVS°-MCCCC-LXXXX-IIII°
Legend in six horizontal lines occupying entire field

VII-7 **Antegnate Lordship**
Mint: Bologna
Giovanni (John) II, Bentivoglio, 1494-1509
1494 Pattern Testone Bronze
R2 *12.70 g*
Frey 423B, CNI 33, Gnecchi 106

IOANNES°BENTIVO-LVS-II°BONONIENSIS
Renaissance bust of duke facing right wearing berretto

MA-XIMILIANI-IMPERATORIS-MVNVS-MCCCCLXXXX-IIII
Legend in six horizontal lines occupying entire field

This is the earliest Anno Domini dated Italian copper coin. It is cast from the same dies as the 4 ducat piece and the silver double testone.

1497

VII-8a **Milan Duchy**
Mint: Milan
Ludovico Maria Sforza (the "Moor"), 1494-1500
1497 Pattern Testone Bronze
R5 *6.60 g*
Frey –, CNI V, No. 28, Crippa 7, p. 200, Gnecchi 2832

LVDOVIC' M SF-1497-ANGLV' DVX M
Bare-headed bust of duke facing right, date upside-down and below bust

PP:ANG:Q3:CO:AC:ANVE:D:-L-V
Crowned four-part shield with letters L-V at sides

Struck in bronze by Duke Ludovico Maria Sforza. The reporting of a 1494 date in the Gnecchi supplement is a misreading of the 1497 date.

VII-8b **Milan Duchy**
Mint: Milan
Ludovico Maria Sforza (the "Moor"), 1494-1500
1497 Pattern Testone Bronze
R5-6 *9.71 g*
Frey –, CNI V, No. 5, Crippa 10, p. 202, Gnecchi 2833

LVDOVIC' M SF-1497-ANGLV' DVX M
Bare-headed bust of duke facing right, date upside-down and below bust

BEATRIX:SF:ANGLA:ESTIS:DVCISA:MLI
Bust of duchess facing left

Struck in bronze using the same obverse dies as the preceding pattern coin. A superb example sold at Leu in 1998 for $22,000. Both CNI and Morosini opine that a silver striking of this piece is a forgery, as the weight is not proper.

1500

VII-9 Papal States Pope
Mint: Rome
Alexander VI, 1492-1503
1500 Triple Florin
R6 10.38 g
Frey —, Berman 526, FR. 28a, De Mey d'Or 1849, Biaggi 2226

ALEXANDER-VI:PONT:MAX
Papal arms in shield

IVSTIT:PACIS:Q:CVLT:AN:IVBILEI:MD
Large bust of pope facing left, letters "MD" representing "1500"

This is the only dated Papal coin and the only early dated coin to express the date as "MD." The references in catalogues to other early dated Papal coins are references to regnal dates.

REGION VIII - France

1491

VIII-1 Lorraine Duchy
Mint: Nancy
Rene II, 1473-1508
1491 Double Gros
R6 3.31 g
Frey —, De Saulcy pl. XIII, #3

RENATVS:D-DVX:LOTHO
Elaborate helmeted shield

ADIVVA NOS:DEVS:SALVTARIVS:NR - GROSSVS:NAN-CEI:1Ꝏ91
Sword dividing inner legend with R-R on sides

This unique piece resides in the Museum of Contemporary and Ancient Art in Epinal, France.

1492

VIII-2 Lorraine Duchy
Mint: St. Die
Rene II, 1473-1508
1492 Ducat
R5 Weight unknown
Frey —, FR. 139, De Mey d'Or 1364, De Saulcy PL. XII, No. 14

M*NOVA-FACTA*I*-SCTO DE-ODATO
Long cross with the shield of Anjou in center, with shields of Hungary, Naples, Jerulsalem and Aragon in quarters

S.GIORGIVS-*1492*
St. George standing, behind shield of arms of Lorraine and Bar

1498

VIII-3 Brittany Kingdom
Mint: Nantes
Anne (As Widow), 1498-1499
1498 Ecu d'or
R5-6 3.48 g
Frey —, Poey D'Avant 1398 -99, Duplessy 357-58, De Mey Br 440-41, FR. 97, De Mey d'Or 458

ANA:D:G:FRAN:REGI:ET:BRITON:DVCSSA:N - 1498
Queen on large Gothic throne with date under throne

SIT:NOMEN:DOMINI:BENEDICTVM
Flowery cross with ermine pelts in angles of cross

Undated examples exist as well. Also known as a cadière d'or.

PART III. OVERVIEW OF COINAGE
REGION I - GERMANY

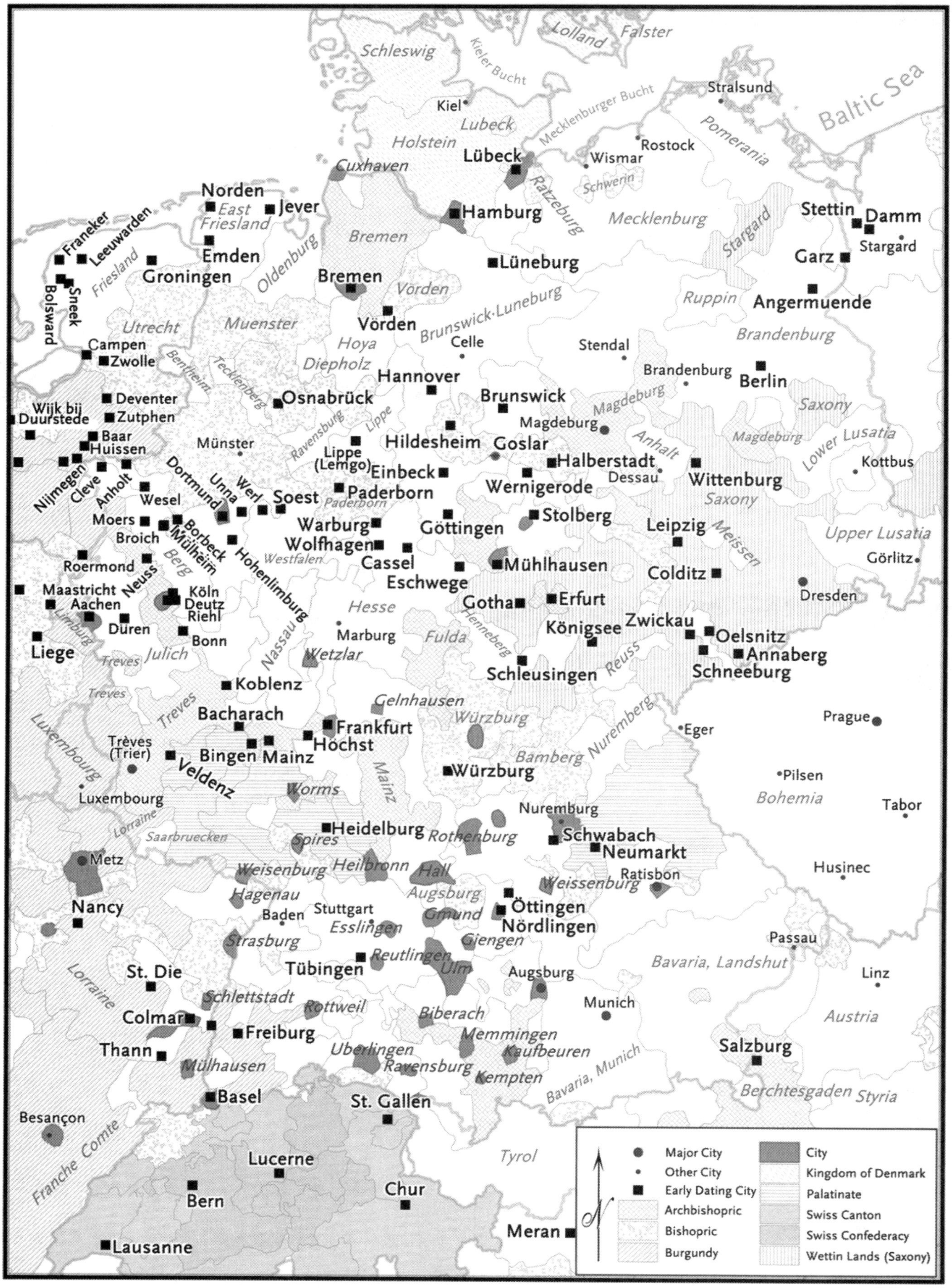

AACHEN (AIX-LA-CHAPELLE) - CITY. MINTS OF JUNGHEIT AND AACHEN*. 1372

Coins of Aachen represent the earliest collectable dated coins. Aachen coins are among the most popular early dated coins to collect for a number of reasons. They are collectable from very early periods (the 1374 groschen, while very rare, is still obtainable), have attractive designs, and are generally well struck. The two collectable 14th century dated pieces, 1374 and 1375, are always in great demand and bring high prices. The series from 1402-1405 are all rare, with the 1405 being the rarest. Groschens dating 1410, 1413, 1425 and 1429 are reliably reported, but all of the greatest rarity or uncollectible, with the latter two dates perhaps unique. The groschens dated 1419-1421 are all common or merely scarce.

There exists substantial confusion and uncertainty as to existing dates, more so than with any other early dated coinage. Frey unreliably reports the existence of a 1406 groschen. Menadier reports a 1409 date and provides a reference which itself does not provide photographic or other verification. The coin cannot be reliably reported. The same is true of the 1430 date. None of these three are listed. The 1425 piece while not photographed is reported by both Menadier and Krumbach, and Krumbach notes the sole piece is in a private collection. There have been numerous examples of false dates reported because of weakness in or misinterpretation of the Roman numeral dating. The common 1419 has been reported as a 1430 date, but upon examination, all such pieces have the middle of the final three digits blundered, so the "XIX" appears as an "XXX."

Beginning 1489, Aachen reissued the groschen for two years and in 1491 struck a Mariengroschen or "Maria" groschen with the Virgin and Child and a "broad Mariengroschen" of twice its value in 1491 and 1492. The latter denomination is exceptionally beautiful and equally rare, with only a few in private hands. Lastly, in 1496 and again in 1498 Aachen issued quarter groschens with the dates in angles of the cross. These last two are both very rare in worn condition, and excessively rare in VF or better.

Standard References: Menadier, Förschner and Krumbach. General Reference: Schulten

Number	Date	Mint	Denomination	Rarity
I-1	1372	Jungheit	Groschen	R6
I-2	1373	Jungheit	Groschen	R6
I-3a	1374	Jungheit	Groschen	R2
I-3b	1374	Jungheit	Groschen	R5
I-4a	1375	Jungheit	Groschen	R2
I-4b	1375	Jungheit	Groschen	R5
I-4c	1375	Jungheit	Groschen	R5
I-5a	1402	Aachen	Groschen	R2
I-5b	1402	Aachen	Groschen	R5
I-5c	1402	Aachen	Groschen	R5
I-6	1403	Aachen	Groschen	R
I-7	1404	Aachen	Groschen	R
I-8	1405	Aachen	Groschen	R2
I-9	1410	Aachen	Groschen	R5
I-10	1411	Aachen	Groschen	VS
I-11	1412	Aachen	Groschen	R
I-12	1413	Aachen	Groschen	R5
I-13	1418	Aachen	Groschen	R
I-14	1419	Aachen	Groschen	C-S
I-15	1420	Aachen	Groschen	S
I-16	1421	Aachen	Groschen	S
I-17	1422	Aachen	Groschen	R
I-18	1425	Aachen	Groschen	R6
I-23	1429	Aachen	Groschen	R5
I-278	1489	Aachen	Turnosgroschen	R2
I-244	1490	Aachen	Turnosgroschen	R3
I-257	1491	Aachen	Broad Mariengros.	R5
I-258	1491	Aachen	Mariengroschen	VS
I-273	1492	Aachen	Broad Mariengros.	R5
I-337a	1496	Aachen	Quarter Groschen	R2
I-337b	1496	Aachen	Quarter Groschen	R4-5
I-372a	1498	Aachen	Quarter Groschen	R4
I-372b	1498	Aachen	Quarter Groschen	R4-5

ANGERMUENDE – SEE BRANDENBURG

ANHOLT-BATENBURG – SEE REGION II, NORTHERN NETHERLANDS

ANNABERG – SEE SAXONY

Number	Date	Mint	Denomination	Rarity

BACHARACH – SEE PALATINATE

BERLIN – SEE BRANDENBURG

BINGEN – SEE MAINZ

BONN – SEE COLOGNE

BORBECK – SEE ESSEN

BRANDENBURG – MARGRAVIATE AND ELECTORATE OF THE HOLY ROMAN EMPIRE. MINTS OF FRANKFURT AM ODER, BERLIN, ANGERMUENDE AND UNCERTAIN MINTS. 1481

Brandenburg, known as Brandenburg-Prussia following the medieval period, was ruled by Margraves and Electors. Its rulers were responsible for a varied and rich numismatic history. From 1496-1500, two different electors, Johann I Cicero and Joachim II Nestor, both in their names and in joint issuance with siblings, struck numerous groschens and half groschens of various types, Johann from 1496-1499 and Joachim (with and without brother Albrecht), from 1498-1500. Brandenburg employed numerous mints to issue its varied coinage, amongst them as Berlin, Stendal and Frankfurt, but only a few types from Frankfurt on the Oder River bear the mint name.

Brandenburg began its dated coinage in 1481 with the issuance of groschens. While Bahrfeldt lists several dies for this coin, it today is of the greatest rarity. Fifteen years later in 1496, Brandenburg began a much more plentiful issuance of groschens and half groschens. While the electors were powerful and influential, the quality of this coinage did not match the glory of the rulers, as both their dated and undated coins were almost always both crudely and poorly engraved and/or often weakly struck. Accordingly, well-struck or high grade examples bring today a substantial premium.

All the dates on Brandenburg coinage from 1496-1500 are collectable, with 1497 being the rarest year for both the groschen and half groschen. Dozens of different die types are reported and the result is that there are many extremely rare or unusual types. From the collector's standpoint, one of the most interesting die types is the 1498 groschen of Johann with the entire reverse engraved backwards, ultimately resulting in a date of "8941"! Other interesting types include the varied date representations on the 1500 groschens and half groschens including "MVC" (1000 + 5 times 100), as well as the mis-or poorly-engraved abbreviations for 1500 represented as either "HVC" or "HV." Excessively crude engraving characterizes many of Brandenburg's early dated coins, so the legends often appear indecipherable or misspelled.

Standard Reference: Bahrfeldt (excellent), Collection Marienburg. Secondary Reference: Weyl. General References: Schulten and Saurma.

I-173	1481	Angermuende	Groschen	R4
I-338	1496	Angermuende	Groschen	R
I-339a	1496	Uncertain	Half Groschen	R
I-339b	1496	Uncertain	Half Groschen	R2
I-356a	1497	Frankfurt	Half Groschen	R5
I-356b	1497	Frankfurt	Half Groschen	R3
I-356c	1497	Frankfurt	Half Groschen	R3
I-357a	1497	Uncertain	Groschen	R2
I-357b	1497	Uncertain	Groschen	R3
I-373	1498	Berlin?	Groschen	R
I-374a	1498	Frankfurt	Half Groschen	R
I-374b	1498	Frankfurt	Half Groschen	R3
I-374c	1498	Frankfurt	Half Groschen	R3
I-375a	1498	Uncertain	Groschen	R2
I-375b	1498	Uncertain	Groschen	VS
I-375c	1498	Uncertain	Groschen	R4
I-394	1499	Berlin?	Groschen	R
I-395	1499	Frankfurt	Groschen	R
I-396a	1499	Frankfurt	Groschen	R
I-396b	1499	Frankfurt	Groschen	R4
I-397a	1499	Frankfurt	Groschen	VS
I-397b	1499	Frankfurt	Groschen	R4
I-398	1499	Frankfurt	Half Groschen	R2
I-399	1499	Uncertain	Groschen	R4
I-400	1499	Uncertain	Half Groschen	R4
I-438a	1500	Frankfurt	Groschen	R
I-438b	1500	Frankfurt	Groschen	VS

Number	Date	Mint	Denomination	Rarity
I-438c	1500	Frankfurt	Groschen	R3
I-439	1500	Frankfurt	Half Groschen	R2
I-440	1500	Frankfurt	Half Groschen	R6
I-441a	1500	Berlin?	Groschen	S
I-441b	1500	Berlin?	Groschen	S
I-441c	1500	Uncertain	Groschen	R3
I-442a	1500	Uncertain	Groschen	R
I-442b	1500	Uncertain	Groschen	R2
I-443a	1500	Uncertain	Half Groschen	R
I-443b	1500	Uncertain	Half Groschen	R4

BRANDENBURG-FRANCONIA (FRANKEN) – MARGRAVIATE. MINT OF SWABIA (SCHWABACH). 1497

The margraves of Brandenburg in Franconia issued a series of goldguldens from 1497-1500 from their mint at Swabia (Schwabach). These coins are plentiful and all the dates are obtainable in high grade, often in XF. The design of these goldguldens did not change over the four years of this run, and the 1497 date is somewhat scarcer than the other dates.

Standard Reference: Von Schrötter. General References: Friedberg, De Mey d'Or and Schulten

I-358a	1497	Swabia	Goldgulden	S
I-358b	1497	Swabia	Goldgulden	VS
I-376	1498	Swabia	Goldgulden	S
I-401	1499	Swabia	Goldgulden	S
I-444	1500	Swabia	Goldgulden	S

BREISACH (BREYSACH) – CITY. 1499

Breisach was a city in the district of Breisgau, in Baden-Württemberg, located on the Rhine in south Germany. The city fathers issued but two early dated coins, an excessively rare 1499 dicken and a likely unique groschen. In style, this dicken resembles the dickens struck by the other cities along the Rhine near Switzerland, such as those of Thann, Colmar and Freiburg in Breisgau.

Standard Reference: Berstett General Reference: Schulten.

I-402	1499	Breisach	Dicken	R5
I-403	1499	Breisach	Groschen	R6

BREMEN – ARCHBISHOPRIC. MINTS OF BREMEN AND VÖRDEN (VÖRDE). 1499

Bremen was a large and prominent archbishopric in one of Germany's most important northern trading cities. The archbishops issued large 4 groten (groschen) coins of good silver in 1499 from their two mints in Bremen and Vörden. Vörden, located southeast of Bremen, was itself was the site of a bishopric, but struck no early dated coins in the name of its own bishop. Bremen's coins from its two mints are essentially identical except for the different obverse legends: "MONETA*NOVA*BREMENSIS"/"MONETA*NOVA*VORDENSIS." Both coins are readily obtainable in high grades and are usually well-struck. Numerous minor die varieties exist.

Primary Reference: Jungk. General Reference: Schulten.

I-404	1499	Bremen	4 Groten	S
I-405	1499	Vörden	4 Groten	S-VS

BROICH – SEE LIMBURG-STYRUM

BRUNSWICK (BRAUNSCHWEIG) – CITY. 1444 (COUNTERMARKED COINAGE) and 1499 (STRUCK COINAGE).

Brunswick, a large city in north-central Germany, issued only a handful of early dated coins of its own, striking them in 1499 and 1500. Brunswick also countermarked local circulating coinage and its lionshield marks are found on 1444 and 1445 Rhineland groschens. All of Brunswick's dated coins are extremely rare, except for the 1499 and 1500 "kleiner" (small) groschens, which are merely rare. Both kleiner groschens are obtainable in high condition, but are often double-struck.

Standard Reference: Jesse. General References: Schulten and Krusy.

I-67	1444	Brunswick	C/M Groschen	R4
I-68	1444	Brunswick	C/M Groschen	R4
I-75	1445	Brunswick	C/M Groschen	R5
I-406	1499	Brunswick	Large Groschen	R5
I-407	1499	Brunswick	Autorgroschen	R5
I-408	1499	Brunswick	Kleiner Groschen	R

Number	Date	Mint	Denomination	Rarity
I-445	1500	Brunswick	Autorgroschen	R5
I-446	1500	Brunswick	Kleiner Groschen	R

CASSEL – SEE HESSE

CLEVE (KLEVE) – DUCHY AND COUNTY. MINTS OF HUISSEN, CLEVE AND WESEL. 1436

Cleve was a large and important duchy in northwestern Germany, bordering Gelderland and Brabant. During the fifteenth century, its dukes were also counts of the Mark, a large county to the east and south, and its coinage carried both titles. Its early dated coinage was very similar to that of the Northern Netherlands, especially Gelderland, with whom the dukes were linked by marriage.

The early dated coinage of Cleve from its mints at Cleve and Wesel was very prolific and over 30 different types of dated coinage were struck between the two with a vast array of different denominations. The lovely "schwanenstübers," (swan stuivers), showing a swan with outstretched wings over the shield of Cleve, are amongst the most attractive of early dated coinage types. The coins struck by the Cleve and Wesel mints are uniform in design. While a few extremely rare types exist, most of the coinage of both Cleve and Wesel mints is still collectable today and specimens still be found in higher grades.

In contrast, all dated coinage from Cleve's small mint of Huissen is of the greatest rarity. Located directly east of the border with the Netherlands and south of the city of Arnheim, the Rhine river city of Huissen struck dated coinage only in 1441, coining blanken and half-blanken using dies similar to Cleve's coinage of the same date. Noss lists the blanken, the monetary equivalent to the groschen, at only .349 fine silver, while the half blanken at only .159 fine silver. No doubt the coin's name derived from "...the white shiny appearance when newly struck." (Frey, *Numismatic Names*).

Primary Reference: Noss (excellent). General Reference: Schulten.

I-27	1436	Cleve	Double Groschen	R-R2
I-55	1441	Cleve	Double Blanken	R6
I-56	1441	Cleve	Blanken	R4-5
I-57	1441	Cleve	Half Blanken	R4-5
I-58	1441	Huissen	Blanken	R5
I-59	1441	Huissen	Half Blanken	R5
I-137	1475	Cleve	Groschen	C
I-138	1475	Cleve	Half Groschen	S
I-167	1479	Cleve	Braspfennig	S
I-168	1479	Cleve	Half Braspfennig	R2
I-176	1482	Cleve	Stüber	R2
I-177	1482	Wesel	Braspfennig	R2
I-186	1483	Cleve	Stüber	R
I-196	1484	Cleve	Stüber	VS
I-199	1485	Cleve	Stüber	VS
I-200	1485	Wesel	Stüber	S
I-204	1486	Cleve	Stüber	VS
I-215	1488	Cleve	Stüber	R
I-216	1488	Wesel	Stüber	R
I-229	1489	Wesel	Half Stüber	R2
I-245	1490	Cleve	Braspfennig	R3
I-246	1490	Wesel	Braspfennig	R3
I-247	1490	Wesel	Stüber	VS
I-248	1490	Cleve	Stüber	VS
I-249	1490	Wesel	Half Albus	R3
I-274	1492	Cleve	6 Stüber	R4
I-275	1492	Cleve	Braspfennig	R
I-276	1492	Wesel	Stüber	VS
I-277	1492	Wesel	Half Stüber	R2
I-A312	1494	Cleve	Braspfennig	R6
I-312	1494	Wesel	4 Möhrchen	R3
I-340	1496	Wesel	Half Albus	R3
I-359	1497	Cleve	Stüber	R2
I-447	1500	Cleve	Stüber	R3

COBLENZ – SEE TRIER

COLDITZ – SEE SAXONY

Number	Date	Mint	Denomination	Rarity

COLMAR – CITY. 1499

Colmar was a mid-sized city in the center of Alsace. Prior to the 15th century, it struck only a handful of coins, mostly small rappen. However, in 1499, in an impressive display of mint vigor, Colmar struck dated dickens, groschens and plapparts, some with more than one die. Large numbers of smaller, undated silver coins were also struck. The dated coinage all featured the imperial eagle on the obverse with either St. Martin on horseback or a cross on the reverse. Only a handful of specimens of any type survive.

Primary Reference: Engel & Lehr and De Mey Alsace. General Reference: Schulten.

I-409	1499	Colmar	Dicken	R4
I-410	1499	Colmar	Groschen	R5
I-411a	1499	Colmar	Plappart	R5
I-411b	1499	Colmar	Plappart	R5

COLOGNE (CÖLN, KÖLN). ARCHBISHOPRIC. MINTS OF BONN, DEUTZ AND RIEHL. 1425

Cologne was the seat of one of the most important archbishoprics of the Middle Ages. It had a long history of coinage and in the late Middle Ages, issued dated coins from 1425 to 1491. Its coins were well-engraved, well-struck and issued in good metal fineness. Except for the groschens of 1425 and 1426, Cologne's early dated coins of the Riehl mint are generally very collectable and can still be found in higher grades.

While Cologne's mint at Bonn ("BVNE") issued large quantities of non-dated coins, it struck only two dated coins types, groschens of 1432 (of the greatest rarity) and of 1450 (excessively rare). Deutz (medieval name "TVICEM") was likewise an important mint of the archbishop, but only struck one early dated coin, an attractive 1482 turnosgroschen. While often listed as very rare, this coin is commonly offered for auction or private sale and is thus listed as very scarce. Struck in good silver, it is readily found in excellent condition.

Standard Reference: Noss (excellent). Secondary Reference: Cappe. General Reference: Saurma

I-19	1425	Riehl	Groschen	R4
I-22	1426	Riehl	Groschen	R5
I-26	1432	Bonn	Groschen	R5
I-28a	1436	Riehl	Goldgulden	R3
I-28b	1436	Riehl	Goldgulden	R5
I-33	1437	Riehl	Goldgulden	VS
I-34	1437	Riehl	Groschen	R
I-43	1438	Riehl	Goldgulden	VS
I-44	1438	Riehl	Groschen	VS
I-63	1443	Riehl	Groschen	R2
I-69a	1444	Riehl	Groschen	C
I-69b	1444	Riehl	Groschen	R2
I-76	1445	Riehl	Groschen	S
I-79	1446	Riehl	Groschen	VS
I-81	1447	Riehl	Groschen	S
I-84	1448	Riehl	Groschen	VS
I-87	1449	Riehl	Groschen	VS
I-89	1450	Bonn	Groschen	R4
I-90	1450	Riehl	Groschen	R
I-178	1482	Deutz	Turnose	VS
I-230	1489	Deutz	Groschen	R
I-231	1489	Deutz	Albus	S
I-259a	1491	Deutz	Goldgulden	R
I-259b	1491	Deutz	Goldgulden	R2

COLOGNE CITY (KÖLN STADT) – CITY. 1493

Cologne city, a member of the Hanseatic League, received its mint rights in the 15th century (Craig P. 62-63). The city issued only two early dated coins, both 1493 blankens of very different styles. Both are excessively rare with no recent auction history. Cologne city also issued a ratzeichen (town token) bearing the date of 1497, one of the tiny handful early dated tokens struck outside of the Lowlands.

Primary Reference; Noss (excellent). Secondary Reference: Cappe. General Reference: Schulten

I-296a	1493	Cologne	Blanken	R5-6
I-296b	1493	Cologne	Blanken	R5

DAMM – SEE POMMERANIA

Number	Date	Mint	Denomination	Rarity

DEUTZ – SEE COLOGNE

DORTMUND (TREMONIA) – CITY. 1489 (COUNTERMARKED COINAGE ONLY)
Dortmund, a city in upper Westphalia, struck no early dated coinage of its own, but instead countermarked local circulating coinage as was popular in Westphalia in the 15th century. Its sole early dated piece is a countermarked host Louvain 1489 4 mites billon coin (No. II-117) with a single-headed eagle. This piece is described in JMP XXXIX 1952 #40, and must be considered of the greatest rarity.

Standard Reference: Berghaus. General Reference: Krusy

I-232	1489	Dortmund	C/M 4 mites	R6

DÜREN - SEE JÜLICH-BERG

EAST FRISIA (OSTFRIESLAND) – COUNTY. MINTS OF EMDEN AND NORDEN. 1473
East Frisia was a county on the most northwestern part of Germany, across the Ems River from West Frisia (Friesland) in the Netherlands. Its coinage copied that of the Northern Netherlands in style, especially that of Groningen, the most successful trading city in the region. While the counts struck early dated coins for a nearly twenty year period from 1473 through 1491, they did so at irregular intervals, skipping years at a time and changing denominations frequently. The coinage was likely struck at both Emden and Norden during the 1470's and at Emden thereafter.

Despite issuing 14 different types, East Frisia's early dated coinage is all very rare to excessively rare. Again, as with most states who copied the coin styles of a larger region, the coins of East Frisia tended to be poorly struck with a high billon content, thus more susceptible to wear. Well-struck pieces in high grade are virtually unobtainable. One 1483 East Frisian stüber was counterstamped for devaluation, the only such example known in early dated coinage.

Primary Reference: Kappelhoff (excellent). General Reference: Schulten.

I-130	1473	Emden?	Witten	R3
I-133	1474	Emden?	Witten	R4
I-139	1475	Emden?	Witten	R3
I-187a	1483	Emden	Stüber	R2
I-187b	1483	Emden	C/S Stüber	R6
I-188	1483	Emden	Groten	R3
I-189	1483	Emden	Half Groten	R2
I-205	1486	Emden	Doppelgroten	R2
I-206	1486	Emden	Half Groten	R3
I-217	1488	Emden	Doppelgroten	R3
I-218	1488	Emden	Half Groten	R3
I-260a	1491	Emden	Stüber	R5?
I-260b	1491	Emden	Stüber	R6
I-261	1491	Emden	Krummsteert	R
I-262	1491	Emden	Half Krummsteert	R4

EINBECK – CITY. 1488
Einbeck was a small city in Hannover, whose nearest large neighbor was the important university town of Göttingen only 15 miles to the south. Einbeck's early dated coinage was a virtual copy of the coinage of Göttingen, except Einbeck used the gothic letter "E" on the obverse and reverse of its simple dies in place of the gothic letter "G" used by Göttingen. Only four different dates are known, the first unique and the rest extremely rare. The 1488 date was not known to Buck and misreported by Schrock as a 1480 date.

Primary References: Buck, Schrock-Einbeck. General Reference: Schulten

I-219	1488	Einbeck	Körtling	R6
I-377	1498	Einbeck	Körtling	R4
I-412	1499	Einbeck	Körtling	R3
I-448	1500	Einbeck	Körtling	R3

EMDEN – SEE EAST FRISIA

ERFURT – CITY. 1468
Erfurt was an important medieval mint of Mainz and of Saxony-Thüringen in central Germany, but its city fathers also issued coins under its own name. Its coins used the design of a wheel with spokes, some with the letter "E" on top. It issued one spectacular large groschen dated 1468, with its patron St. Martin on horseback with a beggar at his feet.

Number	Date	Mint	Denomination	Rarity

Thereafter, the coinage declined (see Craig at p. 75) and all other dated coins were tiny uniface hohlpfennigs or scherfs. All of Erfurt's early dated coins are very rare at the least.

Primary Reference: Leitzmann. General Reference: Schulten

I-115	1468	Erfurt	Groschen	R2
I-134	1474	Erfurt	Hohlpfennig	R4
I-233	1489	Erfurt	Hohlpfennig	R5
I-313	1494	Erfurt	Scherf	R4
I-323	1495	Erfurt	Pfennig	R4
I-324	1495	Erfurt	Scherf	R3
I-341	1496	Erfurt	Pfennig	R3
I-342	1496	Erfurt	Scherf	R3
I-378	1498	Erfurt	Scherf	R3
I-413a	1499	Erfurt	Pfennig	R4
I-413b	1499	Erfurt	Pfennig	R4

ESCHWEGE – SEE HESSE

ESSEN – CONVENT. MINTS OF BORBECK AND ESSEN. 1474

The modern industrial city of Essen, located directly east of Mörs and north of Düsseldorf, was in the Middle Ages the only convent that issued early dated coins. Its dated coinage began in 1474 when Abbess Sophie IV von Gleichen issued a groschen followed by half groschens in 1487 and 1488, all of which copied Southern Netherlands coinage of that period. The former coin is unique and the latter dates are excessively rare.

Primary Reference: Kramer. General Reference: Schulten

I-135	1474	Essen	Groschen	R6
I-211a	1487	Borbeck	Half Groschen	R4
I-211b	1487	Borbeck	Half Groschen	R5
I-220	1488	Borbeck	Half Groschen	R5

FRANKFURT (FRANKFURT AM MAIN, FRANCFORT) – CITY AND IMPERIAL MINT. 1491

Frankfurt, located on the Main River near where it meets the Rhine, was a very large and important city in the Middle Ages as it is today. It was also the location of an important and prolific imperial mint. The city mint struck its own-coinage but issued no early dated coinage in the name of the free city.

Frankfurt's imperial mint struck goldguldens dated consecutively from 1491-1500. These coins were well-struck but used commonplace designs. Each featured the same device: John the Baptist holding the lamb of God on the obverse with the imperial orb on the reverse. Most of the dates are fairly easily collectable. All can still be found in very high grade.

Primary Reference: Joseph and Fellner. General References: Friedberg and Schulten.

I-263	1491	Frankfurt	Goldgulden	R
I-278a	1492	Frankfurt	Goldgulden	VS
I-278b	1492	Frankfurt	Goldgulden	R2
I-297a	1493	Frankfurt	Goldgulden	VS
I-297b	1493	Frankfurt	Goldgulden	R
I-314	1494	Frankfurt	Goldgulden	VS
I-325	1495	Frankfurt	Goldgulden	S
I-343	1496	Frankfurt	Goldgulden	R
I-360	1497	Frankfurt	Goldgulden	VS
I-379	1498	Frankfurt	Goldgulden	VS
I-414	1499	Frankfurt	Goldgulden	VS
I-449	1500	Frankfurt	Goldgulden	VS

FRANKFURT AM ODER — SEE BRANDENBURG

FREIBERG – SEE SAXONY

FREIBURG IN BREISGAU – CITY. 1499

Freiburg was a Habsburg-controlled city in the larger county of Breisgau between Baden in south Germany and Basel in Switzerland (not to be confused with the Saxon mint of Freiberg near the Czech and Polish borders). It issued three early dated coin types in 1499, today all excessively rare. Its coins used denominations and devices typical of Swiss coins of the period. There is little auction history of these elusive pieces.

Number	Date	Mint	Denomination	Rarity
Primary Reference: Berstett and Rommel. General Reference: Schulten				
I-415	1499	Freiburg	Dicken	R5
I-416a	1499	Freiburg	Groschen	R5
I-416b	1499	Freiburg	Groschen	R5

GARZ – SEE POMMERANIA

GOTHA – SEE SAXONY

GÖTTINGEN – CITY. 1429

Göttingen was an important university town in central Germany and was also a member of the Hanseatic League. It was the first German mint outside of the general western Rhineland/Palatinate area to strike early dated coinage, with a relatively plentiful issuance of körtlings dated 1429. Göttingen's early dated coinage was remarkable for several reasons, mainly because it struck its dated coinage as a 70+ year series from 1429 to 1500 (Schrock's listing of a 1410 körtling is an error – it is a mis-engraved 1490). There were intermittent issues at the beginning (the first four dates struck were 1429, 1442, 1446 and 1465, the middle two years currently being unique), and then periodic issuance from 1465-1481, and then coinage was struck dated every year from 1483-1500, the longest such series in all of early dated coinage.

Another remarkable fact about Göttingen's coinage was that it used the same design on all of its early dated coins, the Gothic "G," with legend on both obverse and reverse. Similarly, Göttingen's coinage is notable because its denominations did not vary, as only dated körtlings were struck. Finally, contrary to the practice in most states, Göttingen struck an abundant series of coinage in the first year, 1429. Körtlings struck between 1493 and 1500 are very difficult to find, especially in higher grades. Those issued from 1489–1492 are much easier to obtain.

Primary Reference: Schrock (excellent). General Reference: Schulten

I-24	1429	Göttingen	Körtling	VS
I-61	1442	Göttingen	Körtling	R6
I-80	1446	Göttingen	Körtling	R6
I-94	1465	Göttingen	Körtling	R
I-97	1466	Göttingen	Körtling	VS
I-107	1467	Göttingen	Körtling	R4
I-128	1471	Göttingen	Körtling	R4
I-131	1473	Göttingen	Körtling	R5
I-174	1481	Göttingen	Körtling	R3
I-190	1483	Göttingen	Körtling	R4
I-197	1484	Göttingen	Körtling	R
I-201	1485	Göttingen	Körtling	R2
I-207	1486	Göttingen	Körtling	VS
I-212	1487	Göttingen	Körtling	R5-6
I-221	1488	Göttingen	Körtling	R
I-234	1489	Göttingen	Körtling	S
I-250a	1490	Göttingen	Körtling	S
I-250b	1490	Göttingen	Körtling	R5
I-264	1491	Göttingen	Körtling	VS
I-279	1492	Göttingen	Körtling	S
I-298	1493	Göttingen	Körtling	R2
I-315	1494	Göttingen	Körtling	R2
I-326	1495	Göttingen	Körtling	R3
I-344	1496	Göttingen	Körtling	R4
I-361	1497	Göttingen	Körtling	R3
I-380	1498	Göttingen	Körtling	R3
I-417	1499	Göttingen	Körtling	R3
I-450	1500	Göttingen	Körtling	R

HALBERSTADT – CITY. 1438 (COUNTERMARKED COINAGE ONLY)

Halberstadt was an important early medieval bishopric mint in central-north Germany that issued numerous bracteates of often spectacular designs. The city of Halberstadt was granted the mint right by the bishopric, but issued no early dated coinage of its own. Instead, the city fathers authorized the countermarking of locally circulating coinage, mostly using a lowercase "h" as its mark. Halberstadt countermarks are known on at least nine early dated coins, and all are at least very rare.

Primary Reference: Besser, R./ Brämer, H./Bürger. General Reference: Krusy.

Number	Date	Mint	Denomination	Rarity
I-45	1438	Halberstadt	C/M Groschen	R5
I-70	1444	Halberstadt	C/M Groschen	R4
I-98a	1466	Halberstadt	C/M Horngroschen	R2
I-98b	1466	Halberstadt	C/M Horngroschen	R2
I-98c	1466	Halberstadt	C/M Horngroschen	R3
I-116	1468	Halberstadt	C/M Horngroschen	R4
I-121	1469	Halberstadt	C/M Stüber	R6
I-122	1469	Halberstadt	C/M Horngroschen	R4
I-179	1482	Halberstadt	C/M Bausche	R4

HAMBURG – CITY. 1438 (COUNTERMARKED COINAGE) 1497 (STRUCK COINAGE)

Hamburg, located on the Elbe River about 75 miles southeast of the North Sea, was numismatically one of the important cities of medieval Germany, having been granted the right to strike its own coinage during the 13th century. Despite plentiful coinage issued in its own name, it struck its only early dated coinage in 1497, issuing ducats using two similar die types. Both are relatively common and easy to obtain in high grade. Hamburg also countermarked goldguldens of many types, and a 1438 Palatinate goldgulden of the Bacharach mint has the distinction of being Hamburg's first dated coin, with a thistle ("nesselblatt") as its mark.

Primary Reference: Gaedechens. General References: Schulten, Friedberg, and Krusy.

I-46	1438	Hamburg	C/M Goldgulden	R5
I-362a	1497	Hamburg	Ducat	S
I-362b	1497	Hamburg	Ducat	C

HANNOVER – CITY. 1482

Hannover, a large city in north Germany (later the seat of the electors of Brunswick-Lüneburg), struck dated coins, small groschens, in only 1482 and 1483. These two very attractive coins, both excessively rare, feature a lion marching left on the ramparts of the city castle with the date on the reverse in angles of the cross. Most examples are poorly struck.

Primary Reference: Buck/Meier. General Reference: None

I-180	1482	Hannover	Groschen	R4
I-191	1483	Hannover	Groschen	R6

HEIDELBERG – SEE PALATINATE

HENNEBERG – COUNTY. MINT OF SCHLEUSINGEN. 1499

Henneberg, or "Hen Mountain," located in central-east Germany, was both a county and (later) a mint of Saxony. Its coinage featured a hen facing left as the central device or as part of its shields. Only three early dated coin types were issued, groschens dated 1499 and groschens and half groschens dated 1500. All are at the very least excessively rare with very little auction history.

Primary Reference: Heus (excellent). General Reference: Schulten.

I-418	1499	Schleusingen	Groschen	R5
I-451	1500	Schleusingen	Groschen	R5
I-452	1500	Schleusingen	Half Groschen	R6

HESSE (HESSEN) – LANDGRAVIATE. MINT OF CASSEL (KASSEL) AND ESCHWEGE. 1466

Hesse, also known as Hessen, was a large territory in northwestern Germany ruled by landed counts, or "landgraves." Hesse issued large dated groschens in 1466 and 1467, generally copying the coinage of its larger eastern neighbor, Saxony, which issued similar groschens from 1465-1469. All early dated coinage from Hesse is very rare to extremely rare.

Primary References: Schütz (excellent) and Hoffmeister. General Reference: Saurma.

I-99	1466	Eschwege?	Dreihelmgroschen	R4
I-108	1467	Cassel	Horngroschen	R2
I-109a	1467	Eschwege	Horngroschen	R2
I-109b	1467	Eschwege	Horngroschen	R4

HESSE-MARBURG – LANDGRAVIATE IN LOWER HESSE. MINTS OF MARBURG (?) AND WOLFHAGEN. 1467

Hesse-Marburg was a small landgraviate located southwest of Cassel. Its early dated monetary history was also brief, with dated coins issued in 1467, 1468 and in 1479. It is likely, but unconfirmed, that Marburg was the mint of the first two years. The large groschens of Hesse-Marburg also copied the neighboring Saxony horngroschen coinage, and exhibit little difference to the coins of Hesse.

Number	Date	Mint	Denomination	Rarity

Wolfhagen was a very small mint of Hesse-Marburg, located west of Cassel. The sole type issued from the mint at Wolfhagen was a remarkable tiny (17.5mm!) double-sided pfennig, a denomination not seen since the 1234 Roskilde denier, and bearing an anachronistic early medieval style. The reverse of this marvelous little piece shows the Landgrave standing with a sword and the date occupying the entire legend. Unfortunately, it is excessively rare with no recent auction records.

Primary References: Schütz (excellent) and Hoffmeister. General Reference: Schulten

I-110	1467	Uncertain	Horngroschen	R3
I-117	1468	Uncertain	Horngroschen	R2
I-169	1479	Wolfhagen	Pfennig	R5

HILDESHEIM – CITY. 1469 (COUNTERMARKED COINAGE). 1491 (STRUCK COINAGE)

Hildesheim, located in north-central Germany and west of Brunswick, possessed a lengthy numismatic history as both a bishopric and a city. However, the only early dated coins were a series of small "sechsling" worth six pennies, or half of a groschen, issued only by the city fathers. The coins are all rare and extremely rare in higher grades. A countermarked Deventer stüber dated 1469, (also bearing the countermark of Halberstadt), holds the distinction of being Hildesheim's first dated coin.

Primary Reference: Buck/Bahrfeldt. General Reference: Schulten and Krusy.

I-123	1469	Hildesheim	C/M Stüber	R6
I-265	1491	Hildesheim	Sechsling	R2
I-299	1493	Hildesheim	Sechsling	R2
I-316	1494	Hildesheim	Sechsling	R
I-327	1495	Hildesheim	Sechsling	R

HÖCHST – SEE MAINZ

HÖRDE – SEE MARK

HUISSEN – SEE CLEVE

JEVER (LAND JEVER) – LORDSHIP. 1481

The rulers of Jever were landed lords in the North Sea region at the northeast part of East Frisia (Ostfriesland). Being geographically close to the Netherlands, Jever's early dated coinage copied the typical styles of the Northern Netherlands regions. Although Jever struck a large number of early dated coin types between 1481-1493, all are at least excessively rare and are uniformly found (if at all) poorly struck and in lower grades.

Primary Reference: Kappelhoff (excellent), Merzdorf. Secondary Reference: De Mey Im. General Reference: Schulten.

I-175	1481	Jever	Örtchen	R4
I-181	1482	Jever	Half Witte	R5
I-192	1483	Jever	Groten	R4
I-202	1485	Jever	Groten	R4
I-208	1486	Jever	Groten	R4
I-209	1486	Jever	Half Groten	R4-5
I-210	1486	Jever	Witten	R4
I-213	1487	Jever	Witten	R5
I-222	1488	Jever	Half Groten	R4
I-235	1489	Jever	Stüber	R4
I-236	1489	Jever	Half Witten	R4
I-266	1491	Jever	Groten	R4-5
I-300	1493	Jever	Double Krummsteert	R5

JÜLICH-BERG (JULIERS) – DUCHY. MINTS OF MÜLHEIM, DÜREN and SCHOONVORST. 1441

Jülich-Berg was a duchy in the far western part of Germany near the border of Liège. Its early dated coinage was issued from its mints of Düren, Mülheim and Schoonvorst – none bears the name of the city of Jülich itself. Dated coinage was first issued in 1441 in the name of Duke Gerhard, who was also count of Ravensburg. This coinage was struck in its mint located at the small lordship of Schoonvorst, which in the 14th century had struck its own local coinage (see Schoonvorst-Sichem under Region II, Southern Netherlands). These groschen, also known as "bausche," were dated each year from 1441-1444. Except for the 1444 date, all are excessively rare or of the greatest rarity.

Jülich-Berg's much larger mint of Düren was located on the Ruhr river south of Jülich and east of Cologne. However, it issued only one early dated coin in its mint's name, an excessively rare 1471 bausche. Mülheim, Jülich-Berg's other mint from which early dated coins were struck, was a small Rhine city. Duke William, son of Gerhard, struck a series of bausche and their fractions from 1482 to 1484, and again in 1489 and 1500 at the Mülheim mint. As with most coins

Number	Date	Mint	Denomination	Rarity

struck at Rhineland mints, the coins of Mülheim were well-struck with attractive designs. The exceptions are the poorly-struck half bausche of 1482 and 1483.

Primary Reference: Noss (excellent). General Reference: Schulten

I-60	1441	Schoonvorst	Groschen	R4
I-62	1442	Schoonvorst	Groschen	R5
I-64	1443	Schoonvorst	Groschen	R4
I-71	1444	Schoonvorst	Groschen	R2
I-129	1471	Düren	Groschen	R4
I-182	1482	Mülheim	Bausche	C-S
I-183	1482	Mülheim	Half Bausche	R3
I-193	1483	Mülheim	Bausche	S
I-194	1483	Mülheim	Half Bausche	R5
I-198	1484	Mülheim	Bausche	S-VS
I-237	1489	Mülheim	Double Bausche	S
I-238	1489	Mülheim	Half Weisspfennig	R3
I-453	1500	Mülheim	Groschen	S

JUNGHEIT – SEE AACHEN

KASSEL – SEE HESSE

KLEVE – SEE CLEVE

KOBLENZ – SEE COBLENZ

KÖLN – SEE COLOGNE

KÖNIGSEE – SEE SCHWARZBURG

LEIPZIG – SEE SAXONY

LEMGO – SEE LIPPE

LIMBURG-STYRUM – COUNTY. MINTS OF BROICH AND HOHENLIMBURG. 1438
(Not to be confused with Limbourg in Region II, Southern Netherlands)

Limburg was a county near Berg and close to both the Netherlands and Belgium borders. It struck dated coinage both at the mints of Broich and Hohenlimburg, but neither overlapped the other. Its coinage was highly imitative, not uncommon for a smaller county hoping for good acceptance of its coins in nearby states. Its first dated coin, a remarkable 1438 turnosgroschen of the greatest rarity, copied the earlier Aachen groschens, while its later pieces, struck between 1473 and 1488, copied popular and widely-circulating Netherlands coins such as Groningen stuivers or Nijmegen demi stuivers. Two types were issued dated 1488 containing the obverse legend "MONETA NOVA LIMBORGH" with the reverse legend comprised of the date alone, lending questions to their attribution to this county as opposed to a municipal coinage. All coinage of Limburg is of great degrees of rarity.

Primary Reference: Berghaus/Spiegel (essential). General Reference: Schulten

I-47	1438	Broich	Turnosgroschen	R6
I-132	1473	Broich	Stuiver	R4
I-136a	1474	Broich	Stuiver	R4
I-136b	1474	Broich	Stuiver	R6
I-214	1487	Hohenlimburg	Half Stüber	R4
I-223	1488	Hohenlimburg	Double Stüber	R4
I-224a	1488	Hohenlimburg	Stüber	R4
I-224b	1488	Hohenlimburg	Stüber	R5

LIPPE – LORDSHIP. MINT OF LEMGO. 1498

Lippe was a small lordship (later county in the 16th century) in Westphalia, west of Brunswick and south of Osnabrück. It struck early dated coins in 1498 and 1499 from its mint of Lemgo, both of which are of the greatest rarity. One of these coins sold at Leu for $20,000 in 1995.

Primary Reference: Ihl and Collection Weweler. General Reference: Schulten

I-381	1498	Lemgo	Mite	R6
I-419	1499	Lemgo	Stuiver	R5-6

Number	Date	Mint	Denomination	Rarity

LÜBECK – CITY. 1437 (COUNTERMARKED COINAGE ONLY)

Lübeck, a very powerful and important trading city on the Baltic Sea, struck numerous gold and silver coinage types on its own, but did not date any in the 15th century. However, Lübeck, as with Hamburg to the southwest, countermarked a number of different goldguldens, attesting to these cities' influence in trade, and two such countermarks are known on dated coins. Its countermark was a tiny round shield containing a double-headed eagle. Lübeck's countermark of a 1437 Cologne goldgulden from the Riehl mint is the earliest dated countermarked coin. Lübeck also countermarked its trading rival Hamburg's 1497 goldgulden. Both coins are of the greatest rarity.

Primary Reference: Behrens. General Reference: Krusy.

I-35	1437	Lübeck	C/M Goldgulden	R6
I-363	1497	Lübeck	C/M Goldgulden	R5

LÜNEBURG – CITY. 1493 (COUNTERMARKED COINAGE ONLY)

Lüneburg, a Hanseatic League city southeast of Hamburg, issued no dated coinage but as with its larger northern trading partners Hamburg and Lübeck, countermarked gold coinage. Only a handful of any countermarked Lüneburg coins exist, and the only one dated was on a host 1493 Frankfurt goldgulden. Lüneburg's mark was a tiny round stamp with the letter "A."

Primary Reference: Bahrfeldt Lüneburg. General Reference: Krusy.

I-301	1493	Lüneburg	C/M Goldgulden	R6

MAINZ – ARCHBISHOPRIC AND ELECTORS. MINTS OF MAINZ, HÖCHST AND BINGEN. 1425

Mainz was a very powerful and important archbishopric in the Rhineland with a long history of coinage. It issued early dated coins under both its name and that of its mints, Höchst and Bingen. The early dated coinage of Mainz spanned the period from 1425 to 1499, including a number of goldguldens struck in the decade of 1490. Its early coinage, as with that of the other Rhineland archbishoprics, was well struck and can be collected in higher grades. One reason why the coins of Mainz are relatively plentiful are that Mainz was a member of the Rhineland Monetary Treaty ("Munzvertrag") of 1437. Pursuant to that treaty, a series of goldguldens and groschens of uniform weight and style were struck in the Mainz mints of Höchst and Bingen and struck in other Rhineland jurisdictions from 1436 (employing a date one year prior to the treaty) to 1438.

The mint of Bingen struck early dated coins from 1436-1447. Goldguldens were struck from 1436-1438 and weisspfennige ("white pennies" or groschen) in 1437, from 1443-1445 and again in 1447. The coins of Bingen are generally rarer than those of the other Rhineland mints and not as well struck. Mainz' other mint, Höchst, issued dated gold but no silver. The Höchst 1436 goldgulden is probably the most available of the 1436 goldguldens to collect, being merely "very rare."

Standard References: For Gold – Felke and Schlegel (both excellent). For silver and gold together: Cappe and/or Collection Walther. Secondary Reference: Pr. Alexander. General Reference: Schulten and Saurma.

I-20	1425	Bingen	Groschen	R6
I-25	1431	Bingen	Groschen	R5
I-29	1436	Bingen	Goldgulden	R6
I-30	1436	Höchst	Goldgulden	R2
I-36a	1437	Bingen	Goldgulden	R3
I-36b	1437	Bingen	Goldgulden	R5
I-37	1437	Bingen	Groschen	R3
I-38a	1437	Höchst	Goldgulden	R
I-38b	1437	Höchst	Goldgulden	R5
I-48	1438	Bingen	Goldgulden	R6
I-49	1438	Bingen	Groschen	R3
I-50	1438	Höchst	Goldgulden	R2
I-65	1443	Bingen	Groschen	R2
I-72	1444	Bingen	Groschen	R
I-77	1445	Bingen	Groschen	S
I-82	1447	Bingen	Groschen	R2
I-239	1489	Uncertain	Schilling	R5
I-251	1490	Mainz	Goldgulden	R5
I-267	1491	Mainz	Goldgulden	R3
I-280	1492	Mainz	Goldgulden	R2
I-281	1492	Mainz	Half Groschen	R2
I-302	1493	Mainz	Goldgulden	R2

Number	Date	Mint	Denomination	Rarity
I-303	1493	Mainz	Half Groschen	R2
I-317	1494	Mainz	Goldgulden	R6
I-328	1495	Mainz	Goldgulden	R5-6
I-329	1495	Mainz	Half Groschen	R2
I-330	1495	Mainz	Pfennig	R5
I-345	1496	Mainz	Half Groschen	R
I-364	1497	Mainz	Goldgulden	R5
I-420	1499	Mainz	Goldgulden	R6

MARK (MARCK)– COUNTY. MINTS OF UNNA AND HÖRDE. 1489

Mark was a county near the Belgium border near Liège. It was owned by the dukes of Cleve and its title was included on their coinage. However, the counts of Mark also struck their own coinage from the two small mint cities of Unna and Hörde. Mark issued only three early dated coin types. All copy the typical Cleve and Wesel styles, but are identified by the mint name in the legend. All are of the greatest rarity.

Standard References: Menadier Mark and Collection Weygand. General Reference: Schulten

I-240	1489	Unna	Half Stüber	R6
I-252	1490	Unna	Stüber	R6
I-282	1492	Hörde	Braspfennig	R6

MÖRS – COUNTY. 1476

Mörs was a county in northwestern Germany sandwiched between Jülich, Cleve and Gelderland. Its early dated coinage generally resembled Northern Netherlands coinage, especially that of Groningen. Mörs issued one jager in 1478 (believed unique) and a series of stübers (stuivers) from 1476-1480. All the dated stübers of Mörs are at least extremely rare.

Primary Reference: Noss (excellent). General Reference: None

I-151	1476	Mörs	Stüber	R4
I-152	1477	Mörs	Stüber	R3
I-159	1478	Mörs	Jager	R6
I-160a	1478	Mörs	Stüber	R3
I-160b	1478	Mörs	Stüber	R4
I-172	1480	Mörs	Stüber	R4

MÜHLHAUSEN – CITY. 1496

Mühlhausen was a small city in Thüringia in the center of Germany, east of Hesse. It issued a series of small denomination coinage, three of which contained dates. The dated coins of Mühlhausen were tiny uniface pfennigs struck in 1496, 1497 and 1500, all with the date straddling the winged city shield. All are at least extremely rare and are typically found in lower grades, as is common with small denomination circulating coinage of this period.

Primary Reference: Posern-Klett. General Reference: Schulten

I-346	1496	Mühlhausen	Pfennig	R3
I-365	1497	Mühlhausen	Pfennig	R4
I-454	1500	Mühlhausen	Pfennig	R4

MÜLHEIM (MUHLHEIM) – SEE JÜLICH-BERG

NEUSS – CITY. 1492

Neuss was a Rhineland city just west of Düsseldorf and south of Cleve. It struck one early dated coin copying the style of Cleve coinage, a large and very rare 1492 double groschen. As is typical of most imitative coinage, it was struck with less fineness than the imitated coinage and is generally found well worn.

Primary Reference: Noss (excellent). General Reference: Schulten

I-283	1492	Neuss	Double Groschen	R2

NEWMARKET (NEUMARKT) – SEE PALATINATE-MOSBACH-NEWMARKET AND PALATINATE-UPPER PALATINATE

NORDEN – SEE EAST FRISIA

NÖRDLINGEN – IMPERIAL CITY. 1491

Nördlingen in Bavaria was an imperial city controlled by the Holy Roman Emperor. In the late 15th century, the Emperor sold the mint rights of Nördlingen to the Weinsberg family. On its dated coins, the Emperor's name is always listed, but the obverse shield is that of the Weinsberg family. The larger silver coins featured a portrait of the Emperor,

Number	Date	Mint	Denomination	Rarity

while the imperial eagle appeared on the smaller sizes. The gold followed the typical design standard of St. John with a lamb on the obverse and the imperial orb on the reverse.
An unbroken series goldguldens was struck by Nördlingen from 1491-1500, the same as with Frankfurt. Extremely rare schillings, bearing a portrait of Maximilian as Holy Roman Emperor, were struck from 1496-1498. It is worthwhile to note that in 1497 these schillings were struck from two very dissimilar dies, one with a crude dumpy bust (first struck in 1496) so incompetently engraved that is resembles a caricature, and the other with a lovely Renaissance bust of superb style. The latter replaced the former on the next year's die. Half schillings were also struck ever year from 1495-1500, making early dated coins of Nördlingen some of the most collectable of early dated Germanic coins from the decade of 1491-1500. All Nördlingen gold is collectable in high grade, while the silver less so because of high base metal content.

Primary Reference: Herzfelder (excellent). General Reference: Schulten

I-268	1491	Nördlingen	Goldgulden	R
I-284	1492	Nördlingen	Goldgulden	R
I-304	1493	Nördlingen	Goldgulden	R
I-318	1494	Nördlingen	Goldgulden	R3
I-331	1495	Nördlingen	Goldgulden	R3
I-332	1495	Nördlingen	Half Schilling	R6?
I-347	1496	Nördlingen	Goldgulden	R3
I-348	1496	Nördlingen	Schilling	R4
I-349	1496	Nördlingen	Half Schilling	R3
I-366a	1497	Nördlingen	Goldgulden	R2
I-366b	1497	Nördlingen	Goldgulden	R4
I-366c	1497	Nördlingen	Goldgulden	R3
I-367a	1497	Nördlingen	Schilling	R3
I-367b	1497	Nördlingen	Schilling	R3
I-368	1497	Nördlingen	Half Schilling	S
I-382	1498	Nördlingen	Goldgulden	R
I-383	1498	Nördlingen	Schilling	R3
I-384a	1498	Nördlingen	Half Schilling	VS
I-384b	1498	Nördlingen	Half Schilling	R
I-421a	1499	Nördlingen	Half Schilling	R
I-421b	1499	Nördlingen	Half Schilling	R2
I-455	1500	Nördlingen	Goldgulden	R
I-456	1500	Nördlingen	Half Schilling	R3

ÖLSNITZ - SEE SAXONY

OSNABRÜCK – BISHOPRIC. 1489 (STRUCK COINAGE) 1498 (COUNTERMARKED COINAGE)
Osnabrück was a small bishopric in Westphalia in northwest Germany. It struck only one early dated coin, a half stüber of 1489. It also countermarked a host 1498 Utrecht braspfennig.

Primary Reference: Kennepohl (excellent). General Reference: Schulten.

I-241	1489	Osnabrück	Half Stüber	R6
I-385	1498	Osnabrück	C/M Braspfennig	R4

OSTFRIESLAND – SEE EAST FRISIA

ÖTTINGEN – COUNTY. 1499
Öttingen was a smaller county in Swabia north of Nördlingen. It issued a plentiful series of dated coins in the early 16th century, but struck only two early dated coins, a schilling and half schilling, both dated 1499. Only the half schilling may be extant today, and it is of the greatest rarity. There is no recent auction history of either.

Primary Reference: Löffelholz. General Reference: Schulten.

I-422	1499	Öttingen	Schilling	R6
I-423	1499	Öttingen	Half Schilling	R6

PADERBORN (PADERBORN STADT) – CITY. 1463 (COUNTERMARKED COINAGE ONLY)
Paderborn was a Westphalian bishopric and city, the latter the only one to issue early dated coins. In fact, Paderborn minted no early dated coins from its own dies, but instead countermarked regional circulating coinage with its mark of a cross with three vertical bars below, all inside a shield. Early dated host coins countermarked by Paderborn are 1463 Groningen jagers (itself extremely rare and desirable coins) and 1477, 1478 and 1479 Utrecht jagers. All early dated coinage of Paderborn is very to excessively rare.

Number	Date	Mint	Denomination	Rarity

Primary Reference: Weingaertner   General Reference: Krusy and JMP XXXIX.

I-93	1463	Paderborn	C/M Jager	R5
I-153	1477	Paderborn	C/M Double Stüber	R4
I-161	1478	Paderborn	C/M Double Stüber	R3
I-170	1479	Paderborn	C/M Double Stüber	R4

PALATINATE (PFALZ, RHENISH PALATINATE OR KURPFALZ) – COUNTY AND ELECTORS OF THE HOLY ROMAN EMPIRE. MINTS OF BACHARACH AND HEIDELBERG. 1425

The Palatinate, also known as Pfalz or Kurpfalz, was a very large and important county whose rulers held joint titles as counts and as electors of the Holy Roman Empire. Rhenish Palatinate was one of the four divisions of the Palatinate created for the four sons of Ruprecht III, Duke of Bavaria, after his death. In its mint of Bacharach, the Palatinate struck a number of early dated coins between 1425 and 1448. Early dated coinage was again struck between 1489 and 1500, but mostly without reference to any mint. The coins of Palatinate are generally rare, but due to superior mint standards, can still be obtained in higher grades, especially the gold.

Bacharach was the only mint of the Palatinate that struck early dated coins from 1436-1449. Goldguldens were struck from 1436-1438 and groschens (weisspfennige) were struck from 1437-1438 and again from 1443-1449 except for 1445. The gold of this mint is easily found in high grade, the silver generally so as well, except for the dates 1437 and 1443.

Heidelberg, one of the Palatinate's mints, was an important mint in its own right. However, it struck only one piece in its own name, an excessively rare goldgulden dated 1490. The identification of this coin is made by the title on its reverse: "MONETA:NOVA-AVRE:HEID."

Standard References: For the goldguldens – Felke (Excellent). For silver and gold together – Collection Memmesheimer and Collection Noss. General References: Saurma and Schulten.

I-21	1425	Bacharach	Groschen	R6
I-31	1436	Bacharach	Goldgulden	R2
I-39	1437	Bacharach	Goldgulden	VS
I-40	1437	Bacharach	Groschen	R
I-51	1438	Bacharach	Goldgulden	S
I-52a	1438	Bacharach	Groschen	VS
I-52b	1438	Bacharach	Groschen	R4-5
I-66	1443	Bacharach	Groschen	R2
I-73	1444	Bacharach	Groschen	C
I-78	1445	Bacharach	Groschen	S
I-83	1447	Bacharach	Groschen	S
I-85	1448	Bacharach	Groschen	VS
I-88	1449	Bacharach	Groschen	R
I-242	1489	Heidelberg?	Goldgulden	R6
I-253	1490	Heidelberg	Goldgulden	R5
I-269	1491	Heidelberg	Goldgulden	R2
I-285	1492	Heidelberg	Goldgulden	R2
I-286	1492	Uncertain	Half Groschen	R2
I-287	1492	Uncertain	Half Albus	R
I-305	1493	Heidelberg	Goldgulden	R
I-306	1493	Uncertain	Half Groschen	R
I-319	1494	Uncertain	Half Albus	R3
I-333	1495	Uncertain	Half Albus	VS
I-350	1496	Uncertain	Half Albus	S
I-369	1497	Heidelberg	Goldgulden	R2
I-457	1500	Heidelberg	Goldgulden	R4

PALATINATE (PFALZ)-MOSBACH-NEWMARKET (NEUMARKT) – COUNTY. MINT OF NEWMARKET. 1496

Palatinate-Mosbach-Newmarket was a separate upper Palatinate county in the 15th century, created from the transfer of Newmarket to Mosbach, which was then later absorbed into the Palatinate. In 1496 and in 1498 it struck goldguldens referencing the mint of "NOVIFOREN." Both are excessively rare and command high prices at auction.

Primary Reference: Gotz, Coll. Memmesheimer   General References: Friedberg, De Mey d'Or and Schulten

I-351	1496	Newmarket	Goldgulden	R4
I-386	1498	Newmarket	Goldgulden	R5

Number	Date	Mint	Denomination	Rarity

PALATINATE-UPPER PALATINATE (OBERPFALZ) – ELECTORS. MINT OF NEWMARKET (NEUMARKT). 1500

The patrimony known as "Oberpfalz," or Upper Palatinate, was a short-lived county which was in existence only during the 15th century. Only one early dated coin was struck there, a goldgulden from the Newmarket mint, which also struck coinage for Palatinate-Mosbach.

Primary reference: Gotz. General References: Friedberg, De Mey d'Or and Schulten

I-458	1500	Newmarket	Goldgulden	R3

PALATINATE (PFALZ)-ZWEIBRUECKEN-VELDENZ – COUNTY. MINT OF VELDENZ. 1490

Pfalz-Zweibrueken-Veldenz was one of the four parts of the Palatinate that were divided after the death of Ruprecht III. It was a short-lived county in the western part of the Palatinate, existing but from 1459 to 1514. Only one early dated coin was struck by it, a 1490 schilling of the greatest rarity.

Primary Reference: Coll. Memmesheimer, Collection Noss. General Reference: Schulten

I-254	1490	Veldenz	Schilling	R6

POMMERANIA (POMMERN) – DUCHY. MINTS OF STETTIN, DAMM AND GARZ. 1488

Pommerania was a very large duchy at the far northeastern part of modern Germany, where the German and Polish borders currently meet at the Oder River. Pommerania consisted of several smaller duchies, principally those of Stettin and Wolgast. Stettin, the largest of the duchies, struck early dated coins from its mints in the town of Garz on the island of Rügen, in Stettin, and in the town of Damm, east of Stettin.

Under Bogaslav X of Stettin, Pommerania struck a series of dated coins nearly every year from 1488-1500. The coinage of the duke of Stettin was prolific – nearly twenty different types of early dated coins exist amongst the three mints. Little variety was employed: most were schillings or wittens and each denomination used the identical design, changing only the mint's name. Goldguldens were struck in 1499 and large half mark pieces of half gulden weight were struck in two varieties dated 1500. All three are now excessively rare.

Despite their use of prosaic designs, the three mints of Stettin, especially that of Damm, produced well-struck coinage of good silver which (except as noted above) is collectable in high grades today. Most of the dated schillings are fairly common, with the exception of the single digit dated 1488 schilling of Garz. While numerous catalogues (as well as the primary reference of Bahrfeldt) list a 1497 schilling being struck, all examples seen by the author are of a 1495 schilling using a medieval "5" which appears very much as a modern "7."

Primary References: Bahrfeldt and Dannenberg. General Reference: Schulten

I-225	1488	Garz	Schilling	R4
I-243	1489	Garz	Schilling	C
I-270	1491	Damm	Schilling	R2
I-288a	1492	Damm	Schilling	S
I-288b	1492	Damm	Schilling	VS
I-289a	1492	Garz	Schilling	R
I-289b	1492	Garz	Schilling	R4
I-307	1493	Damm	Schilling	VS
I-320	1494	Damm	Schilling	S
I-334	1495	Damm	Schilling	S
I-352	1496	Damm	Schilling	S
I-370	1497	Damm	Schilling	R5?
I-424	1499	Damm	Schilling	S
I-425	1499	Stettin	Goldgulden	R4
I-426	1499	Stettin	Schilling	VS
I-427	1499	Stettin	Witten	R2
I-459a	1500	Stettin	Half Mark	R5
I-459b	1500	Stettin	Half Mark	R4
I-460a	1500	Stettin	Schilling	VS
I-460b	1500	Stettin	Schilling	VS
I-461	1500	Stettin	Witten	S

SAXONY (SACHSEN) – DUCHY AND ELECTORS OF THE HOLY ROMAN EMPIRE. MINTS OF LEIPZIG, GOTHA, FREIBERG, COLDITZ, WITTENBERG, ÖLSNITZ, ZWICKAU, SCHNEEBERG AND ANNABERG. 1457

Saxony was one of the largest and most important German states in the late Middle Ages and its output of coinage reflected its premier status. Its wealthy monetary history was owed in great part to silver mines in its regions. The successful exploitation of them, which began around the decade of 1460, gave rise to an enormous variety of coinage.

Saxony issued more early dated coin types and denominations than any other German state. Beginning with two different groschen types struck in 1457, the early dated coinage of Saxony continued to be struck, more or less continuously, from 1465 through 1500. Saxony issued denominations from debased half schwertgroschens to half guldiners and goldguldens. To coin this wealth, Saxony engaged mintmasters to run no less than eight different mints.

Not unexpectedly, there are countless reported varieties from numerous mints and the indispensable reference of Krug is necessary to sort them out. Numerous fascinating mules exist of dates and mints and legend types. Adding to the confusion was the decision of the mintmasters to use designs (star, clover leaf, crescent, etc) to identify their product rather than the name of the mint city. Unfortunately, the mintmasters would retain the same design if they traveled to a different mint, as they did periodically. Thus, the mint symbols "traveled" as much as their employing masters. Attribution by mint is not an easy task with some Saxony coinage.

Befitting a great power, Saxony's mints were modern and efficient, and the quality of its coinage was high. Examples in high grade can be collected across nearly all known types. Of great beauty are Saxony's "bartgroschens," featuring the elector with his sword across his shoulder, dated 1492 (very scarce) and 1493 (extremely rare). Two 1457 dated groschens of very different types were also struck by Saxony, and both are extremely or excessively rare. The goldguldens struck from the Leipzig mint from 1498-1500 are all very rare and desirable.

Primary Reference: Krug (excellent and indispensable). Secondary Reference: Haupt. General Reference: Schulten (silver and gold), Friedberg and De Mey d'Or (gold).

Number	Date	Mint	Denomination	Rarity
I-91	1457	Gotha	Groschen	R5
I-92	1457	Leipzig	Turnosgroschen	R3
I-95	1465	Colditz	Horngroschen	S
I-96a	1465	Freiberg	Horngroschen	S
I-96b	1465	Freiberg	Horngroschen	R4
I-100	1466	Colditz	Horngroschen	R
I-101a	1466	Freiberg	Horngroschen	S
I-101b	1466	Freiberg	Horngroschen	R
I-101c	1466	Freiberg	Horngroschen	R5
I-102	1466	Gotha	Horngroschen	R3
I-103a	1466	Leipzig	Horngroschen	C
I-103b	1466	Leipzig/ Colditz	Horngroschen	R5
I-104	1466	Ölsnitz	Horngroschen	R4
I-105	1466	Wittenberg	Horngroschen	R3
I-111	1467	Colditz	Horngroschen	S
I-112a	1467	Freiberg	Horngroschen	S
I-112b	1467	Freiberg	Horngroschen	R4
I-113	1467	Leipzig	Horngroschen	S
I-118	1468	Colditz	Horngroschen	R
I-119	1468	Freiberg	Horngroschen	S
I-120a	1468	Leipzig	Horngroschen	VS
I-120b	1468	Leipzig/ Colditz	Horngroschen	R4
I-124	1469	Colditz	Horngroschen	R
I-125	1469	Freiberg	Horngroschen	VS
I-126	1469	Gotha	Horngroschen	R3
I-127	1469	Leipzig	Horngroschen	S
I-140	1475	Colditz	Spitzgroschen	R
I-141	1475	Colditz	Margaretha Spitzgroschen	R3
I-142	1475	Colditz	Half Spitzgroschen	R
I-143	1475	Colditz	Half Spitzgroschen with Margaretha.	R2
I-144	1475	Colditz	Half Margaretha Spitzgroschen	R4
I-145	1475	Freiberg	Spitzgroschen	C
I-146a	1475	Freiberg	Half Spitzgroschen	VS
I-146b	1475	Freiberg/ Leipzig	Half Spitzgroschen	R4
I-147	1475	Gotha	Half Spitzgroschen	R3
I-148	1475	Leipzig	Spitzgroschen	C
I-149	1475	Leipzig	Half Spitzgroschen	S

Number	Date	Mint	Denomination		Rarity
I-150	1475	Zwickau	Spitzgroschen		R2
I-154	1477	Colditz	Spitzgroschen		R3
I-155	1477	Freiberg	Spitzgroschen		C
I-156	1477	Zwickau	Spitzgroschen		C
I-162	1478	Freiberg	Spitzgroschen		R2
I-163	1478	Zwickau	Spitzgroschen		C
I-164	1478	Zwickau	Half Spitzgroschen		VS
I-184	1482	Freiberg	Half Schwertgroschen		R
I-185	1482	Zwickau/ Schneeberg	Half Schwertgroschen		C
I-226	1488	Freiberg	Half Schwertgroschen		R3
I-227a	1488	Schneeberg	Half Schwertgroschen		C
I-227b	1488	Schneeberg	Half Schwertgroschen		R3
I-227c	1488	Schneeberg	Half Schwertgroschen		R2
I-255a	1490	Freiberg	Half Schwertgroschen		R2
I-255b	1490	Freiberg	Half Schwertgroschen		R4
I-256a	1490	Zwickau	Half Schwertgroschen		S
I-256b	1490	Zwickau	Half Schwertgroschen		R3
I-256c	1490	Zwickau/ Freiberg	Half Schwertgroschen		R4
I-271	1491	Zwickau	Half Schwertgroschen		R3
I-290	1492	Freiberg	Half Schwertgroschen		VS
I-291	1492	Zwickau/ Schneeberg	Bartgroschen	F.I.	VS
I-292	1492	Zwickau/ Schneeberg	Bartgroschen	F.I.G	VS
I-293	1492	Zwickau/ Schneeberg	Half Schwertgroschen		C
I-308	1493	Zwickau/ Schneeberg	Bartgroschen		R3
I-321	1494	Schneeberg	Half Schwertgroschen		R5
I-335a	1495	Freiberg	Half Schwertgroschen		VS
I-335b	1495	Freiberg	Half Schwertgroschen		R5
I-335c	1495	Freiberg/ Schneeberg	Half Schwertgroschen		R5
I-335d	1495	Freiberg/ Schneeberg	Half Schwertgroschen		R4
I-336a	1495	Schneeberg	Half Schwertgroschen		C
I-336b	1495	Schneeberg	Half Schwertgroschen		VS
I-353	1496	Freiberg	Zinsgroschen		R4
I-354	1496	Leipzig	Zinsgroschen		C
I-387	1498	Annaberg	Schreckenberger		R3
I-388	1498	Freiberg	Half Schwertgroschen		R3
I-389	1498	Leipzig	Goldgulden	F.A.I.	R4
I-390	1498	Leipzig	Goldgulden	F.G.I.	R2
I-391a	1498	Schneeberg	Zinsgroschen		C
I-391b	1498	Schneeberg	Zinsgroschen		R3
I-428a	1499	Annaberg	Schreckenberger	F.A.I.	R2
I-428b	1499	Annaberg	Schreckenberger		R2
I-429	1499	Annaberg	Schreckenberger	F.G.I.	R4
I-430	1499	Leipzig	Goldgulden	F.A.I.	R2
I-431	1499	Leipzig	Goldgulden	F.G.I.	R2
I-432	1499	Schneeberg	Zinsgroschen	F.A.I	C
I-433	1499	Schneeberg	Zinsgroschen	F.G.I.	R3
I-434	1499	Schneeberg/ Freiberg	Half Schwertgroschen		R4
I-462	1500	Annaberg	Half Guldiner	F.A.I.	R3
I-463	1500	Annaberg	Half Guldiner	F.G.I.	R3
I-464a	1500	Leipzig	Goldgulden	F.A.I.	R3
I-464b	1500	Leipzig	Goldgulden		R5
I-465	1500	Leipzig	Goldgulden	F.G.I.	R4-5

SCHLEUSINGEN – SEE HENNEBERG

Number	Date	Mint	Denomination	Rarity

SCHNEEBERG – SEE SAXONY

SCHOONVORST – SEE JÜLICH-BERG

SCHOONVORST-SICHEM. LORDSHIP (SEE PART II, UNDER SOUTHERN NETHERLANDS)

SCHWARZBURG – COUNTY. MINT OF KÖNIGSEE. 1493 (Not to be confused with Schwarzenburg)

Schwarzburg was a county in central-east Germany divided into a number of different lineages. However, only the Leutenburg line issued early dated coinage, and that was in only one year, 1493, when a groschen and half groschen were struck. Both are impressive pieces, especially the groschen, which features a standing knight as its reverse device.

Primary Reference: Fischer. General Reference: Schulten.

I-309	1493	Königsee	Groschen	R3
I-310	1493	Königsee	Half Groschen	R2

SOEST – CITY. 1478 (COUNTERMARKED COINAGE ONLY)

Soest was a city in central Westphalia which struck no early dated coins of its own but whose countermarking on local circulating coinage was extremely prolific – perhaps the most widespread of any German state. However, only one early dated coin was known to be countermarked by Soest, a 1478 Utrecht jager, the most common early dated coin countermarked by the Westphalian cities. Soest's countermark was a key whose teeth faced to the right.

Primary Reference: JMP XXXIX. General Reference: Krusy.

I-165	1478	Soest	C/M Double Stüber	R5-6

STETTIN – SEE POMMERANIA

STOLBERG – COUNTY. MINTS OF STOLBERG AND WERNIGERODE. 1483

Stolberg was a county in the Harz mountains of central Germany east of Göttingen and south of Brunswick. Its main device, a stag prancing left, graced all of its early dated coinage. Between 1483 and 1500, Stolberg struck five different double digit and one single digit dated groschen. The notable year for Stolberg coinage was 1492, when both a double digit dated groschen and a single digit dated groschen, with a "Z" representing the date "2," were struck. All early dated coinage of Stolberg is very rare to excessively rare.

Primary Reference: Friederich. General Reference: Schulten.

I-195	1483	Wernigerode	Groschen	R3
I-203	1485	Wernigerode	Groschen	R3
I-294a	1492	Wernigerode	Groschen	R2
I-294b	1492	Wernigerode	Groschen	R3
I-311	1493	Wernigerode	Groschen	R3
I-466	1500	Stolberg	Groschen	R4

SWABIA – SEE BRANDENBURG-FRANCONIA

THANN (TANNENSIS) – CITY. 1499

Thann, located southwest of its larger Alsatian neighbor, Colmar, was an city with a limited monetary history that consisted primarily of the issuance of thalers in the mid-16th century. However, as with Colmar, in 1499 it issued dated dickens and groschens. The coinage featured the shield of Thann on the obverse with the patron St. Theobold on the obverse. All coinage of Thann is extremely or excessively rare.

Primary Reference: Engel & Lehr and De Mey Alsace. General Reference: Schulten.

I-435	1499	Thann	Dicken	R3
I-436	1499	Thann	Groschen	R4

TRIER (TRÈVES)– ARCHBISHOPRIC AND ELECTORS OF THE HOLY ROMAN EMPIRE. MINT OF COBLENZ. 1436

Trier was a powerful archbishopric just east of Luxemburg and was one of the signatories to the Rhineland Monetary Treaty from which standardized gold and silver coinage was issued. Coblenz, the only mint at which Trier's early dated coinage was struck, was a large city at the junction of the Rhine and Mosel Rivers. Between 1436 and 1448 the archbishopric, under the treaty, struck goldguldens and weisspfennige to strict standards. In 1491, 43 years after its last dated coin, Trier struck one more dated type, an excessively rare goldgulden. The coins of Trier were well struck and are collectable in higher grades, but the gold is all very or extremely rare.

Primary References: Felke (excellent) (Gold) and Noss (similarly excellent)(Gold and Silver). General Reference: Saurma.

Number	Date	Mint	Denomination	Rarity
I-32a	1436	Coblenz	Goldgulden	R3
I-32b	1436	Coblenz	Goldgulden	R5
I-41	1437	Coblenz	Goldgulden	R2
I-42	1437	Coblenz	Groschen	R
I-53	1438	Coblenz	Goldgulden	R2
I-54	1438	Coblenz	Groschen	VS
I-74	1444	Coblenz	Groschen	S
I-86	1448	Coblenz	Groschen	VS
I-272	1491	Coblenz	Goldgulden	R4

TÜBINGEN – SEE WÜRTTEMBURG

UNNA – SEE MARK

VELDENZ – SEE PALATINATE-ZWEIBRUECKEN-VELDENZ

VÖRDEN – SEE BREMEN

WARBURG – CITY. 1477 (COUNTERMARKED COINAGE ONLY)
Warburg was a very small city in Westphalia southeast of Paderborn. It struck no early dated coins of its own, but countermarked host Utrecht jagers dated from 1477-1479. Its countermark was a double lily in a diamond, and two different varieties are known for the 1477 pieces, one with a tiny diamond and one with a larger one.

Primary Reference: Collection Hennig, Collection Kayser. General Reference: Krusy and JMP XXXIX.

I-157	1477	Warburg	C/M Double Stüber	R4
I-166	1478	Warburg	C/M Double Stüber	R3
I-171	1479	Warburg	C/M Double Stüber	R4

WERL – CITY. 1477 (COUNTERMARKED COINAGE ONLY)
Werl was a small city in Westphalia near Soest. As with the other small Westphalian cities, it did not possess the right to coin silver money so it instead countermarked circulating coinage from larger regions, typically (and in this case as well) the coinage of Utrecht. There are two early dated coins displaying the Werl countermark of a cross-in-shield. One is on a host 1478 Utrecht jager and the other on a host 1498 Utrecht braspfennig. Both are of the greatest rarity.

Primary Reference: JMP XXXIX. General Reference: Krusy

I-158	1477	Werl	C/M Double Stüber	R5
I-392	1498	Werl	C/M Braspfennig	R6

WERNIGERODE – TOWNSHIP WITH MINT AND MINT OF STOLBERG. 1466 (COUNTERMARKED COINAGE ONLY)
Wernigerode, a mint of Stolberg where early dated Stolberg coinage was struck, was also a small township whose town fathers countermarked a tiny handful of coins in the mid-15th century. Among them were two horngroschens of Saxony, dated 1466 and 1467 with the countermark of a crowned "W." Both are likely unique.

Primary Reference: None. General Reference: Krusy

	1466	Wernigerode	C/M Horngroschen	R6
	1467	Wernigerode	C/M Horngroschen	R6

WESEL – SEE CLEVE

WITTENBERG – SEE SAXONY

WOLFHAGEN – SEE HESSE-MARBURG

WORMS – BISHOPRIC. MINT OF MAINZ 1492
Worms was a bishopric located on the Rhine River between Mainz and Mannheim. It had very a lengthy history of medieval coinage, but struck only one early dated coin, a 1492 schilling in the style of those struck in nearby Mainz and Pfalz. The coin is possibly uncollectible and has no recent auction history.

Primary Reference: Joseph. General Reference: Schulten

I-295	1492	Mainz	Schilling	R5

Number	Date	Mint	Denomination	Rarity

WÜRTTEMBERG – COUNTY. MINT OF TÜBINGEN 1494

Württemberg was a large county in south Germany which was elevated to a duchy a year after its only early dated coin was struck in 1494. This coin, a schilling, had a fascinating reverse field with the date divided by a palm tree. Although more than one die is known, the coin is of the greatest rarity.

Primary Reference: Klein/Raff. Secondary Reference: Collection Ebner. General Reference: Schulten.

I-322	1494	Tübingen	Schilling	R5

WÜRZBURG – BISHOPRIC. 1496

Würzburg was a large bishopric in central-south Germany, southeast of Frankfurt and west of Bamberg. Beginning 1496, the year after Bishop Lorenz von Bibra took office, it struck an unbroken series of early dated schillings through 1500 with a goldgulden dated 1500 as well. The early dated coinage of Würzburg is especially attractive, with a full length standing figure of St. Kilian on the reverse. Although all early dated coinage of Würzburg is of varying degrees of rarity, the 1497 and 1498 dates are still possible to locate with the benefit of time and patience. Being a larger coin of billon composition, the early dated schillings of Würzburg are generally found well worn.

Primary Reference: Helmschrott. Secondary Reference: Collection Piloty. General Reference: Schulten

I-355	1496	Würzburg	Schilling	R3
I-371	1497	Würzburg	Schilling	R
I-393	1498	Würzburg	Schilling	R
I-437	1499	Würzburg	Schilling	R3
I-467	1500	Würzburg	Goldgulden	R4
I-468	1500	Würzburg	Schilling	R4

ZWICKAU – SEE SAXONY

REGION II - SOUTHERN NETHERLANDS

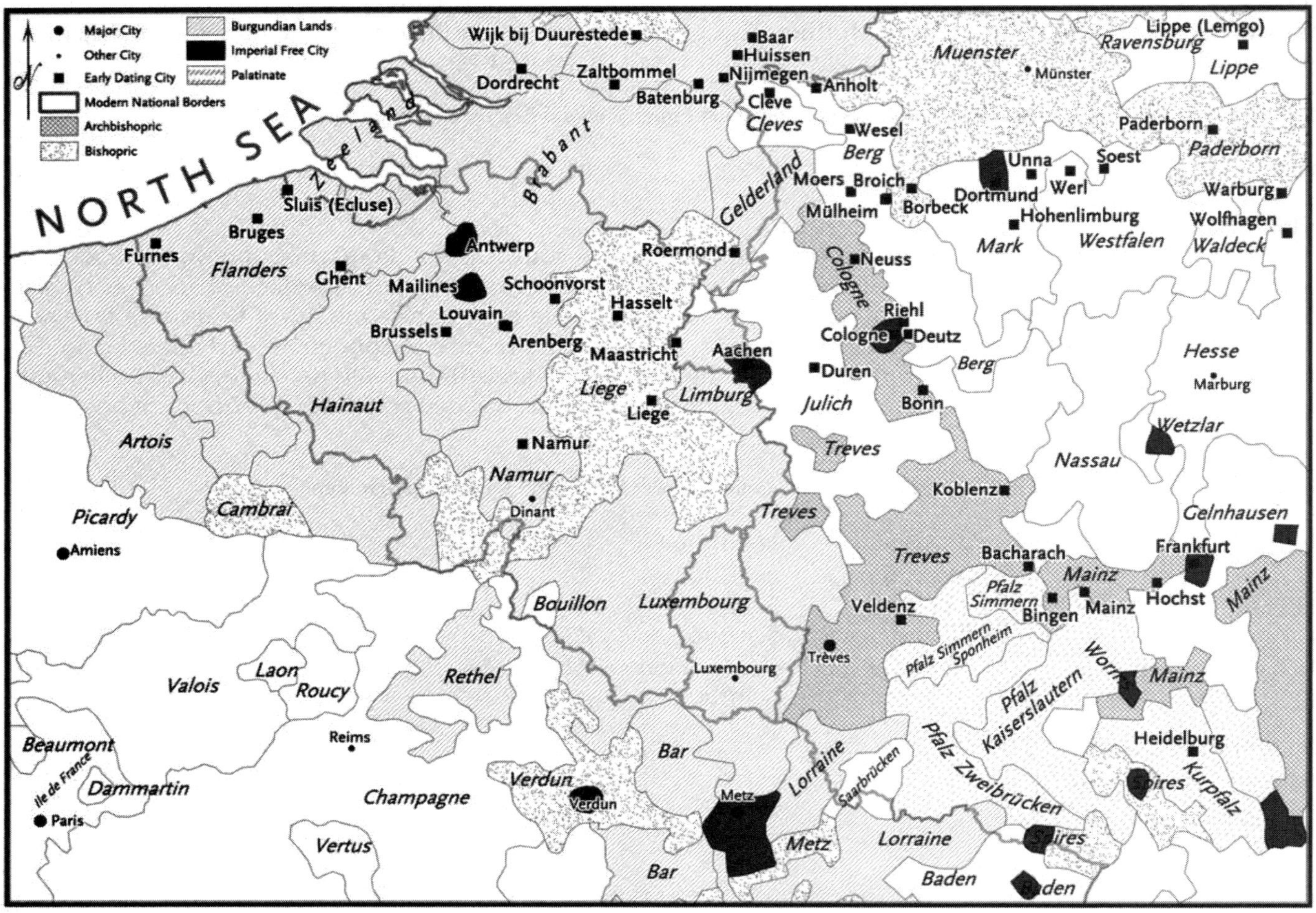

ANTWERP (ANVERS) - SEE BRABANT

BRABANT - DUCHY. OFFICIAL MINTS OF ANVERS (ANTWERP), MALINES (MECHELEN) AND MAESTRICHT (MAASTRICHT) AND UNOFFICIAL MINTS OF BRUSSELS (BRUXELLES) AND LOUVAIN (LEUVEN) IN REVOLT. 1474

The duchy of Brabant, located in what is today the central-west area of Belgium, was by far the most prolific issuer of early dated coins in the entire Netherlands, both in quantity issued, different dates and types. The duchy's status as one of the centers of Europe's northern trade meant that vast quantities of specie passed through its lands, mostly from the sale of woolen clothing, tapestries and paintings. Successful trade meant abundant coinage and Brabant's Burgundian Netherlands' mints excelled in all facets of coinage, both in quantity and quality.

Staggering amounts of coins were struck from the large mint at Anvers (Antwerp), numbering in the millions according to the well-preserved mint records of the Burgundian Netherlands as summarized in van Gelder-Hoc. The quantity of coinage struck in Brabant far exceeded that of the important neighboring county of Flanders (Flandre), containing the premier trading city of Bruges (Brugge), also ruled by the Burgundian dukes. For example, during the period of 1474-1477: 4 million double briquets were struck for Brabant versus 2 million for Flanders; 1.5 million briquets versus .9 Million and 2.2 million demi briquets versus .3 million (all numbers rounded). These numbers generally stayed consistent, until later when Flanders became the premier issuer of small denomination coinage, demi gros and smaller fractions. The other Burgundian Netherlands territories of Holland, Gelderland and Namur struck much smaller quantities.

While the coinage of Brabant was incredibly prolific, its designs and that of the other Burgundian Netherlands territories were prosaic and generally immobilized up to 1487. Prior to that date, the larger silver coinage featured as an obverse device two lions, one lion or one-half lion, each corresponding to its relative denomination as a double, sin-

Number **Date** **Mint** **Denomination** **Rarity**

gle or half briquet. The reverse device was either a cross or the shield of Burgundy until Marie of Burgundy's untimely death in 1482. Thereafter the shield represented Austria-Burgundy, given the unification of those territories under Philip the Fair, the son of Marie of Burgundy and Archduke (later Emperor) Maximilian, who was born in 1478. Maximilian remained regent for his infant son until 1492. Overlap minting also occurred, with coins in the name Marie continuing to be struck well after her death.

During the period of regency, the coinage was radically influenced by Maximilian's needs and ego. As Maximilian needed the revenues from his rich Netherlands territories to fund his expansionist efforts, he began to heavy tax the region. Devaluation through recall of existing coinage and accompanying recoinage added to the Emperor's coffers. Seven separate series of coinage were struck during Philip's rule from 1482-1506, both in the name of Maximilian as Regent and in the name of Philip as Archduke of Austria. Additionally, Maximilian wanted to use the coinage to show his (effective) control over the Burgundian Netherland territories. Contrary to the devaluation efforts with the great body of coinage, he commissioned small numbers of large denomination coinage from 1487-1489, gold and silver, struck to high fineness standards.

Beginning 1487, Maximilian introduced these new denominations whose size and style were meant to be a glorious as his reign. Premier among these for Brabant were the magnificent 1487 dated "grand real d'argent" (great silver real), featuring a half-length figure of Maximilian in armor holding a sword and orb on a crown sized (35mm) planchet. Dated pieces were also struck for Holland and Gelderland and undated ones for Flanders. Struck in 1489 was a new 4 patard, an equally impressive (albeit smaller) coin featuring a very young Philip as archduke wielding a sword behind a large shield of Austria-Burgundy. Large gold coins were struck at other mints in 1487, but not Brabant. However, in 1488, Brabant (as well as Gelderland and Holland) struck dated demi nobles d'or (half nobels of gold), modeled after British gold noble coinage, that featured the ruler in a ship.

In opposition to the high taxes imposed by Maximilian, a revolt in Brabant and Flanders in 1487 spurred the striking of new dated coinage by the cities of Brussels and Louvain beginning in 1488. Maximilian's rival, the King of France, had granted these cities the right to mint coinage in the name of the boy Archduke Philip. Dated coins of ordinary denominations bearing extraordinary designs were struck from 1488-1489 by these cities.

After the quelling of the revolt in 1492, all dated coinage disappeared until 1496. At that time, the official mint at Anvers (Antwerp) began striking rather bland double and single patards, as well as a new coinage, attractive toisons d'argent (silver lambs of God) worth three patards. A tiny quantity of stunning toisons d'or (lambs of gold) were struck dated 1499 and 1500, all excessively rare. In 1500 a mint at Maestricht (Maastricht) was opened and struck the same three former denominations but in very different styles.

As befitting a mighty duchy, Brabant possessed excellent mints which struck its coinage to high standards using strict official measures of fineness. However, recognizing that medieval mints were still entrepreneurial enterprises (see generally *Spufford Money*), the silver coins of Brabant (as with those of Flanders) bear numerous overdates, the fingerprints of thrifty mintmasters attempting to save on engraving costs. Still, the coins of Brabant were for the most part very well struck and can be obtained in high grades today. The very large denomination silver coinage from 1487-1489 is all quite rare, as the high standards of fineness to which they were struck promoted their melting and recoining.

Primary References: van Gelder-Hoc (essential and excellent) and de Witte (also excellent). General Reference: van der Chijs

II-11	1474	Antwerp	Double Briquet	C
II-12	1474	Antwerp	Briquet	S
II-13	1474	Antwerp	Demi Briquet	VS
II-17	1475	Antwerp	Double Briquet	C
II-18	1475	Antwerp	Briquet	VS
II-19	1475	Antwerp	Demi Briquet	VS
II-22	1476	Antwerp	Double Briquet	C
II-23	1476	Antwerp	Briquet	S
II-24	1476	Antwerp	Demi Briquet	VS
II-27	1477	Antwerp	Double Briquet	C
II-28	1477	Antwerp	Briquet	S
II-32	1478	Antwerp	Double Briquet	C
II-33	1478	Antwerp	Briquet	S
II-38	1479	Antwerp	Double Briquet	C
II-39	1479	Antwerp	Briquet	VS
II-45	1480	Antwerp	Double Briquet	S
II-46	1480	Antwerp	Briquet	S
II-47	1480	Antwerp	Gros	R
II-48	1480	Antwerp	Demi Gros	R3
II-54	1481	Antwerp	Double Briquet	C
II-55	1481	Antwerp	Briquet	VS

Number	Date	Mint	Denomination	Rarity
II-56	1481	Antwerp	Gros	VS
II-57	1481	Antwerp	Demi Gros	R4
II-58	1481	Antwerp	4 Mites	R
II-63	1482	Antwerp	Florin d'or	R4
II-64a	1482	Antwerp	Double Briquet	R
II-64b	1482	Antwerp	Double Briquet	VS
II-64c	1482	Antwerp	Double Briquet	R4
II-65a	1482	Antwerp	Briquet	R2
II-65b	1482	Antwerp	Briquet	R
II-67	1483	Antwerp	Florin d'or	R4
II-68a	1483	Antwerp	Double Briquet	R
II-68b	1483	Antwerp	Double Briquet	R3
II-69	1483	Antwerp	Briquet	R2
II-70	1483	Antwerp	Gros	R3
II-71	1483	Antwerp	Demi Gros	R4
II-75	1484	Antwerp	Gros	R
II-82	1485	Antwerp	Double Briquet	VS
II-83	1485	Antwerp	Briquet	R2
II-92	1487	Antwerp	Florin d'or	R6
II-93	1487	Antwerp/ Malines	Silver Real	R3
II-94	1487	Antwerp	Double Griffon	R2
II-A94	1487	Malines	Double Griffon	R2
II-100	1488	Louvain	Double Patard	R6
II-101	1488	Malines	Demi Noble d'or	R
II-102	1488	Malines	Double Patard	R
II-108	1489	Antwerp	Florin d'or	R5
II-109	1489	Antwerp	Demi Florin d'or	R5
II-110	1489	Antwerp	Quadruple Patard	R3
II-111	1489	Antwerp	Double Patard	R4
II-112	1489	Antwerp	Patard	R3
II-113	1489	Antwerp	Gros	VS
II-114	1489	Antwerp	Demi Gros	R4
II-125	1490	Antwerp	Double Florin d'or	R6
II-126	1490	Antwerp	Gros	R
II-127	1490	Antwerp	Four Mites	R3
II-129	1492	Antwerp	Florin d'or	R5
II-130a	1492	Antwerp	Double Briquet	VS
II-130b	1492	Antwerp	Double Briquet	R3
II-131	1492	Antwerp	Briquet	VS
II-136	1496	Antwerp	Toison d'argent	VS
II-137	1496	Antwerp	Double Patard	S
II-138	1497	Antwerp	Toison d'argent	R
II-139	1497	Antwerp	Double Patard	R
II-141	1498	Antwerp	Toison d'argent	VS
II-142	1498	Antwerp	Double Patard	C
II-143	1499	Antwerp	Toison d'or	R4
II-144	1499	Antwerp	Florin d'or	VS-R
II-145	1499	Antwerp	Toison d'argent	VS
II-146a	1499	Antwerp	Double Briquet	C
II-146b	1499	Antwerp	Double Briquet	C
II-151	1500	Antwerp	Toison d'or	R5
II-152	1500	Antwerp	Toison d'argent	VS
II-153a	1500	Antwerp	Double Patard	VS
II-153b	1500	Antwerp	Double Patard	C
II-154	1500	Maestricht	Florin d'or	R4
II-155	1500	Maestricht	Demi Florin d'or	R4
II-156	1500	Maestricht	Toison d'argent	R
II-157	1500	Maestricht	Double Patard	S
II-158	1500	Maestricht	Patard	VS

BRUGES - SEE FLANDERS

BRUSSELS (BRUXELLES) - CITY IN BRABANT UNDER REVOLT. 1488

Number	Date	Mint	Denomination	Rarity

Brussels was a city mint of Brabant. In 1488 and in 1489 it struck patards of single, double and quadruple sizes, all with the spectacular design of its patron St. Michael either killing dragons or holding city shields. Only the three coin types noted above were dated and all are excessively rare.

Primary Reference: van Gelder-Hoc. General Reference: Van der Chijs.

II-98	1488	Brussels	Quadruple Patard	R5-6
II-99	1488	Brussels	Double Patard	R5
II-114	1489	Brussels	Patard	R5

ECLUSE - SEE GHENT

FLANDERS (FLANDRE) - COUNTY. OFFICIAL MINTS OF BRUGES AND FURNES AND UNOFFICIAL MINTS OF GHENT AND ECLUSE IN REVOLT. 1474

Flanders was a very large and powerful county in the center-north of Belgium which had a very significant history of medieval coinage. After acquiring Flanders through marriage, Duke Philip the Good of Burgundy (Philippe Le Bon) issued an edict in 1434 standardizing coinage throughout his Netherlands realm, which then included Brabant, Namur, Limburg, Hainaut, Holland and Zeeland. From that point on, the coinage of the Burgundian Netherlands circulated to recognized standards throughout Medieval Europe.

Simultaneous with a series of new coinage types struck in 1474 by Charles the Rash, Flanders, Brabant and Gelderland all began dating their coinage. The reasons for commencing dating, according to Professor Spufford are unknown. The well-preserved mint records of the Netherlands give no clue. However, given the dates' concurrent appearance, it would appear at first blush to be triggered by an edict issued from the Archduke, such as those standardizing weights and general designs. However, as with the other Burgundian Netherlands territories, Flanders' mint was operated semi-autonomously - dies were not standardized and Flanders' coinage, as with that of Gelderland and later Holland, contained distinctions in its execution of designs and legends. Moreover, far more than any of the other territories, Flanders' mint issued undated coinage where those of the other Burgundian Netherlands territories were dated. Thus the dating "edict," if there were one, was not as compelling or strict as that governing weights and fineness.

The well-struck coinage of Flanders is generally plentiful and many dates are collectable in very high grades, with coinage struck during the revolt from 1488-1492 being the exception. Coins struck from the earliest times, 1474-1475, can be readily found in superior grades. As with Brabant, Flanders' mints were run as entrepreneurial enterprises, so recut dies and overdates are plentiful in this series. A fascinating 1478/1748 overdate is even known. As was typical when dozens of dies were used, numerous die variations exist. The name of Flanders can be found engraved on its early dated coins in any of the following abbreviations: "FLAND, FLAN, FLAD, FLA, FL, or F."

Primary Reference: Deschamps de Pas. Secondary Reference: De Mey Flanders. General Reference: van Gelder-Hoc (highly recommended)

II-14	1474	Bruges	Double Briquet	C
II-15	1474	Bruges	Briquet	S
II-16	1474	Bruges	Demi Briquet	VS
II-20a	1475	Bruges	Double Briquet	C
II-20b	1475	Bruges	Double Briquet	R2
II-21	1475	Bruges	Briquet	VS
II-29a	1477	Bruges	Double Briquet	C
II-29b	1477	Bruges	Double Briquet	R5
II-30	1477	Bruges	Briquet	R5
II-31	1477	Bruges	Briquet	R5
II-34	1478	Bruges	Double Briquet	C
II-35	1478	Bruges	Gros	C
II-40	1479	Bruges	Double Briquet	S
II-41	1479	Bruges	Gros	C
II-49	1480	Bruges	Double Briquet	VS
II-50a	1480	Bruges	Briquet	R
II-50b	1480	Bruges	Briquet	R4
II-51	1480	Bruges	Gros	VS
II-59	1481	Bruges	Double Briquet	R
II-60	1481	Bruges	Gros	R
II-95a	1487	Bruges	Gold Real	R5-6
II-95b	1487	Bruges	Gold Real	R5-6
II-96	1487	Bruges	Double Griffon	R6
II-97	1487	Bruges	Griffon	R6
II-118	1489	Furnes	Quadruple Patard	R6

Number	Date	Mint	Denomination	Rarity

FURNES - SEE FLANDERS

GHENT (GAND) - CITY IN FLANDERS UNDER REVOLT. MINTS OF GHENT AND ECLUSE (SLUIS). 1488

Ghent (Gand) was a major trading city in medieval Europe and one of the centers of commerce of Northern Europe. Given its high profile as a wealthy city, along with other Flemish trading towns, it was eyed by the tax collectors of Maximilian as a ready source of revenue. The burden on the city and its neighbors caused a revolt against his authority and a number of cities in both Brabant and Flanders, led by Ghent, issued their own coinage during the revolt. In keeping with the medieval mind, whereby minting rights were not to be usurped (despite rebellion!) but had to be authorized, the city looked to Maximilian's rival, the King of France, to support the uprising and he authorized Ghent to strike coinage in the name of the young Archduke Philip, at that time an 11 year old boy.

Ghent then struck a number of dated and undated coins, from a gold florin of St. Jean of .800 fineness to a billon double mite of 1.5 % silver. Generally, the city's name was engraved as "GAND" or "GANDA" around the shield of Flanders. Notable for their beauty (but unfortunately of the greatest rarity) are the 1492 double patards and patards of the mint of the castle of Ecluse, (medieval Flemish name "Sluis"), where the coinage of Ghent was struck after its fall to Maximilian's troops. These coins feature as their reverse design the city castle with its towers boldly engraved. There is no recent auction history of these magnificent pieces.

Primary Reference: van Gelder-Hoc. General Reference: Van der Chijs.

II-103	1488	Ghent	Florin St. Jean	R3
II-104	1488	Ghent	Patard	R
II-119	1489	Ghent	Double Briquet	R2
II-120	1489	Ghent	Double Mite	R
II-128	1491	Ghent	Patard	R3
II-132	1492	Ecluse	Double Patard	R5
II-133	1492	Ecluse	Patard	R5

HASSELT - SEE LIÈGE (ALSO A MINT OF UTRECHT, REGION III)

LIÈGE (LUIK, LÜTTICH) - BISHOPRIC AND PRINCIPALITY. MINTS OF HASSELT, LIÈGE, ARENBERG TERRITORIES AND UNCERTAIN MINTS. 1437

The bishopric of Liège was an affluent and influential independent see in the southeastern Netherlands which was also granted secular rights as a principality by the Holy Roman Emperor Otto II in the 10th century. Liège had a lengthy and extensive history of coinage in the medieval times. That tradition continued throughout the fifteenth century, and Liège was responsible for issuing some of the most varied, interesting and unusual of all coinage in this period. Mainly responsible for this numismatic diversity was the constant state of warfare over control of the bishopric and its riches, and a series of competing coinage struck by the two warring factions, the Hornes and Mark families.

Until 1484, Liège's dated coinage was fairly straightforward. One of the earliest of all states to date its coins, Liège commenced dating in 1437 on double and fractional gros, which it struck for a two year period. The next coins were dated in 1476, when the bishop struck imitative briquets and double briquets from 1476 through 1483, modeled after the coinage of the Burgundian Netherlands. That was all to change by 1483.

France was the longtime rival of Burgundy for control of Liège, and did not forgive Duke Philip the Good for installing his nephew Louis de Bourbon (1456-1482) as Liège's bishop. With help from the king of France, the lords of the Mark, a family with longtime ties to Liège and to Arenberg, began a revolt in 1480 against the Burgundian-imposed Bishop Louis. Leading the revolt was William of the Mark (Guillaume de la Marck). William was a brutal warrior whose lower nobility gave him the mere title of "Mambour," a knight who was allowed to administer property on behalf of the bishop. William's war was successful, albeit for a brief period of time, and he deposed and executed Louis in 1482, installed his son Jean of the Mark as bishop-elect in 1483, and usurped secular power over the city of Liège.

As with all medieval rulers, William took advantage of the mints to advertise and proclaim his successes, and issued a short series of coin types, dated 1483-1485. Most were minted in Liège with his title of Mambour (administrator) but two came from Arenberg family territories outside of Liège with neither his title nor the name of Liège in the legend. Most of his coins were struck with realistic portraits of William, a fierce-looking, full bearded warrior. They are the first dated coins of the Netherlands to be struck bearing a realistic portrait. The double patard featured a highly unusual ¾ length full-facing figure of the warrior and another portrayed William in profile with a Renaissance-style bust. In contrast are those coins struck by his son, the bishop-elect, whose styles copied the banal ones of his deposed predecessor.

Alas for the numismatist, William's reign was all-too brief. Maximilian, who had inherited the Burgundian Netherlands from his marriage to Marie of Burgundy, was not going to permit his Burgundian-imposed bishop to be deposed by a usurper. In 1485, his troops invaded Liège, deposed Jean (who fled the bishopric) and captured William, executing him that year. As might be expected, all coinage of both William and Jean is excessively rare, and the dou-

Number	Date	Mint	Denomination	Rarity

ble patard of William, one of the most visually appealing medieval coins ever struck, is thought to be unique.

The coinage that followed William's removal was a testament to the troubled times in the bishopric. Immediately following the retaking of Liège by Maximilian's troops, bishop Jean de Horn (1484-1505) was installed and struck a number of dated coins, most with the family shield of three hunting horns. However, the revolt against Maximilian continued and the family of Mark continued guerrilla warfare in the principality. Everard of the Mark, William's nephew, issued his competing dated coinage in 1488 and 1489, all pieces being extremely or excessively rare. Unlike the coinage of his illustrious uncle, the coinage of Everard copied typical Southern Netherlands styles and exhibited little charm.

Because of the war, the normally tight controls over the mints in Liège became lax. As the mint's operations were already in the hands of entrepreneurs, they saw this lack of oversight as an opportunity to excessively devalue the monies and ignore the quality of the coinage. During this period, nominally silver coinage was struck in base metals and numerous counterfeiters took advantage of the opportunities. All in all, while the coinage was abysmal to those who had to use it or be paid with it, half a millennium later it provides a fascinating numismatic source of study.

The location of the primary mint of Liège is uncertain. While most of William's coinage was struck at a city mint in Liège, the coinage of Liège did not identify its place of manufacture. The exception was coinage struck in Hasselt, northwest of Liège. While only a few early dated coin types were struck there, Hasselt did mint a remarkable 1494 dated pure copper "brule," a very rare circulating non-billon copper coin. Coins of Hasselt, as with most Liège coinage, tended to be weakly struck and are rarely found in high grade.

Primary References: Dengis and Chestret (both excellent)

II-7	1437	Uncertain	Double Gros	R4
II-8	1438	Uncertain	Double Gros	R3
II-9	1438	Uncertain	Demi Gros	R4-5
II-10	1438	Uncertain	Quarter Gros	R5
II-25	1476	Uncertain	Double Patard	R2
II-26	1476	Hasselt	Patard	R2
II-36	1478	Uncertain	Double Patard	R
II-37	1478	Hasselt	Patard	R
II-42a	1479	Uncertain	Double Patard	R
II-42b	1479	Uncertain	Double Patard	R
II-43	1479	Uncertain	Patard	R2
II-44	1479	Hasselt	Patard	R
II-52a	1480	Uncertain	Double Patard	R
II-52b	1480	Uncertain	Double Patard	R3
II-53	1480	Uncertain	Patard	R2
II-61a	1481	Uncertain	Double Patard	VS
II-61b	1481	Uncertain	Double Patard	R2
II-62	1481	Uncertain	Patard	R
II-66	1482	Uncertain	Double Patard	R2

LIÈGE, FAMILY OF HORNES

II-76	1484	Uncertain	Double Patard	R5
II-77a	1484	Uncertain	One-Third Patard	R2
II-77b	1484	Uncertain	One-Third Patard	R5
II-77c	1484	Uncertain	One-Third Patard	R5-6
II-84	1485	Hasselt	Patard	R6
II-85	1485	Uncertain	One-Third Patard	R4
II-88	1486	Uncertain	Double Patard	R2
II-89	1486	Uncertain	Patard	R
II-90a	1486	Uncertain	Double Heaume	R
II-90b	1486	Uncertain	Double Heaume	R5
II-91a	1486	Uncertain	One-Third Patard	R3
II-91b	1486	Uncertain	One-Third Patard	R2
II-A105	1488	Uncertain	One-Third Patard	R5
II-121	1489	Uncertain	Double Patard	R
II-122a	1489	Uncertain	Double Heaume	R2
II-122b	1489	Uncertain	Double Heaume	R3
II-134a	1494	Hasselt	Brulé	R2
II-135a	1494	Liège	Patard	R
II-135b	1494	Liège	Patard	R2
II-A135	1494	Liège	Brulé	R5

Number	Date	Mint	Denomination	Rarity

LIÈGE, FAMILY OF MARK

II-72	1483	Liège	Double Patard	R5
II-A72	1483	Liège	Demi Stoeter	R5-6
II-73	1483	Liège	Patard	R5–6
II-74	1483	Liège	Demi Patard	R5
II-78	1484	Liège	Double Briquet	R6
II-79	1484	Liège	Stoeter	R4
II-80	1484	Liège	Demi Stoeter	R4
II-A81	1484	Liège	Demi Patard	R6
II-81	1484	Liège	Demi Patard	R4
II-86	1485	Uncertain	Stoeter	R6
II-87	1485	Uncertain	Demi Stoeter	R6
II-105	1488	Liège	Double Patard	R4
II-A106	1488	Liège	Patard	R6
II-106	1488	Liège	Demi Patard	R5
II-107	1488	Liège	Gros	R4
II-123	1489	Liège	Double Patard	R4
II-124	1489	Liège	Patard	R5

LIMBURG (LIMBOURG) - DUCHY AND CITY (SEE ALSO LIMBURG-STYRUM IN GERMANY, REGION I)

Limburg was a large province of both medieval and modern Netherlands and was the easternmost part of Belgium. The ancient duchy was absorbed by the dukes of Brabant (see Craig at p. 117) and did not issue coins in its own name. However, the Burgundian Netherland rulers placed the title of this duchy in the legends, such as that found on the 1474 double briquets of Charles the Rash: "KAROL:DEI:GRA:DVX:BRA:Z'LI" ("Charles by the Grace of God, Duke Brabant & Limburg"). Most of the dated coinage of the Burgundian Netherlands up through 1487 carried this title.

Confusingly, the name of Limburg was also given 1) to a large province in the Netherlands ;2) to the name of Limbourg city in Belgium just south of Aachen and east of Liège; 3) to a German city east of Coblenz (Limburg on the Lahn River), and 4) also to the name of a county, Limburg-Styrum, which did strike early dated coins. Some attribution of those coins to Limburg-Styrum (or its mints), as opposed to the Belgium province of Limbourg, may be in question, since the name of the city is used on those coins instead of the county. The modern spellings of "Limbourg" for the Netherlands regions versus "Limburg" for the German region is but a convenience - the medieval names were the same, adding to the confusion.

LOUVAIN (LEUVEN) - CITY IN BRABANT UNDER REVOLT. 1489

Prior to 1400, Louvain was the defacto capital of the duchy of Brabant, but by 1350 lost that status to nearby Brussels. Louvain remained a trading city of secondary importance, but as with many Lowland cities whose livelihood depended upon commerce, it was heavily taxed by Maximilian. In 1489 it joined the revolt and was granted the right by the French King to strike coinage in the name of the young Archduke Philip. Three coin types were struck dated 1488 and 1489, the only Brabant coinage to use Roman numerals. All coins are of the greatest rarity.

Primary Reference: de Witte (excellent). General Reference: van Gelder-Hoc (excellent)

II-100	1488	Louvain	Double Patard	R6
II-116	1489	Louvain	Double Patard	R5
II-117	1489	Louvain	4 Mites	R5

MAESTRICHT - SEE BRABANT

MALINES - SEE BRABANT

NAMUR (NAMEN) - COUNTS. 1497

Namur was a large county in southern Belgium between Luxembourg and Hainaut. Coinage began there in the 11th century and the county was acquired by the dukes of Burgundy in 1429. After this acquisition, however, its mint fell into disuse. Early dated coinage did not begin until 1497 when coinage was ordered struck in the name of Philip the Fair. The mint struck four different denominations - gold coins (florins d'or dated 1499), silver coins (double patards and patards dated 1499) and billon coins of .026 fineness (double mites dated 1497 and 1499). All can still be collected today, although as a rule, the smaller denomination coinage of Namur is the most difficult to obtain and certainly so in higher grades.

II-140a	1497	Namur	Double Mite	R2
II-140b	1497	Namur	Double Mite	R5

Number	Date	Mint	Denomination	Rarity
II-147	1499	Namur	Florin d'or	R
II-148	1499	Namur	Double Patard	S
II-149	1499	Namur	Patard	S
II-150	1499	Namur	Double Mite	R3

SCHOONVORST AS MINT OF JÜLICH-BERG - SEE REGION I

SCHOONVORST-SICHEM - LORDSHIP. 1372

Schoonvorst-Sichem was a small lordship ten kilometers southeast of Aachen with a limited but highly distinctive history of early dated coinage. In the 14th century, it struck six different early dated groschens at the mint at Schoonvorst, one dated 1372 and the rest in a series from 1390-1394. As such, Schoonvorst-Sichem struck the earliest dated coins of the Netherlands and struck more 14th century dated coin types than Aachen, Charlemagne's capital, which is considered the birthplace of dated coinage.

Schoonvorst-Sichem's 14th century coinage was highly recognizable with its nine pellet shield on the obverse, while the reverse bore a typical long cross (as the Aachen coinage). Given the limited quantities of coinage available from this small lordship, both dated and undated types command top prices when they appear at auction. While the dates of 1372, 1390 and 1394 are likely uncollectable, the 1391 groschen, while very rare, does appear with some regularity at auction. The 1393 groschen is also still collectable, but extremely rare at best, while the 1392 is excessively rare. In the early 15th century, Schoonvorst alone was sold to Jülich-Berg, whose dukes operated a mint at the lordship. A discussion of the early dated coinage from the Jülich-Berg mint at Schoonvorst is found in Region I.

Primary Reference: Lucas (excellent) and Menadier. General Reference: Van der Chijs

II-1	1372	Schoonvorst	Groschen	R6
II-2	1390	Schoonvorst	Groschen	R5-6
II-3	1391	Schoonvorst	Groschen	R
II-4	1392	Schoonvorst	Groschen	R4-5
II-5	1393	Schoonvorst	Groschen	R3
II-6	1394	Schoonvorst	Groschen	R6

TOURNAI (TOURNAY) - CITY. 1499 (Countermarked coinage only)

Tournai was a city in the northeast part of France which during the late Middle Ages became a source of conflict between France and Burgundy. It was a mint of both France and the Burgundian Netherlands and its coinage reflects the styles of its contemporaneous rulers. The city struck no early dated coins on its own but instead countermarked circulating coinage with its mark of a castle tower. The coins listed here under Tournai have sometimes been attributed to the Northern Netherlands city of Campen due to the similarity of their castle marks.

II-A150a	1499	Tournai	C/M Patard	R5?
II-A150b	1499	Tournai	C/M Patard	R5?
II-B150	1499	Tournai	C/M Patard	R5?
II-159	1500	Tournai	C/M Patard	R5?

REGION III - NORTHERN NETHERLANDS

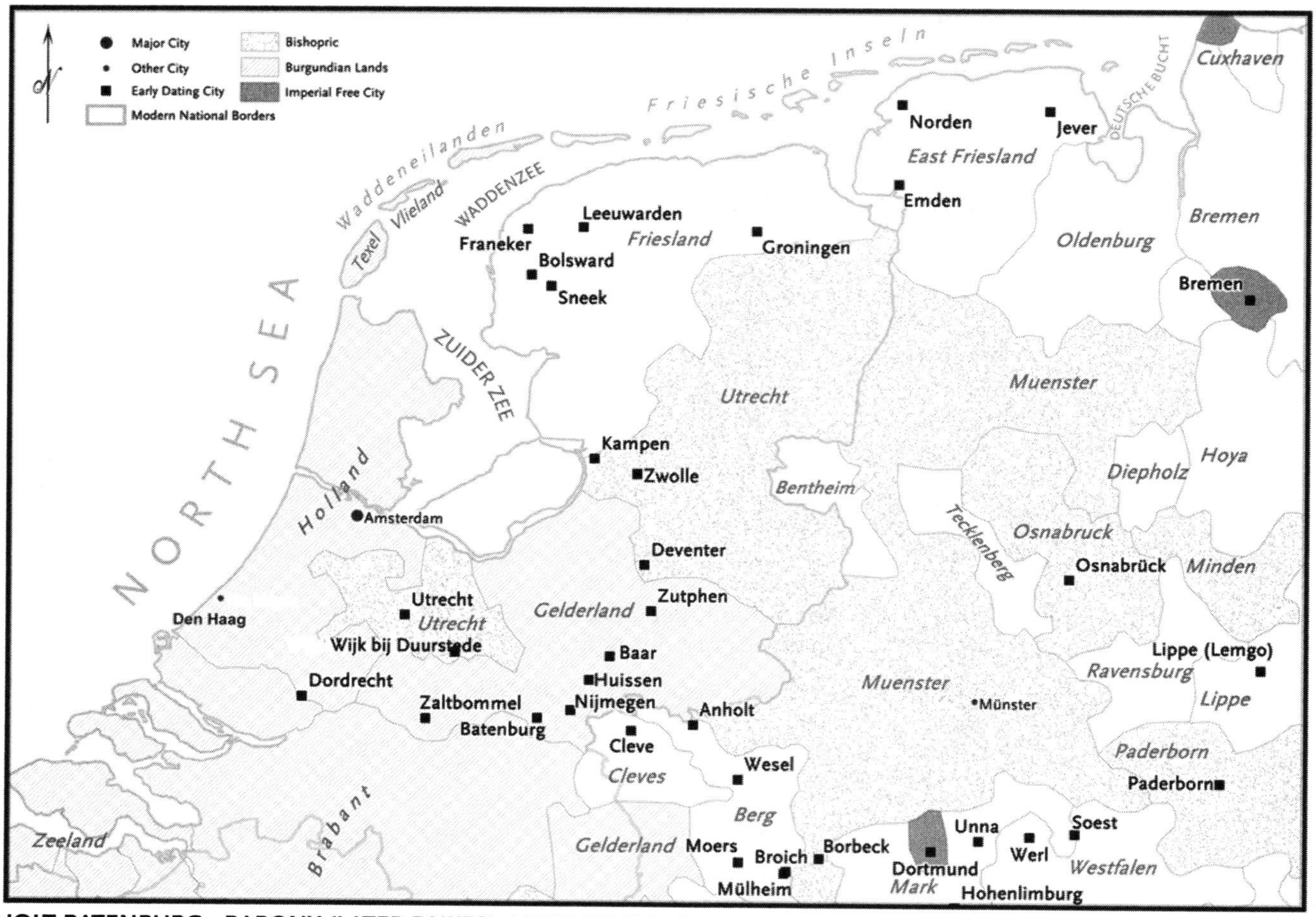

ANHOLT-BATENBURG - BARONY (LATER DUKES). MINT OF ANHOLT. 1424

Anholt, Batenburg and Gronsfeld were small nobilities in central-south Netherlands, all formerly part of the Bronkhorst family possessions (See Craig at p. 54). In the mint at Anholt (not to be confused with the German duchy of Anhalt), Gijsbert I of Anholt & II of Bronkhorst and his successor Theodore of Brokkhorst, struck three remarkable very early dated groschens under the Batenburg name, all copying the style of the Aachen groschens of the same period. Only four pieces are extant for the known dates of 1424, 1427 and 1436; all are believed to reside in museum collections. These coins are so rare that none were known to Van der Chijs.

Primary Reference: RBN 1870, Blätter fur Muenzefreunde, 1913.

Number	Date	Mint	Denomination	Rarity
III-1	1424	Batenburg	Groschen	R6
III-2	1427	Batenburg	Groschen	R6
III-3	1436	Batenburg	Groschen	R6

BAAR (BAER OR BAR-MÖRS) - BARONY. 1445

Baar (not to be confused with Bar in Lorraine) was a barony in Utrecht and a possession of Walram of Mörs, the rival of the named bishop of Utrecht and a relative of the powerful count of Mörs. Walram was one of the contestants for the Utrecht bishopric and when his rival Rudolfe of Diepholz was instead confirmed, Walram carried on his candidacy with the aid of the Anti-Pope until the latter's death in 1449 (see De Mey Ut. at P. 80-81). During this contestancy period, Walram issued a 1445 dated goldgulden, copying the standards and design of Rhineland Monetary Treaty coins. This coin is the Netherlands' first early dated gold coin, and it was not until 1482 that the next one was struck, this time by Brabant in the Southern Netherlands. No other early dated coins were struck for Baar. While this coin is still collectable, it is excessively rare and perhaps only five or six are believed to be in private hands.

Primary Reference: none. General Reference: Friedberg, De Mey d'Or and Delmonte.

III-10	1445	Baar or Cologne	Goldgulden	R4

BOLSWARD - CITY. 1455

Bolsward was a small city in the western tip of Friesland and southwest of Leeuwarden. Although diminutive in size, it was a productive issuer of early dated coins. From the city mint five different denominations were struck bearing nine different dates, comprising fifteen types in total, the most issued during the very earliest period of Northern Netherlands dated coinage. As with most cities which struck coinage during this period, Bolsward coinage was designed to copy the coinage of its larger neighbors, in this case Groningen to the northeast. Typically, Bolsward

Number	Date	Mint	Denomination	Rarity

coinage is found (if at all) in lower grades, attributed to inferior die preparation and higher billon content. Nearly all the coinage of Bolsward is excessively rare.

Primary Reference: Puister Friesland (excellent). General Reference: Van der Chijs.

III-13	1455	Bolsward	Stuiver	R5
III-14	1455	Bolsward	Quarter Stuiver	R5-6
III-15	1455	Bolsward	Plak	R5
III-19	1456	Bolsward	Stuiver	R5
III-20	1456	Bolsward	Half Stuiver	R4-5
III-22	1457	Bolsward	Jager	R4
III-23	1457	Bolsward	Stuiver	R5
III-57	1472	Bolsward	Stuiver	R3
III-66	1474	Bolsward	Stuiver	R4
III-67	1474	Bolsward	Half Stuiver	R5
III-74	1475	Bolsward	Stuiver	R4
III-80	1476	Bolsward	Stuiver	R4
III-87	1477	Bolsward	Stuiver	R4
III-95	1478	Bolsward	Stuiver	R4-5
III-96	1478	Bolsward	Half Stuiver	R5

CAMPEN (KAMPEN) - CITY AND MINT OF MONETARY ALLIANCE. 1480

Campen (not to be confused by the imperial city of Kempten in Bavaria) was the northernmost part of the "Driesteden" (three city) monetary alliance between the free cities of central-east Netherlands. Located near the mouth of the IJssel River (Deventer and Zwolle located up river), Campen struck joint coinage as well as coinage in its own name. Its own coinage consisted of tiny denomination pieces, all of which are today of the greatest rarity and found only in poor condition. Countermarked coins of 1499 and 1500 sometimes attributed to Campen will be found under Tournai.

Primary Reference: None. General Reference: Van der Chijs.

III-118	1480	Campen	One-Eighth Stuiver	R5
III-146	1485	Campen	One-Eighth Stuiver	R6
III-154	1486	Campen	Quarter Stuiver	R5-6
III-176	1488	Campen	Quarter Stuiver	R5
III-177	1488	Campen	One-Eighth Stuiver	R5

DEVENTER - CITY AND MINT OF MONETARY ALLIANCE. 1458

While today a small city in the central Dutch province of Overijssel, Deventer's city mint during the late Middle Ages was a powerhouse of early dated coinage production, striking over 50 different types, with 22 different dates and 9 denominations, more than almost all other medieval states. Coinage struck in Deventer's name conformed to the standards used by its larger neighbor, Groningen: jagers valued at two stuivers, stuivers (double gros), gros, plak, and fractionals. The coinage of Deventer is somewhat unusual in that its earlier coinage (except for that struck in 1458) is significantly easier to obtain than its later coinage. Since the Bishop of Utrecht had governing rights to Deventer, the latter's coinage were struck under his authority.

The coinage of Deventer, struck more or less continuously from 1466-1500, retained the basic city-shield/cross or eagle/cross design throughout most of its coinage. The exceptions to this are two goldguldens issued under the Emperor's name in 1488 and 1498 bearing the typical reverse design of the imperial orb to signify the grant of the right to mint gold. Additionally, two silver stuivers struck in 1499 and 1500 brought new artistry to the otherwise ordinary coinage. Each stuiver featured a haloed, full-length portrait of Saint Lebuinus holding his mitre, his face the very picture of religious piety, beyond doubt one of the most stunning medieval coin types ever struck. Only a tiny handful exist today. Deventer coins as a whole were struck to high standards so its early dated coinage can still be collected today in high grade.

Primary Reference: JFD. General Reference: Van der Chijs.

III-25	1458	Deventer	Plak	R5
III-26	1458	Deventer	Half Plak	R5
III-A34	1462	Deventer	Quarter Stuiver	R6
III-40	1466	Deventer	Jager	R3
III-41	1466	Deventer	Gros	VS
III-42	1466	Deventer	Plak	R
III-43	1466	Deventer	Half Plak	R3
III-44	1466	Deventer	Quarter Plak	R4-5
III-47	1468	Deventer	Stuiver	R
III-48	1469	Deventer	Stuiver	23

Number	Date	Mint	Denomination	Rarity
III-50	1470	Deventer	Stuiver	R
III-51	1470	Deventer	Gros	R2
III-53	1471	Deventer	Stuiver	VS
III-54	1471	Deventer	Gros	R
III-58	1472	Deventer	Stuiver	VS
III-59	1472	Deventer	Gros	R2
III-62	1473	Deventer	Stuiver	R
III-63	1473	Deventer	Gros	R
III-68	1474	Deventer	Stuiver	VS
III-81	1476	Deventer	Half Plak	R3
III-88	1477	Deventer	Half Plak	R6?
III-97	1478	Deventer	Half Plak	R6?
III-106	1479	Deventer	Half Plak	R3
III-119	1480	Deventer	Half Plak	R6
III-128	1481	Deventer	Stuiver	R4
III-129	1481	Deventer	Half Stuiver	R4
III-130	1481	Deventer	Plak	R4
III-131	1481	Deventer	Half Plak	R4-5
III-178	1488	Deventer	Goldgulden	R2
III-179	1488	Deventer	Quarter Stuiver	R4
III-180	1488	Deventer	One-Eighth Stuiver	R5
III-219	1492	Deventer	Stuiver	R4-5
III-241	1495	Deventer	Plak	R4
III-255	1498	Deventer	Goldgulden	R5-6
III-264	1499	Deventer	Double Stuiver	R4
III-265	1499	Deventer	Stuiver	R5
III-278	1500	Deventer	Double Stuiver	R4
III-279	1500	Deventer	Stuiver	R5

DEVENTER, CAMPEN, GRONINGEN - MONETARY ALLIANCE OF THREE CITIES. MINTS IN DEVENTER, CAMPEN AND GRONINGEN. 1479

In 1479, Deventer, Campen and Groningen agreed to issue coins to a monetary standard to circulate equally throughout their provinces. Just as the Rhineland Münzvertrag had dictated some 40 years earlier with the coinage of Cologne, Trier, the Palatinate and Mainz, coins struck to this standard were to circulate freely in the other's state with full acceptance. Additionally, as with the prior treaty, each featured the shields of the participating states - Deventer, Campen and Groningen - with the legend listing the particular mint. In 1479, the only year in which these coins were struck, Deventer struck stuivers and half stuivers in its name and Campen struck stuivers in its name, with a letter "C" in the center of the three conjoined shields. All such coinage is excessively rare.

Primary Reference: JFD DKZ General Reference: Van der Chijs.

III-107a	1479	Campen	Stuiver	R3
III-107b	1479	Campen	Stuiver	R5
III-108	1479	Deventer	Stuiver	R4
III-109	1479	Deventer	Half Stuiver	R4

DEVENTER, CAMPEN, ZWOLLE - MONETARY ALLIANCE OF THREE CITIES. MINTS OF DEVENTER, CAMPEN AND ZWOLLE. 1488

In 1488, Deventer, Campen and Zwolle agreed to continue the monetary alliance with Zwolle instead of Groningen. At the same time, these small cities were free to continue striking their own municipal coinage and did. The 1488 alliance saw the issuance of a variety of types, with each participating state coining stuivers, half stuivers and quarter stuivers in their own name but with the shields of all three. These attractive coins are differentiated by the wording of the obverse legend and by a mintmark in the center of the conjoined shields, either a "D", "C" or a "Z" depending upon at which city mint the coin was struck. The coinage of this alliance is generally extremely rare and almost unknown in higher grades.

Primary Reference: JFD DKZ. General Reference: Van der Chijs.

III-181	1488	Campen	Stuiver	R3
III-182	1488	Campen	Half Stuiver	R3
III-183	1488	Campen	Quarter Stuiver	R5
III-184a	1488	Deventer	Stuiver	R3
III-184b	1488	Deventer	Stuiver	R6
III-185	1488	Deventer	Half Stuiver	R2
III-186	1488	Deventer	Quarter Stuiver	R4

Number	Date	Mint	Denomination	Rarity
III-187	1488	Zwolle	Stuiver	R4
III-188	1488	Zwolle	Half Stuiver	R4
III-189	1488	Zwolle	Quarter Stuiver	R5

DORDRECHT - SEE HOLLAND

FRANEKER - CITY. 1485

Franeker was a very small upper Frisian city located about 15 kilometers west of Leeuwarden. For its small size, Franeker struck a fair number (ten in total) of early dated coins, from 1480-1490, (eight silver and two gold). All silver coinage was struck in the style of the large states to the south, such as Utrecht, Liège and the Burgundian Netherlands states. In 1491 and 1492, Franeker struck two dated goldguldens in the name of the Emperor. These goldguldens are substantially similar to those issued by Frankfurt with the exception of a lion at the feet of St. John the Baptist. All coins of Franeker are excessively rare and the silver likely found (if at all) in very poor grade.

Primary Reference: Puister Friesland (excellent). General Reference: Van der Chijs (silver), Friedberg, De Mey d'Or (gold).

III-147	1485	Franeker	Half Stuiver	R5
III-155	1486	Franeker	Half Stuiver	R5-6
III-162a	1487	Franeker	Half Stuiver	R4
III-162b	1487	Franeker	Half Stuiver	R5
III-190	1488	Franeker	Half Stuiver	R5
III-202	1489	Franeker	Double Stuiver	R5
III-211	1490	Franeker	Double Stuiver	R5
III-212	1490	Franeker	Half Stuiver	R6
III-213	1491	Franeker	Goldgulden	R4-5
III-220	1492	Franeker	Goldgulden	R5

FRANEKER-FRISIA - GOVERNORSHIP UNDER SAXONY. MINT OF FRANEKER. 1498

Rights to Frisia were claimed by Albrecht, Duke of Saxony, whose center of power was in Dresden, many miles to the east. In 1498 he attacked both Friesland and Groningen. In that endeavor, he was successful only as to the former and installed himself as Governor or "Stadhouder" of Frisia thereafter. At that time, independent coinage ended in Franeker. Under Albrecht's governorship, three dated coins were struck in Franeker, all in his name as governor of Frisia, a 1498 thaler (of which it is not certain that it is contemporary) and 1500 dated double stuivers and stuivers.

Primary Reference: Puister Friesland (excellent). General References: Van der Chijs.

III-256	1498	Franeker	Thaler	R6?
III-280	1500	Franeker	Double Stuiver	R4-5
III-281	1500	Franeker	Stuiver	R3

GELDERLAND (GUELDRES) - DUCHY OF THE BURGUNDIAN NETHERLANDS' RULER. MINTS OF NIJMEGEN, ZALTBOMMEL AND MALINES (MECHELEN). 1474

Gelderland was a large duchy in southeastern Netherlands bordering the Rhine and German states. The duchy was successfully claimed by Charles the Rash in 1473 and beginning 1474 a ducal mint was established there. Dated coins conforming to the normal Burgundian Netherlands standards of weight, fineness and engraving were intermittently struck at the Gelderland mint by the Burgundian Netherlands rulers until 1492.

Gelderland coinage is distinguished from that of the other Burgundian Netherlands mints by the abbreviations at the end of the obverse legend, such as "GEL" or "GELRIE" or "GELR." Very minor punctuation differences distinguish the larger denomination coinage. The coinage of Gelderland, while generally quite rare when compared to that of Flanders or Brabant, is mostly obtainable in high grade. In part the rarity of Gelderland coinage resulted from the constant warring between the Burgundian Netherlands and the counts of Egmont, who claimed the duchy for themselves, which necessitated moving the mint several times. The coinage of the Egmont family is discussed immediately below.

Primary Reference: Roest (outdated). General Reference: van Gelder-Hoc (essential) and Van der Chijs.

III-69a	1474	Nijmegen	Double Briquet	R3
III-69b	1474	Nijmegen	Double Briquet	R6?
III-70	1474	Nijmegen	Briquet	R3
III-71	1474	Nijmegen	Half Briquet	R2
III-75	1475	Nijmegen	Double Briquet	R-R2
III-76	1475	Nijmegen	Briquet	R4
III-77	1475	Nijmegen	Half Briquet	R2
III-82	1476	Nijmegen	Half Briquet	R2
III-89	1477	Nijmegen	Half Briquet	R5

Number	Date	Mint	Denomination	Rarity
III-120	1480	Uncertain	Gros	R2
III-163	1487	Zaltbommel	Gold Real	R6?
III-164	1487	Zaltbommel	Silver Real	R5
III-165	1487	Zaltbommel	Double Griffon	R4
III-166	1487	Zaltbommel	One-Sixth Griffon	R6
III-191	1488	Zaltbommel	Half Noble d'or	R5
III-192	1488	Zaltbommel	Double Griffon	R5
III-193	1488	Zaltbommel	Double Patard	R2
III-203	1489	Zaltbommel	Gros	R5
III-221	1492	Malines	Double Briquet	R
III-222	1492	Malines	Briquet	R

GELDERLAND - DUCHY UNDER THE EGMONT FAMILY. MINTS OF ROERMOND AND ZUTPHEN. 1478

Vying for the rights to the duchy of Gelderland was Charles v. Egmont, whose uncle Adolf had been deposed by Charles the Rash of Burgundy. With the help of the French (the longtime rival of the powerful dukes of Burgundy), Charles v. Egmont issued his own competing series of dated coinage between 1478 and 1480, with an additional coin type struck in 1496. The Gelderland coinage of Charles v. Egmont is uniformly poorly struck with questionable fineness, no doubt attributable to the wartime conditions. Well-struck and high condition pieces of Charles v. Egmont are excessively rare.

Primary Reference: Roest (outdated). General Reference: Van der Chijs.

III-98	1478	Roermond	Jager	R5-6
III-99	1478	Roermond	Stuiver	R
III-110	1479	Zutphen	Stuiver	R2
III-121	1480	Zutphen	Stuiver	R
III-245	1496	Uncertain	Double Briquet	VS

GRONINGEN - CITY AND MINT OF MONETARY ALLIANCE. 1437

Groningen was the dominant city in the Northern Netherlands whose coinage set the standards to which numerous other small city-states or provinces in the Netherlands and in Germany sought to copy. Groningen began dating its coinage at nearly the earliest times for Northern Netherlands coinage, 1437. Today, its coinage represents for four different dates - 1439, 1440, 1454 and 1461 - the only known early dated coin types.

Groningen's coinage was standardized in design, with the imperial double-headed eagle (symbol of a free city) and shield below on the obverse, and a cross on the reverse. Groningen's long history of well-accepted coinage was possible because of its political and military strength. In the 15th century, Groningen repulsed several attacks upon it by larger neighbors in its successful quest to remain truly independent from either the Burgundian dukes or the large and powerful bishoprics to its south. The cost of such independence was considerable, and Groningen began devaluing its coinage in the 1470's, and pieces issued in the decades from 1480-1490 were clearly inferior to its prior coinage. Groningen's independence ended early in the 16th century.

Groningen's coinage was issued in denominations of jagers (double stuivers) and their fractionals. With the exception of an extremely rare goldgulden of 1488 issued in the name of the Emperor, Groningen's coinage, even in the earliest dated years, is generally still obtainable and usually can be found in higher grades. As an exception to the rule that the decade of 1451-1460 saw the production of highly inferior coinage, the coinage of Groningen, especially the jagers of 1455, can still be collected in exceptional condition for that period.

Primary Reference: Puister (excellent). General Reference: Van der Chijs.

III-4	1437	Groningen	Jager	R4
III-5	1437	Groningen	Half Jager	R5
III-6	1438	Groningen	Jager	R3
III-7	1439	Groningen	Jager	R2
III-8	1439	Groningen	Half Jager	R5
III-9	1440	Groningen	Jager	R5
III-11	1454	Groningen	Stuiver	R3
III-12	1454	Groningen	Half Stuiver	R4
III-16	1455	Groningen	Jager	R2
III-17	1455	Groningen	Stuiver	R3
III-18	1455	Groningen	Half Stuiver	R4
III-21	1456	Groningen	Jager	R3
III-24	1457	Groningen	Half Stuiver	R5
III-27	1458	Groningen	Jager	R4-5
III-28	1458	Groningen	Half Stuiver	R5

Number	Date	Mint	Denomination	Rarity
III-29	1459	Groningen	Jager	R4
III-30	1459	Groningen	Half Stuiver	R5
III-31	1460	Groningen	Jager	R4
III-33	1461	Groningen	Jager	R4
III-34	1462	Groningen	Jager	R2
III-36	1463	Groningen	Jager	R3
III-38	1465	Groningen	Jager	R2
III-39	1465	Groningen	Half Stuiver	R4
III-45	1467	Groningen	Stuiver	R4
III-46	1467	Groningen	Half Stuiver	R4
III-49	1469	Groningen	Stuiver	R3
III-52	1470	Groningen	Stuiver	R2
III-55	1471	Groningen	Stuiver	R
III-60	1472	Groningen	Stuiver	VS
III-64	1473	Groningen	Stuiver	R
III-72	1474	Groningen	Stuiver	VS
III-78	1475	Groningen	Stuiver	VS
III-83	1476	Groningen	Jager	R4-5
III-84	1476	Groningen	Stuiver	VS
III-90	1477	Groningen	Jager	VS
III-91	1477	Groningen	Stuiver	R3
III-135	1482	Groningen	Stuiver	VS
III-148a	1485	Groningen	Jager	R
III-148b	1485	Groningen	Jager	R
III-149	1485	Groningen	Stuiver	VS
III-156	1486	Groningen	Jager	R
III-157	1486	Groningen	Stuiver	VS
III-167	1487	Groningen	Jager	R5
III-194	1488	Groningen	Goldgulden	R4
III-195	1488	Groningen	Half Plak	R6
III-204	1489	Groningen	Plak	R4
III-214	1491	Groningen	Stuiver	R3
III-215	1491	Groningen	Half Stuiver	R4
III-216	1491	Groningen	Plak	R4
III-217	1491	Groningen	Half Plak	R4-5
III-223	1492	Groningen	Stuiver	R5
III-224	1492	Groningen	Kromstaart	R3
III-257	1498	Groningen	Jager	R
III-258	1498	Groningen	Stuiver	S
III-259a	1498	Groningen	Kromstaart	R2
III-259b	1498	Groningen	Kromstaart	R4
III-260	1498	Groningen	Plak	R3
III-261	1498	Groningen	Half Plak	R4
III-266	1499	Groningen	Jager	VS
III-267	1499	Groningen	Stuiver	S
III-268a	1499	Groningen	Kromstaart	R3
III-268b	1499	Groningen	Kromstaart	R3

HASSELT - SEE UTRECHT

HOLLAND - COUNTY. MINT OF DORDRECHT. 1478

Holland was a large and powerful county in the western Netherlands which was obtained by the duke of Burgundy in 1433. Prior to that time, the independent counts of Holland had an extensive history of coinage dating back to as early as the 11th century, and their coinage, principally struck at the mint of Dordrecht, circulated widely. In 1478, the mint at Dordrecht reopened and began striking dated coins in large numbers, issuing dated coins every year from 1478-1489 and sporadically thereafter. As with the coinage issued from other Burgundian Netherlands mints, the coinage was well-executed and high grade specimens are available to collectors today.

Holland's late 15th century coinage was not particularly distinctive but followed the styles and designs as dictated by its Burgundian Netherlands rulers. As with its sister-territories, the legends on Holland's coinage were rather generic and its location was identified at the end of the legend by one of many abbreviations, in Holland's case: "HOLLA", "HOLL", "HOL", "HO" or "H." The designs were identical to those used for the other territories.

Holland's late 15th century coinage was not without some merit. A product of the Dordrecht mint, as indicated by its

Number	Date	Mint	Denomination	Rarity

rose mintmark, was the gold real, or more aptly-named grand real d'or of 1487, a crown-sized gold coin of extraordinary fineness (.992) struck as part of new series of coinage which also saw the issuance of a companion 1487 grand real d'argent of similar (.93) fineness. Unfortunately, their purity was their undoing and most were melted, leaving only a tiny handful existing today. Overall, Holland's coinage is much rarer than that of Brabant or Flanders, except for its double stuivers and stuivers dated 1499, which are among the most common of early dated coins found today.

Primary Reference: van Gelder-Hoc (excellent). General Reference: Van der Chijs.

III-100	1478	Dordrecht	Double Briquet	VS
III-101	1478	Dordrecht	Briquet	R
III-102	1478	Dordrecht	Gros	VS
III-111	1479	Dordrecht	Double Briquet	VS
III-112	1479	Dordrecht	Briquet	R
III-113	1479	Dordrecht	Gros	S
III-122	1480	Dordrecht	Double Briquet	VS
III-123	1480	Dordrecht	Briquet	R3
III-124	1480	Dordrecht	Gros	VS
III-132	1481	Dordrecht	Double Briquet	VS
III-133	1481	Dordrecht	Briquet	VS
III-134	1481	Dordrecht	Gros	R
III-136a	1482	Dordrecht	Double Briquet	R
III-136b	1482	Dordrecht	Double Briquet	R
III-137	1482	Dordrecht	Briquet	R
III-141	1483	Dordrecht	Double Briquet	R2
III-144	1484	Dordrecht	Gros	R2
III-150	1485	Dordrecht	Double Briquet	R2
III-151	1485	Dordrecht	Half Briquet	R3
III-158	1486	Dordrecht	Double Briquet	R2
III-159	1486	Dordrecht	Briquet	R2
III-160	1486	Dordrecht	Half Briquet	R
III-168	1487	Dordrecht	Gold Real	R3
III-169	1487	Dordrecht	Ducat	R5
III-170	1487	Dordrecht	Silver Real	R4
III-171	1487	Dordrecht	Double Griffon	R3
III-172	1487	Dordrecht	Half Gros	R5-6
III-196	1488	Dordrecht	Half Noble d'or	R2
III-197	1488	Dordrecht	Double Griffon	R3
III-198	1488	Dordrecht	Double Patard	R4
III-205	1489	Dordrecht	Florin d'or	R6
III-206	1489	Dordrecht	Patard	R3
III-207	1489	Dordrecht	Gros	R2
III-225	1492	Dordrecht	Double Briquet	R
III-226	1492	Dordrecht	Briquet	R2
III-227	1492	Dordrecht	Gros	R4-5
III-242	1495	Dordrecht	Briquet	R4
III-246	1496	Dordrecht	Toison D'Argent	R
III-247	1496	Dordrecht	Double Patard	S
III-248	1497	Dordrecht	Double Patard	R4
III-249	1497	Dordrecht	Patard	R5
III-269a	1499	Dordrecht	Toison D'Argent	VS
III-269b	1499	Dordrecht	Toison D'Argent	R2
III-270a	1499	Dordrecht	Double Stuiver	C
III-270b	1499	Dordrecht	Double Stuiver	C
III-271a	1499	Dordrecht	Stuiver	C
III-271b	1499	Dordrecht	Stuiver	C

LEEUWARDEN - CITY. 1471

Leeuwarden, a city in Friesland west of Groningen, issued an infrequent run of dated coinage from 1471-1493. While a strong free city (becoming the capital city of the Friesland area in 1504), its coinage designs were uninspired, designed solely to imitate those of larger neighbors such as Groningen and Utrecht. As with most smaller states of the Northern Netherlands, Leeuwarden's coinage is notable for its extreme rarity and poor condition. In 1487, the most difficult year in the period of 1465-1500 to find dated collectable coinage, Leeuwarden issued four different dated coin

Number	Date	Mint	Denomination	Rarity

types. As a result, a 1487 coin of Leeuwarden, while still excessively rare, is likely the only collectable date for the Leeuwarden series.

Primary Reference: Puister Friesland (excellent). General Reference: Van der Chijs.

III-56	1471	Leeuwarden	Stuiver	R5-6
III-61	1472	Leeuwarden	Stuiver	R5
III-65	1473	Leeuwarden	Stuiver	R5
III-173	1487	Leeuwarden	Jager	R5-6
III-174a	1487	Leeuwarden	Stuiver	R4
III-174b	1487	Leeuwarden	Stuiver	R5
III-175	1487	Leeuwarden	Half Stuiver	R4
III-218	1491	Leeuwarden	Half Stuiver	R6
III-228a	1492	Leeuwarden	Stuiver	R5
III-228b	1492	Leeuwarden	Stuiver	R5
III-229	1492	Leeuwarden	Quarter Stuiver	R6
III-236	1493	Leeuwarden	Stuiver	R6

MALINES - SEE GELDERLAND

MÖRS (MOERS) - SEE REGION I GERMANY

NIJMEGEN (NIMÈGUE, NOVIOMAGEN) - CITY AND MINT OF GELDERLAND. 1460

Nijmegen, located on a tributary of the Rhine river near the German city of Cleve, was named after the Roman city Noviomagus ("new market"), and its early dated coins bear that ancient name. Despite its very long history as a free city, it did not appoint its first mintmaster until 1457 and its first known coin, a tiny billon one-eighth stuiver of 1460, was also its first dated coin. Nijmegen's coinage all consisted of smaller denomination coinage, from stuiver down to one-eighth stuiver, and four of that latter rare denomination were struck, more than with any other state.

Nijmegen's first dated coin also contained its first major error, for its date is actually expressed: "MCC-CCIX" instead of "MCC-CCLX." These errors were all too common on late medieval coinage, where the engravers may not have recognized the numbers as being a date. Nijmegen's small denomination coinage of the 1460's is all excessively rare, while its later coinage, while still quite rare, is collectable.

Primary Reference: Nijmegen Museum Catalogue (essential). General Reference: Van der Chijs.

III-32	1460	Nijmegen	One-Eighth Stuiver	R6
III-35	1462	Nijmegen	One-Eighth Stuiver	R5
III-37	1463	Nijmegen	One-Eighth Stuiver	R5
III-92	1477	Nijmegen	Quarter Stuiver	R4
III-114	1479	Nijmegen	Quarter Stuiver	R4
III-145	1484	Nijmegen	Half Stuiver	R2
III-152	1485	Nijmegen	Half Stuiver	R
III-161	1486	Nijmegen	Half Stuiver	R
III-199	1488	Nijmegen	Half Stuiver	R3
III-208	1489	Nijmegen	Stuiver	R4
III-209	1489	Nijmegen	Half Stuiver	R2
III-210	1489	Nijmegen	Quarter Stuiver	R4-5
III-272	1499	Nijmegen	Half Stuiver	R3
III-273	1499	Nijmegen	One-Eighth Stuiver	R5

ROERMOND - SEE GELDERLAND

SNEEK - CITY. 1476

Sneek, a small but important city in Friesland south of Leeuwarden, derived its name from "Ter Snake" or "headlands," referring to its location at the headland of lakes and rivers in the Friesland Lake district, with canals and waterways connecting it to the open sea. This waterway access led to its success as a trading city, and not surprisingly, coinage in its own name followed. Sneek's coinage all featured its divided city-shield on the obverse, a lovely design of a half-eagle on the left and three vertical crowns on the right. Unfortunately for the collector, Sneek's issuance of dated coins was most brief - stuivers dated 1477-1478, a jager dated 1492 and a half stuiver dated 1493 which may no longer be extant. All of Sneek's highly-desirable coinage, dated or not, is excessively rare to uncollectable.

Primary Reference: Puister Friesland (excellent). General Reference: Van der Chijs.

III-85	1476	Sneek	Stuiver	R5

Number	Date	Mint	Denomination	Rarity
III-93	1477	Sneek	Stuiver	R5
III-103	1478	Sneek	Stuiver	R5
III-230	1492	Sneek	Jager	R5
III-237	1493	Sneek	Half Stuiver	R6

UTRECHT (TRAJECTUM) - BISHOPRIC. MINTS OF WIJK-BIJ-DUURSTEDE, HASSELT AND UTRECHT CITY. 1474

Utrecht, an ancient Roman city located near the center of the Netherlands, was the seat of a bishopric whose rulers in the early to mid-15th century, much as with Liège to the south, relied on the power of the duchy of Burgundy to prop up their own questionable claim of power. In 1455, after the death of Bishop Rudolfe of Diepholz, Philip the Good installed his son, David, as bishop against the will of the city council. This fostered unrest, but David was an able administrator and slowly gained acceptance. However, in the medieval mindset rights taken were never to be forgotten and the revolt against David's appointment was never fully quelled.

In 1482, the city of Utrecht rose again in rebellion and expelled the pro-Burgundian residents. At that time, the city brought in a foreign regent, Engelbert of Cleve, who of course immediately struck coinage in his name, a large braspenning dated 1482. The next year, Burgundian troops arrived, expelled Engelbert, and the rest of David's term was fairly uneventful. Mindful that his power rested in places other than the city of Utrecht itself, David's mints were located outside of the city; only the potential usurper, the regent Engelbert, coined his money in the city.

The early dated coinage of Utrecht was both prolific and diverse. Twenty five different types exist issued from three different mints. Best known of Utrecht's dated coinage is a series of large jagers struck every year between 1474-1479, most of which are still collectable in high grades. Amongst the most interesting (and rare) of Utrecht's coins are a 1492 florin d'or and half florin d'or featuring King David playing a harp, and a highly unusual denomination, a ¾ Stuiver struck in 1485 which used a medieval "5" often mistaken for a "7."

Primary Reference: De Mey Ut., Pietersen. General Reference: Van der Chijs.

III-73	1474	Wijk-bij-Duurstede	Jager	R2
III-79	1475	Wijk-bij - Duurstede	Jager	R5
III-86	1476	Wijk-bij - Duurstede	Jager	R
III-94	1477	Wijk-bij - Duurstede	Jager	VS
III-104	1478	Wijk-bij - Duurstede	Jager	S
III-115	1479	Wijk-bij - Duurstede	Jager	R2
III-138	1482	Utrecht City	Braspenning	R4-5
III-139	1482	Wijk-bij - Duurstede	Double Briquet	R2
III-140	1482	Wijk-bij-Duurstede	Briquet	R2
III-142	1483	Wijk-bij Duurstede	Briquet	R3-4
III-153	1485	Wijk-bij-Duurstede	¾ Stuiver	R3
III-231	1492	Wijk-bij-Duurstede	Florin d'or	R4
III-232	1492	Wijk-bij-Duurstede	Half Florin d'or	R4
III-233	1492	Wijk-bij - Duurstede	Briquet	R
III-234	1492	Wijk-bij - Duurstede	Gros	R
III-238	1494	Hasselt	Gros	R2
III-239	1494	Hasselt	Half Gros	R2
III-240	1494	Hasselt	Quarter Gros	R3
III-250	1497	Uncertain	Stuiver	R4
III-251	1497	Uncertain	Half Stuiver	R6
III-252	1497	Uncertain	Duit	R5-6
III-262	1498	Uncertain	Braspenning	VS
III-263	1498	Uncertain	Duit	R5-6
III-274	1499	Uncertain	Quarter Stuiver	R3
III-282	1500	Uncertain	Quarter Stuiver	R4

Number	Date	Mint	Denomination	Rarity

UTRECHT CITY (UTRECHT STAD) - CITY. 1478

As with several other bishoprics or other religious states, a secular town coinage of Utrecht coexisted with the episcopal coinage. This civic coinage was struck in the name of the city and not in the name of the bishop or any authorizing entity. (This coinage is not to be confused with the coinage struck in his own name by Engelbert, the potential usurper, during the revolt of 1482-1483). The city of Utrecht struck two early dated coins, in 1478 and in 1483, the latter a spectacular and exceptionally rare St. Martin stuiver showing the Saint on horseback riding to the left, reminiscent of the 1468 groschen of Erfurt.

Primary Reference: De Mey Ut. General Reference: Van der Chijs.

III-105	1478	Utrecht	Muter	R4-5
III-143	1483	Utrecht	Stuiver	R5-6

WIJK-BIJ-DUURSTEDE - SEE UTRECHT

ZALTBOMMEL - SEE GELDERLAND

ZUTPHEN - CITY AND MINT OF EGMONT FAMILY OF GELDERLAND. 1479

Zutphen, located in central Gelderland on the IJssel River, was a small city whose early dated coinage was limited to coinage struck in 1479 and 1480 (its next coinage was struck over 100 years later). Zutphen's coinage was issued in the denomination and fractionals of the albus, or groschen, rather resembling that of Nijmegen's. Its 1480 dated coinage, while all very rare, is somewhat more common than that of other small free cities of the Netherlands such as Franeker, Sneek, Bolsward and Leeuwarden.

Primary Reference: Beek. General Reference: Van der Chijs.

III-116	1479	Zutphen	Albus	R6
III-117	1479	Zutphen	Half Albus	R4
III-125	1480	Zutphen	Albus	R2
III-126	1480	Zutphen	Half Albus	R3
III-127	1480	Zutphen	One-Eighth Albus	R4

ZWOLLE - CITY. 1488

Zwolle, the capital city of Overijssel in central-north Netherlands, had a fairly extensive history of early dated coinage, striking both city coinage and coinage for the triple monetary alliance. Notable about the city coinage was not only that eight of the ten known coin types used mixed numeral dating, itself a rare technique, but that its dating technique followed no particular pattern. Mixed numeral dating was employed at the mint at the same time as Roman numeral dated coins were being struck.

Zwolle's larger silver coinage types, a double stuiver and two types of stuivers, are among the most attractive of all the Northern Netherlands coinage. Each featured an obverse theme of St. Michael slaying a monster. Unfortunately, each is of the greatest rarity. The smaller fractional denominations featuring banal designs are collectable, but are extremely rare. As is so common with the small denomination coinage of the small city states, these fractionals are found principally in very poor condition.

Primary Reference: Wiel. General Reference: Van der Chijs.

III-200	1488	Zwolle	Plak	R4
III-201	1488	Zwolle	Quarter Plak	R5
III-235	1492	Zwolle	Stuiver	R5
III-243	1495	Zwolle	Half Plak	R3
III-244	1495	Zwolle	Quarter Plak	R5
III-253	1497	Zwolle	Half Plak	R3
III-254	1497	Zwolle	Quarter Plak	R4-5
III-275	1499	Zwolle	Double Stuiver	R4-5
III-276	1499	Zwolle	Stuiver	R5
III-277	1499	Zwolle	Half Plak	R5

REGION IV - HABSBURG HEREDITARY TERRITORIES AND NEIGHBORING LANDS

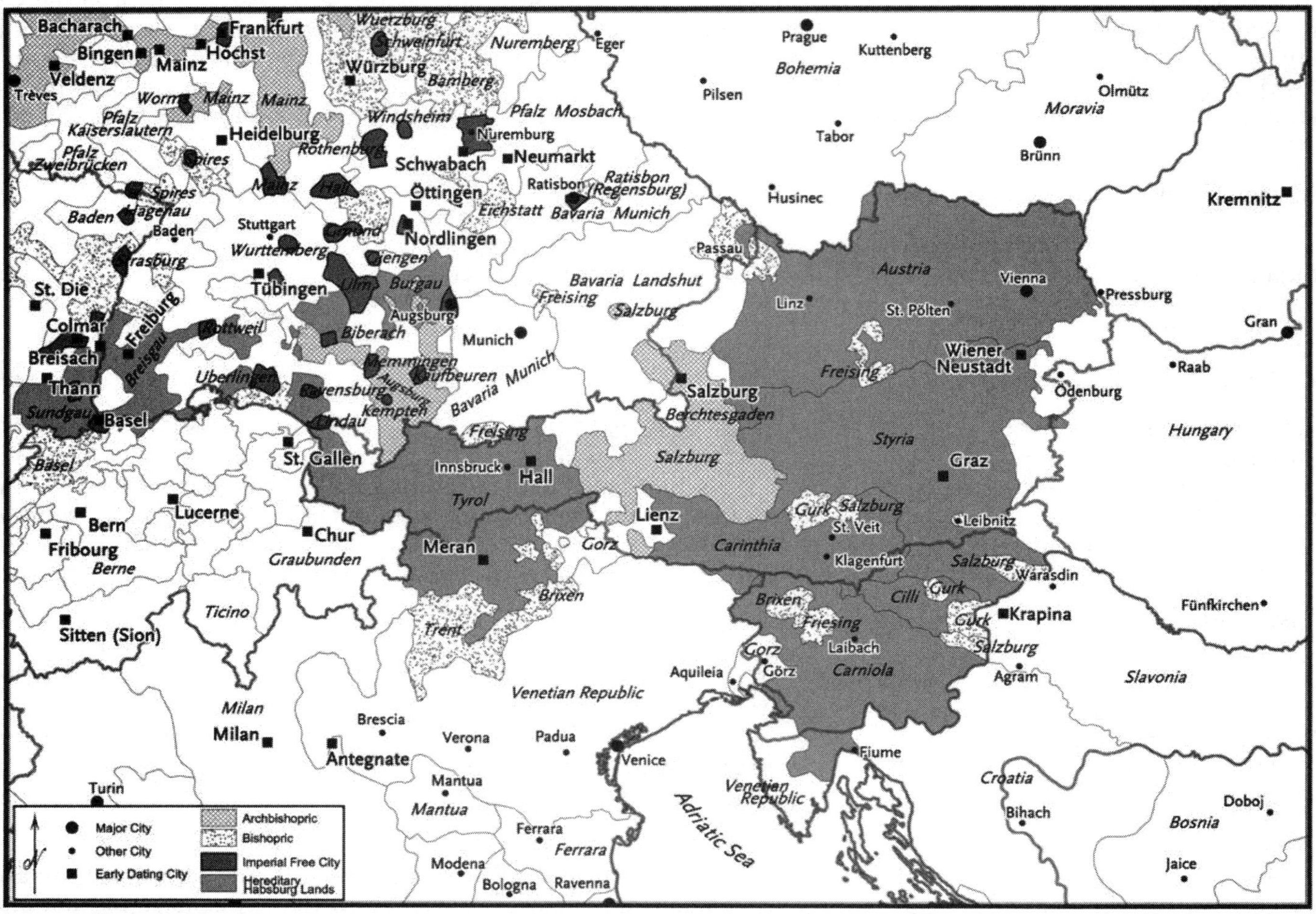

THE AUSTRIAN IMPERIAL DISTRICT OF HOLY ROMAN EMPIRE -
ARCHDUCHY AND POSSESSION OF THE HABSBURG FAMILY. MINTS OF VIENNA AND WIENER NEUSTADT. 1456

The Austrian district of the Holy Roman Empire in the late Middle Ages was not a contiguous region or country but instead a patchwork linking of large and powerful hereditary territories which had earlier been conjoined and split apart as patrimonies. During the 15th century, the Austrian district of the Holy Roman Empire consisted primarily of the archduchy of Austria (Österreich), the duchies of Carinthia (Kärten), Styria (Steiermark) and Krain, the counties of Tyrol (Tirol) and Görz (Goricia) the margraviate of Moravia (Maehren) the bishops of Trient (Triento), and the kingdom of Bohemia (Boehmen). This vast and widespread territory was ruled by Holy Roman Emperor Friedrich III, King of the Germans and later by his son Maximilian.

Friedrich, son of Duke Ernst of Austria, ruled (together with his brother Albrecht) from 1435 as Friedrich V of Styria, Carinthia and Krain. He was elected German king in 1440 and crowned Roman Emperor Friedrich III in 1452, but did not inherit the entire archduchy of Austria until 1463. Later added to the his empire were the Burgundian Netherlands, which his son Maximilian inherited from his deceased widow, Marie of Burgundy, in 1482.

Despite the immense size and power of the empire, the coins struck by the Emperor in the Austrian mints of Vienna and Wiener Neustadt lacked any of the magnificence of their patron issuer. Moreover, with the exception of common Wiener Neustadt kreuzers dated 1470 and 1471 and Viennese kreuzers dated 1482 through 1485, the coins for the most part were poorly struck. Compounding the problems, the coins were often struck (or offstruck) on uneven planchets, with designs and engravings remarkable for their crudeness.

To collectors, the desirability of Austria's mid-15th century coinage stems from the large and varied number of types and dates issued in the latter half of the decade of 1451-1460. With the possible exception of the decade of 1401-1410, where Aachen coinage alone is available, this is the most difficult 15th century decade of coinage to collect. Compounding this challenge is that the designs and lettering of the mid-century Viennese and Wiener Neustadt coins struck from 1456-1460 are exceptionally crude, and examples with all digits clear are most rare.

The mint at Wiener Neustadt struck an unbroken series of four-digit dated kreuzers from 1456-1460, and a second series from 1470-1472. The former are all very to excessively rare and uniformly found in abysmal condition, while the

Number	Date	Mint	Denomination	Rarity

later are well struck, easily collectable in higher grade and are very common, except for the extremely rare 1472. The mint at Vienna, despite its host city's size and importance, struck small sized early dated coinage, primarily pfennigs and kreuzers, except for two exceptionally rare groschens dated 1481 and 1482.

Friedrich III did not lack the resources to strike magnificent coins - witness the diverse and stunning coinage issued in 1487 by his son Maximilian from his Burgundian Netherlands territories. Instead, it appears that inadequate attention was paid to have the local mints in the Habsburg seat of power to produce the top-quality coinage which its satellite possessions so regularly struck. It must be remembered that in the 15th century the Holy Roman Empire was a military power, not a trading power. Still, it is surprising that it took so long for the Emperor to insist that the local Habsburg coinage be struck to appropriate standards.

Primary Work: CNA (excellent). Secondary Work: Luschin and Szego. General Work: Schulten and Saurma

Number	Date	Mint	Denomination	Rarity
IV-1a	1456	Wiener Neust.	Kreuzer	R3
IV-1b	1456	Wiener Neust.	Kreuzer	R4
IV-3	1457	Wiener Neust.	Kreuzer	R6
IV-4	1458	Wiener Neust.	Kreuzer	R2
IV-7	1459	Wiener Neust.	Kreuzer	R3
IV-10a	1460	Vienna	Pfennig	R4
IV-10b	1460	Vienna	Pfennig	R4
IV-11	1460	Wiener Neust.	Kreuzer	R4
IV-15	1467	Vienna	Kreuzer	R2
IV-18	1468	Vienna	Kreuzer	R2
IV-21	1470	Wiener Neust.	Kreuzer	C
IV-24	1471	Wiener Neust.	Kreuzer	C
IV-27	1472	Wiener Neust.	Kreuzer	R3
IV-30	1474	Vienna	Pfennig	R6
IV-35	1481	Vienna	Groschen	R4
IV-36	1481	Vienna	Kreuzer	R2
IV-37	1482	Vienna	Groschen	R6
IV-38	1482	Vienna	Kreuzer	S
IV-40	1483	Vienna	Kreuzer	S
IV-42	1484	Vienna	Kreuzer	R
IV-46	1485	Vienna	Kreuzer	S

GÖRZ (GORIZIA, GORICI) - COUNTY. MINT OF LIENZ. 1477

Görz was a county in the southwestern regions of the Habsburg lands, south of Carinthia. It is currently located on the border between Italy and Slovenia. The ancestors of the counts in the 15th century were also counts of Tyrol, the lines splitting earlier in the 14th century. In its mint at Lienz, Görz struck four early dated coins, three kreuzers and one triple kreuzer. The kreuzers are collectable but still very or extremely rare. The triple kreuzer, bearing a realistic portrait of Count Leonard V, is excessively rare. When last sold in 1998, an attractive specimen of this coin brought $20,000.

Görz is also listed by many numismatic works as an Italian state, as its current location is in modern-day Italy with the old castle of Görz in Slovenia right across the border. Its coins are both listed in Corpus Nummorum Italicorum and Corpus Nummorum Austriacorum. However, its early dated coinage is correctly placed under the listing of Habsburg Territories, since Görz's creation as a county stemmed from its ownership by the Andechs-Meran Family, who were also counts of Tyrol. Its early dated coinage also employed the typical Habsburg device of a double cross on the reverse, the same as kreuzers from Styria or Wiener Neustadt.

Primary References: CNA, CNI. General References: Moser-Tursky and Schulten

IV-31	1477	Lienz	Kreuzer	R3
IV-32a	1478	Lienz	Kreuzer	R
IV-32b	1478	Lienz	Kreuzer	R3
IV-33	1479	Lienz	Kreuzer	R3
IV-58	1498	Lienz	Triple Kreuzer	R5

GRAZ (GRECZ). SEE STYRIA.

HALL. SEE TYROL.

Number	Date	Mint	Denomination	Rarity

HUNGARY (VNGARIE). MINT OF KREMNITZ (KREMNICA) - KINGDOM. 1499

Medieval Hungary was an independent kingdom during the 15th century adjoining the Habsburg territories. During the steady administration of Matthias I Corvinus from 1458-1490, Hungary had been wealthy, powerful and influential. Under the weak leadership of Wladislav II, though, Hungary in 1526 lost its independence in the battle of Mohács, at which time its eastern portion was conquered by the Turks and the Habsburgs claimed the empty throne and occupied western Hungary. Hungary's only early dated coins were issued in 1499 and 1500, during the last few years of its independence.

Hungary had a long history of striking large quantities of both gold and silver coins of several denominations. Its little silver deniers featuring the Madonna and Child are amongst the most common of all 15th century coinage. Despite this extensive coinage history, Hungary struck but three early dated coins, two thalers and a pattern silver gulden, all equally stunning and excessively rare. Ironically, the weakest and least successful of all the Hungarian monarchs ended up issuing the most magnificent coinage in the history of the realm. Gold strikes of the greatest rarity from those two thalers are also extant. Many fakes of the thalers are reported and genuine pieces are near uncollectible.

Primary Work: CNH and Huszar. General Works: Egg and Davenport.

IV-59	1499	Kremnitz	Thaler	R4
IV-60	1500	Kremnitz	Thaler	R4
IV-61	1500	Kremnitz	Pattern Silver Gulden	R6

KRAPINA - BARONY. 1459

Krapina was a barony located in what is now modern day Croatia. In 1459 Krapina's ruler, Jan von Vitovec, was granted by Friedrich III the right to strike coinage in the name of the Emperor. Acting upon that grant, which lasted barely six months, Vitovec had 1459 dated kreuzers struck in the name of Friedrich III with the Habsburg eagle on the obverse and the Habsburg shield on the reverse. Only the reverse legend "MONETA: IN: KRAPINA" distinguishes these coins from other Friedrich III coinage from the Graz mint in Styria.

Two dies are known for the Krapina 1459 dated kreuzers, one with the date engraved as "59" and the other as "9"; unexpectedly, the double digit die is not reported in CNA and likely only one specimen exists. As might be anticipated, all coinage of the barons of Krapina is of the greatest rarity. The few pieces known all tend to be both very weakly struck and off-centered as well. No other coins of Krapina, dated or not, are known.

Primary Work: None. General Work: CNA (essential and excellent)

IV-8a	1459	Krapina	Kreuzer	R5
IV-8b	1459	Krapina	Kreuzer	R6

KREMNITZ (KREMNICA). SEE HUNGARY. 1499

LIENZ. SEE GÖRZ. 1477

MERAN. SEE TYROL. 1460

SALZBURG - ARCHBISHOPRIC. 1500

Salzburg was a very rich and powerful archbishopric located in what is currently central-western Austria southeast of Munich, surrounded on three sides by the Habsburg territories. It was formerly part of the Bavarian District of Germany and maintained its independence from Austria until the early 19th century. It had a history of coinage 500 years before the 15th century, but struck its early dated coins only at the end of the century in the year of 1500. That date was likely immobilized for some years, especially for that of the very common batzens, whose next listed date was 1508.

Salzburg in 1500 struck two gold and three silver denomination coins. The designs were rather ordinary, with the larger denominations all featuring the family shields on the obverse and patron St. Rupert on the reverse. Of the five, the smallest denomination, a billon heller worth one-half pfennig, is the most difficult to find. With that exception, all the rest of Salzburg's coinage, being abundantly struck, is readily collectable in high grade. A unique piefort of half guldiner weight struck from batzen dies is known and recently sold for over $15,000.

Primary Work: Probszt. General Work: Schulten

IV-62	1500	Salzburg	Ducat	R2
IV-63	1500	Salzburg	Goldgulden	R
IV-64	1500	Salzburg	Batzen	C
IV-65	1500	Salzburg	Uniface Pfennig	S
IV-66	1500	Salzburg	Heller	R2

Number	Date	Mint	Denomination	Rarity

STYRIA (STEIERMARK) - DUCHY. MINT OF GRAZ. 1456

Styria was one of the largest of the duchies comprising the Habsburg Empire. Located in central-south Austria, Styria was once an independent duchy, but by the 15th century was ruled exclusively by the Habsburg family. In fact, during the time that Styria's Graz mint struck dated coinage, the ruler of Styria was also the Holy Roman Emperor. Friedrich V, Duke of Styria became Emperor Friedrich III from 1440-1493 and all of Styria's early dated coins bore his title.

As with the Habsburg Austrian lands, the coinage of Styria was notable for its abysmal manufacturing techniques - excessively poor striking and crude die engraving. With the exception of the smaller kreuzers struck in the period from 1480-1493, the coinage is Styria is rarely found fully or sharply struck, with better condition pieces commanding a substantial premium the few times they are offered for sale. Full two or four digit strikes of the pfennigs and kreuzers during the decade of 1451-1460 are excessively rare, as are well-centered or well-struck achters and sechzehners from the following two decades.

Primary Work: CNA (essential). Secondary Work: Pichler. General Work: Saurma and Schulten

IV-2	1456	Graz	Uniface Pfennig	R
IV-5a	1458	Graz	Kreuzer	VS
IV-5b	1458	Graz	Kreuzer	R3
IV-5c	1458	Graz	Kreuzer	R4
IV-5d	1458	Graz	Kreuzer	R5
IV-5e	1458	Graz	Kreuzer	R5
IV-6	1458	Graz	Uniface Pfennig	R4
IV-9	1459	Graz	Uniface Pfennig	R4
IV-13	146?	Graz	Groschen	R5
IV-14	146?	Graz	Kreuzer	R5
IV-16	1467	Graz	Sechzehner	R3
IV-17	1467	Graz	Achter	R2
IV-19	1468	Graz	Achter	R
IV-20	1469	Graz	Sechzehner	R3
IV-22	1470	Graz	Sechzehner	R3
IV-23	1470	Graz	Achter	R?
IV-25	1471	Graz	Sechzehner	R2
IV-26	1471	Graz	Achter	R2
IV-28	1472	Graz	Achter	R2
IV-29	1473	Graz	Achter	R3
IV-A30	1474	Graz	Achter	R6
IV-34a	1480	Graz	Kreuzer	R3
IV-34b	1480	Graz	Kreuzer	R5
IV-39	1482	Graz	Kreuzer	C
IV-41	1483	Graz	Kreuzer	VS
IV-43a	1484	Graz	Kreuzer	R
IV-43b	1484	Graz	Kreuzer	R
IV-43c	1484	Graz	Kreuzer	R
IV-47	1485	Graz	Kreuzer	VS
IV-48a	1486	Graz	Kreuzer	R
IV-48b	1486	Graz	Kreuzer	R3
IV-50	1487	Graz	Goldgulden	R6
IV-51a	1487	Graz	Kreuzer	R3
IV-51b	1487	Graz	Kreuzer	R2
IV-51c	1487	Graz	Kreuzer	R5
IV-52	1488	Graz	Kreuzer	R
IV-53	1489	Graz	Kreuzer	S
IV-54	1490	Graz	Kreuzer	R
IV-55	1491	Graz	Kreuzer	R-R2
IV-56	1493	Graz	Kreuzer	R3

TYROL (TIROL) - COUNTY. MINTS OF HALL AND MERAN. 1460

Tyrol, located in what is now western Austria just south of Germany, was one of the large Habsburg hereditary lands which were part of the Holy Roman Empire. Making good use of the products of Tyrolean mines, Count Sigismund of Tyrol authorized the production of large silver guldiner and their fractionals, the guldiner being a thick silver coin worth one goldgulden. Prior to this time, large silver coins had not been issued in Europe. However, the bullion famine of Europe had ended by the 1460's with the discovery of large silver mines and silver was then plentiful.

Number	Date	Mint	Denomination	Rarity

In 1484 Tyrol struck from its mint at Hall dated half guldiners, worth one-half a goldgulden, and thick ("dickstuck") pieces from the same dies of full guldiner weight. These two types are among the earliest dated coins with realistic portraits of the rulers, the others being several types by William of the Mark of Liège. In 1486, Sigismund authorized the production of a silver guldiner, which later became known as the gulden-thaler, the world's first dated thaler. The guldiner was a highly impressive coin with the archduke in full regalia on the obverse, and on the reverse, a galloping knight surrounded by armorial shields with the date in the center. Three subtypes are known. In the early 16th century, a tiny handful of guldiners were also struck in gold from original dies with the weight of 7 ducats.

The dated coins of Tyrol, with one exception, were all large silver coins which did not normally circulate in commerce. They are often found in high grade and with excellent striking characteristics, giving testament to a superbly run mint. Unfortunately, perhaps close to half of all known specimens were mounted at one time, as the impressive die work on these pieces was equal to any contemporaneous medal. While listed as rare in most auction catalogues, the most common of the major guldiner die types is actually one of the more common of early dated coin types known and is offered multiple times each year in auction sales.

A very rare type of Tyrolean kreuzer, struck in the mint at Meran, bears the numerals "60" on the reverse. Dozens of types of Tyrolean kreuzers are known, so numerous that they do not have separate numbers in CNA, but 4 of the 46 varieties noted have this mysterious double digit numeral. The "60" is not a reference to a denomination, such as 60 kreuzers to the gulden, as that standard of weight did not exist until an edict from Emperor Ferdinand in the mid-16th century. Recent authority supports the interpretation of the “60” as the date of 1460. As these kreuzers were struck in the mid-15th century, and other Habsburg coinage also used the two digit date of "60," the listing of this coin as a dated piece seems well-grounded.

Primary Work: Moeser-Dworschak, Moser-Tursky and Egg. General Work: CNA, Schulten and Davenport.

IV-12	1460	Meran	Kreuzer	R2
IV-44	1484	Hall	Dick Half Guldiner	R4
IV-45a	1484	Hall	Half Guldiner	R
IV-45b	1484	Hall	Half Guldiner	R3-4
IV-49a	1486	Hall	Guldiner	VS
IV-49b	1486	Hall	Guldiner	R3
IV-49c	1486	Hall	Guldiner	R5
IV-57	1495	Hall	Königsguldiner	R5

WIENER NEUSTADT - SEE AUSTRIAN IMPERIAL DISTRICT

VIENNA (WIEN) - SEE AUSTRIAN IMPERIAL DISTRICT

REGION V - SWITZERLAND

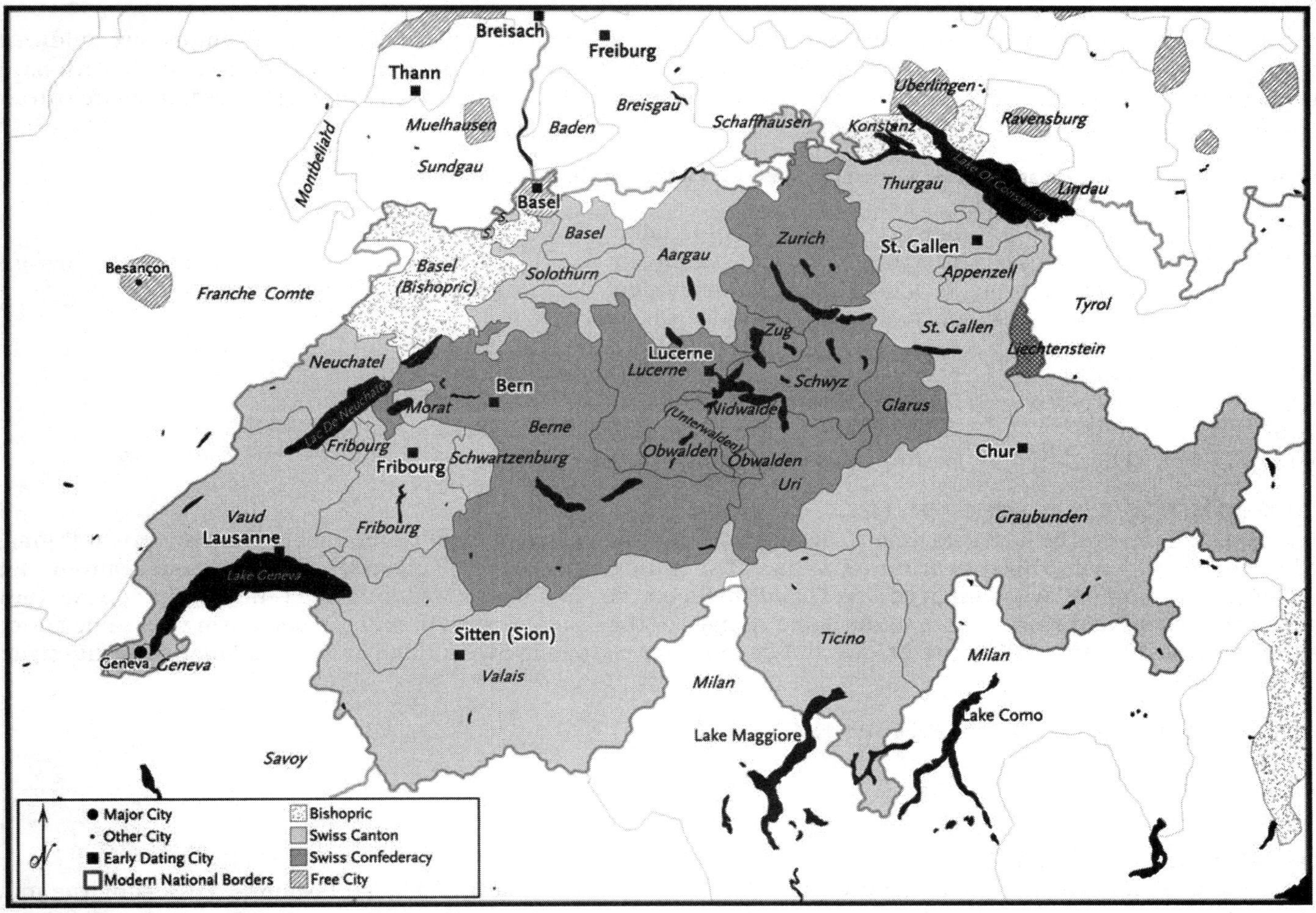

BASEL (BASLE, BALE) - CITY AND IMPERIAL MINT. 1491

Basel, located in north-central Switzerland, was the site of a bishopric and a free city containing an imperial mint. While the bishopric did not strike dated coins in the 15th century, both the city and imperial mint did. The city mint struck large and impressive silver coins of three different denominations and the separate imperial mint struck goldguldens dated from 1491-1493, all issued in the name of either Friedrich or Maximilian. All the early dated coins of Basel were minted to high standards and were well struck.

The gold coins of Basel used rather ordinary designs of the Madonna and Child/imperial orb approved for imperial coinage and while very rare, they are still collectable today in high grades as with much early dated gold. The rare silver coins, a product of the city mint where the die cutters were free from imperial controls, were struck from beautifully-rendered artistic dies. All command high prices today. As was typical with larger denomination coinage such as dickens, the coins were not used much in ordinary daily transactions and thus did not circulate extensively, preserving their condition.

Primary References: Ewig and Winterstein. General References: HMZ and Friedberg

Number	Date	Mint	Denomination	Rarity
V-5	1491	Basel	Goldgulden	R2
V-6	1492	Basel	Goldgulden	R2
V-13	1493	Basel	Goldgulden	R2
V-14	1493	Basel	Goldgulden	R4
V-20	1499	Basel	4 Ducats	R5
V-21	1499	Basel	Heavy Thaler	R5
V-22	1499	Basel	Dicken	R2
V-23	1499	Basel	Heavy Groschen	R5
V-24	1499	Basel	Turnosgroschen	R4

BERN (BERNE) - CITY. 1492

Berne, the capital of modern Switzerland, was a large city whose early dated coinage, as with Basel, consisted solely of gold and large silver coins. The gold coins, issued in multiples from two through four goldguldens, were all struck from 1492 dicken dies. The gold did not feature the typical imperial title or orb device, as the coins were authorized by Papal rather than imperial edict.

Number	Date	Mint	Denomination	Rarity

In addition to the 1492 dated goldgulden multiples and dickens, in 1493 and 1494 Berne struck impressive guldiners, whose legendless reverses contained a circle of 20 shields of counties under the Bernese government. As with Basel, the coinage of Berne, while today rare or very rare, was exceptionally well-struck and high grade examples are still collectable.

Primary References: Geiger and Lohner. General References: HMZ, Friedberg and De Mey D'Or

V-7	1492	Bern	4 Goldgulden	R4
V-8	1492	Bern	3 Goldgulden	R5
V-9	1492	Bern	2 Goldgulden	R5
V-10	1492	Bern	Double Dicken	R5
V-11	1492	Bern	Dicken of 1/3 Gulden	R4
V-12	1492	Bern	Dicken of 1/4 Gulden	R2
V-15	1493	Bern	Guldiner	R2
V-16	1494	Bern	Heavy Guldiner	R4
V-17	1494	Bern	Guldiner	R

CHUR (CVRIENCIS, CVR.) - BISHOPRIC. 1488

Chur was the site of a bishopric in eastern Switzerland and the primary city of Graubunden. The bishopric was granted the mint right over 500 years prior to the time it struck two early dated plapparts, one in 1488 and again in 1495. Employing a common Swiss design of a cross and shield on the obverse and Madonna and Child on the reverse, these plapparts bear similar resemblance to the dated coinage of the bishopric of Würzburg issued during the same period. Both of the dated coins of Chur are unique and lie in museums, one in Switzerland and one in Milan. The city struck no early dated coinage.

Primary Reference: Trachsel General Reference: HMZ

V-4	1488	Chur	Plappart	R6
V-18	1495	Chur	Plappart	R6

LAUSANNE (LAVS.)- BISHOPRIC. 1477

Lausanne was an ancient Roman city in western Switzerland and the seat of a small bishopric. Possessing the mint right from the late 14th century, the bishops struck a handful of coins, most extremely rare, copying French-Savoyen styles. In 1477, bishop Benoit de Montferrand struck dated parpaiolles (10 denier pieces worth about one groschen) from at least two distinct dies, one with a small shield (only two known) and one with a large shield (almost as rare). Both dies employed the modern "4" for the first time on a coin.

Primary Reference: Dolivo. General Reference: HMZ

V-2a	1477	Lausanne	Parpaiolles	R5-6
V-2b	1477	Lausanne	Parpaiolles	R5

LUCERNE (LUZERN) - CITY. 1484

Lucerne, in central Switzerland, was first a monastery and then a Habsburg city. By the 15th century, it had become a free and independent city and later a canton. Its early dated monetary history is limited to a sole 1484 spagürli, a small base silver coin valued at three heller. Despite the extreme rarity of this coin, its original dies, two obverses and one reverse, are still preserved and are located in the Historisches Museum of Lucerne.

Primary Reference: Wielandt and Tobler. General Reference: HMZ

V-3	1484	Lucerne	Spagürli	R6

SITTEN (SION, SEDVNENS) - BISHOPRIC AND COUNTY. 1498

Sitten was a bishopric in the county (later canton) of Wallis (Valais). The bishops of Sitten began minting coins only in the second half of the 15th century, and struck but one early dated coin, a splendid large guldiner dated 1498. The guldiner's obverse shows the donation of the county of Wallis by Charlemagne to bishop Theodul while the reverse is a legendless design of the bishop's shield surrounded by 16 smaller shields. This lovely thaler is highly medallic in design and the few surviving pieces are nearly always found in very high grade.

Primary Reference: M. de Palézieux - Du Pan. General Reference: HMZ

V-19	1498	Sitten	Thaler	R3

ST. GALLEN (SANCTI GALLI) - FREE CITY. 1424

St. Gallen, in northeast Switzerland, was originally the site of a monastery with a mint right, but the town of St. Gallen broke away from religious control and became a secularized free city in the 14th century. It gained its own mint right

Number **Date** **Mint** **Denomination** **Rarity**

from Emperor Sigismund in 1415, but was allowed to only strike smaller denomination coinage until 1500.

St. Gallen struck early dated coins in only two years, and those were 76 years apart. However, its coinage is of supreme importance, as its 1424 plapparts (1/24 of a goldgulden) were the first early Anno Domini coins struck using modern positional (Arabic style) numerals. Less than 10 pieces are extant, mostly in museums, struck from two known die types. In 1500, in celebration of its right to coin larger denomination monies, St. Gallen struck dated dickens, batzens (double plapparts) and plapparts, the latter two being excessively rare.

Primary Reference: Iklé-Steinlin and Hahn. General Reference: HMZ

Number	Date	Mint	Denomination	Rarity
V-1	1424	St. Gallen	Plappart	R4
V-25	1500	St. Gallen	Dicken	R3
V-26	1500	St. Gallen	Batzen	R4
V-27	1500	St. Gallen	Plappart	R4

VALAIS - SEE SITTEN

WALLIS - SEE SITTEN

REGION VI - SCANDINAVIA

COPENHAGEN - SEE DENMARK

DENMARK (DANEMARK, DANOR) - KINGDOM. MINT OF COPENHAGEN. 1496

The medieval kingdom of Denmark in the 15th century was far larger than today, encompassing Sweden, Norway, parts of Finland, Greenland, Iceland and the Faeroe Islands. Joined together in the Union of Kalmar in 1397, the kingdom encompassed all of Scandinavia until the Swedish revolt in 1523, although each of the three countries of Denmark, Norway and Sweden had still maintained their own rulers, laws and coinage.

Despite the size and power of medieval Denmark, its coinage was fairly primitive. No early dated coins were struck by the kingdom until 1496 when King Hans (John) issued two extraordinary high gothic-style dated gold coins. These two coins, a gold noble and triple noble, loosely copied the style of the 1487 grand real d'or of Maximilian. Sadly, these were apparently presentation pieces or patterns only, as but two examples exist of the noble and the triple noble is unique. While these coins are sometimes listed as Swedish (by Frey, for example), Hans did not become king of Sweden until a year later and the legends reference his Danish title only.

Primary Reference: Schou.
General Reference: Friedberg and De Mey D'Or.

Number	Date	Mint	Denomination	Rarity
VI-4	1496	Copenhagen	Gold Triple Noble	R6
VI-5	1496	Copenhagen	Gold Noble	R6

ROSKILDE - BISHOPRIC. 1234

The dated 1234 deniers of Bishop Niels Stigsen of Roskilde are credited with being the first European Anno Domini dated coins not using Islamic script. The bishopric of Roskilde, located in the center of Zealand in modern-day Denmark, apparently minted these remarkable coins as a statement of rights to the mint revenue. Other coins struck by the bishop referenced the king and/or were struck with portraits, making these small and crude deniers, with a crown on the obverse and a bishop's hat on the reverse most extraordinary. Two different dies are reported, one with capital letters and one with lower case letters.

Number	Date	Mint	Denomination	Rarity

Bishopric coinage was struck fairly consistently at the Roskilde mint, one of Denmark's two largest medieval mints, Lund being the other. Examples of bishopric-issued coinage are known from as early as 1080. However, the 1234 coins are the only dated examples, and no trend arose from their issuance, as the next dated European coins were struck in both Aachen and Schoonvorst-Sichem 138 years later in 1372. Only seven examples of this remarkable denier, Europe's first Anno Domini dated coin struck for European circulation, are currently known. All reside in museums and none have ever been offered at public sale.

Primary Reference: Lindahl (article). General Reference: Frey 1978

VI-1	1234	Roskilde	Denier	R6

STOCKHOLM. SEE SWEDEN

SWEDEN (SCS, SVECIE)- KINGDOM. MINT OF STOCKHOLM. 1478

In the 15th century Sweden was forcibly linked to Denmark by a formal union, yet it retained its own rulers, laws and (thankfully) coinage. Pursuant to a 1478 monetary decree or mint contract specifying the weight and silver content, Sweden, under King Sten Sture the Elder, authorized the issuance of dated ortugs and half ortugs of fine silver worth eight and four pennies respectively. The date of 1478 reflected the date of the decree, not necessarily the date of fabrication, as the decree stayed current until the next one was issued in 1497. Thus, the 1478 date was an immobilized date, with the actual coinage being struck anytime from 1478-1497.

When an immobilized date was used, the same general die types were utilized for many years, in this case nearly twenty. Numerous new dies were required as the old ones wore out or broke. If the engravers were not careful, variations, small and large, could occur between the old and new dies. In the case of the Swedish early dated coinage, both for ortugs and half ortugs, profound variations occurred in the expression of the (original) four digit date of 1478 - some of the variations intended, others clearly not.

Most of Sweden's early dated coinage subtypes exist because of significant unintended engraving errors. The (presumed) original dies of the ortug and half ortug had careful spacing allowing for full four digit dates. As dies wore out and new dies were prepared, subsequent engravers left inadequate space on the legend to reflect the full date. Medieval engravers were craftsmen and artists, but were not necessary literate, and therefore the shortening or altering of dates did not strike them as a forbidden alteration. Hence, dates were altered to make them fit in the legend, but sometimes this alteration took a bizarre path because the engraver had no idea that he was changing a date.

The "standard" die of the ortug contained the king's portrait on the obverse with a full four digit date above the bust. In a major variety, a subsequent die dropped the first three digits, leaving the number "8" ambiguously placed next to a large annulet used as a spacing device and appearing all the more as a "0." No wonder numerous auction catalogues and references, including Frey, referred erroneously to a "1480" dated ortug. Adding to the confusion was the appearance of the annulet in two different sizes, large and small.

The die engravings for the half ortugs were even stranger, with the standard 1478 date engraved on more common examples with either a two digit or single digit date. Both of these have been misreported as either 1480 or 1488 dates because of the ubiquitous annulets or double annulets, the latter appearing all the more as an "8," causing Frey (and others) to believe that a 1488 date existed. Three excessively strange dies, caused by mis-engraving and/or muling or both, have dates reflected as "17/78," "14" and "8/78!" The early dated coins of Sweden, despite their peculiar engraving oddities, were well struck and thus can be still be collected (if available at all) in higher grades.

Primary Reference: Lagerqvist (essential). General Reference: none needed

VI-2a	1478	Stockholm	Ortug	R
VI-2b	1478	Stockholm	Ortug	R2
VI-2c	1478	Stockholm	Ortug	R5
VI-3a	1478	Stockholm	Half Ortug	R2
VI-3b	1478	Stockholm	Half Ortug	R
VI-3c	1478	Stockholm	Half Ortug	R4
VI-3d	1478	Stockholm	Half Ortug	R6
VI-3e	1478	Stockholm	Half Ortug	R
VI-3f	1478	Stockholm	Half Ortug	R6

REGION VII - ITALY

ANTEGNATE - LORDSHIP.
MINT OF BOLOGNA. 1494

Antegnate was a lordship in southern Lombardy, southeast of Milan. It was ruled by the Bentivoglio family of Bologna from 1494-1509, whose patriarch, Giovanni II Bentivoglia, ruled Bologna from 1463-1506 before being ousted by the Pope Julius. Antegnate had no history of coinage before 1494, but in that year Giovanni was granted the mint right for Antegnate by Emperor Maximilian. Making utmost use of this right, Giovanni lost no time in issuing numerous dated and undated coins of various denominations and metals, gold, silver and bronze.

The coins of Antegnate are highly desirable for their craftsmanship. The mintmaster of Bologna, where these coins were struck, was the artist-medallist Francesco Raibolini, also known as Francesco Francia. Melding superior artistic design techniques with Italian high Renaissance medallic art, Francia created dies featuring a capped bust of Giovanni on the obverse, with the 1494 date in Roman numerals on the reverse. This die was utilized for most of Antegnate's dated coinage. The prolific issuance of this small lordship's dated coinage exceeds all other Italian states combined, with six distinct denominations and seven distinct types. Numerous undated coins were issued as well. The bronze pattern ("prova") testone is the sole example of the dated coins that is offered intermittently, all others being excessively rare, or of the greatest rarity.

Primary Reference: General References: CNI, Biaggi, Friedberg and De Mey D'Or (gold only)

Number	Date	Mint	Denomination	Rarity
VII-2	1494	Bologna	4 Ducats	R5
VII-3	1494	Bologna	Mezzo Ducato	R5
VII-4	1494	Bologna	Double Testoni	R5
VII-5	1494	Bologna	Mezzo Testone	R5
VII-6a	1494	Bologna	Guilio	R4
VII-6b	1494	Bologna	Guilio	R5
VII-7	1494	Bologna	Pattern Bronze Testone	R2

BOLOGNA - SEE ANTEGNATE

FORLI (FORLIV) - LORDSHIP. 1480

Forli, located southeast of Bologna between Rimini and Ravenna, had a very brief history of coinage. In 1480, the ruling lord, Pino Ordilaffi, died without legitimate descendents and Pope Sixtus IV appointed his nephew, Hieronymus (Italian "Gerolamo") Riaria, lord of nearby Imola, to be lord of Forli as well. The mint right had been previously granted by the Pope to Hieronymus as lord of Imola, but no coins are extant from that mint grant.

Later in 1480, Lord Hieronymus, in commemoration of his appointment to the Forli lordship, struck a gold ducat in the name of the joint titles of lord of Forli and Imola. This coin is so rare that both CNI and Friedberg have but a crude line drawing of this noteworthy piece. This coin obtains the title of the first Italian early Anno Domini dated coin, as the dated coins from Görz (Goriza), a medieval county located now part in modern-day Italy and part in Slovenia, were struck under Habsburg authority. A tiny handful of silver coins were also issued by the lordship, all undated. They are nearly of equal rarity. All coinage of this small lordship ceased by the end of the 15th century.

Primary Reference: none. General Reference: CNI, Friedberg, De Mey D'Or

VII-1	1480	Uncertain	Ducato d'Oro	R6

Number	Date	Mint	Denomination	Rarity

MILAN (MAILAND, MILANO) - DUCHY. 1497
Milan was a large and prosperous duchy at the center of Renaissance revival in northern Italy. From 1450 on, it was controlled by the Sforza family, whose military heritage belied the artistic patronship bestowed on numerous Renaissance artists in residence, foremost amongst these being Leonardo da Vinci. While Milan was a prolific issuer of undated coinage, including many lovely large silver and gold coins, Milan's output of early dated coinage was limited to two types of bronze pattern ("provo") testones. However, these two bronze patterns are among the most beautiful of all early dated coinage.

Both of Milan's early dated coin types were issued by Ludovico Moro, known as "the Moor." Each featured a medallic-like rendering of the Duke on the obverse with the date of 1497 upside down below his bust. The reverse on the first piece bore the armorial shield of the Sforza family, which was the same shield and design used on several generations of silver testones. The obverse die was the same on the second piece, but the reverse was a commemorative design bearing the lovely portrait of the Duke's beloved young wife, Beatrice D'Este, who tragically died at the age of 22 in January 1497. The first is all but uncollectible; the second, when last sold in 1998 at Leu Numismatik, brought over $20,000 and may have been the last such specimen in private hands.

Primary Reference: Morosini, Gnecchi. General Reference: CNI.

VII-8a	1497	Milan	Pattern Bronze Testone	R5
VII-8b	1497	Milan	Pattern Bronze Testone	R5-6

PAPAL STATES - MINT OF ROME (ROMA). 1500
The Papal States were headquartered in Rome at the seat of the Pope but had mints in numerous additional cities, including Bologna, Ancona, Spoleto and Mantua. Despite an unbroken line of coinage extending back more than 600 years, Rome and the Papal States dated their coins, if at all, only with regnal (year of the reign) dates. The one exception was in 1500, when Pope Alexander VI struck a magnificent triple "fiorino di camera" (or triple florin) with his portrait on the reverse, and the Roman numeral date of "MD" at the end of the reverse legend. What is also remarkable about this coin that it is the only example of any Anno Domini dated coin where the date of 1500 is expressed as "MD". All other examples of this date were shown as "MCCCCC" or "MVC" in various forms of lettering (representing 1000 + 5 x 100) or "1500."

Primary Reference: Berman. General Reference: CNI.

VII-9	1500	Rome	Triple Florin	R6

ROME - SEE PAPAL STATES

REGION VIII - FRANCE

BRITTANY (BRETAGNE) - DUCHY. MINT OF NANTES. 1498
Brittany, located at the most northwestern part of France, was first an independent kingdom and later a duchy. In the Middle Ages its lands were alternately claimed by first Viking invaders, then by England and finally by France. During the 15th century, the kingdom was closely allied with France, as the English claims upon it ceased with the Plantagenet kings. Its duchess Anne was married to Charles VIII of France in 1491, but no sons emerged from the marriage by the time of Charles' death in 1498.

In 1498, during Anne's widowhood, as a testament to a hoped for independent Brittany, Anne struck magnificent high gothic-style ecus d'or (alternatively known as cadières d'or or florins d'or) in her joint titles as Queen of France and Duchess of Brittany. Both dated and undated specimens are known, with the date found beneath the throne. It is quite possible that all known dated coins are now in museums. The last known privately held example was offered for sale at a French auction in 1997. At that time, it was sold but then was immediately claimed by right - a process by which the French government grants the power to government institutions to trump at auction any desired specimen.

Primary Reference: De Mey Br. General Reference: Poey d'Avant, Friedberg and De Mey d'Or

VIII-3	1498	Nantes	Ecu d'Or	R6

LORRAINE (LOTHRINGEN, LOT) - DUCHY. MINTS OF NANCY AND ST. DIE. 1491
Lorraine was a large and strategically located duchy at the central-east part of France just north of Colmar and south of Luxembourg. Lorraine was both allied with and coveted by France; France first protected it from the territorial designs of Charles the Rash, who was attempting to recreate the ancient kingdom of Lotharingia by merging his Burgundian territories with his Netherlands territories. With France's aid, Charles was not only defeated but killed in battle in 1477, ending his reign. Beginning in 1552, France turned the tables on its former ally and began to incorpo-

rate it, piece by piece, into its kingdom.

As a wealthy duchy, Lorraine had maintained active mints for centuries, the largest being at Nancy. Lorraine struck numerous coins during the 15th century, but only two were dated. The first is France's earliest dated coin, a unique large double gros of splendid style dated 1491, presently located at the Museum of Contemporary and Ancient Arts in Epinal. The second is an excessively rare ducat dated 1492 from the smaller mint at St. Die. No recent auction records appear for either.

The title of this duchy appears in two other early dated coins. In 1482 and 1483 double briquets with three different legend forms were struck in the name of Marie of Burgundy. These were a posthumous series, as she died in 1482. The rarest of those three subtypes, perhaps as an honor to her father's ambitious but foolish goals (hence the label "Charles the Rash"), bears the legend by which he laid claim to the Duchy: "MONETA:DVC:AVST:LOT:BRA:LI:ZC".

Primary Reference: De Saulcy. General Reference: Friedberg and De Mey d'Or.

Number	Date	Mint	Denomination	Rarity
VIII-1	1491	Nancy	Double Gros	R6
VIII-2	1492	St. Die	Ducat	R5

NANCY - SEE LORRAINE

NANTES - SEE BRITTANY

ST. DIE - SEE LORRAINE

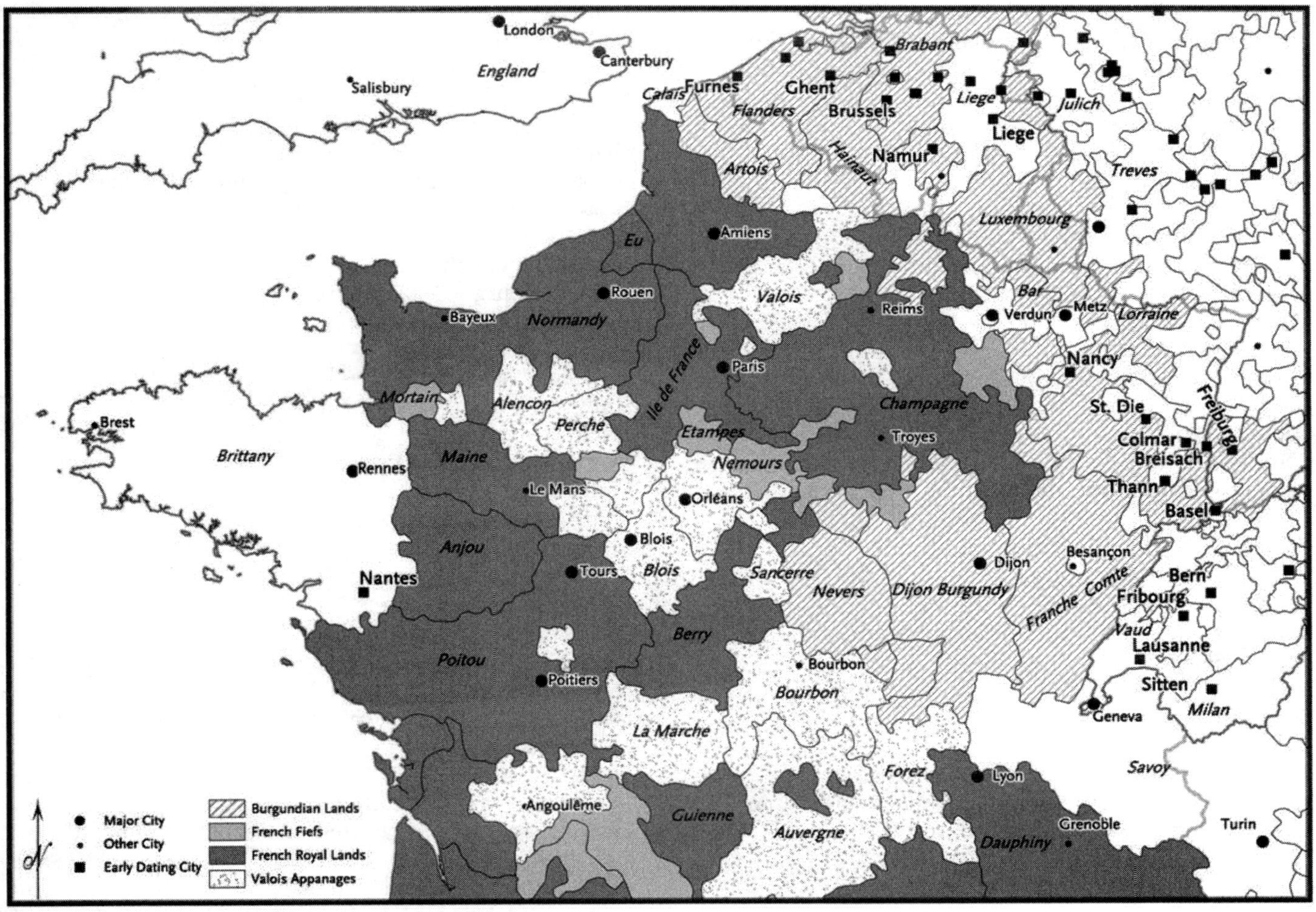

APPENDIX 1
ALPHABETICAL LISTING OF STATES AND THEIR MINTS STRIKING EARLY DATED COINAGE

Aachen (Aix la Chapelle). City mint
Angermuende – See Brandenburg
Anholt-Batenburg. Mint of Anholt
Annaberg – See Saxony
Antegnate. Mint of Bologna
Antwerp (Anvers) – See Brabant
Arenberg territories – See Liège
Austria (Habsburg Hereditary Territories) Mints of Wiener Neustadt and Vienna
Baar- See Mörs-Baar
Bacharach – See Palatinate
Basel (Basle). City Mint (silver), imperial mint (gold)
Berlin – See Brandenburg
Bern (Berne). City Mint
Bingen – See Mainz
Bologna – See Antegnate
Bolsward. City Mint
Bonn – See Cologne
Borbeck – See Essen
Brabant under Burgundian Netherlands and Habsburg control. Mints of Anvers. Malines and Maestricht
Brabant in revolt. Independent mints in Brussels and Louvain
Brandenburg. Mints of Angermuende, Berlin, Frankfurt and uncertain mints
Brandenburg-Franconia (Brandenburg-Franken). Mint of Swabia (Schwabach)
Breisach. City mint
Bremen. Mints of Bremen and Vörden
Brittany (Bretagne). Mint of Nantes
Broich – See Limburg
Bruges – See Flanders
Brunswick (Braunschweig). City mint
Brussels (Bruxelles) – See Brabant in revolt
Campen (Kampen). City mint
Cassel – See Hesse
Chur. Bishopric mint
Cleve (Kleve). Mints of Cleve, Wesel and Huissen
Coblenz – See Trier
Colditz – See Saxony
Colmar - City mint
Cologne Archbishopric (Köln). Mints of Riehl, Bonn and Deutz
Cologne City (Köln Stadt). City mint
Copenhagen - See Denmark
Damm – See Pommerania
Denmark (Danmark). Mint of Copenhagen
Deutz – See Cologne
Deventer. City Mint
Dordrecht – See Holland
Dortmund. City Mint
Düren – See Jülich-Berg
East Frisia (Ostfriesland). Mints of Emden and Norden
Ecluse (Sluis) – See Ghent, city in revolt
Einbeck. City mint
Emden - See East Frisia
Erfurt. City mint
Eschwege – See Hesse
Essen. Mints of Essen and Borbeck
Flanders (Flandres) under Burgundian Netherlands and Habsburg control. Mints of Bruges (Brugge) and Furnes
Flanders in revolt. Independent mints at Ghent and Ecluse (Sluis)
Forli. City mint?
Franeker. City mint
Frankfurt am Main. City mint and Imperial mint
Frankfurt am Oder - See Brandenburg
Freiberg – See Saxony
Freiburg im Breisgau. City Mint
Furnes – See Flanders
Frisia. Mint of Franeker
Garz – See Pommerania
Gelderland under Burgundian Netherlands (Guelders). Mints of Nijmegen (Nimègue), Zaltbommel and Malines (Mechelen)
Gelderland under Family of Egmont. Mints of Roermond and Zutphen
Ghent (Gent, Gand) – See Flanders in revolt
Gotha – See Saxony
Görz (Gorizia). Mint of Lienz
Göttingen. City mint
Graz – See Styria
Groningen. City mint
Halberstadt. City mint
Hall – See Tyrol
Hamburg. City mint
Hannover. City mint
Hasselt – See Liège and Utrecht
Heidelberg – See Palatinate
Henneberg. Mint of Schleusingen
Hesse (Hessen). Mints of Eschwege and Cassel (Kassel)
Hesse-Marburg. Uncertain mints and Wolfhagen
Hildesheim. City mint
Höchst – See Mainz
Hohenlimburg – See Limburg
Holland. Mint of Dordrecht
Hörde – See Mark
Huissen – See Cleve
Hungary. Mint of Kremnitz (Kremnica)
Jever. City mint
Jülich-Berg (Juliers). Mints of Schoonvorst, Düren and Mülheim
Königsee – See Schwarzburg
Krapina. City mint
Kremnitz (Kremnica) – See Hungary
Lausanne. Bishopric mint
Leeuwarden. City mint
Leipzig – See Saxony
Lemgo – See Lippe
Liège (all factions) (Lüttich, Luik). Hasselt, Liège or uncertain mints
Lienz – See Görz
Limbourg – See Region II
Limburg-Styrum - See Region I. Mints of Broich and Hohenlimburg
Lippe. Mint of Lemgo
Lorraine (Lothringen). Mints of St. Die and Nancy
Louvain (Leuven) – See Brabant in revolt
Lübeck. City mint
Lucerne. City mint

Lüneburg. City mint
Maestricht (Maastricht) – See Brabant
Mainz (Mayennes, Maynence). Mints of Bingen, Höchst and Mainz
Malines (Mechelen) – See Brabant and Gelderland
Mark (Marke). Mints of Hörde and Unna
Meran – See Tyrol
Milan (Milano). City mint
Mörs (Moers). City mint
Mörs-Baar. Mint of Baar
Mühlhausen. City mint
Mülheim – See Jülich-Berg
Namur (Namen). City mint
Nancy – See Lorraine
Nantes – See Brittany
Neuss. City mint
Newmarket – See Palatinate-Mosbach-Newmarket and Upper Palatinate
Nijmegen (Nimègue). City mint and mint of Gelderland
Norden – See East Frisia
Nördlingen. Imperial mint
Ölsnitz – See Saxony
Osnabrück. Bishopric mint
Öttingen. City mint
Paderborn. Bishopric mint
Palatinate (Pfalz). Mints of Bacharach and Heidelberg
Palatinate-Mosbach-Newmarket (Neumarkt). Mint of Newmarket
Palatinate-Upper Palatinate (Oberpfalz). Mint of Newmarket
Palatinate-Zweibrueken. Mint of Veldenz
Papal States. Mint of Rome (Roma)
Pommerania (Pommern). Mints of Garz, Stettin and Damm
Riehl – See Cologne
Roermond – See Egmont family of Gelderland
Rome – See Papal States
Roskilde. Bishopric mint
Salzburg. Bishopric mint
Saxony (Sachsen). Mints of Leipzig, Gotha, Freiberg, Colditz, Wittenberg, Ölsnitz, Zwickau, Schneeberg and Annaberg
Schleusingen – See Henneberg
Schneeberg – See Saxony
Schoonvorst – See Jülich-Berg
Schoonvorst-Sichem - Mint of Schoonvoorst
Swabia (Schwabach) – See Brandenburg-Franconia
Schwarzburg . Mint of Königsee
Sitten (Sion). Bishopric mint
Sneek. City mint
Soest. City mint
St. Die – See Lorraine
St. Gallen. City mint
Stettin – See Pommerania
Stockholm – See Sweden
Stolberg. Mints of Wernigerode and Stolberg
Styria (Steiermark). Mint of Graz
Sweden. Mint of Stockholm
Thann. City mint
Tournai (Tournay). City mint
Tri-City Monetary Alliance (De Driesteden Muntslag)
Mints of Deventer, Groningen, Campen and Zwolle
Trier (Trèves)
Mint of Coblenz (Koblenz)
Tübingen – See Württemberg
Tyrol (Tirol)
Mint of Hall and Meran
Unna – See Mark
Utrecht - Mints of Utrecht, Wijk-bij-Duurestede and Hasselt
Utrecht City (Utrecht Stadt) - Mint of Utrecht
Wijk-bij-Duurestede – See Utrecht
Veldenz – See Palatinate-Zweibrueken
Vienna – See Austria
Vörden (Vörde) – See Bremen
Wallis – See Sitten
Warburg. City mint
Weiner Neustadt – See Austria
Werl. City mint
Wernigerode. City mint and mint of Stolberg
Wesel – See Cleve
Wittenberg – See Saxony
Wolfhagen – See Hesse-Marburg
Worms. Mint of Mainz
Württemberg. Mint of Tübingen
Würzburg. Bishopric mint
Zaltbommel – See Gelderland
Zutphen. City mint and mint of Egmont family of Gelderland
Zwickau – See Saxony
Zwolle. City mint

APPENDIX 2
COMMON LATIN WORDS AND ABBREVIATIONS USED IN EARLY DATED COINAGE

The following are the Latin words and their abbreviations commonly used on early dated coinage to describe the date, the ruler and the money, along with the English translation:

ABTISSA, ABDIEE - Abbess [1]
A.E.I.O.V – All Honors Belong to Austria [2]
ANNO, ANN, ANO, ANI, AN, A - Year
ARCHIDVCIS, ARCHIDVCV, ARCHIDVC, ARCHIDV, ARCIDVX, ARCHIC, ARCHID, ARCHD, ARCID, ARDVC, ARDV, ARC– Archduke
ARCHIEPI, ARCHEPIS, ARCHIPS, ARCHIE, ARCEPI, ARCPI, ARCEP, AREP, ARCP, AEPI – Archbishop
ARGENTEA, ARGT, ARGE, AR – Silver
AVREA, AVRE, AVR, AV – Gold
COMIT, COMES, COME, COM, CO – Count
DEVS, DEI, DEV, DI, D – God
DOMINVM, DOMINI, DOMINO, DOMINE, DOMI, DNS, DNE, DYN, DNI, DN, D - Lord
DVCES, DVCVM, DVCIS, DVCS, DVX, DV, DX, D – Duke or Dukes
DVCISSA, DVCSSA, DVCISS, DVCISA – Duchess
ELECT, ELEC, ELE- Elector
EPISCO, EPIS, EPVS, EPS, EPI, EP – BISHOP
ET, Z, 9 – And
FACTA, FACT, FAC – Made or manufactured
GRACIA, GRAC, GRA, GR, G – Grace
GROSSVS, GROS – Groschen (standard monetary unit)
IMPERATOR, IMPERATO, IPERATO, IPERAT, IMPERAT, IMPE'ATO, IMPAT, IMP-ARA, IMPERA, IMPER, IMPR, IMPE, IMP - Emperor
LANTGRAVIVS, LANTG, LANG – Landgrave (landed count, roughly equivalent to an earl)
MAB (MABMOUR) - Lay administrator[3]
MAGNVS, MAG - The Great
MARCHIO, MARCHI, MARCH, MAR – Margrave or Marques
MILLESIMO, MILESIMO, M – Thousand (referring to date in Roman numerals)
MONETA, MONET, MONE, MON, MO – Money
NOVVS, NOVA, NOV, NO – New
PATRONVS, PATRON, PATRO, PATER, PATE, PATO, PAT – Patron
PRINC, PIN, PRI, PR – Prince
REGINA, REGI – Queen
REGIS, REGI, REG, RE – Regent
REX, RE, R – King
ROMANORVM, ROMANORV, ROMANOR, RAMONO, ROMA, ROM, RO - Roman
SANCTVS, SANTTVS, SANCTI, SANCT9, SANT, SACT, SAC, SCS, S – Saint
VRBIS, VRBS, VRB - City

[1] Found only on the coinage of Essen, under the rule of Abbess Sophie IV von Gleichen.

[2] Found only on Habsburg coinage. Szego, in his work, *The Coinage of Medieval Austria,* provides a different translation which he cites was a favorite cliche of Emperor Fredrich III, "all earth is Austria's ultimately."

[3] Found only on the coinage of Liège struck by the usurper William of the Mark

APPENDIX 3
MOST COMMONLY USED LATIN RELIGIOUS MOTTOS ON EARLY DATED COINAGE

The most common Latin religious mottos used on early dated coinage are the examples listed below.[1] Most were heavily abbreviated and liberally misspelled as was common for late medieval coinage. Moreover, to fit the motto into the space allowed by the coin, many words were separated to fit into different quadrants of the legend; hence, a wide variation of spelling, punctuation and presentation is to be expected. The mottos listed below are as found on the coinage, although the actual translations are from the full (and correctly spelled) versions:

AB INIMICIS MEIS LIBE(ra) ME D(omin)E – From mine enemies deliver me, O Lord.
AMA IVSTICIA(m) PACE(m) Z (=ET) DEFENDE P(o)P(u)L(u)M TVVM – Love justice, peace, and defend thy people.
AVE MARIA GRACIA P(lena) – Hail Mary full of Grace.
AVE (Maria) PLEN(a) GRACIA – Hail (Mary), full of Grace.
AVE REG(i)NA C(a)ELORV(m) MATER REGIS A(n)GELOR(um) – Hail, Queen of Heaven and Mother of the King of the Angels.
BA(p)TISTA PROSPER(e) ADESTO – Thou shalt be fortuitously at hand, O Baptist.
BE(ne)DICTA SIT SANCTA TRINIT(as) – Blessed be the Holy Trinity.
BENEDIC(at) A(n)I(m)A MEA D(omi)NO – May my soul bless the Lord.
BENEDIC(at) HEREDITATI TVAE – Bless thy inheritance.
BENEDICTVS SIT DEVS IN S(a)ECVLA S(a)ECV(lorum) – Blessed be God forever.
CONCORDIA RES PARVAE CRESCVNT – Through harmony little things increase.
CONSERVA NOS DOMINA – Preserve us, O Lady.
CUSTODIAT CREATOR O(m)NIV(m) HVMILE(m) SERVV(m) SVV(m) – May the Creator of All protect his humble servant.
DA PACEM DOMINE IN DIEBVS NOSTRIS – Grant (us) peace in our days, O Lord.
DET TIBI IN TER(R)IS VIRTVTE(m) ET IN C(a)ELIS GLORIAM – May he grant thee virtue on Earth and glory in Heaven.
DEVM PLVS AMA QVAM ARGENTVM – Love God more than money (lit. silver).
DEXTERA D(omi)N(i) EXALTAVIT ME DEXTRA D(omi)NI FECIT VIRTV(tem) – The right hand of the Lord has lifted me up; the right hand of the Lord made made virtue.
DILICITE IVSTICIA QVI IVDICATIS TERRAM – Delight in justice, ye who judge the earth.
ELEGIT DAVID S(er)VVM SVV(m) – He hath chosen David his servant.
FIAT MISERICOR(dia) TVA DOMIN(e) – Let there be your mercy, O Lord.
FIAT PAX IN VIRTVTE TVA – Let there be peace in thy strength.
IASP(ar) MELCHIOR BALTHAS(ar) – Iaspar (Caspar), Melchior, Balthasar (the Magi).
IN DOMINO CONFIDO – In the Lord put I my trust.
INICIVM (=Initium) SAPIENCIE (=Sapientiae) TIMOR DOMINI – The fear of the Lord is the beginning of wisdom.
IN N(OMINE) DOMINI ADIVT(orium) MEVM–In the name of the Lord is my aid.
IN NOMINE DOMINI – In the Name of the Lord.
INVENI DAVID SE(r)VV(m) MEV(m) – I have found David my servant.
IVSTIT(ia) PAXQ(VE) EXOSCULENT(UR SESE) – Righteousness and peace have kissed each other.
MEMENTO DOMINE DAVID – Thou shalt remember David, O Lord.
MEMOR ESTO VERBI TVI – Thou shalt be mindful of thy word.
MISER(ere) N(ost)RI Q(ui) PASSUS ES P(ro) NOB(is) – Have mercy on us, you who have suffered for us.
OMNIS SPIRITVS LAVDET DOMINVM – Let every soul praise the Lord.
REDDITE DEO Q(uae) D(ei) SV(NT) – Render unto God the things which are God's.
REFORMATIO GVERR(a)E PAX EST – The reformation of war is peace.
REGINA C(a)ELI L(a)ETARE ALLE(luia) – Queen of Heaven, rejoice. Alleluia!
SALVE REGINA MISERICORDI(a)E – Hail, Queen of Mercy.
SALVV(m) FAC P(o)P(u)L(u)M TVVM – Make safe thy people.
SALVVM FAC POPVLV(m) TVV(m) D(omi)NE[2] – Make safe thy people, O Lord.
SI DEUS NOBISCU(m) QUIS CO(n)T(r)A NOS – If God be with us, who be against us?
SIGNO CRVCIS SALVEMVR – By the Sign of the Cross let us receive salvation.
SIT NOMEN DOMINI BENEDICTVM – Blessed be the name of the Lord.
TENE MESVRAM ET RESPICE FINEM – Hold moderation and look to the end.
XC (=Christus) VINCI(t) XC (=Christus) REGN(at) – Christ conquers, Christ reigns.

---

[1] For many of the translations in this section, I am indebted to Scott van Horn, PhD. for his kind efforts in providing the bulk of these translations. I have also used in this appendix the ANA publication, *Coin Mottoes and Their Translations,* by Stuart Mosher.

[2] Numerous abbreviations occur for this inscription

APPENDIX 4
PATRON SAINTS ON EARLY DATED COINAGE

St. Andreas —	Brabant, mint of Anvers (1482-83 and 1487 and 1489 florins, 1489 demi florins d'or Holland, mint of Dordrecht (1487 ducats)
St. Autor —	Brunswick (1499 and 1500 Autorgroschens, 1499 large groschens)
St. Bernward —	Hildesheim (1491, 1493-95 sechslings)
St. Gallus —	St. Gallen (1424 plapparts)
St. George —	Lorraine, mint of St. Die (1492 ducats)
St. Hubert —	Jülich-Berg, mint of Mülheim (1489 half weisspfennige)
St. John —	Basel (1491-93 goldguldens) Flanders, mint of Ghent (1488 florins St. Jean) Franeker (1491-92 goldguldens) Brandenburg Franconia, mint of Swabia (1497-1500 goldguldens) Frankfurt (1491-1500 goldguldens) Groningen (1488 goldguldens) Nördlingen (1491-1500 goldguldens) Saxony, mint of Annaberg (1500 half guldiners)
St. Kilian —	Würzburg (1496-1500 schillings, 1500 goldguldens)
St. Ladislaus —	Hungary (1499 and 1500 thalers and guldiners)
St. Lebuinus —	Deventer (1488 goldguldens, 1498 goldguldens and 1499-1500 stuivers)
St. Martin —	Colmar (1499 dickens, groschens and plapparts) Erfurt (1468 groschens) Utrecht City (1483 stuivers)
St. Michael —	Brabant, mint of Brussels (1488 quadruple and double patards, 1489 patards) Zwolle (1492 and 1499 stuivers, 1499 double stuivers)
St. Othmar —	St. Gallen (1500 dickens, batzens and plapparts)[1]
St. Peter —	Bremen, mints of Bremen and Vörden (1499 4 grotens) Cologne, mint of Deutz (1437-38, 1443-50 groschens, 1489 turnosgroschens and albus) Mainz, mint of Bingen (1437-38, 1443-45 and 1447 groschens, 1489 schillings and 1492, 1493, 1495 and 1496 half groschens) Palatinate, mint of Bacharach (1437-38, 1444-45, 1447-49 groschens, 1492-94 half groschens, 1492, 95-96 half albus) Palatinate-Zweibruecken, mint of Veldenz (1490 schillings) Saxony, mint of Leipzig (1498-1500 goldguldens) Trier, mint of Coblenz (1437-38, 1444 and 1448 groschens) Worms, mint of Mainz (1492 schillings)
St. Philip —	Brabant, mint of Anvers (1499 florins d'or) Brabant, mint of Maestricht (1500 florins d'or and demi florins d'or)
St. Stephen —	Breisach (1499 dickens)
St. Theobald —	Thann (1499 dickens and groschens)
St. Vincent —	Bern (1492 goldgulden multiples and dickens of various weight, 1493-94 guldiners of multiple weights)

[1] St Othmar is referred to on the legend but is not portrayed on these coins.

APPENDIX 5
PHOTOGRAPHIC GLOSSARY

To aid in identifying the descriptions of the coinage in Part II, this section is designed to show, through photographic examples, a number of common devices and forms of dates engraved on medieval coins. Given that most of the early dated coins the reader will actually encounter are in far less-than-perfect condition (a most common and unavoidable ailment afflicting medieval numismatics), it is hoped that this "photographic glossary" will assist users in their own attribution efforts:

1. Long cross
(1481 Brabant copper 4 mites - II-58)

2. Double-stranded long cross
(1483 East Frisia groten - I-188)

3. Triple-stranded flowery long cross
(1480 Liège double patard - II-52a)

4. Long cross with object in center
(1473 Groningen stuiver - III-64)

5. Triple-stranded flowery short cross
(1474 Flanders briquet - II-15)

6. Ornate triple-stranded short cross
(1484 Nijmegen half stuiver III-145)

7. Long cross with inner and outer legends
(1375 Aachen groschen - I-4a)

8. Shield on long cross
(1489 Brabant 4 patards - II-110)

9. Middle length cross
(1402 Aachen groschen - I-5a)

10. Short cross
(1444 Jülich-Berg groschen - I-71)

11. Double cross
(1488 Styria kreuzer - IV-52)

12. Arms occupying entire field
(1438 Liège double gros - II-8)

13. Shield on flowery cross
(1476 Brabant double briquet - II-22)

14. Shields forming a cross
(1489 Cologne albus - I-231)

15. Long cross with shields in angles
(1426 Cologne groschen - I-22)

16. Designs/devices in angles of cross
(1492 Neuss groschen - I-283)

17. Imperial orb in trefoil
(1496 Frankfurt goldgulden - I-343)

18. Design/shield in trefoil
(1392 Schoonvorst-Sichem groschen - II-4)

19. Quatrefoil
(1492 Stolberg groschen - I-294b)

20. Polyfoil
(1429 Göttingen körtling - I-24)

21. Conjoined shields
(1445 Mainz groschen - I-77)

22. Helmeted shields
(1441 Cleve blanken - I-56)

23. Shield with small shields at triangle points
(1493 Palatinate goldgulden - I-305)

24. Shield not interrupting legend
(1499 Brabant double patard - II-146b)

25. Shield interrupting legend
(1499 Brabant double patard - II-146a)

26. Quartered arms
(1493 Mainz half groschen - I-303)

27. Dates at sides of devices
(1493 Saxony bartgroschen - I-308)

28. Date above shield
(1496 Würzburg schilling - I-355)

29. Date in angles of cross
(1482 Hannover groschen - I-180)

30. Single digit date
(1459 Krapina kreuzer - IV-8a)

31. Number "2" appearing as a "Z"
(1492 Stolberg groschen - I-294b)

32. Backwards "2"
(1492 Damm schilling - I-288b)

33. Medieval "4"
(1499 Basel dicken - V-22)

34. Backwards "4"
(1484 Pommerania kreuzer - IV-43c)

35. Medieval "5"
(1495 Pommerania schilling - I-334)

36. Sideways "5"
(1456 Styria pfennig - IV-2)

37. Lightning Strike "5"
(1495 Nördlingen goldgulden - I-331)

38. Backwards "6"
(1486 Styria kreuzer - IV-48b)

39. Medieval "7"
(1477 Brabant double briquet - II-27)

40. Backwards "7"
(1487 Graz kreuzer - IV-51b)

41. Upside-down "7"
(1487 Styria kreuzer - IV-51c)

42. Tiny "0"
(1490 Saxony half schwertgroschen - I-256a)

43. Large annulet
(1478 Sweden ortug - VI-2b)

44. Small annulet
(1478 Sweden half ortug - VI-3e)

45. Overdate
(1475/1455 Brabant double briquet - II-17)

46. Renaissance bust
(1494 Antegnate guilio - VII-6a)

47. Figure behind shield
(1483 Mülheim bausche - I-193)

48. Figure enthroned
(1491 Cologne goldgulden - I-259a)

49. Monogram
(1487 Brabant silver real - II-93)

50. Countermark
(1478 Warburg double stüber - I-166).

APPENDIX 6
EARLY ANNO DOMINI DATED COINS USING ARABIC WORDS[1]

Sicily, 1198 AD

Sicily issued the first coin showing an Anno Domini date, 1198 AD. Philip Grierson suggested that the coin perhaps celebrated the investiture granted to Frederick and Constance by Pope Innocent III. Since Constance died on November 27, 1198, and the AH calendar year for 595 started in November, Grierson noted that the coin must have been struck in November 1198. In return, the pope received an annual gift of a thousand schifati.[2]

Sicily (Malfi)
Obverse: Outer Ring, Arabic Words, Struck at Malfi the year 594 (AH)
Inner ring, FRE REX SICILIE +
Central design, Palm leaves
Reverse: Outer ring, 1198 (AD) in Arabic Words Using Kufic Script
Inner ring in Arabic words, Constance imperatrix of the Romans
Cross in center, Debased gold, 25 mm

AD Date	Arabic Words for Date	Literal Translation of Arabic Words	Catalogue Number
1198		One-hundred [One thousand] ninety and eight	MEC Volume 14 Italy

Crusader Coinage of Acre, 1251 - 1258

Michael Mitchiner commented that striking of these Christian coins in Akka (modern Acre, Israel) appeared to have been a response to the Papal interdict of 1250 AD on the striking of coins bearing the names of Islamic rulers or Islamic professions of Faith.[3] These coins are inscribed with the AD date in Arabic words rather than numerals. On the obverse around the edge is "Struck at Akka in the year," followed by the year in Arabic words, which are often poorly written on the coins. The translation of the Arabic inscription within the square on the reverse is "One single God, one single Faith, one single Baptism." Virtually all the Akka half dirhem varieties in silver are undated while one is dated for year 1251. The silver dirhem exists in several varieties with date 1251. While Paul Balog and Jacques Yvon cited collections for all dates of gold dinars from 1251 through 1258, they are all rare.[4] The date appears around the edge. Another cited reference is to Gustave Schlumberger.[5]

AD Dated Crusader Coinage, 1251 AD
Obverse: Arabic date and mint around edge.
Small cross, spade, and fleur-de-lis within square
Reverse: Similar to obverse but no cross.
Half Silver dirhem, 17 mm.
Akka (Acre) mint

AD Date	Arabic Words for Date	Literal Translation of Arabic Words (r. to l.)		Catalogue Number
1251	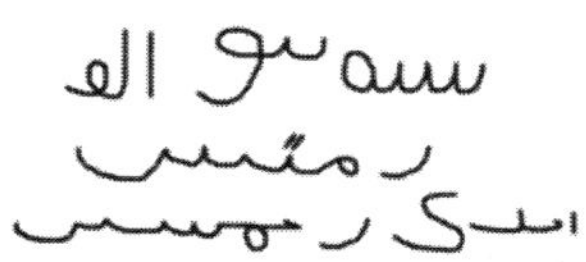	Year onethousand two-hundred and fifty and one	Small Cross	BY 46

[1] The author is indebted to Edward Cohen for Appendix 6 and its accompanying photographs.
[2] Philip Grierson and Lucia Travaini, *Medieval European Coinage, Volume 14, Italy (III) South Italy, Sicily, Sardinia.* Cambridge Press, 1998, Pages 165-166, ISBN 0-521-58231-8 [Cited as MEC]
[3] Michael Mitchiner, *The World of Islam.* Hawkins Publications, London 1977, ISBN 0-904173-15-1 [Cited as MWI]
[4] Paul Balog and Jacques Yvon, *Monnaies A Legendes Arabes De L'Orient Latin.* Revue Numismatique, 6th Series, t.1, 1958, pages 133 - 168, plates 11 - 16 [Cited as BY]
[5] Gustave Schlumberger, *Numismatique de L'Orient Latin.* 2 volumes, and supplement, Paris, 1878, 1882, Graz Reprint 1954 [Cited as Sch]

Obverse: Arabic date and mint around edge. Square with or without cross inside.
Reverse: Similar to obverse but only Arabic Words.
Silver dirhem, 22 mm.
Akka (Acre) mint

AD Date	Arabic Words for Date	Literal Translation of Arabic Words (r. to l.)		Catalogue Number
1251	سنه ثنو مئتين الف ر خمسين ر احدى	Year two-hundred one-thousand and fifty and one 	Cross in circle	BY 42, 43, MWI 2455, Sch Plate V.28
1251	سنه ثنو مئتين الف ر خمسين ر احدى	Year two-hundred one-thousand and fifty and one 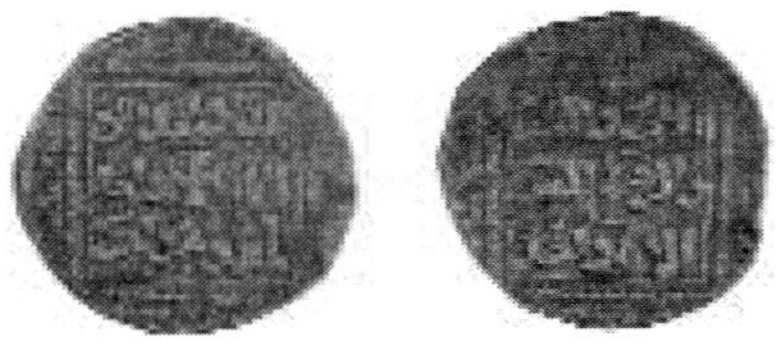	Cross	BY 45, MWI 2456, Sch Plate V.31
1251	سنه ثنو مئتين ر الف خمسين ر احدى	Year two-hundred and one-thousand fifty and one?	No symbols	BY 47a, 47b
1251	سنه ثنو مئتين الف ر خمسين ر احدى	Year two-hundred one-thousand and fifty and one 	Small Fleur de Lis	BY 47c

The next photograph shows an enlargement of the gold dinar of 1256. In the right photo, the date inscription can be read counter-clockwise on the outer ring from the 11 o'clock position. The inscription reads "Struck at Akka, year thousand and two-hundred fifty and six." The Arabic word for six is in the 3 o'clock position, the typical location for the last digit of the date. Since the dates on these coins are usually worn or incomplete on the planchets, this part of the coin is useful for confirming the date.

AD Dated Crusader Coinage, 1251 - 1258 AD

Obverse: Arabic date and mint around edge. Three concentric circles, each containing Arabic Words. A cross is in each of the outer two circles (two crosses in all).
Reverse: Three concentric circles, each containing a cross (three crosses in all) and Arabic Words. The center cross is larger.
Gold dinar, 23 mm.
Akka (Acre) mint

AD Date	Arabic Words for Date	Literal Translation of Arabic Words (r. to l.)	Catalogue Number
1251	سنه ثنو الف ر مئتين احدى ر خمسين	Year one-thousand and two hundred one and fifty	BY 40
1252	سنه ثنو الف ر مئتين ثنتينا ر خمسين	Year one-thousand and two hundred two and fifty	BY 40
1253	سنه ثنو الف ر مئتين ثلث ر خمسين	Year one-thousand and two hundred three and fifty	BY 40
1254	سنه ثنو الف ر مئتين اربع ر خمسين	Year one-thousand and two hundred four and fifty	BY 40
1255	سنه ثنو الف ر مئتين خمس ر خمسين	Year one-thousand and two hundred five and fifty	BY 40, Sch Plate V.27
1256	سنه ثنو الف ر مئتين ست ر خمسين	Year one-thousand and two hundred six and fifty	BY 40
1257	سنه ثنو الف ر مئتين سبع ر خمسين	Year one-thousand and two hundred seven and fifty	BY 40
1258	سنه ثنو الف ر مئتين ثمان ر خمسين	Year one-thousand and two hundred eight and fifty	BY 40

Crusader Coinage of Damascus, 1253

The town of Damascus in Syria struck a silver dirhem in 1253. It struck no other AD-dated coins.[6]

AD Dated Crusader Coinage, 1253 AD
Obverse: Arabic date and mint around edge. Square containing more Arabic words inside.
Reverse: Similar to obverse.
Silver dirhem, 22 mm.
Dimeshk mint (Damascus)

AD Date	Arabic Words for Date	Literal Translation of Arabic Words (r. to l.)	Catalogue Number
1253	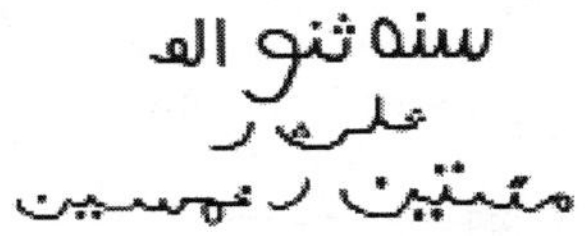	Year one thousand three and two hundred and fifty	B 77-82

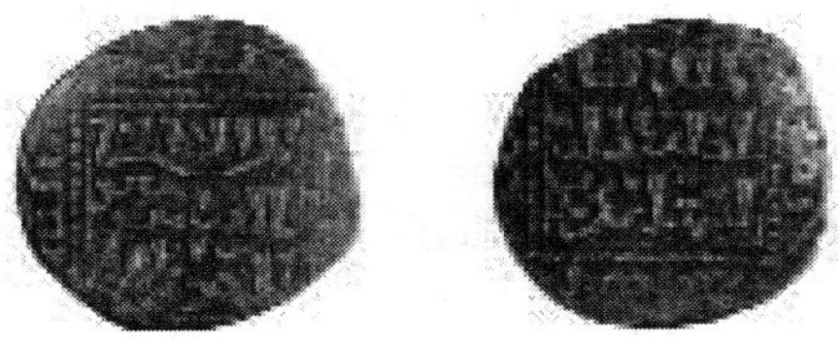

[6] Paul Balog, Etudes Numismatiques De L'Egypte Musulmane, Bulletin De L'Institut D'Egypte, Volume 34, 1952, pages 17 - 55, plates 1 - 14 [Cited as B]

APPENDIX 7
ERRORS OR INACCURATE CITATIONS IN *FREY*

Frey #	State	Date	Denomination	Commentary
16n	Aachen	1406	Groschen	Neither Frey nor Saurma provide descriptions or other references.
17n	Aachen	1409	Groschen	The Menadier reference is unreliable and no other sources confirm its existance.
29	Göttingen	1433	Körtling	Körtlings are reported for the dates of 1429 and 1442, none in between.
60	Coblenz	1443	Groschen	The citation is to a 1444 groschen, misread by Bohl.
60A	Styria	1443	Vierer	This coin is likely a misreading of a 1458 kreuzer.
66A	Utrecht	1444	Goldgulden	A misreading of a 1445 Bar-Mörs goldgulden.
72	Graz	1445	Vierer	The coin shown is a partially dated 1458 Graz kreuzer with the "8" not engraved. The misreading of the date of this coin is discussed in CNA 6b at page 327.
74	Riehl	1446	Goldgulden	This coin does not exist with a date. While this coin is referenced in Cappe #1073, no illustrations appear and no other work verifies its existence.
86	Freiburg	1455	Kreuzer	The reference in Frey is likely for a 1555 dated coin.
91	Habsburg	1456	Achter	The citation does not match; the description is for a kreuzer. The referenced coin is likely a weakly-dated 1458 kreuzer.
91B	Graz	1456	Pfennig	Only one type of Graz pfennig is known for this date, which presumably is Frey 91a.
101A	Austria	1460	Weisspfennig	Only a half groschen or kreuzer is known for this date.
103A	Deventer	1462	¼ Groschen	Only a quarter stuiver is known.
106	Graz	1463	Vierer	This coin is probably a Styria 1468 achter with the last digit weakly struck, appearing as a "3" instead of an "8".
108	Bolsward	1464	Half Escalin	No Bolsward coins were struck dated between 1457 and 1472.
129	Groningen	1468	Jager	The reference in Van der Chijs is to a 1469 jager.
148	Brabant	1472	Double Briquet	Brabant started dating its coins in 1474 only.
152E	Wiener Neustadt	1473	Kreuzer	Wiener Neustadt kreuzers were struck dated 1470-1472 only.
153A	Utrecht	1474	Gros	The reference is likely instead to a 1474 jager.
168	Gelderland	1476	Double Briquet	The reference in Van der Chijs is to a 1475 double briquet instead. Demi briquets were the only dated Gelderland coinage in 1476.
169	Nijmegen	1476	Sou	The reference in Van der Chijs is to a 1477 quarter stuiver instead.
174A	Flanders	1476	Briquet	Flanders did not date coins in 1476.
176	Wiener Neustadt	1476	Kreuzer	The date on this coin has been misread. It is instead dated 1456. See CNA Fa 33.

Frey #	State	Date	Denomination	Commentary
179	Habsburg	1477	Thaler	This is a medaillic piece struck in the early 16th century and is not properly classified as a coin.
183A	Deventer	1477	Half Jager	Deventer did not date larger coins in 1477.
184	Gelderland	1477	Double Briquet	This type is undated. See Van Gelder-Hoc 39-2.
184E	Styria	1477	Kreuzer	Styria did not issue dated kreuzers in the decade of 1470.
185B	Brabant	1478	Gros	Gros for Marie of Burgundy were dated only in 1480 and 1481. See Van Gelder-Hoc 41-1.
185D	Flanders	1478	Briquet	This type is dated for 1477 and 1480 only.
189B	Sneek	1478	Jager	Chijs 20.1 refers to a 1477 stuiver (one half jager) instead.
189C	Graz	1478	Kreuzer	This is undoubtedly the misreading of the date of 1458 on a Styria kreuzer with a medieval "5".
191	Wiener Neustadt	1478	Half Groschen	This is a 1458 kreuzer with the date misread.
192	Graz	1478	Groschen	This is a 1458 Graz kreuzer with the date misread. See CNA Fb 6.
195B	Graz	1478	Kreuzer	This is a 1458 Graz kreuzer with the date misread. See CNA Fb 6.
195C	Liège	1478	Briquet	The mint is instead Hasselt. See Frey 195, which is correctly attributed. Liège struck only double briquets in this year.
196	Tyrol	1479	Thaler	This piece, more properly known as a "Hochzeit Schauguldiner" (marriage show-guldiner) is really a medal of thaler weight struck in 1506 or later.
197	Tyrol	1479	Thaler	This piece, more properly known as a "Hochzeit Schauguldiner" (marriage show-guldiner) is really a medal of thaler weight struck in 1506 or later.
204	Wiener Neustadt	1479	Half Groschen	This coin is a 1459 kreuzer with the date misread. See CNA Fa 36.
205B	Brabant	1479	Gros	Gros for Marie of Burgundy were dated in Brabant only in 1480 and 1481. See Van Gelder-Hoc 41-1
205D	Flanders	1479	Briquet	Briquets were dated for Flanders for 1477 and 1480. See Van Gelder-Hoc 40-3.
208D	Gelderland	1479	Gros	Gros were dated for Gelderland in 1480. See Van Gelder-Hoc 41-2a.
213	Göttingen	1480	Körtling	The closest reported date is 1481.
214	Saxony	1480	Groschen	No references exist to support this claim. Perhaps Frey was confused by a 1482 half schwertgroschen with a weak date.
217	Hasselt	1480	Briquet	The correct reference is to Liège. See Frey 222b.
219	Garz	1480	Schilling	The "9" on a 1489 Garz schilling, which contains a tiny tale, often appears as a blundered "0".
220	Wiener Neustadt	1480	Kreuzer	Perhaps the reference is an 1489 kreuzer from Graz. The "9," with a tiny tale, often appears as a blundered "0".
222	Sweden	1480	Ortug	This is a misreading of the single digit date of 1478, with a large annulet after the 8.

Frey #	State	Date	Denomination	Commentary
222A	Sweden	1480	Half Ortug	This is a misreading of the single digit date of 1478, with a large annulet after the 8. See the commentary in Lagerqvist.
223A	"N.R.E."	1481	Kreuzer	Presumably this is a typographical error for H.R.E., or Holy Roman Empire. The Emperor as Duke of Austria struck kreuzers with this date.
225D	Flanders	1481	Briquet	Only double briquets and gros exist for this date. See Van Gelder-Hoc 40-3.
230	Hasselt	1481	Briquet	The mint for this coin is Liège. See Chestret 354.
232A	Saxony	1482	Spitzgroschen	The reference is probably to a half schwertgroschen.
239	Wiener Neustadt	1482	Kreuzer	Only Vienna and Styria struck dated kreuzers in 1482.
244C	Graz	1482	Double Groschen	Only kreuzers were struck with this date.
247	Utrecht	1483	Double Groschen	The reference is instead to a single briquet, Chijs 18.32.
251	Wiener Neustadt	1483	Kreuzer	The piece described is from the Vienna mint.
253E	Flanders	1483	Briquet	No Flanders briquets are dated 1483. See Van Gelder-Hoc 53-5.
262	Wiener Neustadt	1484	Kreuzer	The piece described is from the Vienna mint.
265	Holland	1484	Briquet	The coin described in Chijs 17.7 is a gros. Holland did not strike dated briquets in 1484. See Van Gelder-Hoc 53-6.
265C	Saxony	1484	Furstengroschen	The "2" in the 1482 date can appear as a blundered "4." The 1484 date does not exist.
265E	Brabant	1484	Kreuzer	No such coin exists. Perhaps the reference is to a gros of this date?
266A	Holland	1485	Briquet	No briquets dated 1485 were struck for Holland. See Van Gelder-Hoc 53-6.
266B	Holland	1485	Gros	The Holland gros during this period were dated 1484. See Van Gelder-Hoc 55-6.
273D	Essen	1485	Half Groschen	No records exist of this coin. It is probably a misread 1487 date
276	Wiener Neustadt	1486	Kreuzer	This reference is likely to a Styria 1486 kreuzer instead.
282C	Campen	1486	Stuiver	The only dated 1486 Campen coin is a quarter stuiver.
286	Utrecht	1487	Double Gros	This is a ¾ stuiver, whose medieval "5" date has been misread to be a "7."
289	Wiener Neustadt	1487	Kreuzer	This coin is most likely a 1485 Vienna kreuzer with a medieval "5" in the date being misread as a "7."
294B	East Frisia	1487	Stüber	Dated stübers exist for 1486 and 1488 only.
294D	Nuremberg	1487	Token	This is not a coin. It is a counting token from Würzburg misattributed to Nuremberg and the date has also been misread. The correct date is 1485. See Neumann 33002.
296A	Holland	1488	Briquet	The Chijs reference is instead to a double patard. See Van Gelder-Hoc 77-1.
303	Franker	1488	Stuiver	The correct reference is to a half stuiver. See Frey 303a.

Frey #	State	Date	Denomination	Commentary
310	Flanders	1488	Demi Noble d'Or	Flanders did not strike these dated gold coins. See Van Gelder-Hoc 75.
310A	Flanders	1488	6 Gros	Perhaps the reference is to an 1488 quadruple patard, worth 6 sols or 12 gros, struck by the city of Brussels in revolt.
316	Sweden	1488	Ortug	Large conjoined double annulets next to the last digit made the date appear to be "88." Frey and other writers apparently did not recognize the medieval "7" on this coin next to the first digit and thus ignored it!
318	Deutz	1488	Groschen	The reference from Saurma shows a blundered date, and 1488 is not a listed date in either Noss or Cappe.
319A	Saxony	1488	Spitzgroschen	Spitzgroschens were dated 1475, 1477 and 1478. Perhaps the reference is to a 1488 half schwertgroschen.
320D	Zwolle	1488	Half Stuiver	This coin is instead properly classified as part of a joint coinage by Deventer, Campen and Zwolle. See JFD DKZ #9.
320E	Zwolle	1488	Quarter Stuiver	This coin is instead properly classified as part of a joint coinage by Deventer, Campen and Zwolle. See JFD DKZ #12.
332C	Flanders	1489	Briquet	Flanders did not strike dated briquets in 1489. See Van Gelder-Hoc 84-5.
333A	Brabant	1498	Patard	Only double patards were struck in this year. This is likely a typographical error for a 1489 patard.
335	Holland	1489	Double Stuiver	Van Gelder-Hoc lists this coin as a patard. While Chijs lists the coins referenced 19.37 and 20.38 as double stuivers, the weight listed in Chijs as 2.95 grams would instead indicate that they are stuivers.
336A	Franeker	1489	Stuiver	Franeker struck only dated double stuivers in 1489.
336D	Wiener Neustadt	1489	Kreuzer	Only Styria struck a 1489 kreuzer.
343A	Saxony	1490	Spitzgroschen	This coin does not exist. Perhaps the reference is to a 1490 half schwertgroschen.
345	Hildesheim	1490	Groschen	According to Buck, this date is unknown and Cappe 384 is incorrect.
349	Cologne	1490	Goldgulden	The first dated Cologne goldguldens in this decade were struck in 1491.
349A	Cologne	1490	Groschen	Perhaps the reference is to a 1489 groschen.
349B	Franeker	1490	Stuiver	Only a double stuiver and half stuiver exist for this date.
366	Deutz	1491	Groschen	The reference is to an albus, and none were dated 1491.
379	Hildesheim	1492	Groschen	According to Buck, this date does not exist and Cappe #386 is incorrect.
383A	Saxony	1492	Spitzgroschen	Perhaps the reference is to a half schwertgroschen. See Frey 383.
386A	Neuss	1492	Half Groschen	No references exist for this coin.
412B	Garz	1493	Quarter Groschen	This is probably a reference to a Damm mint schilling – no schillings were dated by the mint of Garz for this date.

Frey #	State	Date	Denomination	Commentary
412G	Zwickau	1493	Half Zinsgroschen	The Zwickau mint dated only bartgroschen in 1493.
412H	Zwickau	1493	Half Schilling	The Zwickau-Schneeberg mint struck numerous half schwertgroschens in 1492. Perhaps this is the intended reference.
413	Holland	1494	Briquet	The reference in Chijs is to a 1495 date instead. See Chijs 22.18.
418A	Hasselt	1494	Half Patard	The mint for this coin is Liège, not Hasselt. See Chestret 417.
420D	Utrecht	1494	Double Stuiver	Utrecht struck only gros and fractionals of the gros in 1494.
429	Basel	1495	2 Goldgulden	This coin is not listed in Friedberg, Winterstein or in De Mey d'Or.
431A	Saxony	1495	Spitzgroschen	This coin is a misidentified half schwertgroschen.
439	Aachen	1496	Half Groschen	Aachen struck only dated 1496 quarter-groschens in 1496.
448C	Holland	1496	Double Sou	This is the same coin as Frey #443, also known in Flemish as a "Zilveren Vlies."
453	Cleve	1497	Groschen	Only stübers (swanstübers) were struck this year.
455	Saxony	1497	½ Schwertgroschen	This reference is likely to 1495 date with a medieval "5."
461A	Utrecht	1497	Goldgulden	Utrecht struck dated gold in 1492, not 1497.
464	Cologne	1497	Rathszeichen	This piece is a town token and should not be referenced as a dated coin.
464C	Gofnat	1497	Pfennig	Neither this coin nor this mint exists.
471A	Sitten	1498	Dicken	No references are available for this coin. It is likely a misclassified guldiner, the same coin as Frey 471.
480	Garz	1498	Schilling	No 1498 Garz schillings have been reliably reported. This coin is likely a 1492 Garz schilling with a blundered date.
491A	Nijmegen	1499	Stuiver	Only fractional stuivers exist for this date.
515B	Gelderland	1499	Double Briquet	Gelderland did not date coins between 1497 and 1500.
515F	Palatinate	1499	Schilling	No references are available for this coin.
515G	Holland	1499	Real Espagne	This coin was first struck in 1505. See Van Gelder-Hoc 165-1.
519	Utrecht	1500	Florin d'Or	No references exist for this coin.

BIBLIOGRAPHY

GENERAL PUBLICATIONS:

Blätter fur Münzfreunde. Leipzig 1865-1900, Dresden 1900-1908, Munich 1908-1915. Periodical on German coin subjects with good scholarly work on obscure coinage.

Clain-Stefanelli, E.: *Numismatic Bibliography*. Augsburg 1985. The single best numismatic bibliography available, yet one more outstanding publication from the remarkable Elvira Clain-Stefanelli.

Craig, W.: *Germanic Coinages*. Mountain View, California 1954. An extremely useful book, a necessary addition to every library. Long out of print, it features history of states, guides to legends, translations, denominations, abbreviations, rulers, etc.

Davenport, J.: *German Talers 1500-1600*. Frankfurt 1979. The standard work on thalers. Individual pieces lack detailed explanation, but still a necessary work in any library given the breadth of coverage.
-, *European Crowns 1484-1600*. Frankfurt 1977.

de Mey, J.R.: *Le Moyen-Age d'Or*. Brussels 1984 ("De Mey d'Or"). An excellent listing of medieval European coinage, most with legends and photos. A fine and very helpful companion to Friedberg.
-: *European Crown Size Coins and Their Multiples, volume 1, Germany 1486-1599*, Amsterdam 1975. A good companion work to Davenport.
-: Numismatic Pocket series:
-: *Les Countremarques sur les monnaies*, Brussels 1986.
-: *Les Monnaies d' Alsace*. Brussels/Paris 1976 ("De Mey Al").
-: *Les Monnaies de Bourgogne*. Brussels/Paris 1973.
-: *Les Monnaies des Ducs de Brabant I-III*. Watermael/Amsterdam 1966-1974. Coauthored with A. van Keymeulen.
-: *Les Monnaies de Bretagne*. Brussels/Paris 1970 ("De Mey Br").
-: *Les Monnaies des Comtes de Flandre*, Brussels 1986 (De Mey Fl").
-: *Les Monnaies des Evêques et de la Ville d'Utrecht*. Wemmel 1981 ("De Mey Ut").
-: *Les Monnaies de Namur*. Brussels 1971.
-: *Les Monnaies de cuivre liègeoise*. Brussels/Amsterdam 1968 ("De Mey MCL").
-: *Répertoire des Imitations des Types monétaires Belges du Moyen-Age*. Brussels 1988 ("De Mey Im").
-: *Répertoire de la Numismatique des Pays d'en- Bas (1419-1714)*. Brussels 1982.
All part of the fine Numismatic Pocket series of books, quite inexpensive compared to the standard references but with decent research and photography. The subject matters are not covered in depth, so best used along with the standard works, most of which are significantly older.

Dugniolle, J.: *Le jeton historique des dix-sept provinces des Pays-Bas*, 4 volumes. Brussels 1876-1880. The standard and comprehensive work on the jetons of the Lowlands. Essential for any collector in this area, with all varieties listed as well. A single volume of plates is available separately and is very useful.

Egg, E.: *Die Münzen Kaiser Maximilians I*. Innsbruck 1971. Excellent overview on the coins of Emperor Maximilian with top quality photos and descriptions. Covers coinage from all Habsburg territories, including those in Germany, Northern and Southern Netherlands and Italy.

Engel, A./Serrure, R.: *Traité de Numismatique du Moyen Age*, 3 vol. Paris 1890 (reprinted 1964). A three volume series of treatises on the production of coinage in the Middle Ages. Now being replaced by Grierson's work, but still retains merit.

Frey, A.: *The Dated European Coinage prior to 1501*. New York 1915. Reprinted, edited and annotated by David Cervin. Rockville Center 1978, supplemented 2000. The original (and solitary) work on early dated coinage prior to this book. Sorely out-of-date, despite its updates and with numerous errors unbecoming a major work. Most legends are not provided.
-: *Dictionary of Numismatic Names*. New York 1917 (reprinted London 1947). Excellent dictionary of numismatic names and terms, much more thorough than his other work. The reprint contains a very useful five-language guide as well.

Friedberg, A.: *Gold Coins of the World*, 7th ed. Clifton, New Jersey 2003. The standard and indispensable reference on gold coinage of the world, vital to any library.

Grierson, P. and Blackburn, M.: *Medieval European Coinage*. Cambridge 1986. Wonderful study on medieval coinage by the leading scholar of our days. This book focuses on coin types while Spufford's focuses on the use of money, so the works complement each other.

-- *Coins of Medieval Europe.* London 1991. A single volume overview of medieval coinage from the Dark Ages to the 15th century. As with all Grierson works, a masterpiece of scholarly research without being dry or dull. Yet one more marvelous work from the greatest numismatist of the 20th century.

Hazlitt, W.C.: *The Coinage of the European Continent, Middle Age-20th Century.* London 1893 (reprinted Chicago 1974). A fine overview with still useful information on individual states and mints. Provides complementary coverage to Craig.

Jaarboek voor Munt-en Penningkunde. Amsterdam 1914-1964 ("JMP"). Very fine series of articles on coinage, many of which discuss early dated coinage.

Levinson, R.: "Early Anno Domini Dated Copper Coins." *The Numismatist*, May 1996. An introductory to the history of dating and a focus on the ever elusive few known early dated copper coins.
-: "Single Digit Dated Coins, an Anomaly of the Late Middle Ages." *The Celator*, July 2003. A focus on early dated coinage struck with a single digit for the date.
-: "The Rediscovery of Einbeck's First Dated Coin, the Unique 1488 Körtling." Künker Auction Catalogue #90, March 11, 2004 at pp 220-223. A short article on the discovery of the correct date of the first dated coin of Einbeck, which all references hitherto had incorrectly dated as 1480.
-: "A Guide to the Elusive Coinage of the Decade of 1451-1460." *The Celator*, February 1998.

Lucas, P.: *Monnaies Seigneuriales Mosanes.* Walcourt 1982. Excellent large single volume work on the coinage of the small lordships in the Mosane region, containing the best coverage on the coins of Schoonvorst-Sichem and later Schoonvorst as a mint of Jülich-Berg.

Mayhew, N.: *Coinage in the Low Countries (880-1500).* British Archeological Reports, International Series LIV. Oxford 1979. Very interesting set of scholarly studies, a couple of which discuss issues during the time of early dated coinage.

Mosher, S.: "Coin Mottoes and their Translations." *The Numismatist* 1948. Helpful article on the obscure Latin legends found on medieval and early modern coinage.

Neumann, J.: *Kupfermünzen*, 7 vol.. Prague 1858 ff. The standard (seven volume) reference on world copper tokens and jetons, an amazing 150 year old achievement given its world-wide coverage. Best used today for Germanic tokens. The full set usually costs at least $500.

Revue Belge de Numismatique. Bruxelles 1845-1964 ("RBN"). Superb collection of articles on numismatics bound into book form, many of which first identified previously unknown dated coinage.

Saurma-Jeltsch, H. von: *Die Saurmasche Münzsammlung.* Berlin 1892. Catalogue of one of the largest medieval coin collections ever assembled, concentrating on Germanic coinage in the period from 1300-1600. While it has become a reference work by its sheer size and numbers, it is in the form of a catalogue, and thus no legends or descriptions. Good photographs for the period. Still a most useful work which should be in all medieval coin libraries. Now available for free on the internet.

Schlickeysen, F.W.A./Pallmann, R.: *Erklärung der Abkuerzungen auf Münzen der neueren Zeit, des Mittelalters und des Altertums sowie auf Denkmünzen und münzartigen Zeichen.* Berlin and Stuttgart 1896. Guide to the translations of titles and abbreviations on medieval coinage. Helpful and easy to use.

Schulten, W.: *Deutsche Münzen aus der Zeit Karls V.* Frankfurt 1974. One of the finest single volume references in numismatics, an ambitious and fully realized effort to catalogue the Germanic and related coinage issued during the times of Emperor Charles V, but more accurately with coverage from the time of Maximilian; hence, a very great number of early dated coins are referenced. The breadth of coverage did not allow for legends or full descriptions, and a minority of the coins referenced are photographed, but this is still an indispensable and remarkable work.

Spufford, P.: *Monetary Problems and Policies in the Burgundian Netherlands 1433-1496.* Leiden 1970 ("Spufford Policies"). Excellent scholarly work providing an in-depth study of this key area in early dated numismatics. Its only drawback is its liberal use of quotations in numerous languages without translations.
-: *Money and Its Use in Medieval Europe.* Cambridge 1988 ("Spufford Money"). Probably the finest single volume work of its type by Grierson's most talented student, himself a professor (now emeritus) of Cambridge. No library on medieval numismatics is complete without it. Wonderful analysis on the bullion famine of the mid-15th century.
-: *Handbook of Medieval Exchange.* London 1986. A very technical work on the exchange rates between the states of Europe in the Middle ages, fascinating for tracking the devaluation of the centuries and across the regions.

Stephanik, J.: *Cabinet de Monnaies.* Amsterdam 1904. The catalogue of the largest private collection of medieval Lowlands coins ever formed, including hundreds of early dated pieces. A collection of staggering proportions; unfortunately, few are pictured and the descriptions leave very much to desire.

REGION I, GERMANY

Bahrfeldt, E.: *Das Münzwesen der Mark Brandenburg*. Berlin 1889. ("Bahrfeldt").
Old but very thorough standard work on Brandenburg-Prussian coinage with superb line drawings. Essential for this very confusing area. Available now on CD.
-: *Die Münzen- und Medaillensammlung in der Marienburg*, Vol. 1-7. Danzig 1901-1910. The famous Brandenberg Collection Marienberg.
-: *Zur Mittelalterlichen Münzkunde Pommerns*, Berlin 1893. A monograph containing the famous numismatist's commentary to Dannenberg's work on Pommeranian coinage. Important for the discussion of the single digit first dated coin of Pommerania.

Behrens, H.: *Münzen und Medaillen der Stadt und des Bistums Lübeck*. Berlin 1905 (reprinted Hamburg 1972). Standard work on the coinage of Lübeck.

Berghaus, P.: *Die Münzen der Grafen von Limburg*. Münster/Westf. 1968. Fine recent work, well-researched and easy to use. The new standard reference.

Berlin *Blätter für Münz-Siegel-und Wappenkunde, 1863-1873*. Fine German periodical published in the 19th century discussing new discoveries.

Besser, R./ Brämer, H./Bürger, V.: *Halberstadt. Münzen und Medaillen im Spiegel der Geschichte* (2 vols.) Magdeburg 2001 und Halberstadt 2003. New standard work on the coinage of Halberstadt.

Binder, Chr.: *Württembergische Munz- und Medaillenkunde*. Stuttgart 1986. Thorough work for the one early dated type known.

Buck, H.: Die *Münzen der Stadt Einbeck*. Hildesheim/Leipzig 1939 ("Buck"). The standard work for this state. Much more thorough than Schrock, but missing the reference to the earliest dated Einbeck coin, which Schrock pictures and discusses but misidentifies.

Buck, H. und Bahrfeldt, F.: *Die Münzen der Stadt Hildesheim*. Hildesheim and Leipzig 1937 ("Buck/B"). Standard work on Hildesheim coinage, thoroughly researched but poorly photographed.

Buck, H./Meier, 0.: *Die Münzen der Stadt Hannover*. Hannover 1935 ("Buck/M").
Standard work on Hannover coinage. Easy to use but only one of two known types photographed.

Cappe, H.: *Beschreibung der Mainzer Münzen des Mittelalters*. Dresden 1856. Well-known 150 year old work on Mainz coinage, a difficult and confusing area. Badly needs updating.
-: *Cölnischen Münzen des Mittelalters*. Dresden 1853. The standard reference prior to Noss. Still with some usefulness.

Cunz, R.: *Kleine Münzgeschichte der Stadt Hannover*. Hannover 1991. Small museum pamphlet covering the history of Hannover coinage. Good quality photos.

Dannenberg, H.: *Münzgeschichte Pommerns im Mittelalter*. Berlin 1893. Still useful work on Pommeranian coinage with the typical thorough research of the 19th century coupled with wholly inadequate plates or line drawings.

Diepenbach, W.: *Geldwesen und Münzprägung in Bingen*. Mainz 1949. A focus on the Mainz mint at Bingen.

Ebner, J. und Binder, C.: *Württembergische Münz- und Medaillenkünde*. Stuttgart 1904. Early work on Württemberg coinage, now outdated. Poor photos.

Engel, A./Lehr, E.: *Numismatique de L'Alsace*. Paris 1887 ("E & L"). Standard reference on Alsatian coinage which is still very useful despite its age. Best when supplemented with De Mey's more recent work on Alsatian coinage.

Felke G.: Die *Goldprägungen der Rheinischen Kürfursten 1346-1478*. Sohren 1989. Outstanding reference on the gold coinage struck under the Rhineland monetary treaties, covering early dated gold coinage of Cologne, Mainz, Trier and the Palatinate. Highly recommended.

Förschner G.: *Deutsche Münzen, Mittelalter bis Neuzeit der münzpragenden Stande von Aachen bis Augsburg*. Melsungen 1984. An ambitious (intended) series on the Frankfurt museum medieval coinage, the finest collection in Germany other than Berlin. Unfortunately, this project ended after one volume by the untimely death of Ms. Förschner. Still extremely useful for Aachen, the one state with early dated coinage covered in this sole volume.

Fischer, E.: *Die Münzen des Hauses Schwarzburg*. Heidelberg 1904. Fine study on the subject but with inadequate photos.

Friederich, K.: *Die Münzen und Medaillen des Hauses Stolberg*. Dresden 1911. A typical early Germanic work from the turn of the century, wonderfully researched with infuriatingly few photos or drawings.

Gaedechens, O.: *Hamburgische Münzen und Medaillen*, 3 vol. Hamburg 1843-1876. Excellent work on Hamburg coinage, still the standard after more than 150 years. Fine line drawings for the two early dated types struck by Hamburg, but no discussion of the countermarked coinage of Hamburg.

Götz, E: *Die Münzprägung der Oberpfalz*. Nürnberg 1992. Very fine recent work on the Palatinate state of Mosbach. Excellent photos.

Grote, H.: *Münzstudien (Essen), Band III*. Leipzig 1863. A series of studies on Germanic state coinages, well-researched but now quite outdated with very inadequate photography.

Herzfelder, H.: *Die Reichmünzstätten Nördlingen und Augsburg unter den Häusern Weinsberg und Königstein*. Mitteilungen der Bayerischen Numismatischen Gesellschaft 52,1924. A monograph comprising the standard work on Nördlingen coinage, very thorough but with wholly inadequate photography.

Helmschrott, K. u. R.: *Würzburger Munzen und Medaillen*. Kleinrinderfeld 1977. Of limited use with dated coinage, as only one early dated silver coin type out of five is described and photographed.

Haupt, W.: *Sachsische Münzkunde*. Hamburg 1974. Good two volume work (text + plates) as a complement to Krug.

Heus, D.: *Münzwesen und Münzen der Grafschaft Henneberg von den Anfängen bis zum Erlöschen des gräflichen Hauses 1583*. Leipzig 1999. Very fine new work on medieval Henneberg with thorough coverage of its few early dated pieces.

Hoffmeister, J.: *Historisch-Kritische Beschreibung aller bis jetzt bekannt gewordenen Hessischen Münzen, Medaillen und Marken in genealogisch-chronologischer Folge*. Leipzig and Hannover 1862-1880. Older work on Hessen coinage, published in several parts, hard to use and with only a few line drawings. Schutz is far better although more limited in scope.

Ihl, H.: Die *Münzpragung der Edelherrn zur Lippe, Münzstätte Lemgo*. Lemgo 1991. Standard work on the coinage of Lippe but the photos could be better.

Jesse, W.: *Die Münzen der Stadt Braunschweig von 1499 bis 1680*. Braunschweig 1962. Very fine standard work on Brunswick coinage. Thorough coverage.

P. Joseph/E. Fellner.: *Die Münzen von Frankfurt am Main*. Frankfurt/M. 1896-1920. (J&F). The standard work on coinage of Frankfurt, a multi-volume work. Several supplements were published, and all are needed for completeness.

Joseph, P.: *Die Münzen von Worms*. Darmstadt 1906. Standard work and useful for the only early dated coin of Worms.

Jungk, H.: *Die Bremischen Münzen des Erzbisthums und der Stadt Bremen*. Bremen 1875. Old but first rate standard work on the coinage of Bremen. Few drawings but very thorough coverage.

Kappelhoff, A.: *Die Münzen Ostfrieslands*. Aurich 1982. The new standard work on East Frisian coinage, superbly researched with fine photography. Covers not only the coinage of East Frisia (Ostfriesland) but that of Jever as well, some of the 25 most difficult early dated coins to collect.

Kennepohl, K.: *Die Münzen von Osnabrück*. Munich 1938 (reprinted 1967). Standard work on coinage of Osnabrück, very thorough and well researched, easy to read.

Klein, U./Raff, A.: *Die Württembergischen Münzen 1374-1873*. 3 vol. Stuttgart 1991-1992. The standard work on Württemberg coinage, thorough and easy to use, although covering but one dated coin.

Kramer, H.: *Das Stift Essen. Münzen und Medaillen*. Münster 1993. Fine recent work on the coinage of the convent (nunnery) of Essen. Photographs are not the best.

Krug, G.: *Die Meissnisch-Sachsischen Groschen*. Berlin 1974. The standard reference on Saxony late medieval coinage, an outstanding work, absolutely indispensable for referencing the 90 early dated coin types and subtypes of the Saxony dukes and electors. Almost all types are photographed. The focus is on cataloging, not commentary.

Krumbach, G.: *Aachener Münzen des Mittelalters*. Aachen 1995. A recent and useful book providing updated information to Menadier with much better photos than Menadier.

Krusy, H.: *Gegenstempel auf Münzen des Spätmittelalters*. Frankfurt 1974. Standard reference on countermarked Germanic coinage. No photographs, but a still essential and a wonderfully researched work, completely indispensable.

Leitzmann, J.: *Das Münzwesen und die Münzen Erfurts*. Weissensee 1862. Very old and outdated standard work on Erfurt coinage. Sorely in need of good photographs or drawings.

Löffelholz von Kolberg, W.: *Oettingiana*. Nördlingen 1883. Very outdated work on the coinage of Öttingen, poor and missing photographs. Unfortunately, it still is the only single reference of this state available for the 15th century coinage.

Menadier, J.: *Die Aachener Münzen* (2 vols). Berlin 1913. The standard work on the coinage of Aachen and Schoonvorst-Sichem. In need of an update as several of the dated coins are incorrectly attributed, the photos are very poor and new hoard and other evidence is available. Best used with combined with Förschner and Krumbach.

Menadier, J.: *Die Münzen der Grafschaft Mark*. Dortmund 1909. (Menadier Mark). Menadier's article on the coinage of Mark. Useful but in need of updating.

Merzdorf, J.F.: *Die Münzen und Medaillen Jeverlands*. Oldenburg 1862. Previous standard work on Jever coinage. Kappelhoff is better for early dated coinage.

Moers in Nummis – See Slg. Vielhaber.

Noss, A.: *Die Münzen von Trier I*, 2. Bonn 1916.
-, *Die Münzen der Erzbischofe von Köln, Band I*. Cologne 1913.
-, *Die Münzen von Berg und Jülich-Berg, Band I und II*. Munich 1929.
-, *Die Münzen der Grafen und Herzoge von Kleve*. Munich 1931.
-: *Die Münzen von Jülich, Mörs und Alpen*. Munich 1927.
A monumental series of books by the leading German numismatist of the early part of the twentieth century. His books not only contain excellent research and meticulous descriptions but (for the time) rather fine photographs as well. A must for the serious collector.

Pr. Alexander v. Hessen.: *Mainzisches Münzkabinett des Prinzen Alexander von Hessen*. Darmstadt 1882 ("Pr. Alexander"). The catalogue of one of the largest collection of Mainz coinage assembled, still useful given the lack of other references for this important state, but very out of date with no photographs or line drawings

Posern-Klett, C.F.: *Münzstatten und Münzen der Stadte und Geistlichen Stifter Sachsens im Mittelalter*. Leipzig 1846. Standard work on Mühlhausen coinage, wholly inadequate descriptions of the coinage but at least each piece has a line drawing, albeit a poor one.

Rein, B.: *Schwarzburger Münzen und Medaillen, Sammlung des Schlossmuseums in Rudolstadt*. Halle 1930. Museum collection of Schwarzburg coinage, well-described but very lacking in photos.

Riechmann, A.: *Die Mittelalterlichen Münzen des Hessischen Landesmuseums in Kassel*, Auktion No. XXIX, Halle 1924. An sale of medieval coins from a major museum in Cassel, amazing for the quality and rarity of the coins offered.

Rommel, K.: "Die Münzen von Freiburg im Breisgau." *Freiburger Münzblatter* Nr. 2, January 1991. Fine overview of the very rare coinage of Freiburg im Breisgau.
-: "Die Münzen und Medaillenstempel des Augustinermuseums in Freiburg im Breisgau," *Freiburger Münzblatter* Nr. 6 2000. An interesting counterpart to the first work, in this case concentrating on the different dies used in the production of this coinage. Excellent photographs.

Schrock, U.: *Münzen der Stadt Göttingen*. Bremen 1987. The fine standard work on Göttingen coinage, very easy to use and read with excellent photographs. A very important reference, given the 27 different types of Göttingen early dated coins known.
-: *Von der Kunst gutes Geld zu Machen, Die Münzprägung der Stadt Einbeck* ("Schrock Einbeck"). A history of the coinage of Einbeck, not as thorough as Buck.

Schutz, A.: *Die Hessischen Münzen des Hauses Brabant, 5 Teile*. Kassel/Frankfurt 1993-2000. The first volume of this excellent work is all that is needed for the 15th century coverage. Easy to use and well researched, but the photographs could be better.

Schlegel, A.: *Die Kurmainzische Münzstatte Höchst*. Frankfurt 1991. A very specific and thorough work on the medieval mint of Höchst, which issued coinage for bishopric of Mainz.

Schrötter, Frhr. von: *Brandenburg-Frankisches Münzwesen*. Halle 1927 and 1929. Standard work on the gold coinage of Brandenburg-Franconia, easy to use and well-researched.

von Berstett, A.: *Münzgeschichte des Zähringen-Badischen Fürstenhauses*, Freiburg im Breisgau 1846. Old and very outdated standard work on Freiburg in Breisgau and Breisach coinage. Of limited usefulness.

Weingaertner, J.: *Die Gold- und der Silbermünzen des Bisthums Paderborn nebst historischen Nachrichten*. Munster 1882, 1890 (reprinted Hamburg 1977). Standard work on the coinage of Paderborn.

(The next group of references are important published collections or "sammlung," abbreviated in German as "Slg.")

Slg. Dr. E. Bahrfeldt, Münzen des Deutschen Mittelalters. Auktion A. Hess Nachf. 171, Frankfurt. 1921.

Slg. Brand, Medieval Coins of All Europe. Bank Leu Auktion 46, May 1988 Zürich, Auktion 47, October 1988 Zürich, Auktion 67, May 1996, Auktion 69, June 1997 Zürich, Auktion 70, October 1997 Zürich (Coll. Brand). A "small" portion of the greatest collection of medieval coins ever assembled, unrivaled for its quality and quantity. Unfortunately, only a small percentage of the entire collection was ever catalogued. Other Brand coins were sold at other auction companies – this is the most useful series.

Slg. Ebner, Württembergische Münzen. Leo Hamburger, Frankfurt 1917 (Coll. Ebner).

Slg. Hennig (Warburg). Auction Button 89. Frankfurt/M. 1942.

Slg. Kayser (Rheinland). A. Riechmann. Halle 1912.

Slg. Krug, Sachsische Münzen. Auktion Schulten + Co. GmbH, Frankfurt 1980. Extremely important collection, but very few photos.

Slg. Lejeune (Mark). Dr. Busso Peus Nachf. 262, Frankfurt 1961 (Coll. Lejeune). Extraordinary collection of coins of this county, excellent photographic coverage.

Slg. Prof. A. Memmesheimer, Pfalz. Münz Zentrum Auktion 35, Köln 1979.(Coll. "Mem."). Important collection, but lacking enough photos.

Slg. Merseburger, Münzen und Medaillen von Sachsen. Leipzig 1894. Widely cited but very outdated for medieval coins, Krug is far better.

Slg. Noss, Münzen der Pfalz 1. Teil: Die Kur-Linie. In: Auktion 255 Münzenhandlung Dr. B. Peus, Frankfurt 1956. 2. Teil: Die Nebenlinien. In: Auktion 256 Münzenhandlung Dr. Busso Peus, Frankfurt 1957. (Coll. Noss). Professor Noss' collection. Very important.

Slg. Piloty, Würzburg. Auktion Helbing, Munich 1927.

Slg. Pogge, Sammlung des Herrn Commerzienrath C. F. Pogge in Greifswald, Münzen und Medaillen von Pommern, Russland, Polen, Danemark, Schweden und Mecklenburg. Auktion L. & L. Hamburger, Frankfurt 1903.

Slg. Roeper, (German states). Hans Meuss, Hamburg 1937.

Slg. Vielhaber, Moers in nummis, Moers, Nassau, Orange, Jülich, Cleve, Berg, Palatinate. S. Rosenberg, Frankfurt 1920. (Moers in Nummis). Outstanding for the coinage of Mörs.

Slg. Theodor Voltz, Elsass. Münzen und Medaillen AG, Auktion 82, Basel 1996. (Coll. Voltz). Excellent collection of Alsatian coinage.

Slg. Dr. Walther, Mainz. Auktion Dr. Busso Peus Nachf. 275, Frankfurt 1971. (Coll. Walther).

Slg. Weweler, Lippia in Nummis. Auktion 63 Leu Numismatik, Zürich 1995. (Coll. Weweler). The catalogue of the finest collection of Lippe coinage ever sold, superbly presented.

Slg. Weygand, Rheinland, Westfalen. A. Hess, Frankfurt 1917. (Coll. Weygand). One of the finest collection of Rhineland coinages ever assembled.

Slg. Weyl, Die Paul Henckelsche Sammlung Brandenburg-Preussischer Münzen und Medaillen. Berlin 1876-1877.

REGION II, SOUTHERN NETHERLANDS

Chalon, R.: *Recherches sur les monnaies des comtes de Namur.* Brussels 1860 (supplement 1870). Standard work on coinage of Namur. Easy to use with very good line drawings.

Chestret de Haneffe, Baron J.: *Numismatique de la Principauté de Liège.* Brussels 1890. *Supplement Liège 1900* ("Chestret or Ch."). First-rate standard work on coinage of Liège. Updated by Mignolet in 1986, itself a very useful work. Being over 100 years old, though, a new work was needed in this fascinating area and that has now been supplied by Dengis (see below).

Collection (Sammlung) Weygand – see Germany.

Crab, J.: *Munt te Leuven.* Leuven 1967. Small publication on the coins of Louvain, good photographs.

de Coster, L.: *Atlas contenant toutes les Monnaies du Brabant 1000-1506.* Brussels 1888 (reprinted 1979). A helpful overview catalogue, good as an inexpensive volume for those who do have access to de Witte.

Delmonte, A.: *Le Benelux d'Or.* Amsterdam 1964. Very fine and useful single volume work on gold coinage in the Lowlands. Its companion volume from 1967, "*Le Benelux d'Argent,*" does not cover the medieval times.

de Mey - see general references.

Dengis, J-L.: *Les Monnaies de la Principauté de Liège, Tomes I-III.* Wetteren 2006. The outstanding three volume new work on the coinage of Liège, bringing to print a century of numismatic research and discovery since the publication of Chestret. This marvelous book will undoubtedly replace Chestret.

Deschamps de Pas, L.: "Essai sur l'histoire monétaire des comtes de Flandre de la maison de Bourgogne [and] de la maison d'Autriche (1482-1556)." *Revue Numismatique,* new series, VI (1861), VII (1862), XI (1866), XIV (1869), XV (1874), and *Revue Belge de Numismatique, XXXII* (1876) ("D.d.P"). Still the standard reference on Flanders coinage in the 15th century, a collection of essays rather than a book. Sorely in need of updating, but still the only existing major work providing the many varieties in this area. Van Gelder-Hoc is more useful, but lists only main types.

de Witte, A.: *Histoire monétaire des comtes de Louvain, ducs de Brabant.* 3 vols, Antwerp, 1894-99 ("De Witte" or "DW"). The marvelous standard work on Brabant coinage, very easy to use and with excellent line drawings. A wonderful complement to van Gelder-Hoc and very much needed given that the early dated coinage of Brabant represents seven percent of all known types and subtypes listed.

Dugniolle – see General References.

Jaarboek voor Munt-en Penningkunde (JMP) - see General References.

Lucas – see General References.

Menadier - see Germany.

Mignolet, A.: *Les Monnaies de la Principauté de Liège.* Maastricht 1986. Fine update to Chestret, using Chestret's numbering system but adding commentary. Both works should be used together. Inexpensive and with great line drawings, but Dengis will make this work obsolete as well.

Revue Belge de Numismatique – see General References.

Stadsmuseum-Hasselt.: Hasselt Munten. Hasselt 1980. A good museum catalogue of the coinage of one of Liège's principal mints.

Taelman, J.: *Munten en Penningen in Bourgondisch Vlaanderen*. Bruges 1982. A beautifully photographed work on the coinage of Flanders from 1400-1700. More of a historical catalogue than a research study such as Deschamps de Pas.

van der Chijs - see Northern Netherlands.

van Gelder, E/ Hoc, M.: *Les Monnaies des Pays-Bas Bourguignons et Espagnols 1434- 1713.* Amsterdam 1960 ("van Gelder-Hoc" or "GH"). One of the finest references ever written covering the period in which early dated coins were struck. Extremely easy to use, but the photos are lacking some clarity. Essential in every library.

Vanhoudt, H.: *Atlas der Munten van België*. Herent 1996. An ambitious work attempting to cover in a single volume all Belgium coinage from all Southern Netherlands' states from the medieval times up to independence. The line drawings, taken from a number of sources, are excellent and worth the price alone.

REGION III, NORTHERN NETHERLANDS

De Beeldenaar. Utrecht 1977 + Useful articles on Dutch coinage.

Delmonte - see General References.

de Mey d'Or - see General References.

de Voogt, W.: *Bijdragen tot de Numismatiek van Gelderland*, Arnhem 1867. Original work on the coinage of Nijmegen, now very much outdated.

Egg - see General References.

Fortuyn Drooglever, J.: *De Vorstelijke en de Stedelijke Muntslag te Deventer*. Deventer 1982 ("JFD"). Standard work on Deventer coinage, Dutch text but easy to use.
-: *De Driesteden Muntslag Deventer-Kampen-Zwolle*, Den Haag (the Hague) 1986 ("JFD DKZ"). Standard work on the Tri-City coinage. As with his book on Deventer, wonderfully researched and easy to use even with Dutch text.

Jaarboek voor Munt-en-Penningkunde - see General References.

"Notes of Prof. Enno van Gelder." 's-Gravenhage (the Hague) 1977. The correspondence between the renowned numismatic scholar Prof. Enno van Gelder and David Cervin, now in possession of the author through the kindness of Mr. Cervin's family. Given the many year consolidation of the three Netherlands coin museums with the resultant limits on any access, these notes have been most helpful to assessing the holdings of the museums.

Passon, T.: *De Stedelijke Munt van Nijmegen*. Nijmegen 1980 ("Nijmegen Museum"). The standard work on the coinage of Nijmegen, undertaken by the Commander St. John Museum in Nijmegen, now part of the Museum Het Valkhof in Nijmegen. Very thorough work but could use more photos.

Puister, A.: "Groningse Stedelijke Munten," *Jaarboek voor Munt-en Penningkunde, #73,* Amsterdam 1986 ("Puister"). The best work on Groningen coinage, easily surpassing Van der Chijs. Written as a monograph in a Dutch numismatic journal. Hard to find but well worth the effort.
-: "Friese Stedelijke Munten," *Jaarboek voor Munt-en Penningkunde*, 1981 page 27-46 ("Puister- Fr"). another article by Puister, this one the best available work on the exceedingly obscure Frisian coinage of Leeuwarden, Sneek, Bolsward and Franeker. Far better than Van der Chijs.

Revue Belge de Numismatique – see General References.

Roest, T.: "Essai de classification des monnaies du comté puis duché de Gueldre." *RBN* 1891-1893. Articles on Gelderland coinage, well out of date.

Stephanik – see General References.

Tijdschrift van het Koninklijk Nederlandsch Genootschap voor Munt-en Penningkunde. Amsterdam 1893-1913 ("TMP"). Scholarly articles on coinage, including the medieval period.

van Beek, E.J.A./Droogleever, J.F.: *Geslagen te Zutphen*. Zutphen 1990 ("Beek"). Helpful small work on the coinage of the tiny Dutch city of Zutphen, better than Van der Chijs.

Van der Chijs, P. O. : *De Munten der voormalige Hertogen, Graven, Heeren en Steden van de vroegste tijden tot aan de Pacificatie van Gand*, 9 vol. Haarlem 1854 ("Van der Chijs"). The standard 150 year old, nine volume work on coinage of the Southern and Northern Netherlands. Still a vital work, although in the old Dutch text, difficult to use, and naturally somewhat outdated, given its age. The plates, all line drawings, are excellent and can be obtained in a separate volume, which is an outstanding value given the typical cost of the full set.

van der Wee, H.: *The Low Countries in the Early Modern World.* Cambridge 1993. Good historical overview of Low Country commerce.

van der Wiel, Dr. H. J.: *De Stedelijke Muntslag van Zwolle.* Vriezenveen 1994. Standard reference on coinage of Zwolle. Dutch text, easy to follow, but lacking in sufficient photos.

van Gelder-Hoc - see Southern Netherlands.

REGION IV, HABSBURG TERRITORIES

Corpus Nummorum Austriacorum, Band I Mittelalter. (Koch, B editor). Vienna 1994 ("CNA"). The indispensable work on medieval Habsburg coinage, with photographs of every coin, including many subtypes. A wonderful reference book which sets the standards for excellence, especially with such a large coverage area. While the work will eventually span five or more volumes, only the first is needed for the 15th century coinage.

Corpus Nummorum Hungarie. 1899-1907, German translation, (Rethy, L. editor). Graz 1958 ("CNH"). Standard work on medieval Hungarian coinage in just one volume. Easy to use.

Egg – see General References.

Huszár, L.: *Münzkatalog Ungarn von 1000 bis Heute.* Munich 1979. Very fine recent work on Hungarian coinage, much more thorough in descriptions than CNH.

Moeser, K./ Dworschak, F.: *Die grosse Münzreform unter Erzherzog Sigismund von Tirol.* Vienna 1936 ("M.D."). Very scholarly work on the larger coinage which began under Sigismund of Tyrol. Hard to find now, but essential for this area.

Moser, H./ Tursky, H.: *Die Münzstatte Hall in Tirol 1477 -1665.* Innsbruck 1977 ("M-T"). Fine work on the larger coinage of Tyrol.
-:*Tiroler Münzbuch.* Innsbruck 1984. Overview of all Tyrolean coinage. Very good photos.

Pichler, F.: *Repertorium der Steierischen Münzkunde.* Graz 1875 (reprinted 1974). While perhaps still the standard work on the coinage of Styria, it has limited usefulness except for scholars and catalogers since the publication of CNA. Difficult to read and use, an inadequate few line drawings.

Pohl, A.: *Die Grenzland-Prägung, Münzprägung in Österreich und Ungarn im 15. Jahrhundert.* Graz 1972. Very good book on the small coinage in Austria-Hungary bordering areas in the 15th century. Somewhat outdated by CNA now.

Probszt, G.: *Die Münzen Salzburgs.* 2d ed. Basel/Graz 1975. One of the standard references on the coinage of Salzburg, but not the most detailed. Easy to use and inexpensive.

Slg. Morosini. *Steiermark, Kärnten, Krain etc.* Auktion XLIV Brüder Egger, Wien 1912. Important auction of Tyrolean coinage.

Szego, A.: *Coinage of Medieval Austria 1156-1521,* Oakdale 1970. A very useful small pamphlet providing a solid summary of earlier works. Good line drawings. Now made obsolete by CNA, as have so many other notable works.

REGION V, SWITZERLAND

Coll. Brand – see Germany.

Coll. Swiss – see Slg. Schweiz below.

de Palezieux-du Pan, M.: *Numismatique de l'eveche de Sion.* Geneva 1909. Standard catalogue on the coinage of Sion (Sitten). Contains one early dated coin reference, that of the famous 1498 thaler.

Dolivo, D.: *Les monnaies de l'évêché de Lausanne. Schweizerische Münzkataloge Band 2.* Bern 1961. Standard work on medieval Lausanne coinage, well-described but needing more photos.

Ewig A.: *Katalog der Basler Münzen und Medaillen der im Historischen Museum zu Basel*, Basel 1899. Very useful catalogue on the many Basel coinage types.

Geiger, H-G.: *Der Beginn der Gold-und Dickmünzenpragung in Bern.* Bern 1968. Fine work on the coinage of Berne.

Helvetische Münzenzeitung ("HMZ Bulletin"). Hilterfingen 1966 +. Articles on Swiss coinage.

HMZ Katalog Schweiz Liechtenstein. Zürich 1995 ("HMZ"). The widest used single reference on Swiss coinage. As with most catalogues, an emphasis on breadth, not depth. Still obligatory for the collector of Swiss coinage, and each edition contains more photos than the previous.

Ikle-Steinlin, A.: *Die Münzen der Stadt St. Gallen*. Schweizerische Numismatische Rundschau, 16-18, 1910-1912. Standard work on coinage of St. Gallen

Jahresbericht 1978 des Rätischen Musems Chur. Chur 1979 ("Museum Chur"). A yearbook of the City Museum of Chur, containing an article regarding the unique 1488 plappart of Chur.

Kapossy, B.: *Monnaies et Médailles du Musee d'Histoire de Berne.* Bern 1969. A useful reference on Bernese coinages with fine photographs.

Lohner, C.: *Die Münzen der Republik Bern.* Zürich 1846. Nachtrag Zürich 1858. Difficult to use older work on Bernese coinage.

Slg. Schweiz. Teils 1-4. Leu Numismatik AG, Zürich, Auktion 82, 84, 88 and 94 ("Coll. Swiss"). The indispensable four-part sale of the finest collection of Swiss coins ever assembled, containing 18 of the reported 27 early dated Swiss types. The superb quality of the collection is matched by that of the catalogue, in scholarship, presentation, photography and layout. A major achievement with the added benefit of both German and English text.

Slg. Righetti: *Katalog der Sammlung Jean-Pierre Righetti im Bernischen Historischen Museum.* Bern 1993. Important collection of Swiss coins.

Voltz, T.: *Die Basler Groschen und Dicken. SD aus dem Jahresbericht des Historischen Museums 1949.* Basel 1950. Very thorough work on the die types of the larger coinage of Basel.

Wielandt, F.: *Münz- und Geldgeschichte des Standes Luzern.* Lucerne 1969. Standard catalogue on the coinage of Lucerne. Easy to use.

Winterstein, C.: *Die Goldgulden von Basel.* Basel 1977. In-depth study on Basel's gold coinage, helpful for the 15th century.
-: *Die Taler von Basel.* Basel 1983. Likewise good coverage for the thalers of Basel.

REGION VI, SCANDINAVIA

Lagerqvist, L.: *Svenska mynt under Vikingatid och Medeltid (ca. 995-1521) samt Gotländska mynt (ca 1140-1565).* Stockholm 1970. Indispensible work on Swedish coinage with thorough coverage (and photos) of the dated ortugs and half-ortugs.

Bengtsson, K.: "Ett Nytt exemplar av Eropas första årtalsdaterade mynt Nordisk," *Numismatisk Unions medlemsblad.* Copenhagen August 2003. Short article on the discovery of the seventh known example of the famous 1234 Roskilde denier.

Galster, G.: *Unionstidens udmøntninger Danmark og Norge 1397-1540, Sverige 1363-1521.* Copenhagen 1972. Work on the coinage of the time of the Scandanavian Union. Good overview, but Lagerqvist is much better for the early dated coins of Sweden.

Jensen, J.: *Nationalmuseets Arbejdsmark 1997.* Copenhagen 1997 ("National Museum Yearbook"). Small publication by the Royal Collection of Coins and medals featuring a section on the 1234 Roskilde denier and the unique Danish triple noble of 1496.

Lindahl, F.: "Valdemarernes mønter, isaer Anno Domini MCCXXXIIII-mønten, belyst ved løsfund fra Kirkerne," *Nordisk Numismatisk Årsskrift 1963.* Lund 1964. Excellent article by one of Scandanavia's leading numismatists on the subject of the first Anno Domini dated European coin, the 1234 Roskilde denier. Provides the best history of the discovery and analysis of this coin type.
Slg. Bruun, *Schwedische Münzen, 2 Teile.* Adolphe Hess 1914 ("Coll. Bruun"). Leading sale of Swedish coinage. Not as helpful as Lagerqvist.

REGION VII, ITALY

Berman, A: *Papal Coins*, South Salem 1991. In just a short period of time, this remarkably useful single volume book has become the standard reference on Papal coinage. Well-illustrated and very easy to use.

Biaggi, E: *Moneta e Zecche Medievali Italiane Dal Sec. VIII al Sec. XV*. Turin 1992. The best overall single volume work on gold and silver Italian medieval coinage. Photographs and line drawings are very useful.

Corpus Nummorum Italicorum, Vols. 1-20. Rome 1910-1943 (Reprint 1961) ("CNI"). The monumental 20 oversized volume work on Italian medieval coinage, based on the Italian national collection. Covers coins issued in all metals. A work of immense scholarship, full with descriptions of coins never before seen or known. Very expensive, usually over $5,000.00, but for the serious collector it is incomparable.

Crippa, C.: *La moneta di Milano II, dai Visconti agle Sforza dal 1329 al 1535* (Milan 1986). The first-rate standard work on Milanese coinage which corrects errors in Gnecchi.

Gnecchi, F and E.: *Le monete di Milano*. Milan 1884, Supplement 1894. Fine old work on Milanese coinage, but it misidentifies a key early dated piece (out of only two known types). CNI or Crippa is more useful.

Muntoni, F. *Le Monete dei Papi e degli Stati Pontifici*, Roma 1972-1973, 4 voll.

Sekulich, L.: "Shedding light on a Renaissance Trial Piece," *The Numismatist*, Oct 2004. Interesting article from an artistic viewpoint on the 1494 Antegnate pattern bronze testone.

REGION VIII, FRANCE

de Mey *Brittany* – see General References.

Duplessy, J.: *Les Monnaies Francaises Féodales, Tome I.* Paris 2004. The first of a widely-anticipated multi-volume work intended to replace Poey d'Avant. Very easy to use and containing fine line drawings.

de Saulcy, F.: *Recherches sur les monnaies des ducs héréditaires de Lorraine*. Metz 1841. The standard work on the coinage of Lorraine, sorely out of date yet still useful. For an early 19th century reference guide it is easier to use than most and the research is solid.

Poey d'Avant, F.: *Monnaies Féodales de France*, 3 vol. Paris 1858-1862 (reprinted reprinted Graz 1961 and Bologna 1976). Still the leading work on French feudal coinage, wonderfully detailed and with fine line drawings. Still available today as a result of two different reprints.

INDEX

III-168 *Holland 1487 Gold Real*

II-134 *Liège 1494 Brulé*

III-164 *Gelderland 1487 Silver Real*

II-143 *Brabant 1499 Toison d'or*

II-22 *Brabant 1476 Double Briquet*

II-144 *Brabant 1499 Florin d'or*

II-78 *Liège 1484 Double Patard*

III-80 *Bolsward 1476 Stuiver*

II-97 *Flanders 1487 Griffon*

III-279 *Deventer 1500 Stuiver*

II-110 *Brabant 1489 Quadruple Patard*

VIII-3 *Brittany 1498 Ecu d'or*

VIII -1 *Lorraine 1491 Double Gros*

IV-63 *Salzburg 1500 Goldgulden*

IV-7 *Austria 1459 Kreuzer*

V-22 *Basel 1499 Dicken*

VII-8a *Milan 1497 Pattern Bronze Testone*

I-3a *Aachen 1374 Groschen*

III-40 *Deventer 1466 Jager*

III-220 *Franeker 1492 Goldgulden*

III-231 *Utrecht 1492 Florin d'or*

III-1 *Anholt-Batenburg 1424 Groschen*

I-449 *Frankfurt 1500 Goldgulden*

I-428a *Saxony 1499 Schrenkenberger*

I-411a Colmar 1499 Plappart

I-259a Cologne 1491 Goldgulden

II-117 Brabant 1489 4 Mites

I-98a Countermarked, Halberstadt 1466 Horngroschen

I-134 Erfurt 1474 Uniface Hohlpfennig

I-171 Countermarked, Warburg 1479 Double Stüber

II-B150 Countermarked, Tournai 1499 Patard

I-56 Cleve 1441 Blanken

I-77 Mainz 1445 Groschen or Weisspfennig

I-28a Cologne 1436 Goldgulden

I-28b Cologne 1436 Goldgulden

II-129 Brabant 1492 Florin d'or

II-58 Brabant 1481 4 Mites

III-232 Utrecht 1492 Half Florin d'or

II-79 Liège 1484 Stoeter

II-67 Brabant 1483 Florin d'or

II-94 Brabant 1487 Double Griffon

I-268 Nördlingen 1491 Goldgulden

II-101 Brabant 1488 Demi Noble d'or

I-362b Hamburg 1497 Ducat

II-108 Brabant 1489 Florin d'or

I-282 Mark 1492 Braspfennig

II-112 Brabant 1489 Patard

IV-10a Austria 1460 Pfennig

I-278a Frankfurt 1492 Goldgulden

III-61 Leeuwarden 1472 Stuiver

III-255 Deventer 1498 Goldgulden

I-379 Frankfurt 1498 Goldgulden